Research Methods, Design, and Analysis

ELEVENTH EDITION

Larry B. Christensen
University of South Alabama

R. Burke Johnson
University of South Alabama

Lisa A. Turner
University of South Alabama

Allyn & Bacon

Boston   Columbus   Indianapolis   New York   San Francisco   Upper Saddle River
Amsterdam   Cape Town   Dubai   London   Madrid   Milan   Munich   Paris   Montreal   Toronto
Delhi   Mexico City   Sao Paulo   Sydney   Hong Kong   Seoul   Singapore   Taipei   Tokyo

Executive Acquisitions Editor: Jeff Marshall
Editorial Assistant: Amy Trudell
Marketing Manager: Nicole Kunzmann
Marketing Assistant: Amanda Olweck
Production Manager: Fran Russello
Manager, Visual Research: Beth Brenzel
Manager, Rights and Permissions: Zina Arabia
Image Permission Coordinator: Joanne Dippel
Editorial Production and Composition Service: Hemalatha/Integra Software Services, Ltd.
Art Director: Jayne Conte
Cover Designer: Suzanne Behnke
Text Printer: Courier Companies, Inc.
Cover Printer: Lehigh Phoenix Color

Library of Congress Cataloging-in-Publication Data
Christensen, Larry B.,
    Research Methods, Design, and Analysis / Larry B. Christensen,
R. Burke Johnson, Lisa Turner. —11th ed.
        p. cm.
Rev. and updated ed. of : Experimental methodology.
Includes bibliographical references and index.
ISBN-13: 978-0-205-70165-0
ISBN-10: 0-205-70165-5
    1. Psychology, Experimental—Textbooks.   2. Psychology—Experiments—
Textbooks.   3. Experimental design.   I. Johnson, Burke.   II. Turner, Lisa.
III. Christensen, Larry B., 1941– Experimental methodology.   IV. Title.
BF181.C48 2010
150.72'4—dc22

                                                    2010004679

10 9 8 7 6 5 4 3 2 1-CRW-13 12 11 10 09

Allyn & Bacon
is an imprint of

www.pearsonhighered.com

ISBN-10:   0-205-70165-5
ISBN-13: 978-0-205-70165-0

◼ Brief Contents

■ Contents

CHAPTER 2   **Research Approaches and Methods of Data Collection | 28**

PART III   Foundations of Research | 139

  CHAPTER 5   Measuring Variables and Sampling | 139

PART IV   **Experimental Methods | 199**

CHAPTER 7   **Control Techniques in Experimental Research | 199**

CHAPTER 10   ## Quasi-Experimental Designs | 281

CHAPTER 11   ## Single-Case Research Designs | 306

CHAPTER 15 Inferential Statistics | 423

■ Preface

For the past 10 editions of this textbook, I (Larry Christensen) have dedicated myself to writing a research methods book that conveys the primary research method used by psychologists in the conduct of their research. However, I felt that it was time to bring additional authors into the process to continue to reflect the broad scope of methods used in the research process. Toward this end, I have asked two excellent researchers, Burke Johnson and Lisa Turner, to contribute to the 11th edition of this textbook. Both have made excellent contributions, and I believe the book is much better as a result of their contributions. In addition to including Burke and Lisa in this revision of the textbook, we decided to change the title of the book to reflect its broader scope. When the first edition of the book was written, the zeitgeist was a dominant focus on the experimental method. While considerable research is still conducted using the experimental method, a significant percentage of research uses methods other than the experimental method. Prior editions of the book did include nonexperimental methods, but these nonexperimental methods comprised only one chapter of the book. The current edition, while maintaining detailed coverage of the experimental method, has expanded coverage on nonexperimental methods as well as on data analysis.

Although the title and a significant portion of the content, as well as the authors contributing to the 11th edition, have changed, the overarching goals of the book have *not*. First, we have focused on writing a book that provides an understanding of the research methods used to investigate human thought and behavior. Research methods tend to change very slowly, but they do change. For example, the last edition incorporated information on the increased use of the Internet not only in soliciting subjects but in the actual conduct of research studies. In the present edition, information is included on "mixed methods." This is a relatively new but important addition to the arsenal of research methods an investigator might use to answer a research question, and it represents just one example of the changes incorporated into the 11th edition in an effort to insure that the content of the book is current.

A second overarching goal that has been maintained throughout all editions of the textbook is to present information in a way that is understandable to students. We have attempted to meet this goal by presenting material in as simple and straightforward a manner as possible and by accompanying complex material with illustrations taken from the research literature. We believe that such illustrations not only assist in clarifying the presented material but also bring the material to life when it is placed in the context of actual research studies. This allows the student not only to learn the material but also to see how it is used in a research study.

Overview and Organization of the Textbook

Research Methods, Design, and Analysis is written at the undergraduate level and is intended for use in the undergraduate methods course. The book provides an introduction to all aspects of research methodology, and assumes no prior knowledge. The chapters are divided into seven major parts, as follows:

Part I. Introduction (Chapters 1 and 2)

This section begins with a discussion of knowledge and science in an effort to provide students with an understanding of the nature, goals, and outcomes of science. We believe that most students have an incomplete understanding of science and that they must understand its goals and limitations in order to appreciate and understand the nature of the research process. This is followed by a discussion of the major types of research used to investigate mind and behavior in an attempt to make sure that the students connect the various research approaches with science. We also discuss the major methods of data collection to help students see how empirical data are obtained.

Part II. Planning the Research Study (Chapters 3 and 4)

In this section, the focus of the book moves to some general topics involved in all research studies. First, we explain how to come up with a research idea, conduct a literature review, and develop a research question and hypothesis. Second, we explain the key ethical issues that must be considered when planning and conducting a research study. We explain the ethical guidelines sanctioned by the American Psychological Association.

Part III. Foundations of Research (Chapters 5 and 6)

In Part III, we cover some concepts that the researcher must understand before critiquing or conducting a research study. We begin with a discussion of measurement. We define measurement, and explain how measurement reliability and validity are obtained. Next, we explain how researchers obtain samples of research participants from targeted and accessible populations. We explain the different methods of random and nonrandom sampling, and we show the important distinction between random selection and random assignment. We also briefly explain the sampling methods used in qualitative research. Next, we explain how research validity (i.e., valid results) is obtained. This includes discussions of the major kinds of research validity (internal, external, statistical conclusion, and construct) that must be addressed and maximized in empirical research.

Part IV. Experimental Methods (Chapters 7–11)

Part IV is focused on, perhaps, the most prominent approach to research in psychology and related disciplines (i.e., experimental research). The section includes (a) a chapter explaining the control techniques required to obtain valid research results, (b) a chapter explaining how to select and/or construct a strong experimental research design, (c) a chapter explaining the procedure and details of carrying out an experimental study, (d) a chapter explaining how to select and/or construct a quasi-experimental research design when needed, and (e) a chapter explaining when single-case designs are needed and how to select and/or construct an appropriate single-case design.

Part V. Exploratory and Descriptive Methods (Chapters 12 and 13)

This section includes chapters on additional major research methods used in psychology and related disciplines. First, the student is introduced to the goals, design, and conduct of survey research. The student will also learn how to correctly construct a questionnaire and/or interview protocol to be used in survey research. Second, the book includes a full chapter on qualitative and mixed methods research. The relative strengths and weaknesses of quantitative, qualitative, and mixed methods research are discussed, the different qualitative and mixed methods approaches and designs are explained, and information is provided about how to conduct a defensible and rigorous qualitative or mixed methods study.

Part VI. Analyzing and Interpreting Data (Chapters 14 and 15)

This section explains descriptive and inferential statistics in a way that is both rigorous and fully accessible to students with no prior background in statistics. The descriptive statistics chapter explains the graphic representation of data, measures of central tendency, measures of variability, measures of relationship between variables, and effect size indicators. The inferential statistics chapter explains how researchers obtain estimates of population characteristics based on sample data and how researchers conduct statistical hypothesis testing. In an effort to connect design and analysis, the appropriate statistical tests for the experimental and quasi-experimental research designs covered in earlier chapters are discussed. The student will also learn how to present the results of significance tests using APA style.

Part VII. Writing the Research Report (Chapter 16)

In this final section, we explain the basics of writing a professional, informative, and accurate research manuscript that can be submitted for publication. The guidelines from the latest edition of the *Publication Manual of the American Psychological Association* are explained.

Pedagogical Features

The pedagogical features incorporated in the 10th edition have been retained in the 11th edition. Each chapter has a concept map that presents the main concepts and ideas that are discussed. This is followed by a short vignette that illustrates a main topic discussed in the chapter. The vignettes are taken from current events reported in newspapers or magazines not only to illustrate the chapter topic but also to demonstrate to the student that real events are related to the material they are to learn in the chapter. Each chapter highlights important terms and concepts and includes definitions of these in the chapter margins. These terms and concepts are highlighted not only to point out to students that they are important but also to increase the ease with which students can learn these terms and concepts. Study questions are spaced throughout each chapter to help students review the material after they have finished reading a section; this feedback system will assist students in learning the material and assessing whether they understand the material. Each chapter ends with several learning aids. First, a summary of the material, a list of the key terms, and a set of useful Internet sites are provided. Next, to help students access their knowledge of the chapter material, a Practice Test is provided at the end of each chapter. These tests include several multiple choice questions that students can use to assess their knowledge of the chapter material. The Practice Test is followed by a set of Challenge Exercises; these are designed to provide students with exposure to and experiences with activities required in the conduct of a research study.

In addition to the pedagogical aids included in the book, there is an accompanying Web site maintained by Allyn & Bacon. This Web site includes many materials and activities that will further assist the student in learning the material. Included on the Web site are flash cards for each of the highlighted chapter terms, a practice examination, and answers to the study questions included in the chapters.

New to the Eleventh Edition

Many important changes have been made to the 11th edition. Some were suggested by external reviewers, and many were made in an attempt to expand the book's coverage. The primary changes made are as follows:

1. Many of the previous chapters have been shortened and made a little simpler. An attempt was made to do this without sacrificing the book's well-known rigor.

2. A new chapter is included on quantitative and mixed methods research.

3. A new chapter is included on survey research.

4. A new chapter is included on measurement and sampling.

5. There are two new chapters on statistics: one focuses on descriptive statistics and the other on inferential statistics.

6. The chapter on writing the research report incorporates the material from the most recent sixth edition of the APA *Publication Manual*. This chapter also includes a more recent and shorter sample research article demonstrating the APA guidelines.

Acknowledgments

As with all previous editions, we offer our sincere appreciation and gratitude to our editor and all of our reviewers. Jeff Marshall was our editor, and our reviewers for this edition included the following:

John Vessey, Wheaton College
Daniel McElwreath, William Patterson University
Judith Horowitz, Medaille College
Tammy Zacchilli, Saint Leo University
Nicholas Palomares, University of California, Davis
Trellis Jones, Bowie State University
Sandra Trafalis, San Jose State University
Eileen Anderson, Virginia Tech
Melanie Deckert Pelton, University of West Florida

CHAPTER

Introduction to Scientific Research

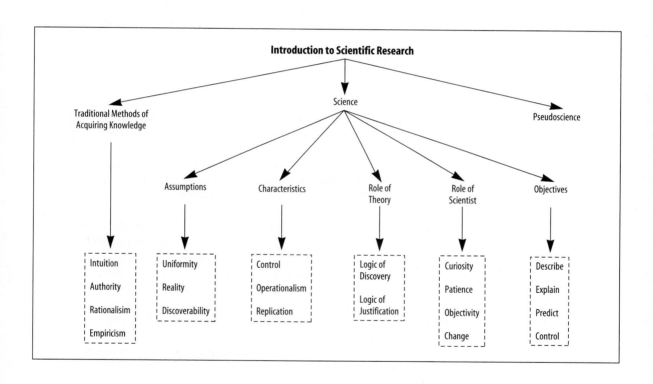

On July 5, 1998, the *Los Angeles Daily News* ran an article under the headline "Handwriting Analyst Reads Human Nature." In this article, Sheila Lowe, a handwriting analyst for 31 years, stated that "you are what you write." According to Ms. Lowe, handwriting always tells the truth because it is a projective behavior that reflects all the experiences of a person's life. Lowe has gained considerable attention for her comments to the media on criminal and civil trials such as the O. J. Simpson trial and the JonBenet Ramsey murder case. She has even appeared on NBC's *Unsolved*

Mysteries. She states that when she analyzes handwriting, she tries to focus on small details, such as how Ts are crossed, as well as the larger picture, such as the arrangement and balance on the page and whether anything stands out. From a handwriting analysis of individuals such as former president Bill Clinton and Elvis Presley, she drew the following conclusions. "Bill Clinton is a combination of strength and flexibility. He can stand firm and build a consensus." Elvis Presley's handwriting indicated that he was in ill-health and depressed.

Is there anything to handwriting analysis? Are you what you write, as claimed by Ms. Lowe? It would be wonderful if we could tell what a person was like just from analyzing a sample of an individual's handwriting. There are, however, many skeptics of handwriting analysis. Handwriting analysis has typically been criticized by scientists as something akin to fortune-telling and palm reading. In spite of this, some individuals and companies are turning to individuals such as Ms. Lowe to assist them in identifying desirable employees and in providing guidance in child rearing. Law enforcement agencies have employed her to assist in background investigations, as have individuals involved in romantic entanglements. Ms. Lowe has even sold a computer program that analyzes handwriting because of the demand for her services.

There seems to be little question that there is an interest in handwriting analysis. The important question is whether handwriting analysis really does provide a window into the personality of an individual. Obviously many individuals think it does because they use it in making some very important decisions. But how do we know for sure? In order to determine if handwriting analysis can provide an accurate and reliable assessment of personality, we must conduct a scientific study. You might wonder how something that seems as subjective as handwriting analysis can be scientifically investigated. Many people do not understand the nature of a scientific investigation or the need to conduct such an investigation in situations like this. This lack of understanding might be because scientists are often conceptualized as people in white coats who work in a laboratory, conducting experiments on complex theories that are far beyond the comprehension of the average person. Actually studying the validity of something like handwriting analysis seems very mysterious. This is probably because the actual process by which scientists uncover the mysteries of the universe eludes many people. It is as if the research process were encompassed in a shroud of secrecy and could be revealed only to the scientist. Research, however, is not a mysterious phenomenon! Rather, it is a very logical, creative, and rigorous set of methods for obtaining facts and making warranted generalizations.

Introduction

In our daily lives, we continually encounter problems and questions relating to thoughts and behavior. For example, one person might have a tremendous fear of taking tests. Others might have problems with alcoholism or drug abuse or problems in their marriage. People who encounter such problems typically want to eliminate them, but often need help. Consequently, they seek out professionals, such as psychologists, to help them remediate such difficulties. Likewise, business professionals might enlist the assistance of psychologists in understanding the thinking and behavior of others. For example, salespeople differ greatly in their ability to understand customers and sell merchandise. One car salesperson might be capable of selling twice as many cars as another salesperson. If the sales manager could discover why such differences in ability exist, he or she might be able to develop either better training programs or more effective criteria for selecting the sales force.

In an attempt to gain information about mental processes and behavior, people turn to the field of psychology. As you should know by now, a great deal of knowledge about information processing and the behavior of multiple types of organisms has been accumulated. We have knowledge that enables us to treat problems such as test anxiety and depression. Similarly, we have identified many of the variables influencing persuasion and aggression. Although we know a great deal about mental processes and behavior, there is still much to be learned. In order to learn more about such psychological phenomena, we must engage in scientific research.

The course in which you are now enrolled will provide you with information about conducting scientific research. Some students might feel that understanding research is important only for professional scientists. But, as Table 1.1 reveals, there are many reasons why students should take a research methods course. One reason identified in Table 1.1 is to help students become more informed and critical consumers of information. We are all bombarded by the results of scientific and pseudoscientific research, and we all need tools to interpret what is being reported. For example, saccharin has been demonstrated to cause cancer in laboratory animals, yet there are many people who consume saccharin and do not contract cancer. You as a consumer must be able to resolve these discrepancies in order to decide whether or not you are going to eat foods containing saccharin. Similarly, television commercials often make claims of "scientific proof" regarding the effectiveness of their products. First of all, science does not provide "proof" for general laws; instead, it provides evidence, often very strong evidence. Second, upon closer examination, almost all of the "scientific tests" reported in television commercials would likely be shown to be flawed.

TABLE 1.1
Reasons for Taking a Research Methods Course

- Learn how to conduct psychological research.
- Provides a foundation for topic-specific courses such as abnormal, social, cognitive, biopsychology, and developmental psychology.
- Can be a more informed and critical consumer of information.
- Helps develop critical and analytical thinking.
- Provides information needed to critically read a research article.
- Necessary for admission into most graduate programs in psychology.

Methods of Acquiring Knowledge

There are many procedures by which we obtain information about a given phenomenon or situation. We acquire a great deal of information from the events we experience as we go through life. Experts also provide us with much information. We will briefly discuss four ways by which we acquire knowledge, and then we will discuss the scientific approach to acquiring knowledge. You should be able to see that each successive approach represents a more acceptable means of acquiring knowledge. You will also see that although the earlier approaches do not systematically contribute to the accumulation of scientific knowledge, they are used in the scientific process. The scientific approach is a very special hybrid approach to generating and justifying knowledge claims and to accumulating this knowledge over time.

Intuition

Intuition
An approach to acquiring knowledge that is not based on a known reasoning process

Intuition is the first approach to acquiring knowledge that we examine. *Webster's Third New International Dictionary* defines intuition as "the act or process of coming to direct knowledge or certainty without reasoning or inferring." Such psychics as Edgar Cayce seem to have derived their knowledge from intuition. The predictions and descriptions made by psychics are not based on any known reasoning or inferring process; therefore, such knowledge would appear to be intuitive. Intuition relies on justification such as "it feels true to me" or "I believe this point, although I can't really tell you why." The problem with the intuitive approach is that it does not provide a mechanism for separating accurate from inaccurate knowledge.

The use of intuition is sometimes used in science (Polanyi & Sen, 2009), and it is probably seen most readily in the process of forming hypotheses. Although most scientific hypotheses are derived from prior research, some hypotheses arise from hunches and new ways of looking at the literature. You might, for example, think that women are better at assessing the quality of a relationship than are men. This belief might have been derived from things others told you, your own experience, or any of a variety of other factors. Somehow you put together prior experience and other sources of information to arrive at this belief. If someone asked you why you held this belief, you probably could not identify the relevant factors—you might instead say it was based on your intuition. From a scientific perspective, this intuition could be molded into a hypothesis and tested. A scientific research study could be designed to determine whether women are better at assessing the quality of a relationship than are men.

Authority

Authority
A basis for acceptance of information, because it is acquired from a highly respected source

Authority as an approach to acquiring knowledge represents an acceptance of information or facts stated by another because that person is a highly respected source. For example, on July 4, 1936, the Central Committee of the Communist Party of the Soviet Union issued a "Decree Against Pedology" (Woodworth & Sheehan, 1964), which, among other things, outlawed the use of standardized tests in schools. Because no one had the right to question such a decree, the need to eliminate standardized tests had to be accepted as fact. The problem with the authority approach is that the information or facts stated by the authority might be inaccurate.

If the authority approach dictates that we accept whatever is decreed, how can this approach be used in science? In the beginning stages of the research process, when the problem is being identified and the hypothesis is being formed, a scientist might consult someone who is considered "the" authority in the area to assess the probability that the hypothesis is one that is testable and addresses an important research question. Virtually every area of endeavor has a leading proponent who is considered the authority or expert on a given topic. This is the person who has the most information on a given topic.

Although authority plays a part in the development of hypotheses, it is not without its problems. A person who is perceived as an authority can be incorrect. For example, Key (1980) has been a major proponent of the claim that advertisers resort to "subliminal advertising" to influence public buying and has been perceived by some as being the authority on this topic. He has stated, for instance, that implicitly sexual associations in advertisements enhance memorability. Fortunately, such claims by authority figures are subject to assessment by research studies. The claims made by Key (1980) are readily testable and were tested by Vokey and Read (1985) in their study of subliminal messages. Vokey and Read demonstrated that Key's claims were unfounded.

Authority is also used in the design stage of a study. If you are unsure of how to design a study to test a specific variable, you might call someone who is considered an authority in the area and get his or her input. Similarly, if you have collected data on a given topic and you are not sure how to interpret the data or how they fit with the other data in the field, you might consult with someone who is considered an authority in the area and obtain input. As you can see, the authority approach is used in research. However, an authority is an expert whose facts and information are subject to testing using the scientific process.

Rationalism

Rationalism
The acquisition of knowledge through reasoning

A third approach to gaining knowledge is **rationalism**. This approach uses reasoning to arrive at knowledge and assumes that valid knowledge is acquired if the correct reasoning process is used. During the sixteenth century, rationalism was assumed to be the dominant mode by which one could arrive at truth. In fact, it was believed that knowledge derived from reason was just as valid as, and often superior to, knowledge gained from observation. Its leading advocate was the philosopher René Descartes (1596–1650). Descartes, who famously claimed, "I think, therefore I am", argued that "clear and distinct ideas" must be true, and from those foundational ideas one should deduce all other beliefs. One danger of relying solely on rationalism for acquiring knowledge is that it is not unusual for two well-meaning and honest individuals to reach different conclusions.

This does not mean that science does not use reasoning or rationalism. In fact, reasoning is a vital element in the scientific process. Scientists make use of reasoning not only to derive some hypotheses but also to identify the outcomes that would indicate the truth or falsity of the hypotheses. Mathematics, which is a type of rationalism, is used extensively in many areas of science such as physics. There is also a well-developed line of research in mathematical psychology. In short, rationalism can be very important for science, but by itself it is insufficient.

Empiricism

Empiricism
The acquisition of knowledge through experience

A fourth approach to gaining knowledge is through **empiricism**. In its naïve form, this approach would say, "If I have experienced something, then it is valid and true." Therefore, facts that concur with experience are accepted, and those that do not are rejected. This approach was used by some individuals in the 1960s who stated that satanic messages were included on some records. These individuals had played the records backward and had heard messages such as "Oh Satan, move in our voices." Because these individuals had actually listened to the records and heard the messages, this information seemed to be irrefutable. Therefore, naïve empiricism can be problematic; however, empiricism in its more realistic form can be very useful, and, as you will see, it is an important part of the scientific approach.

Empiricism as a systematic and well-developed philosophy is traced to John Locke (1632–1704) and David Hume (1711–1776). These philosophers argued that virtually all knowledge is based on experience. Locke put it well when he claimed that each person is born a *tabula rasa* (i.e., individuals' minds are blank slates or tablets upon which the environment or nature writes). The *origin* of all knowledge is from our senses (sight, hearing, touch, smell, and taste). Our senses imprint ideas in our brains that then are further worked upon (combined, related) through cognitive processes. The early system of psychology known as associationism arose out of empiricist philosophy, and one might view it as the first "school of psychology" (Heidbreder, 1933). Although the empirical approach is very appealing and has much to recommend it, several dangers exist if it is used alone. Our perceptions are affected by a number of variables. Research has demonstrated that such variables as past experiences and our motivations at the time of perceiving can drastically alter what we see. Research has also revealed that our memory for events does not remain constant. Not only do we tend to forget things, but at times an actual distortion of memory might take place.

Empiricism is probably the most obvious approach that is used in science. Science is based on observation, and empiricism refers to the observation of a given phenomenon. The scientific studies investigating the satanic messages that supposedly existed when certain records were played backward made use of the same empirical observations as did the unscientific approach. Greenwald (mentioned in Vokey & Read, 1985), for example, played records backward and asked people to hear for themselves the satanic messages that appeared on the records. In doing so, Greenwald relied on empiricism to convince the listeners that satanic messages were actually on the records. Scientific studies such as those conducted by Vokey and Read (1985) and Thorne and Himelstein (1984) make use of the same type of data. These studies also ask people to identify what they hear on records played backward. The difference is the degree of objectivity that is systematically imposed on the observation. Greenwald proposed to the listeners that the source of the messages was Satan or an evil-minded producer, thereby generating an expectation of the type of message that might exist on the records. In science, researchers avoid setting up such an expectation unless the purpose of the study is to test such an expectation. Vokey and Read (1985), for example, used religious as well as meaningless passages played backward and asked participants to try to identify messages. These research participants were not, however, informed of the probable source of the messages. Interestingly, Vokey and Read discovered that messages were identified in both meaningless and religious passages played backward, and subjects found that some of these messages had satanic suggestions.

Empiricism is a vital element in science, but in science, empirical observations must be conducted under controlled conditions and systematic strategies must be used to minimize researcher bias and to maximize objectivity. The later chapters in this book will carefully explain how to carry out empirical research that is scientific and, therefore, reliable and trustworthy.

STUDY QUESTION 1.1 | **Explain each of the approaches to acquiring knowledge and how these methods are used in science.**

Science

Science
The most trustworthy way of acquiring reliable and valid knowledge about the natural world

The word *science* had its ancient origins in the Latin verb *scire*, meaning "to know." However, the English word "science," with its current meaning, was not coined until the nineteenth century by William Whewell (1794–1866). Before that time, scientists were called "natural philosophers" (Yeo, 2003). **Science** is a very important way of acquiring knowledge. Although it is a hybrid of the forms discussed earlier, it is superior in the sense that it is designed to systematically produce reliable and valid knowledge about the natural world. One might think that there is only one method by which scientific knowledge is acquired. While this is a logical thought, Proctor and Capaldi (2001) have pointed out that different scientific methods have been popular at different points in time. That's because science continues to develop and improve all the time. We now take a brief historical tour of scientific methods.

Induction and Deduction

Induction
A reasoning process that involves going from the specific to the general

As classically defined by Aristotle (384–322 BCE), **induction** is a reasoning process that involves going from the specific to the general.[1] For example, if on a visit to a daycare center you see several children hitting and kicking other children, you might infer that many children in that center are aggressive or even infer that children in daycare centers across the country tend to be aggressive. This inference is

[1]In the philosophy of logic, induction and deduction have slightly different meanings from what is presented here. In philosophy of logic, inductive reasoning refers to drawing of a conclusion that is probably true, and valid deductive reasoning refers to the drawing of a conclusion that is necessarily true if the premises are true (Copi & Cohen, 2005).

an example of induction, because you moved from the particular observations to a much broader and general claim. Induction was the dominant scientific method used from the late seventeenth century to about the middle of the nineteenth century (Proctor & Capaldi, 2001). It was during this time that scientific advances were made by careful observation of phenomena with the intent to arrive at correct generalizations. Both Francis Bacon (1561–1626) and Isaac Newton (1642–1727) advocated this approach. Newton, for example, has stated that "principles deduced from phenomena and made general by induction, *represent* (italics ours) the highest evidence that a proposition can have . . . " (Thayer, 1953, p. 6).

While induction is not the primary scientific method used today, it is still used very frequently in science. For example, Latané (1981) observed that people do not exert as much effort in a group as they do when working alone and inferred that this represented the construct of social loafing. When Latané made this generalization of social loafing from the specific observation that less effort was expended in a group, he was engaged in inductive reasoning. Inductive reasoning is also seen in the use of statistical analysis in psychological research. When researchers rely on samples and generalize to populations, they are using inductive reasoning. Inductive reasoning is, therefore, an integral part of science. It is not, however, the only reasoning process used in science. Deductive reasoning is also used.

Deduction
A reasoning process that involves going from the general to the specific

Deduction, as classically defined by Aristotle, refers to going from the general to the specific. For example, Levine (2000) predicted that a person who views the group's task as important and does not expect others to contribute adequately to the group's performance will work harder. Here, Levine was logically moving from the general proposition of social loafing and deducing a specific set of events that would reduce social loafing. Specifically, Levine deduced that viewing the group's task as important and not expecting others to contribute adequately would cause a person to work harder or counter the social loafing effect. Today, when researchers develop hypotheses, they routinely deduce the observable consequences that must occur if they are going to claim (after collecting data) that the hypothesis is supported or not supported. As mentioned earlier, deduction is also routinely used in mathematical psychology.

Science, therefore, makes use of *both* inductive and deductive thinking. However, neither of these approaches represents the only or primary approach to current science.

Hypothesis Testing

Hypothesis testing
The process of testing a predicted relationship or hypothesis by making observations and then comparing the observed facts with the hypothesis or predicted relationship

Hypothesis testing refers to a process by which an investigator formulates a hypothesis to explain some phenomenon that has been observed and then compares the hypothesis with the facts. Around 1850, induction was considered to be inadequate for the task of creating good scientific theories. Scientists and philosophers suggested that hypothesis testing should be formally added to induction as the appropriate scientific method (Proctor & Capaldi, 2001). According to Whewell (1847/1967), "The process of scientific discovery is cautious and rigorous, not by abstaining from hypothesis, but by rigorously comparing hypothesis with facts, and by resolutely rejecting all which the comparison does not confirm" (p. 468). According to this approach, scientific activity involves the testing of hypotheses derived from theory or experience. Whewell suggested that science should focus on the confirmation of predictions derived from theory and experience.

Proctor and Capaldi (2001) argue that the era of hypothesis testing extended from approximately 1850 to about 1960. However, an examination of the psychological research literature shows that hypothesis testing has been, and still is, a very important part of scientific activity in psychology. For example, Fuller, Luck, McMahon, and Gold (2005) investigated cognitive impairments in schizophrenic patients. They hypothesized that schizophrenics' working memory representation would be abnormally fragile, making them prone to being disrupted by distracting stimuli. They then designed a study to collect data that would test the adequacy of this hypothesis.

Hypothesis testing as a scientific methodology was associated with the logical positivist movement. **Logical positivism** was the outgrowth of a group of scholars at the University of Vienna with a scientific background and a philosophical bent. This group became known as the Vienna Circle and espoused a logical positivism philosophical position (Miller, 1999). One of the central views of the Vienna Circle was that a statement is meaningful only when it is verifiable by observation or experience. Logical positivists believed that the most important aspect of science was the verification of hypotheses by objective observation or experience. Logical positivist Moritz Schlick (1882–1936) said in 1934 "Science makes prophecies that are tested by 'experience' " (in Ayer, 1959, p. 221). For the logical positivists, hypothesis testing was an inductive approach that moved from experiential "facts" (i.e., from particulars) to general propositions. They ultimately hoped to show that the natural world followed scientific laws.

Although logical positivism had many supporters, it was also criticized. One of the most severe critics was the philosopher of science Karl Popper (1902–1994). Popper pointed out that the (inductive) verification approach of the logical positivists was based on a logical fallacy (known as affirming the consequent). To fix this "error," Popper argued that science should rest on a deductively valid form of reasoning (1968). One can claim conclusively using deductive reasoning that a general law is falsified if the data do not support the hypothesis, and this deductively valid approach is what Popper advocated. He argued that science should focus on stating bold hypotheses followed by attempts to falsify them. Popper's approach is known as **falsificationism**.

A major strength of Popper's approach is that it helps eliminate false theories from science. However, Popper's approach also was criticized because it focused *only* on falsification and completely rejected induction. Popper stated "There is no induction; we never argue from facts to theories, unless by way of refutation or 'falsification' " (Popper, 1974, p. 68). Unfortunately for Popper, induction is required in order to claim what theories are supported and what theories we should believe. Popper's approach was also criticized because even if the data appear to falsify a hypothesis, one still cannot conclude that the theory is necessarily false. That's because many assumptions have to be made during the hypothesis testing process, and one of those assumptions might have been false rather than the hypothesis. This idea that a hypothesis cannot be tested in

Logical positivism
A philosophical approach that focused on verifying hypotheses as the key criterion of science

Falsificationism
A deductive approach to science that focuses on falsifying hypotheses as the key criterion of science

Duhem–Quine principle
States that a hypothesis cannot be tested in isolation from other assumptions

isolation (i.e., without making additional assumptions) is called the **Duhem–Quine principle**. Today, psychologists rely on a hybrid approach to hypothesis testing that includes probabilistic thinking, preponderance of evidence, and a mixture of the logical positivists' verification approach *and* Popper's falsification approach. It is important to remember that hypothesis testing produces evidence but does not provide proof of psychological principles.

Naturalism

Naturalism
Position popular in behavioral science stating that science should justify its practices according to how well they work rather than according to philosophical arguments

Empirical adequacy
Present when theories and hypotheses closely fit empirical evidence

Since the 1960s we have entered a methodological era in science that has evolved from a movement in the philosophy of science called naturalism (Proctor & Capaldi, 2001). Naturalism rejects what is called *foundational epistemology*, which assumes that knowledge is a matter of deductive reasoning and that knowledge is fully certain, much like a mathematical or geometrical proof. Instead, **naturalism** takes the position that science should be studied and evaluated empirically, just like a science studies any other empirical phenomenon. Naturalism is a *pragmatic* philosophy of science that says scientists should believe what is shown to work. When it comes to judging scientific beliefs, naturalism says we should evaluate our theories based on their **empirical adequacy**. That is, do the empirical data support the theory, does the theory make accurate predictions, and does the theory provide a good causal explanation of the phenomenon that you are studying?

If you look at the history of science, you can see that scientific advances exhibit a structure that is not captured singularly by hypothesis testing or induction. Science uses many approaches that have been shown to be helpful to the advancement of valid and reliable knowledge. Naturalism takes a practical approach to methods and strategies. Next we briefly mention several historical influences since about 1960 that were precursors to today's scientific naturalism.

Normal science
The period in which scientific activity is governed and directed by a single paradigm

Paradigm
A framework of thought or beliefs by which reality is interpreted

Revolutionary science
A period in which scientific activity is characterized by the replacement of one paradigm with another

Kuhn and Paradigms   Thomas Kuhn (1922–1996) conducted a historical analysis of science and, in 1962, published his famous book *The Structure of Scientific Revolutions*. His research suggested that science reflects two types of activities: normal science and revolutionary science. **Normal science** is governed by a single paradigm or a set of concepts, values, perceptions, and practices shared by a community that forms a particular view of reality. A **paradigm**, therefore, is a framework of thought or beliefs by which you interpret reality. Mature sciences spend most of their time in "normal science." However, over time anomalies and criticisms develop, and **revolutionary science** occurs. During this more brief period (compared to normal science), the old paradigm is replaced by a new paradigm. Replacement of one paradigm with another is a significant event because the belief system that governs the current view of reality is replaced with a new set of beliefs. After a revolutionary period, science enters a new period of normal science, and this process, according to Kuhn, has continued throughout history.

Lakatos and Research Programs   Another philosopher of science named Imre Lakatos (1922–1974) took an approach similar to that of Kuhn by attempting to

Research program

Lakatos's term for a paradigm. It includes a set of "hard-core" beliefs and an outer "protective belt" of additional beliefs

portray scientific activity as taking place within a framework. Kuhn labeled this framework a paradigm, but Lakatos coined the phrase **research program** to represent this framework (Lakatos, 1970). According to Lakatos, a research program involves a succession of theories that are linked by a set of *hard-core* beliefs; this is in contrast to Kuhn who saw each paradigm being replaced by an entirely new paradigm. For example, one of the core principles of the Copernican program was that the earth and the planets orbit a stationary sun. Lakatos's hard-core beliefs or principles are the defining characteristics of a research program, but a research program also includes a *protective belt* of additional beliefs, principles, assumptions, and so on. Lakatos argued that scientists would not allow the hard-core principles to be falsified as Popper had assumed; Lakatos argued that when a hard-core hypothesis is not supported, the researcher would simply modify something in the protective belt. This certainly makes it very difficult for a theory to be falsified or rejected.

A development within the field of psychology of learning provides an example of what Kuhn would have called paradigms and Lakatos would have called research programs. In the early 1930s, a "mechanistic" paradigm or research program had developed in the psychology of learning. The basic set of concepts and beliefs or the fundamental principle of this mechanistic view was that learning is achieved through the conditioning and extinction of specific stimulus–response pairs. The organism is reactive in that learning occurs as a result of the application of an external force known as a reinforcer.

A competing paradigm at this time was an "organismic" paradigm or research program. The basic set of concepts and beliefs or the fundamental principles of the organismic view were that learning is achieved through the testing of rules or hypotheses and organisms are active rather than reactive. Change or learning occurs by some internal transformation such as would be advocated by Gestalt theory, information processing, or cognitive psychology (Gholson & Barker, 1985). Piaget's theory of child development is an example of the organismic view. Other paradigms, research programs, or research traditions (Laudan, 1977) in psychology include associationism, behaviorism, cognitive psychology, and neuropsychology.

Feyerabend's Anarchistic Theory of Science   Paul Feyerabend (1924–1994) was a philosopher of science who looked at the various methodological approaches to science that had been advocated and was not surprised to see that each had been criticized and was lacking. For example, both the verification approach advocated by the logical positivists and the falsification approach advocated by Popper floundered because of the logical problems mentioned earlier. As a result of the failure to identify any single distinguishing characteristic of science, Feyerabend (1975) argued that there is no such thing as the method of science. According to him, science has many methods. Most psychologists would argue, however, that Feyerabend went too far when he claimed that the single unchanging principle of scientific method is that "anything goes." Feyerabend also argued that science included many irrational practices and was partially the result of the operation of power. He concluded that scientific knowledge was not nearly as secure as scientists would have the public believe. As you can see, Feyerabend offered a relatively severe critique of normal science. Perhaps the key conclusion to draw from his critique is that science might not be as simple and formulaic as it sometimes is made to appear. In short, it is true that scientific practice includes many complexities. Nonetheless, in this book, we will do our best to explain some of the complexities and provide a clear explanation of the current best practices in psychological research.

What Exactly Is Science?

Philosophers have, for many years, been trying to provide an exact demarcation of science from nonscience. The logical positivists had hoped verificationism would be the criterion. They also hoped a single, universal method could be identified. Popper claimed the criterion was falsificationism (i.e., only scientists attempted to falsify hypotheses). For Kuhn, it was the values, interactions, and activities of scientists that identified science. Some philosophers of science seek a relatively secure basis for science in experimentation or what Robert Ackermann (1989) calls "the new experimentalism." According to this approach, experimentation can have a life of its own independent of theory, and scientific progress is seen as the steady buildup of experimental knowledge (Chalmers, 1999) or knowledge acquired from experimentation. In many ways, the experiment is the strongest and best of the scientific methods. It is probably better to conclude, however, that the multiple methods and practices used by the many highly trained scientists can contribute in complementary ways to the development of secure scientific knowledge.

As you can see, there is no perfect definition of science that applies to every part of every field in science (e.g., physics, psychology, or molecular biology). Science just does not seem to run according to a *single* set of fixed and universal rules or activities. Identifying a single rule or activity probably would be detrimental to science because it would neglect the complex character of science; it also would make it less adaptable and more dogmatic. Still, one needs a working definition of science. According to Chalmers, "a science will consist of some specific aims to arrive at knowledge of some specific kind, methods for arriving at those aims together with the standards for judging the extent to which they have been met, and specific facts and theories that represent the current state of play as far as the realization of the aim is concerned" (Chalmers, 1999, p. 168). This is consistent with our view of science as the preferred way of acquiring reliable, valid, and practical knowledge about the natural world, but to continue to be successful, it must always practice research ethically, must critically self-examine its practices to determine what is working and what is not working, and must engage in ongoing learning and improvement. If science does this, scientific knowledge also will continue to advance.

STUDY QUESTIONS 1.2

- **What is science, and how have the methods of science changed over time?**
- **What is the difference between induction and deduction?**
- **What is naturalism?**
- **What are the similarities between Kuhn's and Lakatos's approach to science?**
- **Why has Feyerabend argued that there is no such thing as a method of science?**

Basic Assumptions Underlying Scientific Research

In order for scientists to have confidence in the capacity of scientific research to achieve solutions to questions and problems, they make several working assumptions so that they can get on with the day-to-day practice of science.

Uniformity or Regularity in Nature

Determinism
The belief that mental processes and behaviors are fully caused by prior natural factors

Probabilistic causes
A weaker form of determinism that indicates regularities that usually but not always occur

Science searches for regularities in nature. If there were no uniformity or regularity, science would only amount to a historical description of unrelated facts. B. F. Skinner (1904–1990) put it well when he stated that science is "a search for order, for uniformities, for lawful relations among the events in nature" (1953, p. 13). If there were no uniformity in nature, there could be no understanding, explanation, or knowledge about nature. Without regularity, we could not develop theories or laws or generalizations. Implicit in the assumption of uniformity is the notion of a rather strong form of **determinism**—the belief that there are causes, or determinants, of mental processes and behavior. In our efforts to uncover the laws of psychology, we attempt to identify the variables that are linked together. What we have found thus far are **probabilistic causes** (i.e., causes that usually produce outcomes), but the search for more certain, fuller causation will continue. We construct experiments that attempt to establish the determinants of events. Once we have determined the events or conditions that usually produce a given outcome, we have uncovered probabilistic causes.

Reality in Nature

Reality in nature
The assumption that the things we see, hear, feel, smell, and taste are real

A related assumption is that there is **reality in nature**. For example, as we go through our daily lives we see, hear, feel, smell, and taste things that are real, and these experiences are real. We assume that other people, objects, or social events like marriage or divorce are not *just* creations of our imagination, and we assume that many different types of "objects" can be studied scientifically. Stating that something is true or real because we say it is real does not work in science. In science, researchers check the reality in many ways to obtain objective evidence that what is claimed is actually true. In short, researchers interact with a natural world (that includes social objects such as attitudes, beliefs, institutions), and this reality must have primary say in our claims about reality and truth. This is why we collect data. Again, science makes the assumption that there is an underlying reality, and it attempts to uncover this reality.

Discoverability

Discoverability
The assumption that it is possible to discover the regularities that exist in nature

Scientists believe not only that there is regularity and reality in nature but also that there is **discoverability**—that is, it is possible to discover the regularities and reality. This does not mean that the task of discovering the regularities will be simple. Nature is very reluctant to reveal its secrets. Scientists have been working on discovering the cause and cure for cancer for decades. Although significant progress has been made, we still do not know the exact cause of all forms of cancer or the contributors to the development of cancer. Similarly, a complete cure for cancer still does not exist. An intensive effort is also taking place within the scientific community to identify a cure for AIDS. However, scientists have yet to fully uncover nature's secrets in this arena.

The intensive effort that has existed to uncover the cause of such diseases as cancer and AIDS or, within the field of psychology, such disorders as schizophrenia and depression reveals one of the basic processes of research. The research process is similar to putting a puzzle together: You have all the pieces of the puzzle in front of you, which you try to put together to get the overall picture. Scientific research includes the difficult task of first discovering the pieces of the puzzle. Each study conducted on a given problem has the potential of uncovering a piece of the puzzle. Only when each of these pieces has been discovered is it possible for someone to put them together to enable us to see the total picture. Consequently, discoverability incorporates two components: The first is discovery of the pieces of the puzzle, and the second is putting the pieces together, or discovery of the nature of the total picture.

Characteristics of Scientific Research

We have argued that science is the preferred way to obtain reliable and valid knowledge about the natural world. In order to produce reliable and justified knowledge, the scientific process relies on several important characteristics. Three of the most important characteristics of scientific research are control, operationalism, and replication.

Control

Control
Elimination of the influence of extraneous variables

Control refers to holding constant or eliminating the influence of extraneous variables so that an unambiguous claim about cause and effect can be made. One of the most important tasks of the psychological researcher is to identify causal relationships, and without control for extraneous variables, this is not possible. It is important that you remember this point: experiments are the preferred research method whenever you need to address the issue of cause and effect. Experiments are conducted in an attempt to answer questions, such as why forgetting occurs, what reduces the symptoms of schizophrenia, or what treatment is most effective for depression. In order to provide unambiguous answers to such questions, researchers must rely on control.

Placebo Effect
Improvement due to partcipants' expections for improvement rather than the actual treatment

For example, when testing the effectiveness of a new drug on depressive symptomology, researchers must control for participants' expectations that the drug will help their symptoms. That's because in some cases, participants will experience improvement in symptoms as a result of thinking that they have received a useful treatment, even when the treatment condition has no value (e.g., a sugar pill). This type of improvement is referred to as the **placebo effect**. Therefore, well-designed experiments testing the effectiveness of new drugs include a control condition where participants receive a treatment in which the "drug" looks like the actual drug, when in fact it does not have the active ingredient of the new drug. If participants receiving the real drug report more improvement than participants receiving the placebo, the researcher can be more confident that the new drug is the actual cause of the improvement. Without the control condition, the researcher would not know whether the cause of the improvement was the drug or the placebo effect.

Operationalism

Operationalism
Representing constructs by a specific set of operations

The principle of **operationalism** was originally set forth by the physicist Percy Bridgman (1882–1961). Bridgman (1927) argued that science must be specific and precise and that each concept must be defined by the steps or operations used to measure them. Length, for example, would be defined as nothing more than the set of operations by which it was measured. If length was measured with a ruler or tape measure graded in terms of inches, length would be defined as a specific number of inches. If length was measured with a ruler or tape measure graded in terms of centimeters, length would be defined as a specific number of centimeters. This type of definition came to be known as an **operational definition**. Operational definitions were initially embraced by research psychologists because they seemed to provide the desired level of specificity and precision. However, using a strict operational definition of psychological concepts didn't last long because of the limitations it imposed.

Operational definition
Defining a concept by the operations used to represent or measure it

One of the early criticisms of operational definitions was that their demands were too strict. For example, it would be virtually impossible to formulate a problem concerning the functional relationships among events. Instead of stating a relationship between hunger and selective perception, one would have to talk about the relationship between number of hours of food deprivation and inaccurate description of ambiguous stimuli presented for 500 milliseconds.

Another criticism was that a single operational definition could not completely specify the *meaning* of a term. Any change in the set of operations would specify a new concept, which would lead to a multiplicity of concepts. Such a strict operational definition notion suggests that there is no overlap among the operations—that, for example, there is no relationship among three different operational measures (responses to a questionnaire, galvanic skin response [GSR] readings, and heart rate change) of a concept such as anxiety.

Multiple operationalism
Using multiple measures to represent a construct

The prominent research methodologist Donald Campbell (1916–1996) criticized operational definitions on the grounds that any set of operations will always be incomplete (Campbell, 1988). For example, aggression has been defined in different research studies as honking of horns, hitting a BoBo doll, delivering electric shocks to another, and the force with which a pad is hit. However, none of these indicators represents a complete definition of aggression. Campbell suggested that a more accurate representation of a construct could be obtained by representing it in several different ways. The use of multiple measures of a construct is called **multiple operationalism**. An advantage of using several different operationalizations of a construct is that confidence in the result is increased if the findings across the different operationalizations are similar. Campbell (1988) also criticized the term *operational definition*. He recommended that the word "definition" be removed from "operational definition" and that researchers simply talk about constructs being *"operationalized"* rather than being literally *defined* by the operations. According to Campbell, an operational definition should be called an **operationalization**.

The criticisms presented do not mean that operationalism is not important. What is essential for science is that constructs are clearly and effectively represented by a specific set of operations, and this information must be provided when researchers publish their results. Consider the construct of "good car salesperson." How would you operationalize a good car salesperson? What empirical referents would you use to characterize this construct? In Figure 1.1, we suggest that these empirical referents might consist of selling many cars, pointing out a car's good features, helping the customer to find financing, and complimenting the customer on an excellent choice. Once such indicators have been clearly identified, meaning can be communicated with minimal ambiguity and maximum precision.

Operationalization
Campbell's term for an operational defintion

Replication

Replication
The reproduction of the results of a study in a new study

Scientific knowledge is greatly advanced by replication. **Replication** refers to the reproduction of the results obtained from one study in additional studies. It is important to remember this key point: Before you can trust the findings of a single research study, you must determine whether the observed results are reliable. You should always be cautious when interpreting findings from a single study in isolation from other research. To make a general claim, you must know whether the same results will be found if the study is repeated. If the observations are not repeatable, the observations were either due to chance or they operate differently in different contexts. If the variables of interest operate differently in different contexts, then contextual factors must be systematically examined in additional research.

Failure to replicate the results of a previous study can be interpreted in several ways because there are many possible reasons why it might occur. The first and most obvious possibility is that the results of the prior study were due entirely to chance, which means that the phenomenon that was previously identified did not really exist. If the phenomenon did not exist, it obviously cannot be reproduced in a replication study. The second reason is that the replication experiment

FIGURE 1.1
Example of an operationalization of a good car salesperson.

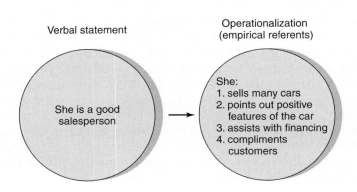

Verbal statement

She is a good salesperson

Operationalization (empirical referents)

She:
1. sells many cars
2. points out positive features of the car
3. assists with financing
4. compliments customers

might have altered some seemingly nonsignificant element of the experiment, and this element in turn produced an altered response on the part of the research participants. The third reason is that the relationship under investigation might vary across context. In this case, the initial finding does not apply in the new group, time, setting, and so on. For example, social psychological research on gender stereotypes has yielded different findings across the last four decades. These changes in findings (failures to replicate) are very informative.

Although the need for replication is accepted as a characteristic of scientific research, Campbell and Jackson (1979) have pointed out that an inconsistency exists between the acceptance of this characteristic and researchers' commitment to actually conduct replication research. Few researchers conduct exact replication research, primarily because it is difficult to publish such studies. Nonetheless, partial replication of research is readily produced when the key variables are included in multiple research studies. The results of this sort of replication are frequently reported in **meta-analysis** research. Meta-analysis is a quantitative technique that is used to integrate and describe the relationships between variables across multiple research studies. Earlier we noted that you should not place too much trust in the findings of a single research study. You should, however, place significant trust in the results of a meta-analysis because the finding is shown to apply across multiple related research studies. Whenever you review the research literature on a topic of interest, you should be sure to search for meta-analysis research studies!

Meta-analysis
A quantitative technique for describing the relationship between variables across multiple research studies

STUDY QUESTION 1.3

List and define the characteristics of scientific research. Then, explain why each is a characteristic of the research process.

The Role of Theory in Scientific Research

Use of the research process in making objective observations is essential to the accumulation of a highly reliable set of facts. Accumulating such a body of facts, however, is not sufficient to answer many of the riddles of human nature. For example, research has revealed that individuals who are paid less than someone else for doing the same job are more likely to get angry and upset than workers who feel they are fairly compensated. Research has also shown that increases in pay are associated with increases in job satisfaction. Once facts such as these have been accumulated through the use of the research process, they must somehow be integrated and summarized to provide more adequate explanations of psychological phenomena. This is one of the roles that theory plays in the scientific enterprise. Equity theory, for example, summarized and integrated a large portion of the data related to the notion of fairness and justice to provide a more adequate explanation of interpersonal interactions. A **theory** helps to explain how and why a pheonomenon operates as it does.

Theories are not created just to summarize and integrate existing data, however. A good theory must also suggest new hypotheses that are capable of being

Theory
An explanation of how and why something operates

FIGURE 1.2
Illustration of the relationship between theory and research.

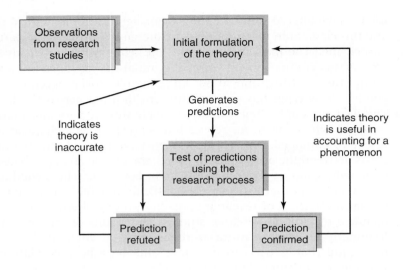

tested empirically. Consequently, a theory must have the capacity to guide research as well as to summarize the results of previous research. This means that there is a constant interaction between theory and empirical observation, as illustrated in Figure 1.2. From this figure you can see that theory is originally based on empirical observations obtained from research; this is called the **logic or context of discovery;** it's the inductive part of science. Once the theory has been generated, it must direct future research; this is called the **logic or context of justification;** it's the deductive part of science where predictions are derived and empirically tested. The outcome of the future research then feeds back and determines the usefulness of the theory, and this process continues again and again. If the predictions of the theory are confirmed by subsequent research, evidence exists that the theory is useful in accounting for a given phenomenon. If the predictions are refuted by subsequent research, the theory has been demonstrated to be inaccurate and must either be revised so as to account for the experimental data or be thrown out. In short, Figure 1.2 shows that theory *generation* and theory *testing* are valuable parts of the scientific enterprise.

Logic of discovery
The inductive or discovery part of the scientific process

Logic of justification
The deductive or theory-testing part of the scientific process

STUDY QUESTIONS 1.4

- **List the basic assumptions of scientific research, and explain why these assumptions are needed.**
- **Explain the role theory plays in scientific research.**

The Role of the Scientist in Psychological Research

One very significant component in research is the scientist—the individual who employs the scientific approach. A scientist is any individual who rigorously employs the scientific research process in the pursuit of knowledge. Is the scientist just any person, or does he or she possess special characteristics? As might be expected, some characteristics are especially important. Because nature's secrets are revealed reluctantly, scientists must actively search and probe nature to uncover orderly relationships, and he or she must strive to be curious, patient, objective, and tolerant of change.

Curiosity

The scientist's goal is the pursuit of knowledge and the uncovering of regularities in nature. Scientists attempt to answer the following questions: What? When? Why? How? Under what conditions? With what restriction? These questions are the starting point of scientific investigation, and they continue to be asked throughout each study and throughout the researcher's career. To adddress these questions, the scientist must be inquisitive, must exhibit curiosity, and must never think that the ultimate solution has been reached. If questions cease, then so does the scientific process.

Scientists must maintain an open mind, never becoming rigid in orientation or in method of research. Such rigidity could cause him or her to become blinded and incapable of capitalizing on, or even seeing, unusual events. Curiosity and careful observation enable Skinner's "fifth unformalized principle of scientific practice . . . serendipity—the art of finding one thing while looking for another" (1956, p. 227). The sort of curiosity suggested here also enables what Louis Pasteur (1822–1895) is believed to have said in 1854: "Chance favors the prepared mind." If scientists were not inquisitive and open to new and different phenomena, they would have never made many of the discoveries of the past.

Patience

The reluctance of nature to reveal secrets is seen in the slow progress made in scientific inquiry. When individuals read or hear of significant advances in some field of scientific inquiry, they might marvel at the scientists' ability and think of the excitement and pleasure that must have surrounded the discovery. Although moments of excitement and pleasure do occur, research often includes many months or years of tedious, painstaking work. Many failures usually precede a success, so the scientist must be patient and be satisfied with rewards that are few and far between. For example, note the many years of effort that have gone into cancer research; many advances have been made, but a cure is still not available.

Objectivity

Objectivity
Goal in science to eliminate or minimize opinion or bias in the conduct of research

One of the goals of the research process is **objectivity**. Ideally, the scientist's personal wishes and attitudes should not affect his or her observations. Realistically, however, perfect objectivity cannot be attained, as scientists are only human. Even if perfect objectivity cannot often be achieved, it is essential to use it as a goal of research. The idea is to minimize the influence of the researcher on the conduct and outcomes of the research process. In order to be objective, however, one must also be critical and reflective because we often cannot "see" our biases. Throughout this book, we will be providing methods and strategies to help you conduct research in ways that strive to maximize objectivity and understanding.

Change

Scientific investigation necessitates change. The scientist is always devising new methods and new techniques for investigating phenomena. This process typically results in change. When a particular approach to a problem fails, a new approach must be devised, which also necessitates change. Change does not require abandoning all past facts and methods; it merely means the scientist must be appropriately critical of the past and constantly alert to new facts and techniques to enable new advances in scientific knowledge. Despite the need for the scientist to accept change as part of the research process, it seems that new ideas are sometimes resisted if they do not somehow fit in with current knowledge. Polanyi (1963), for example, relayed his own experience of the reaction to his theory of the absorption (adhesion) of gases on solids following its publication in 1914. He was chastised by Albert Einstein for showing a "total disregard" for what was then known about the structure of matter. Polanyi, however, was later proved to be correct. The moral is to continually self-examine and to attempt to be open to new ways of viewing the facts and not be blinded or hindered by one's beliefs.

STUDY QUESTION 1.5 | **What are the characteristics a person has to have to be a good scientist, and why are these characteristics necessary?**

Objectives of Psychological Research

Ultimately, the objective of scientific research is to understand the world in which we live. Scientific research demands a detailed examination of a phenomenon. Only when a phenomenon is accurately described and explained—and therefore predictable and, in most cases, capable of being controlled—will a scientist say that it is understood. Consequently, scientific understanding requires four specific objectives: description, explanation, prediction, and control.

Description

Description
The portrayal of a situation or phenomenon

The first objective, **description**, requires that the phenomenon be accurately portrayed. One must identify the characteristics of the phenomenon and then determine the degree to which they exist. For example, Piaget's theory of child development arose from detailed observations and descriptions of his own children. Any new area of study usually begins with the descriptive process, because it identifies the variables that exist. Only after we have some knowledge of which variables exist can we begin to explain why they exist. For example, we would not be able to explain the existence of separation anxiety (an infant's crying and visual searching behavior when the caretaker departs) if we had not first identified this behavior and the age at which it occurs. Scientific knowledge typically begins with description.

Explanation

Explanation
Determination of the cause or causes of a given phenomenon

The second objective is the **explanation** of the phenomenon, and this requires knowledge of why the phenomenon exists or what causes it. Therefore, we must be able to identify the antecedent conditions that result in the occurrence of the phenomenon. Assume that separation anxiety existed only when an infant was handled by few adults other than its parents and that it did not exist when the infant was handled by many adults other than parents. We would conclude that one of the antecedent conditions of separation anxiety was frequency of handling by adults other than the parents. Note that frequency was only *one* of the antecedents. Scientists recognize that most phenomena are multidetermined and that new evidence might necessitate replacing an old explanation with a better one or expanding an explanation to include new information. As the research process proceeds, we acquire more and more knowledge concerning the causes of phenomena. With this increasing knowledge comes the ability to predict and possibly control what happens.

Prediction

Prediction
The ability to anticipate the occurrence of an event

Prediction refers to the ability to anticipate an event prior to its actual occurrence. We can, for example, predict very accurately when an eclipse will occur. Making this kind of accurate prediction requires knowledge of the antecedent conditions that produce such a phenomenon. It requires knowledge of the movement of the moon and the earth and of the fact that the earth, the moon, and the sun must be in a particular relationship for an eclipse to occur. If we knew the combination of variables that resulted in academic success, we could then predict accurately who would succeed academically. To the extent that we cannot accurately predict a phenomenon, we have a gap in our understanding of it.

Control or Influence

Control
(1) A comparison group, (2) elimination of the influence of extraneous variables, or (3) manipulation of antecedent conditions to produce a change in mental processes and behavior

Control refers to the manipulation of the *conditions that determine a phenomenon*. Control, in this sense, requires knowledge of the causes or antecedent conditions of a phenomenon. When the antecedent conditions are known, they can be manipulated to produce the desired phenomenon.

Once psychologists understand the conditions that produce an outcome, the outcome can potentially be controlled by either allowing or not allowing the conditions to exist. Consider the hypothesis that frustration leads to aggression. If we knew that this hypothesis were completely correct, we could control aggression by allowing or not allowing a person to become frustrated. Control, then, refers to the manipulation of conditions that produce a phenomenon, not of the phenomenon itself.

At this point, it seems appropriate to provide some additional insight into the concept of control. So far, control has been discussed in two slightly different ways. In the discussion of the characteristics of scientific research, control was referred to in terms of holding constant or eliminating the influence of extraneous variables in an experiment. In the present discussion, control refers to the antecedent conditions determining a behavior. An experimental psychologist and a historian of psychology, Edwin Boring (1886–1968) noted (1954) that the word *control* has three meanings. First, control refers to a check or verification in terms of a standard of comparison (such as use of a placebo with a control group in a medical experiment). Second, it refers to a restraint—keeping conditions constant or eliminating the influence of extraneous conditions from the experiment. Third, control refers to manipulating conditions to produce an exact change or a specific attitude or behavior. The second and third meanings identified by Boring are those used in this book so far. Because all of these meanings will be used at various times, it would be to your advantage to memorize them.

STUDY QUESTION 1.6 | **List and define the objectives of research. Then explain why each is an objective of the research process.**

Pseudoscience

We have introduced you to science in this chapter. We pointed out that science is the approach to acquiring and establishing the type of knowledge that is relied upon in psychology. Scientific knowledge has a special status in our society because this type of knowledge claim is not made by scientists until a high degree of reliability and validity has been obtained. Now we will take another look at science by examining what it is not. Science is contrasted with pseudoscience.

Pseudoscience
Set of beliefs or practices that are not scientific but claim to be scientific

Pseudoscience is an approach that claims to be scientific but is based on methods and practices that violate many tenets of science. Pseudoscientific claims often are made in an attempt to gain legitimacy. For example, commercials often claim that their products' effectiveness has been "scientifically proven," when the claim is based on no credible evidence. Other examples of pseudoscience are found in astrology, ESP, fortune-telling, flat-earth claims, and superstitions. In Table 1.2, we list some strategies commonly relied upon in pseudoscience. You should avoid these faulty strategies when conducting research because they show what science is not.

STUDY QUESTIONS 1.7 | • **What is pseudoscience?**
• **What are the faulty strategies used in pseudoscience?**

TABLE 1.2
Strategies Used in Pseudoscience

- Creating new (ad hoc) hypotheses in order to explain away negative findings.
- Exclusive use of confirmation and reinterpretation of negative findings as supporting the claim.
- Absence of self-correction through continual and rigorous testing of the claim.
- Reversed burden of proof (i.e., stating that the onus of proof is on the critics).
- Overreliance on testimonials and anecdotal evidence supporting a claim.
- Use of obscurantist language to make a claim sound as if it has survived scientific scrutiny.
- Absence of any connection to other disciplines that study issues related to the claim.

Summary

This chapter provides an introduction to psychological research and science. The key ways that people acquire knowledge are intuition (i.e., based on preconscious processes), authority (i.e., based on what authorities say), rationalism (i.e., based on reasoning), and empiricism (i.e., based on experience). Science is a very special mixture of the approaches just mentioned, and it is the most trustworthy way to acquire reliable and valid knowledge about the natural world.

During its history, science has emphasized different inquiry approaches. From the seventeenth century to about the middle of the nineteenth century, induction was the primary scientific methodology. From about 1850 to about 1960, hypothesis testing was the primary scientific methodology. During this period, the logical positivists emphasized verification of hypotheses. Popper, who was not a logical positivist, emphasized attempting to falsify hypotheses and theories. Both the logical positivists' principle of verificationism and Popper's principle of falsification have some problems when taken singularly. In the current period, a mixture of verificationism and falsificationism is used. Since 1960, we have entered a methodological era of *naturalism* that says we should justify science empirically rather than through philosophical argument. Science during the periods of naturalism is marked by a mixture of ideas from previous periods; it is a pragmatic approach that is focused on the empirical adequacy of our hypotheses and theories and focuses on finding what works in practice. Naturalism was also influenced by the ideas of Thomas Kuhn (who talked about paradigms) and Imre Lakatos (who focused on research programs). Paul Feyerabend took a "radical position" and argued that science used so many different approaches that it could be viewed as anarchistic.

Although it is true that there is no single, simple definition of science that distinguishes it from nonscience, we offered a working definition: Science is the preferred way of acquiring reliable and valid knowledge about the natural world, including methods for obtaining scientific knowledge, standards for judging whether the knowledge is warranted or justified, and, finally, a set of facts and theories constituting the current status of the science. The primary assumptions of science are as follows: (1) there is uniformity or regularity in nature, (2) nature is real including our experiences of it, and (3) discoverability (i.e., it is possible to discover regularities in nature).

Three major characteristics of science are control, operationalism, and replication. *Control* is the most important characteristic because it enables the scientist to identify causation; without control, it would be impossible to identify the cause of a given effect. *Operationalism* means researchers must clearly represent their constructs according to the operations used during measurement. Perhaps the best way to operationalize a concept is through multiple operationalism (i.e., the use of multiple measures to represent a construct). *Replication* occurs when the results of a study are shown to occur again in future studies. Meta-analysis is an excellent way to summarize the results across multiple studies.

Theory is an important part of science. When relying on the logic of discovery, theories are generated, discovered, and developed. When relying on the logic of justification, theories are systematically tested with new empirical data to determine how well they operate. Science continually moves back and forth between theory discovery and theory testing (or induction and deduction), as shown in Figure 1.2.

Scientists should be curious, must have patience, must try to be objective, and must be open to change. The four major objectives of psychological research are description, explanation, prediction, and control or influence. Pseudoscience is a set of beliefs or practices that claim scientific status but are not scientific. You should avoid the strategies listed in Table 1.2, which characterize bad science or pseudoscience.

Key Terms and Concepts

Authority
Control
Deduction
Description
Determinism
Discoverability
Duhem–Quine principle
Empirical adequacy
Empiricism
Explanation
Falsificationism
Hypothesis testing
Induction
Intuition
Logic of discovery
Logic of justification
Logical positivism
Meta-analysis
Multiple operationalism

Naturalism
Normal science
Objectivity
Operational definition
Operationalism
Operationalization
Paradigm
Placebo effect
Prediction
Probabilistic causes
Pseudoscience
Rationalism
Reality in nature
Replication
Research program
Revolutionary science
Science
Theory

Related Internet Sites

http://www.pbs.org/wgbh/aso/databank/humbeh.html
This Internet site gives a short summary of the training and scientific contributions made by 11 scientists who figure very prominently in the history of psychology. This site also gives a brief discussion of a number of discoveries made by scientists from the early 1900s to 1993 that have significantly impacted the field of psychology.

http://quasar.as.utexas.edu/BillInfo/Quack.html
This Internet site has an entertaining discussion on a number of flaws that characterize "bogus" theories.

http://psychology.wadsworth.com/workshops/workshops.html
This Internet site gives a link to a workshop in statistics and research methods. For Chapter 1, go to this Internet site and click on the Web page link corresponding to the workshop titled "Research Methods Workshops." Then click on the "What Is Science?" link.

http://www.chem1.com/acad/sci/pseudosci.html
This Internet site discusses pseudoscience and how to recognize it.

Practice Test

Five multiple choice questions are included at the end of each chapter to enable you to test your knowledge of the chapter material. If you would like a more extensive assessment of your mastery, you can go to the Allyn and Bacon Web site accompanying this textbook, where you will find additional review questions. Prior to taking these sample tests, you should study the chapter. When you think you know the material, take the practice test to get some feedback regarding the extent to which you have mastered the material.

The answers to these questions can be found in Appendix.

1. Empiricism is a vital element in scientific studies. What does empiricism refer to?
   a. acquiring knowledge through experience
   b. A person's personal opinions about phenomena in the world
   c. Tenacious determination to hold onto one's current beliefs
   d. Accepting information because it comes form an authority

2. Scientific activities have included
   a. Induction
   b. Hypothesis testing
   c. Paradigms
   d. Research programs
   e. All of the above

3. Professor Albert was conducting an experiment investigating the influence of "status" on a person's persuasive influence. In this study, he manipulated the variable of status by presenting different dress styles. In particular, a high-status person was dressed in an expensive business suit and carried a briefcase. The low-status person was dressed in faded jeans and torn shirt. The difference in dress styles of the high- and low-status person was used to
   a. Control for the influence of extraneous variables
   b. Operationalize the construct of status

    c. Enable him to replicate the results of his study

    d. Control for the type of dress the participants wore

4. If you conducted a study in which you wanted to determine why help is not given to people who obviously need it, with which of the following objectives would you have conducted the study?

    a. Description

    b. Explanation

    c. Prediction

    d. Control

5. Scientists usually make several assumptions in order to have confidence in the scientific research process. Which of the following is *not* one of these assumptions?

    a. There is an underlying reality in nature including what we see, hear, feel, touch, and taste.

    b. It is possible to discover the regularities in nature.

    c. There is uniformity or regularity in nature.

    d. Psychology studies only psychologically constructed reality.

Challenge Exercises

In addition to the review questions, each chapter ends with challenge exercises. These exercises will encourage you to think about the concepts discussed in the chapter to give you an opportunity to apply what you have learned.

1. Psychology makes use of many concepts when explaining mental processes and behavior and when conducting research. Consider each of the following concepts, and identify a set of operations that will be representative of each concept.

    a. Depression

    b. Aggression

    c. Child abuse

    d. Attitude

    e. Leadership

2. The medical community has repeatedly expressed concern about the fact that the average weight among Americans is increasing. The concern focuses on the health risks of people who are overweight. Think about each of the four major objectives of science, and apply each of these objectives to this concern of the medical community.

3. What would happen to the science of psychology if none of the assumptions underlying science existed? What would happen in our daily lives if these assumptions did not exist?

4. Identify an area that would be considered to be pseudoscientific, such as astrology, palm reading, and ESP. Find evidence for claims made by these fields, and explain why this evidence is pseudoscientific.

5. Are the following fields scientific or pseudoscientific? Justify your answer.

a. Chiropractic medicine
b. Faith healing
c. Homeopathy
d. Acupuncture
e. Parapsychology

Research Approaches and Methods of Data Collection

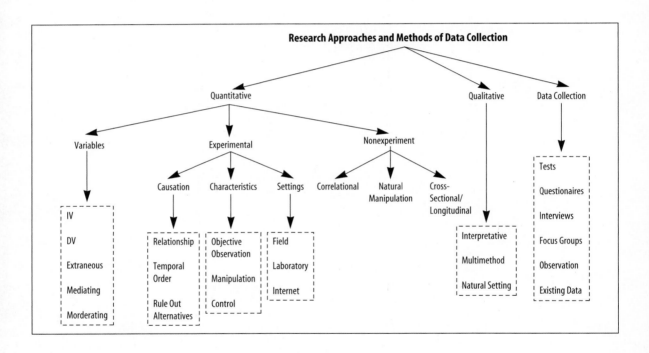

On July 7, 2005, Michael Henning, a 39-year-old banker, was reading the morning paper while making his morning commute to work on the London underground transit system. At about 8:50 a.m., a bomb exploded on the train he was riding on, blinding him with a yellow light and throwing him to the floor. Everything went pitch black, and Henning felt blood on his face as he realized that he was at least alive. A few seconds later, about two miles away, a second blast occurred as another train with several hundred passengers descended into a 12-foot-wide tunnel deep into the heart of London. The train cars were immediately plunged into darkness, and the air was filled with acrid smoke. Breathing became difficult, and passengers began to shout, cry, and bang on windows. After 10 or 15 minutes had passed, the passengers realized that no immediate help was on the way, so they slowly climbed out of the train and moved down the dark tunnel into Russell Square Station. As they walked down the tunnel, they passed people mutilated from the blast.

In central London, a double-decker bus was diverted away from the second bombing, causing the driver to take several detours. One of the passengers on the bus appeared agitated at the detours and kept reaching into his knapsack, fiddling with something. Police suspect that this man was trying to reset the timer on the bomb contained in the knapsack. At 9:47 a.m., nearly an hour after the London tube (subway) bombings, the bus exploded. Metal, glass, and body parts blew up and out of the rear of the bus.

Following the explosions, many questions were asked. Why did the bombings occur, who was responsible, what was the motive for blowing up the subway trains and bus, and why would someone do this? The bombings appeared to be timed to coincide with the meeting of the leaders of the world's greatest industrial nations, known as the G8, in an attempt to undermine the conference. But who would commit such a heinous crime, and what would be the impact on Londoners and the economy of Britain? British Prime Minister Tony Blair stated that "we are simply not going to be terrorized by terror in this way" (Terror, 2005). Later he said that such terrorist acts would not change the way of life of the British people. However, such events do have an impact on individuals' lives. While it is impossible to identify all the effects of such events, it is possible to provide a descriptive account of them and some evidence on how they have impacted and altered individuals' lives.

Introduction

Experimental research
The research approach in which one attempts to demonstrate cause-and-effect relationships by manipulating the independent variable

Descriptive research
Research that attempts to describe some phenomenon, event, or situation

Quantitative research study
A research study that is based on numerical data

Numerical data
Data consisting of numbers

Qualitative research study
A research study based on nonnumerical data

Nonnumerical data
Data that consist of pictures, words, statements, clothing, written records or documents, or a description of situations and behavior

The various approaches to conducting psychological research traditionally have been categorized as experimental or descriptive. This categorization was based on the goals of the various research approaches. **Experimental research** attempts to identify cause-and-effect relationships by conducting controlled psychological experiments. **Descriptive research** focuses on describing some phenomenon, event, or situation. Consequently, the experimental–descriptive dichotomy was a very useful way of presenting the various types of research approaches used in psychology.

More recently, another way of dichotomizing research approaches has appeared in the psychological literature. This approach is the quantitative–qualitative research dichotomy, which is based on the type of data collected in a study.

A **quantitative research study** is one that collects some type of **numerical data** to answer a given research question. For example, a study that collects information such as a person's ratings of attractiveness, the number of times a child hits another child, the number of times a rat presses a bar, or the score a person makes on a personality test is a quantitative study. Quantitative research is, by far, the most popular type of research in psychology. A **qualitative research study** is a study that collects some type of **nonnumerical data** to answer a research question. Nonnumerical data consist of data such as the statements made by a person during an interview, written records, pictures, clothing, or observed behavior. A number of individuals, for example, Creswell (1998) and Patton (1990), feel that research that collects only quantitative data often provides an incomplete analysis or picture of the phenomenon, event, or situation being investigated and that the addition of qualitative data provides an added level of understanding.

In this chapter, we provide an overview of quantitative research and qualitative research. We also introduce you to the major methods of data collection used in psychological research.

STUDY QUESTION 2.1 | **Distinguish between experimental and descriptive research and between quantitative and qualitative research.**

Variables in Quantitative Research

Variable
A characteristic or phenomenon that can vary across or within organisms, situations, or environments

Categorical variable
Variable that varies by type or kind

Quantitative variable
Variable that varies by degree or amount

Independent variable
Variable that is presumed to cause changes in another variable

Dependent variable
Variable that is presumed to be influenced by one or more independent variables

The basic building blocks of quantitative research are variables. A **variable** is something that takes on different values or categories, and it is the opposite of a **constant**, which is something that cannot vary, such as a single value or category of a variable. For example, gender is a variable that takes on the values of male or female. Male is a constant because it does not vary; female also is a constant.

Many of the important types of variables used in quantitative research are shown, with examples, in Table 2.1. One useful distinction for variables is to determine if they are categorical or quantitative. A **categorical variable** is a variable that varies by type or kind. A **quantitative variable** is a variable that varies by degree or amount. For example, the variable gender is categorical because its levels represent types (male vs. female), and the variable reaction time might be operationalized as number of milliseconds required to react to a stimulus and is, therefore, a quantitative variable. Additional examples of categorical variables are religion, college major, political party identification, personality type, type of memory strategy, and method of therapy. Additional examples of quantitative variables are height, self-esteem level, age, anxiety level, rate of cognitive processing. Although we introduce you to a four-level system for classifying variables for their level of measurement, this two-level system (i.e., categorical vs. quantitative) is sufficient for many purposes.

The other set of variables in Table 2.1 (under the heading "Role Taken by the Variable") are the kinds researchers use when describing and explaining how the world operates and when designing a quantitative research study. As you can see in Table 2.1, **independent variables** (symbolized by "IV") are the presumed *cause* of another variable. **Dependent variables** (symbolized by "DV") are the presumed effect or *outcome*. Dependent variables are influenced by one or more independent variables. For example, what are the IV and the DV in the relationship between smoking and lung cancer? As you know, smoking is the IV and lung cancer is the DV; that's because smoking causes lung cancer. In experimental research, the independent variable is the variable manipulated by the experimenter; for example, one level of the manipulated independent variable might be administration of a new therapy, and the other level is the "no therapy" control condition.

TABLE 2.1

Types of Variables Classified by Level of Measurement and by Role of Variable

Variable Type	Key Characteristic	Example
Level of Measurement[*]		
Categorical variable	A variable that varies by type or kind or categories of a phenomenon.	The variable *gender* is made up of the categories of male and female.
Quantitative variable	A variable that varies in amount or degree of a phenomenon.	The variable *reaction time* is often measured in milliseconds and can vary from just a few milliseconds to minutes or longer.
Role Taken by the Variable		
Independent variable (symbolized by "IV")	A variable that is presumed to cause changes to occur in another variable; it's the causal variable.	Amount of anxiety (IV) affects performance on a memory task (DV).
Dependent variable (symbolized by "DV")	A variable that changes because of another variable; it's the effect or outcome variable; it's the variable that measures the effect of the IV.	Amount of anxiety (IV) affects performance on a memory task (DV).
Mediating variable	A variable that operates in between two other variables. It delineates the intervening process through which one variable affects another variable.	Amount of anxiety (IV) leads to cognitive distraction (mediating variable), which affects performance on a memory task (DV).
Moderator variable	A variable that specifies how a relationship of interest changes under different conditions or circumstances.	Perhaps the relationship between anxiety (IV) and memory (DV) changes according to the different levels of fatigue (moderator).
Extraneous variable	A variable that can compete with the independent variable in explaining an outcome.	Perhaps an observed relationship between coffee drinking (IV) and cancer (DV) is actually due to smoking cigarettes.

[*]A four-level measurement system will be provided in Chapter 5.

Cause-and-effect relationship
Relationship in which changes in one variable produce changes in another variable

Extraneous variable
Variable that might compete with the IV in explaining the outcome

Whenever you want to make a claim about **cause and effect** (i.e., that changes in an IV cause changes in a DV), you must be careful, especially in nonexperimental research, about what are called extraneous variables. An **extraneous variable** is a variable that competes with the independent variable in explaining the outcome. (Extraneous variables are also called *third variables* and *confounding variables*). When attempting to identify an extraneous variable, you should consider this question, "Could my DV have changed values not because of the IV, but because of an extraneous variable that I did not consider?" For example, researchers have shown that there is a statistical relationship between coffee drinking and heart attacks (i.e., greater coffee consumption is associated with more heart attacks and lower coffee consumption with fewer heart attacks). Is this a causal relationship? Additional research showed that this was not a causal relationship, and that the reason was the extraneous variable of smoking. High coffee consumers are more likely to smoke than low coffee consumers; it is the smoking that causes heart attacks and not the consumption of great amounts of coffee. Smoking, therefore, was a confounding extraneous variable because this variable influences the DV of heart attacks. You will learn how to "control for" these kinds of extraneous variables in several places in this book.

Sometimes we want to understand the process or variables through which one variable affects another variable. This brings us to another type of variable. It is the idea of a mediating variable (also called an *intervening variable*). A **mediating variable** is a variable that occurs in-between two other variables in a causal chain. For example, tissue damage is an intervening variable in the smoking and lung cancer relationship. We can use arrows (which mean causes) and draw this relationship as follows: smoking→tissue damage→lung cancer.

Sometimes a relationship between two variables will not generalize to everyone, and you will need another type of variable to study this possibility. Specifically, psychologists use **moderator variables** to determine how the relationship between an IV and a DV changes across the levels of an additional variable (which is called a moderator variable because it "moderates the relationship"). For example, if behavioral therapy worked better for males and cognitive therapy worked better for females, then gender would be a moderator variable. That's because the relationship between the IV (type of therapy) and the DV (client mental health) varies across the levels of the moderator variable (gender). In this case, we would say that the relationship between type of therapy and mental health is moderated by gender. As you can imagine, there are many moderator variables working in the natural causal world because this world tends to be quite complex.

Be sure to remember all of the variable types just defined and summarized in Table 2.1, because the language of variables is a very powerful language, and it is the "language" used in quantitative research. When you think about how things that interest you are related in the world, try to translate them to this new language, and you will be ready to carry out some quantitative research. You will find that this language will also help you to clarify your meaning.

Mediating variable
Variable that occurs between two other variables in a causal chain; it's an intervening variable

Moderator variable
Variable that changes or "moderates" the relationship between other variables

STUDY QUESTIONS 2.2

- **What is the difference between an independent variable and a dependent variable?**
- **What is the difference between a quantitative variable and a categorical variable?**
- **What is the difference between a mediating variable and a moderator variable?**

Experimental Research

The experimental research approach is a quantitative approach designed to discover the effects of presumed causes. The key feature of this approach is that one thing is deliberately varied to see what happens to something else (i.e., to determine the effects of presumed causes). This is something that people do all the time. For example, individuals try different diets or exercise to see if they will lose weight. Others might get an education to see if that will lead to a better job. As you can see, both scientists and nonscientists use experimentation to try to identify causal relationships. However, scientific experimentation differs from practical experimentation in that the scientist makes a deliberate attempt to make observations that are free of bias and that have controlled for extraneous variables. Both approaches attempt to identify causal relationships. We therefore begin by exploring the concept of causation and then discuss scientific experimentation and the nature of causation that experiments systematically test.

Causation

Causation
A term whose meaning is debated by philosophers, but in everyday language implies that manipulation of one event produces another event

Causation is one of those terms that people frequently use but don't always carefully consider. People ask questions like "What causes cancer?" "What causes a person to murder someone else?" What do they really mean? Common sense suggests that causality refers to a condition in which one event—the cause—generates another event—the effect. However, causality is more complex.

When individuals discuss causation, they tend to use the words *cause* and *effect* rather informally. If you think about it, you will see that manipulation is often implicit in the concept of causation. If we manipulate or do something, we expect something else to happen. If something does happen, the thing or event we manipulate is called the *cause* and what happens is called the *effect*. For example, if a parent punished a child for coloring on a wall and then observed that the child no longer colors on the wall, the parent would assume that the punishment caused the child to stop the coloring. This temporal relationship between events such as punishment and ceasing a behavior such as coloring on a wall gives an intuitive sense of the meaning of cause and effect. Using the language of variables, the causal variable is the independent variable and the effect or outcome variable is the dependent variable.

Cause

The intuitive definition of cause is too simplistic because most causal relationships are dependent on many factors, including contextual factors. For example, depression can occur in many different ways. Eating a diet that does not contain the precursor of the central neurotransmitter serotonin, having a baby, being fired from a job, getting a divorce, and numerous other events can cause an onset of depression. However, none of these events by itself is sufficient to cause depression. For some individuals, losing a job causes depression, whereas others view it as an opportunity to develop another stimulating career. The point is that many factors are usually required for an effect to occur, and we rarely know all of them and how they relate to each other. This means that any causal relationship occurs within the context of many factors, and, if any of these other factors change, the causal relationship previously identified might or might not be replicated. This is why causal relationships are not fully

Cause
The factor that makes
something else exist
or change

deterministic but are probabilistic (Shadish, Cook, & Campbell, 2002). In spite of the difficulty with identifying the cause of some event, it is still useful to think of **cause** as something that produces something else. We will stress throughout this book that when you want to study cause and effect, your first choice should be to conduct an experiment.

Effect

Effect
The difference
between what would
have happened and
what did happen
when a treatment
is administered

An **effect** is the difference between what would have happened without the manipulation of the IV and what did happen with the manipulation of the IV. In an experiment, the effect is the difference between what did happen when a treatment was administered and what would have happened to *this same group of individuals* if the treatment had not been administered. The emphasis is on the *same group* of individuals. However, it is impossible for the same group of people to both have and not have a treatment, so perfectly identifying a true effect is not possible. What we attempt to do within the context of an experiment is to obtain an imperfect measure of this difference by doing such things as working with two different groups of individuals and administering the treatment to one group and not to the other group; the group not receiving the treatment is used as the estimate of what the group that received the treatment would have been like if it had not received the treatment. The point is that it is never possible to obtain a true measure of an effect, because this requires participants to both be exposed to something and not be exposed to something, and that is not possible.

Required Conditions for Making the Claim of Causation

Throughout this book we will refer to the three required conditions for making a justified claim of cause and effect (i.e., that changes in an independent variable cause the changes in a dependent variable). These required conditions are shown in Table 2.2. First, the researcher has to demonstrate that the independent variable and the dependent variable are related. Second, the researcher must demonstrate that the changes in the independent variable occurred before the changes in the

TABLE 2.2
Required Conditions for Claiming that a Causal Relationship Exists

Researchers must establish the following conditions if they are to make a justified claim that changes in variable A *cause* changes in variable B:

Condition 1: Variable A (the presumed causal or independent variable) and variable B (the presumed effect or dependent variable) must be associated or related. This is called the relationship condition.

Condition 2: Changes in variable A must precede the changes in variable B. This is called the temporal order condition.

Condition 3: No plausible alternative explanations exist for the relationship between variable A and variable B. This is called the no alternative explanation condition.

dependent variable. Third, the researcher has to demonstrate that the relationship between the independent and dependent variables is not due to some other variable. For example, there is a correlation between coffee drinking and likelihood of having a heart attack. Condition 1 is met simply because these variables are related. Condition 2 is met because coffee drinking precedes heart attacks. The problem with claiming that coffee drinking *causes* heart attacks is with condition 3; there are plausible alternative explanations for the observed relationship. One big problem with concluding that coffee drinking causes heart attacks is that cigarette smoking is related to *both* of these variables (i.e., we have a condition 3 problem). People who drink little coffee are less likely to smoke cigarettes than are people who drink a lot of coffee. Therefore, perhaps the observed relationship between coffee drinking and heart attacks is due to the extraneous variable of smoking. The researcher would have to "control for" smoking in order to determine if this alternative explanation accounts for the original relationship.

STUDY QUESTIONS 2.3

- **What is experimental research?**
- **What is a cause-and-effect relationship?**
- **What are the three required conditions for making the claim of cause and effect?**
- **Why can't you claim cause and effect from just the relationship between two variables?**

The Psychological Experiment

Psychological experiment

Objective observation of phenomena that are made to occur in a strictly controlled situation in which one or more factors are varied and the others are kept constant

The three required conditions for cause and effect (shown in Table 2.2) mirror what happens in the psychological experiment. Zimney (1961, p. 18) provides a classical definition of a **psychological experiment** as the "objective observation of phenomena which are made to occur in a strictly controlled situation in which one *or more* factors are varied and the others are kept constant." This definition seems to be a good one because of the components that it includes, each of which is examined separately in the next sections. The following analysis of this definition should provide an understanding of the concept and components of an experiment:

1. Objective Observation   Impartiality and freedom from bias on the part of the investigator, or objectivity, was previously discussed as a characteristic that the scientist must strive to exhibit. In order to be able to identify causation from the results of the experiment, the experimenter must avoid doing anything that might influence the outcome. Many psychologists have demonstrated that the experimenter is probably capable of greater biasing effects than one would expect. We will discuss this in detail in later chapters. In spite of this, and recognizing that complete objectivity is probably unattainable, the investigator must continually strive for freedom from bias.

Zimney (1961) presents three rules that investigators should follow to minimize recording and observation errors. The first rule is to accept the possibility that mistakes can occur—that we are not perfect and that our perceptions and therefore our responses are influenced by our motives, desires, and other biasing factors. Once we accept this fact, we can then attempt to identify where the mistakes are likely to occur—the second rule. To identify potential mistakes, we must carefully analyze and test each segment of the entire experiment in order to anticipate the potential sources and causes of the errors. Once the situation has been analyzed, then the third rule can be implemented—to take the necessary steps to avoid the errors. Every effort should be expended to construct the experiment so that accurate observations are recorded.

2. Of Phenomena That Are Made to Occur In psychological experimentation, *phenomenon* refers to any publicly observable behavior, such as actions, appearances, verbal statements, responses to questionnaires, and physiological recordings. Focusing on such observable behaviors is a must if psychology is to meet the previously discussed characteristics of science. Only by focusing on these phenomena can we satisfy the demands of operationalism and replication of experiments.

Defining a phenomenon as publicly observable behavior would seem to exclude the internal or private processes and states of the individual. In the introductory psychology course, such processes as memory, perception, personality, emotion, and intelligence are discussed. Is it possible to retain these processes if we study only *publicly* observable behavior? The answer is yes. In studying these processes, researchers investigate publicly observable behavior and infer from their observations the existence of internal processes. It is the behavioral manifestation of the inferred processes that is observed. For example, intelligence is inferred from responses to an intelligence test, and self-esteem is inferred from responses to an inventory completed by the participant that asks a series of questions designed to tap the construct of self-esteem.

Manipulation
Active intervention by researcher that is expected to produce changes in the dependent variable

When conducting an experiment, the psychologist precisely **manipulates** one or more independent variables and objectively observes the phenomena *that are made to occur* by this manipulation. This part of the definition of experimentation refers to the fact that the experimenter is manipulating the conditions that cause a certain effect. In this way, experimenters identify the cause-and-effect relationships from experimentation by noting the effect or lack of effect produced by their manipulations.

3. In a Strictly Controlled Situation in Which One or More Factors Are Varied and the Others Are Kept Constant The researcher must control the experimental situation so that the only things varied in the experiment are the experimental conditions. The groups must be the same on everything except for their experimental condition that is manipulated by the researcher. At the start of an experiment, the best way to construct equivalent groups (i.e., groups that are the same on all variables) is by randomly assigning participants to the experimental conditions. Then, during the experiment, you administer the conditions, and at the same time, you must make sure that no extraneous variables enter that might threaten the study. You must control the situation so that nothing is different for the groups other than the administration of the experimental conditions. If this is done, then at the end of the experiment you will be able to attribute the difference in outcome to the experimental conditions.

Example of an Experiment and Its Logic

Now we want you to see what a basic experimental design looks like. Here is a depiction of an experiment for testing the effectiveness of a new drug that is hypothesized to reduce generalized anxiety:

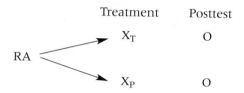

Where:

- O denotes observation/measurement of the dependent variable
- X denotes the independent variable
- Subscript T denotes the treatment condition of the IV (i.e., the treatment group that gets the drug with the active agent)
- Subscript P denotes the placebo condition of the IV (i.e., the control group that gets the drug without the active ingredient)
- RA stands for random assignment of participants to the two groups in this experimental design

As random assignment is the best way to make the two groups similar on all possible variables at the beginning of an experiment (i.e., the groups will not systematically differ), we have used it in the above research design. (You will learn exactly how to perform random assignment in Chapter 6.) Let's assume that we have a convenience sample of 100 people experiencing generalized anxiety and that we randomly assign them to form two groups with 50 participants in each group.

Here is the logic of this experiment. First, we made the groups approximately the same at the start of the study on all variables by using random assignment (i.e., the groups are "equated"). If you randomly assign the participants, there should be no systematic difference between the groups on any variable, including anxiety level. Second, you manipulate the independent variable by administering the new drug to the participants in the treatment condition and a placebo to the control condition. Next (after giving time for the drug to operate), you measure the participants' anxiety levels after the manipulation of the independent variable. Let's say that the people in the treatment group show lower anxiety after receiving the new drug than those in the control group who only received a placebo (i.e., a pill that looks similar to the real drug but does not include the active ingredient). What would you conclude? Is the drug effective? In this case, you would be able to conclude that there is a *causal* relationship between the independent variable type of drug (active vs. placebo) and the dependent variable anxiety level. We can make this conclusion because (1) we made objective observations (i.e., we used standardized and calibrated measurement instruments to measure anxiety), (2) we made the key phenomena occur (i.e., we administered the two conditions), and (3) we varied only the independent variable (drug vs. placebo) and held all other variables constant (by equating the groups at the start of the study via random assignment and treating the participants in the two groups the same in every way during the study except administering a different type of pill). Again, because the only difference between the two groups was the ingredient in the pill, we are able to conclude that the drug was the cause of the superior decrease in anxiety in the treatment group.

Now, let's say that in the above experiment we could not use random assignment to equate our groups. Assume that some of the participants have a fear of medication, but they, nonetheless, volunteered and consented. Finally, assume that most of the participants who feared medication ended up in the treatment condition. (If you don't use random assignment, you should assume that your groups are different on variables in addition to your independent variable.) At the end of the study, perhaps the two groups did not differ in anxiety level. What can you conclude? Since you would not be aware of the fear of medication problem, you would probably conclude that the drug was ineffective. However, the drug might have actually been effective but the negative effect of fear of medication in the treatment group participants was greater in increasing their anxiety than was the drug's effect in decreasing their anxiety.

It is important to remember the definition of an *extraneous variable* because extraneous variables can destroy the integrity of a research study that claims to show a cause-and-effect relationship. An *extraneous variable* is a variable that might compete with the independent variable in explaining the outcome. Remember this, if you are ever interested in identifying cause-and-effect relationships, you must always determine whether there are any extraneous variables you need to worry about. If an extraneous variable really is the reason for an outcome (rather than the IV), then researchers sometimes like to call it a **confounding variable** because it has confused or confounded the relationship we are interested in. In our previous example, the confounding variable was fear of medication, and it made the study appear that the drug had no effect when it really did have some positive effect.

Confounding variables
An extraneous variable that if not controlled for will eliminate the researcher's ability to claim that the IV causes changes in the DV

Advantages of the Experimental Approach

1. Causal Inference   The psychological experiment is the best method for identifying causal relationships. However, in looking at this advantage, it is important to distinguish between causal description and causal explanation because the most immediate strength of an experiment is for demonstrating causal description (Shadish et al., 2002). **Causal description** refers to describing the consequences attributable to deliberately varying a treatment. For example, many studies have demonstrated that drugs such as Prozac help ameliorate depression. Such a study is

Causal description
Description of the consequences of manipulating an independent variable

causal description because it describes the causal connection between administering the drug and the consequence of amelioration of depression. However, this study does not provide an explanation of why the drug worked. This is the purview of causal explanation.

Causal explanation

Explaining the mechanisms through which a causal relationship operates

Causal explanation refers to clarifying the mechanisms or processes by which a causal relationship holds. In other words, causal explanation involves taking a causal relationship and identifying the mediating and moderating variables that produce the causal relationship. (Definitions of mediating and moderating variables were given earlier in Table 2.1.) For example, identifying a causal descriptive relationship between Prozac and amelioration of depression is not sufficient. After identifying this causal descriptive relationship, we also want to know why the relationship holds. For example, we want to know how Prozac works to reduce depression. Currently we know that it has an influence on the central neurotransmitter serotonin and that serotonin is involved in depression. But how is serotonin involved, and why does it take some time for Prozac to reduce depression symptoms when its effect on increasing serotonin is rather immediate? There are too many questions whose answers still remain unknown for us to have a full explanation of how the treatment (Prozac) produces its influence on the outcome, the amelioration of depression. The practical importance of causal explanation is seen when a person with depression does not obtain relief from taking Prozac. It is important to know why and determine what can be done next. Such instances not only emphasize the importance of causal explanation but also help explain why much scientific research is directed toward explaining how and why something happens. Although causal description is easier to obtain, ultimately scientific research areas tend to move toward causal explanation.

2. Ability to Manipulate Variables   Experimental research is the only research method in which the researcher is able to actively manipulate one or more independent variable and observe the outcome. If a researcher is interested in studying the effects of the independent variable of crowding on a dependent variable such as social comfort, crowding can be manipulated in a very precise and systematic manner by varying the number of people in a constant amount of space (e.g., low, medium, and high crowding conditions). If the researcher is interested in the effects of crowding *and* homogeneity of the groups on social comfort, then the experimenter could construct the following experimental conditions: crowded–homogeneous, crowded–heterogeneous, noncrowded–homogeneous, and noncrowded–heterogeneous. In this way, the experimenter can precisely manipulate two independent variables: degree of crowding and group homogeneity.

3. Control   Not only does experimental research include active manipulation of the independent variable, but it is also the method in which the researcher exercises the most control over extraneous variables (typically by holding them constant). Control can be achieved by bringing the experiment into the laboratory, thereby eliminating noise and other potentially distracting stimuli. Control is also achieved by using such techniques as random assignment and matching to equate the groups on all variables except for the independent variable, which is purposively varied to create different experimental conditions for comparison.

Disadvantages of the Experimental Approach

1. Does Not Test Effects of Nonmanipulated Variables   Although the experimental research approach is the best method we have for identifying causal relationships, it is limited to testing the effect of independent variables that can be manipulated, such as the amount of a drug administered and the type of therapy used to treat people with depression. The world in which we live includes many independent variables that cannot be controlled by an experimenter and, therefore, are not capable of being deliberately manipulated. For example, we cannot deliberately manipulate people's ages, their raw genetic material, gender, the weather, past events, or terrorists' activities. This does not mean that we cannot or should not investigate the effects of nonmanipulable events. We not only can but do investigate these nonmanipulable variables; however, to do this we must use nonexperimental research designs.

2. Artificiality   The most frequently cited and probably the most severe criticism leveled against the experimental approach is that laboratory findings are obtained in an artificial and sterile atmosphere that precludes generalization to real-life situations. The following statement by Bannister (1966) views artificiality quite negatively:

> In order to behave like scientists we must construct situations in which subjects are totally controlled, manipulated and measured. We must cut our subjects down to size. We must construct situations in which they can behave as little like human beings as possible and we do this in order to allow ourselves to make statements about the nature of their humanity. (p. 24)

Is such a severe criticism of experimentation justified? It seems to us that Bannister overstated the problem. Underwood (1959) views the problem much more positively:

> One might view the laboratory as a fast, efficient, convenient way of identifying variables or factors which are likely to be important in real-life situations. Thus, if four or five factors are discovered to influence human learning markedly, and to influence it under a wide range of conditions, it would be reasonable to suspect that these factors would also be important in the classroom. But, one would *not* automatically conclude such; rather, one would make field tests in the classroom situation to deny or confirm the inference concerning the general importance of these variables. (pp. 107–117)

The artificiality issue is a problem only when an individual makes a generalization from an experimental finding without first determining whether the generalization can be made. Ideally, competent psychologists rarely blunder in this fashion because they realize that laboratory experiments are contrived situations.

Realistically, psychologists seem to frequently make risky generalizations from their work, although there are times when such generalizations are warranted. Additional difficulties of the experimental approach include problems in designing the experiment and the fact that the experiment might be extremely time consuming. It is not unusual for an experimenter to have to go to extreme lengths to set the stage for, motivate, and occasionally deceive the research participant. Then, when the experiment is actually conducted, the experimenter and perhaps one or two assistants are often required to spend time with each participant.

3. Inadequate Method of Scientific Inquiry   A final criticism that has been aimed at the experimental research approach is that it is inadequate if one views it as the only method for studying humans. Gadlin and Ingle (1975) believe that the experimental approach is an inappropriate paradigm because it promotes the view that humans are manipulable mechanistic objects. It appears that this criticism has been satisfied through the use of qualitative and mixed research methodologies (Camic, Rhodes, & Yardley, 2003; Teddlie & Tashakkori, 2009).

STUDY QUESTIONS 2.4

- **What is a psychological experiment?**
- **What are the advantages and disadvantages of the psychological experiment?**

Experimental Research Settings

The experimental research approach is not just used in laboratory settings. It is also used in field settings, and, increasingly, on the Internet. Manipulation of the independent variable is present in all three cases because this is a defining characteristic of experimental experiments. There are, however, some other differences.

Field Experiments

Field experiment
An experimental research study that is conducted in a real-life setting

A **field experiment** is an experimental research study that is conducted in a real-life setting. The experimenter actively manipulates variables and carefully controls the influence of as many extraneous variables as the situation will permit. Regan and Llamas (2002), for example, wanted to find out if a female shopper's appearance influenced the amount of time it took for an employee of a store to approach and acknowledge her. (Note: A "confederate" is someone working with the experimenter, which is not known by the participants.) The basic procedure they used was to have a female confederate dress either in formal work clothes and grooming (skirt, blouse, and dress shoes, with makeup and her hair down) or informal sports clothes and grooming (tights, T-shirt, and tennis shoes, with no makeup, and her hair in a ponytail) and then enter a randomly selected set of women's stores between the hours of 3:00 and 4:00 p.m. on two consecutive Thursdays. Upon entering the store, the confederate activated

FIGURE 2.1
Amount of time for a store employee to approach and acknowledge the confederate.

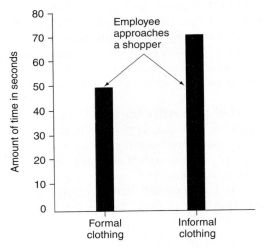

(Adapted from "Customer Service as a Function of Shopper's Attire" by P. C. Regan & V. Llamas (2002), *Psychological Reports, 90*, pp. 203–204.)

a stopwatch and proceeded down the first open aisle, giving the appearance of shopping for clothing. As soon as an employee approached and spoke to her, she stopped the timer. As Figure 2.1 indicates, females dressed in formal work clothes were approached more quickly by store employees than were females dressed in informal sports clothing.

This is an example of a field study because it was conducted in the natural setting of a mall while engaging in daily activities. It also represents an experimental research study because variable manipulation was present (type of dress). Field experiments like this one are not subject to the artificiality problem that exists with laboratory experiments, so field experiments are excellent for studying many problems. Their primary disadvantage is that control of extraneous variables cannot be accomplished as well as it can be in laboratory experiments. For example, in field settings, the researcher cannot prevent participants in comparison groups from communicating, and the researcher cannot prevent participants from engaging in other activities that might affect their scores on the dependent variable.

Tunnell (1977) states that field experimentation should be conducted in a manner that makes all variables operational in real-world terms. The Regan and Llamas (2002) study included the three dimensions of naturalness identified by Tunnell: natural behavior, natural setting, and natural treatment. The natural behavior investigated was a store employee approaching a shopper. The setting was natural because the study took place in a mall; the natural treatment was type of dress. In reality, the treatment was imposed by a confederate, but it mirrored a behavior that could have occurred naturally. These are the types of behaviors Tunnell says we must strive for when we conduct field experimentation.

Laboratory Experiments

The **laboratory experiment** is a research study that is conducted in the laboratory, and the investigator precisely manipulates one or more independent variables and controls the influence of all, or nearly all, extraneous variables. For example, Kassin and Kiechel (1996) realized that there were police reports of individuals who confessed to crimes that they had not committed. They realized that there was no scientific evidence of this phenomenon and were interested in determining if they could experimentally demonstrate that vulnerable individuals, under the right circumstances, would confess to an act that they did not commit and internalize this confession to the point that they would confabulate details in memory consistent with the confession. To investigate this phenomenon, Kassin and Kiechel constructed a situation in which they manipulated the vulnerability of the research participants as well as the presence of a person falsely incriminating them. In addition, they controlled other variables such as the presence of witnesses and other individuals refuting or confirming the false accusation. To precisely manipulate vulnerability and the presence of a witness and to control for the impact of extraneous variables, Kassin and Kiechel created a situation within the context of a laboratory setting in which the research participants had to perform a task at either moderate or rapid speed. A rapid-speed completion of the task created a vulnerable condition because the more rapidly the participants had to respond, the greater the likelihood of making a mistake. The results of this study revealed that individuals were more likely to confess to making a mistake they had not made in the vulnerable condition when a confederate, or witness, said that the research participant had made the error. More important, these vulnerable individuals were more likely to internalize the false confession and tell others that they had committed the error.

In contrast to the field experiment, the laboratory experiment epitomizes the ability to control or eliminate the influence of extraneous variables. This is accomplished by bringing the problem into an environment apart from the participants' normal routines. In this environment, outside influences (such as the presence of others and of noise) can be eliminated. However, the price of this increase in control is the artificiality of the situation created. Even though precise results can be obtained from the laboratory, the applicability of these results to the real world must always be verified.

Internet Experiments

An **Internet experiment** is an experimental study that is conducted over the Internet. As with all types of experiments, the investigator precisely manipulates one or more variables and controls for as many extraneous confounding variables as possible.

The precursor to conducting experiments over the Internet was probably the incorporation of computer automation in experimental research in psychology. As early as the 1970s, researchers were making use of computers in psychological experiments to perform tasks such as delivering a standardized and controlled presentation of stimuli and making accurate recordings of responses. This trend is not only continuing, but, currently, most human experimental research in psychology is aided by computer automation.

The move to conduct human psychological experimentation on the Internet was made possible by the development, in 1990, of a new protocol, http, or hypertext transfer protocol. This allowed an Internet browser, such as Netscape Navigator or Internet Explorer, to get a document it located on a server. This document, or Web page, is coded in a language known as hypertext markup language, or HTML, and this language permits the display of text, graphics, or other information on a Web page. With the ability to display such a combination of words, pictures, and sounds on Web pages, the Web grew at an astonishing rate. In 1997, Krantz, Ballard, and Scher conducted an Internet experiment investigating the determinants of female attractiveness and published it in a scientific journal (Musch & Reips, 2000). This was one of the first published Internet experiments.

Since that time the number of Internet experiments has grown considerably, and this growth rate is expected to continue because the advantages seem to outweigh the disadvantages compared to other types of experiments (Birnbaum, 2001). Some advantages identified by Reips (2000, p. 89) include the following:"(1) ease of access to demographically and culturally diverse participant populations, including participants from unique and previously inaccessible target populations; (2) bringing the experiment to the participant instead of the opposite; (3) high statistical power by enabling access to large samples; (4) the direct assessment of motivational confounding *by noting the differential dropout rate between treatment conditions because participants in Web experiments are not induced to stay due to, for example, course credit* (the italics are ours); (5) cost savings of lab space, person-hours, equipment, and administration." The disadvantages identified by Reips (2000, p. 89) include issues "such as (1) multiple submissions, (2) lack of experimental control, (3) self-selection, and (4) dropout." Of these disadvantages, the most significant is lack of experimental control. However, as we will emphasize in later chapters, random assignment to experimental conditions is the most important technique to be included in the design of an experimental study. Reips (2000) points out that this technique can be incorporated into the design of an experiment with the use of "so-called CGIs, small computer programs that cooperate with the Web Server" (p. 107).

STUDY QUESTION 2.5 | **What are the different research settings in which experimental research is conducted, and what are the advantages and disadvantages of each setting?**

Nonexperimental Quantitative Research

Nonexperimental quantitative research
Type of quantitative research in which the independent variable is not manipulated by the researcher

The defining characteristic of **nonexperimental quantitative research** is that there is no manipulation of an independent variable. Typically, this is a descriptive type of research in which the goal is to provide an accurate description or picture of a particular situation or phenomenon or to describe the size and direction of relationships among variables. More advanced and sophisticated nonexperimental approaches attempt to identify causal relationships through attempting to establish time ordering of the independent and dependent variables and controlling for extraneous variables identified by the researcher.

When initially investigating a new area, scientists frequently use nonexperimental quantitative research to identify existing factors and relationships among them. Such knowledge is later used to formulate hypotheses to be used either in more advanced forms of nonexperimental quantitative research such as path analysis (defined below) or in experimental research.

Correlational Study

Correlational study
Nonexperimental research study based on describing relationships among variables and making predictions

In its simplest form, a **correlational study** consists of measuring two variables and then determining the degree of relationship that exists between them. Consequently, a simple correlational study can be incorporated into other quantitative research approaches. A relatively old, but still interesting, study commonly cited in introductory and developmental texts is a study by Conrad and Jones (1940) regarding the relationship between the IQ scores of parents and those of their offspring. To accomplish the goals of this study, Conrad and Jones measured the IQs of the parents and correlated them with those of their children. In this way, a quantitative index was obtained that described the relationship between these two variables. Because a correlational study is, by definition, a nonexperimental research approach, it lacks manipulation of the independent variable. The researcher simply measures variables in their natural state and determines if they are related.

The correlational approach is quite effective in enabling us to accomplish the research objectives of description and prediction. If a reliable relationship is found between two variables, we not only have described the relationship but also have gained the ability to predict one variable from knowledge of the other variable. Frequently, multiple variables are used in correlational studies to improve the researcher's ability to make predictions. Here are several dependent variables that psychologists have used in prediction studies: major affective disorders in adolescents (Aebi, Metzke, & Steinhausen, 2009), recidivism for sexual offenders (Hanson & Morton-Bourgon, 2009), relapse in depression (Lethbridge, & Allen, 2008), supervisory ratings of employees (Hermelin, Lievens, & Robertson, 2007), social withdrawal in elementary school children (Booth-LaForce & Oxford, 2008), recovery after mild traumatic brain injury (Stulemeijer, van der Werf, Borm, & Vos, 2008), functional outcomes in schizophrenia (Wittorf, Wiedemann, Buchkremer, & Klingberg, 2008), and self-harm and suicide by adolescents (Larsson & Sund, 2008). As you can see in the list of studies provided, prediction studies have an important place in psychological research.

The primary weakness of the correlational approach is present when someone assumes that simply because two variables are related that one *causes* the other. As discussed earlier, there are three required conditions for claiming that two variables are causally related, and relationship is just one of those. In short, you cannot claim causation unless the other two conditions in Table 2.2 are realized, and this is very difficult in correlational research. Mastering the remainder of this book will be easier if you will take a moment and memorize the three required conditions for causation provided in Table 2.2.

An example of the difficulty of claiming causation from mere relationship between two variables is seen in a study by Sears, Whiting, Nowlis, and Sears

(1953). These researchers found that there was a positive relationship between severity of weaning and later psychological adjustment problems. Given the study's results, some individuals might claim that severity of weaning was the agent causing later psychological maladjustment. But, because of the so-called third variable problem, such an inference is not justified. The **third variable problem** refers to the fact that two variables might be correlated not because they are causally related but because some third variable caused both of them to vary. As Figure 2.2 illustrates, the degree of severity with which a child is weaned and his or her later psychological adjustment might both be influenced by the parents' child-rearing skills. If the parents are unskilled, they might both wean their child in a severe manner and inflict verbal or physical abuse, contributing to later adjustment problems. If the parents are skilled at child rearing, weaning might take place with little or no trauma, and the child might have a healthy relationship with his or her parents, leading to stable psychological adjustment. The key point is that in such a situation, although a correlation exists between severity of weaning and later psychological adjustment, these variables are not causally related. Rather, both are caused by an underlying third variable: the parents' parenting skills.

It is very important that you understand that you cannot jump to a conclusion of cause and effect from only knowing that two variables are related. Here is another interesting example. Did you know that there is a relationship between the number of fire trucks responding to a fire and the amount of fire damage? There is a correlation between these two variables: As the number of fire trucks increases, so

Third variable problem

Occurs when observed relationship between two variables is actually due to a confounding extraneous variable

FIGURE 2.2
Illustration of the third variable problem in correlations.

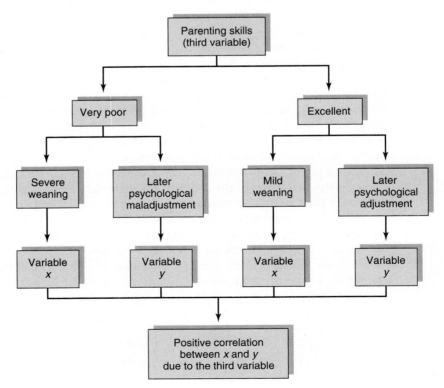

does the amount of fire damage. Should we conclude that increasing the number of fire trucks causes increased fire damage? No! There is a third variable operating here: It is the size of fire. As the size of fire increases, so does the number of fire trucks. It is the size of the fire that is actually causing the amount of fire damage not the number of trucks. Here is one more example. Tea drinking is correlated with lung cancer; people who drink more tea are less likely to get lung cancer. It is the tea preventing lung cancer? No. Tea drinkers have a lower risk for lung cancer because they smoke less. It is very important to remember that *you cannot conclude that two variables are causally related based only on correlation or association.*

Whenever there is the issue of causation (i.e., "Do changes in variable A cause changes in variable B?"), researchers must always consider all three of the required conditions listed earlier in Table 2.2. Relationship is not enough evidence. In Chapter 15, we explain two statistical techniques for controlling for extraneous or third variables, but you can't know whether you have controlled for all of the third variables that might be operating. Another correlational procedure for obtaining some evidence of causation is known as **path analysis**. The idea is to develop a theoretical model describing how a set of variables are related and then to empirically test the theoretical model.

For example, Turner and Johnson (2003) proposed a theoretical model of children's motivation, which is shown in Figure 2.3. Moving from left to right in the model, you will see that parenting characteristics (i.e., parents' education, income, and self-efficacy) were hypothesized to impact parenting beliefs and parent–child relationships. Next, parenting beliefs and parent–child relationships were hypothesized to impact children's mastery motivation (labeled child's mastery). Last, children's motivation was hypothesized to impact children's' academic performance. Remember from Table 2.1 that a mediating variable is a variable that comes in between two variables; given this definition, you can see that the variables in the middle of the figure operate as mediating variables because they are placed between the parent's characteristic variables on the left and child's mastery and achievement on the right. The theoretical model shows several

Path analysis
Type of research in which a researcher hypothesizes a theoretical causal model and then empirically tests the model

FIGURE 2.3
Theoretical child mastery "path model." Each single arrow shows a hypothesized direct effect. Two or more arrows in a causal line show a hypothesized indirect effect, where one variable is hypothesized to affect a later variable by operating through one or more mediating variable(s).

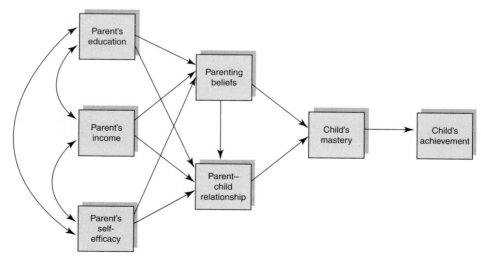

Direct effect

An effect of one variable directly on another variable; depicted as a single arrow in a path model

Indirect effect

An effect occurring through a mediating variable

hypothesized **direct effects** where one variable has an arrow going from it directly to another variable. The theoretical model also shows several **indirect effects**, where one variable affects another variable by going through a mediating variable.

Turner and Johnson tested the theoretical model with data collected from 169 African American children and their teachers and parents. The final path analysis model, shown in Figure 2.4, only includes the statistically significant paths. The paths that were not supported were removed. You can see in this "trimmed model" which hypothesized paths were supported by the empirical data. The final model suggests that parenting characteristics affect children's mastery motivation through the mediating variable of parent–child relationships. In other words, it suggests that parenting characteristics affect the type of parent–child relationships present, and these parent–child relationships affect children's mastery motivation. The results also suggest that mastery motivation mediates the relationship between parent–child relationships and children's achievement. In other words, the parent–child relationships have an effect on children's mastery motivation, and this mastery motivation has an effect on the children's achievement.

The strength of path analysis models (when properly conducted) is that the researcher carefully develops a theoretical model and then empirically tests the model. The primary weakness is that the models usually are based on nonexperimental data rather than experimental research data. Therefore, you should not place too much faith in these models. They provide more evidence of causation than is present in a mere correlation between two variables; however, if you want the strongest evidence of causation, you should conduct an experimental research study (if possible).

F I G U R E   2 . 4

The trimmed child mastery path model. It is the theoretical path model with the nonsignificant paths eliminated (i.e., it is the model that the data support). The numbers on the lines are called path coefficients, and they show the strength and direction of the relationship (i.e., the closer the numbers are to $+1.00$ or to -1.00, the stronger the relationship; if the number is positive, then as one variable increases, so does the other variable; if the number is negative, then as one variable increases, the other variable decreases).

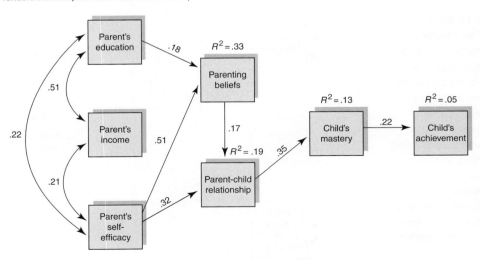

Natural Manipulation Research

Natural manipulation research[1] is another type of nonexperimental research study that examines possible causes that are not usually manipulatable by a researcher, but the causal variable is one that "describes a naturally-occurring contrast between a treatment and a comparison condition" (Shadish et al., 2002, p. 12). In other words, the independent variable maps onto what one might view as a natural manipulation occurring in the world. For example, the destruction of the twin trade towers in New York City on September 11, 2001, had a significant psychological impact on many individuals' lives. You might hypothesize that the impact will be greater for people who were near the twin towers when they collapsed than for individuals who were far away. The causal or independent variable would be closeness to attack, and the levels of this variable are "near the towers" versus "farther away." You might operationalize the levels of the independent variable as within two miles (for the near condition) versus more than 100 miles away (for the faraway condition). Obviously it would not be possible for an experimenter to manipulate such an event, but one might view it as a naturally occurring experiment.

In practice, the difference between the kinds of predictor or independent variables examined in correlational and natural manipulation research is small (it is a matter of degree). The difference is one of "degree of manipulation." In correlational research no manipulation is present, but in natural manipulation research an event occurs that one might view as an approximation of a manipulation. On the one hand, one might argue that a study based on trait variables (e.g., intelligence, extraversion, anxiety, submissiveness) and characteristic variables (e.g., height, weight, ethnicity, political affiliation) should be called a correlational study, because these kinds of variables cannot be changed; they are characteristics that remain relatively constant throughout someone's life. On the other hand, a study based on experience variables (e.g., death of a loved one, experience of an earthquake, winning the lottery, divorce, experience of a hurricane) can be treated as naturally manipulated variables if individuals' status on these variables change.

If you believe the independent variable approximates a natural manipulation then call the study a natural manipulation study, but if the independent variable seems like one that is not naturally manipulated, then call it a correlational study. Also, if your research purpose is predictive, then call your study a predictive study. In practice, the best advice might be to call both correlational and natural manipulations "nonexperimental" studies to emphasize the point that the researcher did not manipulate the independent variable or control the conditions surrounding the manipulation. Remember that whenever you want to draw a conclusion about cause and effect, you must meet the three required conditions provided in Table 2.2. In both correlational and natural manipulations, you will find yourself in trouble on condition 3 shown in Table 2.2. To the degree that a researcher has attempted to determine proper time order of the

Natural manipulation research
Type of research in which the independent variable approximates a naturally occurring manipulation, but it is not manipulated by the researcher

---

[1]This type of research was formally labeled *ex post facto research*, a term that has become obsolete. The newer term is *natural experiment*; however, we believe the term *natural manipulation* more clearly communicates the essential idea of this type of research. Some authors will prefer to classify natural manipulation research as a quasi-experimental approach than a nonexperimental approach.

variables (condition 2) and has systematically controlled for extraneous variables (condition 3), you can upgrade your evaluation of the nonexperimental research study. Also, generally speaking, when the nonexperimental study is based on longitudinal data rather than cross-sectional data (discussed in the next section), the researcher is better able to establish time order, and you can upgrade your evaluation of the research study.

An example of a natural manipulation research study is demonstrated in Richards, Hardy, and Wadsworth's (1997) investigation of the relationship between divorce and psychological functioning of adults. One might view divorce as a natural manipulation independent variable because it marks a categorical change in individuals' status from married to divorced. The researchers hypothesized that adults who had been divorced would report higher rates of anxiety and depression than those who had not (after equating the two groups on several extraneous variables for control). The study included data from the participants at ages 13 and 43. Richards et al. found that the adults at age 43 who had been divorced reported more anxiety and depression than those who had not been divorced. This relation between divorce and depression and anxiety was present after controlling for measures of psychological functioning at age 13.

STUDY QUESTIONS 2.6

- **What is nonexperimental quantitative research?**
- **What is the difference between correlational research and natural manipulation research?**
- **In what ways is correlational research and natural manipulation research similar?**

Cross-Sectional and Longitudinal Studies

Cross-sectional study
Study conducted at a single time period, and data are collected from multiple groups; data are collected during a single, brief time period

Longitudinal study
Data are collected at two or more points in time

In a **cross-sectional study**, the data are collected from research participants during a single, relatively brief period. The "single" time period is just long enough to collect data from all of the participants. In a **longitudinal study**, the data are collected at two or more points in time. Cross-sectional and longitudinal studies are frequently used in developmental psychology and are used to study changes that take place over time. The primary independent variable might or might not be a manipulated independent variable. In other words, these studies are sometimes experimental studies, but perhaps more commonly are nonexperimental studies. Age is a nonmanipulatable variable, so if it is the primary independent variable, then the study will be nonexperimental.

In developmental research, a longitudinal study involves choosing a single group of participants and measuring them repeatedly at selected time intervals to note changes that occur over time in the specified characteristics. For example, Gathercole and Willis (1992) measured a group of children's phonological memory and their vocabulary knowledge at 4, 5, 6, and 8 years of age to determine if the relationship between these two variables changed as the children got older. On the other hand, in developmental research, a cross-sectional study involves identifying representative samples of individuals that differ on some characteristic, such as age, gender, ethnic group, or religion, and measuring these different samples of individuals on the same variable or variable(s) at one point in time. Wagner, Torgesen, Laughon, Simmons, and Rashotte (1993) used the cross-sectional approach in their study of the nature and development of young children's phonological processing abilities. They randomly selected a group of 95 kindergarten and 89 second-grade students from three elementary schools and administered a number of phonological tasks to both groups to determine whether phonological processing abilities differ among these two age groups.

Although the longitudinal and cross-sectional research approaches are frequently used in developmental research, this type of study is not confined to this specific area. For example, Moskowitz and Wrubel (2005) took a longitudinal approach to gaining a more in-depth understanding of the meaning of having contracted HIV. To accomplish the purpose of this study, Moskowitz and Wrubel identified 57 gay men testing positive for HIV and then conducted bimonthly interviews over the course of 2 years to identify how these individuals appraise their HIV changes over time. Andersen, Franckowiak, Christmas, Walston, and Crespo (2001) took a cross-sectional approach to assess the relationship between not participating in leisure time physical activity and body weight among various ethnic groups of older U.S. adults. To accomplish the goal of the study, these investigators surveyed a national representative cross-section of the U.S. population (e.g., Hispanic Americans, African Americans, Caucasian Americans) of individuals aged 60 and older regarding their weight and participation in leisure time activity.

There has been discussion of the relative advantages and disadvantages of longitudinal and cross-sectional approaches to developmental research. One important point is that these two approaches have not always produced similar results. The classic example of this discrepancy is seen in the development of intelligence during adulthood. As seen in Figure 2.5, cross-sectional studies have suggested that adult intelligence begins to decline around the age of 30, whereas longitudinal studies

FIGURE 2.5

Change in intellectual performance as a function of the longitudinal versus the cross-sectional method.

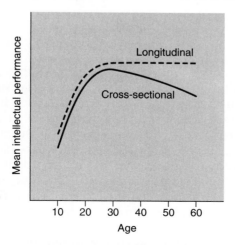

show an increase or no change in intellectual performance until the age of 50 or 60 (Baltes, Reese, & Nesselroade, 1977). Why? The difference has been attributed to what is called an *age-cohort effect.* Longitudinal studies follow just one group or age cohort of individuals over time, so all individuals within this cohort experience similar environmental events. However, cross-sectional studies investigate a number of different groups of individuals or different age cohorts. Because of changes in environmental events, these cohorts have not been exposed to similar experiences. For example, members of a 50-year-old cohort would not have been exposed to video games or computers when they were 10 years old, but a group of 11-year-olds would have. Such differences are confounded with actual age differences in cross-sectional studies, where you compare individuals who are of different ages at one point in time.

Because of the constraints of time, attrition of participants (i.e., participants dropping out of the study), and costs involved in conducting a longitudinal study, the cohort-sequential design has been suggested as an alternative approach. This approach is a hybrid of longitudinal and cross-sectional approaches. The **cohort-sequential design** is a design in which different age groups are tested longitudinally. For example, Chouinard and Roy (2008) were interested in the changes that occur in students' academic motivation during adolescence. They recruited a group of seventh graders and a group of ninth graders and followed them until they completed 9th and 11th grade, respectively. Use of the cohort-sequential design allowed these researchers to gather data from 7th to 11th grade in less time than would be required by a fully longitudinal study. The cohort-sequential design typically results in less cost, time, and attrition than a fully longitudinal study.

Cohort-sequential design
Design that combines cross-sectional and longitudinal elements by following two or more age groups over time

STUDY QUESTIONS 2.7

- **What are cross-sectional and longitudinal designs?**
- **How are cross-sectional and longitudinal designs different?**
- **How does the cohort-sequential design combine characteristics of cross-sectional and longitudinal designs?**

Qualitative Research

Qualitative research
Interpretive research approach relying on multiple types of subjective data and investigation of people in particular situations in their natural environment

Qualitative research is an interpretive research approach that relies on multiple types of subjective data and investigates people in particular situations in their natural environment (Denzin & Lincoln, 1994). This definition has three primary components that are essential to understanding the nature of qualitative research. The first component is that qualitative research is *interpretive*. Qualitative data consist of words, pictures, clothing, documents, or other nonnumerical information. During and after the data are collected, the researcher continually attempts to understand the data *from the participants' subjective perspectives*. The most important task of the qualitative researcher is to understand the insiders' views. Then the research also takes the role of "objective outsider" and relates the interpretive–subjective data to the research purpose and research questions. In qualitative research, the research questions are allowed to evolve, or possibly change, during the study because qualitative research is usually focused on exploring phenomena; in contrast, quantitative research typically does not allow changes of this sort because the focus usually is on hypothesis testing. Qualitative research tends to be most useful for understanding and describing local situations and for theory *generation*; in contrast, quantitative research tends to be most useful for hypothesis *testing*.

Starting with the interpretive component, let's examine a qualitative research study in which the researchers (i.e., Schouten & McAlexander, 1995) became participant observers of the subculture of consumerism associated with Harley-Davidson motorcycles. In their words: " . . . with the excitement and trepidation of neophytes, we tiptoed into our fieldwork as naïve nonparticipant observers. At the time of this writing, we have spent the last year deeply immersed in the lifestyle of the HDSC [Harley-Davidson sub culture], 'passing,' as bikers . . . " (p. 44). It was essential that the researchers understand the subculture from the *insider's perspective*, rather than from the perspective of an ethnocentric outsider. The researchers noted the general appearance and clothing worn by the Harley-Davidson bikers. Many of the bikers had massive bellies, large biceps, and enjoyed loud, aggressive behavior. They adorned their bikes with chrome and leather and wore leather clothing, heavy boots, and gauntlets as well as wallet chains, conches, chrome studs, and other similar hardware. Their motto was "Live to ride, ride to live." The members were "brothers." Their core values included total personal freedom, liberation from confinement, patriotism and American Heritage, and machismo. What did this mean? This is where the interpretive component comes in. The concept of *real Harley–Davidson men* seemed to pervade and help explain many aspects of the biker experience from the clothing they wore to their general behavior and appearance. Members selected this subculture, became socialized, and then continued the tradition by rewarding other members when they displayed the cultural values and behaviors. The most-valued Harley-Davidson bikes were the biggest, heaviest, and loudest ones, which meant that they were the manliest, even though they were not the fastest. All of this was interpreted as conveying a sense "of power, fearsomeness, and invulnerability to the rider" (p. 54).

The second component is that qualitative research is *multimethod*. This means that a variety of methods are used to collect data. These include such diverse data collection methods as an individual's account of a personal experience, introspective analysis, an individual's life story, interviews with an individual, observation of an individual or individuals, written documents, photographs, and historical information. In many qualitative studies, several of these data collection methods might be used to try to get the best description of an event and the meaning it has for the individual or individuals being studied. This use of several methods is referred to as **triangulation**, because it is believed that the use of several methods provides a better understanding of the phenomenon being investigated. For example, Schouten and McAlexander (1995) collected their data from formal and informal interviews, observations, and photographs of the Harley-Davidson bikers.

The third component of qualitative research is that it is conducted in the field or in the person's *natural setting* and surroundings, such as a school classroom, the playground, a board meeting, or a therapy setting. To meet this component of conducting the research in the natural surroundings of the research participants,

Triangulation
Use of multiple data sources, research methods, investigators, and/or theories/perspectives to cross-check and corroborate research data and conclusions

Schouten and McAlexander attended rallies of the Harley Owners Group (HOG), as well as biker swap meets and certain club meetings. The final step involved purchasing Harley-Davidson bikes and the appropriate clothing (jeans, black boots, and black leather jackets), followed by wearing the clothing and using the bikes as their primary means of transportation. This heightened personal involvement increased the frequency of contact with other "bikers" and allowed the researchers to gain an empathic understanding of the bikers' identity, psyche, and everyday social interactions.

From this description of qualitative research, you should be able to see that it is an approach that uses many data collection methods requiring the interpretation of nonnumerical data. The strength of qualitative research is the description and understanding of individuals and groups of individuals with a common identity. Another strength is providing data from which researchers can generate and develop theoretical understandings of phenomena. It is useful for the "logic of discovery" defined in the last chapter.

Qualitative research has its limitations just as every other research method does. One weakness of qualitative research is that it is difficult to generalize because the data are based on local, particularistic data. Another weakness is that different qualitative researchers might provide very different interpretations of the phenomena studied. Another weakness is that objective hypothesis testing procedures are not used. Nonetheless, qualitative data can provide a useful complement to quantitative data and are very useful when the research purpose is exploration and description.

The argument that adding qualitative data to psychological studies is beneficial has been compelling because during the last decade we have witnessed an increase in research that makes use of this type of data. For example, a burgeoning literature has developed in organizational management, social psychology, aging, education, and family studies (Denzin & Lincoln, 1994; Gilgun, Daly, & Handel, 1992; Gubrium & Sankar, 1993; Silverman, 1993) that focuses on the collection and analysis of qualitative data.

STUDY QUESTIONS 2.8

- **What is qualitative research, and explain each of the components included in this definition.**
- **What are the strengths and weaknesses of qualitative research?**

Major Methods of Data Collection

Method of data collection
Technique for physically obtaining the data to be analyzed in a research study

In empirical research, researchers collect data, analyze the data, and report and interpret the results. The term **method of data collection** refers to how the researcher obtains the empirical data to be used to answer his or her research questions. We contend that there are six major methods of data collection and that these methods incorporate more specific methods of data collection. We now describe these following major methods of data collection: tests, questionnaires, interviews, focus groups, observations, and existing or secondary data.

Tests

Tests
Standardized or researcher-constructed data collection instruments designed to measure personality, aptitude, achievement, and performance

Tests are commonly used data collection instruments or procedures designed to measure personality, aptitude, achievement, and performance. Many tests are standardized and come with information on their reliability, validity, and norms for comparison. Tests also are frequently constructed by experimental researchers for specific variables examined in research studies. Some strengths and weaknesses of tests are provided in Table 2.3.

As a general rule, you should *not* construct a new test if one is already available. For psychological research purposes, the best source of information about the tests you should be using to address your research questions is found in the published psychological research literature. You should always examine the best research in the research area and locate the measures that they use. Another useful source of tests and measures is *The Directory of Unpublished Experimental Mental Measures* (2003), edited by Goldman and Mitchell and published by the American Psychological Association. We discuss standardized tests in detail in Chapter 5, and we explain the psychometric properties of reliability and validity and provide some additional sources for locating tests and reviews of tests.

TABLE 2.3
Strengths and Weaknesses of Tests

Strengths of tests (especially standardized tests)
- Can provide measures of many characteristics of people.
- Often standardized (i.e., the same stimulus is provided to all participants).
- Allows comparability of common measures across research populations.
- Strong psychometric properties (high measurement reliability and validity).
- Availability of reference group data.
- Many tests can be administered to groups, this saves time.
- Can provide "hard," quantitative data.
- Tests are usually already developed.
- A wide range of tests is available.
- Response rate is high for group-administered tests.
- Ease of data analysis because of quantitative nature of data.

Weaknesses of tests (especially standardized tests)
- Can be expensive if test must be purchased for each research participant.
- Reactive participant effects such as social desirability can occur.
- Test might not be appropriate for a local or unique population.
- Open-ended questions and probing not available.
- Tests are sometimes biased against certain groups of people.
- Nonresponse to selected items on the test.
- Some tests lack psychometric data.

In addition to the tests discussed in Chapter 5, however, researchers must sometimes develop a new test to measure the specific knowledge, skills, behavior, or cognitive activity that is being studied. For example, a researcher might need to measure response time to a memory task using a mechanical apparatus or develop a test to measure a specific mental or cognitive activity (which obviously cannot be directly observed). Again, the best source for this information is the psychological research literature.

Questionnaires

Questionnaire
Self-report data collection instrument completed by research participants

The second method of data collection is the questionnaire. A **questionnaire** is a self-report data collection instrument that is filled out by research participants. Questionnaires measure participants' opinions and perceptions and provide self-reported demographic information. They are usually paper-and-pencil instruments (i.e., participants fill them out), but are increasingly being placed on the Web for participants to go to and "fill out." Questionnaires can include closed-ended items (where respondents must select from the responses given by the researcher) and open-ended items (where respondents provide answers in their own words). We discuss the questionnaire method of data collection extensively in Chapter 12 and explain how to construct a questionnaire. The strengths and weaknesses of questionnaires are provided in Table 2.4.

Interviews

Interview
Data collection method in which an interviewer asks the interviewee a series of questions, often with prompting for additional information

The third method of data collection is the interview method. An **interview** is a situation where the interviewer asks the interviewee a series of questions. Interviews are conducted in face-to-face situations and over the telephone. It is also possible to conduct interviews electronically, such as over the Internet. These interviews can be asynchronous (interaction occurs over time) or synchronous (interaction happens in real time). The strengths and weaknesses of interviews as a method of data collection are provided in Table 2.5. In Chapter 12 you will learn how to construct interview protocols, which have much in common with questionnaires. Also in Chapter 12, we provide practical information on how to conduct interviews.

Focus Groups

Focus group
Collection of data in a group situation where a moderator leads a discussion with a small group of people

The fourth method of data collection involves the use of focus groups. A **focus group** is a situation where a focus group moderator keeps a small and homogeneous group (of 6–12 people) focused on the discussion of a research topic or issue. Focus group sessions generally last between 1 and 3 hours and are recorded using audio and/or videotapes. A focus group should not be viewed as a group interview because the emphasis is on small-group interaction and in-depth discussion among the participants about the issues being studied. Focus groups are especially useful for exploring ideas and obtaining in-depth information about how people think about an issue. The strengths and weaknesses of focus groups as a method of data collection are provided in Table 2.6.

TABLE 2.4
Strengths and Weaknesses of Questionnaires

Strengths of questionnaires

- Good for measuring attitudes and eliciting other content from research participants.
- Inexpensive (especially mail questionnaires and group-administered questionnaires).
- Can provide information about participants' subjective perspectives and ways of thinking.
- Can administer to probability samples.
- Quick turnaround for group-administered questionnaires.
- Perceived anonymity by respondent can be high if situation is carefully controlled.
- Moderately high measurement validity (i.e., high reliability and validity) for well-constructed and validated questionnaires.
- Closed-ended items can provide exact information needed by researcher.
- Open-ended items can provide detailed information in respondents' own words.
- Ease of data analysis for closed-ended items.
- Useful for exploration as well as hypothesis testing research.

Weaknesses of questionnaires

- Usually must be kept short.
- Reactive effects might occur (e.g., respondents might try to show only what is socially desirable).
- Nonresponse to selective items.
- People filling out questionnaires might not recall important information and might lack self-awareness.
- Response rate may be low for mail and e-mail questionnaires.
- Open-ended items may reflect differences in verbal ability, obscuring the issues of interest.
- Data analysis can be time consuming for open-ended items.
- Measures need validation.

Observation
Researcher watches and records events or behavioral patterns of people

Naturalistic observation
Observation conducted in real-world situations

Laboratory observation
Observation conducted in lab setting set up by the researcher

Observation

The fifth method of data collection is the observation method, in which the researcher looks at what people do. Often, it is important to collect observational data (in addition to attitudinal data) because what people say is not always what they do! Researchers can observe participants in natural and/or structured environments. The former is called **naturalistic observation** because it is done in real-world settings. The latter is called **laboratory observation** because it is conducted in a lab or other controlled environment set up by the researcher.

In quantitative research, the researcher standardizes the procedures and collects quantitative data. Specifically, the researcher standardizes who is observed, what is observed, when and where the observations are to take place, and how the observations are to take place. Standardized instruments (e.g., checklists) are often used in quantitative observation. Sampling procedures are sometimes used so that the researcher does not have to make continuous observations. For example, a researcher might use time-interval sampling to obtain a representative

TABLE 2.5
Strengths and Weaknesses of Interviews

Strengths of interviews

- Good for measuring attitudes and most other content of interest.
- Allows probing and posing of follow-up questions by the interviewer.
- Can provide in-depth information.
- Can provide information about participants' subjective perspectives and ways of thinking.
- Closed-ended interviews provide exact information needed by researcher.
- Telephone and e-mail interviews usually provide very quick turnaround.
- Moderately high measurement validity (i.e., high reliability and validity) for well-constructed and well-tested interview protocols.
- Can use with probability samples.
- Relatively high response rates are often attainable.
- Useful for exploration as well as hypothesis-testing research.

Weaknesses of interviews

- In-person interviews usually are expensive and time consuming.
- Reactive effects (e.g., interviewees might try to show only what is socially desirable).
- Investigator effects might occur (e.g., untrained interviewers might distort data because of personal biases and poor interviewing skills).
- Interviewees might not recall important information and might lack self-awareness.
- Perceived anonymity by respondents might be low.
- Data analysis can be time consuming for open-ended items.
- Measures need validation.

Time-interval sampling
Observations are recorded during preselected time intervals

Event sampling
Observations are recorded every time a particular event occurs

sample of possible observations. **Time-interval sampling** is conducted by observing during preselected time intervals, such as during the first 5 minutes of each 30-minute time interval. Conversely, in **event sampling** the researcher conducts observations every time that a particular event takes place (e.g., observe every time a participant asks another participant a question). Event sampling is an efficient method of sampling when you want to observe a particular event that occurs infrequently.

In qualitative research, observation procedures usually are exploratory and open ended, and the researcher takes extensive field notes. It is helpful to consider qualitative observation as falling on a continuum originally developed by social scientist Raymond Gold (1958). Following are the types from least-qualitative (complete observer) to the most-qualitative observation (complete participant) in nature:

- *Complete observer*. Here the researcher observes from the "outside" and, if the setting is a public one, the researcher does not inform the participants that he or she is studying them.

TABLE 2.6
Strengths and Weaknesses of Focus Groups

Strengths of focus groups
- Useful for exploring ideas and concepts.
- Provides window into participants' internal thinking.
- Can obtain in-depth information.
- Can examine how participants react to each other.
- Allows probing.
- Most content can be tapped.
- Allows quick turnaround.

Weaknesses of focus groups
- Sometimes expensive.
- Might be difficult to find a focus group moderator with good facilitative and rapport-building skills.
- Reactive and investigator effects might occur if participants feel they are being watched or studied.
- Might be dominated by one or two participants.
- Difficult to generalize results if small, unrepresentative samples of participants are used.
- Might include large amount of extra or unnecessary information.
- Measurement validity might be low.
- Usually should not be the only data collection methods used in a study.
- Data analysis can be time consuming because of the open-ended nature of the data.

- *Observer-as-participant.* Here the researcher spends a limited amount of time "inside" the situation and obtains informed consent to observe the participants for a research study.
- *Participant-as-observer.* Here the researcher spends extensive time "inside" the group or situation and always informs the participants that they are being studied and obtains informed consent.
- *Complete participant.* Here the researcher becomes a full participating member of the group. In most cases, the group must be informed and permission granted.

If you ever collect observational data, remember the following: (1) Make sure everyone is well trained; (2) be sensitive to your appearance and how people being observed react to you; (3) establish rapport but do not promise anything you cannot deliver; (4) be reflexive, unobtrusive, empathetic, and alert at all times; (5) find an effective way to record what is observed (e.g., note taking, tape recordings); (6) try to validate and corroborate what you think you are seeing; (7) make observations in multiple settings; and (8) spend enough time in the "field" to obtain sufficient information. The strengths and weaknesses of observational data are provided in Table 2.7.

T A B L E   2 . 7
Strengths and Weaknesses of Observational Data

Strengths of observational data

- Allows one to directly see what people do without having to rely on what they say they do.
- Provides firsthand experience, especially if the observer participates in activities.
- Can provide relatively objective measurement of behavior (especially for standardized observations).
- Observer can determine what does *not* occur.
- Observer might see things that escape the awareness of people in the setting.
- Excellent way to discover what is occurring in a setting.
- Helps in understanding importance of contextual factors.
- Can be used with participants with weak verbal skills.
- Might provide information on things people would otherwise be unwilling to talk about.
- Observer might move beyond selective perceptions of participants in the setting.
- Good for description.
- Provides moderate degree of realism (when done outside of the laboratory).

Weaknesses of observational data

- Reasons for observed behavior might be unclear.
- Reactive effects might occur when respondents know they are being observed (e.g., people being observed might behave in atypical ways).
- Investigator effects (e.g., personal biases and selective perception of observers).
- Observer might "go native" (i.e., overidentifying with the group being studied).
- Sampling of observed people and settings might be limited.
- Cannot observe large or dispersed populations.
- Some settings and content of interest cannot be observed.
- Collection of unimportant material might be moderately high.
- More expensive to conduct than questionnaires and tests.
- Data analysis can be time consuming.

Existing or secondary data
Collection of data that were left behind or originally used for something different than the current research study

Document
Personal and official documents that were left behind

Physical data
Any material thing created or left behind by humans that might provide clues to some event or phenomenon

Existing or Secondary Data

The sixth and last major method of data collection is the collection of **existing or secondary data**. This means that the researcher collects or obtains "data" that were originally left behind or used for some purpose other than the new research study. The most frequently used existing data are **documents**, physical data, and archived research data. Personal documents are documents that were written or recorded for private purposes, such as letters, diaries, and family pictures. Official documents are documents that were written or recorded for public or private organizations, such as newspapers, annual reports, yearbooks, and meeting minutes. **Physical data** are any material thing created or left by humans that might provide information about a phenomenon of interest to a researcher, such as the

Archived research data
Data (usually quantitative) originally used for a different research project

contents of someone's trash, wear on the tiles in museums, wear on library books, and soil and DNA on clothes. **Archived research data** are secondary research data that were collected by other researchers for other purposes. When data are saved and archived, others researchers can later use the data. The largest repository of archived quantitative data is the Interuniversity Consortium for Political and Social Research (ICPSR), which is located at the University of Michigan in Ann Arbor, Michigan. The strengths and weaknesses of existing/secondary data are provided in Table 2.8.

TABLE 2.8
Strengths and Weaknesses of Existing Data

Strengths of documents and physical data
- Can provide insight into what people think and what they do.
- Unobtrusive, making reactive and investigator effects very unlikely.
- Can be collected for time periods occurring in the past (e.g., historical data).
- Provides useful background and historical data on people, groups, and organizations.
- Useful for corroboration.
- Grounded in local setting.
- Useful for exploration.

Strengths of archived research data
- Archived research data are available on a wide variety of topics.
- Inexpensive.
- Often are reliable and valid (high measurement validity).
- Can study trends.
- Ease of data analysis.
- Often based on high quality or large probability samples.

Weaknesses of documents and physical data
- Might be incomplete.
- Might be representative only of one perspective.
- Access to some types of content is limited.
- Might not provide insight into participants' personal thinking for physical data.
- Might not apply to general populations.

Weaknesses of archived research data
- Might not be available for the population of interest to you.
- Might not be available for the research questions of interest to you.
- Data might be dated.
- Open-ended or qualitative data usually not available.
- Many of the most important findings have already been mined from the data.

STUDY QUESTIONS 2.9

- **What are the six methods of data collection?**
- **What are two strengths and weaknesses of each of the six methods of data collection?**

Summary

The two major research approaches of quantitative and qualitative research were introduced. Quantitative research (e.g., experimental research and nonexperimental research) relies on numerical data and qualitative research on nonnumerical data. Experimental research is the best type of research for demonstrating cause-and-effect relationships. In experimental research, the researcher actively manipulates the independent variable (IV) and holds all other variables constant so that a difference between the treatment and control groups found on the dependent variable after the manipulation can be attributed to the independent variable. For example, the researcher might randomly assign participants with a common cold to two groups in order to form two probabilistically equivalent groups at the start of the experiment. The researcher "manipulates the independent variable" by giving a pill with the active ingredient (supposed to cure the cold) to one group and a placebo (pill without the active ingredient) to the other group. The only difference between the two groups is that one received the real pill and the other received the placebo. If the group receiving the pill with the active ingredient improves, but the group receiving the placebo does not improve, then the researcher can conclude that the pill worked (i.e., it caused the treatment group participants to improve). Another way of stating this is to say that the researcher concludes that changes in the IV caused the changes in the dependent variable (DV). The three required conditions for making a claim of cause and effect are as follows: (1) There must be a relationship between the IV and DV, (2) changes in the IV must occur before the changes in the DV, and (3) the relationship between the IV and DV must not be due to any extraneous or third variable (i.e., there must not be any alternative explanation for the relationship observed between the IV and DV). When you want to study cause and effect, the experimental research approach should always be your first choice because it is the strongest type of research for this purpose. Experiments can be conducted in field settings, in the laboratory, or on the Internet.

In nonexperimental quantitative research, the researcher is not able to manipulate the IV, and the required causal condition 3 (eliminating alternative explanations) is always a concern. Two types of nonexperimental quantitative research are correlational research (measuring relationships among variables) and natural manipulation research (when the independent variable approximates a natural manipulation in the world). Correlational research is often used for predictive purposes, but it is also used for testing theoretical models (in a technique called path analysis).

Cross-sectional studies (where data are collected during a single time period) and longitudinal studies (where data are collected at two or more time periods) are sometimes used in experimental research, but they are more often used in nonexperimental quantitative research. Longitudinal studies are especially popular in developmental psychology. Longitudinal studies are helpful in establishing causal condition 2 (establishing time ordering of the IV and DV).

Qualitative research is an interpretive research approach that relies on multiple types of subjective data and is used to investigate people in particular situations in natural environments. It is interpretive (i.e., it attempts to understand the insiders' subjective perspectives), multimethod (i.e., it uses multiple data collection methods such as life stories, participant observation, in-depth interviewing, open-ended questionnaires), and conducted in natural real-world settings (i.e., it studies behavior as it naturally occurs rather than manipulating independent variables).

Last, the six major methods of data collection (i.e., ways to obtain empirical data) were described. They are as follows: (1) tests (instruments or procedures for measuring personality, achievement, performance, and other more specific experimental outcome variables), (2) questionnaires (i.e., self-report data collection instrument filled out by research participants), (3) interviews (i.e., situation in which an interviewer asks the interviewee a series of questions and probes for clarification and detail when needed), (4) focus groups (i.e., small-group situation, where a group moderator keeps a group of participants focused on discussion of research topics of interest), (5) observation (i.e., the researcher looks at what people do rather than asking them), and (6) existing or secondary data (i.e., collection of data left behind for other purposes, such as documents, physical data, and archived data).

Key Terms and Concepts

Archived research data
Categorical variable
Causal description
Causal explanation
Causation
Cause
Cause-and-effect relationship
Cohort-sequential design
Confounding variables
Correlational research
Cross-sectional study
Dependent variable
Descriptive research
Direct effect
Documents
Effect
Event sampling
Existing data
Experimental research
Extraneous variable

Field experiment
Focus group
Independent variable
Indirect effect
Internet experiment
Interviews
Laboratory experiment
Laboratory observation
Longitudinal study
Manipulation
Mediating variable
Method of data collection
Moderator variable
Natural manipulation research
Naturalistic observation
Nonexperimental quantitative research
Nonnumerical data
Numerical data
Observation
Path analysis

Physical data	Tests
Psychological experiment	Third variable problem
Qualitative research	Time-interval sampling
Quantitative research	Triangulation
Quantitative variable	Variable
Questionnaire	

Related Internet Sites

http://www.pitt.edu/~super1/lecture/lec7741/
This site gives a discussion on the processes used to identify cause and effect.

http://www.acenet.edu/bookstore/pdf/2002_access&persistence.pdf
This site contains the results of a longitudinal study focusing on college students.

http://www.pitt.edu/~pittcntr/About/links.htm
This site has links to philosophy of science pages.

http://www.apa.org/
Link to the American Psychological Association. Students can join at a reduced price.

http://www.socialpsychology.org/methods.htm
Link to the Social Psychology Network. Has lots of good stuff.

http://davidakenny.net/cm/mediate.htm
This site has a discussion of mediating variables.

http://www.qualitativeresearch.uga.edu/QualPage/
This site has links to lots of materials on qualitative research.

Practice Test

1. A variable that varies in type or kind is called a(n)

   a. Categorical variable
   b. Dependent variable
   c. Independent variable
   d. Intervening variable

2. The variable that is presumed to cause a change in another variable is called a(n)

   a. Categorical variable
   b. Dependent variable
   c. Independent variable
   d. Intervening variable

3. A mediating variable is

   a. An intervening variable
   b. A variable that moderates a relationship
   c. Extraneous variable
   d. Interaction variable

4. Why is it important to control extraneous variables (to the best extent possible)?

    a. An uncontrolled extraneous variable (variable "X") can cause doubt as to whether changes in one variable (variable "A") cause changes in another variable (variable "B").

    b. An uncontrolled extraneous variable (variable "X") can act as an alternative explanation for the claim that changes in one variable (variable "A") cause changes in another variable (variable "B").

    c. Uncontrolled extraneous variables rarely have an impact on empirical research and therefore it is not important to carefully control them most of the time.

    d. Both A and B are correct

5. The strongest evidence for causality comes from which of the following research methods?

    a. Experimental research

    b. Natural manipulation research

    c. Correlational research

    d. All of the above provide strong evidence for making cause-and-effect claims

6. In what kind of research are "words and pictures" common forms of data?

    a. Quantitative research

    b. Qualitative research

Challenge Exercises

The challenge exercises included in this chapter represent topics for discussion. Included are a couple of Web sites (see the section "Related Internet Sites") that address the topic of causation. You might want to log in to these Web sites to get more information on this topic.

1. Consider a field experiment conducted after a severe hurricane. Imagine that the findings indicated that aggression was higher among children who had to change schools after the storm (due to their school being damaged and closed). Identify the independent and dependent variables in this study. Describe possible mediating and moderating variables.

2. When we conduct our experiments, we attempt to identify a cause-and-effect relationship. Is it more accurate to say that any relationship we find is deterministic or probabilistic? In other words, would it be more accurate to state that the presumed cause determined the effect or that the presumed cause increased the probability of the effect occurring? Make sure that you explain and defend your answer.

3. Consider each of the following situations and identify the presumed cause and the presumed effect. Then discuss the likelihood that the presumed cause actually did produce the observed effect. Explain why someone might think these two variables were causally related and then consider the fact that other variables could also have produced the effect.

   a. The Republicans passed a law giving a tax break that benefits wealthy Americans. Shortly after the tax break went into effect, the stock market went down, and the economy went into a recession. The Democrats claimed that the tax break caused the economic decline and attempted to repeal the tax break.

   b. Bill purchased a new piece of software for his computer and installed it immediately. The next time he started his computer, it froze up on him, so Bill concluded that it was the software that caused the computer to freeze.

4. There are many beliefs about events in the world that different people hold, such as the following:

   - When bones ache, rain is coming.
   - Blondes aren't very smart.
   - People who live in the country move more slowly than people in the city.
   - People who live in the South are not very smart.

   Think about each of these beliefs and the various quantitative research designs. Identify the type of quantitative research design or designs (more than one design could be used to test some of these beliefs) that could be used to test each of these beliefs. Then explain why the design or designs you selected could test the belief. Also explain why the designs you did not select could not be used to test the beliefs.

5. We discussed six major ways to collect data. Compare and contrast interviews and observations. What are the strengths and weaknesses of interviews and observations? What are the advantages of collecting multiple types of data?

C H A P T E R

Problem Identification and Hypothesis Formation

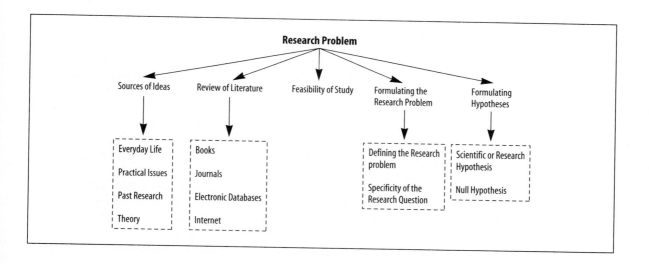

September 11, 2001, started as a typical Tuesday morning with every promise of being just another work day, one that few would remember or think much about. But what started out as an uneventful morning became a tragic event, claiming thousands of innocent lives as 19 suicide hijackers attacked the United States in one of the biggest enemy attacks on American soil since Pearl Harbor.

It all began uneventfully when Mohammed Atta and several other suicide hijackers boarded American Airlines flight 11, scheduled to depart Boston's Logan Airport at 8 a.m. Flight 11 was a Boeing 767 capable of carrying more than 24,000 gallons of aviation fuel, enough to fill a swimming pool 22 feet in diameter to a depth of 8 feet. Shortly after takeoff, men armed with box cutters and plastic knives hijacked flight 11. At 8:46 EDT, flight 11, traveling at nearly 500 mph, crashed into the north tower of the World Trade Center. The impact ripped a huge hole in the tower from the 94th to the 98th floor and spilled thousands of gallons of fuel from the aircraft wreckage, which ignited, cascading through vents and elevator shafts, and setting the building on fire.

Morning news programs immediately switched to live coverage of the tower, showing the gaping black hole in its upper floors, the thick smoke billowing out across lower Manhattan. At first, there was no thought that this was an attack on America. Rather, people wondered how such a thing could happen. Did the pilot have a heart attack? Did the plane's mechanical system fail? Eighteen minutes later, the answer became crystal clear as United Airlines flight 175, another Boeing 767, bound from Boston's Logan Airport to Los Angeles, banked in a graceful curve and slammed into the south tower impacting the 78th through 84th floors.

Instant replays showed the plane's last moments over and over, and the realization grew that this was not an accident but an attack on America. The horror grew as some of the victims trapped above the fires apparently decided that death by jumping was preferable to being burned by the fires. One by one, hand in hand, they jumped, falling for 10 seconds or more before striking the ground.

At 9:59 a.m., the structural steel holding the north tower erect had become soft and pliable from the heat of the fire and was no longer able to support the building's weight. The steel buckled under the load, and the floors containing the fire began to fall, each one smashing into the floor beneath it until the weight was more than the steel inner structure could bear. The collapsed floors drove the entire 110 stories of the north tower to the ground, trapping and killing all those who had not escaped as well as rescue workers. At 10:28 a.m., the south World Trade Center tower shuddered and fell, creating a gaping wound in the air where once there had been tall buildings. At the same time that these events were taking place in New York, a Boeing 757 slammed into the west wing of the Pentagon and a United Airlines flight bound from Newark, New Jersey, to San Francisco crashed in a field in rural Pennsylvania.

These repeated and coordinated crashes clearly demonstrated that America was under attack and that this was a planned attack by a group of terrorists. Throughout the day, people repeatedly asked, "Why?" "What?" and "How?" Why would anyone want to do this? What had motivated them to engage in such a destructive act? How had they orchestrated such an event? As the investigation of these terrorist acts continued, it became clear that they were orchestrated by a group of fanatical Muslims headed by Osama bin Laden and his al Qaeda fighters. However, if you were a social psychologist, you might want to search for reasons *why* such tragic events could take place. What would prompt a person to become a suicide terrorist? What would motivate a person to kill thousands of innocent people? What would a person hope to gain from acts such as these? What has America done to anger people halfway around the world so much that they want to destroy Americans? These are just some of the research questions that could be asked and that could become the topic of a research study.

Introduction

Up to this point in the text, we have discussed the general characteristics of scientific research. Using this approach, however, requires that we first have a problem in need of a solution. In the field of psychology, identification of a research idea should be relatively simple because psychology is the scientific study of behavior—including human behavior. Our behavior represents the focus of attention of a great deal of psychological investigation. To convert our observations of behavior into legitimate research questions, we must be inquisitive and ask ourselves why certain types of behavior occur. For example, assume that you hear a person express an extremely resentful, hostile, and prejudiced attitude toward Russians. The next day you see this person interacting with a Russian and note that she is both being very polite and courteous. You have seen a contradiction between the attitude expressed by this individual and her behavior. Two well-founded research questions are "Why is there a lack of correspondence between attitude and behavior?" and "Under what circumstance do attitudes *not* predict behavior?"

Let us now look at the major sources that can be used to generate research questions.

Sources of Research Ideas

Where do ideas or problems originate? Where should we look for a researchable problem? In all fields, there are a number of common sources of problems, such as existing theories and past research. In psychology, we are even more fortunate; we have our own personal experience and everyday events to draw from. The things we see, read about, or hear about can serve as ideas to be turned into research topics. But identifying these ideas as research topics requires an alert and curious scientist. Rather than just passively observing behavior or reading material relating to psychology, we must actively question the reasons for the occurrence of an event or behavior. If you ask, "Why?" you will find many researchable topics. Typically, problems originate from one of four sources: everyday life, practical issues, past research, and theory.

Everyday Life

As we proceed through our daily routine, we come into contact with many questions in need of solution. Parents want to know how to handle their children; students want to know how to learn material faster. When we interact with others or see others react, we note many individual differences. If we observe children on a playground, these differences are readily apparent. One child might be very aggressive and another much more reserved, waiting for others to encourage interaction. The responses of a particular person also vary according to the situation. A child who is very aggressive in one situation might be passive in another. Why do these differences exist? What produces these varying responses? Why are some people leaders and others followers? Why do we like some people and not others? Many such researchable questions can be identified from everyone's interactions and personal experiences.

Practical Issues

Many research problems arise from practical issues that require solutions. Private industry faces such problems as low employee morale, absenteeism, turnover, selection, and placement. Work has been and continues to be conducted in these areas. Clinical psychology is in need of a great deal of research to identify more efficient modes of dealing with mental disturbances. Units of the federal and state governments support experimentation designed to solve practical problems, such as finding a cure for cancer. Large expenditures are also being directed toward improving the educational process.

Law enforcement agencies are concerned not only with obtaining accurate eyewitness testimony but also with extracting leads or clues from eyewitnesses. To that end, these agencies now use hypnosis, under the assumption that hypnosis can extract accurate evidence that otherwise would not be available. The validity of such an assumption was not tested until Sanders and Simmons (1983) asked eyewitnesses, some of whom were hypnotized and some of whom were not, to identify a thief from a lineup. As Figure 3.1 reveals, hypnotized subjects, contrary to expectations, identified the thief *fewer* times than did the subjects who were not hypnotized. Such evidence suggests that hypnosis is not an effective technique for extracting accurate evidence.

FIGURE 3.1

Accuracy of eyewitness identification as a function of being hypnotized.

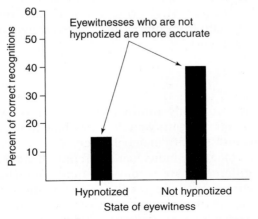

(Based on data from "Use of hypnosis to enhance eyewitness accuracy: Does it work?" by G. S. Sanders and W. L. Simmons, 1983, *Journal of Applied Psychology, 68*, pp. 70–77.)

Past Research

Previously conducted research is an excellent source of research ideas. This might sound like a contradiction because research is designed to answer questions, but one of the interesting features of research is that it tends to generate more questions than it answers. Although each well-designed study does provide additional knowledge, phenomena are multidetermined. In any experiment, only a limited number of variables can be studied. Investigation of these variables might lead to hypotheses about the effects of other variables. The multidimensional nature of phenomena is also frequently the cause of a lack of agreement among research results. An unidentified variable might be the source of conflict among various studies on a given problem, and research must be conducted to uncover this variable and thereby eliminate the apparent contradiction.

To illustrate this, consider the study conducted by Mellgren, Seybert, and Dyck (1978). They investigated the influence of presenting different orders of schedules of continuous reinforcement, nonreinforcement, and partial reinforcement on resistance to extinction. Previous research had revealed conflicting results when the resistance to extinction of participants who had received continuous reward and then partial reward was compared with that of participants given only partial reward schedules. Some studies indicated that resistance to extinction decreased, others indicated that it increased, and still others showed that the existence of an increase or decrease in resistance to extinction depended on the stage of extinction. Mellgren et al. attempted to resolve this inconsistency. The results of their study revealed that the greatest resistance to extinction occurred when a large number of nonreinforced trials preceded a partial reinforcement schedule. Although this study showed which schedule produced the greatest resistance to extinction, it left other questions unanswered. For example, it did not provide an explanation of why resistance to extinction increases if a large number of nonreinforced trials precedes partial reinforcement. This led to another study, which attempted to answer this new question. As you can see, each study leads to a subsequent study, so people can spend their whole lives investigating one particular area. Research is an ongoing process.

Theory

Theory
A group of logically organized and deductively related laws

A **theory**, defined by M.H. Marx (1963, p. 9) as "a group of logically organized (deductively related) laws," is supposed to serve a number of distinct functions. Marx states that theory is both a tool and a goal. The *goal* function is evidenced by the proposition that laws or generalizations are ordered and integrated by theories; theories summarize and integrate existing knowledge. The *tool* function, evidenced by the proposition that theories guide research, is the function of interest to us here. A good theory goes beyond the goal function to suggest new relationships and make new predictions. Thus, it serves as a source of researchable ideas.

Leon Festinger's (1957) theory of cognitive dissonance is an example of a theory that stimulated an extraordinary amount of research in the decade that followed its publication. From this theory, Festinger and Carlsmith (1959) hypothesized and validated the less-than-obvious prediction that, after completing a boring task, participants who were given $1 to tell a "stooge" that the boring task was interesting and fun actually stated that they had enjoyed the task more than did the participants who were given $20 to do the same thing.

The four sources of research ideas—everyday life, practical issues, past research, and theory—barely scratch the surface of circumstances that can inspire a creative idea. The important issue is not the identification of sources of ideas but the generation of these ideas as illustrated in Exhibit 3.1. This is

---

EXHIBIT 3.1

Finding the Cause and Treatment of Peptic Ulcer Disease

In the early part of the twentieth century, peptic ulcer disease was believed to be caused by stress and dietary factors. Treatment for the disease involved hospitalization, bed rest, and prescription of special bland foods. Later in the twentieth century, gastric acid was blamed for the disease. Antacids and medications that block acid production became the standard therapy. However, the incidence of peptic ulcer disease remained high, and victims of this disease continued to battle it in spite of this treatment.

The real cause and an effective treatment did not appear on the medical scene until 1982 when Australian physicians Robin Warren and Barry Marshall (2002) first identified a link between *Helicobacter pylori* (*H. pylori*) and ulcers. These investigators concluded that the bacterium, not stress or diet, causes ulcers. However, the medical community was slow to accept this novel finding, and it was not until over 10 years later that the National Institutes of Health Consensus Development Conference concluded that there was a strong association between *H. pylori* infections and ulcer disease. At this time, the conference also recommended that ulcer patients with *H. pylori* infection be treated with antibiotics. In 1996, the Food and Drug Administration approved the first antibiotic for treatment of ulcer disease (Centers for Disease Control, 2001).

Although we now know the cause and the effective treatment of peptic ulcer disease, this knowledge came only with Dr. Barry Marshall's boundless conviction that he was right when

others doggedly pronounced him wrong. Marshall's initial investigation into this disease began when he was a medical resident at Royal Perth Hospital. He searched the literature and discovered that the presence of the spiral bacterium in the stomach had been reported as far back as the late 1800s and became convinced that this bacterium was the key to the cause and treatment of gastritis and ulcers. As a result of this conviction, he collaborated with Robin Warren, a staff pathologist at Royal Perth Hospital. Both of these individuals knew that the spiral bacterium was present in over half their patients but had not been recognized as a common occupant of human gastric mucosa. This further stimulated their investigations into the relationship between this bacterium and peptic ulcer disease. At one point, Marshall even infected himself with the ulcer-causing bacteria to create an experimental model to substantiate his hypothesis and challenge the accepted belief that mental or emotional disturbance or diet was responsible for peptic ulcer disease.

Persevering against the almost universal skepticism of his peers, Marshall's investigations proved the significance of *H. pylori* in peptic ulcer disease. And finally, in 1996, the Food and Drug Administration officially approved the first drug therapy for the treatment of this disorder, a combination of bismuth and the antibiotic tinidazole. Marshall continues to investigate the significance of this bacterium and has focused on its relationship to stomach cancer, which is also gaining acceptance.

the initial stage in the context of science. To develop these researchable ideas requires the development of a way of thinking. You have to develop a questioning and inquisitive approach to life. For example, Edwin H. Land invented the Polaroid Land Camera after his 3-year-old daughter asked him why a camera could not produce pictures instantly. He could have dismissed this question and merely told her that this was not possible. However, Land asked himself why it couldn't be done. While out for a stroll he thought about this issue and came up with the ideas for a camera that could produce developed photographs.

Bias in Research Ideas

Although there are many sources of ideas in psychology, it is important that we not overlook significant topics. To do so would lead us to develop a knowledge base that is incomplete. All scientists probably agree that we need to conduct research on all important topics. However, scientists are human, and the questions and particular topics they think are most significant can be affected by their personal and demographic characteristics such as gender, social class, ethnicity, sexual orientation, religiosity, age, and so forth. For example, in past years there was a lot of research focusing on the influence of mothers' working outside the home on their children's psychological welfare. Much less attention focused on whether fathers' commitment to their work endangers their children's welfare or if the mothers' employment might even benefit their children (Hare-Mustin & Marecek, 1990). It appears that personal characteristics have influenced the selection of research questions and have led scientists to overlook important aspects of human behavior. To correct for potential bias and ensure that all topics of importance receive attention, it is imperative that the scientific community include scientists of many different personal and demographic characteristics.

Ideas Not Capable of Scientific Investigation

Researchable ideas, as you have just seen, originate from a variety of sources. However, it is important to realize that not all ideas are subject to scientific investigation. One of the criteria that a scientific study must meet is that the research idea must be capable of being confirmed or refuted. There are some ideas that are very important, are debated vigorously, and consume inordinate amounts of time and energy but are not subject to scientific investigation. These ideas typically revolve about issues of morality and religion. Consider, for example, the issue of abortion. This is an issue that has been debated for decades and has polarized the population. A large segment of the population advocates a pro-choice position; another large segment advocates a prolife position. Science can investigate the genesis of these positions and mechanisms for changing them, but it cannot resolve the issue of which position is the best or correct one.

- **Where can you get ideas for a research study?**
- **Explain why some ideas you might have cannot be subjected to a scientific investigation.**

Review of the Literature

After a topic of research has been obtained from one of the sources just mentioned, the next step in the research process is to become familiar with the information available on the topic. For example, assume that you want to conduct research on the impact of environmental stress on AIDS. Before beginning to design such a research project, you should first become familiar with current information on both of these topics. Prior work has been conducted on practically all psychological problems, and the topics of AIDS and environmental stress are no exceptions.

At this point you might be asking yourself, "Why should I review the literature on my selected topic? Why not just proceed to the laboratory and find an answer to the problem?" There are several good reasons why you should do your homework in the form of a literature review before conducting any experiments. The general purpose of the library search is to gain an understanding of the current state of knowledge about the selected topic. Specifically, a review of the literature

1. Will tell you whether the problem you have identified has already been researched. If it has, you should either revise the problem in light of the experimental results or look for another problem, unless there is a good reason to replicate the study.

2. Might give you ideas as to how to proceed in designing the study so that you can obtain an answer to your research question.

3. Can point out methodological problems specific to the research question you are studying.

4. Can identify whether special groups or special pieces of equipment are needed and perhaps give clues as to where to find the equipment or how to identify the particular groups of participants needed.

5. Will provide needed information for preparing the research report, because this research report requires that you not only set your study in the context of prior studies but also that you discuss the results in relation to other studies.

These are just a few of the more salient reasons for conducting a literature review.

Assuming you are convinced of the necessity of a literature review, you now need to know how to conduct such a review. Frequently, students don't know what kind of literature search is expected, where to start, how to get the best results from a search, what resources are available, or when to stop the search. To help in this process, Marques (1998) has provided a number of guidelines such as those discussed next.

Getting Started

Before doing an effective search, you should know how to use the library. If you are unfamiliar with effective use of the library, you should ask your librarian to give you a guided tour and explain where and how to find documents related to psychology. You also need to define your topic area before beginning the search. This definition needs to be relatively narrow and specific to conduct an appropriate search. For example, you might be interested in depression. However, the topic of depression is very broad and would be unmanageable because it includes everything about depression from causes to treatment. If you narrow this topic to something like relapse of depression, you have a more manageable topic.

In conducting the search, be prepared to spend considerable time and effort. Effective searches frequently take many hours. When you search for journal articles, you will see abstracts of these articles. Do not rely only on the information in these abstracts. Abstracts should be used only to give you information about the content of the actual article so you can tell if you need to select that article for further reading. When you get an actual journal article, take detailed notes of its content as you read it. This includes a complete reference, details about the methodology, important findings, strengths and weaknesses, and any other thoughts or comments that might arise as you are reading the article.

Defining Objectives

Before starting the literature search, it is helpful to define your objectives. For example, is the literature search being conducted to familiarize you with the topic area you want to investigate, or are you doing the literature search to help develop the methodology you need to use in conducting your research study? Identifying your objectives will show you that there are different reasons for doing a literature search and give you a focus when reading the literature.

Doing the Search

After you have developed some knowledge of how to find documents in your library and have defined the objectives of your search, you should be ready to do your literature search. There are many resources at your disposal that will give you more information than you ever thought existed. These resources consist of books, journal articles, computer databases, and the World Wide Web.

Books   Books have been written about most, if not all, areas in psychology. This is actually a good place to start your literature search because it will provide you with an introduction to your research topic and a summary of the literature published up to the time of the writing of the book. One book that is often very useful is the *Annual Review of Psychology*. Published yearly since 1950, it presents an expert's in-depth discussion of the principal work done during the preceding year on a variety of topics. One of the topics might relate to your own, so it is worthwhile to check this source. Other relevant books and chapters can be identified from a search of *Psychological Abstracts* or PsycINFO (discussed later). After you have identified the book or books relating to your topic of interest from a search of PsycINFO, you should connect to your library's online catalogue to see if your library holds the book or books you are interested in. You should be able to connect to your library's online catalogue through the Internet. If your library does not have the books you are interested in, you should be able to request them through interlibrary loan.

Most books do not, however, provide a comprehensive review of all research conducted on a topic. The author has to be selective and present only a small portion of the literature. To be sure that the author has not presented a biased orientation, you should select and read several books on your chosen research topic.

Psychological Journals   Most of the pertinent information about a research topic is usually found in the psychological journals. Frequently, a review that has started with books leads to the journals. Because books are generally the outgrowth of work cited in journals, this progression from books back to journals is a natural one.

How should one proceed in reviewing the work cited in the journals? There are so many psychological journals that it would be impossible to go through each and every one looking for relevant information.

PsycINFO
An electronic bibliographic database of abstracts and citations to the scholarly literature in psychology

Computerized or Electronic Databases   **PsycINFO** is an electronic bibliographic database providing abstracts and citations to the scholarly literature in the behavioral sciences and in mental health. It is a department of the American Psychological Association and has the mission of locating and summarizing psychologically relevant documents from a variety of disciplines and disseminating these summaries in a form that is easy to access and retrieve. This mission was initially accomplished by publishing *Psychological Abstracts*. Although *Psychological Abstracts* remains a staple of library reference collections, PsycINFO is the electronic database and contains the same references as those found in *Psychological Abstracts*, plus some additional references.

The PsycINFO database contains more than 2 million references to the psychological literature accumulated from 1887 to the present day. It covers publications from approximately 50 countries and literature written in more than 29 languages. The database is updated weekly and more than 100,000 new records were added in 2007. Because of its depth and breadth of coverage, PsycINFO is the database of choice for a search of psychologically relevant material. For additional up-to-date information on PsycINFO, you can check out the Web site at http://www.apa.org/psycinfo/. This Web site will also give you information about other electronic products such as those listed in Table 3.1.

TABLE 3.1

Additional Electronic Products from PsycINFO

Product	Description
PsycARTICLES	Database containing full-text articles from 66 journals published by APA and allied organizations
PsycBOOKS	Full-text database of scholarly titles published by APA

In searching PsycINFO, the basic procedure is to identify a list of search terms, enter them, and let the computer conduct the search for articles focusing on the issues relating to those terms. For example, if you were interested in literature focusing on the effect of food on a person's mood, you might select terms such as food and mood, carbohydrates and mood, and carbohydrate cravings. There are times when you might not know which terms to select for your search or you might think that there are more terms that should be used than you can think of. This is where the *Thesaurus of Psychological Index Terms* is helpful. This is an index of psychological terms as well as terms that describe interrelationships and related categories. For example, if you were interested in child welfare, the *Thesaurus of Psychological Index Terms* would provide a list of additional terms (adoption advocacy, child abuse, child day care, child neglect, child self-care, foster care, social casework, and social services) relevant to the topic of child welfare. These additional terms could also be searched to provide references to additional journal articles and books on the topic of child welfare. The thesaurus is available in a hardbound copy in most libraries. However, it can also be accessed from the PsycINFO main menu, so if you have access to PsycINFO, you can first access the thesaurus to identify a list of appropriate search terms and then have PsycINFO conduct your search using these terms.

Once you have identified the terms you want to use in your search, you are ready to conduct your search. PsycINFO gives you the option of searching for articles that contain your key search terms in the title, in the author, in the subject, or anywhere. You could also do an author search if you know the author of a journal article of interest to you. In addition to searching by using relevant search terms, PsycINFO allows you to limit your search in a number of ways, such as searching only journal articles and not books or searching only animal literature and not human literature. These are specific things you can do to insure that you identify relevant literature. You will develop proficiency in using these options as you gain experience doing PsycINFO literature searches.

Assume you are interested in road rage and want to identify the literature on this topic area. You connect to PsycINFO and search the literature for the years 2000–2009, and your search identifies 77 articles. Your next step is to read the abstracts of these articles and identify the ones that are of interest to you. Exhibit 3.2 presents the information provided by PsycINFO for one of

---

EXHIBIT 3.2

"Example of PsycINFO Result for an Article

Record: 1

Title: Is road rage increasing? Results of a repeated survey.

Author(s): Smart, Reginald G., Social, Prevention and Health Policy Research
Department, Centre for Addiction and Mental Health, Toronto, ON, Canada,
reg_smart@camh.net
Mann, Robert E., Social, Prevention and Health Policy Research
Department, Centre for Addiction and Mental Health, Toronto, ON,
Canada
Zhao, Jinhui, Social, Prevention and Health Policy Research Department,
Centre for Addiction and Mental Health, Toronto, ON, Canada
Stoduto Gina, Social, Prevention and Health Policy Research Department,
Centre for Addiction and Mental Health, Toronto, ON, Canada

Address: Smart, Reginald G., Social, Prevention and Health Policy Research
Department, Centre for Addiction and Mental Health, 33 Russell St., Toronto,
ON, Canada, M5S 2S1, reg_smart@camh.net

Source: *Journal of Safety Research*, Vol. 36(2), 2005, pp. 195–201.

Publisher: The Netherlands: Elsevier Science
Publisher URL: http://elsevier.com

ISSN: 0022-4375 (Print)

Digital Object Identifier: 10.1016/j.jsr.2005.03.005

Language: English

Keywords: road rage; victimization; perpetration; demographics

Abstract: Problem: We report on trends in road rage victimization and perpetration
based on population survey data. Method: Based on repeated cross-
sectional telephone surveys of Ontario adults between July 2001 and
December 2003, logistic regression analyses examined differences
between years in road rage victimization and perpetration in the
previous year controlling for demographic characteristics. Results: The
prevalence of any road rage victimization in the previous year decreased
significantly from 47.5% in 2001 to 40.6% in 2003, while prevalence of
any road rage perpetration remained stable (31.0–33.6%). Logistic regression analyses revealed that the odds of experiencing any road rage
victimization was 33% higher in 2001 and 30% higher in 2002 than in
2003. Discussion: Survey data provide a valuable perspective on road
rage trends, but efforts to track road rage incidents are also needed.
Summary: In Ontario, the proportion of adults experiencing any road

rage victimization decreased from 2001 to 2003, while the proportion reporting any road rage perpetration remained stable. Impact on industry: None. (PsycINFO Database Record © 2005 APA, all rights reserved)(journal abstract)

Subjects: Aggressive Driving Behavior; Demographic Characteristics; Harassment; Highway Safety; Victimization

Classification: Transportation (4090)

Population: Human (10)
Male (30)
Female (40)

Location: Canada

Age Group: Adulthood (18 years and older) (300)
Young Adulthood (18–29 years) (320)
Thirties (30–39 years) (340)
Middle Age (40–64 years) (360)
Aged (65 years and older) (380)
Very Old (85 years and older) (390)

Tests and Measures: Computer Assisted Telephone Interview

Form/Content Type: Empirical Study (0800)
Study (0890)
Article (2400)

Publication Type: Peer Reviewed Journal (270); Print Format(s) Available: Print; Electronic

Release Date: 20050718

Accession Number: *2005-06225-010*

Number of Citations in Source: 20

Database: PsycINFO

these 77 articles. If this abstract indicates that the article contains information of importance to you, then you retrieve the article. The information given identifies the author(s), title, and journal in which the article appeared, allowing you to seek and obtain a copy of the entire article. As you read the article, take notes to get as much as you can out of it. Scholarly articles are written for professionals, so there might be some parts that are difficult for you to understand. Table 3.2 gives some guidelines for reading journal articles.

You might want to search other databases (see Table 3.3) in addition to PsycINFO that incorporate psychological literature. This is particularly valuable if your research topic bridges other areas, such as medicine.

TABLE 3.2
Guide for Reading Journal Articles

When you read scholarly articles, you might have a difficult time comprehending much of the material. If you follow these simple steps, you will get the most out of the article:

1. Read and remember the title because it tells you what is being investigated in the article.

2. Read the abstract very carefully because it summarizes what is being investigated as well as what was found in the study.

3. As you read the introduction to the article, pay particular attention to the first paragraph because this typically gives a general statement of the topic area and problem being studied.

4. Toward the end of the introduction, typically in the last paragraph, the author(s) usually state the purpose of the study and, perhaps, the hypotheses being tested in the study. Keep these two in mind as you read the rest of the article, and see how the author(s) go about testing the hypotheses or meeting the purpose of the study and what the results have to say about them.

5. As you read the Method section, make note of the type of research participants used and then pay particular attention to the Procedure section because this section tells you how the author(s) designed the study to test their hypotheses and meet the purpose of the study. Pay attention to what was done to the participants and what the participants were asked to do and then ask yourself if this tested the hypotheses of the study.

6. The Results section might be the hardest for you to read and comprehend because the author(s) might have used statistical procedures unfamiliar to you. Rather than spending time trying to understand the statistical analysis, look at what the authors say about the results of the statistical analysis. Look at any tables and figures presented, and try to relate the information in them to the hypotheses and purpose of the study.

7. If you have difficulty with the Results section, read the first paragraph of the Discussion section. This typically summarizes the results of the study in a form that is easier to understand. In addition to helping understand the results, the Discussion section is where the author(s) explain why the study turned out as it did: Did it support the hypotheses? As you read this section, think about the purpose and hypotheses and look for the explanation of why the study did or did not support the hypotheses and fulfill the purpose of the study.

Internet Resources The Internet is an additional resource that can be used to acquire psychological information. The Internet is best described as a "network of networks" consisting of millions of computers and tens of millions of users all over the world, all of which are joined into a single network to promote communication. It is probably an understatement to say that the Internet is revolutionizing communications much the way the telephone did many years ago. Now we can connect to the Internet and communicate with someone in another country just as easily as we can with our neighbor next door. The Internet has a number of tools that are of

TABLE 3.3
Databases Incorporating Psychological Publications

Database	Subject Coverage	Internet Address
PsycINFO	Psychology, mental health, biomedicine	Connect through your university library
MEDLINE	Medicine, biomedicine, health care	http://www.ncbi.nlm.nih.gov
SocINDEX	Sociology and related disciplines	Connect through your university library

value to both the student and psychologists. In addition to the resources discussed here, there are conferences, debates, journals, and lists of references, as well as complete studies, on the Internet.

Electronic Mail.   E-mail, or electronic mail, is probably one of the most frequent uses of the Internet. E-mail is an electronic means of sending messages as well as files and documents to another person over the Internet. It provides an unprecedented means of communication that avoids the problems of playing phone tag when trying to reach another person. Most, if not all, colleges and universities have connections to the Internet and provide a means for students to either become connected using their own computers or provide access to computers that are connected to the Internet. Regardless of the means of access to the Internet, once you have access, you must have a user ID, which is your Internet address. This address identifies your location on the Internet and allows e-mail to get to you. Similarly, to send an e-mail message to another person, you must have their user ID or their address. Once you have a person's address, you can communicate with them regardless of where they are in the world.

Listserv.   Discussion groups are also used for communication among researchers, students, and others interested in a particular topic, such as depression. Within psychology, there are many topics that are of interest to a particular group of individuals. These special interest groups use a variation of e-mail called a Listserv to communicate among all members of the group. A Listserv is a program that automatically distributes messages to all members of the list so it can be viewed as a discussion group organized around a particular topic. To become a participant in a Listserv, you must first join or subscribe to the list. Once you have joined the list, the Listserv sends you all the messages posted by other subscribers. You can just read these messages, reply to them, or send your own message. For example, if you are having difficulty finding information on a topic of interest, you might post a message on a Listserv asking for information relating to that topic. In a short period of time, you should get many replies from other participants giving you valuable, or not so valuable, information.

World Wide Web.   Probably the most popular part of the Internet is the World Wide Web. The Web consists of hundreds of thousands of computers, each containing information, some of which might be useful and much of which is not. There is a wealth of information on the Web, and students and faculty alike enjoy surfing the Web. However, the giant waves of information typically contain only a few drops of relevant information. This is why the Web can be a frustrating and time-consuming place to search for information. Therefore, you need a clear idea of what you are looking for to be able to mine the Web effectively.

One thing you need to know prior to beginning your search of the Web is that it will not search subscription or proprietary databases such as PsycINFO, SocINDEX, or ERIC. Although some databases, such as MEDLINE, are free and can be accessed by anyone, other databases, such as PsycINFO, are not and have to be accessed through your library because your library has paid the fee to permit your access. But remember that you can access your university library via the web. Another source for published research via the web is Google Scholar (http://scholar.google.com/). In addition to these approaches for locating scholarly research, there is a vast amount of other kinds of information available on the Web.

To access material on the Web you need to make use of a browser such as Internet Explorer, Netscape, Safari, Opera, or Firefox. Browsers such as these allow a user to access Web pages stored on servers around the world and display them on the screen of their computer. If you know the address (the uniformed resource locator, or URL) of the Web page you are seeking, all you have to do is type in the address, and the browser you are using will locate and display the Web page on your computer screen. In case you didn't know, the URL is the global address of documents and other resources on the World Wide Web.

In many instances, you would not know the address, or URL, of Web pages containing information you desire. For example, if you were seeking information about support groups for people suffering from depression, you probably would not know the address of such groups. To find Web pages with information about depression support groups, you need to use a search engine. A **search engine** is a program that is designed to help find information stored on servers that are part of the World Wide Web. A listing of some of the search engines that can be used to search for information on the Web are listed in Table 3.4.

In spite of the vast amount of information provided by these search engines, none of them has a database that even approaches all of the information on the

Search engine
A software program that seeks out Web pages stored on servers throughout the World Wide Web

TABLE 3.4
Internet Search Tools

Major Search Engines	Internet Address
Google	http://www.google.com
Yahoo!	http://www.yahoo.com
Ask Jeeves	http://www.ask.com
Metacrawlers or Meta Search Engines	**Internet Address**
Dogpile	http://www.dogpile.com
Vivisimo	http://vivisimo.com/
Kartoo	http://www.kartoo.com
Mamma	http://mamma.com
SurfWax	http://surfwax.com

Web. This is why for the most comprehensive search you must use several search engines; each search engine will have visited different Web pages and have a slightly different database.

In an attempt to provide a more comprehensive search of the information on the Web, meta search engines have been developed. These are search engines that submit your search to several search engine databases at the same time. The results are then blended together into one page.

The World Wide Web is a potentially valuable resource, giving you a wealth of information. Its tremendous advantage is that it is accessible 24 hours a day and can be accessed from the comfort of your own home, apartment, office, or dorm room. However, there are some significant disadvantages to conducting a Web search. It can be very time consuming because much of the information is disorganized. Because the database of search engines consists of information gleaned from Web pages, a lot of the information you get will be irrelevant. Also, there is no controlling authority ensuring the accuracy or credibility of the information, so you must judge each Web site to determine if the information contained is reliable and accurate. Table 3.5 provides some guidelines for evaluating the accuracy of information obtained from the Web.

The World Wide Web is potentially a valuable resource. The challenge is to learn how to mine the Web to effectively use its vast information. There are books that describe the Internet and provide some instruction in searching for information. However, the best way to learn more about the Internet is to use it. As you spend more and more time navigating the Internet, you will become proficient at locating information and maximizing the tremendous resources available at your fingertips.

Obtaining Resources

Once you have obtained the list of books, journal articles, and other resources relevant to your topic of interest, you must obtain a copy of them. Obviously, the first choice is to search your library. Libraries purchase many books and subscribe to many journals and other documents, and it is possible that the books and journal articles you need are in your library. However, few libraries will contain all the resources you have selected, and in such cases, you must use alternative means of securing documents.

Your first choice for securing documents not in your library should be through the interlibrary loan department. This is a department maintained by the library dedicated to obtaining documents from other locations, such as other libraries. In most instances, they are reasonably efficient and can obtain documents within several weeks. Journal articles are often sent to you as pdf files; therefore, you don't have to go to the library to pick them up. The downside to using the interlibrary loan method is that you might be assessed a small fee for copies of journal articles. Rather than using interlibrary loan, you can contact the author of a journal article and request a reprint of that article. When authors publish journal articles, they typically receive a number of reprints that they distribute to individuals requesting copies.

TABLE 3.5
Evaluating Web Pages

The main problem with the information received from the World Wide Web is its validity because anyone can establish a Web site and produce a Web page. The following criteria can help you differentiate good information from bad.

1. **Authority**: Authority exists if the Web page lists the author and his or her credentials, and the address has a preferred domain such as .edu, .org, or .gov. Therefore, to assess the authority, you should:

   a. Find the source of the document. A URL ending with .edu is from an institution of higher education, .gov is from some branch of the federal government, .org is from some nonprofit organization such as the American Psychological Association, .com is from a commercial vendor, and .net is from anyone who can afford to pay for space on a server.

   b. Identify the qualifications of the publisher of the Web document. You can get some of this information from the Web site itself by reading the "about us," "mission," or "Who we are" sections.

2. **Accuracy**: Accuracy is best when the Web page lists the author and institution that publishes the page and provides a way of contacting him or her. This means that you should do the following:

   a. Look at the credentials of the person who wrote the Web page and check for a link or an e-mail address that will permit you to contact this person.

   b. Identify the purpose of the information. Is it a public service announcement, advertising, sales, news, or a published research study? The purpose might suggest that a certain bias exists in the information.

   c. Determine if there is an acknowledgment of the limitations of the information, particularly if the information is the report of some study.

3. **Objectivity**: Objectivity is best when the Web page has little or no advertising and provides accurate and objective information. Therefore, you should do the following:

   a. Identify if there is any evidence of some sort of bias in the information presented.

      i. Is the information traceable to factual information presented in some bibliographic or Internet reference? Such information might be less biased.

      ii. Do the authors express their own opinions? Authors' opinions suggest bias.

4. **Currency**: Currency exists when the Web page and any links it provides are updated regularly. This means that you should determine

   a. When the Web page was produced.

   b. When the Web page was updated and how up to date the links (if any) are.

5. **Coverage**: Coverage is good when you can view the information on the Web page without paying fees or having additional software requirements.

There is also an increasing trend for libraries to provide a full-text electronic copy of journal articles and books. If your library provides full-text copies of journal articles you are interested in, there will be a link, frequently at the end of the abstract, that says something like "linked full-text" or "check for full-text." If there is a "linked full-text" statement and you click on this link, you will retrieve the complete article, which you can then print.

Additional Information Sources

The regional and national psychological association meetings are an excellent source of *current* information. We emphasize *current* because of the publication lag

TABLE 3.6
Psychological Associations

National	Regional	Selected Others
American Psychological Association	New England Psychological Association Southwestern Psychological Association	Psychonomic Society Association for Behavioral And Cognitive Therapies
American Psychological Society	Eastern Psychological Association Southeastern Psychological Association Western Psychological Association Midwestern Psychological Association Rocky Mountain Psychological Association	National Academy of Neuropsychologists International Neuropsychological Society

that exists in journals and books. A research study that appears in a book might be several years old, whereas studies presented at professional meetings are typically much more recent. An additional advantage of securing information at professional meetings is that frequently you can interact with the investigator. Exchanging ideas with the researcher is likely to generate added enthusiasm and many more research ideas.

Many times, the beginning researcher returns from meetings with renewed confidence in his or her developing research skills. Novices often feel that researchers at other institutions are more skilled or more adept, but when they attend professional meetings, they find out that others use the same techniques and skills. It is recommended that psychology majors try to attend one of these national or regional meetings. Table 3.6 lists the various regional psychological associations, as well as a variety of other, more specialized psychological associations.

Information can also be gained from direct communication with colleagues. It is not unusual for researchers to call, write, or e-mail one another to inquire about current studies or methodological techniques.

STUDY QUESTIONS 3.2

- **What is the purpose of a literature review?**
- **How you would go about conducting a literature review?**
- **What resources are available for conducting a literature review?**

Feasibility of the Study

After you have completed the literature search, you are ready to decide whether it is feasible for you to conduct the study. Each study varies in its requirements with respect to time, type of research participants, expense, expertise of the experimenter, and ethical sensitivity.

For example, you might want to study the effect of being sexually abused as a child on the stability of a person's later marital relationship. Although this is an excellent research question and one that has been investigated and needs further investigation, it is a difficult study to conduct and one that is not feasible for most students. This study requires the identification of sexually abused children, which would be difficult in the best of circumstances. In addition, it requires following the abused children for years until they marry, which would take an inordinate amount of time. Then an assessment of the couple's marital stability has to be obtained, which might require a level of expertise you do not have. In addition, this is an ethically sensitive topic, because just revealing the fact that a person has been sexually abused could have a variety of consequences.

Contrast this with the study conducted by DePaulo, Dull, Greenberg, and Swaim (1989), in which they attempted to determine whether shy individuals seek help less frequently than people who are not shy. In conducting this study, the researchers administered a four-item shyness survey to introductory psychology students, and shy and not-shy individuals were selected on the basis of their survey scores. All participants were then given the impossible task of standing a stick on end when the end was slightly rounded. The number of times shy and not-shy individuals asked for help was recorded. This study was relatively simple to conduct, did not require any special skills on the part of the experimenters or the research participants, was relatively inexpensive, took only a moderate amount of time, and did not violate the participants' rights.

These two studies represent opposite ends of the continuum with respect to the issues of time, money, access to participant sample, expertise, and ethics. Although most studies fall somewhere between the two extremes, these examples serve to emphasize the issues that must be considered in selecting a research topic. If the research topic you have selected will take an inordinate amount of time, require funds that you don't have or can't acquire, call for a degree of expertise you don't have, or raise sensitive ethical questions, you should consider altering the project or selecting another topic. If you have considered these issues and find that they are not problematic, then you should proceed with the formulation of your research problem.

Formulating the Research Problem

You should now be prepared to make a clear and exact statement of the specific problem to be investigated. The literature review has revealed not only what is currently known about the problem but also the ways in which the problem has been attacked in the past. Such information is a tremendous aid in formulating the problem and in indicating how and by what methods the data should be collected. Unfortunately, novices sometimes jump from the selection of a research topic to the data collection stage, leaving the problem unspecified until after data collection. They thus run the risk of not obtaining information on the problem of interest. An exact definition of the problem is very important because it guides the research process.

Defining the Research Problem

What is a **research problem**? Kerlinger (1973, p. 17) defines a problem as "an interrogative sentence or statement that asks: 'What relation exists between two or more variables?' " For example, Milgram (1964a) asked, "Can a group induce a person to deliver punishment of increasing severity to a protesting individual?" This statement conforms to the definition of a problem, because it contains two variables—group pressure and severity of punishment delivered—and asks a question regarding the relationship between these variables.

Are all problems that conform to the definition good research problems? Assume that you posed the problem: "Do space creatures influence the behavior of college students?" This question might meet the definition of a problem, but it obviously cannot be tested. Kerlinger (1973) presents three criteria that good problems must meet. First, the variables in the problem should express a relationship. This criterion was contained in the definition of a problem. The second criterion is that the problem should be stated in question form. The statement of the problem should begin with "What is the effect of . . . ," "Under what conditions do . . . ," "Does the effect of . . . ," or some similar form. Sometimes only the purpose of a study is stated, which does not necessarily communicate the problem to be investigated. The purpose of the Milgram (1964a) study was to investigate the effect of group pressure on a person's behavior. Asking a question has the benefit of presenting the problem directly, thereby minimizing interpretation and distortion. The third criterion, and the one that most frequently distinguishes a researchable from a nonresearchable problem, states, "The problem statement should be such as to imply possibilities of empirical testing" (p. 18). Many interesting and important questions fail to meet this criterion and therefore are not amenable to empirical inquiry. Quite a few philosophical and theological questions fall into this category. Milgram's problem, on the other hand, meets all three criteria. A relation was expressed between the variables, the problem was stated in question form, and it was possible to test the problem empirically. Severity of punishment was measured by the amount of electricity supposedly delivered to the protesting individual, and group pressure was applied by having two confederates suggest increasingly higher shock levels.

Specificity of the Question

In formulating a problem, **specificity of the research question** is an important consideration. Think of the difficulties facing the experimenter who asks the question "What effect does the environment have on learning ability?" This question meets all the criteria of a problem, and yet it is stated so vaguely that the investigator could not pinpoint what was to be investigated. The concepts of *environment* and *learning ability* are vague (what environmental characteristics? learning of what?). The experimenter must specify what is meant by *environment* and by *learning ability* to be able to conduct the experiment. Now contrast this question with the following: "What effect does the amount of exposure to words have on the speed with which they are learned?" This question specifies exactly what the problem is.

The two examples of questions presented here demonstrate the advantages of formulating a specific problem. A specific statement helps to ensure that the experimenters understand the problem. If the problem is stated vaguely, the experimenters probably do not know exactly what they want to study and therefore might design a study that will not solve the problem. A specific problem statement also helps the experimenters make necessary decisions about such factors as participants, apparatus, instruments, and measures. A vague problem statement helps very little with such decisions. To drive this point home, go back and reread the two questions given in the preceding paragraph and ask yourself, "What research participants should I use? What measures should I use? What apparatus or instruments should I use?"

How specific should one be in formulating a question? The primary purposes of formulating the problem in question form are to ensure that the researcher has a good grasp of the variables to be investigated and to aid the experimenter in designing and carrying out the experiment. If the formulation of the question is pointed enough to serve these purposes, then additional specificity is not needed. To the extent that these purposes are not met, additional specificity and narrowing of the research problem are required. Therefore, the degree of specificity required is dependent on the purpose of the problem statement.

STUDY QUESTIONS 3.3

- **What is meant by research problem, and what are the characteristics of a good research problem?**
- **Why should a research problem be stated in very specific and precise terms?**

Formulating Hypotheses

Hypothesis
The best prediction or a tentative solution to a problem

After the literature review has been completed and the problem has been stated in question form, you should begin formulating your **hypothesis.** For example, if you are investigating the influence of the number of bystanders on the speed of intervention in emergencies, you might hypothesize that as the number of bystanders increases, the speed of intervention will decrease. From this example, you can see that hypotheses represent predictions of the relation that exists among the variables or tentative solutions to the problem. The formulation of the hypothesis logically follows the statement of the problem, because one cannot state a hypothesis without having a problem. This does not mean that the problem is always stated explicitly. In fact, if you survey articles published in journals, you will find that most of the authors do not present a statement of their specific problem. It seems that experienced researchers in a given field have such familiarity with the field that they consider the problems to be self-evident. Their predicted solutions to these problems are not apparent, however, and so these must be stated.

The hypothesis to be tested is often a function of the literature review, although hypotheses are also frequently formulated from theory. As stated earlier, theories guide research, and one of the ways in which they do so is by making predictions of possible relationships among variables. Hypotheses also (but less frequently) come from reasoning based on casual observation of events. In some situations, it seems fruitless even to attempt to formulate hypotheses. When one is engaged in exploratory work in a relatively new area, where the important variables and their relationships are not known, hypotheses serve little purpose.

More than one hypothesis can almost always be formulated as the probable solution to the problem. Here again the literature review can be an aid because a review of prior research can suggest the most probable relationships that might exist among the variables.

Regardless of the source of the hypothesis, it *must* meet one criterion: A hypothesis must be stated so that it is capable of being either refuted or confirmed. In an experiment, it is the hypothesis that is being tested, not the problem. One does not test a question such as the one Milgram posed; rather, one tests one or more of the hypotheses that could be derived from this question, such as "group pressure increases the severity of punishment that participants will administer." A hypothesis that fails to meet the criterion of testability, or is nontestable, removes the problem from the realm of science. Any conclusions reached regarding a nontestable hypothesis do not represent scientific knowledge.

Research hypothesis
The predicted relationship among the variables being investigated

Null hypothesis
A statement of no relationship among the variables being investigated

A distinction must be made between the **research hypothesis** and the null hypothesis. The research hypothesis represents the researcher's predicted relationship among the variables being investigated. The **null hypothesis** represents a statement of no relationships among the variables being investigated. For example, Hashtroudi, Parker, DeLisi, and Wyatt (1983) wanted to explore the nature of the memory deficits that occur due to the influence of alcohol. One of the research questions these investigators asked was whether the memory deficit induced by alcohol is decreased when intoxicated individuals are forced to generate a meaningful context for a word that is to be recalled. Although not specifically stated, these investigators' research hypothesis was that the generation of a meaningful context reduces the memory deficit produced by the alcohol. The null hypothesis predicted that no difference in recall is found between intoxicated participants who generated the meaningful context and those who did not.

Although a research study would seem to be focused on directly testing the research hypothesis, this is not the case. In any study that relies on statistical hypothesis testing, it is the null hypothesis that is tested, because the research hypothesis does not specify the exact amount of influence that is expected. To obtain support for the research hypothesis, you must collect evidence and determine if it enables you to reject the null hypothesis. Consequently, support for the research hypothesis is obtained *indirectly* by rejecting the null hypothesis. The exact reason for testing the null hypothesis as opposed to the research hypothesis is based on statistical hypothesis-testing theory, which is discussed in Chapter 15.

Why should research hypotheses be set up in the first place? Why not just forget about hypotheses and proceed to attempt to answer the question? Hypotheses serve a valuable function. Remember that hypotheses are derived from knowledge obtained from the literature review of other research, theories, and so forth. Such prior knowledge serves as the basis for the hypothesis. For example, if an experiment confirms the hypothesis, then, in addition to providing an answer to the question asked, it gives additional support to the literature that suggested the hypothesis. But what if the hypothesis is not confirmed by the experiment? Does this invalidate the prior literature? If the hypothesis is not confirmed, then the hypothesis is false, or some error exists in the conception of the hypothesis, or some other assumption made was false. If there is an error in conceptualization, it could be in any of a number of categories. Some of the information obtained from prior experiments might be false, or some relevant information might have been overlooked in the literature review. It is also possible that the researcher misinterpreted some of the literature. These are a few of the more salient errors that could have taken place. In any event, failure to support a hypothesis might indicate that something is wrong, and it is up to the researcher to discover what it is. Once the researcher uncovers what he or she thinks is wrong, a new hypothesis is proposed that can be tested. The researcher now has another study to conduct. Such is the continuous process of science. Even if the hypothesis is false, knowledge has been advanced, because, for now, an incorrect hypothesis can be ruled out. Another hypothesis must be formulated and tested in order to reach a solution to the problem.

STUDY QUESTIONS 3.4

- **What is a hypothesis and what specific criterion must a hypothesis meet?**
- **Distinguish between the research and null hypothesis.**
- **Explain how you would obtain support for the research hypothesis.**

Summary

In order to conduct research, it is first necessary to identify a problem in need of a solution. Psychological problems arise from several traditional sources: theories, practical issues, and past research. In addition, in psychology, we have our personal experience to draw on for researchable problems, because psychological research is concerned with behavior. Once a researchable problem has been identified, the literature relevant to this problem should be reviewed. A literature review will reveal the current state of knowledge about the selected topic. It will indicate ways of investigating the problem and will point out related methodological problems. The literature review should probably begin with books written on the topic and progress from there to the actual research as reported in journals. In surveying the past research conducted on a topic, the scientist can make use of an electronic database, one of which is operated by the American Psychological Association. In addition to using these sources, the researcher can search the World Wide Web and obtain information by attending professional conventions or by calling, writing, or e-mailing other individuals conducting research on the given topic.

When the literature review has been completed, the experimenter must determine whether it is feasible for him or her to conduct the study. This means that an assessment must be made of the time, research participant population, expertise, and expense requirements, as well as the ethical sensitivity of the study. If this assessment indicates that it is feasible to conduct the study, the experimenter must make a clear and exact statement of the problem to be investigated. This means that the experimenter must formulate an interrogative sentence asking about the relationship between two or more variables. This interrogative sentence must express a relation and be capable of being tested empirically. The question must also be specific enough to assist the experimenter in making decisions about such factors as participants, apparatus, and general design of the study.

After the question has been stated, the experimenter needs to set down the hypotheses. These must be formalized because they represent the predicted relation that exists among the variables under study. Often, hypotheses are a function of past research. If they are confirmed, the results not only answer the question asked but also provide additional support to the literature that suggested the hypotheses. There is one criterion that any hypothesis must meet: It must be stated so that it is capable of being either refuted or confirmed. Always remember that it is actually the null hypothesis, and not the research hypothesis, that is being statistically tested in a study.

Key Terms and Concepts

Hypothesis
Null hypothesis
PsycINFO
Research hypothesis

Research problem
Search engine
Specificity of the research question
Theory

Related Internet Sites

http://www.apa.org/science/lib.html
This site provides instruction on how to find relevant information on psychological topics in outlets ranging from newspaper articles to scientific journals. It also includes links to information about PsycINFO, PsycARTICLES, PsycBOOKS, and so on.

http://library.albany.edu/usered/
This is a great site containing links to information relevant to just about anything you want to know about searching the World Wide Web, as well as links to information regarding evaluating information on the Web.

Practice Test

Answers to these questions can be found in Appendix.

1. Assume that you have just been to a demonstration by the psychic Uri Geller and watched him apply his psychic powers to do such things as bend spoons. Let's further assume that you are a skeptic and doubt that this was done by psychic powers. You want to conduct a study to determine if Uri Geller really has the ability to bend a spoon through use of his psychic powers. This research idea has originated from

   a. Everyday life
   b. A practical issue
   c. Past research
   d. Theory

2. Dr. Skeptic was interested in the following questions:

- Is it ethical to experiment with animals?
- Is there an afterlife?

The common element of these two questions is that they
a. Arise from everyday life experience
b. Arise from practical issues
c. Arise from past research
d. Arise from theory
e. Are not capable of scientific investigation

3. If you are doing a literature search, you can log on to the World Wide Web and conduct your search using one of the available search engines. Using this procedure to do your literature search has the disadvantage of

a. Not providing any relevant information
b. Being too slow
c. Not providing enough information
d. Providing too much information with questionable credibility
e. Being accessible only through the university library

4. Consider the research question: "Does excessive drinking occur in animals other than rats?" This is considered a good research question because it

a. Asks a question
b. Focuses on a relationship between two variables
c. Can be empirically tested
d. Is stated specifically enough to specify the variables being tested and to aid in the design of the study
e. All of the above

5. If you have stated your hypothesis in such a way that you predict no relationship between the variables being investigated, you have stated a

a. Research hypothesis
b. Null hypothesis
c. Rival hypothesis
d. Formal hypothesis
e. Experimental hypothesis

Challenge Exercises

1. Construct a research problem that could be experimentally investigated and then provide the following information about this research problem.

a. My research problem is _____

_____

b. The relation expressed in my research problem is _____

   c. Does the research problem ask a question? If it does not, restate it in question form. _____

_____

   d. The research problem can be empirically tested because _____

_____

_____

   e. The hypothesis I want to test is _____

_____

2. Now that you have a research problem, you should conduct a literature review. Conduct this literature review using the databases specified here. You should get very different results, and this should illustrate to you the advantages and limitations of each.

   a. Conduct a mini-literature review of the information relating to your research topic using the PsycINFO database. Use the following approach when doing this literature review:

     1) List the search terms you want to use when searching PsycINFO.

     2) Identify five articles related to your research problem. For each of these articles, provide the following information:

       a) Author(s)

       b) Title

       c) Journal

       d) Study hypothesis or purpose

       e) Results, or what the study found

   b. Conduct a mini-literature review using the World Wide Web. Use the following approach when conducting this search:

     1) Specify a search engine.

     2) Identify two Web pages that you think you can use for your literature review, and answer the following questions regarding each Web page:

       a) What is the source of the information?

       b) What is the purpose of the Web page?

       c) Is the information accurate, and how can you tell that it is accurate?

       d) Does the Web page report the results of a study or a summary of several studies? Does it provide some acknowledgment of the limitations of the information?

       e) What type of information is being provided (scholarly, popular, trade, etc.)?

CHAPTER 4

Ethics

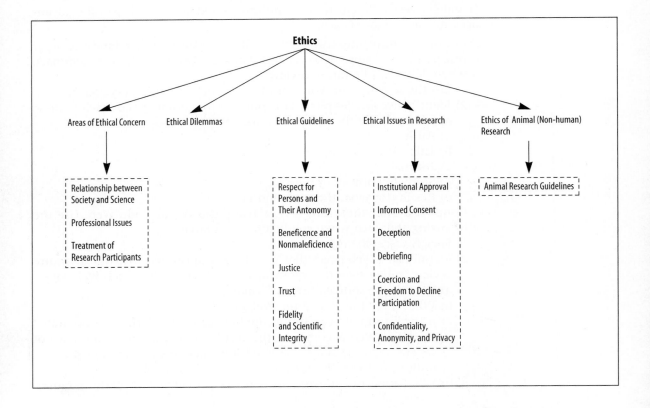

Riddick Bowe was the youngest of 13 children raised by his mother, Dorothy Bowe, in an impoverished and violent neighborhood. However, he had an extraordinary gift as a fighter. As a youngster, he won three Golden Gloves, and later won a silver medal at the Olympics in Seoul, South Korea, in October 1988. He easily charmed almost everyone and was very protective of his mother, suggesting to some that he possessed a lot of character. His high school sweetheart described him as distinctive, partially because he did not seem to be like the other guys in their neighborhood—the drug dealers and fast talkers with girls all over the place. On April 27, 1988, when she was 21, she married Bowe. Everyone, however, was not taken in by Bowe's charm. Several of his trainers saw through his charm and correctly concluded that he was a difficult individual with a discipline and control problem. However, because of his enormous talent, they continued to function as his trainers. Their efforts were not unrewarded. Four years after turning pro, Bowe was a champion, winning a 12-round decision over Evander Holyfield in November 1992. His agent produced a lucrative HBO contract and a multimillion dollar endorsement deal with Fila, an athletic apparel company, and the media embraced him partly because reporters and broadcasters were weary of the unabashedly violent Mike Tyson.

Riddick Bowe's personal life, however, had a dark side. He was physically abusive to his wife. On one occasion, he knocked her out in front of their 3-year-old son. He could be a strict disciplinarian. One incident involved his ripping the cord from the television in his hotel suite, and, after using duct tape to bind his son's hands and feet, whipping him with the cord.

In 1997, Judy and Riddick Bowe separated. However, after a 5-month separation, Riddick Bowe decided he wanted to reunite with his family and set about doing that in his own way. Armed with a buck knife, pepper spray, a flashlight, and duct tape, he and his brother drove to his wife's new home and abducted her and their five children during the early morning hours of February 1998.

Domestic violence such as is illustrated in the case of Riddick Bowe is not an isolated incident but one that is repeated multiple times every day in the United States and in virtually every other country in the world. It is also a research area that has attracted the attention of researchers, many of whom are psychologists. These individuals are trying to provide answers to questions such as why do people engage in domestic violence, what are the causes of such violence, and how can the incidence of such violence be reduced. Engaging in research such as this generates a variety of ethical concerns. One of the most serious ethical issues is the potential harmful effect the research might have on the participants. This could take the form of, for example, enraging either the husband or wife and causing an escalation of the already violent relationship by virtue of the fact that the abusive behavior is being reported to the researcher. In the course of conducting the research, an investigator might uncover a seriously abusive relationship in which the safety of the research participant is in jeopardy. In such an instance, the investigator has the responsibility to protect the research participant, which might mean that the abusive behavior becomes public. Although this would be the appropriate behavior for the investigator, the researcher would have invaded the privacy of the couple.

Introduction

Once you have constructed your research problem and formulated the hypothesis, you are ready to begin to develop the research design. The design will specify how you will collect data that will enable you to test your hypothesis and arrive at some answer to the research question. However, at the same time that you are designing the research study, you must pay attention to ethical issues involved in research.

In their pursuit of knowledge relating to the behavior of organisms, psychologists conduct surveys, manipulate the type of experience that individuals receive, or vary the stimuli presented to individuals and then observe the research participants' reactions to these stimuli. Such manipulations and observations are necessary in order to identify the influence of various experiences or stimuli. At the same time, scientists recognize that individuals have the right to privacy and to protest surveillance of their behavior carried out without their consent. People also have the right to know if their behavior is being manipulated and, if so, why. The scientific community is confronted with the problem of trying to satisfy the public demand for solutions to problems such as cancer, arthritis, alcoholism, child abuse, and penal reform without infringing on people's rights. For a psychologist trained in research techniques, a decision *not* to do research is also a matter of ethical concern.

In order to advance knowledge and to find answers to questions, it is often necessary to impinge on well-recognized rights of individuals. Consideration of ethical issues is, therefore, integral to the development of a research proposal and to the conduct of research (Sieber & Stanley, 1988). It is very difficult to investigate such topics as child abuse, for example, without violating the right to privacy, because it is necessary to obtain information about the child abuser and/or the child being abused. Such factors create an ethical dilemma: whether to conduct the research and violate certain rights of individuals for the purpose of gaining knowledge or to sacrifice a gain in knowledge for the purpose of preserving human rights. Ethical principles are vital to the research enterprise because they assist the scientist in preventing abuses that might otherwise occur and delineate the responsibilities of the investigator.

Research Ethics: What Are They?

Research ethics
A set of guidelines to assist the researcher in conducting ethical research

When some people think of ethics, they think of moralistic sermons and endless philosophical debates. However, **research ethics** is a set of principles that assist the community of researchers in deciding how to conduct ethical research. Within the social and behavioral sciences, ethical concerns can be divided into three areas (Diener & Crandall, 1978): (1) relationship between society and science, (2) professional issues, and (3) treatment of research participants.

Relationship Between Society and Science

The ethical issue concerning the relationship between society and science revolves about the extent to which societal concerns and cultural values should direct the course of scientific investigation. The federal government spends millions of dollars each year on research, and it sets priorities for how the money is to be spent. To increase the probability of obtaining research funds, investigators orient their research proposals toward these same priorities, which means that the federal government at least partially dictates the type of research conducted. AIDS (acquired immunodeficiency syndrome) research provides an excellent illustration. Prior to 1980, AIDS was virtually unheard of. Few federal dollars were committed to investigating this disorder. But when AIDS turned up within the U.S. population and its lethal characteristic was identified, it rapidly became a national concern. Millions of dollars were immediately earmarked for research to investigate causes and possible cures. Many researchers reoriented their interests and investigations to the AIDS problem because of the availability of research funds.

In the past 30 years, corporate support for research has increased from less than $5 million a year to hundreds of millions of dollars (Haber, 1996). Although this is substantial support, it frequently comes with a set of biases and restrictions. For example, most of the research sponsored by drug companies has focused on the development of variants of existing drugs with the goal of improving sales rather than developing new drugs. When comparisons are made between a new drug and a traditional therapy, 43% of the studies funded by a drug company and only 13% of the studies funded by other sources supported the new drug (Davidson, 1986). Drug companies obviously want their new patented drugs to turn out to be superior because this leads to sales of the new drug and increases the profit that can be made by the company.

Because funding is the lifeblood of scientists, they attempt to identify the priorities of various funding sources and then slant their proposals toward these priorities. In this way, corporate support drives a significant portion of the research that is conducted.

Societal and cultural values also enter into science to the extent that the phenomenon a scientist chooses to investigate is often determined by that scientist's own culturally based interests (e.g., a female psychologist might study sex discrimination in the workforce or a black psychologist might study racial attitudes). The scientific enterprise is not value free; rather, society's values as well as the scientist's own can creep into the research process in subtle and unnoticed ways.

Professional Issues

Research misconduct
Fabricating, falsifying, or plagiarizing the proposing, performing, reviewing, or reporting of research results

The category of professional issues includes the expanding problem of research misconduct. In December 2000, the U.S. Office of Science and Technology Policy (OSTP) defined **research misconduct** as "fabrication, falsification, or plagiarism (FFP) in proposing, performing, or reviewing research, or in reporting research results" (OSTP, 2005). The attention fabrication, falsification, and plagiarism has received is understandable, given that a scientist is trained to ask questions, to be skeptical, and to use the research process in the search for truth. This search for truth is completely antithetical to engaging in any type of deception. The most serious crime in the scientific profession is to cheat or present fraudulent results. Although fraudulent activity is condemned on all fronts, in the past decade there has been an increase in the number of reports of scientists who forge or falsify data, manipulate results to support a theory, or selectively report data, as illustrated in Exhibit 4.1. In the past 20 years, the federal government has confirmed 200 cases of fraud, which works out to 1 case per 100,000 active researchers per year. However, this statistic might underrepresent the actual number; a 1987 study found that one-third of the scientists interviewed suspected that a colleague had committed plagiarism. However, 54% of these did not report their suspicions to university officials (Brainard, 2000).

The cost of such fraudulent activity is enormous, both to the profession and to the scientist. Not only is the whole scientific enterprise discredited, but the professional career of the individual is destroyed. Breuning (see Exhibit 4.1) pleaded guilty to scientific misconduct in a plea bargain and was sentenced to 60 days in a halfway house, 250 hours of community service, and 5 years of probation. There is no justification for faking or altering scientific data.

Although fraudulent activity is obviously the most serious form of scientific misconduct, there is a broader range of less serious, although still unacceptable, practices that are receiving attention. These include such practices as overlooking others' use of flawed data; failing to present data contradicting one's own work; changing the design, methodology, or results of a study in response to pressure from a funding source; or circumventing minor aspects of human-participant requirements. While

---

EXHIBIT 4.1

Two Cases of Reportedly Fraudulent Research

Although most known cases of fraudulent research have occurred in the field of medicine, several very significant instances have recently been identified in the field of psychology. Two of the most infamous cases are described in this exhibit.

Cyril Burt, the first British psychologist to be knighted, received considerable acclaim in both Great Britain and the United States for his research on intelligence and its genetic basis. A biographical sketch published upon his death depicted a man with unflagging enthusiasm for research, analysis, and criticism. Shortly after his death, however, questions about the authenticity of his research began to appear. Ambiguities and oddities were identified in his research papers. A close examination of his data revealed that correlation coefficients did not change across samples or across sample sizes, suggesting that he might have fabricated data. Attempts to locate one of Burt's important collaborators were unsuccessful. Dorfman (1978) conducted an in-depth analysis of Burt's data and showed beyond a reasonable doubt that Burt fabricated his data on the relationship between intelligence and social class.

More recently, the National Institute of Mental Health (NIMH) conducted an investigation of alleged research fraud by one of its grantees, Steven E. Breuning. Breuning received his doctorate from the Illinois Institute of Technology in 1977 and several years later obtained a position at the Coldwater Regional Center in Michigan. At Coldwater, Breuning was invited to collaborate on an NIMH-funded study regarding the use of neuroleptics on institutionalized mentally disabled people. In January 1981, he was appointed director of the John Merck program at Pittsburgh's Western Psychiatric Institute and Clinic, where he continued to report on the results of the Coldwater research and even obtained his own NIMH grant to study the effects of stimulant medication on participants with mental disabilities. During this time, Breuning gained considerable prominence and was considered one of the field's leading researchers. In 1983, however, questions were raised about the validity of Breuning's work. The individual who had initially taken Breuning on as an investigator started questioning a paper in which Breuning reported results having impossibly high reliability. This prompted a further review of Breuning's published work, and contacts were made with personnel at Coldwater, where the research had supposedly been conducted. Coldwater's director of psychology had never heard of the study and was not aware that Breuning had conducted any research while at Coldwater. NIMH was informed of the allegations in December 1983. Following a 3-year investigation, an NIMH team concluded that Breuning "knowingly, willfully, and repeatedly engaged in misleading and deceptive practices in reporting his research." He reportedly had not carried out the research that was described, and only a few of the experimental subjects had ever been studied. It was concluded that Breuning had engaged in serious scientific misconduct (Holden, 1987).

these practices do not approach the seriousness of fabrication, falsification, or plagiarism, they are of concern to the profession, especially as Martinson, Anderson, and de Vries (2005) have revealed that more than a third of U.S. scientists surveyed admitted to engaging in one or more of these practices in the past 3 years. This does not necessarily mean that the structure of the research process has eroded. However, these problems deserve attention, as they do represent a form of research misconduct.

The increased frequency and interest in scientific misconduct have naturally stimulated discussion about its cause and the type of action that needs to be taken to reduce the frequency of misconduct (Hilgartner, 1990; Knight, 1984). One of the best deterrents is probably the development of an institutional culture in which key faculty members model ethical behavior, stress the importance of research integrity, and translate these beliefs into action (Gunsalus, 1993). Prevention strategies that make it difficult to engage in scientific misconduct, such as checking and verifying that data are collected as well as those listed in Table 4.1, must be instituted.

Additionally, the National Institutes of Health (NIH) require that all investigators who receive funding from NIH, as well as other key personnel such as coinvestigators and study coordinators, complete an education module on the protection of human participants. The National Science Foundation (NSF) has recently mandated that any research projects supported by NSF funds provide appropriate training and oversight in the responsible and ethical conduct or research for undergraduates, graduate students, and postdoctoral researchers. Starting January 25.2010, NIH requires similar training in the Responsible Conduct of Research for NIH supported career development awards, research education grants, and dissertation research grants. Most universities extend these requirements to all investigators, including other key personnel such as graduate and undergraduate students who are conducting research with human participants whose research does not receive NIH funding.

Treatment of Research Participants

The treatment of research participants is the most fundamental issue confronted by scientists. The conduct of research with humans can potentially create a great deal of physical and psychological harm. For example, in September 1995, *U.S. News &*

TABLE 4.1

Information That Must Be Presented in a Research Protocol Presented to the IRB

- Purpose of the research
- Relevant background and rationale for the research
- Participant population
- Experimental design and methodology
- Incentives offered, if any
- Risks and benefits to the participants and precautions to be taken
- Privacy and confidentiality of the data collected

World Report (Pasternak & Cary, 1995) published an article on once-secret records of government-sponsored or -funded radiation experiments carried out between 1944 and 1974. During this time, more than 4000 radiation experiments were conducted on tens of thousands of Americans for the dual purpose of learning more about the effects of radiation on humans and the potential medical benefits of radiation on cancer.

In one of the most controversial experiments, cancer patients receiving radiation treatments were told that the radiation might cure their cancer. Documents, however, suggested that many of these treatments were conducted only to gather data on the effect of radiation on humans. Other radiation studies were conducted on patients with cancer resistant to radiation. In these experiments, the principal investigator even stated that he was experimenting and not treating the patients' disease. There was a 25% mortality rate. Such experiments are clearly unethical and should not be conducted.

Experiments designed to investigate important psychological issues might subject participants to humiliation, physical pain, and embarrassment. In planning an experiment, a scientist is obligated to consider the ethics of conducting the necessary research. Unfortunately, some studies cannot be designed in such a way that the possibility of physical and psychological harm is eliminated. Hence, the researcher often faces the dilemma of having to determine whether the research study should be conducted at all. Because it is so important, we will consider this issue in some detail.

STUDY QUESTIONS 4.1
- **What is meant by the term *research ethics*?**
- **What are the major areas of ethical concern in the social and behavioral sciences?**
- **What are the ethical issues in each of these areas, and which area is of most concern?**

Ethical Dilemmas

The scientific enterprise in which the research psychologist engages creates a special set of dilemmas. On the one hand, the research psychologist is trained in the scientific method and feels an obligation to conduct research; on the other hand, doing so might necessitate subjecting research participants to stress, failure, pain, aggression, or deception. Thus, there arises the **ethical dilemma** of having to determine if the potential gain in knowledge from the research study outweighs the cost to the research participant (see Exhibit 4.2). In weighing the pros and cons of such a question, the researcher must give primary consideration to the welfare of the participant. Unfortunately, there is no formula or rule that can help investigators. The decision must be based on a subjective judgment, which should not be made entirely by the researcher or his or her colleagues, because such individuals might become so involved in the study that they might tend to exaggerate its scientific merit and potential contribution. Investigators must seek the recommendations of others, such as scientists in related fields, students, or lay individuals.

Ethical dilemma
The investigator's conflict in weighing the potential cost to the participant against the potential gain to be accrued from the research project

EXHIBIT 4.2

Documenting That Stuttering Can Be a Learned Disorder: Did the Benefit of This Study Outweigh the Harm to the Participants?

In 1939, an experimental study was conducted demonstrating that stuttering could be created by constantly badgering a person about the imperfections in his or her speech (Monster experiment, June 2001). This experiment led to a theory that helped thousands of children overcome their speech impediment. However, the experiment affected the participants negatively, creating significant lifelong pain and suffering.

The experiment was designed by Dr. Wendell Johnson, who theorized that stuttering was not an inborn condition but something children learned from parents who seized on minor speech imperfections. As children became aware of their speech, he believed, they could not help but stutter. To validate his theory, he experimented with 22 orphans at an Iowa orphanage. Half of the orphans were given positive speech therapy, and the other half were induced to stutter by his graduate assistant Mary Tudor. Tudor induced stuttering by badgering the orphans about their speech even if it was nearly flawless. Through this process, 8 of the 11 orphans who were constantly badgered became chronic stutterers. One of the orphans who had developed stuttering wrote Tudor a letter in 2001 and called her a "monster" and "Nazi." She stated that Tudor had destroyed her life and left her nothing. Fortunately, she had married a man who helped her piece together her self-confidence.

However, after he died in 1999, she resumed stuttering and placed a Do Not Disturb sign on her door, rarely venturing outdoors.

Clearly, this experiment caused significant grief and pain for the orphans who developed stuttering. It is also something that has bothered Tudor while and after she conducted the experiment. At the time she conducted the experiment, she didn't like what she was doing. After the conclusion of the experiment, Tudor returned to the orphanage three times to try to reverse the orphans' stuttering with little success. Since that time, she has remained extremely ambivalent of her participation in the study because the results have helped countless individuals but, at the same time, the study caused considerable pain for the participants. She remembers how the orphans greeted her, running to her car and helping her carry in materials for the experiment. She got them to trust her and then she did this horrible thing to them. However, countless individuals have overcome their stuttering problems as a result of the knowledge acquired from this experiment.

There are tremendous benefits and costs that have accrued from this study. This is the reason for Tudor's current ambivalent feelings. She conducted an experiment that created a knowledge base that was very beneficial. It is also very clear that the cost was considerable to the participants.

At the present time, the recommendations regarding the cost–benefit relationship in a study comes from the Institutional Review Board (IRB). This is a board that exists at all institutions that receive federal funds for research and reviews research proposals involving human participants.

In reviewing the research proposals, members of the IRB are required to make judgments regarding the ethical appropriateness of the proposed research by ensuring that protocols are explained to the research participants and that the risks of harm are reasonable in relation to the hoped-for benefits. To make this judgment, the IRB members must have sufficient information about the specifics of the research protocol. This means that the investigator must submit a research protocol that the IRB can review. This research protocol must provide the information listed in Table 4.1. A sample research protocol submitted to an IRB appears in Exhibit 4.3.

EXHIBIT 4.3

Sample Research Protocol

Title of Protocol: The Relationship of Attributional Beliefs, Self-Esteem, and Ego Involvement to Performance on a Cognitive Task.

Primary Investigator: Doe
Psychology
Address Psychology Bldg.
Phone Number 123-4567

Purpose of the Research: The present investigation is designed to determine the potential individual differences in the ego-involvement effect. It is possible that some people are more at risk for the debilitating effects of ego-involving instructions than others. It is predicted that individuals with low self-esteem and negative attributional beliefs will be influenced negatively by ego-involving instructions.

Relevant Background for the Research: Recent research suggests that the way in which a cognitive task is presented influences performance on the task. Nicholls (1985) suggested that ego involvement often resulted in diminished task performance. He described ego involvement as a task orientation in which the goal is to either demonstrate one's ability relative to others or avoid demonstrating a lack of ability. This ego orientation is in contrast to task involvement in which the goal is simply to learn or improve a skill. In support of the Nicholls position, Graham and Golan (1991) found that ego-involving instructions resulted in poorer recall in a memory task than task-involving instructions. Apparently, the focus on performance detracted from the necessary information processing.

Participant Population: Two hundred students will be recruited from the Department of Psychology research participant pool. The pool consists of students enrolled in Psychology 120 who choose to participate in the research option to fulfill a course requirement.

The Experimental Design and Methodology: The research will be conducted in a large group setting (approximately 30 students) in a classroom on campus. Students choosing to participate in the research will first read and sign the consent from. Students will then complete an attributional questionnaire and a self-esteem questionnaire. These materials will then be collected, and a cognitive task will be distributed. Students will be given 1 minute to read the instructions and 3 minutes to solve 20 anagrams. (The experimenter will announce when to start and end each activity.) The packets containing the instructions and the anagrams will be randomly ordered so that half of the participants in each session will receive the ego instructions and half will receive the task instructions. The ego instructions explain that the anagram task is a test of ability and that the researchers want to see how each person rates in comparison to his or her peers. The task instructions explain that the anagram task is an opportunity to learn how to solve anagrams and that practice helps people improve. The attributional questionnaire is designed to assess the students' beliefs about the importance of different causal factors (e.g., effort, ability, luck, and powerful others) in academic performance. The self-esteem questionnaire is designed to measure global self-worth.

The data will be analyzed through multiple regression with attributions, self-esteem, gender, and instructional format as predictors of the criterion variables (number of anagrams solved, number of codes completed).

Potential Benefit to Participant, Humankind, or General Knowledge: The present literature on ego and task involvement indicates that ego instructions can negatively affect performance. It is important to determine the individual differences in this phenomenon. It is possible that females, individuals with low self-esteem, and individuals with negative attributional beliefs might be especially at risk for the debilitating effects of ego-involving instructions. If this is the case, one

EXHIBIT 4.3 (continued)

could reduce these individual differences in performance (and support optimal learning) by presenting tasks primarily in a task-involvement format.

Risks, Hazards, and Precautions to Be Taken:
The risks are minimal. It is possible that students will be discouraged by not having time to complete all of the tasks. However, at the end of the session, we will make it clear to the group of students that the tasks were designed so that no one could complete them in the time allotted.

Assurance of Confidentiality, Including Description of Means of Such Assurance:
Participants will remain anonymous. Each packet (questionnaires and cognitive tasks) will have a number. Participants will be identified only by this number. Students will not be asked to put their name on any form (other than the consent form). All data will be stored securely. Only the principal investigator and her assistants will have access to the data.

Sample Consent Form
Consent to Participate in Research

Primary Investigator: Doe
Department: Psychology
Telephone Number: 123-4567

The purpose of this research is to determine the role of beliefs about success and failure and about self-esteem in cognitive tasks. If you agree to participate in this research, you will be asked to complete two questionnaires. The attributional questionnaire includes 60 questions concerning the possible causes of academic success and failure. The self-esteem questionnaire includes 10 questions designed to measure an individual's global sense of self-worth or self-acceptance.

After completing both questionnaires, you will be asked to read a set of instructions and then try to solve as many anagrams as possible in a limited amount of time. Anagrams are jumbled letters that can be reordered to form a word (e.g., rlyibar = library).

Your participation in this research is entirely voluntary. You can change your mind and withdraw at any time without affecting your grade in the class.

The information gathered from this study will be strictly confidential, and your privacy will be carefully protected. Code numbers will be used to record all test results and responses to questionnaires. Your name will not be used. Should the results of this research be published or presented in any form, your name or other identifying information will not be revealed.

This research has been approved by the chair of the Department of Psychology and the Institutional Review Board of the University of USA. Any questions you might have should be directed to Dr. Jane Doe, who can be reached at 123-4567. Should you have unresolved questions relating to your rights as a research participant, you can contact the Institutional Review Board at 246-8910.

I have read or have had read to me and understand the above research study and have had an opportunity to ask questions that have been answered to my satisfaction. I agree voluntarily to participate in the study as described.

_____
Participant's Name

_____
Date

_____
Signature of Consenting Party

_____
Date

_____
Signature of Investigator

From the information contained in the research protocol, IRB members must make a judgment as to the ethical acceptability of the research. In making this judgment, the primary concern of the IRB is the welfare of the research participants. Specifically, the IRB will review proposals to ensure that research participants provide informed consent (see sample in Exhibit 4.3) for participation in the study and that the procedures used in the study do not harm the participants. This committee has particularly difficult decisions to make when a procedure involves the potential for harm. Some procedures, such as administering an experimental drug, have the potential for harming participants. In such instances, the IRB must seriously consider the potential benefits that might accrue from the study relative to the risks to the participant. Figure 4.1 presents a decision plane that provides a conceptual view of how the cost–benefit analysis should work. Studies falling in the areas labeled A and D can be easily decided on. Area A studies have high costs and low benefits and would *not* be approved. Area D studies would have high benefit and low cost and would be approved. The difficulty in deciding to approve or disapprove a study increases as a study moves into the areas labeled B and C. Studies in area C create difficulty because, although they create little potential cost to the participant, they are also likely to yield little benefit. Studies in area B create difficulty because, although the benefit accruing from the study is high, costs to the participants are also high. An example of such a study appears in Exhibit 4.2.

Sometimes the board's decision is that the risks to the research participants are too great to permit the study; in other instances, the decision is that the potential benefits are so great that the risks to the research participants are deemed to be acceptable. Unfortunately, the ultimate decision seems to be partially dependent on the composition of the IRB; Kimmel (1991) has revealed that males and research-oriented individuals who worked in basic areas were more likely to

FIGURE 4.1
A decision-plane model representing the costs and benefits of research studies.

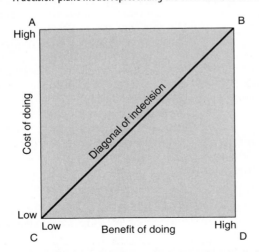

(From "Hedgehogs, foxes and the evolving social contract in science: Ethical challenges and methodological opportunities" by R. L. Rosnow, 1997, *Psychological Methods, 2,* pp. 345–356. Copyright by the American Psychological Association. Reprinted by permission of the author.)

approve research proposals than were women and individuals who worked in service-oriented contexts and were employed in applied areas.

Even if the IRB approves the research protocol prepared, the investigator must always remember that no amount of advice or counsel can alter the fact that the final ethical responsibility lies with the researcher conducting the study.

STUDY QUESTION 4.2 | **What is the ethical dilemma researchers are faced with in psychology, and how is this dilemma resolved?**

Ethical Guidelines

Nazi scientists during World War II conducted some grossly inhumane experiments that were universally condemned as being unethical. For example, they immersed people in ice water to determine how long it would take them to freeze to death, performed mutilating surgery, and deliberately infected many individuals with lethal pathogens. In 1946, 23 of the physicians went on trial at Nuremberg for the crimes they committed against these prisoners of war. During this trial, the fundamental ethical standards for the conduct of research were set forth in what has become known as the Nuremberg Code. This code set forth 10 conditions that must be met to justify research involving human participants. Of the 10 conditions, the two most important were voluntary informed consent and a valid research design that had the potential of yielding valuable results.

One would logically think that the Nuremberg trial and the ethical standards resulting from this trial would have led to the conduct of ethical research with human participants. However, this was not the case, although the abuses (e.g., falsifying data) were not as profound as those committed by the Nazi physicians. In the 1960s, there was not only an increase in funding for medical research and a corresponding increase in human participants but also an increase in the attention given to human rights and the publicizing of research abuses.

In the medical field, Pappworth (1967) cited numerous examples of research that violated the ethical rights of human participants. The Tuskegee experiment (Jones, 1981), described in Exhibit 4.4, probably epitomizes the type of unethical experimentation that was conducted within the medical field. There was an equal concern about the violation of the rights of human participants in psychological research. Kelman (1967, 1968, 1972) has been by far the most outspoken on this issue, although others, such as Seeman (1969) and Beckman and Bishop (1970), have also contributed. Entire books have been devoted to this issue (e.g., Kimmel, 1996). This widespread concern led to the development of several sets of guidelines, such as the Belmont Report (Office for Protection from Research Risks OPRR, 1979) and the American Psychological Association's *Ethical Principles of Psychologists and Code of Conduct* (APA, 2002), one section of which is for researchers to use when conducting their research. There are five basic moral principles (respect for persons and their autonomy, beneficence and nonmaleficence, justice, trust, and fidelity and scientific integrity) that should be adhered to when conducting research with human participants (Sales & Folkman, 2000).

EXHIBIT 4.4

The Tuskegee Syphilis Experiment

In July 1972, the Associated Press released a story that revealed that the U.S. Public Health Service (PHS) had for 40 years been conducting a study of the effects of untreated syphilis on black men in Macon County, Alabama. The study consisted of conducting a variety of medical tests (including an examination) on 399 black men who were in the late stages of the disease and on 200 controls. Although a formal description of the experiment could never be found (apparently one never existed), a set of procedures evolved in which physicians employed by the PHS administered a variety of blood tests and routine autopsies to learn more about the serious complications that resulted from the final stages of the disease.

This study had nothing to do with the treatment of syphilis; no drugs or alternative therapies were tested. It was a study aimed strictly at compiling data on the effects of the disease. The various components of the study, and not the attempt to learn more about syphilis, made it an extremely unethical experiment. The participants in the study were mostly poor and illiterate, and the PHS offered incentives to participate, including free physical examinations, free rides to and from the clinic, hot meals, free treatment for other ailments, and a $50 burial stipend. The participants were not told the purpose of the study or what they were or were not being treated for. Even more damning is the fact that the participants were monitored by a PHS nurse, who informed local physicians that those individuals were taking part in the study and that they were not to be treated for syphilis. Participants who were offered treatment by other physicians were advised that they would be dropped from the study if they took the treatment.

As you can see, the participants were not aware of the purpose of the study or the danger it posed to them, and no attempt was ever made to explain the situation to them. In fact, they were enticed with a variety of inducements and were followed to ensure that they did not receive treatment from other physicians. This study seems to have included just about every possible violation of our present standard of ethics for research with humans.

(From Jones, 1981.)

Respect for Persons and Their Autonomy

An autonomous person is one who is capable of making decisions and following through on those decisions. Within the context of research, this means that a prospective research participant has the right to choose to participate in a research study. Denial of this choice shows a lack of respect for that person. This principle is adhered to in research studies by obtaining the prospective participant's informed consent. This means that the prospective participant is given all the information about a research study that might influence his or her willingness to participate. Once they have this information, they can make an informed choice whether to participate. Although adherence to this principle seems simple and straightforward, difficulties arise when the target population of a research study has limited or diminished capacity to understand the consent agreement, as might exist with young children or individuals with a mental disorder. In these instances, the interests of the participant must be appropriately represented and an assurance must be provided that they will not be placed at risk. This assurance is typically obtained by having a proxy, such as a parent or guardian, provide the informed consent.

Although informed consent is the standard that must be followed in most studies, there are situations in which informed consent is not required, for example, in the limited situation where participation in the study is deemed to involve no risk. However, the judgment of no risk can be difficult. These issues surrounding informed consent are discussed in more detail later in the chapter.

Beneficence and Nonmaleficence

Beneficence means doing good and *nonmaleficence* means doing no harm. This principle states that we should design and conduct our research studies in a way that minimizes the probability of harm to the participant and maximizes the probability that the participants receive some benefit. This is obviously a laudable goal, and one that we should strive for. However, the costs and benefits of research studies vary considerably and seldom can we, in advance, anticipate all the costs and benefits that might accrue from a particular study. However, this is the task that is given to the IRB. Remember that a researcher planning to conduct a study using human participants must prepare and submit a proposal to the IRB detailing the elements of the research. From reading this proposal, the IRB members attempt to determine the costs and benefits of the research and then either approve or disapprove the research based on this determination.

There are actually three categories of review that a proposal can receive from the IRB. These categories relate directly to the potential risk of the study to the participant. Studies can receive exempt status, expedited review, or review by the full IRB (OPRR, 2001). Exempt studies are studies that appear to involve no known physical emotional, physiological, or economic risk to the participants and do not require review by the IRB. However, studies involving special populations such as minors, pregnant women, or prisoners are never exempt. Also, children involved in surveys, interview procedures, or the observation of their public behavior are never exempt unless the study involves observing them in the absence of any type of intervention. In making the decision to place a study in the exempt category, the IRB staff makes use of the exempt categories set forth in the OPRR (2001) reports and listed in Table 4.2.

The second category of review, expedited review, is a process whereby a study is rapidly reviewed by fewer members than constitute the full IRB. Studies receiving expedited review are typically those involving no more than minimal risk, where minimal risk means that the discomfort or harm expected from participation in the research is not greater than would be expected in daily life or from physical or psychological tests. Expedited studies would include the following:

1. Research involving data, documents, records, or specimens that have been collected or will be collected solely for nonresearch purposes.

2. Research involving the collection of data from voice, video, digital, or image recordings made for research purposes.

3. Research on individual or group characteristics or behavior (e.g., perception, cognition, motivation, and social behavior) or research employing survey, interview,

TABLE 4.2
Exempt Categories

1. Research conducted in established or commonly accepted educational settings, involving normal educational practices, such as (a) research on regular and special education instructional strategies or (b) research on the effectiveness of or the comparison among instructional techniques, curricula, or classroom management methods.

2. Research involving the use of educational tests (cognitive, diagnostic, aptitude, achievement), or observation of public behavior, unless:
   a. information obtained is recorded in such a manner that the participants can be identified, directly or through identifiers linked to the participants;
   b. any disclosure of this information outside the research could reasonably place the participant at risk of criminal or civil liability or be damaging to the participants' financial standing, employability, or reputation.
   c. the research focuses on behaviors such as illegal conduct, drug use, sexual behavior, or use of alcohol.

3. Research involving the use of educational tests, survey, interview procedures, or observation of public behavior or when participants are elected or appointed public officials or candidates for public office, or observation of public behavior that is not exempt under item 2 above if
   a. the participants are elected or appointed public officials or candidates for public office, or
   b. federal statute(s) require(s) without exception that the confidentiality of the personally identifiable information will be maintained throughout the research and thereafter.

4. Research involving the collection or study of existing data, documents, records, pathological specimens, or diagnostic specimens if these sources are publicly available or if the information is recorded by the investigator in such a manner that participants cannot be identified, directly or through identifiers linked to the participants.

oral history, focus groups, program evaluation, human factors evaluation, or quality assurance methodologies when they present no more than minimal risk to participants.

Many of the studies conducted by students and psychology faculty fall into the minimal risk category and should receive expedited review.

The third category of review is full board review. This is a review by all members of the IRB. Any proposal that involves more than minimal risk (e.g., experimental drugs, stressful psychological testing, and specific populations) raises red flags and must receive full board review.

Justice

The moral principle of justice is perhaps one of the more difficult ones to accomplish and is unlikely to be fully achieved (Sales & Folkman, 2000) in our imperfect world. In the research arena, justice asks the question: Who should receive the benefits of the research and who should bear its burdens? Go back and reread Exhibit 4.2. In this study, the research participants not only did not benefit from participation in the study but were also harmed. It seems clear that there was not a sense of fairness in the distribution of the benefits of this study. This brings up a difficult question for researchers. How should the benefits that might accrue from a study be distributed? Should all research participants receive equal benefits, and should the research participants benefit as much as nonparticipants? It seems fair that they should. However, the benefits from participation in the various components of a study are not known prior to the completion of the study, just as the benefits that might accrue from the research study are not known prior to its completion.

Trust

The moral principle of trust states that researchers should establish and maintain a relationship of trust with the research participants. This should not only be an obvious relationship but one that should be easy to accomplish. In fact, the necessity of requiring the research participants' informed consent would seem to dictate that participants be told what they are getting into. However, in our society, there has developed a mistrust of science and public institutions (Sales & Folkman, 2000). This mistrust has probably been precipitated by the disclosures in the media of studies such as the Tuskegee study in Exhibit 4.4 and the stuttering study summarized in Exhibit 4.2. In 2002, there was a repeated disclosure of fraudulent activity by executives of corporations such as Enron and World Com, and the financial crisis of 2009 probably further contributed to this mistrust.

Within the context of the psychological experiment, the principle of trust can be compromised in several ways. Some studies incorporate deception to maximize the probability that valid unbiased data are collected. Whenever deception is incorporated, the principle of trust is violated. The principle of trust can also be violated when the confidentiality of the information collected from research participants is not maintained. Safeguards need to be incorporated into each study to deal with these issues to reduce compromising the principle of trust. These two issues are discussed later in this chapter.

Fidelity and Scientific Integrity

The principle of fidelity and scientific integrity refers to the goal of discovering valid knowledge. Behavioral scientists conduct studies to uncover the mysteries of behavior—to acquire knowledge that will advance our understanding of behavior. To accomplish this goal, the scientist must not only conduct quality research but must also truthfully report the research he or she conducts. Both of these components are integral to the discovery and promulgation of truth. Poorly designed and executed studies lead to questionable information, whereas well-designed studies lead to valid information that contributes to the psychological knowledge base. Truthfully reporting the results of research also contributes to a valid knowledge base. This moral principle speaks directly to the issue of presenting fraudulent results that we discussed earlier in this chapter. As stated earlier, faking or altering scientific results has no place in science.

APA Ethical Standards for Research

Any psychologist conducting research must ensure that the dignity and welfare of the research participants are maintained and that the investigation is carried out in accordance with federal and state regulations and with the standards set forth by the American Psychological Association (APA).

The code of ethics, first published in 1953 (APA, 1953), was the outcome of about 15 years of discussion within APA. Since that time, the code has been revised several times. The most recent revision was approved in October of 2002. Exhibit 4.5 presents the section of the code of ethics pertaining to research and publication.

EXHIBIT 4.5

Ethical Standards Pertaining to Research and Publication

Section 8 of the code of ethics gives the standards psychologists are to adhere to when conducting human and animal research and publishing the results of this research. These standards are as follows.

8.01 Institutional Approval

When institutional approval is required, psychologists provide accurate information about their research proposals and obtain approval prior to conducting the research. They conduct the research in accordance with the approved research protocol.

8.02 Informed Consent to Research

(a) When obtaining informed consent as required in Standard 3.10, Informed Consent, psychologists inform participants about

(1) the purpose of the research, expected duration, and procedures

(2) their right to decline to participate and to withdraw from the research once participation has begun

(3) the foreseeable consequences of declining or withdrawing

(4) reasonably foreseeable factors that might be expected to influence their willingness to participate such as potential risks, discomfort, or adverse effects

(5) any prospective research benefits

(6) limits of confidentiality

(7) incentives for participation

(8) whom to contact for questions about the research and research participants' rights. They provide opportunity for the prospective participants to ask questions and receive answers.

(b) Psychologists conducting intervention research involving the use of experimental treatments, clarify to participants at the outset of the research

(1) the experimental nature of the treatment

(2) the services that will or will not be available to the control group(s) if appropriate

(3) the means by which assignment to treatment and control groups will be made

(4) available treatment alternatives if an individual does not wish to participate in the research or wishes to withdraw once a study has begun

(5) compensation for or monetary costs of participating, including, if appropriate, whether reimbursement from the participant or a third-party payer will be sought.

8.03 Informed Consent for Recording Voices and Images in Research

Psychologists obtain informed consent from research participants prior to recording their voices or images for data collection unless

(1) the research consists solely of naturalistic observations in public places, and it is not anticipated that the recording will be used in a manner that could cause personal identification or harm

E X H I B I T   4 . 5 (continued)

(2) the research design includes deception, and consent for the use of the recording is obtained during debriefing.

8.04 Client/Patient, Student, and Subordinate Research Participants

(a) When psychologists conduct research with clients/patients, students, or subordinates as participants, psychologists take steps to protect the prospective participants from adverse consequences of declining or withdrawing from participation.

(b) When research participation is a course requirement or opportunity for extra credit, the prospective participant is given the choice of equitable alternative activities.

8.05 Dispensing with Informed Consent for Research

Psychologists might reasonably dispense with informed consent only

(a) Where research would not reasonably be assumed to create distress or harm and involves

(1) the study of normal educational practices, curricula, or classroom management methods conducted in educational settings

(2) only anonymous questionnaires, naturalistic observations, or archival research for which disclosure of responses would not place participants at risk of criminal or civil liability or damage their financial standing, employability, or reputation, and confidentiality is protected

(3) the study of factors related to job or organization effectiveness conducted in organizational settings for which there is no risk to participants' employability, and confidentiality is protected.

(b) Where otherwise permitted by law or federal or institutional regulations.

8.06 Offering Inducements for Research Participation

(a) Psychologists make reasonable efforts to avoid offering excessive or inappropriate financial or other inducements for research participation when such inducements are likely to coerce participation.

(b) When offering professional services as an inducement for research participation, psychologists clarify the nature of the services, as well as the risks, obligations, and limitations.

8.07 Deception in Research

(a) Psychologists do not conduct a study involving deception unless they have determined that the use of deceptive techniques is justified by the study's significant prospective scientific, educational, or applied value and that effective nondeceptive alternative procedures are not feasible.

(b) Psychologists do not deceive prospective participants about research that is reasonably expected to cause physical pain or severe emotional distress.

(c) Psychologists explain any deception that is an integral feature of the design and conduct of an experiment to participants as early as is feasible, preferably at the conclusion of their participation, but no later than at the conclusion of the data collection, and permit participants to withdraw their data.

8.08 Debriefing

(a) Psychologists provide a prompt opportunity for participants to obtain appropriate information about the nature, results, and conclusions of the research, and they take reasonable steps to correct any misconceptions that participants might have of which the psychologists are aware.

(b) If scientific or humane values justify delaying or withholding this information, psychologists take reasonable measures to reduce the risk of harm.

(c) When psychologists become aware that research procedures have harmed a participant, they take reasonable steps to minimize the harm.

8.09 Humane Care and Use of Animals in Research

(a) Psychologists acquire, care for, use, and dispose of animals in compliance with current federal, state, and local laws and regulations, and with professional standards.

(b) Psychologists trained in research methods and experienced in the care of laboratory animals supervise all procedures involving animals and are

(continued)

EXHIBIT 4.5 (continued)

responsible for ensuring appropriate consideration of their comfort, health, and humane treatment.

(c) Psychologists ensure that all individuals under their supervision who are using animals have received instruction in research methods and in the care, maintenance, and handling of the species being used, to the extent appropriate to their role.

(d) Psychologists make reasonable efforts to minimize the discomfort, infection, illness, and pain of animal subjects.

(e) Psychologists use a procedure subjecting animals to pain, stress, or privation only when an alternative procedure is unavailable and the goal is justified by its prospective scientific, educational, or applied value.

(f) Psychologists perform surgical procedures under appropriate anesthesia and follow techniques to avoid infection and minimize pain during and after surgery.

(g) When it is appropriate that an animal's life be terminated, psychologists proceed rapidly, with an effort to minimize pain and in accordance with accepted procedures.

8.10 Reporting Research Results

(a) Psychologists do not fabricate data.

(b) If psychologists discover significant errors in their published data, they take reasonable steps to correct such errors in a correction, retraction, erratum, or other appropriate publication means.

8.11 Plagiarism

Psychologists do not present portions of another's work or data as their own, even if the other work or data source is cited occasionally.

8.12 Publication Credit

(a) Psychologists take responsibility and credit, including authorship credit, only for work they have actually performed or to which they have substantially contributed.

(b) Principal authorship and other publication credits accurately reflect the relative scientific or professional contributions of the individuals involved, regardless of their relative status. Mere possession of an institutional position, such as department chair, does not justify authorship credit. Minor contributions to the research or to the writing

for publications are acknowledged appropriately, such as in footnotes or in an introductory statement.

(c) Except under exceptional circumstances, a student is listed as principal author on any multiple-authored article that is substantially based on the student's doctoral dissertation. Faculty advisors discuss publication credit with students as early as is feasible and throughout the research and publication process as appropriate.

8.13 Duplicate Publication of Data

Psychologists do not publish, as original data, data that have been previously published. This does not preclude republishing data when they are accompanied by proper acknowledgment.

8.14 Sharing Research Data for Verification

(a) After research results are published, psychologists do not withhold the data on which their conclusions are based from other competent professionals who seek to verify the substantive claims through reanalysis and who intend to use such data only for that purpose, provided that the confidentiality of the participants can be protected and unless legal rights concerning proprietary data preclude their release. This does not preclude psychologists from requiring that such individuals or groups be responsible for costs associated with the provision of such information.

(b) Psychologists who request data from other psychologists to verify the substantive claims through reanalysis can use shared data only for the declared purpose. Requesting psychologists obtain prior written agreement for all other uses of the data.

8.15 Reviewers

Psychologists who review material submitted for presentation, publication, grant, or research proposal review respect the confidentiality of and the proprietary rights in such information of those who submitted it.

STUDY QUESTIONS 4.3

- **What are the five basic moral principles that psychologists should follow when conducting research? Explain what is meant by each of these principles.**
- **What are the categories of review that a research proposal can receive, and what are the criteria used to determine in which category a research proposal falls?**

Ethical Issues to Consider When Conducting Research

Section 8 of the code of ethics was adopted by the APA in October 2002 as its official position on research and publication and, therefore, represents the standards to be used by psychologists conducting animal and human research. Included in these standards are a number of important issues focusing on research with human participants that are worthy of further discussion. These include the issues of institutional approval, informed consent, deception, and debriefing. In addition to these issues are the issues of freedom to decline to participate in or to withdraw from the study at any time and of confidentiality and anonymity. There is also the issue of the ethics of Internet research that has not been addressed by the APA code of ethics.

Institutional Approval

Most, if not all, institutions that have active research programs have a requirement that all human research is reviewed by an IRB. The requirement that all human research be reviewed by an IRB dates back to 1966. At the time there was a concern for the way in which medical research was designed and conducted. As a result of this concern, the surgeon general initiated an institutional review requirement at the Department of Health, Education, and Welfare (DHEW). This policy was extended to all investigations funded by the Public Health Service that involved human participants, including those in the social and behavioral sciences. By 1973, the DHEW regulations governing human research required a review by an IRB for all research receiving Public Health Service funds. This meant that virtually all institutions of higher education had to establish an IRB and file an assurance policy with the OPRR of the Department of Health and Human Services. This assurance policy articulates the responsibilities and purview of the IRB within that institution. Although the Public Health Service mandated only that federally funded projects be reviewed by an IRB, most institutions extended the scope of the IRB to include all research involving human participants, even those falling into the exempt category. Once this assurance policy is approved, it becomes a legal document to which the institution and researchers must comply. If your institution receives funds from one of the federal granting agencies, such an assurance policy probably exists, which means that any research involving human participants must be submitted to and approved by your institution's IRB prior to conducting the research.

Ethical Standard 8.01 of the code of ethics specifies that, when such institutional approval is required, psychologists must provide accurate information about their research proposal (see Table 4.2), receive approval from the IRB, and then conduct the research in accordance with the approved protocol.

Informed Consent

Informed consent refers to fully informing the research participants about all aspects of the study. Standards 8.02 to 8.04 of the code of ethics (Exhibit 4.5) state that fully informing the research participants means that you inform them of all aspects of the research, from the purpose and procedures to any risks and benefits, including such things as incentives for participation. With this information, the research participant can make an informed decision and choose to either decline to participate in the study or give his or her informed consent.

Gaining a participant's informed consent is considered to be vital because of the sacredness of the principle that individuals have a fundamental right to determine what is done to their minds and bodies. Once a person is provided with all available information, it is assumed that he or she can make a free decision as to whether to participate, and in this manner, participants can avoid experimental procedures they consider objectionable. In this way, the basic principle of "respect for persons and their autonomy," discussed early in this chapter, is achieved.

Dispensing With Informed Consent   Although the ideal procedure is to fully inform research participants of all features of the study that might affect their willingness to participate, the current code of ethics recognizes that there might be times when it is appropriate to dispense with informed consent. There is a good reason to dispense with informed consent in some studies because the integrity of the data can be compromised. Consider the study by Resnick and Schwartz (1973). These investigators attempted to determine the impact of following the informed consent principle to its logical extreme in a simple but widely used verbal conditioning task developed by Taffel (1955). The control, or noninformed, group was given typical instructions, which gave them a rationale for the study and informed them of the task that they were to complete. The experimental, or informed, group received *complete* instructions regarding the true reason for conducting the experiment and the *exact* nature of the Taffel procedure. Figure 4.2 depicts the results of the data obtained from the 14 participants in each treatment condition. The uninformed participants performed in the expected manner, demonstrating verbal conditioning. The informed group, however, revealed a reversal in the conditioning rate. Such data show that maintaining maximum ethical conditions alters the knowledge that we accumulate. This altered information might represent inaccurate information, which would create a *lack* of external validity.

Federal guidelines as well as the APA's code of ethics, Standard 8.05, recognize the necessity of sometimes forgoing the requirement of informed consent. However, the code of ethics specifies that informed consent can be dispensed with only under specific and limited conditions in which the research will not reasonably be assumed to create distress or harm or where dispensing with informed consent is permitted by law or federal or institutional regulations. This is consistent with federal regulations, which state that investigators can waive the requirement of informed consent if signing the consent form would be the only thing linking the participant to the research and the research presents no more than minimal risk of harm to the participant.

FIGURE 4.2

Verbal conditioning data obtained by Resnick and Schwartz.

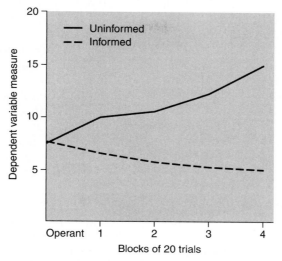

(Adapted from "Ethical standards as an independent variable in psychological research" by J. H. Resnick and T. Schwartz, 1973, *American Psychologist, 28*, p. 136. Copyright 1973 by the American Psychological Association. Reprinted by permission of the author.)

Informed Consent and Minors   The principle of informed consent refers to the fact that a person, once given the pertinent information, is competent and legally free to make a decision as to whether to participate in a given research study. Minors, however, are presumed to be incompetent and cannot give consent. In such instances, Standard 3.10(b)(4) states that permission must be obtained from a legally authorized person, if this substitute consent is permitted or required by law. In most instances, the substitute consent is obtained from the minor's parents or legal guardians after they have been informed of all the features of the study that might affect their willingness to allow their child to participate. In addition to obtaining informed consent from the minor's parents or legal guardians, Standard 3.10(b)(1 & 2) of the code of ethics specifies that the minor be given an appropriate explanation of the study and that he or she give his or her assent. **Assent** means that the minor agrees to participate in the research after receiving an appropriate explanation. By appropriate, we mean that the explanation is one that is in language that the minor can understand.

Federal regulations (OPRR, 2001) state that provisions should be made for soliciting the assent of a minor, when, in the judgment of the IRB, the minor is capable of providing assent. However, the age at which a person is capable of providing assent can differ among children. To provide assent, the child must be able to understand what is being asked, to realize that permission is being sought, and to make choices free from outside constraints. This depends on the cognitive capabilities of the child. Unfortunately, the cognitive capabilities of children develop at different rates, making it difficult to state an age at which a child is capable of providing assent. Individuals over the age of 9 generally

Assent
Agreement from a minor to participate in research after receiving an age-appropriate explanation of the study

have sufficient cognitive ability to make a decision concerning participation in research, and individuals over the age of 14 seem to make the same decisions as adults (Leikin, 1993). This should not be taken to mean that assent should definitely be obtained from individuals over age 14, possibly from individuals over age 9, and not from individuals age 9 or less. Rather, most individuals (e.g., Leikin, 1993) and the ethical guidelines provided by the Society for Research in Child Development (2003) state that assent should be obtained from all children. Assent occurs when "the child shows some form of agreement to participate without necessarily comprehending the full significance of the research necessary to give informed consent" (Society for Research in Child Development, 2003). Not only is it ethically acceptable to obtain the assent of minors, but it might also enhance the validity of the study. Insisting that minors participate when they have clearly stated that they do not want to alter their behavioral responses and represent a confounding influence on the data collected.

Active consent
Verbally agreeing and signing a form consenting to participate in research

Passive Versus Active Consent   The discussion of consent has, up to this point, focused on active consent. **Active consent** involves consenting to participate in a research study by verbally agreeing and signing a consent form. When minors are used as research participants, consent is typically obtained from the minor's parent or legal guardian. If consent is desired from school-age children, a common way in which consent is obtained is to provide the parent or legal guardian with a consent form by some means, such as mailing the consent form or sending it home with the minor. Ideally, the parent reads the consent form and either gives or refuses consent and returns the consent form to the researcher. However, studies (e.g., Ellickson, 1989) have revealed that only 50–60% of parents return consent forms even when follow-up efforts are made. One interpretation of the failure to return consent forms is that the parents have denied consent. However, there are a number of other reasons why parents might not return consent forms. They might not have received the consent form, might forget to sign and return the form, or might not take enough time to read and consider the request. The existence of any or all of these possibilities will reduce the sample size and possibly bias the results.

Passive consent
Consent is received from a parent or guardian by not returning the consent form

To increase participation in research studies, Ellickson (1989) recommended the use of passive consent. **Passive consent** is a process whereby parents or legal guardians give consent by not returning the consent form. They return the consent form only if they do *not* want their child to participate in the research. Passive consent has been promoted by some investigators as a legitimate means of securing parental consent. Ethical concerns have been raised when passive consent procedures are used, because these studies might include children whose parents actually oppose their participation in the research but did not return the consent form or perhaps did not receive it. However, studies (e.g., Ellickson & Hawes, 1989; Severson & Ary, 1983) have revealed that active and passive consent procedures yield comparable rates of participation when the active consent procedures used extensive follow-up techniques. This suggests that nonresponse to passive consent represents latent consent. When this is combined with the fact that the use of the active consent process, in the absence of extensive follow-up, results in a lower level of participation of low socioeconomic status and minority participants, the use of passive consent seems legitimate. This conclusion seems to be particularly true because the lower participation stems primarily from a failure to respond rather than an explicit desire to not participate. Requiring active consent would, therefore, run counter to federal guidelines to increase minority participation in research. In addition, passive consent, because it increases low socioeconomic status and minority participation, leads to less biased results than does the use of active consent. Exhibit 4.6 provides an example of a passive consent form.

Although there seems to be a place for passive consent and some cogent arguments for its use in certain situations, we recommend that you use active consent

---

EXHIBIT 4.6

Example of a Passive Consent Form

Dear Parent or Legal Guardian:

I am a faculty member in the Psychology Department at Excel University. I am interested in finding the best method of teaching mathematical concepts. To identify the best method, I am planning a study that will compare two different methods of teaching mathematical concepts. Both teaching methods are acceptable and standard methods of teaching these concepts, but we do not know which is the more effective method. My research will identify the more effective method.

To identify the more effective method, during the next 6 weeks I will be presenting material in two different ways to separate classes. To test the effectiveness of each method, I will measure students' performance by giving them a standard math test.

Your child's responses will remain confidential and will be seen only by me and my research assistant.

No reports about this study will contain your child's name. I will not release any information about your child without your permission.

Participation in this study is completely voluntary. All students in the class will take the test. If you do **not** wish your child to be in this study, please fill out the form at the bottom of this letter and return it to me. Also, please tell your child to hand in a blank test sheet when the class is given the mathematics test so that he or she will not be included in this study.

I will also ask the children to participate and tell them to hand in a blank test sheet if they do not want to be included in the study. Your child can choose to stop participating at any time.

If you have any questions about the study, please contact professor John Doe, Excel University, Department of Psychology, Good Place, AL 12345, Phone 251–246–8102. You can also contact me at (provide address and phone number).

Thank you,

Joh Doe

Return this portion only if you do not want your child to participate in the study described above.

I do not wish for my child _____ to be in the research study on the teaching of math concepts being conducted in his/her classroom.

_____
Parent's Signature

_____
Date

whenever possible. This is the best form of consent. Passive consent should be considered only when the integrity of the study would be seriously compromised by requiring active consent. The APA code of ethics does not directly address passive consent so it is imperative that you inform the IRB whenever you want to use passive consent and receive their approval prior to making use of this technique.

- **What is meant by *informed consent,* and why is this considered a vital component of a research protocol?**
- **When is it appropriate for you to dispense with informed consent?**
- **What is meant by *assent,* and when should it be obtained?**
- **What is the difference between active consent and passive consent?**
- **When should you try to obtain passive consent, and what ethical issues are associated with it?**

Deception

Deception refers to deceit. The use of deception in psychological research is counter to the requirement of fully informing the research participants of the nature of the research in which they are asked to participate. It also runs counter to the basic moral principle of trust that psychologists should adhere to when conducting research with humans. However, psychologists must also conduct their research with fidelity and scientific integrity. This means that they must conduct well-designed and executed studies to advance our understanding of behavior. To conduct such studies requires, in some instances, the use of deception. This requirement is acknowledged by the code of ethics. However, the code of ethics does not permit the unfettered use of deception. Rather, the use of deception is limited to studies in which alternative procedures are not available and the study has the potential of producing important knowledge. If deception is used, the participants are informed of its use as early as is feasible. In addition, deception cannot be used in studies that can be expected to cause harm or severe emotional distress.

In social and behavioral research, deception can be either active or passive deception (Rosnow & Rosenthal, 1998). **Active deception** refers to deception by commission, when the researcher deliberately misleads the research participants such as when they are given false information about the purpose of the experiment or when they are deliberately led to believe that a confederate is a research participant. **Passive deception** refers to deception by omission, when certain information is withheld from the research participants, such as not giving the research participants all the details of an experiment. Both active and passive deception are incorporated in the design of many psychological experiments. In fact, a number of investigators have attempted to determine the extent to which deception is used in psychological studies. These surveys reveal that the use of deception increased from the late 1940s to the late 1960s. This increase occurred primarily within the fields of personality and social psychology. From 1969 to 1987, the percent of deception studies declined, suggesting that initial increase was followed by a more recent decline in the use of deception.

Active deception
Deliberately misleading research participants by giving them false information

Passive deception
Withholding information from the research participants by not giving them all the details of the experiment

If this suggested trend is true, it might imply that the objections to deception and the more rigid ethical standards (Nicks, Korn, & Mainieri, 1997) have been acknowledged by researchers, and they have turned to alternative methods for investigating important psychological phenomena. Unfortunately, this does not seem to be the case. Sieber, Iannuzzo, and Rodriguez (1995) have revealed that any change in the percentage of studies using deception has been an outgrowth of the type of study conducted. Such topic areas as attribution, environmental psychology, and sex roles were popular in 1978 and 1986. These are topic areas in which deception is seldom used and corresponds to the years in which the percentage of deception studies declined. In 1992, there were fewer studies focusing on these topic areas, and the result was that the percentage of deception studies increased.

Given that deception is here to stay and that alternatives to deception, such as role playing (Kelman, 1967), are inadequate substitutes (Miller, 1972), we need to take a look at the effect of deception on research participants because it has been stated that deception will affect their behavior in unintended ways (Ortmann & Hertwig, 1997). More than four decades ago Kelman (1967) predicted that the persistent use of deception would cause research participants to become distrustful of psychologists and undermine psychologists' relations with them. Fortunately, this prediction has not come true. Sharpe, Adair, and Roese (1992) revealed that current research participants are as accepting of arguments justifying the use of deception as they were 20 years ago. Soliday and Stanton (1995) found that mild deception had no effect on attitudes toward researchers, science, or psychology. Fisher and Fyrberg (1994) even found that most of the student research participants in their study believed that the deception studies they evaluated were scientifically valid and valuable. Most also believed that the use of deception was an important methodology to retain even when other methodologies, such as role playing or questionnaires, were available.

Christensen (1988) summarized the results of studies investigating the reactions of participants to deception experiments. The literature consistently revealed that research participants do not perceive that they were harmed and do not seem to mind having been misled. For example, in a follow-up investigation of people who had participated in a series of studies that included deception and potential physical and mental stress, Pihl, Zacchia, and Zeichner (1981) found that only 19% of those contacted reported being bothered by any aspect of the experiment and only 4% said they were bothered by the deception. The components that upset the participants were mostly rather trivial (one participant felt that using a cloth holder for a drinking glass was unsanitary). The greatest distress surrounded the type of alcohol consumed, the dose, and the speed with which it had to be consumed. One participant reported being bothered for several days because "laboratory and not commercial alcohol was consumed" (Pihl et al., 1981, p. 930). Interestingly, this participant was in a placebo group that had not even consumed alcohol. It is also interesting to note that the distress surrounding the deception and averse stimuli variables lasted less time than did the distress surrounding other seemingly

FIGURE 4.3

Average length of distress for four categories of complaints.

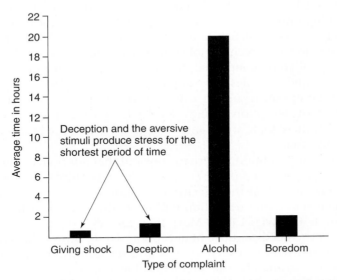

(Based on data from "Follow-up analysis of the use of deception and aversive contingencies in psychological experiments" by R. D. Pihl, C. Zacchia, and A. Zeichner, 1981, *Psychological Reports, 48,* pp. 927–930.)

trivial variables such as boredom. As is illustrated in Figure 4.3, the duration of distress over the deception or shock was only 1 hour or less, whereas the dissatisfaction with the alcohol lasted an average of 20 hours.

Smith and Richardson (1983) found that the participants who had taken part in deception experiments reported enjoying the experiment more, felt that they had received more educational benefit from the experiment, and perceived their participation in the research as being more satisfactory than did other participants. Not only did Smith and Richardson not find support for the notion that deception is harmful but they also provided data suggesting that deception might be advantageous. Kimmel (1998) concludes that deception does not negatively influence participants' perception of psychology or science in general.

Although research participants consistently report that they do not mind having been misled and were not harmed by deception experiments, a case could be made for the view that the detrimental effects of deception depend on the type of study being conducted. Christensen (1988) pointed out that deception is viewed as less acceptable ethically if the study investigates private behaviors such as sexual experiences or if the experimental procedure has significant potential to harm the research participant. Deception research raises special ethical concerns when it involves private behaviors or behaviors that are perceived as negative and might result in harm to the research participant (Sieber et al., 1995). This is consistent with the code of ethics, which states that deception should not be used in research expected to cause pain or severe emotional distress.

Debriefing

Debriefing
A postexperimental discussion or interview about the details of the study, including an explanation for the use of any deception

Debriefing refers to a postexperimental interview or discussion with the participant about the purpose and details of the study, including an explanation for the use of any deception. APA code of ethics Standard 8.08 specifies that psychologists must debrief participants as soon as possible following completion of a study and that if this information must be delayed, measures must be taken to reduce any risk of harm. In addition, if the research procedures might have harmed the participant, steps must be taken to minimize the harm. Debriefing participants is not only required by the code of ethics but can also be beneficial to the researcher in many ways. We elaborate on the beneficial use of debriefing in Chapter 9. Here we focus on deception and the use of debriefing because considerable attention has been focused on this issue.

The evidence shows that deception is not necessarily the harmful component many individuals assume it to be. This does not mean that the potentially harmful effects of deception can be forgotten, however. One of the primary modes used to eliminate any harmful effects of deception is debriefing. All the studies that investigated the impact of deception incorporated a debriefing procedure, and, if such a procedure does in fact eliminate any harmful effects of deception, this might explain the positive findings of these experiments.

Milgram (1964b) reported that, after extensive debriefing, only 1.3% of his participants reported any negative feelings about their experiences in the experiment. Such evidence indicates that the debriefing was effective in eliminating the extreme anguish that these participants apparently experienced. Ring, Wallston, and Corey (1970), in their quasi-replication of Milgram's (1964a) experiment, found that only 4% of the participants who had been debriefed indicated they regretted having participated in the experiment and only 4% believed that the experiment should not be permitted to continue. On the other hand, about 50% of the participants who had not been debriefed responded in this manner. Berscheid, Baron, Dermer, and Libman (1973) found similar ameliorative effects of debriefing on consent-related responses. Holmes (1973) and Holmes and Bennett (1974) took an even more convincing approach and demonstrated that debriefing reduced the arousal generated in a stress-producing experiment (expected electric shock) to the prearousal level, as assessed by both physiological and self-report measures.

Smith and Richardson (1983) asserted that their deceived participants received better debriefings than did their nondeceived participants and that this more effective debriefing might have been the factor that caused the deceived participants to have more positive responses than did the nondeceived participants.

This suggests that debriefing is quite effective in eliminating the stress produced by the experimental treatment condition. However, Holmes (1976a, 1976b) has appropriately pointed out that there are two goals of debriefing and both must be met for debriefing to be maximally effective: dehoaxing and desensitizing. **Dehoaxing** refers to debriefing the participants about any deception that the researcher might have used. In the dehoaxing process, the problem is one of convincing the participant that the fraudulent information given was, in fact,

Dehoaxing
Debriefing the participants about any deception that was used in the experiment

Desensitizing
Eliminating any undesirable influence that the experiment might have had on the participant

fraudulent. **Desensitizing** refers to debriefing the participants about their behavior. If the experiment has made participants aware that they have some undesirable features (e.g., that they could and would inflict harm on others), then the debriefing procedure should attempt to help the participants deal with this new information. This is typically done by suggesting that the undesirable behavior was caused by some situational variable rather than by some dispositional characteristic of the research participant. Another tactic used by researchers is to point out that the research participants' behavior was not abnormal or extreme. The big question is whether or not such tactics are effective in desensitizing or dehoaxing the participants. In Holmes's (1976a, 1976b) review of the literature relating to these two techniques, he concluded that they were effective. Fisher and Fyrberg (1994) support this conclusion. Over 90% of their student research participants were of the opinion that the dehoaxing would be believed.

This only means that effective debriefing is *possible*. These results hold only if the debriefing is carried out properly. A sloppy or improperly prepared debriefing session might very well have a different effect. In addition, the beneficial impact of debriefing can be experienced only if the experimental procedure includes a debriefing session. Adair, Dushenko, and Lindsay (1985), in their survey of the literature, found that only 66% of all the deception studies reported in the *Journal of Personality and Social Psychology* in 1979 included debriefing. This suggests that researchers should be more diligent about debriefing their research participants.

However, Campbell (1969) suggested that debriefing be eliminated when the experimental treatment condition falls within the participant's range of ordinary experiences. This recommendation has also been supported by survey data collected by Rugg (1975).

STUDY QUESTION 4.5 | **What is deception, and what are the ethical issues involved with the use of deception in psychological research? In answering this question, consider the effect of deception on the research participant and the use of debriefing.**

Coercion and Freedom to Decline Participation

Standard 3.08 of the code of ethics explicitly states that psychologists should not exploit the individuals over whom they have some authority. This includes students and clients/patients. The concern with coercion has probably been expressed most frequently over the widespread use of research participant pools and the nature of the relationship between professors and students. Professors might present situations where students might feel coercive pressure to participate, such as providing extra-credit for participation. Leak (1981) found that students who were induced to participate by means of an offer of extra-credit points were divided on their perception of the coercive nature of the means used for attaining participation. However, they did not resent or object to being offered the extra credit for participation and, overall, viewed the research experience as being worthwhile.

In addition to the issue of coercion, individuals must always feel free to decline to participate in or free to withdraw from the research at any time. This principle seems quite reasonable and relatively innocuous. Gardner (1978), however, has asserted that such a perception, although ethically required, can influence the outcome of some studies. The subtle influence of telling research participants that they were free to discontinue participation was discovered quite accidentally. Gardner had been experimenting on the detrimental impact of environmental noise. Prior to the incorporation of a statement informing potential participants that they could decline to participate without penalty, he always found that environmental noise produced a negative aftereffect. After he incorporated this statement, however, he could not produce the effect. In order to verify that a statement regarding freedom to withdraw was the factor causing the elimination of the negative aftereffect of environmental noise, Gardner replicated the experiment, telling participants in one group that they could decline to participate at any time without penalty and not making this statement to participants in another group. As Figure 4.4 illustrates, the environmental noise caused a decline in performance under the old procedures but not under the new procedures. This study indicates the very subtle effects that ethical principles can have and suggests that such effects should be considered when prior results are not replicated, and the only difference in procedure is the incorporation of the ethical principles.

Confidentiality, Anonymity, and the Concept of Privacy

Privacy
Having control of others access to information about you

Privacy refers to controlling other people's access to information about a person. There are two aspects to privacy that must be considered (Folkman, 2000). The first involves a person's freedom to identify the time and circumstances under which information is shared with or withheld from others. For example, a person might

FIGURE 4.4
Accuracy of performance of participants during silence or environmental noise conditions after being instructed or not instructed that they can decline to participate.

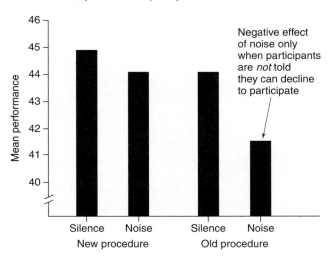

(Based on data from "Effects of federal human subjects regulations on data obtained in environmental stressor research" by G. T. Gardner, 1978, *Journal of Personality and Social Psychology, 36*, pp. 628–634.)

not want information about his or her sexual behavior shared with others, or he or she might agree to share this information only if it is aggregated with others' information so they cannot be identified. The second is the person's right to decline receiving information that he or she does not want. For example, a person might not want to know if he or she performed worse on a task than the average person.

While respecting the privacy of research participants is at the heart of the conduct of ethical research, constitutional and federal laws have not been passed that would protect the privacy of information collected within the context of social and behavioral research. So how do we protect the privacy of research information? Researchers attempt to ensure the privacy of research participants by either collecting anonymous information or ensuring that information collected is kept confidential. Anonymity is an excellent way of protecting privacy because **anonymity** refers to keeping the identity of the research participants unknown. In the context of a research study, anonymity is achieved if the researcher cannot connect the data collected with any specific participant. For example, if you were conducting a survey of the sexual behavior of college students, you might ask every person taking a psychology course during the fall semester to complete the survey. If the research participants did not put any identifying information on the survey, anonymity would be obtained. However, Picou (1996) has revealed that removing all identifiers from data files might not be sufficient to maintain research participants' anonymity because a careful examination of participant responses might allow a third party to deduce a participant's identity. This was a hard lesson he learned during a year in federal court.

Anonymity
Keeping the identity of the research participant unknown

Confidentiality is the other means that researchers use to protect the privacy of research participants. **Confidentiality**, in the context of a research study, refers to an agreement with research investigators about what might be done with the information obtained about a research participant. Typically, this means that the information obtained, although known to the research group, will not be revealed to anyone other than the researcher and his or her staff. The APA code of ethics is very explicit in stating that information obtained about a research participant must be kept confidential because to do otherwise represents a violation of the right to privacy.

Confidentiality
Not revealing information obtained from a research participant to anyone outside the research group

This promise to keep information confidential is provided in the context of the informed consent. However, investigators must be careful about what they promise for several reasons. The APA code of ethics permits disclosure of confidential information without consent to protect others from harm; some states, such as California, mandate that therapists protect potential victims from harm. Also, all states have mandatory reporting of child abuse or neglect, and many mandate reporting of elder abuse or neglect. This means that researchers should be familiar with state and federal laws to determine what can and cannot be kept confidential, and this information should be included in the informed consent.

Because information collected by researchers is not protected by law, confidentiality can be difficult to maintain. Research records can be subpoenaed by a court to be turned over to the party that wants them. However, courts have typically been willing to protect the identity of participants who have been promised confidentiality (Holder, 1993). Also, research data are rarely subpoenaed because they typically do not provide information central to the issue being litigated. If you think your data might be subject to litigation and subpoenaed, you could obtain a "certificate of confidentiality" from the U.S. Department of Health and Human Services. Obtaining such a certificate provides immunity from the requirement to reveal names or identifying information in a legal proceeding.

As the above indicates, ensuring the privacy of research participants is littered with obstacles, some of which are not under the control of the researcher. This means that researchers should carefully consider the nature of the study they are conducting and the probability of the data collected being the subject of some type of litigation and incorporate as many controls as seems prudent to ensure the privacy of the research participants. It is also incumbent upon the researcher to inform the research participants of the limits of their ability to maintain the privacy of the information collected.

Ethical Issues in Electronic Research

Over the past decade, researchers have increasingly turned to the Internet as a medium for conducting research investigating important psychological issues. For example, Smucker, Earleywine, and Gordis (2005) made use of the Internet in their study examining the relationship between alcohol consumption and cannabis use. The increasing use of the Internet in the conduct of psychological studies is logical, given the advantages it offers. Internet studies can access not only a large number of individuals in a short period of time but also those with diverse backgrounds. This is contrasted with numerous psychological studies that are limited to their universities' "subject or participant pool" consisting primarily of college sophomores. Psychology experiments conducted on the Internet are also much more cost-effective and capable of reaching individuals anywhere in the world.

The ease with which many studies can be conducted with the Internet medium also raises ethical issues. These issues focus on topics such as informed consent, privacy, and debriefing. While these issues are recognized and have been discussed by organizations such as the American Association for the Advancement of Science (see http://www.aaas.org/spp/sfrl/projects/intres/report.pdf) and the Association of Internet Research (see http://www.aoir.org/reports/ethics.pdf), the development of a firm set of guidelines has not been established. Although these guidelines have not been established, we do want to elaborate on some of the ethical issues surrounding Internet research.

Before getting into the thorny and difficult issues, we do want to point out that the absence of an experimenter in Internet research removes the probability of coercion (Nosek, Banaji, & Greenwald, 2002) as a source of concern, which is an advantage. Because Internet studies are not conducted in a face-to-face environment and the researcher has no obvious power over the potential participant, there is little possibility for the participant to feel coerced into participating. In fact, it is extremely easy for the potential participant to hit the "delete" button on his or her computer if they do not want to participate.

Informed Consent and Internet Research

Obtaining the informed consent of participants is one of the vital components of conducting ethical research, because this is the component that recognizes the autonomy of research participants. Obtaining informed consent and answering questions participants might have regarding consent is a relatively simple process in the context of most experiments. However, when conducting research over the Internet, there are a variety of issues that must be confronted, such as when is informed consent required, how should informed consent be obtained, and how can you make sure that the participant actually provided informed consent.

The issue of when informed consent should be obtained is complicated because it involves a determination of what is public and what is private behavior. Informed consent might not be needed with data collected from the public domain. For example, data collected from television or radio programs or from books or conferences are definitely within the public domain. However, are the data that could be obtained from newsgroups, listservs, and chat rooms within the public or private domain? Some see these components of cyberspace as being in the public domain because they are there for anyone to read. Others disagree because, although the communications are public, the cyberspace participants might perceive and expect a degree of privacy in their communications. This is one of those issues that have not been resolved.

If it is determined that a study requires informed consent, there is the issue of how it should be obtained. Informed consent has three components: providing the information to participants, ensuring that they comprehend it, and then obtaining their voluntary consent to participate. Obviously a consent form can be placed online with a request that the participant read it and then check a box next to a statement such as "I agree to the above consent form." However, there are the accompanying issues of ensuring that the participant comprehends the information contained in the consent form and answering any questions he or she might have. If a study is online, it is accessible 24 hours a day, but researchers are not. To try to deal with this issue, Nosek et al. (2002) suggested that consent forms be accompanied by FAQs (frequently asked questions) that anticipate potential questions and concerns.

Privacy and Internet Research

Maintaining the privacy of the research data collected from participants is essential to the conduct of an ethical study, as participants can be harmed when their privacy is invaded or when there is a violation of confidential information. This is an important issue when conducting research over the Internet because there are limits to the ability to maintain the privacy and confidentiality of information collected. Privacy and confidentiality can be compromised during data transmission and storage in a multitude of ways—from hackers to someone sending an e-mail to the wrong address. However, Nosek et al. (2002) point out that it might be possible to guarantee a greater degree of privacy of research data collected over the Internet than in standard studies. Data transmitted over the Internet can be encrypted, and if no identifying information is collected, the only connection that could possibly lead to a participant is the Internet protocol (IP) address. However, IP addresses identify machines and not individuals, so the only way an IP address could be connected to a participant is if the participant is the sole user of the machine or computer. If identifying data are obtained, assurance of privacy and confidentiality is not as great if the information is stored in a file that is on an Internet-connected server. However, most of the data collected in psychological studies would be of little interest to hackers, so we suspect that these data would run little risk of being compromised. In spite of this, individuals conducting Internet research must consider such a possibility and take as many precautions as necessary to prevent it.

Debriefing and Internet Research

To conduct an ethical study, it is necessary to debrief participants following its completion. To be most effective, debriefing should be interactive, with the researcher providing a description of the study, including its purpose and the way in which it was conducted. The researcher is also available to answer any questions the participant might have, and, more importantly, to ensure that the participant is adequately dehoaxed if deception is used and desensitized if made to feel uncomfortable. However, the Internet can create difficulties in effectively debriefing participants for a variety of reasons. The study could be terminated early because of a computer or server crash, a broken Internet connection, or a power outage. Also, the participant might become irritated with the study or decide to voluntarily terminate due to boredom or frustration. All of these are real possibilities that could preclude the possibility of conducting debriefing. Nosek et al. (2002) anticipated such difficulties and have identified several options researchers can use to maximize the probability of debriefing in the event that a study is terminated early.

1. Require the participant to provide an e-mail address so that a debriefing statement can be sent to them.

2. Provide a "leave the study" radio button on every page that will direct them to a debriefing page.

3. Incorporate a debriefing page into the program driving the experiment that directs the participant to this page if the study is terminated prior to completion.

As you can see, researchers conducting research on the Internet encounter a number of ethical issues that do not have a perfect solution. If you are going to conduct a study using the Internet you must consider the issues of privacy, informed consent, and debriefing just discussed and identify the best way to accomplish each. In doing this, you must keep the general principles of the code of ethics in mind. Also keep in mind that data collected over the Internet are potentially available to anyone if they are not encrypted.

Ethical Issues in Preparing the Research Report

Throughout this chapter we have concentrated on various ethical issues that must be considered in designing and conducting an ethical study. After you have completed the study, the last phase of the research process is to communicate the results of the study to others. Communication most frequently takes place through professional journals in a field. This means that you must write a research report stating how the research was conducted and what was found. In writing the research report, the two moral principles of justice and fidelity and scientific integrity are involved. Justice involves the decision of authorship, or who receives credit for the research. Fidelity and scientific integrity in the preparation of the research report refers to the accurate and honest reporting of all aspects of the study.

Authorship

Authorship is important because it is used to identify the individual or individuals who are responsible for the study. It is also important because it represents a record of a person's scholarly work and, for the professional, relates directly to decisions involving salary, hiring, promotion, and tenure. For the student, it can have direct implications for getting into a graduate program or for securing a job upon completion of doctoral studies. Authorship, therefore, has serious implications for all those involved. However, everyone who makes a contribution to the research study should not receive authorship. The person or persons who receive authorship should be confined to individuals who have made a substantial contribution to the conceptualization, design, execution, analysis, or interpretation of the study being reported. The order of authorship of these individuals is typically such that the person who made the most substantial contribution is listed as the first author. Anyone who has made a contribution of a technical nature, such as collecting, coding, entering data into a computer file, or running a standard statistical analysis under the supervision of someone else does not warrant authorship. These individuals' contributions are generally acknowledged in a footnote.

Writing the Research Report

The primary ethical guideline that must be followed in writing the research report is honesty and integrity. You should never fabricate or falsify any information presented, and you should report the methodology used in collecting and analyzing the data as accurately as possible and in a manner that allows others to replicate the study and draw reasonable conclusions about its validity. In writing this research report, it is necessary to make use of the work of others both in the introduction section where you set down the rationale for the study and in the discussion section where you discuss your study's findings and relate them to the findings of others.

When making use of the contributions of others, it is essential that you give credit to them. To make use of the contributions of others without giving them credit constitutes plagiarism. **Plagiarism** occurs when you copy someone else's work but do not give them appropriate credit. When you do not give them credit, you are giving the reader the impression that the work you have copied is yours. This constitutes a type of scholarly thievery and is totally unethical.

To appropriately give credit to a person whose work you are using, you could make use of quotation marks or you could indent the material and then give a

Plagiarism
Using work produced by someone else and calling it one's own

citation for the material you have quoted. If you were using some of the material presented in the Nosek et al. (2002) article discussing many issues involved in Internet research, you could put the material you were using in quotation marks and then give the authors credit as follows: Nosek et al. (2002) have stated that "The potential of the information highway to advance understanding of psychological science is immense . . . " (p. 161). If you wanted to use a longer quote you would indent the quoted material as follows: Nosek et al. (2002) have stated that

> The potential of the information highway to advance understanding of psychological science is immense, and it is likely that the Internet will decisively shape the nature of psychological research. Yet as any researcher who has attempted to use the Internet to obtain data will have discovered, a host of methodological issues require consideration because of differences between standard laboratory research and Internet-based research concerning research methodology. (pp. 161–162)

While we have only addressed plagiarism with regard to the written work, it is equally important that you give appropriate credit if you use tables or figures taken from someone else's work, including something you find on the Internet. The basic principle you must use is that if you use something someone else has done, you must give them credit for that work.

STUDY QUESTIONS 4.6

- **Define or refute the position that participants in most psychological research studies are coerced to participate.**
- **Explain privacy and how confidentiality and anonymity relate to privacy.**
- **What are the ethical issues involved in conducting research on the Internet?**
- **What is the difference between privacy, confidentiality, and anonymity?**

Ethics of Animal (Nonhuman) Research

Considerable attention has been devoted to the ethics of human research. In about 7–8% of the studies they conduct, however, psychologists use animals as their research participants in order to gain control over many potentially contaminating factors (Gallup & Suarez, 1985) or to investigate the influence of a variable that might be judged too dangerous to test on humans or to increase our knowledge of the species being studied. Of the animals used by psychologists, 90% have been rodents and birds. Only about 5% are monkeys and other primates. Dogs and cats are rarely used.

Safeguards in the Use of Animals

There are many safeguards that have been instituted to ensure that laboratory animals receive humane and ethical treatment. The Animal Welfare Act, enforced by the Department of Agriculture, governs the care and use of many research animals and conducts unannounced inspections of both public and private animal research facilities. In addition, institutions conducting animal research, and covered by the act, are required to have an Institutional Animal Care and Use Committee (IACUC) that reviews each research protocol. This committee reviews the researcher's rationale for the proposed experiment, the conditions of animal care during the experiment, the rationale for the number of animals that will be used, as well as the researcher's assessment of the pain and suffering that might be involved in the experiment and the approach that the researcher uses for alleviating any pain and suffering.

Professional societies whose members conduct animal research also have a set of ethical standards and guidelines to which their members must adhere. The APA code of ethics (see Exhibit 4.5, section 8.09) includes principles for the humane and ethical treatment of research animals. All APA members are committed to upholding these principles.

Animal Research Guidelines

Animal welfare
Improving the laboratory conditions in which animals live and reducing the number of animals used in research

Animal rights
The belief that animals have rights similar to humans and should not be used in research

In reading the guidelines in Exhibit 4.5, you should be aware of the fact that they focus primarily on animal welfare and not animal rights. **Animal welfare** is concerned with improving laboratory conditions and reducing the number of animals needed in research (Baldwin, 1993). **Animal rights** focuses on the rights of animals. This position states that animals have the same rights as humans and should not be used in research. Because there is often no substitute for the use of animals as research participants, the focus of attention is on animal welfare, which concerns the humane treatment of animals.

The acquisition, care, housing, use, and disposition of animals should be in compliance with the appropriate federal, state, local, and institutional laws and regulations and with international conventions to which the United States is a party. APA authors must state in writing that they have complied with the ethical standards when submitting a research article for publication. Violations by an APA member should be reported to the APA Ethics Committee, and any questions regarding the guidelines should be addressed to the APA Committee on Animal Research and Ethics (CARE) at science@apa.org.

I. Justification of the Research

Research using animals should be undertaken only when there is a clear scientific purpose and a reasonable expectation that the research will increase our knowledge of the processes underlying behavior, increase our understanding of the species under study, or result in benefits to the health or welfare of humans or other animals. Any study conducted should have sufficient potential importance to justify the use of animals, and any procedure that produces pain in humans should be assumed to also produce pain in animals.

The species chosen for use in a study should be the one best suited to answer the research question. However, before a research project is initiated, alternatives or procedures that will minimize the number of animals used should be considered. Regardless of the type of species or number of animals used, the research cannot be conducted until the protocol has been reviewed by the IACUC. After the study has been initiated, the psychologist must continuously monitor the research and the animals' welfare.

II. Personnel

All personnel involved in animal research should be familiar with the guidelines. Any procedure used by the research personnel must conform with federal regulations regarding personnel, supervision, record keeping, and veterinary care. Both psychologists and their research assistants must be informed about the behavioral characteristics of their research animals so that unusual behaviors that could forewarn of health problems can be identified. Psychologists should ensure that anyone working for them when conducting animal research receives instruction in the care, maintenance, and handling of the species being studied. The responsibilities and activities of anyone dealing with animals should be consistent with his or her competencies, training, and experience regardless of whether the setting is the laboratory or the field.

III. Care and Housing of Animals

The psychological well-being of animals is a topic that is currently being debated. This is a complex issue because the procedures that promote the psychological well-being of one species might not be appropriate for another. For this reason, the APA does not stipulate any specific guidelines but rather states that psychologists familiar with a given species should take measures, such as enriching the environment, to enhance the psychological well-being of the species. For example, the famous Yerkes Laboratory and New York University's Laboratory for Experimental Medicine and Surgery in Primates (LEMSIP) have constructed wire-mesh tunnels between the animals' cages to promote social contact.

In addition to providing for the animals' psychological well-being, the facilities housing the animals should conform to current U.S. Department of Agriculture ([USDA], 1990, 1991) regulations and guidelines and are to be inspected twice a year (USDA, 1989). Any research procedures used on animals are to be reviewed by the IACUC to ensure that they are appropriate and humane. This committee essentially supervises the psychologist who has the responsibility for providing the research animals with humane care and healthful conditions during their stay at the research facility.

IV. Acquisition of Animals

Animals used in laboratory experimentation should be lawfully purchased from a qualified supplier or bred in the psychologist's facility. When animals are purchased from a qualified supplier, they should be transported in a manner that provides adequate food, water, ventilation, and space and that imposes no unnecessary stress on the animals. If animals must be taken from the wild, they must be trapped in a humane manner. Endangered species should be used only with full attention to required permits and ethical concerns.

V. Experimental Procedures

The design and conduct of the study should involve humane consideration for the animals' well-being. In addition to the procedures governed by guideline I, "Justification of the Research," the researcher should adhere to the following points:

1. Studies, such as observational and other noninvasive procedures, that involve no aversive stimulation and create no overt signs of distress are acceptable.

2. Alternative procedures that minimize discomfort to the animal should be used when available. When the aim of the research requires use of aversive conditions, the minimal level of aversive stimulation should be used. Psychologists engaged in such studies are encouraged to test the painful stimuli on themselves.

3. It is generally acceptable to anesthetize an animal prior to a painful procedure if the animal is then euthanized before it can regain consciousness.

4. Subjecting an animal to more than momentary or slight pain that is not relieved by medication or some other procedure should be undertaken only when the goals of the research cannot be met by any other method.

5. Any experimental procedure requiring exposure to prolonged aversive conditions, such as tissue damage, exposure to extreme environments, or experimentally induced prey killing, requires greater justification and surveillance. Animals that are experiencing unalleviated distress and are not essential to the research should be euthanized immediately.

6. Procedures using restraint must conform to federal guidelines and regulations.

7. It is unacceptable to use a paralytic drug or muscle relaxants during surgery without a general anesthetic.

8. Surgical procedures should be closely supervised by a person competent in the procedure, and aseptic techniques that minimize risk of infection must be used on warm-blooded animals. Animals should remain under anesthesia until the procedure is ended, unless there is good justification for doing otherwise. Animals should be given postoperative monitoring and care to minimize discomfort and prevent infection or other consequences of the procedure. No surgical procedure can be performed unless it is required by the research or it is for the well-being of the animal. Alternative uses of an animal should be considered when they are no longer needed in a study. Multiple surgeries on the same animal must receive special approval from the IACUC.

9. Alternatives to euthanasia should be considered when an animal is no longer required for a research study. Any alternative taken should be compatible with the goals of the research and the welfare of the animal. This action should not expose the animal to multiple surgeries.

10. Laboratory-reared animals should not be released because, in most cases, they cannot survive or their survival might disrupt the natural ecology. Returning wild-caught animals to the field also carries risks both to the animal and to the ecosystem.

11. Euthanasia, when it must occur, should be accomplished in the most humane manner and in a way that ensures immediate death and is in accordance with the American Veterinary Medical Association panel on euthanasia. Disposal of the animals should be consistent with all relevant legislation and with health, environmental, and aesthetic concerns and should be approved by the IACUC.

VI. Field Research

Field research, because of its potential for damaging sensitive ecosystems and communities, must receive IACUC approval, although observational research might be exempt. Psychologists conducting field research should disturb their populations as little as possible and make every effort to minimize potential harmful effects on the population under investigation. Research conducted in inhabited areas must be done so that the privacy and property of any human inhabitants are respected. The study of endangered species requires particular justification and must receive IACUC approval.

VII. Educational Use of Animals

Discussion of the ethics and value of animal research in all courses is encouraged. Although animals can be used for educational purposes after review of the planned use by the appropriate institutional committee, some procedures that might be appropriate for research purposes might not be justified for educational purposes. Classroom demonstrations using live animals can be valuable instructional aids—as can videotapes, films, and other alternatives. The anticipated instructional gain should direct the type of demonstration.

STUDY QUESTIONS 4.7

• **What is the distinction between animal welfare and animal rights?**
• **What basic guidelines have been adopted by APA for the care and use of research animals?**

Summary

The ethical concerns surrounding the conduct of psychological research can be divided into three areas: relationship between society and science, professional issues, and treatment of research participants. The area involving the relationship between society and science focuses on the extent to which societal concerns and cultural values direct scientific investigations. Because research is an expensive enterprise, both federal and corporate funding directs a large portion of the research that is conducted.

Professional issues include a variety of areas such as overlooking others' use of flawed data. However, the most serious professional issue is research misconduct—scientists must not forge or falsify data. The treatment of research participants is the most important and fundamental ethical issue confronted by scientists. Research participants have certain rights, such as the right to privacy, that must be violated if researchers are to attempt to arrive at answers to many significant questions. This naturally poses a dilemma for the researcher as to whether to conduct the research and violate the rights of the research participant or abandon the research project. To address the ethical concerns of researchers, the APA has developed a code of ethics that includes a set of standards that psychologists must adhere to when conducting research studies. Inherent in the code of ethics are five basic moral principles that should be adhered to when conducting research with human participants: respect for persons and their autonomy, beneficence and nonmaleficence, justice, trust, and fidelity and scientific integrity. The specific issues addressed by Section 8 of the code of ethics include getting institutional approval, informed consent, deception, and debriefing.

Approval must be obtained from the IRB prior to conducting any study involving human participants. If the research falls into the exempt category, the research protocol must still be submitted to the IRB because this is the board that must approve its exempt status.

The code of ethics requires that research participants be fully informed about all aspects of the study so that they can make an informed decision to choose or to decline to participate. However, the code of ethics recognizes that there are instances in which it is appropriate to dispense with informed consent. This occurs only under specific and limited conditions in which it is permitted by law or federal or institutional regulations. If the research participant is a minor, informed consent must be obtained from the minor's parent or legal guardian. If consent is given, assent must be obtained from the minor. Although most consent involves active consent, some individuals recommend the use of passive consent in certain situations, such as when the research participants are school-age children and the research is conducted in the school. This is an issue that the APA code of ethics has yet to address.

Some studies require the use of deception to insure the integrity and fidelity of their research study. Although deception runs counter to the necessity of informed consent, the code of ethics recognizes that, in some studies, deception is necessary.

A number of individuals have suggested alternatives to deception, such as role playing, but research studies have shown that such alternatives are poor substitutes. Therefore deception remains a part of numerous psychological studies, and its potential effects must be considered. It is generally assumed that deception creates stress and that this stress or invasion of privacy is ethically objectionable and perhaps harmful to the research participants. Yet research indicates that participants do not view deception as detrimental and that those who have been involved in deceptive studies view their research experience as more valuable than do those who have not. This phenomenon might be due to the increased attention given in deception studies to debriefing, which seems to be effective in eliminating the negative effects of deception as well as any stress that might have occurred.

Although there does not seem to be a negative effect resulting from deception or from the use of research participant pools, it has been demonstrated that informing participants that they are free to withdraw at any time without penalty can influence the outcome of some experiments.

Investigators are also quite concerned about coercing students to become research participants. Experiments investigating the perceptions of research participants drawn from a research participant pool reveal that they generally view their research experience quite positively.

A significant ethical concern involves ensuring the privacy of the information obtained from research participants, because privacy is at the heart of conducting ethical research. Anonymity is an excellent way of ensuring privacy because the identity of the research participant is unknown. If anonymity is not possible, the information obtained must be kept confidential. However, the information collected by researchers is not protected by law, so confidentiality might be difficult to maintain if researchers are subpoenaed by a court of law. If this is a possibility, a researcher could obtain a "certificate of confidentiality" that would provide immunity from the requirement to reveal names or identifying information.

In recent years, there has been an increasing use of the Internet as a medium for conducting psychological research. Use of this medium has many advantages such as reduced cost, access to many individuals, and the reduction of feeling of being coerced into participation. However, there are many ethical issues that accompany use of this medium such as obtaining informed consent from the participants, ensuring the privacy of the data collected, and debriefing the participants following completion of the study.

When preparing a research report of a completed study, ethically, only those individuals who made a substantial contribution should receive authorship. Also, honesty and integrity should be followed when writing the research report. This means that you should not plagiarize, because this is a form of scholarly thievery.

There is concern for the ethical treatment of animals in research. Recent efforts have resulted in the development of institutional animal care and use committees and a set of guidelines adopted by the APA for use by psychologists working with animals. These guidelines address various issues, ranging from where the animals are housed to how the animals are disposed of. Psychologists using animals for research or educational purposes should be familiar with these guidelines and adhere to them.

Key Terms and Concepts

Active consent
Active deception
Animal rights
Animal welfare
Anonymity
Assent
Confidentiality
Debriefing
Dehoaxing

Desensitizing
Ethical dilemma
Informed consent
Passive consent
Passive deception
Plagiarism
Privacy
Research ethics
Research misconduct

Related
Internet Sites

http://www.nap.edu/readingroom/books/obas/
This site reproduces a book online that includes a discussion of most of the topics relating to the ethical conduct of research.

http://www.apa.org/ethics/
This is the American Psychological Association's site for information on ethics. It contains links to the code of ethics and information on ethics in the use of animals.

http://www.psychologicalscience.org/teaching/tips/tips_0902.cfm
This site is maintained by the American Psychological Society and provides information relevant to teaching ethics. There are many brief cases at this site that can be used for the discussion of ethics in the conduct of research and in the delivery of psychological services.

http://www.psychology.org
To get to the site that is applicable to this chapter, you must, when the home site opens, click on the "Resources" link and then the "Ethical Issues" link. This will bring you to a site with links to online books and other discussions of ethical issues involved in the conduct of psychological research.

Practice Test

The answers to these questions can be found in Appendix.

1. The National Institutes of Mental Health funded Dr. Doom's study of the effect of treating obsessive-compulsive disorder with a new drug produced by one of the biotechnology companies. Dr. Doom reported that his research found that the new drug was more effective than any prior treatment of this disorder. However, a detailed investigation of Dr. Doom's research revealed that he fudged and manipulated some of the data to show these results. This ethical issue falls under which of the following areas:
   a. The relationship between society and science
   b. Professional issues
   c. Treatment of research participants
   d. Trust
   e. Autonomy

2. Obtaining informed consent meets the moral principle of
   a. Respect for persons and their autonomy
   b. Beneficence and nonmaleficence
   c. Justice
   d. Trust
   e. Fidelity and scientific integrity

3. Assume that you are a member of the IRB and are presented with a research protocol stating that the researcher wants to test a new treatment for autistic children. Although the new treatment holds out a promise of benefiting the children in the study and yielding new knowledge, it also includes some troublesome components that might create severe emotional stress for the

children. Having to consider the benefits of the research as well as the distress that it might cause

a. Involves the moral principle of trust
b. Involves the moral principle of fidelity and scientific integrity
c. Creates an ethical dilemma
d. Will result in disapproval because the children could be harmed
e. Will result in approval because the children might benefit from the research

4. When you are proposing a research study that uses minors as the research participants, you must

a. Gain their trust
b. Get the informed consent of their parent or guardian
c. Get the child's assent to participant in the research study
d. Incorporate additional safeguards to insure that the child is not harmed
e. Both b and c

5. The committee that reviews the care and use of nonhuman animals in research is the

a. IRB
b. IACUC
c. PETA
d. AEA

Challenge Exercises

1. This challenge exercise is intended to give you some practice and experience in recognizing and dealing with scientific fraud. For this exercise, we will focus on the case of Steven E. Breuning. Read the article

   Holden, C. (1987). NIMH finds a case of "serious misconduct." *Science, 235*, 1566–1567.

   Read some of the other articles that are provided in the reference section as well, and then answer the following questions.

   a. What evidence led to the exposure of Breuning's scientific misconduct?
   b. What ethical principles were violated by Bruening's behavior?
   c. What were the consequences to Bruening of his behavior?
   d. What are the possible consequences of his misconduct to his colleagues, to the organization in which he worked, to other scientists, and to the general public?

2. This challenge exercise is intended to give you some practice reviewing a research protocol and then acting like an IRB member, scrutinizing the protocol and making a decision as to whether the research should receive approval. Assume that you received a protocol having the following characteristics:

   Dr. Smith is interested in studying the resilience of some individuals to the effects of exposure to maladaptive environments. The basic research question she poses is: Why are some individuals able to fend off the negative consequences of adverse environmental conditions, whereas others are not? Dr. Smith proposes to study sixth, seventh, and eighth graders who have been exposed to violent and stressful home and community environments.

The research participants will be assessed at 6-month intervals for the next 3 years by means of surveys and individual interviews. These outcome measures will assess the extent and frequency of exposure to violence and stress both in the home and in the community. Additional outcome measures will assess psychological stability (anxiety, depression, suicidal thoughts, and social support), academic achievement, and psychological and behavioral coping responses.

Dr. Smith has received the approval of the local school system as well as the principal of the school in which the study is to be conducted. She proposes to obtain passive consent from the students' parents and to provide the school system with a summary of the outcome of the study.

As an IRB member, evaluate this study from the perspective of

a. The investigators—what are the important items to consider?
b. The nature of the study—what are the important aspects of the study design that must be considered?
c. The research participants—what are the important considerations regarding who they are and how they are recruited?
d. Confidentiality—what information should be kept confidential, and what can be revealed?
e. Debriefing—what should these children be told about the study?

3. This challenge exercise pertains to an aspect of research that is new and has been given little consideration even by the current APA code of ethics. However, it is becoming a common event and one that should be considered—it is research conducted over the Internet. Think about a study that is being conducted via the Internet regardless of whether this is a survey or an experimental study.

a. What are the ethical issues that must be considered and that might create difficulty in conducting such a study? In answering this question, consider the five moral principles discussed in this chapter as well as the code of ethics presented in Exhibit 4.5.
b. Is the current code of ethics sufficient to cover research conducted in cyberspace?

4. This challenge exercise involves more of a debate than a specific exercise. There has been considerable emotion devoted to the issue of the use of animals in research. The basic questions are: Should they be used, and is the harm and suffering inflicted on them justified by the benefit achieved? Animal rights people say no to both, but researchers say yes. For this exercise, form two groups, one to argue the animal rights' and one to argue the researchers' point of view. Take about 10 minutes to form your positions and then debate the issue for another 10 minutes. After the debate, consider this general issue: What limits should we place on our scientific curiosity in our use of animals in research?

CHAPTER 5

Measuring Variables and Sampling

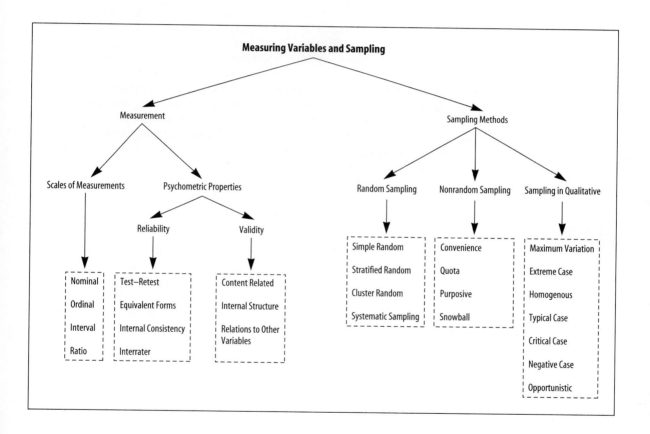

Every year many people have a limb amputated as a result of disease or an accident. When they awake from surgery and recover from the anesthesia, many of these individuals have the feeling that the surgery has not been performed. This feeling is so vivid that they are frequently shocked when they try to look at the limb that seems to be there, only to see that it has indeed been amputated. This realization does nothing to subdue the sensation of the presence of the limb, a phenomenon known as *phantom limb*. The phantom limb experience is often accompanied by a presence or absence of pain. The nonpainful variety is typically accompanied by a tingling or pins and needles experience. However, more than 70% of amputees experience phantom limb pain, described as pain traveling up and down the limb, a cramped or unnatural posture of the limb causing pain, or an intense burning pain. Unfortunately, this pain typically lasts for decades.

In the last century, numerous psychological and neurological explanations have been proposed to account for phantom limbs and particularly the pain associated with them. Katz (1992) has summarized these explanations as well as his own. Katz has suggested that the central nervous system is extremely plastic and can change in response to various sensory inputs. Specifically, Katz believes that phantom limb experience is a biopsychosocial phenomenon consisting of the neural integration of a variety of sensory processes including cognitive and emotional processes.

If you were interested in assessing Katz's biopsychosocial explanation of phantom limb pain, you would design a psychological experiment to test one or more components of this explanation. Designing the study would require you to make a variety of decisions. You would have to choose the variables to be investigated. For example, you would have to identify the cognitive or emotional variables to investigate. You would also have to identify the sample of research participants to include in your study and the techniques to eliminate the influence of any confounding variables. Only after making such decisions can you describe the final design of your study.

Introduction

Variable
A condition or characteristic that can take on different values or categories

One can say that psychology uses the language of variables. That is because psychologists study variables and how they are related. As you know from earlier chapters, a **variable** is a condition or characteristic that can take on different values or categories. A key point now is that many variables are difficult to accurately measure, and if psychologists do not measure the variables they study accurately, then their research is flawed. It's like the GIGO principle: garbage in, garbage out. If you fail to measure your variables accurately, you will obtain useless data and, therefore, useless results.

Defining Measurement

Measurement
The assignment of symbols or numbers to something according to a set of rules

When we measure, we attempt to identify and characterize the dimensions, quantity, capacity, or degree of something. More formally, **measurement** refers to the act of measuring, and it is conducted by assigning symbols or numbers to something according to a specific set of rules. This definition is based on the work of the famous Harvard psychologist Stanley Smith Stevens (1906–1973). For an example of measurement, you could place the starting point of a ruler at one end of your textbook and determine its length by noting the number on the ruler corresponding to the other end of the book. You would assign the number taken from the ruler to represent your book's length. "Length of books" is a variable because different books can take on different values (i.e., they can vary).

Scales of Measurement

In addition to helping define measurement, Stevens (1946) showed that measurement can be categorized by the type of information that is communicated by the symbols assigned to the variables of interest. Based on his work, we usually identify four levels of measurement, which provide different kinds and amounts of information. Stevens called these following four levels of measurement the "scales of measurement": nominal scale, ordinal scale, interval scale, and ratio scale. You can also refer to these as variables: nominal variables, ordinal variables, interval variables, and ratio variables. We now explain the characteristics of each of Stevens' four scales of measurement. The key ideas are summarized in Table 5.1.

Nominal Scale

Nominal scale
The use of symbols, such as words or numbers, to classify or categorize measurement objects into groups or types

The simplest and most basic type of measurement is what Stevens called a nominal scale. It is a nonquantitative scale of measurement because it identifies *types* rather than amounts of something. A **nominal scale** uses symbols, such as words or numbers, to classify or categorize the values of a variable (i.e., nominal scaled variables) into groups or types. Numbers can be used to label the categories of a nominal variable, but these numbers serve only as markers, not as indicators of amount or quantity. For example, you might mark the categories of the variable "gender" with 1 = female and 2 = male. Some other examples of nominal-level variables are personality type, country you were born in, college major, and research group (e.g., experimental group or control group).

TABLE 5.1
Stevens' Four Scales of Measurement

Scale*	Characteristics	Examples
Nominal	Used to name, categorize, or classify.	Gender, marital status, memory strategy, personality type, type of therapy, experimental condition (treatment vs. control).
Ordinal	Used to rank order objects or individuals.	Order of finish in race, social class (e.g., low, medium, high), ranking of need for therapy, letter grade (A, B, C, D, F).
Interval	Used to rank order, plus has equal intervals or distances between adjacent numbers.	Celsius temperature, Fahrenheit temperature, IQ scores, year.
Ratio	Fully quantitative, includes rank ordering, equal intervals, plus has an absolute zero point.	Kelvin temperature, response time, height, weight, annual income, group size.

*The first letters of the four scales spells **NOIR** (which means black in French). You can use this acronym to help you remember the order of the four scales of measurement, from least quantitative to the most quantitative.

Ordinal Scale

Ordinal scale
A rank order measurement scale

An **ordinal scale** is a *rank-order* scale of measurement. Any variable where the levels can be ranked (but you don't know if the distance between the levels is the same) is an ordinal variable. It allows you to determine which person is higher or lower on a variable of interest, but it does not allow you to know exactly how much higher or lower a person is compared to another. Some examples of ordinal-level variables are the order of finish in a marathon, social class (e.g., high, medium, and low), rank ordering of applicants for a job, and rank ordering of need for special services. In a marathon, for example, the distance between the first-place and second-place runners might be different from the distance between the second-place and third-place runners.

Interval Scale

Interval scale
A scale of measurement with equal intervals of distance between adjacent numbers

The third level of measurement, the **interval scale**, has equal distances between adjacent numbers on the scale (called *equal intervals*) as well as the characteristics of the lower-level scales (i.e., marking/naming of levels and rank ordering of levels). For example, the difference between 1° and 2° Fahrenheit is the same amount of temperature as the distance between 50° and 51° Fahrenheit. Other examples of interval-level variables are Celsius temperature, year, and IQ scores.

Although the distance between adjacent points on an interval scale is equal, an interval scale does not possess an absolute zero point. The zero point is somewhat arbitrary. You can see this by noting that neither 0° Celsius nor 0° Fahrenheit means no temperature. Zero degrees Celsius (0°C) is the freezing point of water, and zero degrees Fahrenheit (0°F) is 32 degrees below freezing.

Ratio Scale

Ratio scale
A scale of measurement with rank ordering, equal intervals, and an absolute zero point

The fourth level of measurement, the ratio scale, is the highest (i.e., most quantitative) level of measurement. A **ratio scale** has an *absolute zero point* as well as the characteristics of the lower-level scales. It marks/names the values of the variable (as in nominal scales), provides rank ordering of the values of the variable (as in ordinal scales), and has equal distances between the values of the variable (as in interval scales). In addition, only ratio scales have a true or absolute zero point (where 0 means none).

Some examples of ratio-level variables are weight, height, response time, Kelvin temperature, and annual income. If your annual income is zero dollars, then you earned no annual income. You can buy absolutely nothing with zero dollars. On the Kelvin temperature scale, zero is the lowest possible temperature; zero means no molecular movement or no heat whatsoever. (In case you are curious: 0°Kelvin = −459 °F = −273 °C.)

| • **What are the distinguishing characteristics of the four levels of measurements?**

Psychometric Properties of Good Measurement

Good measurement is fundamental for research. If a research study is not based on good measurement, then the results cannot be trusted. So, what is needed to obtain good measurement? The two major properties of good measurement are reliability and validity.

Overview of Reliability and Validity

Reliability refers to the consistency or stability of the scores of your measurement instrument. Validity refers to the extent to which your measurement procedure is measuring what you think it is measuring (and not something else) and whether you have used and interpreted the scores correctly. If you are going to have validity, you must have some reliability, but reliability is not enough to ensure validity.

Here's the idea: Assume you weigh 125 pounds. If you weigh yourself five times and get scores of 135, 134, 134, 135, and 136, then your scales are reliable, but they are not valid. The scores were consistent, but wrong! If you weigh yourself five times and get scores of 125, 124, 125, 125, and 126, then your scales are reliable and valid. Researchers want their measurement procedures to be both reliable and valid.

Reliability

Reliability
The consistency or stability of scores

Reliability refers to consistency or stability of scores. In psychological testing, it refers to the consistency or stability of the scores that we get from a test or assessment procedure. In psychological research, it refers to the consistency or stability of the scores that we get from our research apparatus and instruments used to produce our variables. There are four primary types of reliability test–retest, equivalent forms, internal consistency, and interrater reliability. Frequently, reliability coefficients are obtained as quantitative indexes of reliability. A **reliability coefficient** is a type of correlation, and it should be strong and positive (i.e., > 0.70) to indicate strong consistency of relationship.

Reliability coefficient
Type of correlation coefficient used as an index of reliability

Test–Retest Reliability   The first type of reliability, **test–retest reliability**, refers to the consistency of scores over time. To determine the test–retest reliability of a test or research instrument, you administer the test, wait for a week or so, and administer it again. The two sets of scores (scores at time one and scores at time two) are correlated to determine the strength of relationship. A strong relationship indicates consistency across time [people with high (or low) scores at time one tended to be the same people with high (or low) scores at time two]. A primary issue is identifying the appropriate time interval between the two testing occasions because, generally speaking, the longer the time interval between the two testing occasions, the lower the reliability coefficient will be.

Test–retest reliability
Consistency of a group of individuals' scores on a test over time

Equivalent-forms reliability
Consistency of a group of individuals' scores on two versions of the same test

Equivalent-Forms Reliability   The second type of reliability, **equivalent-forms reliability**, refers to the consistency of scores obtained on two equivalent forms of a test or research instrument designed to measure the same thing.

Examples of tests with equivalent forms are seen in college entrance exams (SAT, GRE, ACT). This type of reliability is measured by correlating the scores obtained by giving two forms of the same test to a single group of people. This correlation should be very strong and positive, indicating that the people with high (low) scores on form one tend to have high (low) scores on form two. The success of this method hinges on the equivalence of the two forms of the test.

Internal consistency reliability
Consistency with which items on a test measure a single construct

Internal Consistency Reliability The third type of reliability, **internal consistency reliability**, refers to the consistency with which items on a test or research instrument measure a single construct. For example, psychological research is conducted on constructs such as learning, shyness, love, or any of various personality dimensions such as dominance or extraversion. To obtain a measure of these constructs, we typically devise a test or scale composed of multiple items. No single item is assumed to be able to provide a sufficient measure of the construct, so multiple items are constructed—each of which is assumed to contribute to the measure of the construct. Internal consistency reliability is affected by the length of the test—as the test gets longer, it becomes more reliable. Your goal is to obtain high reliability with relatively few items for each construct.

Estimation of internal consistency only requires one administration of a test or scale, which is probably one reason it is commonly reported in journal articles. The most commonly reported index of internal consistency is **coefficient alpha** (also called **Cronbach's alpha**). Coefficient alpha should be .70 or higher, and a high value is evidence that the items are consistently measuring the same thing. Researchers use coefficient alpha when they want an estimate of the reliability of a homogeneous test or scale. When a test or scale is *multidimensional* (i.e., measures more than one construct or trait), coefficient alpha should be reported for each dimension separately. For example, if your instrument includes 5 sets of items measuring 5 different constructs, then you should report 5 coefficient alphas in your research write-up.

Coefficient alpha
The most frequently used index of internal consistency

Cronbach's alpha
Another name for coefficient alpha

Interrater reliability
The degree of consistency or agreement between two or more scorers, judges, observers, or raters

Interrater Reliability The fourth and last major type of reliability, **interrater reliability**, refers to the consistency or degree of agreement between two or more scorers, judges, observers, or raters. For example, you might have two judges rate a set of 35 student essay papers. You would correlate the two judges' ratings of the papers and obtain the interrater reliability coefficient, which is an index of the degree of consistency of the two judges' ratings. This reliability coefficient should be strong and positive, indicating strong agreement or consistency between the judges. Interrater reliability is also measured by **interobserver agreement**, which is the percentage of times different raters agree. For example, you might have two individuals observe children and record the incidence of violent behavior. Each observer would record a child's behavior as being either violent or not violent. The measure of reliability would be the percentage of time that the two observers agreed.

Interobserver agreement
The percentage of time that different observers' ratings are in agreement

STUDY QUESTION 5.2 | • **How does one obtain evidence of relability in measurement?**

Validity

According to current thinking by measurement experts, **validity** refers to the accuracy of the inferences, interpretations, or actions made on the basis of test scores (Messick, 1989). We are using the word "test" broadly to include any measurement procedure or device (standardized test, survey instrument, multi-item scale, experimental apparatus, observational coding). Sometimes researchers claim that a particular test or instrument is valid; however, technically speaking, that is not quite correct. It is the interpretations and actions taken based on the test scores that are valid or invalid. Here's how Anastasi and Urbina (1997, p. 113) put it: "The validity of a test concerns what the test measures and how well it does so. It tells us what can be inferred from test scores. . . . [Test] validity must be established with reference to the particular use for which the test is being considered." Cronbach (1990, p. 145) states that "validation is inquiry into the soundness of the interpretations proposed for scores from a test."

Because tests and research instruments always involve the measurement of constructs (e.g., intelligence, gender, age, depression, self-efficacy, personality, eating disorders, pathology, and cognitive styles), measurement experts (called psychometricians) generally agree that all validity types are part of construct validity (Anastasi & Urbina, 1997; Messick, 1995). For example, when we talk about individuals diagnosed with schizophrenia, obsessive-compulsive disorder, or an eating disorder, we are dealing with the constructs of these disorders. Constructs could also characterize a field experimental setting such as an impoverished setting, enriched setting, or a poverty neighborhood. For example, if you are investigating the effect of being depressed on marital discord among disadvantaged people living in an impoverished neighborhood, you have a construct representing the research participants (disadvantaged people), the independent variable (depression), the dependent variable (marital discord), and the setting of the experiment (a poverty neighborhood). For each of these constructs, you must identify a set of operations that represent the construct. The difficulty arises in identifying the set of operations that will best and most efficiently allow you to infer each of the constructs accurately from the data collected.

An **operationalization** (also called an *operational definition*) is the particular measurement procedure used in a research study to represent the constructs of interest. For example, disadvantaged people might be operationally defined as individuals who have had incomes below the poverty level for the past 6 months and who participate in government welfare programs. The independent variable depression might be operationalized as persons scoring above 20 on the Beck Depression Inventory (Beck, Ward, Mendelson, Mock, & Erbaugh, 1961). The dependent variable of marital discord might be operationalized by a count of the number of arguments the couple had per day, and the setting of a poverty neighborhood might be based on the type and condition of the homes and other buildings in the neighborhood in which the participants lived.

The important issue with respect to validity is whether the operations produce a correct or appropriate representation of the intended construct. Are persons who have had an income below the poverty level for the past 6 months and who participate in government welfare programs really representative of disadvantaged persons? Are participants who score above 20 on the Beck Depression

Inventory really depressed? These are the questions that must be asked to determine if claims of validity can be made.

Validity is based on evidence revealing that the target construct can correctly be inferred from the particular operations of measurement. **Validation** is the gathering of evidence supporting inferences to be made on the basis of the scores obtained from the operations of measurement. Evidence of validity is obtained by developing a theory about how a test or instrument should operate if it is working correctly, and then the theory is tested to obtain the evidence. Validation should be viewed as a continual or never-ending process. Researchers should never stop asking whether their measures are working validly with their particular research participants. The more validity evidence a researcher provides, the more confidence you can place in the interpretations based on measurement scores. Now we describe three major ways to collect evidence of validity.

Validity Evidence Based on Content   **Content-related evidence (or content validity)** is based on a judgment of the degree to which the items, tasks, or questions on a test or instrument adequately represent the construct's domain. You need to be an expert on the construct of interest to make these judgments. Therefore, the judgment of multiple experts is typically used to obtain evidence of content validity. When making decisions about content-related evidence, experts collect the necessary data to answer the following kinds of questions:

1. Do the items appear to represent the thing a researcher is attempting to measure? (This prima facie judgment is sometimes called **face validity**.)

2. Does the set of items underrepresent the construct's content (i.e., did the researcher exclude any important content areas or topics)?

3. Do any of the items represent something other than what the researcher is trying to measure (i.e., were any irrelevant items included)?

If, in the judgment of the experts, the test adequately samples the content domain and meets the three criteria suggested above (i.e., the test has face validity, it does not underrepresent the construct, and no irrelevant items are included), then the test is said to have content validity.

Validity Evidence Based on Internal Structure   Some tests/instruments are designed to measure one general construct, but others are designed to measure several dimensions of a **multidimensional construct**. The Rosenberg Self-Esteem Scale is a 10-item scale, which measures the single construct of global self-esteem. In contrast, the Harter Self-Esteem Scale, which, if often used with children, is used to measure global self-esteem and five dimensions including social acceptance, scholastic competence, physical appearance, athletic competence, and behavioral conduct.

Sometimes researchers use a statistical technique called **factor analysis** to determine the number of dimensions in a set of items. The researcher collects data on the items, enters the data into a statistical program, and runs the factor analysis procedure, and the results indicate whether the items are all interrelated or whether there are subsets of items that are closely related to one another. The

---

Validation
Gathering of evidence regarding the soundness of inferences made from test scores

Content-related evidence or content validity
Judgment by experts of the degree to which items, tasks, or questions on a test adequately represent the construct

Face validity
Prima facie judgment of whether the items appear to represent the construct and whether the test or instrument looks valid

Multidimensional construct
Construct consisting of two or more dimensions; contrasted with a unidimensional construct

Factor analysis
A statistical analysis procedure used to determine the number of dimensions present in a set of items

number of subsets of items indicates the number of dimensions (also called "factors") that are present. The key point is that the factor analysis results tell you whether a test is unidimensional (i.e., it just measures one factor) or multidimensional (i.e., it measures two or more factors). It is important that a researcher know how many dimensions or factors are represented by the items because, otherwise, incorrect interpretations of the results would follow.

Indexes are also used to indicate the degree of homogeneity of each dimension or factor. **Homogeneity** is the degree to which a set of items measures a single construct or trait. The two primary indices of homogeneity are the *item-to-total correlation* (i.e., correlate each item with the total test score) and coefficient alpha (discussed above under "Internal Consistency Reliability"). The larger the value on these indices, the more strongly the items are related to one another, which provides evidence that they measure the same unidimensional construct or dimension of a multidimensional construct. As you can see, evidence based on the internal structure of a test or instrument is based on how the items are related to one another. The next source of validity evidence comes from relating the items to other criteria.

Validity Evidence Based on Relations to Other Variables   This form of evidence is obtained by relating your test scores with one or more relevant and known criteria. A *criterion* is the standard or benchmark that you want to correlate with or predict accurately on the basis of your test scores. If we use a correlation coefficient for validity evidence, we call it a **validity coefficient**. The key is that the test scores should be related to the criterion in the predicted direction and magnitude.

There are several different kinds of relevant validity evidence based on relations to other variables. The first is **criterion-related validity** evidence, which is validity evidence based on the extent to which scores from a test can be used to predict or infer performance on some known or standard criterion, such as an already established test or future performance. There are two different types of criterion-related validity: predictive validity and concurrent validity. The only difference between these two types is time. **Predictive validity** involves using your procedures or behavioral measures to predict some future criterion performance; **concurrent validity** involves using your procedures or behavioral measures to predict some concurrent criterion performance on either the same construct or a related construct. For example, if you were testing the concurrent validity of a new depression scale, you could administer your new scale and administer the Beck Depression Inventory (the known criterion) to a set of research participants (some of which are expected to be depressed). The scores from your scale and the Beck scale should be strongly and positively correlated if your new scale is valid. If you were testing the predictive validity of a new scale that you developed to measure success in college, then you could administer your scale, and at a later time measure how well the participants perform in college. The two sets of scores should be strongly and positively related.

Evidence of validity based on relations to other variables can also be obtained by collecting convergent and discriminant evidence. Similar to concurrent validity just discussed, **convergent validity evidence** is evidence based on the relationship between the focal test scores (i.e., the test you are developing and checking for validity) and independent measures of the same construct.

Homogeneity
The degree to which a set of items measures a single construct

Validity coefficient
The type of correlation coefficient used in validation research

Criterion-related validity
Degree to which scores predict or relate to a known criterion such as a future performance or an already-established test

Predictive validity
Degree to which scores obtained at one time correctly predict the scores on a criterion at a later time

Concurrent validity
Degree to which test scores obtained at one time correctly relate to the scores on a known criterion obtained at approximately the same time

Convergent validity evidence
Validity evidence based on the degree to which the focal test scores correlate with independent measures of the same construct

TABLE 5.2
Summary of Methods for Obtaining Evidence of Validity

Type of Evidence	Procedures
Evidence based on content	Experts on the construct examine the test/scale content and determine whether the content adequately represents the construct.
Evidence based on internal structure	Use *factor analysis*, which indicates how many constructs are present in the set of items. Also, examine the *homogeneity* of each set of unidimensional items by calculating *item-to-total correlation* and *coefficient alpha*.
Evidence based on relations to other variables	Determine whether the scores are related to known criterion by collecting *concurrent* and *predictive* validity evidence. Also determine if the test/scale scores are strongly correlated with participants' scores from other measures of the same construct (*convergent* validity evidence) and are NOT correlated with scores from measures of different constructs (*discriminant* validity evidence). Last, determine if groups that are known to differ on the construct are accurately classified by the scale under consideration (*known groups* validity evidence).

Discriminant validity evidence
Validity evidence based on the degree to which the focal test scores do *not* correlate with measures of *different* constructs

Discriminant validity evidence is evidence that the scores on your focal test are not related to the scores from other tests that are designed to measure theoretically different constructs. Convergent and validity evidence are used together in testing how well a new scale or test operates. The key point is that both convergent and divergent evidence are desirable.

The last type of validity evidence discussed here is **known groups validity evidence**. This is evidence that groups that are known to differ on the construct are said to differ (in the hypothesized direction) on the test being used to classify the participants into groups. For example, if you develop a test of gender roles, you would hypothesize that females will score higher on femininity and males will score higher on masculinity. Then you would test this hypothesis with females and males to see if you have evidence of validity.

Known groups validity evidence
Degree to which groups that are known to differ on a construct actually differ *according to the test* used to measure the construct

We have listed several kinds of validity evidence here, but we reiterate our point that the more validity evidence, the better. You must develop a theory of how a scale or test should operate, and test the theory in multiple ways. For your convenience, the three major methods for obtaining evidence of validity are summarized in Table 5.2.

STUDY QUESTION 5.3 | • **How does one obtain evidence of validity in measurement?**

Using Reliability and Validity Information

Norming group
The reference group upon which reported reliability and validity evidence is based

You must be careful when interpreting the reliability and validity evidence provided with standardized tests and when judging empirical research journal articles. With standardized tests, the reported validity and reliability data are typically based on a **norming group** (which is an actual group of people). If the people you intend to use a test with are very different from the people in the norming group, then the validity and reliability evidence provided with the test become questionable. That is because you need to know if the test or scale is valid with the people in *your* research study.

When reading journal articles, you should view an article positively to the degree that the researchers provide reliability and validity evidence for the measures that they use with their research participants. Two related questions to ask when reading and evaluating an empirical research article are as follows: "Did the researchers use appropriate measures?" and "How much evidence did the writers provide for measurement validity?" If the answers are positive, then give the article high marks for measurement. If the answers are negative, then you should significantly downgrade your assessment of the research.

Sources of Information About Tests

The two most important sources of information about standardized tests are the *Mental Measurements Yearbook* (MMY) and *Tests in Print* (TIP); you can find both of these at your college library. Another very important source is the empirical research literature found on databases such as PsycINFO, PsycARTICLES, SocINDEX, MEDLINE, and ERIC. When trying to determine how to measure a construct, you should carefully study the measures currently being used by the top researchers in the top journals in the research area. Then try to obtain permission to use the best measures of the constructs you hope to study. Some additional sources are provided: Miller's (1991) *Handbook of Research Design and Social Measurement*, Maddox's (1997) *Tests: A Comprehensive Reference for Assessment in Psychology, Education, and Business*, Fields' (2002) *Taking the Measure of Work: A Guide to Validated Scales for Organizational Research and Diagnosis*, and Robinson, Shaver, and Wrightsman's (1991) *Measures of Personality and Social Psychological Attitudes*.

Sampling Methods

Whenever you review published research, it is important to critically examine the sampling methods used (i.e., how the researcher obtained the research participants) so that you can judge the quality of the study. Furthermore, if you ever conduct an empirical research study on your own, you will need to select research participants and to use the best sampling method that is appropriate and feasible in your situation. In experimental research, random samples are usually *not* used because the focus is primarily on the issue of causation, and random assignment is far more important than random sampling for constructing a strong experimental research design. Conversely, in survey research, random samples often are used and are quite important if the researcher intends to generalize directly to a population based on his or her single research study results. Political polls are a common example where the researcher needs to generalize to a population based on a single sample. The purpose of this second major part of the chapter is to introduce you to the different kinds of sampling methods that are available to researchers.

Terminology Used in Sampling

Sample
The set of elements selected from a population

Element
The basic unit selected

Population
The full set of elements from which the sample is selected

Sampling
The process of drawing a sample from a population

Representative sample
A sample that resembles the population

Equal probability of selection method (EPSEM)
Sampling method in which each individual element has an equal probability of selection into the sample

Statistic
A numerical characteristic of sample data

Parameter
A numerical characteristic of a population

Sampling error
Differences between sample values and the true population parameter

Before discussing the specific methods of sampling, you need to know the definitions of some key terms that are used in sampling. A **sample** is a set of elements taken from a larger population; it is a subset of the population. An **element** is the basic unit of sampling. The **population** is the full set of elements or people from which you are sampling. **Sampling** refers to drawing elements from a population to obtain a sample. The usual goal of sampling is to obtain a **representative sample**, which is a sample that is similar to the population on all characteristics (except that it includes fewer people, because it is a sample rather than the complete population). Metaphorically, a perfectly representative sample would be a "mirror image" of the population from which it was selected (except that it would include fewer people).

When you want your sample to represent or "mirror" the population, the best way is to use an **equal probability of selection method (EPSEM)**. An EPSEM is any sampling method in which each individual member of the population has an equal chance of being selected for inclusion in the sample. If everyone has an equal chance, then the kinds of people in large groups will be selected more often and the kinds of people in small groups will be selected less often, but every single individual person will have the same chance of inclusion. For example, if the composition of a population is 55% female, 75% young adults aged 18–28, and 80% individuals who have completed an introductory psychology course, then a representative sample would have approximately the same percentages on these characteristics. Approximately 55% of the *sample* participants would be female, approximately 75% would be young adults, and approximately 80% would have completed an introductory psychology course. You will learn presently that there are several equal probability sampling methods, but simple random sampling, perhaps, is the most common (Peters & Eachus, 2008).

Once you collect data from the research participants in your sample, you must analyze the data. During analysis, you will determine characteristics of your sample such as the mean and variance on variables, as well as relationships between variables; these results calculated from your sample data are known as statistics. A **statistic** is a numerical characteristic of the sample data. For example, perhaps the mean income in a particular sample (i.e., the statistic) is $56,000 per year. Oftentimes a researcher also wants to make statements about population characteristics based on the sample results, such as an estimate of the population mean based on the sample mean. In statistical jargon, the researcher wants to make statements about parameters. A **parameter** is a numerical characteristic of a population. Perhaps the mean income in the entire population (i.e., the parameter) is $51,323 per year.

Notice that our sample mean and population mean income levels are different ($56,000 in the sample vs. $51,323 in the population). That's the typical situation in sampling, even when the best sampling methods are used. The term **sampling error** is used to refer to the difference between the value of a sample statistic and the value of the population parameter. In our case of annual income, the sampling error was equal to $4,677 (i.e., 56,000 − 51,323 = 4,677). A key point is that some error is always present in sampling. With random sampling methods, errors are random rather than being systematically wrong (and, potentially, the errors will be relatively small if large samples are drawn). When error is random, as in random

Census
Collection of data
from everyone in the
population

Sampling frame
A list of all the elements
in a population

sampling, the average of all possible samples is equal to the true population para-meter, and the values of the samples vary randomly around the true parameter. This is the best we can hope for with sampling. If you need to have no sampling error, you will have to avoid sampling and conduct a **census**—you will have to col-lect data from everyone in the population. Conducting a census is rarely an option, however, because most populations are very large, and it would be too expensive.

Most sampling methods require that you have a list of the people who are in the population. This list is called a **sampling frame**. An example of a sampling frame is shown in Figure 5.1. This sampling frame includes all the presidents of

FIGURE 5.1
A sampling frame of presidents of the American Psychological Association.*

1. Granville Stanley Hall (1892)
2. George Trumbull Ladd (1893)
3. William James (1894)
4. James McKeen Cattell (1895)
5. George Stuart Fullerton (1896)
6. James Mark Baldwin (1897)
7. Hugo Munensterberg (1898)
8. John Dewey (1899)
9. Joseph Jastrow (1900)
10. Josiah Royce (1901)
11. Edmund Clark Sanford (1902)
12. William Lowe Bryan (1903)
13. William James (1904)
14. Mary Whiton Calkins (1905)
15. James Rowland Angell (1906)
16. Henry Rutgers Marshall (1907)
17. George Malcolm Stratton (1908)
18. Charles Hubbard Judd (1909)
19. Walter Bowers Pillsbury (1910)
20. Carl Emil Seashore (1911)
21. Edward Lee Thorndike (1912)
22. Howard Crosby Warren (1913)
23. Robert Sessions Woodworth (1914)
24. John Broadus Watson (1915)
25. Raymond Dodge (1916)
26. Robert Mearns Yerkes (1917)
27. John Wallace Baird (1918)
28. Walter Dill Scott (1919)
29. Shepard Ivory Franz (1920)
30. Margaret Floy Washburn (1921)
31. Knight Dunlap (1922)
32. Lewis Madison Terman (1923)
33. Granville Stanley Hall (1924)
34. Madison Bentley (1925)
35. Harvey A. Carter (1926)
36. Harry Levi Hollingsworth (1927)
37. Edwin Garrigues Boring (1928)
38. Karl Lashley (1929)
39. Herbert Sidney Langfeld (1930)
40. Walther Samuel Hunter (1931)
41. Walter Richard Miles (1932)
42. Luis Leon Thurstone (1933)
43. Joseph Peterson (1934)
44. Albert Theodor Poffenberger (1935)
45. Clark Leonard Hull (1936)
46. Edward Chace Tolman (1937)
47. John Frederick Dashiell (1938)
48. Gordon Willard Allport (1939)
49. Leonard Carmichael (1940)
50. Herbert Woodrow (1941)
51. Calvin Perry Stone (1942)
52. John Edward Anderson (1943)
53. Garder Murphy (1944)
54. Edwin R. Guthrie (1945)
55. Henry E. Garrett (1946)
56. Carl R. Rogers (1947)
57. Donald G. Marquis (1948)
58. Ernest R. Hilgard (1949)
59. Joy Paul Guilford (1950)
60. Robert R. Sears (1951)
61. Joseph McVicker Hunt (1952)
62. Laurence Frederic Shaffer (1953)
63. O. H. Mowrer (1954)
64. E. Lowell Kelly (1955)
65. Theodore M. Newcombe (1956)
66. Lee J. Cronbach (1957)
67. H. F. Harlow (1958)
68. W. Kohler (1959)
69. Donald O. Hebb (1960)
70. Neal E. Miller (1961)
71. Paul E. Meehl (1962)
72. Charles E. Osgood (1963)
73. Quinn McNemar (1964)
74. Jerome Bruner (1965)
75. Nicholas Hobbs (1966)
76. Gardner Lindzey (1967)
77. A. H. Maslow(1968)
78. George A. Miller (1969)
79. George W. Albee (1970)
80. Kenneth B. Clark (1971)
81. Anne Anastasi (1972)
82. Leona E. Tyler (1973)
83. Albert Bandura (1974)
84. Donald T. Campbell (1975)
85. Wilbert J. Mckeachie (1976)
86. Theodore Blau (1977)
87. M. Brewster Smith (1978)
88. Nicholas A. Cummings (1979)
89. Florence L. Denmark (1980)
90. John J. Conger (1981)
91. William Bevan (1982)
92. Max Siegal (1983)
93. Janet T. Spence (1984)
94. Robert Perloff (1985)
95. Logan Wright (1986)
96. Bonnie R. Strickland (1987)
97. Raymond D. Fowler (1988)
98. Joseph D. Matarazzo (1989)
99. Stanley Graham (1990)
100. Charles Spielberger (1991)
101. Jack Wiggins, Jr. (1992)
102. Frank Farley (1993)
103. Ronald E. Fox (1994)
104. Robert J. Resnick (1995)
105. Dorothy W. Cantor (1996)
106. Norman Abeles (1997)
107. Martin E. P. Seligman (1998)
108. Richard M. Suinn (1999)
109. Patrick H. Deleon (2000)
110. Norine G. Johnson (2001)
111. Philip G. Zimbardo (2002)
112. Robert J. Sternberg (2003)
113. Diane F. Halpern (2004)
114. Ronald F. Levant (2005)
115. Gerald P. Koocher (2006)
116. Sharon Stephens Brehm (2007)
117. Alan E. Kazdin (2008)
118. James H. Bray (2009)

*Year of each president's term is provided in parentheses

the American Psychological Association since its founding in 1892. The population is "Presidents of the APA." This sampling frame also includes an identification number for each population member, starting with 1 (for the first president) and ending with 118 (for the last president). The majority of the people in this sampling frame are no longer alive. Therefore, this population would only be relevant for nonexperimental or historical research. For example, you might have wanted to conduct a descriptive study of the age, gender, and research specialties of past presidents, looking for changes over time (e.g., Hogan, 1994).

Now let's think about another research study. Assume that you work for the APA and the executive director wants you to conduct a telephone survey investigating current APA members' attitudes toward the use and treatment of animals in psychological research. In 2009, there were approximately 150,000 APA members; therefore, the sampling frame would include 150,000 entries. This sampling frame would probably be in a computer file. Next you would randomly select the sample. Perhaps you have enough funds to survey 400 APA members. When you attempt to conduct the telephone survey with the 400 sample members, you will find that not everyone will consent to participate. To indicate the degree of sample participation in research studies, researchers report the response rate. The **response rate** is the percentage of people in the sample selected for study who actually participate. This rate should be as high as possible. If 300 of the 400 members selected in the APA descriptive study sample participate, the response rate would be 75% (i.e., 300 divided by 400).

Response rate
The percentage of people selected to be in a sample and who participate in the research study

Random Sampling Techniques

The two major types of sampling used in psychological research are random sampling and nonrandom sampling. When the goal is to generalize from a specific sample to a population, random sampling methods are preferred because they produce representative samples. Nonrandom sampling methods generally produce **biased samples** (i.e., samples that are not representative of a known population). Any particular research sample might (or might not) be representative, but your chances are much greater if you use a random sampling method (in particular, if you use an equal probability of selection method). It is especially important that the demographic characteristics of nonrandom samples be described in detail in research reports so that readers can understand the exact characteristics of the research participants. Researchers and readers of reports can then make generalizations based on what the famous research methodologist (and past APA president) Donald Campbell (1916–1996) called **proximal similarity**. Campbell's idea is that you can generalize research results to different people, places, settings, and contexts to the degree that the people in the field are similar to those described in the research study.[1]

Biased sample
A nonrepresentative sample

Proximal similarity
Generalization to people, places, settings, and contexts that are similar to those described in the research study

[1]Campbell (1986) recommended that the term *proximal similarity* be used to replace what he originally called *external validity*. However, the label has never caught on.

Simple Random Sampling

The most basic type of random sampling is **simple random sampling**. Simple random sampling is the definitive case of an equal probability of selection method). Remember, to be an EPSEM, everyone in the population must have an equal chance of being included in the final sample. It is the characteristic of equal probability that makes simple random sampling produce representative samples from which you can directly generalize from your sample to the population.

One way to visualize simple random sampling is to think of what we call "the hat model." The idea is to write everyone's name on an equal-sized slip of paper. Then put the slips into a hat, cover the top of the hat, and shake it up so that the slips are randomly distributed. Next, pull out a slip of paper, and place it to the side. You would repeat this procedure until the number of selected slips of paper pulled from the hat equals the desired sample size.

When drawing a simple random sample, sampling experts recommend that you use sampling "without replacement" (as we did in the "hat model" example) instead of sampling "with replacement" (where one would put the selected slip of paper back in the hat to potentially be selected again). That's because sampling without replacement is slightly more *efficient* in producing representative samples (i.e., it requires slightly fewer people and is therefore slightly cheaper). When sampling without replacement, you do not allow anyone to be selected more than once; once a person is selected, you do not put the person back into the pool of people to be potentially selected. Perhaps the easiest way to see the need for sampling without replacement is with a very small sample. If you drew a sample of 10 people from a population, you would want all of them to be different people. If you used sampling with replacement and happened to select a person five times, then you would be estimating the characteristics of the population from just 5 people rather than from 10.

In practice, you would not use a "hat model" for drawing a random sample. Before the widespread availability of computers, a traditional way to obtain simple random samples was to use a table of random numbers from which researchers obtained numbers to be used in identifying people to be included in a sample. Today, the use of random number generators is more common. Here are links to some popular and easy-to-use random number generators that are available on the World Wide Web:

http://www.randomizer.org

http://www.psychicscience.org/random.aspx

http://www.random.org

To find additional random number generators, just search the Web for "random number generator."

If you are using a random number generator, such as the ones just listed, you are actually randomly selecting a set of numbers. Therefore, you must make sure that each person in your sampling frame is associated with a number. Look at Figure 5.1, and you will see that each of the APA presidents was assigned an identification number. We will use these numbers to identify the persons selected for our sample.

With the help of the randomizer.org program, we selected a sample of size 10 from our sampling frame in Figure 5.1. We needed 10 numbers randomly selected from 1 to 118 because there are 118 APA presidents in our sampling frame. We went to the Web site and answered each of the questions as follows:

1. How many sets of numbers do you want to generate?
   - We inserted 1 to indicate that we wanted one set of numbers.
2. How many numbers per set?
   - We inserted 10 to indicate that we wanted 10 numbers in our set.
3. Number range?
   - We inserted 1 and 118 to indicate the range of numbers in our sampling frame.
4. Do you wish each number in a set to remain unique?
   - We clicked "yes" to indicate that we wanted sampling *without replacement*.
5. Do you wish to sort the numbers that are generated?
   - Either yes or no is fine. We clicked "yes."
6. How do you wish to view your random numbers?
   - We left the program at its default value ("place markers off") because we did not want a listing of the order in which the numbers were selected.
7. Next, to obtain our set of random numbers we clicked "Randomize Now!"

The resulting set of numbers from the random number generator was 1, 4, 22, 29, 46, 60, 63, 76, 100, and 117. The last step was to go to the sampling frame in Figure 5.1 to determine who from our population was included in the sample. We did this by locating the people in the sampling frame who were associated with our randomly generated identification numbers. Here is the resulting random sample of 10 APA presidents: 1-Granville Stanley Hall, 4-James McKeen Cattell, 22-Howard Crosby Warren, 29-Shepard Ivory Franz, 46-Edward Chace Tolman, 60-Robert R. Sears, 63-O. H. Mower, 76-Gardner Lindzey, 100-Charles Spieberger, and 117-Alan E. Kazdin.

Stratified random sampling
Division of population elements into mutually exclusive groups and then selection of a random sample from each group

Stratification variable
The variable on which the population elements are divided for the purpose of stratified sampling

Stratified Random Sampling

A second type of random sampling is **stratified random sampling** (or stratified sampling). In stratified sampling, the population is divided into mutually exclusive groups called strata, and then a random sample is selected from each of the groups. The set of groups make up the levels of the **stratification variable**. For example, if gender were the stratification variable, the population sampling frame would be divided into a group of all the females and a group of all the males. Figure 5.2 shows our sampling frame stratified by gender. Stratification variables can be categorical variables (e.g., gender, ethnicity, personality type) or quantitative variables (e.g., intelligence, height, age), and more than one stratification variable can be used.

FIGURE 5.2
Sampling frame stratified by gender.*

Female APA Presidents:

1. Mary Whiton Calkins (1905)
2. Margaret Floy Washburn (1921)
3. Anne Anastasi (1972)
4. Leona E. Tyler (1973)
5. Florence L. Denmark (1980)
6. Janet T. Spence (1984)
7. Bonnie R. Strickland (1987)
8. Dorothy W. Cantor (1996)
9. Norine G. Johnson (2001)
10. Diane F. Halpern (2004)
11. Sharon Stephens Brehm (2007)

Male APA Presidents:

1. Granville Stanley Hall (1892)
2. George Trumbull Ladd (1893)
3. William James (1894)
4. James McKeen Cattell (1895)
5. George Stuart Fullerton (1896)
6. James Mark Baldwin (1897)
7. Hugo Munensterberg (1898)
8. John Dewey (1899)
9. Joseph Jastrow (1900)
10. Josiah Royce (1901)
11. Edmund Clark Sanford (1902)
12. William Lowe Bryan (1903)
13. William James (1904)
14. James Rowland Angell (1906)
15. Henry Rutgers Marshall (1907)
16. George Malcolm Stratton (1908)
17. Charles Hubbard Judd (1909)
18. Walter Bowers Pillsbury (1910)
19. Carl Emil Seashore (1911)
20. Edward Lee Thorndike (1912)
21. Howard Crosby Warren (1913)
22. Robert Sessions Woodworth (1914)
23. John Broadus Watson (1915)
24. Raymond Dodge (1916)
25. Robert Mearns Yerkes (1917)
26. John Wallace Baird (1918)
27. Walter Dill Scott (1919)
28. Shepard Ivory Franz (1920)
29. Knight Dunlap (1922)
30. Lewis Madison Terman (1923)
31. Granville Stanley Hall (1924)
32. Madison Bentley (1925)
33. Harvey A. Carter (1926)
34. Harry Levi Hollingsworth (1927)
35. Edwin Garrigues Boring (1928)
36. Karl Lashley (1929)
37. Herbert Sidney Langfeld (1930)
38. Walther Samuel Hunter (1931)
39. Walter Richard Miles (1932)
40. Luis Leon Thurstone (1933)
41. Joseph Peterson (1934)
42. Albert Theodor Poffenberger (1935)
43. Clark Leonard Hull (1936)
44. Edward Chace Tolman (1937)
45. John Frederick Dashiell (1938)
46. Gordon Willard Allport (1939)
47. Leonard Carmichael (1940)
48. Herbert Woodrow (1941)
49. Calvin Perry Stone (1942)
50. John Edward Anderson (1943)
51. Garder Murphy (1944)
52. Edwin R. Guthrie (1945)
53. Henry E. Garrett (1946)
54. Carl R. Rogers (1947)
55. Donald G. Marquis (1948)
56. Ernest R. Hilgard (1949)
57. Joy Paul Guilford (1950)
58. Robert R. Sears (1951)
59. Joseph McVicker Hunt (1952)
60. Laurence Frederic Shaffer (1953)
61. O. H. Mowrer (1954)
62. E. Lowell Kelly (1955)
63. Theodore M. Newcombe (1956)
64. Lee J. Cronbach (1957)
65. H. F. Harlow (1958)
66. W. Kohler (1959)
67. Donald O. Hebb (1960)
68. Neal E. Miller (1961)
69. Paul E. Meehl (1962)
70. Charles E. Osgood (1963)
71. Quinn McNemar (1964)
72. Jerome Bruner (1965)
73. Nicholas Hobbs (1966)
74. Gardner Lindzey (1967)
75. A. H. Maslow (1968)
76. George A. Miller (1969)
77. George W. Albee (1970)
78. Kenneth B. Clark (1971)
79. Albert Bandura (1974)
80. Donald T. Campbell (1975)
81. Wilbert J. Mckeachie (1976)
82. Theodore Blau (1977)
83. M. Brewster Smith (1978)
84. Nicholas A. Cummings (1979)
85. John J. Conger (1981)
86. William Bevan (1982)
87. Max Siegal (1983)
88. Robert Perloff (1985)
89. Logan Wright (1986)
90. Raymond D. Fowler (1988)
91. Joseph D. Matarazzo (1989)
92. Stanley Graham (1990)
93. Charles Spielberger (1991)
94. Jack Wiggins, Jr. (1992)
95. Frank Farley (1993)
96. Ronald E. Fox (1994)
97. Robert J. Resnick (1995)
98. Norman Abeles (1997)
99. Martin E. P. Seligman (1998)
100. Richard M. Suinn (1999)
101. Patrick H. Deleon (2000)
102. Philip G. Zimbardo (2002)
103. Robert J. Sternberg (2003)
104. Ronald F. Levant (2005)
105. Gerald P. Koocher (2006)
106. Alan E. Kazdin (2008)
107. James H. Bray (2009)

*The 11 female presidents are listed first, followed by the 107 male presidents.

Here is how you obtain a stratified sample with just one stratification variable:

1. Stratify your sampling frame (e.g., divide the list into the males and the females if gender is your stratification variable), and give the elements in each set identification numbers.
2. Draw a random sample from each of the groups (e.g., take a random sample of females and a random sample of males).
3. Combine the sets of randomly selected people (e.g., males and females), and you will have the final sample.

Proportional stratified sampling
Stratified sampling where the sample proportions are made to be the *same* as the population proportions on the stratification variable

There are actually two different kinds of stratified sampling: proportional stratified sampling and disproportional stratified sampling. In **proportional stratified sampling**, the numbers of people selected from the groups (e.g., females and males) are proportional to their sizes in the population. For example, if 60% of the population is female, then you select 60% of your sample to be female. In **disproportional stratified sampling**, the numbers of people selected from the groups are not proportional to their sizes in the population. For example, if 60% of the population is female, you might select only 50% of the sample to be female.

Assume that you want to stratify on the basis of the variable gender, and the large population is 75% female and 25% male. Also assume that you want a sample of size 100. For proportional stratified sampling, you would randomly select 75 females and 25 males from the stratified sampling frame; the final sample would exactly match the population on gender percentages (75%, 25%). Proportional stratified sampling is an EPSEM (each individual has an equal chance of being included in the final sample), and you can directly generalize from the sample to the population.

Disproportional stratified sampling
Stratified sampling where the sample proportions are made to be *different* from the population proportions on the stratification variable

For disproportional stratified sampling, you might randomly select 50 females and 50 males from the gender populations. Disproportional stratified sampling is not EPSEM because everyone does not have an equal chance. In this case, the population is 75% female and 25% male, but the sample is 50% female and 50% male. When you under- or oversample groups like this, your sampling method is no longer an equal probability of selection method. You cannot combine the samples of 50 females and 50 males and directly generalize to the population.[2] Even though disproportional stratified sampling is not EPSEM, it is still used sometimes because small groups might be missed if they are not over sampled.

Proportional stratified sampling is an especially strong type of sampling. Just like simple random sampling, proportional stratified random sampling is EPSEM, which means you will be able to generalize directly from your final combined sample to the population (Kalton, 1983; Kish, 1995). However, proportional stratified sampling is a little more efficient than simple random sampling (which means it requires slightly fewer people and is therefore slightly less expensive). A proportional stratified sample is a slightly improved simple random sample (i.e., it is forced to be representative of the stratification variable; otherwise, it is a random sample). Corporations that spend a lot of money on sampling often prefer stratified sampling because it results in reduced costs.

[2]In this case, sampling experts would weight the females and males back to their appropriate sizes if they wanted to generalize from the sample to the population.

Cluster Random Sampling

In the third major type of random sampling, called **cluster random sampling** (or cluster sampling), the researcher randomly selects *clusters* rather than individual-type units (such as individual people) in the first stage of sampling. A **cluster** is a collective type of unit that includes multiple elements; it has more than one unit in it. Some examples of clusters are neighborhoods, families, schools, classrooms, and work teams. Notice that all of these collective-type units include multiple individual elements or units.

We briefly explain two types of cluster sampling: one stage and two stage. The first type of cluster sampling is **one-stage cluster sampling**. To select a one-stage cluster sample, you randomly select a sample of clusters. You include in your final sample all of the individual units in the randomly selected clusters. For example, if you randomly select 15 psychology classrooms, you would include all of the students in those 15 psychology classrooms in your sample.

The second type of cluster sampling is **two-stage cluster sampling**. In the first stage, you randomly select a sample of clusters (i.e., just like you did in one-stage cluster sampling). However, in the second stage you draw a random sample from the elements in each of the clusters selected in the first stage. For example, in stage one you might randomly select 30 psychology classrooms and in stage two randomly select 10 students from each of the 30 psychology classrooms.

Cluster sampling is an EPSEM if the clusters are approximately the same size. Remember that EPSEM is very important because that is what makes the sampling method produce representative samples. If the clusters are not the same size, there are some advanced techniques beyond the scope of this book that can be used to help make it EPSEM.[3]

Systematic Sampling

Another type of sampling that usually produces samples similar to random samples is **systematic sampling**. Systematic sampling is about as efficient as simple random sampling and, like simple random sampling, systematic sampling is an EPSEM (Kalton, 1983). If you decide to draw a sample using systematic sampling, you must follow three steps. First, determine the **sampling interval**, which is the population size divided by the desired sample size. The sampling interval can be symbolized by "*k*." Second, randomly select a number between 1 and *k*, and include that person in your sample. Third, also include each kth element in your sample. For example, assume your population is 100 in size and you want a sample of 10. In this case, *k* is equal to 10 which is your sampling interval. Next, assume your randomly selected number between 1 and 10 is 5. Last, in addition to person 5, include every 10th person (e.g., the second person will be person 15 because 5 + 10 is 15, and the third person will be person 25 because 15 + 10 is 25, and continue this process). The final sample will include persons 5, 15, 25, 35, 45, 55, 65, 75, 85, and 95. If you follow the three steps, then when you get to the end

---

[3]You can fix this problem by using a technique called "probability proportional to size" (PPS).

of your sampling frame, you will always have all the people to be included in your sample. In systematic sampling, you essentially take a random starting point, and work your way through a list of names.

Let's now select a systematic sample of size 10 from our sampling frame in Figure 5.1. The population size is 118, and the desired sample size is 10; therefore, k is 118 divided by 10, which is approximately equal to 12 ($11.8 \approx 12$). Second, we used the random number generator to select a number between 1 and 12, and we obtained 6. Person 6 is included in the sample. Third, we also took every 12th person to obtain our final sample. The sample includes person 6, 18, 30, 42, 54, 66, 78, 90, 102, and 114. You can use these numbers and identify the 10 APA presidents selected for this sample.[4]

Periodicity

Problematic situation in systematic sampling that can occur if there is a cyclical pattern in the sampling frame

There is one potential (but uncommon) problem in systematic sampling. It is called **periodicity**. Periodicity can occur if there is a cyclical pattern in the sampling frame. It could occur if you attached several ordered lists to one another (e.g., if you take lists from multiple classes in which each class list is ordered according to a variable such as grades), and the length of the separate lists is equal to k. As long as you don't attach multiple lists to one another, periodicity will not be a problem. If you have multiple lists, be sure to organize them into one overall list (i.e., into a new list ordered randomly, or alphabetically, or according to a stratification variable).

STUDY QUESTION 5.4

- **What are the strengths and weaknesses of the major random sampling techniques?**

Nonrandom Sampling Techniques

Convenience sampling

Use of people who are readily available, volunteer, or are easily recruited for inclusion in a sample

The other major type of sampling used in psychological research is nonrandom sampling. These tend to be weaker sampling methods, but sometimes they are necessary because of practical considerations. We briefly explain the four major nonrandom sampling methods: convenience sampling, quota sampling, purposive sampling, and snowball sampling.

When using **convenience sampling**, you simply ask people who are most available or the most easily selected to participate in your research study. For example, psychologists often include college students from the introductory psychology subject pool (i.e., students who are participating in a research project for college credit and to learn what it is like to be a research participant).

Quota sampling

A researcher decides on the desired sample sizes or quotas for groups identified for inclusion in the sample, followed by convenience sampling from the groups

When using **quota sampling**, the researcher sets quotas (which are the numbers of the kinds of people you want in the sample), and then the researcher locates (using convenience sampling) the numbers of people needed to meet the quotas. For example, a set of quotas might be as follows: 25 African American males, 25 European American males, 25 African American females, and 25 European American females. You could use convenience sampling to find the people. The key is to obtain the right number of people for each group quota.

[4]You can also use systematic sampling with a stratified sampling frame such as the one shown in Figure 5.2. In fact, this is slightly better because of the advantage of stratification.

Purposive sampling

A researcher specifies the characteristics of the population of interest and then locates individuals who have those characteristics

When using **purposive sampling**, the researcher specifies the characteristics of the population of interest and then locates individuals who match the needed characteristics. For example, you might decide that you want to conduct a research study with "adolescent boys and girls aged 14–17 who have been diagnosed with obsessive compulsive disorder." You might try to locate 25 boys and 25 girls who meet the inclusion criteria and are willing to participate, and include them in your research study.

Snowball sampling

Each sampled person is asked to identify other potential participants with the inclusion characteristic

Last, in **snowball sampling**, each research participant is asked to identify other potential research participants who have a certain inclusion characteristic (or set of characteristics). You start with one or a few participants whom you can locate; you ask them to participate and also ask them if they know of some other potential participants who meet the inclusion characteristic. You then locate these additional participants, ask them to participate, and ask them for other potential participants. You continue this process until you have a sufficient number of research participants. Snowball sampling is especially useful when you need to select from a hard-to-find population where no sampling frame exists. For example, if you want to conduct a study of people in your city who have a lot of political power (formal and informal power), you might use snowball sampling because there is no sampling frame. You would identify a starting set of people with power, and then you would use the process of snowball sampling just described.

STUDY QUESTION 5.5

- **What are the key characteristics of the different types of non random sampling methods?**

Random Selection and Random Assignment

This chapter is about measurement and sampling techniques. It is not about assignment techniques. However, we need to make sure you understand the important distinction between random selection and random assignment. Random selection is a sampling technique, and random assignment is not. In random selection, you select a sample from a population using one of the random sampling techniques that we have discussed. The purpose of **random selection** is to obtain a sample that represents a population. If you use an EPSEM technique, the resulting random sample will be similar to the population (i.e., it will be representative). For example, if you randomly select (e.g., using simple random sampling) 1000 people from the adult population in Ann Arbor, Michigan, your sample would be similar to the adult population of Ann Arbor. Random selection is very important for survey research in which you need to generalize from a single sample directly to a population.

Random selection

Selection of participants using a random sampling method

Random assignment

Placement of participants into experimental conditions on the basis of a chance process

Random assignment is not used to obtain a sample. Random assignment is used in experimental research to produce treatment and control groups (or comparison groups) that are similar on all possible characteristics. When conducting random assignment, you start with a set of people (typically you will have a *convenience sample*), and then you randomly divide the set of people into two or

Purpose of random selection
To obtain a representative sample

Purpose of random assignment
To produce two or more equivalent groups for use in an experiment

more groups. Then one group can be given the treatment condition, and the other can serve as the control condition (determined randomly), and you conduct the experiment. *The random assignment process is a key element in producing the strongest experimental designs available for the study of causation.* Randomized designs are explained in Chapter 8. As with random selection, researchers typically use random number generators for random assignment (e.g., the program used earlier for random selection can be used for random assignment). It is important to remember that the difference between random selection and random assignment is the purpose. *The **purpose of random selection** is to obtain a representative sample, and the **purpose of random assignment** is to produce two or more probabilistically equivalent groups for use in an experiment.*

Determining the Sample Size When Random Sampling Is Used

When you design a research study, the following key question will inevitably arise: "How many people should I include in my sample?" Although this is a very practical question, it is difficult to answer because sample size is affected by many different factors. We now offer some recommendations and provide some relevant information that will help.

Here are five relatively "simple" answers to the important question about sample size. First, if your population is 100 people or fewer, then include the entire population in your study rather than drawing a sample. In this case, we recommend that you don't take a sample; include everyone. Second, try to get a relatively large sample size when possible for your research study. Larger sample sizes make it less likely that you will miss an effect or relationship that is present in your population. At some point, adding more people adds little benefit and can become cost ineffective; however, we don't expect you to be in that situation very often. Third, we recommend that you carefully examine other research studies in the research literature on your topic and determine how many participants other researchers are selecting. Fourth, for an exact number of people to include in a sample, look at Table 5.3, which shows recommended sample sizes. Table 5.3, however, is only an approximate starting point for consideration, however, because several assumptions were made in determining the sample sizes provided. Fifth, we strongly recommend that you use a **sample size calculator**. You will have to learn a little about inferential statistics in order to use these calculators, but we discuss inferential statistics in detail in Chapter 15. Perhaps the most popular sample size calculation program is G-Power (Erdfelder, Faul, & Buchner, 1996). Here's a link to the program: http://www.psycho. uni-duesseldorf.de/aap/projects/gpower/.

Sample size calculator
A statistical program used to provide a recommended sample size

We complete this section with a few additional points about sample sizes. First, you will need a larger sample size when your population is heterogeneous (i.e., composed of widely different kinds of people). Second, you will need larger sample sizes when you want to break down your data into multiple subcategories. For example, if you want to conduct a separate analysis for males and females (rather than just looking at the overall group) or by ethnic groups, you will need a sufficient sample size for every subgroup. Third, you will need larger sample sizes

TABLE 5.3

Sample Sizes for Various Populations of Size 10–50 Million

N stands for the size of the population. *n* stands for the size of the recommended sample. The sample sizes are based on the 95 % confidence level.

N	n	N	n	N	n	N	n	N	n
10	10	110	86	300	169	950	274	4,500	354
15	14	120	92	320	175	1,000	278	5,000	357
20	19	130	97	340	181	1,100	285	6,000	361
25	24	140	103	360	186	1,200	291	7,000	364
30	28	150	108	380	191	1,300	297	8,000	367
35	32	160	113	400	196	1,400	302	9,000	368
40	36	170	118	420	201	1,500	306	10,000	370
45	40	180	123	440	205	1,600	310	15,000	375
50	44	190	127	460	210	1,700	313	20,000	377
55	48	200	132	480	214	1,800	317	30,000	379
60	52	210	136	500	217	1,900	320	40,000	380
65	56	220	140	550	226	2,000	322	50,000	381
70	59	230	144	600	234	2,200	327	75,000	382
75	63	240	148	650	242	2,400	331	100,000	384
80	66	250	152	700	248	2,600	335	250,000	384
85	70	260	155	750	254	2,800	338	500,000	384
90	73	270	159	800	260	3,000	341	1,000,000	384
95	76	280	162	850	265	3,500	346	10,000,000	384
100	80	290	165	900	269	4,000	351	50,000,000	384

Adapted from R. V. Krejecie and D. W. Morgan, "Determining sample size for research activities," *Educational and Psychological Measurement, 30*(3), 608, copyright © 1970 by Sage publications, Inc. Reprinted by permission of Sage Publications, Inc.

when you want to obtain a relatively narrow (i.e., precise) confidence interval. For example, a confidence interval estimate that 75% of clinical psychologists support a new prescription licensing bill *plus or minus 4%* is narrower (i.e., more precise) than a confidence interval estimate of *plus or minus 5%*. Unfortunately, increased precision will come at a cost: You will need a larger sample if you want increased precision. Fourth, you will need a larger sample size when you expect a weak relationship or a small effect. It takes a larger sample to pick up on weak relationships. There tends to be a lot of random error or "noise" present in data from a small sample, making it difficult to pick up a "weak signal" given by a weak relationship. Fifth, you will need a larger sample size when you use a less-efficient technique of random sampling (e.g., cluster sampling is less efficient than proportional stratified sampling). Sixth, some statistical techniques require larger or smaller sample sizes. We provide a table with recommended sample sizes for several different statistical tests in Chapter 9 (Table 9.1, page 268). You will learn more about this issue when you take a statistics course. Last, you will need a larger sample size when you expect to have a low response rate. As you learned above, the response rate is the percentage of people in your sample who agree to be in your study. If many people refuse to participate in your research study, you will need to select more people in order to obtain the desired sample size.

Sampling in Qualitative Research

Qualitative psychological research usually focuses on understanding the thinking of particular people, groups, places, and contexts. It can also be used to add insights to quantitative research. Qualitative research tends to focus on in-depth understanding of one or a few cases, rather than on the breadth of study of many cases. Therefore, a primary goal in qualitative research is to find information rich cases. As the cases are "selected," data collection methods such as in-depth interviews and field observation are used to obtain open-ended data.

Because of the focus on particular cases, sampling in qualitative research is usually *purposive*. The idea is to identify a particular group or kind of person that you wish to study in-depth to learn about a particular phenomenon. Oftentimes, sampling in qualitative research is *theoretical*. The idea is to select cases during the conduct of a research study (rather than only in the beginning). You continually select people who you believe are information rich and are likely to aid in the development of a theory about how and why some process works. You will continually locate the potential cases and gain permission for study. In Table 5.4, we list several specific sampling methods that are often identified with qualitative research (Miles & Huberman, 1994). One can also use what is called **mixed sampling**. Mixed sampling involves the mixing of qualitative sampling methods (Table 5.4) and quantitative sampling methods (discussed earlier under random and nonrandom sampling methods). The idea of mixed sampling is to develop more complex sampling methods that are tailored to your particular research questions, purposes, and needs.

Mixed sampling
Use of a combination of quantitative and qualitative sampling methods

TABLE 5.4
Sampling Methods Used in Qualitative Research

Maximum variation sampling—Identification and selection of a wide range of cases for data collection and analysis (e.g. locate psychotherapy clients at a college clinic who have high, medium, and low self-esteem).

Extreme case sampling—Identification and selection of cases from the extremes or poles of a dimension (e.g. locate psychotherapy clients at a college clinic who have very high and very low self-esteem).

Homogeneous sample selection—Identification and selection of a small and homogeneous group or a set of homogeneous cases for intensive study (e.g., selection of adolescent girls for a focus group discussion on diet and ideal body images).

Typical-case sampling—Identification and selection of what is believed to be a typical or average case (e.g., selection and in-depth interviews with several college students without health care coverage).

Critical-case sampling—Identification and selection of particularly important cases (i.e., you select cases that are known to be very important).

Negative-case sampling—Identification and selection of cases that you believe will probably disconfirm your generalizations, so that you can make sure that you are not just selectively finding cases to support your personal theory.

Opportunistic sampling—Identification and selection of useful cases during the conduct of a research study, *as the opportunity arises.*

Summary

Measurement is the act of measuring by assigning symbols or numbers to something according to a specific set of rules. Stevens' four "scales of measurement" are nominal ("type" measurement), ordinal (rank measurement), interval (equal distances between adjacent numbers), and ratio (includes an absolute zero). Examples are gender (nominal), order of finish in a race (ordinal), Fahrenheit temperature (interval), and height (ratio). The two primary psychometric characteristics of a test or instrument are reliability (consistency or stability of scores) and validity (correctness of interpretations about constructs made from scores). The key reliability types are test–retest (consistency over time), equivalent forms (consistency across forms), internal consistency (interrelatedness of items or consistency in measuring a single construct), and interrater (consistency of agreement). The key types of validity evidence include content-related evidence, internal structure evidence, and evidence based on relations to other variables (e.g., predictive, concurrent, convergent, discriminant, known groups).

The second major topic was sampling (i.e., selecting a set of people from a population). Important terminology includes sample versus population, statistic versus parameter, representative sample, EPSEM, sampling error, sampling frame, and response rate. Random sampling techniques include simple random sampling, proportional stratified sampling, disproportional stratified sampling, cluster sampling, and systematic sampling. The following are equal probability of selection methods (EPSEM): simple random sampling, proportional stratified sampling, systematic sampling (as long as you have a random start and periodicity is not present), and cluster sampling (when the clusters are of equal size). Major non-random sampling methods include convenience, quota, purposive, and snowball sampling. It is essential to understand the difference between random selection and random assignment; the chapter was about sampling, but the distinction is carefully explained. Multiple factors were discussed for consideration when determining the appropriate sample size. Last, several sampling methods used in qualitative research were briefly discussed.

Key Terms and Concepts

Biased sample
Census
Cluster
Cluster random sampling
Coefficient alpha
Concurrent validity
Content-related evidence or content
  validity
Convenience sampling
Convergent validity evidence
Criterion-related validity
Cronbach's alpha
Discriminant validity evidence
Disproportional stratified sampling

Element
Equal probability of selection
  method (EPSEM)
Equivalent-forms reliability
Face validity
Factor analysis
Homogeneity
Internal consistency reliability
Interobserver agreement
Interrater reliability
Interval scale
Known groups validity evidence
Measurement
Mixed sampling

Multidimensional construct
Nominal scale
Norming group
One-stage cluster sampling
Operationalization
Ordinal scale
Parameter
Periodicity
Population
Predictive validity
Proportional stratified
  sampling
Proximal similarity
Purpose of random assignment
Purpose of random selection
Purposive sampling
Quota sampling
Random assignment
Random selection
Ratio scale
Reliability

Reliability coefficient
Representative sample
Response rate
Sample
Sample size calculator
Sampling
Sampling error
Sampling frame
Sampling interval
Simple random sampling
Snowball sampling
Statistic
Stratification variable
Stratified random sampling
Systematic sampling
Test–retest reliability
Two-stage cluster sampling
Validation
Validity
Validity coefficient
Variable

Related Internet Sites

ftp://ftp.sas.com/pub/neural/measurement.html
Frequently asked measurement questions.

http://www.unl.edu/buros/bimm/html/lesson01.html
How to evaluate a standardized test?

http://www.chime.ucla.edu/measurement/webresources.htm
More measurement links.

http://www.personal.psu.edu/users/d/m/dmr/testing/testlinks.htm
Scale construction.

http://www.randomizer.org
http://www.psychicscience.org/random.aspx
http://www.random.org
These are some random number generators.

http://www.psycho.uni-duesseldorf.de/aap/projects/gpower/
Sample size calculator mentioned in the chapter.

http://www.surveysampling.com/index.php
This is a company that sells samples to corporations and consulting firms that don't have the resources to conduct large scale sampling.

Practice Test

1. Which is the correct order of the scales of measurement?
   a. Nominal, ordinal, interval, ratio
   b. Ordinal, interval, ratio, nominal
   c. Interval, ordinal, ratio, nominal
   d. Ratio, nominal, ordinal, interval

2. Reliability of a test refers to which of the following?
   a. The consistency or stability of test scores
   b. Whether a test measures what it is supposed to measure
   c. Whether a test is valid
   d. Its content sampling

3. _____ is the process of assigning symbols or numbers to objects, events, people, or characteristics according to a specific set of rules.
   a. Assessment
   b. Evaluation
   c. Measurement
   d. Observation

4. Which of the following sampling techniques is an *equal probability selection method* (i.e., EPSEM) in which every individual in the population has an equal chance of being selected?
   a. Simple random sampling
   b. Proportional stratified sampling
   c. Cluster sampling when the clusters are of equal size
   d. All of the above are EPSEM

5. Determining the sample interval (represented by k), randomly selecting a number between 1 and k, and then including every kth element in your sample are the steps for which type of sampling?
   a. Simple random sampling
   b. Three-stage cluster sampling
   c. Stratified sampling
   d. Systematic sampling

6. The purpose of random _____ is to produce a set of groups that are similar on all possible factors at the beginning of an experiment.
   a. Sampling
   b. Assignment

Challenge Exercises

1. Use the randomizer.org random number generator to select a proportional stratified sample of APA presidents. Assume that you want a final sample of size 20 APA presidents. As seen in Figure 5.2, 11 of the APA presidents were women (numbered 1–11) and 107 were men (numbered 1–107); about 9.3% of this population is female, and about 90.7% is male. For your sample, 9.3% of 20 rounds to 2 and 90.7% rounds to 18, so you want 2 female APA presidents and 18 male APA presidents. Therefore, you will want to use the random number generator to select 2 female APA presidents, and use it again to select 18 male APA presidents. Combining the two subsamples, you will have a stratified random sample of APA presidents (with gender as the stratification variable).

2. Professor Christensen develops a test of emotional intelligence. Which of the following represent convergent and discriminant evidence?

   a) The test correlates highly with another test of emotional intelligence and is uncorrelated with self-efficacy.
   b) The test correlates highly with another test of emotional intelligence and is highly correlated with self-efficacy.
   c) The test does not correlate with another test of emotional intelligence, but does correlate with self-efficacy.
   d) The test does not correlate with other tests of emotional intelligence nor with self-efficacy.

Next, explain why your answer is correct. Last, search the published research literature and decide what specific tests would you use in this validation process.

Research Validity

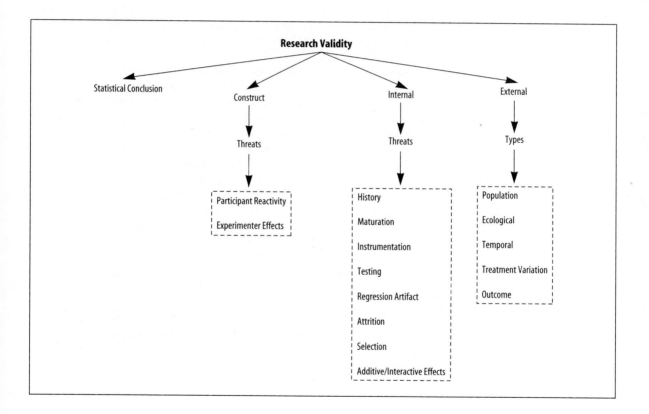

Jacqueline Gavagan was one of those fortunate individuals who seemed to have a perfect life. She had a satisfying profession as a speech pathologist, a loving husband, and two healthy young children with a third due in 7 weeks. On September 11, 2001, her world came tumbling down. Jacqueline's husband was a bond broker working in the World Trade Center on that fatal morning when terrorists crashed hijacked planes into the north and south towers. By midmorning, Jacqueline's husband and many of their closest friends were entombed in a million tons of burning rubble.

The trauma of a loss such as this causes one to grieve and experience feelings of anger, fear, guilt, hopelessness, and chronic fear. For some individuals, these emotions continue for years. Others, such as Jacqueline Gavagan, are more resilient and appear to adjust more quickly. Did Gavagan grieve? Of course she did, and still does. However, some individuals have the ability to bounce back from even the most severe setbacks. In the year after Jacqueline's husband was killed, she managed to restore meaning and even some joy to her life. She began this effort by starting a fund in her husband's name that might save a child's life. Earlier that year, surgeons at New York University Medical Center had successfully repaired a defect in her toddler's heart, and she wanted to sponsor similar operations for families that couldn't afford it. Through her efforts, the money flowed in, and by April 2002, sufficient funds had been donated to allow her to sponsor a similar operation for the son of a woman from Kosovo (Cowley, 2002).

Psychologists have for years expended most of their research efforts on understanding illness and developing treatments for disorders. In doing so, perhaps, they neglected the other side of the spectrum. In the 1990s, a movement was initiated to direct attention to studying positive emotions such as optimism and contentment and why some individuals are so resilient in the face of adversity. This new emphasis has attracted the attention of many psychologists who are uncovering interesting findings, such as that there seems to be a genetic component in one's mood and temperament and that the circumstances in life have less to do with the satisfaction we experience than previously expected. Health, wealth, good looks, and status seem to have only a small effect on what researchers call *subjective well-being*. So what does contribute to happiness? According to Martin Seligman (2002), happiness is not about managing our moods but about outgrowing our concern with how we feel. We need to have some gratification and fulfillment that comes from developing strengths and putting them to positive use, as Jacqueline Gavagan did in developing the fund to assist families with children in need of heart surgery.

Where did we gain this interesting knowledge about positive psychology? We gained it from the efforts of research psychologists who have conducted empirical high-quality research studies that are likely to produce valid conclusions. It is only when high-quality research studies are conducted that we are likely to obtain valid conclusions that should be trusted and believed.

Introduction

Research validity
Truthfulness of inferences made from a research study

Research validity refers to the correctness or truthfulness of an inference that is made from the results of a research study. Research validity is important in all types of research. To conduct a valid research study, you must develop a plan or strategy to use and follow it closely. This plan must involve the use of strategies for obtaining valid results. In this chapter, we will focus on the various types of validity and the key threats to validity in quantitative research, especially experimental research. We address validity in qualitative research in Chapter 13.

Overview of Four Major Types of Validity

The best way to ensure that a quantitative research study yields empirical findings from which accurate inferences can be made is to try to ensure that the study has the four types of validity that are listed in Table 6.1 (Shadish et al., 2002): statistical conclusion validity, construct validity, internal validity, and external validity. We discuss each of these in some depth. However, it is best to think of validity as falling on a continuum rather than into the dichotomous categories of 100% valid versus 0% valid. The goal is to maximize all four validity types as much as possible. However, any single study will do a good job achieving only some of these types of validity. This is because we cannot incorporate all the methods and procedures that would enable us to simultaneously achieve all four types of validity, and, sometimes, incorporating a method to achieve one type of validity will reduce our chances of achieving another type of validity. You will learn that this seems to be particularly true for internal and external validity. In this chapter, we introduce you to the major types of validity in research and explain the major threats that often creep into research studies when a study is not designed and executed well. Later chapters will go into much greater depth on the specifics of designing and executing the research study.

Statistical Conclusion Validity

Statistical conclusion validity
The validity of inferences made about the covariation between the independent and dependent variables

Statistical conclusion validity refers to the validity with which we can infer that the independent and dependent variables covary. By *covary* we mean that with every variation in the independent variable (IV) there is a corresponding variation in the dependent variable (DV); that is, we mean that the IV and DV are statistically related. As a reminder, covariation or relationship between the IV and DV was the first of three required conditions for making a claim of cause and effect (see Table 2.2 in Chapter 2, page 34). We make this inference about covariation, or relationship between the IV and DV, from the results of the statistical analysis computed on the data collected in the research study. You will learn in Chapter 15

TABLE 6.1

Types of Validity in Quantitative Research

Validity Types	Description
Statistical conclusion validity	Validity of the inference made about whether the independent and dependent variables covary.
Construct validity	Validity of the inference about the higher-order constructs from the operations used to represent them.
Internal validity	Validity of the inference that the independent and dependent variables are causally related.
External validity	Validity of the inference about whether the causal relationship holds over people, settings, treatment variables, measurement variables, and time.

that not only do we want to see if the data we collected show a relationship, but we must also determine if the observed relationship is statistically significant. A relationship is **statistically significant** when the analysis procedure described in Chapter 15 (called significance testing) indicates that the observed relationship is probably not due to chance, but is, instead, a real relationship.

Statistically significant
The observed relationship is probably *not* due to chance

If the researcher's inference about the covariation between the variables is correct, then the study has statistical conclusion validity. Sometimes, however, the inferences researchers make from their statistical analysis to the populations of interest are wrong. For example, if a study does not have enough research participants, the statistical test used might not have sufficient power to detect the covariation that really exists between the independent and dependent variables in the population, leading to the wrong conclusion (i.e., that no relationship between the variables exists when it really does). A researcher might also incorrectly conclude that a relationship is large when it actually is small, or vice versa. The lack of a sufficient number of participants in one's sample is one of the many factors that can threaten statistical conclusion validity. However, understanding these threats requires a statistical background and will not be reviewed here; if you are interested in them, see Shadish et al. (2002, p. 45).

STUDY QUESTIONS 6.1
- **What is statistical conclusion validity?**
- **Why is statistical conclusion validity important?**

Construct Validity

Construct validity is the extent to which we can infer higher-order constructs from the operations we use to represent them. As discussed in the previous chapter, creating operations from which we can accurately infer constructs is very important because, in many ways, scientific psychology is the study of constructs. For example, when we talk about individuals diagnosed with schizophrenia, obsessive-compulsive disorder, or an eating disorder, we are dealing with the constructs of these disorders. Constructs are also used to refer to experimental or nonexperimental research settings such as impoverished settings, enriched settings, or poverty neighborhoods. If you are investigating the effect of being depressed on marital discord among disadvantaged people living in an impoverished neighborhood you have a construct representing the research participant (disadvantaged people), the independent variable (depression), the dependent variable (marital discord), and the setting of the study (a poverty neighborhood). For each of these constructs, you must identify a set of operations that adequately represent the construct.

Construct validity
The extent to which a construct is adequately represented by the measures used in a research study

As we explained in the previous chapter, construct validity is the unifying concept for measurement validity, and we provided a section on validity in that chapter that explained how to obtain construct validity. In this chapter, we focus on some key threats to construct validity.

Threats to Construct Validity

Construct validity is concerned with the extent to which operationalizations represent and, therefore, can be used to infer the higher-order constructs they describe. For example, is a person who has had an income below the poverty level for 6 months a good representation of the construct of a disadvantaged person? In other words, is there a match between the construct and the operations used in your study? Sometimes our operationalizations are good representations, and sometimes there are other factors that affect these operationalizations that reduce the accuracy with which the operations represent the intended construct. Shadish et al. (2002) have identified a number of reasons why we might be incorrect in the inferences we make about constructs from our study operations. These reasons, presented in Table 6.2, are considered to be threats to construct validity. For example, the first threat in the table says that if you have an inadequate understanding

TABLE 6.2
Threats to Construct Validity

- *Inadequate explanation of the construct*—if a construct is not adequately explained and analyzed, it can lead to a set of operations that do not represent the construct adequately.
- *Construct confounding*—the operations used in a study represent more than one construct.
- *Mono-operation bias*—a study uses only one operationalization of a construct. This typically results in an underrepresentation of the construct and lowers construct validity.
- *Mono-method bias*—a study uses only one method (e.g., physiological recording) to operationalize a construct. When this occurs, the method used might influence the results.
- *Confounding constructs with level of constructs*—a study investigates only a few levels of a construct (e.g., three doses of a drug), but makes inferences about the overall construct (e.g., the overall effect of the drug).
- *Treatment-sensitive factorial structure*—an instrumentation change that occurs because of the experimental treatment.
- *Reactive self-report changes*—changes that a research participant might make on self-report measures as a result of a motivational shift after being included in the experimental study.
- *Reactivity to the experimental situation*—research participants' perceptions and motives can affect the responses they make to the dependent variable, and these responses can be interpreted as part of the treatment construct being tested.
- *Experimenter effects*—the experimenter's attributes and expectancies can influence the responses made by the research participants, and these responses can be interpreted as part of the treatment construct being tested.
- *Novelty and disruption effects*—research participants usually respond better to a new and novel situation and poorly to one that disrupts their routine. These effects are part of the overall treatment effect.
- *Compensatory equalization*—individuals try to provide the same benefits or services to the control group that are received by the experimental group.
- *Compensatory rivalry*—individuals resent being assigned to the control group and respond more negatively than would be expected, because of the resentment they feel.
- *Treatment diffusion*—individuals in one treatment group receive some or all of another group's treatment.

of the construct then it will be difficult to adequately measure it. According to the second threat, when possible, you should use operations that measure your construct only, rather than measuring more than one construct. You should read the table to learn about some additional ways that construct validity can be threatened.

Two of the threats listed in Table 6.2, participant reactivity to the experimental situation and experimenter effects, are discussed next in more detail because a considerable amount of research has documented the biasing effect that they can have on the outcome of experimental studies.

Participant reactivity to the experimental situation
Research participants' motives and tendencies that affect their perceptions of the situation and their responses on the dependent variable

Participant Reactivity to the Experimental Situation   This threat refers to the fact that participants bring with them motives and tendencies that can influence their perceptions of the experiment and the responses they make on the dependent variable measures. When agreeing to take part in an experiment, a person makes an implicit contract to "play the role" of the participant. Theoretically, this means that the participant will listen to the instructions and perform the tasks requested to the best of his or her ability and as truthfully as possible. In reality, such an ideal situation does not exist because participants are not passive responders to the experimental instructions and manipulations. Kihlstrom (1995) put it well when he stated that participants "are sentient curious creatures, constantly thinking about what is happening to them, evaluating the proceedings, figuring out what they are supposed to do, and planning their responses" (p. 10). These cognitive activities sometimes interact with the experimental procedures and measures and threaten the construct validity of the experimental treatment because the treatment is no longer the pure scientific production aimed for by the researcher.

Participant Effect.   When participants enter an experiment, they are generally naive regarding its purpose or the task required of them. Once they arrive, they receive information from the way the experimenter greets them, the instructions given about the experiment, the task required of them, the laboratory setting (including the visible equipment), and any rumors they might have heard about the experiment. This information, called the **demand characteristics** of the experiment, defines the experimental "demands" from the participants' point of view (Orne, 1962; Rosnow, 2002). Demand characteristics provide the participants with information from which they construct their perceptions of the purpose of the experiment and the task required. Once the participants identify this task, they are motivated to perform it. It is in the performance of the experimental task(s) that the participants' perceptions can influence the outcome of the experiment.

Demand characteristics
Any of the cues available in an experiment, such as instructions, rumors, or setting characteristics, that influence the responses of participants

In the past, it was thought that participants assumed a specific role (Fillenbaum, 1966; Masling, 1966; Orne, 1962; Rosenberg, 1969) and attempted to portray this role when performing the experimental task. Increasingly, this view has been rejected and replaced by the notion that participants often respond to the experimental task as they perceive it (Carlopia, Adair, Lindsay, & Spinner, 1983; Carlston & Cohen, 1980). If the experiment involves a learning task, participants will attempt to learn the material presented. However, participants do not take an uninvolved, neutral approach because often their performance implies something about them. For example, a learning task indirectly says something about the participants' intelligence. If they learn the material rapidly, this suggests that they are intelligent. Most individuals have a desire to appear intelligent, so they will try to learn as rapidly as possible. Similarly, if the task suggests something about emotional stability, participants will respond in such a way as to appear most emotionally stable (Rosenberg, 1969). Consequently, although participants seem to approach an experiment with the motivation to perform the task requested, superimposed on this desire is the wish to make a **positive self-presentation** (Christensen, 1981). This means that participants use their perceptions of the experiment to determine how to respond to the experimental task in such a way that they appear most positive.

Consider the experiment conducted by Christensen (1977). In this experiment, an attempt was made to verbally condition the research participants—to increase the participants' use of certain pronouns such as *we* and *they* by saying "good" whenever the participants used one of them. Some participants interpreted the experimenter's reaction of saying "good" as an attempt to manipulate their behavior. These participants resisted any behavioral manifestation of conditioning. This resistance was caused by their viewing being manipulable as negative—if they did not demonstrate any conditioning, then they would show that they could not be manipulated and, in this way, present themselves most positively. Similarly, Bradley (1978) has shown that individuals often take credit for desirable acts but deny blame for undesirable ones to enhance their self-presentation.

Conditions Producing a Positive Self-Presentation Motive.   It would be advantageous to know the conditions that alter participants' behavior in their attempt to attain favorable self-presentations. Only when such conditions are identified can one construct conditions that control for this threat to construct validity.

Some insight into the general conditions that might determine whether or not the self-presentation motive will exist within an experiment was provided by Tedeschi, Schlenker, and Bonoma (1971). These researchers found that this motive is activated when participants believe that others view their behavior as under the internal control of each participant. If participants believe that others view their behavior as being determined by some external source not under their control, then the positive self-presentation motive is not aroused. However, psychological experiments are usually not constructed so that the research participants will believe that others think their behavior is externally determined. Thus, it seems that the positive self-presentation motive will exist in most research studies.

Implications for Research.   The key implication of the positive self-presentation motive is that experimenters must try to ensure that participant perceptions are held constant across the groups throughout all phases and conditions of the experiment. When such constancy is not maintained, alternative explanations of findings can be expected to occur because of the interaction of the motive of

---

Positive self-presentation Participants' motivation to respond in such a way as to present themselves in the most positive manner

positive self-presentation with the experimental treatment condition. Some individual differences in interpretation of the research situation always will be present. However, it can be helpful to sometimes conduct postexperimental interviews with participants to identify how they viewed the situation and modify your conclusion if a problem is found. Also, postexperiment interviews can provide useful information for writing future experimental instructions and determining how future experiments can be presented that will help minimize participant reactivity.

Experimenter Effects You have just seen that participants in psychological research are neither apathetic nor willing to passively accept and follow the experimenter's instructions. Rather, they have motives that can affect the results and threaten the validity of the inferences you make about the independent variable construct. In a like manner, the experimenter is not just a passive, noninteractive observer but an active agent who can influence the outcome of the experiment. These experimenter influences are called the **experimenter effects.** These effects can be intentional or unintentional. Although we will not go into the literature in depth here, the evidence indicates that experimenter expectancy effects can be large and that precautions should be taken against them.

> **Experimenter effects** Actions and characteristics of researchers that influence the responses of participants

Consider the motives that experimenters might bring to the experiment. First, an experimenter has a specific motive for conducting the experiment. The experimenter is a scientist attempting to uncover the regularities of nature through experimentation. The scientist seeks to understand, control, and predict behavior. To attain this goal, the scientist must eliminate participant effects, and so the researcher hopes for ideal research participants, who are open and honest and unbiased. The experimenter also has expectations about the outcome of the experiment and hopes the hypotheses will be confirmed. In addition, because of the policy of journals, studies supporting hypotheses have a greater chance of being accepted for publication. Can the researcher's desires and expectations bias the results of the experiment and increase the probability of attaining the desired outcome? Consider the fascinating story of Clever Hans. Clever Hans (shown in Figure 6.1) was a remarkable horse that appeared to solve arithmetic problems. Von Osten, the master of Clever Hans, would give Hans a problem, and then Hans would give the correct answer by tapping with his hoof. Pfungst (1911/1965) observed and studied this incredible behavior. Careful scrutiny revealed that von Osten would, as Hans approached the correct answer, look up at Hans. This response of looking up presented a cue for Hans to stop tapping his foot. The cue was unintentional and not noticed by observers, who attributed mathematical skills to the horse.

Observations, going as far back as Pfungst's observations, indicate that researchers' desires and expectancies can somehow be communicated to participants and that participants will respond to them. As discussed, research participants are motivated to present themselves in the most positive manner. If this is true, then the subtle cues presented by the experimenter in an experimental session are picked up by participants and influence their performance in the direction desired by the experimenter. Consequently, the experimenter represents a demand characteristic.

FIGURE 6.1
Picture of Clever
Hans and his owner,
Wilhelm von Osten.

(From Archives of the
History of American
Psychology—The
University of Akron.)

The experimenter can also unintentionally influence the recording of data to support the research prediction. Kennedy and Uphoff (1939) investigated the frequency of misrecording of responses as a function of research participants' orientation. Participants, classified on the basis of their belief or disbelief in extrasensory perception (ESP), were requested to record the guesses made by the receiver. The receiver was supposedly trying to receive messages sent by a transmitter. Kennedy and Uphoff found that 63% of the errors that were in the direction of increasing the telepathic scores were made by believers in ESP, whereas 67% of the errors that were in the direction of lowering the telepathic scores were made by disbelievers. Such data indicate that biased recording, unintentional as it might be, can exist in some experiments.

Experimenter effects can affect research participants. In particular, bias can arise because of experimenter expectancies and attributes of the experimenter. **Experimenter expectancies** are biasing effects that can be attributed to the expectancies an experimenter has about the outcome of an experiment. These expectancies can lead experimenters to behave unintentionally in ways that result in the research participant providing responses that support the experimenter's hypothesis, thus biasing the results of the experiment. **Experimenter attributes** are physical and psychological characteristics of experimenters that can produce changes in performance by research participants. Rosenthal (1966) classified experimenter attributes into three categories. First is *biosocial attributes*, which includes factors such as the experimenter's age, sex, race, and religion. Second is *psychosocial attributes*. These attributes include experimenter characteristics that must be psychometrically determined, such as anxiety level, need for social approval, hostility, authoritarianism, intelligence, and dominance and social behavior of relative status and warmth. The third category is *situational*

Experimenter expectancies

Biasing experimenter effects attributable to the researcher's expectations about the outcome of the experiment

Experimenter attributes

Biasing experimenter effects attributable to the physical and psychological characteristics of the researcher *factors.* This includes whether the experimenter and the participant have had prior contact, whether the experimenter is a naive or experienced researcher, and whether the participant is friendly or hostile.

Although experimenter expectancies and experimenter attributes can alter the nature of the construct presented to the research participants and the results of the study, this does not mean that they will necessarily do so. Sufficient empirical information does not exist to identify exactly when and under what conditions experimenter effects will influence the outcome of an experiment. However, because we know that they can sometimes have an effect, controls for these effects should be incorporated into our studies. We explain some of the control procedures in the next chapter.

STUDY QUESTIONS 6.2

- **What is construct validity, and why is it important?**
- **What are some threats to construct validity?**
- **What is meant by *reactivity to the experimental situation*, and how does this bias the results of a psychological experiment?**
- **What is meant by the *experimenter effect*, and how does this bias the results of a psychological experiment?**

Internal Validity

Internal validity
The correctness of inferences made by researchers about cause and effect

Identifying cause-and-effect relationships is perhaps the most frequent purpose of psychological research, and internal validity is concerned specifically and only with the issue of causation. **Internal validity** is the "approximate validity with which we infer that a relationship between two variables is causal" (Cook & Campbell, 1979, p. 37). It is the degree to which you can justifiably claim from your empirical research study that changes in the independent variable caused changes in the dependent variable.

In Chapter 2, we pointed out that there are three "required conditions" that must be met if you are going to make a claim of cause and effect. You can make a cause-and-effect claim only when (1) you have obtained strong evidence that the presumed cause and effect variables are related, (2) the cause precedes the effect, and (3) no plausible alternative explanation for the relationship exists. These three "required conditions" for making a claim of cause and effect are summarized in Table 2.2 (in Chapter 2, page 34). Please take a moment to look at that table again; it is important that you memorize those three conditions and apply them when you wish to make a claim of cause and effect.

Internal validity boils down to ensuring that the observed effect, as measured by the dependent variable, is caused *only* by the variation in your independent variable. That's another way of stating required condition 3 (no alternative explanation exists for the observed relationship). This requirement is the most difficult to achieve because the dependent variable can be influenced by variables other than the independent variable. For example, you might investigate the influence of tutoring (independent variable) on grades (dependent variable). Assume that you do *not* use the strongest experimental design (which has random assignment to the groups to equate them on all extraneous variables at the start of the study), and you provide tutoring to the students in one class and no tutoring to the students in another class. If the students receiving tutoring show more improvement in their grades than the students not receiving tutoring, you might want to conclude that the difference is due to the tutoring. However, an alternative explanation exists. What if the tutored students were brighter than those who were not tutored? Perhaps the superior performance by tutored students was due to the fact that the tutored students were brighter. In such an instance, intelligence or prior achievement would represent an alternative explanation for the relationship you observed between your independent and dependent variables. This alternative explanation is due to the presence of an *extraneous variable* that could have confounded the results. If a confounding extraneous variable creeps into an experiment, the researcher cannot claim that a causal relationship exists between the independent and dependent variables because an alternative explanation exists.

Confounding

Occurs when an extraneous variable co-occurs with the independent variable and affects the dependent variable

Confounding, therefore, occurs when the research study contains a variable that systematically varies with the independent variable and this variable also affects the dependent variable. This is an important point because extraneous variables might or might not introduce a confound. The only extraneous variables that can introduce a confound are extraneous variables that *systematically* vary with the independent variable and cause changes in the dependent variable. In our example, any difference in the dependent variable of grades could be due to the tutoring, the difference in intelligence levels of the tutored and nontutored students, or some combination of these two variables. The key point is that it is impossible to tell what caused the grade difference because the influence of the extraneous variable of intelligence was confounded with the influence of tutoring, and this leaves you in an ambiguous situation where you have to be silent about causation.

Confounding extraneous variable

An extraneous variable that co-occurs with the independent variable and affects the dependent variable

If the extraneous variable of intelligence did not systematically vary with the independent variable of tutoring, it would not represent a confounding extraneous variable. If the students who received and did not receive tutoring were of the same intelligence level, any difference in grades could not be attributed to intelligence. Intelligence level, in this case, would represent an extraneous variable, but it would not represent a **confounding extraneous variable**. It is necessary to control only for the influence of confounding extraneous variables in order to attain internal validity. Unfortunately, you often will not know if an extraneous variable represents a confound or not. Therefore, you must attempt to control for any and all extraneous variables that you believe might systematically vary with your independent variable and affect the dependent variable. Remember this key point: Good researchers are always looking out for confounding extraneous variables.

Threats to Internal Validity

The purpose of many research studies is to obtain evidence that a cause-and-effect relationship exists. However, extraneous variables that could confound the results of the study must be controlled to achieve internal validity. Because the concept of internal validity was developed in the context of experimental research and because experiments offer the best way to study cause and effect, the remainder of this section focuses on threats to internal validity in experimental research. However, if you ever conduct a nonexperimental study, the same three conditions required to establish cause and effect must be met. When attempting to establish cause and effect in a nonexperimental research study, the key idea is to conduct a nonexperimental study that *approximates* a strong experimental design as closely as possible. This would include using strategies such as theoretical modeling, hypothesis testing, and control strategies that are available (e.g., path analysis, statistical control, matching, longitudinal data).

Controlling for the effect of extraneous variables does not mean totally eliminating their influence because eliminating the influence of many extraneous variables—such as intelligence, past experience, or history of reinforcement—is not possible. The key strategy is to eliminate any *differential* influence that these variables have across the various levels of the independent variable. This means that we must keep the influence of these variables **constant** across the various levels of the independent variable. In other words, your goal is to **equate the groups** (which form the levels of the independent variable) on all extraneous variables that could confound the results. For example, in our tutoring example above, you would need to make sure that the two groups (tutoring group and nontutoring group) were equivalent on intelligence and prior knowledge (and any additional extraneous variables that you are worried about). If you make the two groups the same on these variables, then any difference found on the dependent variable cannot be due to those extraneous variables. Remember: The key idea is to "equate your groups."

How is this constancy achieved? That is, how do we arrange factors so that extraneous variables are equated across the groups and do not differentially influence the results? The only way is through some type of control. Control means exerting a constant influence. Thus, if we wanted to hold constant the trait of dominance, we would attempt to make sure that this trait had an equal influence on all groups of participants.

Control, or achieving constancy, is relatively easy to accomplish if you can identify the potentially confounding extraneous variables. The difficulty frequently lies in identifying the problematic extraneous variables. Shadish et al. (2002) have identified a number of extraneous variables that have been shown to affect a study. We discuss these next. These extraneous variables are threats to the internal validity of a study and must be controlled if the researcher intends to infer that a causal relationship exists between the independent and dependent variables.

History The first threat to internal validity is called **history**. History refers to any event that can produce the outcome, other than the treatment, that occurs after the beginning of the study but before the posttest measurement of the dependent variable. The basic history threat is a problem in a one-group experimental design, such as the design depicted in Figure 6.2(a). Look at the design in the figure and notice that participants are measured on the dependent variable at the pretest and the posttest, and the treatment is administered between these two test points. A history threat exists in this one-group design if an event occurs

Constancy
The influence of an extraneous variable is same on all of the independent variable groups

Equating the groups
Using control strategies to make the influence of extraneous variables constant across the independent variable groups so that the only systematic *difference* between the groups is due to the influence of the independent variable

History
Any event that can produce the outcome, other than the treatment condition, that occurs during the study before posttest measurement

FIGURE 6.2
Demonstration of basic history effect in one-group design and two-group design and differential history effect in two-group design. It is a threat to internal validity in (a) and (c) but not in (b) because in (b) the history event does not cause the groups to become different on the history extraneous variable.

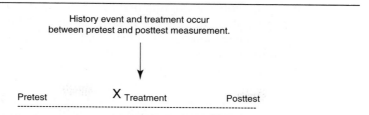

History event and treatment occur between pretest and posttest measurement.

Pretest   X Treatment   Posttest

(a) One group design where history event occurs between pretest and posttest measurement of the dependent variable.

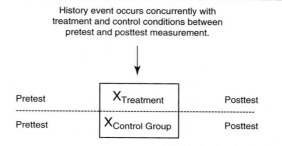

History event occurs concurrently with treatment and control conditions between pretest and posttest measurement.

Pretest   XTreatment   Posttest

Prettest   XControl Group   Posttest

(b) Two group design where history event occurs in both treatment and control conditions.

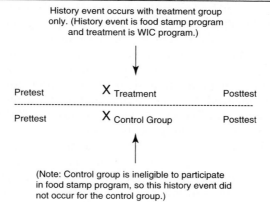

History event occurs with treatment group only. (History event is food stamp program and treatment is WIC program.)

Pretest   X Treatment   Posttest

Prettest   X Control Group   Posttest

(Note: Control group is ineligible to participate in food stamp program, so this history event did not occur for the control group.)

(c) Two group design where history event occurs only with the treatment condition (i.e., it's a differential history event).

(other than the treatment) that can affect the dependent variable. If this situation happens, the treatment and history event would both occur between the pretest and the posttest, and you would not know if a pretest-to-posttest improvement was due to the treatment or history event because you cannot separate their influences.

For example, Schoenthaler (1983) investigated the impact of a dietary change on violent and aggressive behaviors of institutionalized juveniles. A record of such behaviors was maintained for each inmate for 3 months prior to, as well as 3 months after, the dietary change program. The results of this study revealed that the mean number of violent and aggressive behaviors exhibited during the 3 months prior to the dietary change was significantly greater than the mean number of such behaviors exhibited after the dietary change. Schoenthaler concluded that the dietary change program was responsible for the reduction in violent and aggressive behavior. Although this might be true, it is important to realize that 6 months elapsed between the beginning of the pretesting and the completion of the posttesting, and many other events that took place during this time might have accounted for the improvement in behavior. Schoenthaler realized this and considered a variety of alternative explanations, such as system-wide changes that coincided with the introduction of the dietary alteration. Although these rival hypotheses did not seem to be supported by facts and apparently could not explain the observed change in violent and aggressive behavior, there was another alternative explanation that was not controlled and that might explain the observed results. The juveniles who participated in the study were institutionalized for the entire 6-month period. It is reasonable to expect that institutionalization itself should, over time, reduce the frequency of violent and aggressive behavior and that a 6-month period should be sufficient to induce such a reduction.

This history event in the one-group design would have been controlled if Schoenthaler had included a control group in the design. Look at the design depicted in Figure 6.2(b). It is a two-group design that includes a treatment group and a control group. If Schoenthaler had included a control group of participants similar to those in the treatment groups, and if both of these groups were institutionalized, then any difference in the reduction in violent and aggressive behavior could not be attributed to institutionalization because both groups were institutionalized. The key point is that the basic history threat is a problem for the one-group design shown in Figure 6.2(a), but it is not a problem when a control group is added, as long as the history event affects both of the groups in the control-group design, such as the one depicted in Figure 6.2(b). In short, addition of the control group in Figure 6.2(b) fixed the problem shown in Figure 6.2(a).

Unfortunately, we are not out of the woods yet. The problem of differential history is shown in Figure 6.2(c). **Differential history** occurs when one group experiences the history event, but the other group does not. When differential history operates, the groups become different on the history variable, which is problematic because the groups should only differ on the levels of the independent variable; they should not be different on any extraneous variables. Here's an example. Shadish and Reis (1984) revealed that women who participated in the experimental group of the federal Women, Infants, and Children (WIC) program to improve their pregnancy outcome by improving their nutritional intake were also eligible for and probably participated in the food stamps program. Because the food stamps program could also lead to better nutrition and improve pregnancy outcomes, it represented a history threat in studies attempting to demonstrate the efficacy of the WIC program. This idea of a history event affecting only one group in a two-group design (i.e., differential history) is illustrated in Figure 6.2(c).

Differential history
The groups in a multigroup design experience different history events that result in differences on the dependent variable

The women in the experimental group of the WIC program received the WIC treatment condition, *but they also experienced the history event* (i.e., participation in the food stamp program). The women in the control group experienced neither the WIC treatment nor the history event. This means that if the experimental and control groups differed at the end of the experiment, the researcher would not know if the outcome was due to the new treatment or to the food stamps. Therefore, the researcher could not legitimately claim that the new treatment was "the cause" of the improved pregnancy outcomes.

Generally speaking, the longer the time lapse of a research study, the greater the possibility of history becoming a rival explanation. But, it is possible that history effects can occur in short time periods as well. Researchers must always be on the lookout for history effects and should use designs that help neutralize and eliminate the history threat. A key point is that adding a control group to the one-group design is an effective way to eliminate the basic history threat, as shown by moving from the design in Figure 6.2(a) to the improved design in Figure 6.2(b); however, this inclusion of a control group will not fix the problem of differential history, which is shown in Figure 6.2(c).

Maturation

Any physical or mental change that occurs with the passage of time and affects dependent variable scores

Maturation   This threat refers to changes in the internal conditions of the individual that occur as a function of the passage of time. The changes involve both biological and psychological processes, such as age, learning, fatigue, boredom, and hunger that are not related to specific external events but reside within the individual. To the extent that such natural changes affect the individual's performance on the dependent variable measurement, they create internal invalidity.

Consider a study that attempts to evaluate the benefits achieved from a Head Start program. Assume the investigator gave the participants an achievement test at the beginning of the school year (i.e., the pretest) and again at the end of the school year (the posttest). (This is the one-group design just shown in Figure 6.2(a).) In comparing the pretest and posttest achievement measures, the investigator found that a significant increase in achievement existed and concluded that the Head Start program was beneficial. Unfortunately, this study is internally invalid because there was no control for maturational influence. The increased achievement could have been due to the changes that occurred with the passage of time. A group of children who did not participate in Head Start might have progressed an equal amount. In order to determine the effect of a program such as Head Start, a control group that does not receive the treatment (and is very similar to the treatment group participants in every other way) should be included to control for the potential rival influence of maturation.

Instrumentation

Changes from pretest to posttest in the assessment or measurement of the dependent variable

Instrumentation   This threat refers to changes that occur over time (i.e., during the course of the study) in the measurement of the dependent variable. This class of confounding extraneous variables does not refer to participant changes but to changes that occur in the measurement process. For example, the problem will be present if the measurement process at the pretest is different from the measurement process at the posttest in a design lacking a control group such as the one-group design shown in Figure 6.2(a).

Measurement procedures that require use of human observers are the most likely to have instrumentation error. Physical measurements show minor changes, but human observers are subject to such influences as fatigue, boredom, and learning processes. In administering intelligence tests, novice testers typically gain facility and skill over time and collect more reliable and valid data as additional tests are given. Observers and interviewers are often used to assess the effects of various experimental treatments. As the observers and interviewers assess more and more individuals, they gain skill. The interviewers might, for example, gain additional skill with the interview schedule or with observing a particular type of behavior, producing shifts in the response measure that cannot be attributed to either the participant or the treatment conditions. This is why studies that use human observers typically use more than one observer and have each of the observers go through a training program. In this way, some of the biases can be minimized, and the observers can serve as checks on one another to ensure that accurate data are collected. Typically, the data collected by the multiple observers must coincide before they are considered valid.

Testing effect

Changes in a person's score on the second administration of a test resulting from having previously taken the test

Testing   This threat refers to changes in the scores participants make on the second administration of a test that result from having previously taken the test. In other words, the experience of taking a test at the pretest can alter the results obtained on a second administration of the same test at the posttest. Taking a test does a number of things that can alter a person's performance on a subsequent administration of the same test. Taking a pretest can sensitize you to the test topic or issues related to the topic. Taking a test also gives you practice with taking the test and familiarizes you with the content of the test. After taking a test, you might think about the errors you made that could be corrected if the test were taken over. When the test is administered a second time, you are already familiar with it and you might remember some of your prior responses. This can lead to an enhanced performance entirely tied to the initial or pretest administration. Any alteration in performance as a result of a testing effect threatens the internal validity of a study because it serves as an alternative explanation or rival hypothesis to the claim that performance on the second administration of a test was due to the treatment. As with the previous threats, this threat in its basic form is problematic for the one-group design in Figure 6.2(a), but adding a control group as in Figure 6.2(b) usually eliminates this threat.

Regression Artifact   Many psychological studies involve the selection of research participants that have high (or low) scores on a measure. For example, when studying anxiety you might select participants with high anxiety scores. When studying functional illiteracy, you might select participants with very low reading scores. This makes a lot of sense because the purpose of this sort of research is to find ways to improve participants' status on these dependent variables. Unfortunately, the threat to internal validity known as regression artifact operates when participants are selected based on extreme (high or low) scores. Participants with very high scores have a tendency to decrease and participants with very low scores have a tendency to increase *without any treatment from the* *pretest to the posttest measurement.* The participants with the most extreme scores (highest or lowest) at one time of measurement are likely to be different from the participants with the most extreme scores at the next time of measurement. Here is a formal definition from the founder of the threat (Campbell): **Regression artifacts** are "pseudoeffects that appear to be effects due to some supposed causal variable (e.g., an intervention) but are nothing more than regression toward the mean" (Campbell & Kenny, 1999, p. 37). This phenomenon is also called **regression toward the mean** because very high scores and very low scores tend to show the most movement toward the mean from pretest to posttest measurement. More simply, regression artifacts can be viewed as the "*you can only go up (or down) from here phenomenon*" (Trochim, 2001).

Here's an example. You conduct a study investigating the efficacy of a new type of psychotherapy for treating depression. You put up a notice asking participants to volunteer. The study probably will be most attractive to individuals when they are feeling very depressed. Because they come to the study when they are very depressed, they are likely to be less depressed on subsequent occasions. This type of regression artifact is illustrated in Figure 6.3. Such a decline in depression is due to a regression artifact and threatens the internal validity of a study such as this one because the change is not due to the treatment.

If you select participants based on very high or very low scores and use the one-group pretest–posttest design shown earlier in Figure 6.2(a), some or all of the change from pretest to posttest might be due to the regression artifact problem. You will not know if the change is due to the treatment or if it is due to the operation of a regression artifact. There is a solution that usually solves the problem,

Regression artifacts
Effects that appear to be due to the treatment but are due to regression to the mean

Regression toward the mean
A synonym for regression artifacts

FIGURE 6.3
Illustration of a regression artifact.

however. If you use two similar groups in the two-group design shown in Figure 6.2(b), the regression artifact is not problematic, because even if regression occurs, the *difference* between the groups will not be due to a regression artifact. If you ever select participants based on extreme scores, you should be on the lookout for a regression artifact, and you should always include a control group in this situation.

Attrition Some individuals do not complete a research study for a variety of reasons, such as failure to show up at the scheduled time and place or not participating in all phases of the study. This dropping out of the research study is called **attrition**. Most psychological experiments, both human and infrahuman, must contend with this potential source of bias at some time. Physiological experiments involving electrode implantation sometimes experience participant loss because of the complications that arise from the surgical procedures. Human experiments must contend with participants who do not show up for the experiment at the designated time and place or do not participate in all the conditions required by the study. Attrition is not an internal validity problem in the one-group design, although it will negatively affect your ability to generalize the results—you will be able to only generalize to the kinds of people who stayed in the study. The internal validity problem with attrition arises not just because participants are lost, but because the loss of participants might produce *differences* in the groups that cannot be attributed to the experimental treatment—it is a threat to internal validity in the two-group design shown in Figure 6.2(b), and it is called **differential attrition**.

Consider the following example. Assume that you want to test the effect of a certain treatment condition designed to increase participants' conformity to authority. Also assume that past research has demonstrated that females conform to a greater degree than males do, so you control for this factor by assigning an equal number of males and females to two groups. When you actually run the experiment, however, half of the male participants assigned to the group that received the experimental treatment condition (i.e., the treatment group) do not show up and half of the female participants assigned to the group that does not receive the treatment condition (i.e., the control group) do not show up. Because of differential attrition, your treatment group is now heavily female constituted and the control group is heavily male constituted. Statistical analysis reveals that the treatment group, on average, conforms significantly more than does the control group. Can you conclude that this significantly greater degree of conformity in the treatment group is caused by the independent variable administered? Such an inference would be incorrect because the treatment group had a greater percentage of female participants, and past research indicates that females exhibit a greater degree of conformity. This extraneous variable (i.e., gender), and not the independent variable (treatment vs. no treatment), could have produced the observed significant difference. When participants drop out from your study, you should always attempt to determine if your groups have become *different* on an extraneous variable that could confound the results. You must always remember the cardinal rule of experimentation: You want your groups to differ because of exposure to the independent variable and not because of an extraneous variable.

Selection The threat known as **selection** exists when a *differential* selection procedure is used for placing research participants in the various comparison

Attrition
Loss of participants because they don't show up or they drop out of the research study

Differential attrition
In a multigroup design, groups become different on an extraneous variable because of differences in the loss of participants across the groups

Selection
Production of nonequivalent groups because a different selection procedure operates across the groups

groups. Ideally, participants are randomly assigned to the various experimental groups (e.g., to the treatment and control groups). Random assignment is the best procedure for equating groups (i.e., constructing groups that are very unlikely to differ on any extraneous variable). When random assignment to groups cannot be used, there is a high probability that rival hypotheses are introduced ("required condition 3"). Assume that you conduct the conformity study mentioned in the previous paragraph and that you did not randomly assign participants to the treatment and control groups. Also assume that you were not aware of any research literature showing that females are more likely to conform than males. Because of the lack of random assignment of participants to the two groups, the two groups might differ on many extraneous variables *including gender*. After administration of the treatment, you find that the treatment group exhibits more conformity on average than the control-group participants. Can you claim that this difference between the groups is because of the treatment? You should not make this claim. The groups can differ on extraneous variables, which might be the cause of the observed group differences. In this case, if the treatment group had a higher percentage of female participants, then it is quite likely that gender (rather than the treatment) is the cause of the difference between the groups on the dependent variable.

Additive and Interactive Effects   Validity threats do not necessarily operate in isolation. **Additive and interactive effects** refer to the fact that the threats to internal validity can combine to produce complex biases. Of special importance, the selection threat can combine with history, maturation, instrumentation, testing, and regression artifacts. When selection is a problem, your groups are composed of different kinds of people; therefore, the different groups might react differently to the threats. A **selection-history** effect occurs when the groups are exposed to the same history event but react to it differently. This can happen when the groups are composed of different kinds of people. A **selection-maturation** effect occurs if the groups mature at different rates. This can happen when the groups are composed of different kinds of people. For example, if you were testing a literacy treatment, you would not want one group to be composed of 6-year-olds and the comparison group to be composed of 10-year-olds because 6-year-olds naturally improve more on reading (even without the treatment). A **selection-instrumentation** effect occurs if the groups respond differently to an instrumentation effect because they are composed of different kinds of people. A **selection-testing** effect occurs if testing affects the groups differently because they are composed of different kinds of people. A **selection-regression artifact** effect occurs if a regression artifact affects the groups differently because they are composed of different kinds of people.

A key idea here is that when the validity threats operate in combination, such as the ones just mentioned, the groups in a multigroup design will differ not just on the levels of the independent variable (e.g., treatment vs. control), which is what is desired; the groups will also be different because of the operation of extraneous variables, and you will not know if the difference between the groups' scores on the dependent variable at the end of the experiment is due to the independent variable or if it is due to a confounding extraneous variable. Another key point, that we will

---

Additive and interactive effects
Differences between groups is produced because of the combined effect of two or more threats to internal validity

Selection-history
The groups are exposed to the same history event, but they react differently because they were not equated

Selection-maturation
The groups undergo different rates of maturation because they were not equated

Selection-instrumentation
The groups react to changes in instrumentation differently because they were not equated

Selection-testing
The groups react to the pretest differently, because they were not equated

Selection-regression artifact
The groups show different amounts of regression to the mean, because they were not equated

explain in greater detail in later chapters, is that the best solution to the problems caused by the threats to internal validity discussed in this chapter is to construct the groups at the beginning of your experiment using random assignment; this process helps ensure that the groups will not systematically differ on any extraneous variable. When an experimental research study uses random assignment to the groups, you should upgrade your assessment of that study's ability to provide strong evidence of cause and effect.

STUDY QUESTIONS 6.3

- **What is meant by internal validity, and why is it important?**
- **What is the principle of constancy, and why is it important?**
- **What are the threats to internal validity, and how does each threaten internal validity?**

External Validity

External validity
Degree to which the study results can be generalized to and across other people, settings, treatments, outcomes, and times

Internal validity focused on whether you could claim that a cause-and-effect relationship was present for the participants in your single research study. The fourth major type of validity, called **external validity**, focuses on whether a researcher can generalize the research findings to other people, settings, treatments, outcomes, and times. External validity is an inferential process because it involves making broad statements based only on limited information. Stating that a particular study conducted on 100 college students in a psychology laboratory is fully *externally valid* would imply that the results obtained from the experiment are true for all college students responding in a variety of settings to variations in the treatment and outcome measures, and at different times. Researchers hope to make these kinds of inferences because one of the most important goals of psychological research is to identify regularities in human thinking and behavior. Generalization is a major goal of scientific research.

In order to generalize the results of a study, you must identify a target population of people, settings, treatment variations, outcome measures, and times and try to use representative samples of these. In an ideal research world, you would be able to randomly select individuals from these populations so that the sample would be representative of the defined population. For a variety of reasons (e.g., cost, time, accessibility), most experimental research studies are not based on a random sample from the defined population. Failure to randomly select participants means that the study will probably contain characteristics that will threaten its external validity. In short, one reason for lack of generalizability of a set of findings is the lack of random selection. Another reason for the lack of generalizability of the research findings from a single research study is because of chance factors. Findings usually vary slightly from study to study because of the operation of chance, but occasionally this variation will be large simply because of the operation of chance. This is why *replication* is so important in scientific research. Another major reason for the lack of generalizability of research findings is because sometimes the relationship between an independent variable and the dependent variable varies across the levels of another independent variable. For example, if one attitude change procedure works best with females and another works best with males, then the results are specific to each gender. In this situation, the finding does not generalize broadly to everyone (i.e., to males *and* females), and your mission will be to correctly specify to whom a finding does and does not generalize.

Now we cover the major types of external validity and some of the associated threats. The types of external validity fall into five broad categories: population validity, ecological validity, treatment variation validity, outcome validity, and time validity (Bracht & Glass, 1968; Shadish et al., 2002; Wilson, 1981). The key points are going to be that your results might not generalize to other people (population validity), other settings (ecological validity), other treatments (treatment variation validity), other outcomes (outcome validity), or other times (temporal validity). It is essential that a researcher knows how research findings can be generalized and understands the threats to generalization.

Population Validity

Population validity refers to the ability to generalize from the sample on which your study is conducted to the larger population of individuals in which you are interested. The **target population** is the larger population (such as all college students) to whom you hope to generalize the results of your study, and the **accessible population** is the population that is available. For example, you might want to generalize to all young adults in the United States, but you have access only to college students at your university. As illustrated in Figure 6.4, two

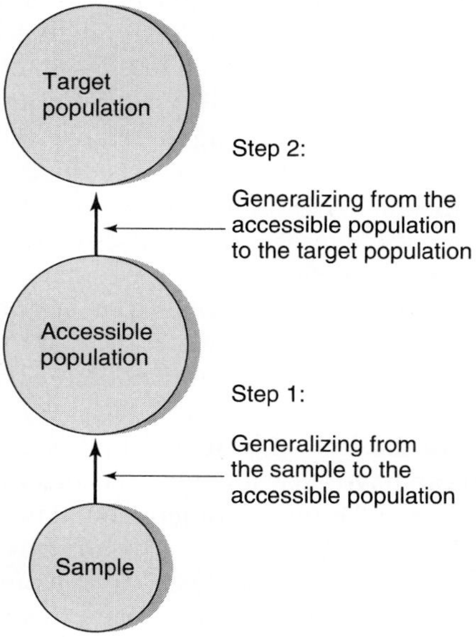

Population validity
Degree to which the study results can be generalized to and across the people in the target population

Target population
The large population to which the researcher would like to generalize the study results

Accessible population
The population of research participants that is practically available to the investigator

FIGURE 6.4
Two-step inferential process involved in generalizing from the sample to the target population.

Target population

Step 2:

Generalizing from the accessible population to the target population

Accessible population

Step 1:

Generalizing from the sample to the accessible population

Sample

inferential steps are involved in making a statistical generalization from the results of a research study to the target population. First, the researcher has to generalize from the sample to the accessible population from which the sample was drawn. This step is easily accomplished if the researcher *randomly* selects the sample from the accessible population. If the sample is randomly selected, it should be *representative*, which means that the characteristics of the accessible population can be inferred from the sample. If you conduct a study with a sample of 250 participants randomly selected from a given university, you can say that the obtained results are characteristic of students at that university.

The second step requires moving from the accessible population to the target population. This ultimate generalization seldom can be made with confidence because often the accessible population will not be representative of the target population. For example, assume that you are conducting a research study using college students as your target population. You want to be able to say that the results of your study will hold for all college students in the United States. To be able to make such a statement, however, you must randomly select your sample from the target population of all college students in the United States! For research, where you must physically meet with the participants, you usually will have to settle for randomly selecting from a nonrepresentative but accessible population. Because many research studies are based on nonrandom samples, generalization of findings usually is obtained through replication instead of directly generalizing from a single sample to a target population.

Most of this discussion about population thus far has been about generalizing the characteristics of a study sample (e.g., sample averages, differences between means in the sample, and correlations between variables based on the sample data) to the characteristics of the target population (e.g., population averages, differences between means in the population, and correlations between variables in the population). This is sometimes called "generalizing *to* a population." Random sampling is especially strong in allowing one to generalize from sample characteristics to population characteristics. However, another major issue in generalizing is to what extent a sample finding generalizes across the different kinds of people in sample and in the population. This is called "generalizing *across* a population" (Cook & Campbell, 1979), and it refers to how broadly a finding applies. For example, perhaps the average on a self-esteem scale is 80 in your sample. Does this mean that all the males and all the females got an 80? Does it mean that everyone in the sample got an 80? Does it mean that everyone in the population would obtain a score of 80 if they were to fill out the scale? The key point here is that some research findings generalize better than other findings *across* all of the people.

Here are some examples of the lack of generalization *across* people. Research shows that men and women can have very different reactions to drugs (Neergaard, 1999). First, morphine controls pain better in women than in men. Second, women reject heart transplants more often than men do, which might be due to the fact that antirejection drugs such as cyclosporine clear out of women's bodies faster. Third, aspirin seems to thin men's blood better than that of women. These gender differences have resulted in the Food and Drug Administration's requiring drug manufacturers to analyze how different sexes respond to experimental therapies. The issue of lack of generalization across people is not a problem that can be solved with random sampling. It is just an empirical fact of our world that some findings generalize only to certain kinds of people. This is frequently examined in research by collecting data on the characteristics of the people and determining for whom the findings apply, and following this with additional research to determine why this happens.

Ecological Validity

Ecological validity
The degree to which the results of a study can be generalized across settings or environmental conditions

Ecological validity refers to the generalizability of the results of a study across different settings or from one set of environmental conditions to another. Laboratory experiments are sometimes criticized for a lack of ecological validity. If the results of a laboratory experiment can be generalized to nonlaboratory settings (such as a therapy setting or a labor relations setting), then the experiment possesses ecological validity. Ecological validity exists to the extent that the treatment effect is independent of the experimental setting. If a treatment effect depends on the experimental setting, then ecological validity does not exist. Kazdin (1992), for example, described a particular treatment for drug abusers that worked for individuals living in rural areas; however, the treatment did not work with individuals living in urban areas. Ecological validity boils down to whether a finding generalizes across different settings.

Temporal Validity

Temporal validity
The degree to which the results can be generalized across time

Temporal validity refers to the extent to which the results of an experiment or other type of research study can be generalized across time. For example, Walster (1964) asked army recruits to rate the attractiveness of ten different jobs to which they could be assigned during their enlistment period. After rating the ten jobs, each recruit was asked to choose between two moderately attractive jobs that had been rated similarly. After selecting one of the two, the recruits were asked to rate the attractiveness of the two jobs once again. For one group of recruits, this second rating took place immediately after the job choice was made. For the other three groups, the choice was delayed for 4, 15, or 90 minutes. In Figure 6.5, you can see that there was a change in attractiveness of the chosen job over these time periods. Immediately after making the choice, the draftees found the chosen job more attractive. Within 4 minutes, however, the recruits apparently experienced some degree of regret or had second thoughts about the jobs they had chosen because they rated the job as less attractive. This regret then dissipated rather rapidly. Ratings of the chosen job reached their highest level after 15 minutes, only to return to their original postchoice level within 90 minutes.

Seasonal variation
Values on the dependent variable vary by season

Some more predictable time patterns of results also have been identified. **Seasonal variation** occurs when the values on a dependent variable tend to vary by season. For example, juvenile delinquency tends to increase every summer. This is because during the summer months adolescents are not in school and

FIGURE 6.5
Illustration of how the attractiveness of a chosen job changes across time.

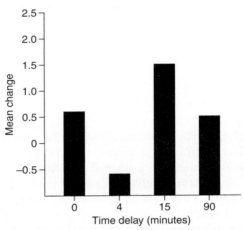

(Based on data from "The Temporal Sequence of Post-Decision Processes" by E. Walster. In L. Festinger (Ed.), *Conflict, decision, and dissonance.* Stanford: Stanford University Press, 1964.)

have more free time to get into trouble. Studies conducted during the summer are, therefore, likely to show more overall juvenile delinquency than studies during other months. Likewise, if you are studying the influence of an advertising campaign on retail sales, you would need to take into account the predictable seasonal variation that sales go up during the December holiday season. Seasonal variation is one type of the more general concept of **cyclical variation**, which can refer to any up-and-down variation that occurs over time. The time period can be short or quite long. A relatively short cyclical variation is the circadian (approximately 24-hour) rhythm on which our pulse rate, temperature, and endocrine and kidney functions operate. Research results might vary on these variables depending on the time of day in which the study is conducted. A longer term and less predictable cyclical variation is the business cycle in which the economy tends to vary between periods of expansion and growth to periods of contraction and recession over multiple years.

Cyclical variation
Any type of systematic up-and-down movement on the dependent variable over time

Treatment Variation Validity

Treatment variation validity refers to the generalizability of results across variations of the treatment. Treatment variation validity is an issue because the administration of a treatment can vary from one administration to the next. For example, many studies have been conducted demonstrating that cognitive-behavior therapy is effective in treating depression. However, these studies have typically been conducted in a way that has provided maximum assurance that the therapists are competent and have delivered the therapy in the prescribed manner. Therapists who administer cognitive-behavior therapy to the general public, however, vary considerably in their competency and the extent

Treatment variation validity
The degree to which the results of a study can be generalized across variations in the treatment

to which they deliver the therapy in the prescribed manner. This means that there is considerable variation in the way the therapy is administered. If cognitive-behavior therapy produces a beneficial effect for the treatment of depression across these different variations in the way it is delivered, treatment variation validity exists. If cognitive-behavior therapy is beneficial only when administered exactly as prescribed and is not beneficial when administered in a slightly different way, then treatment variation validity does not exist.

Outcome Validity

Outcome validity
The degree to which the results of a study can be generalized across different but related dependent variables

Outcome validity refers to the generalizability of results across different but related dependent variables. Many studies investigate the effect of an independent variable on more than one dependent variable. Outcome validity refers to the extent to which the same effect is measured by all related outcome measures. For example, a job-training program is expected to increase the likelihood of a person's getting a job after graduation. This is probably the primary outcome measure of interest. However, an equally important issue is keeping the job. This means that the person must arrive on time, not miss work, work well with others, and demonstrate an acceptable level of performance. The effectiveness of the job-training program might increase the probability of getting a job but have no effect on job retention because it has little impact on these other essential adaptive job skills. If this is the case, the job-training program does not have outcome validity. However, if the job-training program increases the probability of getting a job and also increases the other essential adaptive job skills necessary to keeping a job, the training program has outcome validity.

STUDY QUESTIONS 6.4

- **What is meant by external validity, and why is it important?**
- **What are some factors that can threaten external validity?**
- **What specific sort of generalizability does each of the types of external validity address?**

Relationship between Internal and External Validity

Given our knowledge of the classes of variables that threaten external validity, it would seem logical to design experiments using a diverse sample of research participants, treatment variations, outcome measures, and settings across several different time periods in order to increase external validity. The problem with this strategy is that there tends to be an inverse relationship between internal and external validity. When external validity is increased, internal validity tends to be sacrificed; when internal validity is increased, external validity tends to suffer (Kazdin, 1980).

Experiments tend to have high internal validity (i.e., they provide strong evidence of cause and effect). The researcher conducts the experiment within the confines of a controlled laboratory setting in order to present a specific amount of the treatment condition and to eliminate the influence of extraneous variables, such as the presence of noise or weather conditions. While in the laboratory setting, the research participants receive a set of standardized instructions delivered by one experimenter or perhaps by some automated device and complete outcome measures at one specific point in time. But these same features that maximize the possibility of attaining internal validity—using a restricted sample of research participants and testing them in the artificial setting of a laboratory at one specific time—limit the external validity (Kazdin, 1980) by excluding different people, treatment variations, settings, and times. However, if an experimenter tried to maximize external validity by conducting the experiment on diverse groups of individuals and treatment variations in many settings and at different points in time, control would likely decrease and the experiment's internal validity would decrease. Therefore, external validity of cause-and-effect relationships is often obtained by observing the same cause-and-effect relationship in research studies conducted by different researchers in different settings, with different kinds of people, with slightly different treatments and outcome variables. The type of validity that is most important is a function of the purpose of the research study. If your primary purpose is to determine the relationship between two variables is causal, then internal validity takes priority. However, if prior research has established that a causal relationship exists between the two variables, then the purpose of the study might be to assess the external validity of the causal relationship. In some studies, such as in survey research, your primary research goal might be to make statements about the characteristics of a target population based on a single sample of research participants. In this situation, external validity would be of primary importance.

STUDY QUESTIONS 6.5 | • **How can one maximize internal validity?**
• **How can one maximize external validity?**
• **Why does there tend to be an inverse relationship between internal and external validity?**

Summary

Research validity refers to the truthfulness of the inferences made from a research study. There are four major types of research validity in quantitative research. They are (1) statistical conclusion validity (degree to which a claim about the existence and strength of a reported relationship is correct), (2) construct validity (degree to which a construct is adequately represented by the operations used in the study), (3) internal validity (the correctness of a claim about cause and effect), and (4) external validity (degree to which the results can be generalized to and across other people, settings, treatments, outcomes, and times).

The threats to internal validity (i.e., to one's ability to claim cause and effect) are history, maturation, instrumentation, testing, regression artifacts, attrition, selection, and additive and interactive effects. The threats to internal validity become problematic when they cause the independent variable groups to become different on confounding extraneous variables. A cardinal rule in experimental research is that you want your groups to differ only on the independent variable conditions. The best way to make the groups the same on extraneous variables (called equating the groups) is to use random assignment of participants to the groups. Once you have groups that are similar, you administer the levels of the independent variable and determine if the groups become different on the dependent variable. If they do, you can conclude that the cause was the independent variable.

External validity refers to whether the research can generalize the results. Population validity is present to the degree that you can generalize your results to and across people in the target population. Ecological validity is present to the degree that you can generalize your results to other settings. Treatment variation validity is present to the degree that you can generalize your results to slightly different versions or administrations of the treatment. Outcome validity is present to the degree that you can generalize your results to different but related dependent variables. Last, temporal validity is present to the degree that your results generalize across time.

Key Terms and Concepts

Accessible population
Additive and interactive effects
Attrition
Confounding
Confounding extraneous variable
Constancy
Construct validity
Cyclical variation
Demand characteristics
Differential attrition
Differential history
Ecological validity
Equating the groups
Experimenter attributes
Experimenter effects
Experimenter expectancies
External validity
History
Instrumentation
Internal validity
Maturation

Outcome validity
Participant reactivity to the experimental situation
Population validity
Positive self-presentation
Regression artifacts
Regression toward the mean
Research validity
Seasonal variation
Selection
Selection-history
Selection-instrumentation
Selection-maturation
Selection-regression artifact
Selection-testing
Statistical conclusion validity
Statistically significant
Target population
Temporal validity
Testing
Treatment variation validity

Related Internet Sites

http://www.wadsworth.com/psychology_d/templates/student_resources/workshops/index.html
This site contains a variety of workshops focusing on research methods. To get to the one on reliability and validity, click on the "Research Methods Workshop" link. Then click on the "reliability and validity" workshop link.

http://psych.athabascau.ca/html/Validity/
This site has a tutorial on internal validity. The tutorial exposes the student to each of the threats to internal validity discussed by Campbell and Stanley (1963).

http://www.socialresearchmethods.net/kb/constval.htm
This site discusses construct validity and gives a variety of links that help in understanding construct validity and the threats to construct validity.

http://www.socialresearchmethods.net/kb/external.htm
This site provides a brief discussion of external validity as well as of threats to external validity.

Practice Test

The answers to these questions can be found in the publisher's Web site.

1. When we talk about the validity of psychological research studies we are referring to
   a. Statistical conclusion validity
   b. Internal validity
   c. Construct validity
   d. External validity
   e. All of the above

2. If a research study permits you to accurately infer that the independent variable is the cause of the changes observed in the dependent variable, then you have a study
   a. That is worthwhile
   b. That has internal validity
   c. That has statistical conclusion validity
   d. That has construct validity
   e. That has external validity

3. Dr. Know conducted an experiment on youth violence and found that his treatment was effective when he conducted it at the Strickland Youth Center; so he also tried it at the Boys Club, testing which threat to external validity?
   a. Population validity threat
   b. Ecological validity threat
   c. Temporal validity threat
   d. Outcome validity threat
   e. Treatment variation validity threat

4. If a research study revealed that the independent and dependent variables covary in the study sample, and they really do covary in the population, the study has
   a. Been demonstrated to be worthwhile
   b. Revealed a causal relationship
   c. Internal validity
   d. Statistical conclusion validity
   e. Experimental validity

5. John Brown has signed up for a social psychology study. His friend just completed the study and told him that he experienced smoke coming into the room while they were completing some questionnaires. His friend told him that he thought the study was investigating a reaction to the smoke and not the response to the questionnaires. When John arrived at the experimental site and heard the experimenter's instructions, he evaluated the things he was told to see if the experiment was actually about the reaction to smoke. John's behavior

a. Represents a positive self-presentation attempt
b. Represents an example of demand characteristics
c. Represents experimental curiosity
d. Represents an example of confounding extraneous variables influencing the experiment
e. Represents an inappropriate behavior on the part of John's friend

6. Dr. Prediction conducted an experiment investigating future predictions of violent behavior and found that children who hurt animals are more likely to become spouse abusers. From the results of this study, he wrote a book that had as its thesis the fact that parents should use children's behavior toward pets as an indication of their future behavior toward others, and if they see them consistently abuse pets, they should get their children some help. In suggesting that his experiment applies to other children, Dr. Prediction assumes that his study

a. Has external validity
b. Has construct validity
c. Has experimental reliability
d. Has internal validity
e. Has eliminated all confounding variables

Challenge Exercises

1. For each of the following research examples, identify the threat to internal validity that could also explain the improvement in math performance. Because a pretest–posttest design is used and the same test is used at both pretest and posttest assessment in many of the examples, there is naturally a potential testing threat. However, there is also another potential threat in each example, and it is this other threat that I want you to identify.

a. Dr. Green was investigating the effect of a compensatory education program in mathematics for first-grade students. This study gave a standardized math achievement test to all first-grade students and, based on the results of this test, identified the first-grade students that scored in the lowest quartile on this test. He then placed these students in the compensatory education program and administered the program for the next 6 months. At the end of the 6-week period, he again administered the standardized math achievement test to these students and found that they had significantly increased their math score and concluded that the compensatory program was effective in remediating poor math performance.

b. Dr. Green was investigating the effect of a compensatory education program in mathematics for first-grade students. This study gave a standardized math achievement test to all first-grade students and administered the program to half of the students for the next 6 months; the other half of students were in the control group. During this 6-month period, a number of families moved and withdrew their children from this school. As it turned out, most of the children from families that moved were in the control group. It also turned out that most of the students who were withdrawn from school were poor math students. At the end of the 6-week period, Dr. Green again administered the standardized math achievement test to the treatment and control-group participants who remained in the study and found that the treatment-group students had increased their math score significantly more than the control-group students. Dr. Green concluded that the compensatory program was effective in remediating poor math performance.

c. Dr. Green was investigating the effect of a compensatory education program in mathematics for first-grade students. This study gave a standardized math achievement test to all first-grade students and then placed these students in the compensatory education program and administered the program for the next 6 weeks. At the end of the 6-week period, he again administered the standardized math achievement test to these students. However, the company from which he purchased the standardized math achievement test had developed an updated and revised form, which was supposed to be better, so he used the new form for the posttest and found that the students had significantly increased their math score at posttesting time. Therefore, Dr. Green concluded that the compensatory program was effective in remediating poor math performance.

d. Dr. Green was investigating the effect of a compensatory education program in mathematics for first-grade students. This study gave a standardized math achievement test to all first-grade students and administered the program to these students for the entire year. At the end of the year, he again administered the standardized math achievement test to these students and found that they had significantly increased their math score and concluded that the compensatory program was effective in remediating poor math performance.

e. Dr. Green was investigating the effect of a compensatory education program in mathematics for first-grade students. This study gave a standardized math achievement test to all first-grade students and then placed these students in the compensatory education program and administered the program for the next 6 weeks. During this 6-week period, *Sesame Street* ran a special program on mathematics concepts, which many of the students watched. Dr. Green encouraged the students to watch this program and even used examples from it when he was teaching to emphasize the concepts he used in his compensatory math program. At the end of the 6-month period, he again administered the standardized math achievement test to these students and found that they had significantly increased their math score and concluded that the compensatory program was effective in remediating poor math performance.

2. For each of the following research examples, identify
   a. The independent variable
   b. The dependent variable
   c. The constructs being investigated
   d. The operations used to represent these constructs
   e. How you would collect evidence indicating the construct validity of the operations

A. Logue and Anderson (2001) were interested in determining whether experienced administrators were more likely than individuals training to be administrators to consider the long-term consequences of their actions. The experienced group of administrators consisted of 44 provosts (chief academic officers) of colleges and universities, and the trainees consisted of 14 individuals enrolled in the American Council on Education Fellows Program (a program that trains individuals to be college and university administrators). One of the measures of long-term consequences was that all participants made a series of 59 hypothetical choices between two monetary alternatives. These alternatives always took the form of "The administrator to whom you report will give your unit $X right now or The administrator to whom you report will give you $20,000 in Y time." The $X amounts varied from $20 to $20,000 in increments of $666, and the Y time periods were 1 week, 10 weeks, 5 months, 10 months, 1.5 years, 3 years, 6 years, and 12 years. The participants had to select one of the two alternatives. Interestingly, when given the choice between choosing a smaller but immediate amount of money versus a larger amount to be received at some time in the future, the experienced administrators were more likely to choose the immediate funding, whereas the trainees were more likely to select the larger future funding.

B. Blascovich, Spencer, Quinn, and Steele (2001) wanted to test the hypothesis that stereotype threat causes an increase in blood pressure among African Americans, but not among European Americans. To test this hypothesis, African American and European American participants were randomly assigned to a high-stereotype or low-stereotype threat condition. In the high-stereotype condition, the experimenter was a European American man presumably from Stanford University who informed the participants about the debate regarding standardized tests—whether they were biased toward particular subcultural groups—and that a new test of intelligence had been developed and asked the participants to take the new test to obtain a nationally representative sample. In the low-stereotype condition, the experimenter was an African American man presumably from Stanford University. He noted the debate about the use of standardized tests and said he wanted them to take a new culturally unbiased test. He further noted that prior studies had indicated that the test was unbiased. All participants then completed the Remote Associates Test, which consists of presenting three words and asking the participants to generate a fourth word related to the three they see. Arterial blood pressure of the participants was taken prior to hearing the instructions and continuously while they took the Remote Associates Test.

CHAPTER

Control Techniques in Experimental Research

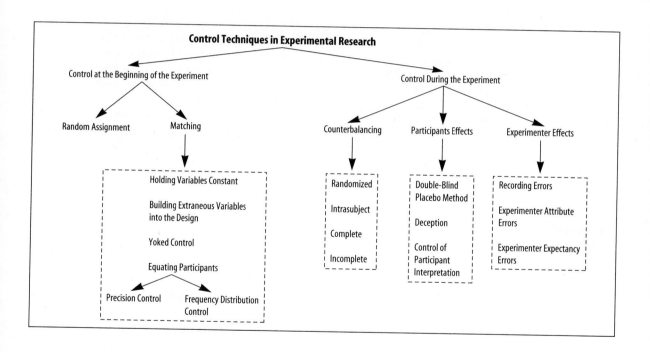

One of the areas that has attracted considerable attention over the past several decades is the effect of diet on behavior. The increased attention and interest have come from both researchers and practitioners. For example, several years ago, the parents of a 4-year-old child found that he would suddenly become extremely disobedient and even rather violent. He would start running around in circles, and, when his parents tried to restrain him, would run away from them as fast as he could, run straight into a wall, bounce off it, pick himself up, and do the same thing again and again until his parents finally caught him and physically restrained him. Eventually it was established that this behavior was elicited when the child consumed Kool-Aid sweetened with NutraSweet (the sugar substitute aspartame). Many parents and teachers believe that the diet their children eat and whether or not they have eaten a decent breakfast have an impact on their later behavior. In fact, a survey of teachers (McLoughlin & Nall, 1988) revealed that 90% of them believed that sugar adversely affected children's classroom behavior and academic performance despite the fact that there is little, if any, evidence to support the notion that restriction of a child's sugar intake is of any benefit. Does this mean that diet does not affect subsequent behavior? Little high-quality research has been done on this question, but the studies that have been conducted indicate that there is such a relationship. For example, Boris and Mandel (1994) revealed that 73% of children with attention-deficit/hyperactivity disorder demonstrated an improvement when placed on a diet restricting a variety of foods such as dairy products, wheat, eggs, and peanuts.

Any investigation into an area like this, however, is littered with variables that must be controlled. For example, a maturational variable, such as the age of the participants, might influence the outcome of a diet–behavior study because younger individuals who are still maturing might be more susceptible to the impact of dietary manipulations. In addition, other variables—previous dietary habits, the food combinations ingested, the personality of the participants, or their metabolic rate—can have an impact on the effect of a specific diet or even on whether skipping meals has any impact. The influence of such extraneous variables must be controlled for us to reach a warranted conclusion about the impact of a specific dietary variable.

Introduction

In Chapter 5, we covered how researchers obtain their samples. We discussed several types of random sampling (e.g., simple random sampling, stratified sampling, and cluster sampling) and nonrandom sampling (e.g., convenience sampling, purposive sampling, quota sampling, and snowball sampling). In this chapter, we will assume that you already have your sample of participants. The ideal situation in experimental research would be to randomly select your sample and then randomly assign the participants to the groups to be used in the experiment (as shown in Figure 7.1). However, random selection is rarely used in experimental research because the focus is much more on obtaining strong evidence for making claims of cause and effect (i.e., internal validity) than on directly generalizing from a single sample to a population (which is a type of external validity). Purposive and convenience samples are typically used in experimental research, and experimenters usually generalize on the basis of replication of experimental findings with different people, places, settings, and conditions. That is, experimenters generalize on the basis of multiple studies. In the remainder of this chapter we want you to assume that you already have your sample of research participants

FIGURE 7.1
Illustration of the ideal procedure for obtaining participants for an experiment.

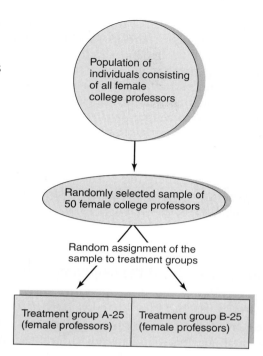

Population of individuals consisting of all female college professors

Randomly selected sample of 50 female college professors

Random assignment of the sample to treatment groups

Treatment group A-25 (female professors)

Treatment group B-25 (female professors)

so that we can focus on control techniques for maximizing internal validity. Although the focus is on internal validity (i.e., causation), external validity (i.e., generalizing) issues will occasionally arise in this chapter because some control procedures have implications for both internal validity and external validity.

The primary goal when conducting a psychological experiment is to determine whether the independent variable causes the changes observed in the dependent variable. To make this causal inference, we must control for the influence of extraneous variables that could serve as rival hypotheses. If we can control for the influence of extraneous variables, internal validity is achieved. Unfortunately, there are many different extraneous variables that can creep into an experiment and threaten internal validity such as those presented in Chapter 6.

The key strategy for eliminating extraneous variables as rival explanations for claims of causation is to produce an experimental situation that holds the extraneous variables constant across the different levels of the independent variable. The experimental groups (e.g., treatment and control) should have the same levels of each extraneous variable to eliminate any **differential influence**. The *only* difference between the experimental groups should be the levels of the independent variable. The nineteenth-century philosopher John Stuart Mill (1806–1873) called this process the **method of difference**. When the only difference between the groups is due to the independent variable, the researcher can confidently conclude that the result of the study is due to the independent variable and not to an extraneous variable.

Differential influence
When the influence of an extraneous variable is different for the various groups

Method of difference
If groups are equivalent on every variable except for one, then that one variable is the cause of the difference between the groups

Many techniques have been developed over the years that enable researchers to control the influence of confounding extraneous variables. In this chapter, we discuss the more commonly used control techniques in experimental research. It is important to remember that experimental research is the strongest research method for obtaining evidence of cause and effect. The strongest experimental designs include randomization (i.e., random assignment of participants to the groups forming the independent variable). This will be our first control technique discussed. After discussing control techniques that are implemented at the beginning of the experiment, we discuss several techniques that are implemented during the experiment. The first key point is that you want to generate equivalent experimental groups at the beginning of the experiment (e.g., treatment and control groups), and during the experiment you need to treat the groups exactly the same except for administering the independent variable conditions.

Control Techniques Carried Out at the Beginning of the Experiment

Randomization

Randomization
Control technique that equates groups of participants by ensuring every member an equal chance of being assigned to any group

Random assignment
Randomly assigning a sample of individuals to a specific number of comparison groups

Randomization (also called **random assignment**) is the most important and basic of all the control methods. It is a probabilistic control technique designed to equate experimental groups at the start of an experiment on all extraneous variables, both known or unknown. Because it "equates groups," there will not be systematic group differences on extraneous variables to bias the study results. Random assignment is the only technique for controlling both known and unknown sources of extraneous variation. As Cochran and Cox (1957) have stated,

> Randomization is somewhat analogous to insurance, in that it is a precaution against disturbances that may or may not occur and that may or may not be serious if they do occur. It is generally advisable to take the trouble to randomize even when it is not expected that there will be any serious bias from failure to randomize. The experimenter is thus protected against unusual events that upset his [or her] expectations. (p. 8).

How does randomization eliminate systematic bias in the experiment? The key word is *random*. The term *random* refers to the statistical characteristic of equiprobability (i.e., equal in probability) of events. Random assignment of participants to the experimental groups assures that each participant has an equal chance of being assigned to each group. In order to achieve equiprobability of events when randomly assigning participants to treatment conditions, it is necessary to use a randomization procedure, such as the one explained in Exhibit 7.1. When such a procedure is used, maximum assurance is provided that systematic differences between the groups that might bias the results will be eliminated. Random assignment produces control by virtue of the fact that all variables present in a group of participants will be distributed in approximately the same manner in all groups. When the distributions of extraneous variables

EXHIBIT 7.1

Procedure for Randomly Assigning Participants to Experimental Treatment Conditions

The traditional procedure for randomly assigning participants to experimental treatment conditions is to use a list of random numbers, such as the following list of two hundred numbers. A larger list of random numbers appears in Appendix B. Our list below consists of a series of 20 rows and 10 columns. The number in each position is random because each of the numbers from 0–9 had an equal chance of occupying that position and the selection of one number for a given position had no influence in the selection of another number for another position. Therefore, because each individual number is random, any combination of the numbers is random.

Now let's look at the procedure you should follow when using this list of random numbers (or the random number table in Appendix B). Let's assume that you want to conduct an experiment. You have 20 research participants, and you need to randomly assign them to two groups: one group to receive the experimental treatment condition and one group to receive the control condition. To *randomly assign* your 20 participants to two groups, you complete the following steps.

Step 1. Number the participants from 0 to 19. This is your list of research participants with their identification numbers.

Step 2. Block the list of random numbers into columns of two, because the maximum number of participants you have is a two-digit number. This blocking has been done in the list of random numbers in this exhibit. The same procedure should be used if you are using the random numbers in Appendix B.

Step 3. Randomly select the first group of 10 participants by reading down the first two columns until you come to a number less than 20. The first number encountered that is less

than 20 is 00. Therefore, the first person in your first group is the participant assigned the number 00 in your list of 20 participants (from step 1). Proceed down the columns until you encounter the other numbers less than 20, which are 18 and 03. Participants numbered 18 and 03 represent the second and third randomly selected participants. When you reach the bottom of the first two columns, start at the top of the next two columns. With this procedure, the participant numbers 05, 06, 09, 10, 01, 14, and 07 are selected, which represent the remaining eight of the first 10 randomly selected participants. Note that if you encounter a number that has already been selected (as we did with the numbers 03, 06, and 14), you must disregard it.

Step 4. If you have to randomly assign the research participants to more than two groups, continue step 3 for the third and subsequent groups. However, the last group will be the remaining participants. In our example, we randomly selected 10 of the 20 participants for one group, so the remaining 10 participants represent the second group as follows:

Group 0		Group 1	
00	01	02	04
03	05	08	11
06	07	12	13
09	10	15	16
14	18	17	19

Step 5. After you have obtained the same number of groups as there are treatment conditions, the groups should ideally be randomly assigned to the treatment conditions. In this case, this is

(continued)

E X H I B I T 7 . 1 (continued)

accomplished by using only one column of the table of random numbers because there are only two groups of participants. The two groups are numbered 0 and 1. If you proceed down the first column, you can see that the first number encountered that is less than 2 is 0, so group 0 (the first group of participants) is assigned to the first treatment group. This means that group 1, the

second group of randomly assigned participants, is assigned to the second treatment group as follows:

Treatment Condition

A_1	A_2
Group 0	Group 1

Random Number List

	1	2	3	4	5	6	7	8	9	10
1	8	1	4	5	5	6	9	8	7	3
2	2	7	9	6	5	4	6	4	8	3
3	0	0	0	5	5	8	9	7	6	9
4	7	8	3	4	7	0	7	7	5	2
5	8	5	8	6	3	5	4	2	2	2
6	7	3	5	3	6	8	0	7	3	3
7	1	8	6	0	1	0	7	4	4	7
8	7	9	5	3	0	1	5	5	5	1
9	5	6	6	7	8	5	8	1	1	9
10	3	0	3	3	9	1	9	9	1	9
11	9	7	4	7	8	4	7	1	0	9
12	5	6	4	5	1	4	5	4	1	1
13	5	7	4	0	4	2	5	9	6	7
14	8	6	0	5	6	9	4	4	3	2
15	6	7	6	7	3	3	7	1	8	9
16	2	6	0	6	7	3	3	0	6	9
17	6	7	5	5	1	4	7	4	1	2
18	6	3	0	9	9	9	5	3	8	0
19	0	3	7	3	0	3	0	6	8	6
20	7	1	6	8	2	0	5	3	2	1

are approximately equal in all groups, the influence of the extraneous variables is held constant because they cannot exert any *differential influence* on the dependent variable. For example, gender cannot be the cause of the difference found between two groups if 58% of the treatment group and 58% of the control group participants are women; likewise, gender cannot be the cause if 30% of the treatment group and 30% of the control group participants are women. Gender could be a problem, however, if 68% of one group and 30% of the other group were women (if gender also affects the dependent variable). The key is not the level of the extraneous variable in the groups, but that *the groups do not differ* on the level of the extraneous variable. It is a cardinal rule in experimental research that you want your groups to be equivalent on any and all extraneous variables!

Will random assignment *always* result in equal distributions of the variables to be controlled? As long as a sufficient sample size is used, a researcher can reasonably assume that random assignment will produce groups that are approximately equal. Although it is possible for random assignment to fail in any particular study, it is a relatively rare event. Consequently, a researcher can reasonably assume that the distribution and influence of the extraneous variables, both known and unknown, will be approximately the same in all groups of participants at the start of the experiment when random assignment is used to form the groups. Because the probability of the groups' being equal is so much greater with randomization than any other control technique, random assignment is considered the most important and most powerful control method in experimental research. And because it is really the *only* method for controlling unknown extraneous variables, it is important to randomize whenever and wherever possible, even when another control technique is being used.

Consider the following example using the random assignment of participants. Professor X was conducting a study on learning. The extraneous variable intelligence is correlated with learning, so this factor must be controlled for, or held constant. Let us consider two possibilities—one that provides the needed control through the use of random assignment and one that does not. Assume first that no random assignment of participants existed (no control), but that the first 10 participants who showed up for the experiment were assigned to treatment Group A, and the second 10 participants were assigned to treatment Group B. Assume further that the results of the experiment revealed that treatment Group B learned significantly faster than treatment Group A. Is this difference caused by the different experimental treatments that were administered to the two groups or by the fact that the participants in Group B *may* have been more intelligent than those in Group A? Suppose the investigator also considers the intelligence factor to be a possible confounding variable and gives all participants an intelligence test. The left-hand side of Table 7.1 depicts the hypothetical distribution of IQ scores of these 20 participants. From this table, you can see that the mean IQ score of the people in Group B is 10.6 points higher than that of those in Group A. Intelligence is, therefore, a potentially confounding variable and serves as a rival hypothesis for explaining the observed performance difference in the two groups. To state that the treatment conditions produced the observed effect, researchers must control for potentially confounding variables such as IQ.

One means of eliminating such a bias is to randomly assign the 20 participants to the two treatment groups. The right-hand side of Table 7.1 depicts the random distribution of the 20 participants and their corresponding hypothetical IQ scores. Now note that the mean IQ scores for the two groups are very similar. There is only a 0.2 point IQ difference as opposed to the prior 10.6 point difference. In addition to similar mean IQ scores, both groups of participants must have a

TABLE 7.1
Hypothetical Distribution of 20 Research Participants' IQ Scores

Group Assignment Based on Arrival Sequence				Random Assignment of Participants to Groups			
Group A		Group B		Group A		Group B	
Participants	IQ Scores	Participants	IQ Scores	Participants	IQ Scores	Participants	IQ Scores
1	97	11	100	1	97	3	100
2	97	12	108	2	97	4	103
3	100	13	110	11	100	6	108
4	103	14	113	5	105	12	108
5	105	15	117	13	110	7	109
6	108	16	119	9	113	8	111
7	109	17	120	15	117	14	113
8	111	18	122	10	118	16	119
9	113	19	128	19	128	17	120
10	118	20	130	20	130	18	122
Mean IQ score	106.1		116.7		111.5		111.3

Mean difference between the two groups: 10.6   Mean difference between the two groups: 0.2

similar distribution of IQ scores, the effect of which is to control for the potential biasing effect of IQ. The IQ scores in Table 7.1 have been rank ordered to show this similar distribution.

So far we have demonstrated the process of random assignment using a table of random numbers. We did this because tables of random numbers are still commonly used for random assignment. Another useful tool for random assignment, which is becoming increasingly popular, is a random number generator. We illustrated the use of a random number generator in Chapter 5 for use in random selection. That same random number generator (http://randomizer.org) can be used for random assignment. If you use this program for random assignment, you will obtain one long list of random numbers organized into blocks (where the block size is equal to the number of groups you desire). If you want two groups, the first two numbers (i.e., block 1) will include 1 and 2 in random order, the next two numbers (i.e., block 2) will also include 1 and 2 in random order, and so forth to the end of the list. If you want three groups, the first three numbers (i.e., block 1) will include 1, 2, and 3 in random order; the next three numbers (i.e., block 2) will include 1, 2, and 3 in random order, and so forth to the end of the list. Therefore, when using this random number generator for random assignment, you do not need to give your participants unique numbers. You just go down your list of names, assigning them to the conditions.

One more example will make this process fully clear. Let's assume that you have 30 participants, and you want to randomly assign them to three groups, with 10 people in each group. Here's how to use the randomizer.org program for random assignment. Go to the Web site and answer the questions as follows:

1. How many sets of numbers do you want to generate?
   - Insert 10 (which is your total number of participants divided by the number of groups; in our case this is 30/3=10).
2. How many numbers per set?
   - Insert 3 (which is the number of groups we want).
3. Number range?
   - Insert 1 and 3 (which will order the list of numbers into blocks, including the numbers 1, 2, and 3).
4. Do you wish each number in a set to remain unique?
   - Click "yes" so that every block of three numbers will include the numbers 1, 2, and 3.
5. Do you wish to sort the numbers that are generated?
   - Click "no."
6. How do you wish to view your random numbers?
   - Leave the program at its default value ("place markers off").
7. To obtain your list of random numbers organized into blocks of 1, 2, and 3, click "Randomize Now!"

Here is the blocked list of random numbers that we obtained when we ran the program: 3,2,1, 1,3,2, 3,2,1, 2,1,3, 2,3,1, 2,1,3, 2,1,3, 1,3,2, 3,1,2, 3,2,1 (we underlined the blocks for clarity). To use these numbers, start with the first block, and place your first participant in group 3, the second participant in group 2, and the third in group 1; then go to the second block and place the fourth participant in group 1, the fifth participant in group 3, and the sixth participant in group 2; continue this process until you have used all of the 30 numbers in the list. The 30 participants will have been randomly assigned to the three groups, and you will have 10 people in each group.

STUDY QUESTIONS 7.1
- **Why is randomization the most important control technique?**
- **How does it control for the confounding effect of extraneous variables?**
- **How does one randomly assign a set of participants to groups to be used in an experiment?**

Matching

Matching
Using any of a variety of techniques for equating participants on one or more variables

Although random assignment is the best control technique available in experimental research, random assignment is not always possible or expedient. When random assignment is not possible, **matching** can be an effective technique to equate groups if the researcher has the information required for matching. If you wish to match participants on intelligence, you will need to know their intelligence scores. The strength of matching is that it ensures that participants in the

Matching variable
The extraneous
variable used in
matching

different groups are equated on the **matching variable**(s). The variables on which participants are matched are controlled because constancy of influence is attained across the treatment conditions. If participants in different treatment conditions are matched on intelligence, then the intelligence level of the research participants will be the same in each treatment group—intelligence is held constant and therefore controlled. The key weakness of matching is that the groups are equated only on the matching variables. If you can combine matching with random assignment (e.g., match pairs of participants, and then randomly assign them to treatment and control groups), this problem is eliminated. In the sections that follow, we present several ways in which matching is accomplished in experimental research.

Matching by Holding Variables Constant

One technique that can be used to control an extraneous variable is to hold the extraneous variable constant for all groups in the experiment. This means that all participants in each treatment group will have the same degree or type of extraneous variable. If we are studying conformity, then gender of participants needs to be controlled because conformity has been shown to vary with the gender of the participant. As illustrated in Figure 7.2, the gender variable can be controlled by using only female (or only male) participants in the experiment. This matching procedure creates a more homogeneous participant sample because only participants

FIGURE 7.2
Illustration of
matching by holding
variables constant.

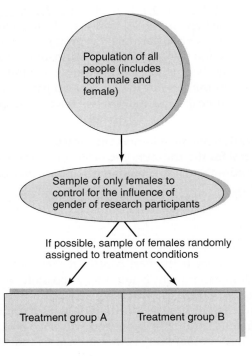

with a certain amount or type of the extraneous variable are included in the participant pool.

Although sometimes used, the technique of holding variables constant has some serious disadvantages. Two are readily identified. The first disadvantage is that the technique restricts the size of the participant population. Consequently, in some cases, it might be difficult to find enough participants to participate in the study. The second disadvantage is more serious. The results of the study can be generalized only to the type of participant who participated in the study. For example, if a study is conducted with only female participants, it cannot be generalized to males. The only way we can find out if the results of one study can be generalized to individuals of another population is to conduct an identical study using representatives of the second population as research participants.

Matching by Building the Extraneous Variable into the Research Design

A second means of controlling extraneous variables through matching is to build the extraneous variable into the research design. (In the psychological literature, this technique sometimes is called "blocking.") Assume that we are conducting a learning experiment and want to control for the effects of intelligence. Also assume that we have considered the previous technique of holding the variable constant by selecting only individuals with IQs of 110–120 but thought its unwise and inexpedient to do so. Instead, we decided to select several IQ levels (e.g., 90–99, 100–109, and 110–119), as illustrated in Figure 7.3, and

FIGURE 7.3
Illustration of matching by building the extraneous variable into the research design.

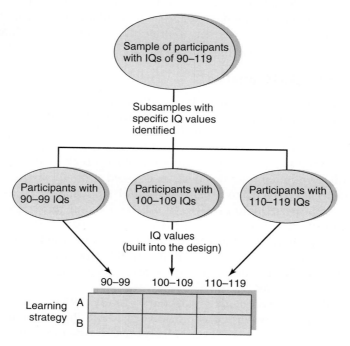

treat them as we would an independent variable. This would allow us to control and detect the influence of the intelligence variable. Differential influence of intelligence is eliminated because the treatment groups are compared within each of the three intelligence levels.

Building the extraneous variable into the research is a good technique for achieving control over the matching variable. The technique is recommended if one is interested in the differences produced by the various levels of the extraneous variable or in the interaction between the levels of the extraneous variable and other independent variables. In the hypothetical learning experiment, one might be interested in the differences produced by the three levels of intelligence and how these levels interact with the learning strategies. When such conditions are of interest, the technique is excellent because it isolates the variation caused by the extraneous variable. This control technique takes a factor that can operate as a confounding extraneous variable and makes it focal in the experiment as an independent variable.

Before moving to the next matching technique, it needs to be pointed out that some experts recommend that a quantitative variable such as intelligence *not* be categorized into a few groups as we did in the previous example (Maxwell & Delaney, 2004). Rather than categorizing intelligence into three groups, these psychologists recommend that the matching variable, such as intelligence, be left in its natural units and then entered into the study during statistical analysis. This form of control is sometimes called **statistical control** because it is done during data analysis. Statistical control is much more important in quasi-experimental designs than in randomized experimental designs because quasi-experimental designs lack random assignment, and it is wise for the researcher to determine the variables the groups might differ on, measure those variables, and then control for those variables during data analysis. We explain how to carry out this type of statistical analysis in the chapter on inferential statistics (i.e., Chapter 15).

Statistical control
Control of measured extraneous variables during data analysis

Matching by Yoked Control

Yoked control
A matching technique that matches participants on the basis of the temporal sequence of administering an event

The **yoked control** matching technique controls for the possible influence of participant-controlled events. For example, if you want to know the effect of students having the freedom to choose snack breaks whenever they want on their classroom productivity, it would be important to know if the effects are due to having the freedom to choose a snack break or due to having a snack break (determined by the teacher). In a yoked control experiment, each control participant is "yoked" to an experimental participant. Therefore, when the experimental participant engages in a behavior and receives an outcome (e.g., taking a self-chosen snack break), the "yoked" participant is given the same outcome (teacher tells the student to take a snack break). If the experimental group scores higher on the dependent variable than the control group, it can be attributed to the freedom to choose and receive the snack rather than just getting a snack break.

Consider the classic study conducted by Brady (1958) in which he investigated the relationship between psychological stress and development of ulcers. Brady trained monkeys to press a lever at least once during every 20-second interval to avoid receiving electric shock. The monkeys learned this task quite rapidly, and only occasionally did they miss a 20-second interval and receive a shock. In order to determine whether the monkeys developed ulcers from the psychological stress rather than the physical stress resulting from the cumulative effect of the shocks, Brady had to include a control monkey that received an equal number of shocks in the same temporal sequence. Brady placed the experimental and the control monkeys in "yoked chain," whereby both monkeys received a shock when the experimental monkey failed to press the lever during the 20-second interval. However, the control animal could not influence the situation and essentially had to sit back and accept the fact that sometimes the shock was going to occur. The only apparent difference between these animals was the ability to influence the occurrence of the shock. If only the experimental monkey got ulcers, as was the case in this experiment, the ulcers could be attributed to the psychological stress.

Matching by Equating Participants

Matching by equating participants is similar to matching by building the extraneous variable into the study design: Both techniques attempt to eliminate the influence of the extraneous variable by creating equivalent groups of participants. The difference lies in the procedure for creating the equivalent groups. The previously discussed method creates equivalent groups by establishing categories of the extraneous variable into which participants are placed, thereby creating another independent variable. The present method does not build the extraneous variable into the design of the study but matches participants on the variable to be controlled. The number of participants must be some multiple of the number of levels of the independent variable. There are two techniques that are commonly used to accomplish this matching, which Selltiz, Jahoda, Deutsch, and Cook (1959) originally labeled the *precision control technique* and the *frequency control technique*.

Precision control
A matching technique in which each participant is matched with another participant on selected variables

Precision Control   As illustrated in Figure 7.4, the technique of **precision control** requires the investigator to match participants in the various treatment groups on a case-by-case basis for each matching variable (i.e., the extraneous variable used in matching). Scholtz (1973) investigated the defense styles used by individuals who attempted suicide versus those used by individuals who did not attempt suicide. All participants were neuropsychiatric patients. The study was an ex post facto study because the participants self-selected themselves (based on prior behavior) to the various categories of interest to the experimenter; the researcher could not randomly assign participants after being paired. The suicide attempter participants were identified as those individuals who, among other things, had attempted suicide during the past year. The other participants had evidenced "no history of a suicide attempt nor marked suicidal ideation" (p. 71). For a non–suicide attempter to be included in the study, the participant had to be of the same age, gender, race, marital status, diagnosis, and education as a suicide attempter. Matching on these variables on a case-by-case basis resulted in 35 pairs of participants.

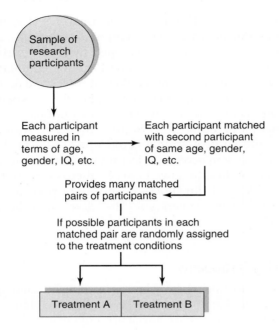

FIGURE 7.4
Illustration of matching by the precision control technique.

The Scholtz study illustrates the advantages and disadvantages of precision control matching. The primary advantage of precision control is that the participants in the various groups are equal on at least the matched variables; that is, *the groups are equated on the matching variables*, which rules out these extraneous variables as rival explanations for the relationship between the independent and dependent variables. In the Scholtz study, a critic would not be able to claim that the relationship observed between suicide attempts and defensive styles was due to the extraneous variables used in matching (i.e., age, gender, race, marital status, diagnosis, and education) because the groups were the same on those variables.

Precision control has three major disadvantages. First, it is difficult to know which matching variables should be used and which of the potential matching variables are most critical. The logic of matching is to identify the variables that comparison groups differ on (and that are related to the dependent variable) and to match on those variables. In many instances, the researcher does not know what extraneous variables the groups differ on, and there often are many potentially relevant variables. In his study, Scholtz selected age, gender, race, marital status, diagnosis, and education, but many other variables could have been selected. From a statistical standpoint, the variables selected should be those that show the lowest intercorrelation but the highest correlation with the dependent variable.

A second problem encountered in precision control matching is that the difficulty in finding matched participants increases disproportionately as the number of matching variables increases. Scholtz matched on six variables, which must have been very difficult. His task would have been much easier if matching had been attempted on only one or two variables, such as gender and age. In order to match individuals on many variables, one must have a large pool of individuals available in order to obtain a few who are matched on the relevant variables.

A third problem is that matching limits the generality of the results of the study because matching can result in some rather unique groups of participants. Assume that you are matching on age and education and that the participants in your final sample of matched participants are between the ages of 20 and 30 and have only high school education. Because this is the type of participant included in the study, you can generalize the results only to other individuals having the same characteristics.

A fourth disadvantage is that some variables are very difficult to use in matching. If having received psychotherapy was considered a relevant variable, an individual who had received psychotherapy would have to be matched with another person who had also received psychotherapy. A related difficulty is the inability to obtain adequate measures of the variables to be matched. If we wanted to equate individuals on the basis of the effect of psychotherapy, we would have to measure such an effect. Matching can only be as accurate as the available measurement of the matching variable.

Frequency Distribution Control   The precision control technique of matching is excellent, but many participants must be eliminated because they cannot be matched. **Frequency distribution control** attempts to overcome this disadvantage while retaining some of the advantages of matching. This technique, as the name implies, matches groups of participants in terms of the overall distribution of the selected variable or variables rather than matching individuals for the groups on a case-by-case basis. If IQ were used in frequency distribution control matching, the two or more groups of matched participants must have the same average IQ *as well as* the same standard deviation and skewness of IQ scores, as illustrated in Figure 7.5. This means that, generally speaking, the investigator would select the first group of participants and determine the mean, standard deviation, and so forth of their IQ scores. Then another group having the same statistical measures would be selected. If more than one extraneous variable was considered to be a relevant variable on which to match participants, the groups of participants would have to have the same statistical measures on these matching variables. The number of participants lost using this technique would not be as great as the number lost using the precision control method because each additional participant would merely have to contribute to producing the appropriate statistical indices rather than be identical to another participant on the relevant variables. Consequently, this technique allows more flexibility in terms of being able to use a particular participant.

The major disadvantage of matching by the frequency distribution control method is that the combinations of variables might be mismatched in the various groups. If age and IQ were to be matched, one group might include old participants with high IQs and young participants with low IQs, whereas the other group might be composed of the opposite combination. In this case, the mean and distribution of the two variables would be equivalent, but the participants in each group would be completely different. This disadvantage obviously exists only if matching is conducted on more than one variable.

Frequency distribution control
A matching technique that matches groups of participants by equating the overall distribution of the chosen variable

FIGURE 7.5
Illustration of the
frequency distribution
control technique.

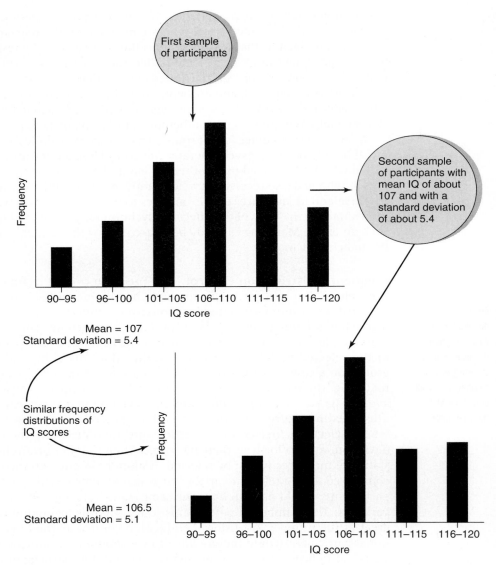

Control Techniques Carried Out During the Experiment

Up to this point, we have explained how to assign participants to experimental groups in ways that equate the groups at the beginning of the experiment on one or more extraneous variables. Unfortunately, extraneous variables also can enter into an experiment during the conduct of the study. A key point here is as follows: *You must treat the different groups in the same way during the conduct of the experiment, except for administration of the different levels of the independent variable.* We now explain the most important control techniques for employment during the experimental study.

Counterbalancing

In most experiments, the different treatment groups are composed of different participants, and our goal has been to make sure the participants in the different groups are similar. In another type of experimental design, called the repeated measures design (or a within-subjects design), all participants receive all treatments. The idea of this type of experiment is depicted in Figure 7.6 (and discussed in depth in Chapter 8). The control method of **counterbalancing** applies only to repeated measures designs (i.e., where all participants receive all levels of at least one independent variable). Counterbalancing is specifically used to control for sequencing effects in repeated measures designs.

Counterbalancing
A technique used to control for sequencing effects

Sequencing effects can occur when participants participate in more than one treatment condition. There are two types of sequencing effects. The first is an **order effect**, which arises from the order in which the treatment conditions are administered to the participants. Changes that occur over time within a repeated measures experiment will result in order effects because the participant has changed somewhat from the first condition to the last condition, regardless of what treatments are administered. Suppose that you are conducting a verbal learning experiment in which the independent variable is rate of presentation of nonsense syllables. The participant has to learn, sequentially, list S (the slow list, in which the syllables are presented at 6-second intervals), then list M (the moderate list, in which the syllables are presented at 4-second intervals), and finally list F (the fast list, in which the syllables are presented at 2-second intervals). In this experiment, there is the possibility that practice with the equipment, learning how to work with nonsense syllables, or just becoming more familiar with the surroundings of the experimental environment might enhance performance.

Order effect
A sequencing effect arising from the order in which the treatment conditions are administered to participants

Let us assume that one or more of these variables does enhance performance and that the increment due to the order effect is 4 units of performance for participants progressing from list order one to order two (S to M) and 2 units of performance for participants progressing from order two to order three (M to F). The left half of Table 7.2 depicts these order effects. As you can see, order effects could affect the conclusions reached because of the performance increments due to the order of the lists. When the increment in performance is caused by order effects, the particular sequence of the nonsense lists would be irrelevant. If the

FIGURE 7.6
Illustration of the type of design that might include sequencing effects.

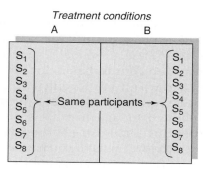

Treatment conditions

TABLE 7.2
Hypothetical Order Effects

	List Learned			Reversed Order of List		
	S	M	F	F	M	S
Increment in performance	0	4	2	0	4	2

order of the lists were reversed, the increments in performance would still occur in the same ordinal position, as is shown in the right half of Table 7.2. Participants' increased familiarity and practice with the whole experimental environment can produce order effects such as the ones shown in the table. Other experimental factors, such as the time of testing (morning, noon, or night), can also produce order effects. Such effects must be controlled to avoid reaching false conclusions.

The second type of sequencing effect that can occur is a carryover effect. A **carryover effect** occurs when performance in one treatment condition is partially dependent on the treatment conditions that precede it. Consider an experiment studying the relative effectiveness of three types of therapy (e.g., client-centered therapy, rational–emotive therapy, and Gestalt therapy). Perhaps participants tend to be relaxed after client-centered therapy and somewhat on edge after rational–emotive therapy, and these effects carry over to any subsequent conditions, changing the apparent effectiveness of the later treatment conditions. One strategy for minimizing carryover effects is to provide a sufficient period between conditions for the effects of the previous condition to wear off. This sometimes is called the "wash out" period. Use of washout periods is especially important in drug studies and learning studies, or any other type of study where the effects linger over some period of time.

Order effects and carryover effects are potential sources of bias in any studies in which the participant partakes of several treatment conditions. In such cases, the sequencing effects need to be controlled, and researchers often resort to counterbalancing. We now discuss several counterbalancing techniques for dealing with sequencing effects.

Carryover effect
A sequencing effect that occurs when performance in one treatment condition affects performance in another treatment condition

Randomized Counterbalancing

If you can counterbalance at the individual level (i.e., give different participants different treatment sequences), then you are in a stronger situation than when you can only counterbalance the treatment sequences received by different groups of participants. In **randomized counterbalancing**, in effect, the experiment is replicated for each participant using different counterbalancing sequences. When counterbalancing at the individual level, the method of choice for controlling for sequencing effects is to randomize the sequence of the treatment conditions across the participants. This is done by randomly generating and assigning a sequence to each research participant. If you have a sufficient number of participants in a study, randomizing the sequences of treatment conditions

Randomized counterbalancing
Sequence order is randomly determined for each individual

ensures that each sequence occurs approximately the same number of times and each condition occurs before and after each other condition approximately the same number of times. As a result, sequencing effects will be equally distributed across the conditions and eliminated as threats to the internal validity of your research study.

For an example, assume that you have an independent variable with three levels (e.g., client-centered therapy, rational–emotive therapy, and Gestalt therapy). In this case, you have three treatment groups. When you have three treatments, there are six possible sequences in which the conditions can be presented to participants: 1,2,3; 1,3,2; 2,3,1; 2,3,2; 3,1,2; and 3,2,1. You could use the same random number generator we used earlier for this process of assigning each participant a random ordering of the numbers 1, 2, and 3. In your research study, participant one might receive sequence 2,3,1; participant two sequence 2,1,3; participant three sequence 3,1,2, and so forth. The randomized procedure is used until you have determined the sequence for the last research participant. It is essential that you remember that you do not decide the sequence; you must use a random process such as a table of random numbers or a random number generator.

Intrasubject Counterbalancing

The next type of counterbalancing, intrasubject counterbalancing, is used when each participant receives all levels of the independent variable *more than one time.* **Intrasubject counterbalancing** controls for sequencing effects by having each participant take the treatment conditions first in one order and then in the reverse order. For example, suppose that you were conducting a Pepsi challenge experiment to find out if people prefer Pepsi or Coke. In this experiment, the treatment conditions would consist of the two colas. Research participants would make an assessment of liking after tasting first the cola A (Pepsi) and then cola B (Coke), in AB order. Participants would then taste the cola B (Coke) a second time, followed by the cola A (Pepsi), and make a liking assessment after each, making the sequence ABBA. In other words, each participant would taste each cola drink twice and make an assessment of liking after each tasting. The results of the liking assessment obtained from the two Pepsi tastings would be combined for each participant, as would the results of the two Coke tastings, once again making the study a two-treatment-condition experiment. The Pepsi-liking average across all participants would then be compared to the Coke-liking average. Any observed difference between the averages would not be attributable to carryover or order effects because they would have been equalized, or held constant, across conditions.

A disadvantage of the intrasubject counterbalancing technique is that each treatment condition must be presented to each research participant more than once. As the number of treatment conditions increases, the length of the sequence of conditions each participant must take also increases. For example, with three treatment conditions A, B, and C, each participant must take a sequence of six treatment conditions—ABCCBA.

Randomized counterbalancing takes place across individuals (different sequences are randomly assigned to different individuals). Intrasubject counterbalancing takes

Intrasubject counterbalancing Administering the treatment conditions to each individual participant in more than one order

Group counterbalancing
Administering different sequences to different groups of participants

place within participants (each participant receives the forward sequence and the reversed sequence). The remaining two types of counterbalancing (complete and incomplete counterbalancing) are **group counterbalancing** techniques because the counterbalancing sequences are varied across two or more groups of participants (participants within each group receive the same sequences).

Complete Counterbalancing

Complete counterbalancing
Enumerating all possible sequences and requiring different groups of participants to take each of the sequences

In **complete counterbalancing**, all possible sequences of the treatment conditions are used in the experiment, and an equal proportion of research participants are randomly assigned to each sequence. When there are two treatment conditions, there are just two possible sequences, which are as follows:

1,2
2,1

If there are three treatment conditions, there are six possible sequences:

1,2,3
1,3,2
2,3,1
2,1,3
3,1,2
3,2,1

When using complete counterbalancing, it is important that an equal proportion of research participants are randomly assigned to each of the sequences.

A limitation of complete counterbalancing is that when the number of treatment conditions is large, the number of possible sequences becomes unwieldy. You can determine the number of possible sequences by calculating $N!$ (called "N factorial").[1] The number of treatment conditions is symbolized by "N," and the "!" symbol means you multiply N by the numbers falling below it: N times $N - 1$ times, $N - 2$, and so on, until you reach 1. For example, if you have three groups, then N is 3 and $N!$ is 3 times 2 times 1 (which is 6). For four groups, $N!$ is 4 times 3 times 2 times 1 (which is 24). For five groups, $N!$ is 5 times 4 times 3 times 2 times 1 (which is 120). As you can see, the possible number of sequences was fully 120 for just five conditions! Because of this problem, complete counterbalancing is rarely used when the researcher has three or more treatment conditions.

Incomplete counterbalancing
Enumerating fewer than all possible sequences and requiring different groups of participants to take each of the sequences

Incomplete Counterbalancing

The most frequently used group counterbalancing technique is **incomplete counterbalancing**. This technique derives its name from the fact that all possible sequences of treatment conditions are *not* enumerated. The first criterion that incomplete counterbalancing must meet is that, for the sequences enumerated,

[1]You can easily find a factorial calculator on the Web. Here is one: http://www.webcalc.net/calc/0504.php

each treatment condition must appear an equal number of times in each ordinal position. Also, each treatment condition must precede and be followed by every other condition an equal number of times.

Assume that you are conducting an experiment to determine whether caffeine affects reaction time. You want to administer 100, 200, 300, and 400 mg of caffeine (conditions A, B, C, and D, respectively) to participants to see whether reaction time increases as the amount of caffeine consumed increases. You know that, if each participant takes all four doses of caffeine, sequencing effects could alter the results of your experiment, so you want to counterbalance the order in which the dosages are administered to the participants. Whenever the number of treatment conditions is even, as is the case with the four caffeine dosages, the number of counterbalanced sequences equals the number of treatment conditions. The sequences are established in the following way. The first sequence takes the form 1, 2, n, 3, $(n - 1)$, 4, $(n - 2)$, 5, and so forth, until we have accounted for the total number of treatment conditions. In the case of the caffeine study with four treatment conditions, the first sequence would be ABDC, or 1, 2, 4, 3. If an experiment consisted of six treatment conditions, the first sequence would be ABFCED, or 1, 2, 6, 3, 5, 4. The remaining sequences of the incomplete counterbalancing technique are then established by incrementing each value in the preceding sequence by 1. For example, for the caffeine study, in which the first sequence is ABDC, the second sequence is BCAD. Naturally, to increment the last treatment condition, D, by 1, you do not proceed to E but go back to A. This procedure results in the following set of sequences for the caffeine study.

Participant	Sequence			
1	A	B	D	C
2	B	C	A	D
3	C	D	B	A
4	D	A	C	B

If the number of treatment conditions is odd, as with five treatment conditions, the criterion that each value must precede and follow every other value an equal number of times is not fulfilled if the above procedure is followed. For example, the foregoing procedure would give the following set of sequences:

Sequence				
A	B	E	C	D
B	C	A	D	E
C	D	B	E	A
D	E	C	A	B
E	A	D	B	C

In this case, each treatment condition appears in every possible position; but, for example, D is immediately preceded by A twice but never by B. To remedy this situation, we must enumerate five additional sequences that are exactly the reverse of the first five sequences. In the five-treatment-condition example, the additional five sequences appear as follows:

Sequence				
D	C	E	B	A
E	D	A	C	B
A	E	B	D	C
B	A	C	E	D
C	B	D	A	E

When these 10 sequences are combined, the criteria of incomplete counterbalancing are met. Consequently, the incomplete counterbalancing technique provides for control of most sequencing effects.

How well does the incomplete counterbalancing technique control for sequencing effects? The influence of sequencing effects are controlled because every treatment condition occurs at each possible position in the sequence. In other words, every condition (A, B, C, and D) precedes and follows every other condition an equal number of times. However, sequencing effects are controlled only if they are linear for all sequences. If they are not, then all types of counterbalancing are inadequate. More specifically, no type of counterbalancing controls for **differential carryover effect**. This problem occurs if an earlier administration of a treatment affects participants' performance in a later treatment condition in one way, but in a different way when followed by a different treatment condition. For example, perhaps the carryover from treatment A is 4 units when it is immediately followed by treatment B, but the carryover from treatment A is 2 units when it is immediately followed by treatment C. To learn more about identifying and dealing with differential carryover effects see Keppel and Zedeck (1989) and Maxwell and Delaney (2004).

Differential carryover effect
A treatment condition affects participants' performance in a later condition in one way and in another way when followed by a different condition

STUDY QUESTION 7.2

- **List and define each of the matching control techniques discussed. How does each technique control for extraneous variables?**

Control of Participant Effects

In Chapter 6, you learned that participants' behavior in an experiment can be influenced by the perceptions and motives they bring with them. We noted the implications of demand characteristics (cues in the experiment that might influence participant behavior) and positive self-presentation (participants' motivation to present themselves in a positive light). For internal validity to be obtained, there must be constancy in participants' effects across treatment groups. Only then can a researcher state with certainty that administration of the independent variable conditions caused the variation in the dependent variable. The experimenter can use a number of control techniques to try to produce identical perceptions in all participants. The following techniques cannot be used in all types of experiments; they are presented so that you can choose the most appropriate technique for the particular study under consideration.

Double-Blind Placebo Method

Double-blind placebo method
Neither the experimenter nor the research participant is aware of the treatment condition administered to the participant

One of the best techniques for controlling demand characteristics is the **double-blind placebo method**. This requires that the experimenter "devise manipulations that appear essentially identical to research participants in all conditions" (Aronson & Carlsmith, 1968) and that the experimenter not know which group received the placebo condition or the experimental manipulation. Both the participant and the experimenter are "blind" to any differences between the conditions.

If you were conducting an experiment designed to test the effect of aspartame on disruptive behavior in young children, you would have to administer this sweetener to one group of children and a placebo to another group. Expectancies would need to be held constant for both groups. To make this a double-blind experiment, the experimenter must not know whether a given participant received the aspartame or the placebo in order to avoid communicating any expectancy of generating disruptive behavior and participants must have the same perceptions of their condition. In short, the experimenter as well as the participant must be blind to the treatment condition that a given participant received. For some time, drug research has recognized the influence of patients' and providers' expectations on their experiences subsequent to taking a drug. Thus, drug research consistently uses this approach to eliminate participant bias.

Use of the double-blind placebo method is a way to eliminate the development of differential participant perceptions because all participants are told the same thing (that they might or might not receive the treatment). And because the researcher does not know which participants have received the experimental treatments, he or she cannot communicate this information to the participants. Therefore, the demand characteristics surrounding the administration of the treatment conditions are controlled by the double-blind placebo model.

Unfortunately, many types of experiments cannot use such a technique because all conditions cannot be made to appear identical in all respects. In such cases, other techniques must be employed.

Deception

Deception
Giving the participant a bogus rationale for the experiment

One of the methods used to solve the problem of participant perceptions is the use of deception in the experiment. **Deception** involves providing all research participants with a hypothesis that is unrelated to or different from the real research hypothesis. Deception can range from minor deceit (an omission or a slight alteration of the truth) to more elaborate schemes. Christensen, Krietsch, White, and Stagner (1985), in their investigation of the impact of diet on mood disturbance, told the research participant that the "food challenge" in which they had just participated had isolated a certain food substance as the causal factor in their mood disturbance. But the particular food mentioned was one that actually had not been investigated in the challenge to which they had participated. Each participant was given bogus information to induce the perception that the offending food had been isolated and that the remaining foods could be eaten without inducing any detrimental effect on mood states. At the other end of the deception continuum, there are experiments in which participants are given unrelated or bogus hypotheses to ensure that they do not discover the real hypothesis.

Is it better to use such deception or simply to refrain from giving any rationale for the tasks to be completed in the experiment? It seems as though providing participants with a false, but plausible, hypothesis is the preferred procedure because the participants' curiosity might be satisfied so that they do not try to devise their own hypotheses. If different participants perceive the study to be investigating different hypotheses, their responses can create a source of bias.

In an experiment with deception, all participants should receive the same false information about what is being done, which should produce relatively constant participant perceptions of the purpose of the experiment. Therefore, deception seems to be an excellent technique for controlling the potential biasing influence that can arise from research participants' differential perceptions regarding the hypothesis of the experiment. The key problem with deception is that it frequently prompts objections on ethical grounds (see Chapter 4).

Control of Participant Interpretation

The techniques just discussed are excellent for controlling some of the demand characteristics of the experiment. "However, these control techniques seem to be limited to ensuring that subjects [research participants] have a unified perception of the treatment condition they are in, whether or not they receive a given treatment, and the purpose of the experiment" (Christensen, 1981, p. 567). There is less recognition of the fact that the participants' perceptions are also affected by the many demand characteristics surrounding the whole procedure. To provide adequate control of participant perceptions and the positive self-presentation motive, one needs to know the types of situations and instructions that will alter participants' perceptions of the experiment. The literature on this issue, however, is in its infancy. At the present time, it is necessary to consider each experiment separately and try to determine if participants' perceptions of the experiment might lead them to respond differentially to the levels of variation in the independent variable.

A variety of techniques that can be used to gain insight into participants' perceptions of an experiment are summarized in Christensen (1981) and Adair and Spinner (1981). These methods can be grouped into two categories: retrospective verbal reports and concurrent verbal reports. A **retrospective verbal report** consists of a technique such as the **postexperimental inquiry**, which is

Retrospective verbal report
An oral report in which the participant retrospectively recalls aspects of the experiment

Postexperimental inquiry
An interview of the participant after the experiment is over

Concurrent verbal report
A participant's oral report of the experiment, which is obtained as the experiment is being performed

Sacrifice groups
Groups of participants who are stopped and interviewed at different stages of the experiment

Concurrent probing
Obtaining a participant's perceptions of the experiment after completion of each trial

Think-aloud technique
A method that requires participants to verbalize their thoughts as they are performing the experiment

exactly what it says it is: questioning the participant regarding the essential aspects of the experiment after completion of the study. What did the participant think the experiment was about? What did he or she think the experimenter expected to find? What type of response did the participant attempt to give, and why? How does the participant think others will respond in this situation? Such information will help to expose the factors underlying the participant's perception and ways that perception might have influenced behavior. The primary disadvantage of retrospective reporting is that participants might fail to recall and report perceptions they had earlier in the experiment.

Concurrent verbal reports include techniques such as Solomon's sacrifice group (Orne, 1973), concurrent probing, and the think-aloud technique (Ericsson & Simon, 1980). In Solomon's **sacrifice groups**, each group of participants is "sacrificed" by being stopped at a different point in the experiment and probed regarding the participants' perceptions of the experiment. You will not have data on the dependent variable from the participants that are "sacrificed," but you will gain insight into how the experiment is understood by the participants. "Sacrificing" can be done at different points in the procedure, not just at the end of the experiment, as in retrospective reporting. **Concurrent probing** requires participants to report at the end of each trial the perceptions they have regarding the experiment. The **think-aloud technique** requires participants to verbalize any thoughts or perceptions they have regarding the experiment while they are performing the experimental task. The obvious disadvantage to concurrent probing and the think-aloud technique is that verbalizing one's thoughts during the experiment might affect participants' behavior and, therefore, the dependant variable (Wilson, 1994). None of the techniques presented here is foolproof or without disadvantages. However, the use of these methods will provide some evidence regarding research participants' perceptions of the experiment and will enable you to design and interpret your experiment in such a way as to minimize the differential influence of the participants' motive of positive self-presentation.

STUDY QUESTIONS 7.3

- **List and describe the control techniques that can be used to create, in the research participants, identical perceptions of the experiment.**
- **Assume you want to identify the research participants' perception of the purpose of the experiment. What are the various ways in which you could accomplish this purpose and how do they operate?**

Control of Experimenter Effects

Experimenter effects
The biasing influence that can be exerted by the experimenter

Experimenter effects are defined in Chapter 6 as the unintentional biasing effects that the experimenter can have on the results of the experiment. The experimenter is not a passive, noninfluential agent in an experiment, but an active potential source of bias. Therefore, potential experimenter effects must be eliminated or minimized.

Control of Recording Errors

Errors resulting from the misrecording of data can be minimized if the person recording the data remains aware of the necessity of making careful observations to ensure the accuracy of data transcription. An even better approach is to use multiple observers or data recorders. If, for example, three individuals independently recorded the data, discrepancies could be noted and resolved to generate more accurate data. Naturally, all data recorders could err in the same direction, which would mask the error, but the probability of this occurring is remote. This procedure could be improved even further if the data recorders were kept blind regarding the experimental conditions in which the participant was responding (Rosenthal, 1978).

The best means for controlling recording errors, although not possible in all studies, is to eliminate the human data recorder and have responses recorded by some mechanical or electronic device. In some research laboratories, the participants' responses are automatically fed into a computer.

Control of Experimenter Attribute Errors

At first glance, there seems to be a simple and logical solution to the problem created by experimenter attributes. Throughout much of this book, we have referred to control in terms of constancy. Because most extraneous variables cannot be eliminated, they are held constant across groups so that no differential influence is present. Remember, if the groups differ only on the independent variable (and not on any extraneous variable), the researcher can conclude that the independent variable is the causal influence of any observed difference. In like manner, the influence of experimenter attributes should be held constant across all treatment conditions. Some experimenters, because of their attributes, produce more of an effect than other experimenters. But this increased effect needs to be constant across all treatment groups.

The influence of experimenter attributes should not significantly affect the *mean differences* among treatment groups. Assume that a cold and a warm experimenter independently conduct the same learning study and that the warm experimenter obtains an average of 3 more units of learning from participants in each of the two treatment groups than does the cold experimenter, as shown in the top half of Table 7.3. Note that the mean *difference* between Groups A and B is identical for both experimenters, indicating that they would have reached the same conclusions even though each obtained different absolute amounts of learning. As long as experimenter 1 administers condition A and condition B, any observed difference between conditions A and B cannot be due to the experimenter (because the experimenter was constant across groups A and B). The same is true for experimenter 2 (as long as this experimenter administers both groups, any difference found cannot be due to this experimenter). In such a situation, the effects of the experimenter attributes do not have any influence on the final conclusions reached. The key point here is to never use one experimenter in one condition and a different experimenter in the other condition; this would make the groups different not just on the independent variable but also on the experimenter.

TABLE 7.3

Hypothetical Data Illustrating the Mean Difference in Learning Obtained from a Warm and a Cold Experimenter

	Experimental Group		
Experimenters	**A**	**B**	**Mean Difference**
Experimenter attributes controlled			
Warm	10	20	10
Cold	7	17	10
Experimenter attributes not controlled			
Warm	8	21	13
Cold	17	17	0

The bottom part of Table 7.3 shows how a more complex experimenter effect might occur. Assume that in the foregoing example a warm experimenter obtained an average of 8 units of performance from participants in group A (imagine that the task was easy but the warmth of the experimenter was seen as condescending because of the easy nature of the task, so participants did not try) and 21 units of performance from participants in group B (imagine that the task was difficult and the warmth of the experimenter was seen as encouraging because of the difficult nature of the task, so participants tried very hard), whereas the cold experimenter obtained identical performance from participants in both treatment groups. In this case, we have an interaction between treatment conditions and experimenter attributes because the experimenter effect varies across the conditions of the experiment. In this case, the two experimenters have produced conflicting results. Unfortunately, we do not know which experimenter attributes interact with numerous independent variables that exist in psychology. Because we do not know how much difference is exerted by various experimenters, a number of experts (e.g., McGuigan, 1963; Rosenthal, 1966) have suggested that several experimenters be employed in a given study. But remember that each experimenter must administer all conditions so that the groups do not become different because they have different experimenters.

If more than one experimenter is employed, evidence can be acquired to determine whether there is an interaction between the treatment conditions and an experimenter's attributes. If identical results are produced by all experimenters, you will have increased assurance that the independent variable and the experimenter attributes did not interact. If the experimenters produced different results, however, you will know that an interaction exists, and you will need to attempt to identify the probable cause of the interaction.

Based on his review of the literature, Johnson (1976) has found that the effect of experimenter attributes can be minimized if the researcher controls for "those experimenter attributes which correspond with the psychological task" (p. 75). In other words, if the experimenter attribute is correlated with the dependent variable, then it should be controlled. On hostility-related tasks, it is necessary to hold the experimenters' hostility level constant. In a weight reduction experiment, the weight of the therapist might be correlated with the success of the program. Therefore, to identify the relative effectiveness of different weight reduction techniques, it would be necessary, at the very least, to make sure the therapists were of approximately the same weight. Such an attribute consideration might not, however, have an influence in a verbal learning study. At the present time, it is necessary for the investigator to use his or her judgment as well as any available research to ascertain whether the given attributes of the experimenters might have a confounding influence on the study.

Control of Experimenter Expectancy Error

Rosenthal and his associates have presented a strong argument for the existence of experimenter expectancy effects in most types of psychological research. Despite the fact that certain individuals, notably Barber and Silver (1968), have presented counterarguments against Rosenthal, it seems important to devise techniques for eliminating potential bias of this type. A number of techniques can be used for eliminating or, at least, minimizing expectancy effects. Generally, they involve automating the experiment or keeping the experimenter ignorant of the condition the participant is in so that appropriate cues cannot be transmitted. Rosenthal (1966) discusses such techniques, several of which are now presented.

Blind technique
A method whereby knowledge of each research participant's treatment condition is kept from the experimenter

The Blind Technique   The **blind technique** actually corresponds to the experimenter's half of the double-blind placebo method. In the blind technique, the experimenter knows the hypothesis but is blind as to which treatment condition the research participant is in. Consequently, the experimenter cannot unintentionally treat groups differently. At present, the blind technique is probably the best procedure for controlling experimenter expectancies. But in many studies, it is impossible to remain ignorant of the condition the participant is in, and in these cases, the next best technique should be employed—the partial blind technique.

Partial blind technique
A method whereby knowledge of each research participant's treatment condition is kept from the experimenter through as many stages of the experiment as possible

The Partial Blind Technique   In cases where the blind technique cannot be employed, it is sometimes possible to use the **partial blind technique**, whereby the experimenter is kept ignorant of the condition the research participant is in for a portion of the study. The experimenter could remain blind while initial contact was made with the participant and during all conditions prior to the actual presentation of the independent variable. When the treatment condition was to be administered to the participant, the experimenter could use some technique (such as pulling a number out of a pocket) that would designate which condition the participant was in. Therefore, all instructions and conditions prior to the manipulations would be standardized and expectancy minimized.

Although this procedure is only a partial solution, it is better than the experimenter's having knowledge of the participant's condition throughout the experiment. If the experimenter can leave the room immediately following administration of the independent variable and allow another person (who is ignorant of the experimental manipulations administered to the participant) to measure the dependent variable, the solution would come closer to approaching completeness. In many experiments, this is not possible because the independent and dependent variables cannot be temporally separated.

Automation   A third possibility for eliminating expectancy bias in animal and human research is total **automation** of the experiment. Indeed, numerous animal researchers currently use automated data collection procedures. Many human studies can also be completely automated by having instructions written, tape recorded, filmed, televised, or presented by means of a computer, and by recording responses via timers, counters, pen recorders, computers, or similar devices. These procedures are easily justified to the participant on the basis of control and standardization, and they minimize the participant–experimenter interaction.

> **Automation**
> The technique of totally automating the experimental procedures so that no experimenter–participant interaction is required

STUDY QUESTIONS 7.4

- **What techniques can be used to control for experimenter recording errors, experimenter attribute errors, and experimenter expectancy errors?**
- **How does each technique produce the necessary control?**

Likelihood of Achieving Control

We have looked at several categories of extraneous variables that need to be controlled and a number of techniques for controlling them. Do these methods allow us to achieve the desired control? Are they effective? The answer to these questions seems to be both yes and no. The control techniques are effective, but not 100% effective. The key is to use the strongest control methods available and to do your best to collect additional data to help determine how well the control techniques have worked. Then you must inform the reader of your research report how well the control techniques seem to have worked, and adjust your interpretations of findings accordingly.

Summary

In conducting an experiment that attempts to identify a causal relationship, the experimenter must accomplish one important task: controlling for the influence of extraneous variables. In experiments that have more than one group (e.g., experimental and control group), the desired outcome is for the groups to be equivalent on all extraneous variables *except* for the independent variable (i.e., the different groups get the levels of the independent variable). When the only difference between the groups is due to the independent variable, the researcher can legitimately claim that differences between the groups found on the dependent variable at the end of the experiment are due to the independent variable. Most control techniques operate by attempting to equate the groups; the idea is to eliminate differential influence of extraneous variables. Following are two main control techniques carried out at the beginning of the experiment: random assignment of participants to groups (which is the best control technique) and matching. Here are the matching techniques covered: matching by holding variables constant (i.e., only use one level of the extraneous variable; e.g., only use females in the study), matching by building the extraneous variable into the research design (e.g., you might make gender a design variable and compare experimental and control conditions for males only and females only), matching by yoked control (matching participants on the basis of the temporal sequence of administering an event), and matching by equating participants (via precision control or frequency distribution control). Control techniques carried out during the experiment were also discussed. They include counterbalancing (randomized counterbalancing, intrasubject counterbalancing, complete counterbalancing, and incomplete counterbalancing), methods for dealing with participant effects (including double-blind placebo method and deception), methods for dealing with participant interpretation (including retrospective verbal reports, postexperimental inquiry, and concurrent verbal reports such as sacrifice groups, concurrent probing, and the think-aloud technique), and methods for dealing with experimenter effects (such as checking for recording errors, controlling experimenter attribute errors, and controlling for experimenter expectancy errors through the blind technique, the partial blind technique, and automation).

Key Terms and Concepts

Automation
Blind technique
Carryover effect
Complete counterbalancing
Concurrent probing
Concurrent verbal report
Counterbalancing
Deception
Differential carryover effect
Differential influence
Double-blind placebo method
Experimenter effects
Frequency distribution control
Group counterbalancing
Incomplete counterbalancing
Intrasubject counterbalancing

Matching
Matching variable
Method of difference
Order effect
Partial blind technique
Postexperimental inquiry
Precision control
Random assignment
Randomization
Randomized counterbalancing
Retrospective verbal report
Sacrifice groups
Statistical control
Think-aloud technique
Yoked control

Related Internet Sites

http://www.randomizer.org
This site permits the user, or student, to randomly sample participants from a defined population or to randomly assign participants to an experimental treatment condition.

http://www.psychology.uiowa.edu/Faculty/wasserman/Glossary/yoke.html
This site has a short tutorial on the yoked control design.

http://skepdic.com/experimentereffect.html
This site gives a good example of experimenter expectancy effects and how they can influence the outcome of a study.

Practice Test   *The answers to these questions can be found in the publisher's Web site.*

1. If you could use only one control technique, which one should you use?
   a. Random assignment of participants to groups
   b. Matching by holding variables constant
   c. Matching by yoked control
   d. Double-blind placebo model
   e. Counterbalancing

2. Assume that you wanted to investigate the effect of caffeine on a person's ability to identify the number of times the letter *q* appeared in a page filled with a random list of letters. To control for the effect of a person's reaction time, you divided people into those that had high and low reaction times and then included this difference in reaction time as another independent variable in the design of your study. By controlling for the possible influence of reaction time in this way you used
   a. Random assignment of participants to reaction time groups
   b. Yoked control by yoking the reaction time to identification of the letter *q*
   c. Counterbalancing by having participants in each reaction-time group
   d. Matching by including the extraneous variable into the design of the study
   e. The blind technique, because the people did not know if their reaction times were fast or slow

3. If you identify extraneous variables that are correlated with the dependent variable and control for them by matching participants on an individual basis and then randomly assign the matched participants to groups, which control technique have you used?
   a. Matching with random assignment
   b. Yoked control
   c. Precision control
   d. Frequency distribution control
   e. Procedural control

4. Assume you wanted to find out if alcohol increased a person's aggressiveness. To test this hypothesis, you wanted to test people's aggressiveness while they were under the influence of alcohol and while they were not. However, you know that you are asking people to perform under two conditions and that performing once might change their performance on the second occasion. To control for this effect you elect to
   a. Randomly select the research participants from the larger group of people who volunteer for the study
   b. Match the people who participate in terms of their sensitivity to alcohol
   c. Administer the alcohol in a double-blind fashion
   d. Assess the participants' perceptions of whether they can tell they are drinking alcohol
   e. Counterbalance the administration of the alcohol and no-alcohol conditions

5. If you wanted to control for the expectancies that the experimenter might have regarding the outcome of the experiment, you might
   a. Use deception
   b. Counterbalance the treatment conditions so that any change due to expectancies is distributed equally across groups of participants
   c. Automate the experimental procedure so that the experimenter does not interact with the research participant
   d. Randomly assign participants to treatment conditions so that the expectancies are distributed equally across groups
   e. Match participants so that the expectancies are the same for all participants

Challenge Exercises

1. You want to conduct an experiment to test the effect of a new drug for treating children with attention deficit disorder. You have decided to test four different amounts of the new drug—5, 10, 15, and 20 mg. The parents of 40 children with attention deficit disorder have volunteered their child to participate in the study. Randomly assign the 40 children to the four drug conditions using the table of random numbers in Appendix B, describing each step taken in this procedure and what you did in each step.
   a. Step 1
   b. Step 2
   c. Step 3
   d. Step 4

Participants Randomly Assigned to Groups

Group 1	Group 2	Group 3	Group 4

   e. Step 5

2. You want to test the effect of a new drug for treating children with attention deficit disorder, but this time you want all the children to take a placebo—5, 10, 15, and 20 mg on different days. You know that using this procedure might result in either carryover or order effects, so you want to counterbalance the order of presentation of the five dosages. Construct the different counterbalanced order of treatment conditions using the incomplete counterbalancing technique.

3. Dr. Know developed a new type of therapy for treating individuals' depression. He wanted to find out if the therapy technique he had developed was effective and resulted in an amelioration of depression. Assume that he enlisted your aid in setting up a study that would test the effectiveness of this therapy. Identify the extraneous variables that could confound the results of this experiment, explain how the confounding would take place, and identify how you would control for these extraneous variables.

CHAPTER 8

Experimental Research Design

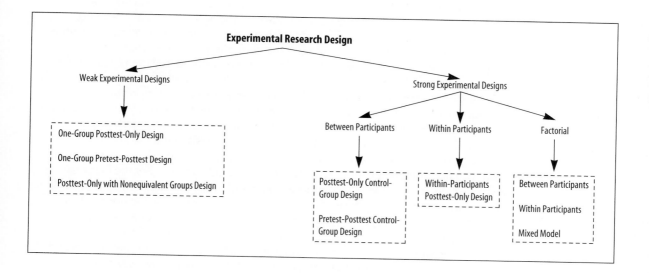

In February 1999, Cathy Hainer (1999) wrote an article for *USA Today* on the ancient art of face reading. This article summarized a book written by Rose Rosetree, a leading face reader, in which she stated that reading a person's face can tell you things such as "how a person spends money, makes decisions, and works." Face reading, which is also called physiognomy, is similar to phrenology (examination of the bumps on the skull of a person's head for personality cues), which was practiced in psychology during the nineteenth century. The difference is that face reading is focused on the outward appearance of the face (rather than bumps on the skull) and does not require touching. Many face readers work from photographs.

According to Rose Rosetree, prominent facial features signal personality characteristics. The position of a person's ears, whether they sit high, low, or in the middle of a person's head, is significant because it reveals the speed with which a person makes decisions. Eyelids provide a clue to a person's emotionality and aggressiveness. Straight lower eyelids indicate wariness, suspicion, and shyness. Curved lower lids indicate an emotionally open person. The fullness of lips is an indication of the degree of comfort in talking about personal issues. People with full lips are more comfortable talking openly about private issues, whereas people with thin lips don't like to share personal details.

In reading such claims, different people will have different reactions. Some will consider it total garbage; others will place considerable faith in it and make decisions based on the conclusions drawn from face readers. Yet others will, perhaps, be skeptical but open enough to consider that it might have some validity. According to Cathy Hainer (1999), face reading is enjoying a renaissance along with several other ancient Chinese arts. However, the real question is this: Does this approach really work? Does it accurately reveal the personality characteristics of individuals? Rose Rosetree is convinced of its accuracy and has written a book advocating this approach. However, just because some individuals are convinced of and believe in a practice does not necessarily make it valid. Many people believe in the accuracy of palm reading, handwriting analysis, tarot cards, and astrology. Most scientists, however, place little faith in the accuracy of these techniques because there is little objective data to support the conclusions drawn. Psychology gave up phrenology many years ago because it did not provide a window into a person's personality.

How do we determine if face reading accurately portrays a person's personality characteristics? We must test experimentally the conclusions drawn from face reading to determine its accuracy. This means that we must formulate a research design that can be used to answer this research question. On the basis of the material presented in the previous chapters, you know that answering such a research question requires that you first identify the independent and dependent variables. For the face reading question, you might test the hypothesis that people with ears located high, low, or in the middle of the head differ in the speed with which they make decisions. In testing this research question, your independent variable is the location of the ears on the head and the dependent variable is the speed of decision making. You also have to identify the variables that must be controlled in order to ensure internal validity and use techniques for controlling for the influence of these extraneous variables. For example, you want to control for the intelligence of the individuals comprising the three levels of the independent variable, which might be accomplished by matching individuals' intellectual levels. Only after these decisions are made would you construct a design that would incorporate the independent and dependent variables and the control techniques. This design would provide a strategy for collecting data that will give an answer to the research question regarding the validity of conclusions drawn from face reading about the location of ears on a person's head.

Introduction

Research design
The outline, plan, or strategy used to investigate the research problem

After a research topic has been selected and decisions have been made about the independent and dependent variables, it is necessary to develop a plan for collecting data and testing the effect of the independent variable(s) on the dependent variable. This plan is the research design of the experiment. The term **research design** refers to the outline, plan, or strategy that specifies the procedure to be used in seeking an answer to your research question(s). It specifies such things as how to collect and analyze the data. Building a research design is often a complicated process because you might encounter constraints on what type of design will work for your research question.

The goal in research is to use the strongest design that is possible, ethical, and feasible for your research question. But what makes a design strong or weak? You will see that strong designs often include pretests (to measure the level of the dependent variable before the start of the experiment), control groups (to allow a comparison of the experimental group to a group that did not receive the treatment), and random assignment (to equate the experimental and control groups at the outset of the experiment).

This chapter is very important because experimental research is the best type of research when you want to make claims about *cause and effect*. We start with a discussion of several weak designs that do not control for important threats to internal validity. We then cover strong designs that provide excellent control for the threats to internal validity and, therefore, provide strong evidence about causal relationships between independent and dependent variables. Next, we discuss factorial designs; these designs are strong and very important because they enable researchers to test for the separate and interactive effects of two or more independent variables. We conclude with comments on choosing or constructing a research design.

STUDY QUESTION 8.1 | **What is a research design, and what is its purpose?**

Weak Experimental Research Designs

In seeking answers to questions about cause and effect, the scientist conducts experiments. Ideally, these experiments control for all threats to internal validity and support a conclusion about whether the independent variable affected the dependent variable. However, sometimes this is not possible, and many threats to internal validity cannot be eliminated. As Shadish et al. (2002) have pointed out, sometimes researchers have to use designs that do not control for various threats to internal validity such as when the focus of attention is on external validity or when ethical considerations preclude including design elements that would control for more threats to internal validity. When these weaker designs are used, it becomes much more difficult to infer a causal relationship between your independent and dependent variables. The first few designs that we discuss are considered **weak experimental designs** because they control for very few threats to internal validity. One should avoid these designs when a strong design can be used.

Weak experimental designs
Designs that do not control for many extraneous variables and provide weak evidence of cause and effect

One-group posttest-only design
Administration of a posttest to a single group of participants after they have been given an experimental treatment condition

One-Group Posttest-Only Design

In the **one-group posttest-only design**, a single group of research participants is measured on a dependent variable after having undergone an experimental treatment. For example, perhaps an institution starts a training program (the experimental treatment condition). The institution wants to evaluate the effectiveness of the program; so upon completion of the program, it assesses knowledge,

FIGURE 8.1

One-group posttest-only design.

Treatment	Posttest measure
X	O

attitudes, and behavioral outcomes of the program participants. If the outcome (i.e., dependent variable) measures are positive and if the individuals' performances are good, the administrator might want to conclude that the program worked.

The design is depicted in Figure 8.1. For this design and for all designs depicted in this chapter, the symbol "O" stands for measurement of the dependent variable(s) of interest to the researcher. The symbol "X" stands for the experimental intervention, where the researcher or professionals working with the experimenter actively provide some condition to the participants that they otherwise would not have experienced. As you can see in Figure 8.1, the structure of the one-group posttest-only design includes an experimental manipulation (X) followed by measurement (O) of the dependent variable(s).

For yielding scientific data, the one-group posttest-only design is rarely useful because the design allows no evidence of what the participants would have scored on the dependent variables had they not received the treatment. Specifically, the design does not have a no-treatment control group (which would allow a comparison of participants' posttest performance with the performance of a similar group that did not receive the treatment) and the design does not have a pretest (which would allow a comparison of participants' posttest performance with their performance prior to treatment). Because this design does not include either of these comparisons, it should be viewed as a faulty design. It is difficult to know if any effect is due to the treatment or to some confounding extraneous variable. Shadish et al. (2002) point out that this design does have merit in the rare cases where specific background information exists on the dependent variable and additional studies have established the mechanism by which the independent variable influences the dependent variable. However, because all of this information is rarely available, this design is rarely used by psychologists.

One-Group Pretest–Posttest Design

One-group pretest–posttest design

Design in which a treatment condition is interjected between a pretest and posttest of the dependent variable

The **one-group pretest–posttest design** improves the one-group posttest design by adding a pretest to measure the dependent variable before the treatment is introduced. Figure 8.2 depicts such a plan, which corresponds to the one-group pretest–posttest design. A group of research participants is measured on the dependent variable, O, prior to administration of the treatment condition. The independent variable, X, is then administered, and O is again measured. The difference between the pretest and posttest scores is taken as an indication of the effectiveness of the treatment condition.

For example, imagine that your school district adopted an expensive new curriculum for reading in first grade. Students' reading was measured at the beginning of the school year (pretest, O), the reading curriculum was employed daily throughout the academic year (treatment, X), and reading was measured

FIGURE 8.2
One-group
pretest–posttest
design.

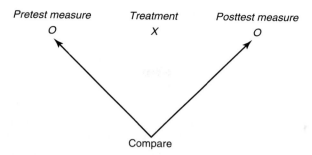

again at the end of the year (posttest, O). Results indicate that students' reading improved by a full grade level. Such a study has intuitive appeal and at first seems to represent a good way to accomplish the research purpose—a change in performance can be seen and documented. In actuality, this design represents only a small improvement over the one-group posttest-only study because of the many uncontrolled rival hypotheses that could also explain the obtained results.

In our example, one academic year elapsed between the pretest and posttest. Consequently, the uncontrolled rival hypotheses of history, testing, regression artifact, instrumentation, and maturation could account for some, if not all, of the observed change in performance. In order to determine conclusively that the observed change was caused by the treatment effect (the experimental curriculum) and not by any of these rival hypotheses, researchers should have included an equated group of first graders who did not receive the new curriculum. This equated group's performance could have been compared with the performance of the children who received the experimental treatment. If a significant difference had been found between the scores of these two groups, it could have been attributed to the influence of the experimental curriculum, because both groups would have experienced any history, testing, regression artifact, instrumentation, and maturation effects that had occurred, and, therefore, these variables would have been controlled. The design of one-group pretest–posttest study is weak, not so much because the sources of rival hypotheses *can* affect the results, but because in most cases we do not know if they did.

Although the one-group pretest–posttest does not allow us to control or to test for the potential influence of these effects, it is not totally worthless. In situations in which it is impossible to obtain an equated comparison group, the design can be used to provide some information. However, the confidence one has in concluding that the treatment produced the observed effect is dependent on the success of identifying the possible threats to internal validity and then collecting data demonstrating that these threats did not influence the outcome.

**Posttest-only design
with nonequivalent
groups**
Design in which the
performance of an
experimental group is
compared with that of
a nonequivalent control
group at the posttest

Posttest-Only Design with Nonequivalent Groups

The primary disadvantage of the previous two designs is that we cannot know if the independent variable influenced the dependent variable. The **posttest-only design with nonequivalent groups** (see Figure 8.3) makes an attempt to remedy this deficiency by including a control group. In this design, one group of

FIGURE 8.3

Posttest-only design with nonequivalent groups. The dashed line indicates nonequivalent groups.

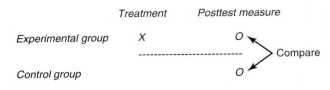

research participants receives the treatment condition (X) and is then compared on the dependent variable (O) with a group that did not receive this treatment condition. This sounds ideal. The problem is that in this design, the comparison group is a nonequivalent group. That is, the participants in the comparison group might differ in important ways from the participants in the experimental group. In Chapter 7, this threat to internal validity was called *selection*.

In our example of the new reading curriculum, let's imagine that some schools adopt the new curriculum and others do not. At the end of the year, we compare reading scores of the schools that adopted the curriculum to those that did not, and we observe that the schools with the new curriculum scored better on the reading test. The problem is that these groups might differ in many important ways including initial reading levels of the students, parental involvement, and parental education levels. The researcher will not know whether the posttest difference in reading level is due to the treatment or due to one of these initial differences between the groups.

The only way to ensure that the groups are equated is to assign participants randomly to the two groups. The dashed line in Figure 8.3 is used to indicate that random assignment is not included in the nonequivalent posttest-only design. In studies in which it is not possible to assign participants randomly, the next best technique is to match on relevant variables. However, matching is no substitute for random assignment because it does not control for other variables. This design, therefore, does not exclude possible selection effects from the treatment effect and should be considered a weak design.

STUDY QUESTIONS 8.2

- **What are the components and structure of the weak experimental research designs?**
- **Explain why the threats to internal validity exist in each of these designs.**

Strong Experimental Research Designs

The designs just presented are weak designs because, in general, they do not provide a way of isolating the effect of the treatment condition; rival hypotheses are not eliminated. How, then, is a strong research design different? Strong experimental research designs have greater internal validity. That is, they provide more assurance that the effect of the independent variable on the dependent variable has been isolated and tested.

In order to achieve internal validity, we must eliminate potential rival hypotheses. This can be accomplished by two primary means: control techniques and a control

Control group
The group of participants that does not receive the active treatment condition and serves as a standard of comparison for determining whether the treatment condition produced any causal effect

Experimental group
The group of participants that receives the treatment condition that is intended to produce an effect

Counterfactual
What the experimental group participants' responses would have been if they had *not* received the treatment

Strong experimental designs
Designs that effectively control extraneous variables and provide strong evidence of cause and effect

group. The most important control technique, as indicated in Chapter 7, is random assignment to groups (also called randomization) because this is the only means by which known *and* unknown variables can be controlled. Randomization is the best control technique because it is the best means for insuring that your groups vary *only* on the variable that you manipulate—your independent variable. The groups should be comparable across all variables other than the independent variable.

The second means of eliminating potential rival hypotheses is the inclusion of a control group. A **control group** is a group of research participants that do not receive the active level of the independent variable; they might either receive zero amount of the independent variable or receive an amount that is in some sense a *standard* value, such as what they would typically receive if they were not participants in research. An **experimental group** (also called a treatment group) is a group of research participants that receive some level of the independent variable that is intended to produce an effect. In our study of the reading curriculum, if we randomly assigned half of the first graders to receive the experimental reading curriculum and the other half to receive the standard reading instruction that was typically used in the school district, we would be able to determine if the reading curriculum really caused an increase in reading scores beyond the standard practice.

A control group serves two functions. First, it serves as a source of comparison. Only by including a control group—assuming all other variables are controlled—can we get a concrete indication of whether the treatment condition produced results different from those that would have been attained in the absence of the treatment. The responses of the control group must stand for the responses that members of the experimental group would have given if they had not received the treatment condition. Stated more technically, the control group is used to estimate the **counterfactual** (i.e., what the participants' responses *would have been had they not received the treatment*). The participants in the two groups must be as similar as possible so that theoretically they would yield identical scores in the absence of the introduction of the independent variable.

Second, the control group serves as a control for rival hypotheses. The experimenter's goal is for all variables to operate on the control and experimental groups identically, except for the one variable (i.e., the independent variable) being manipulated by the experimenter. In this way, the influence of extraneous variables is held constant. If a control group is included and random assignment is used, extraneous variables will equally impact the performance of *both* the control and the experimental participants, effectively holding the influence of the extraneous variables constant. If an extraneous variable affects both groups equally, then the groups will not differ on that variable, enabling the researcher to conclude that the reason the groups differed at the posttest was because of the treatment. The only variable the groups should vary on is the independent variable.

In the next sections of this chapter, we consider several strong experimental research designs. To be a **strong experimental design**, the research design must enable the researcher to maintain control over the situation in terms of assignment of research participants to groups, in terms of who gets the treatment condition, and in terms of the amount of the treatment condition that participants receive. In other words, the researcher must have a controlled experiment in order to have confidence in the relations observed between the independent and dependent variable. Strong research designs can take the form of a between-participants research design in which participants are randomly assigned to different groups and participate in a single condition or a within-participants design where participants serve as their own control group by participating in all of the conditions sequentially. We now discuss these two major types of research designs.

STUDY QUESTIONS 8.3

- **What are the criteria that need to be met to have a strong experimental research design?**
- **What function is served by the control group?**
- **What function is served by random assignment of participants to groups?**

Between-Participants Designs

Between-participants designs
Groups are produced by random assignment, and the different groups are exposed to the different levels of the independent variable

In the strong experimental research designs known as **between-participants designs**, the groups are composed of different people, the participants in the groups are exposed to different experimental conditions, and the participants are randomly assigned to the groups. The use of random assignment of the participants to different groups eliminates most of the threats to internal validity. Because these designs rely on random assignment, they are also called **randomized designs**. We now introduce two basic between-participants research designs, including the posttest-only control-group design, and the pretest–posttest control-group design. These are "basic" designs because they have only one independent variable and one dependent variable. In the section "Factorial Designs," we introduce designs that include more than one independent variable.

Randomized designs
Between-participants designs in which participants are randomly assigned to groups

Posttest-Only Control-Group Design

Posttest-only control-group design
Administration of a posttest to two or more randomly assigned groups of participants that receive the different levels of the independent variable

In the between-participants **posttest-only control-group design**, the research participants are randomly assigned to as many groups as there are experimental conditions. For example, if a researcher was investigating the effects of one independent variable (e.g., social skills training) and the presence-versus-absence form of variation (one group receives the training, one group does not) was being used with this independent variable, participants would be randomly assigned to two groups, as illustrated in Figure 8.4. This design is similar in appearance to the nonequivalent posttest-only design, except for one important difference: The nonequivalent posttest-only design lacks random assignment. Remember that the nonequivalent posttest-only design was criticized primarily because it does not provide any assurance of equality among the comparison groups.

The between-participants posttest-only control-group design provides the necessary equivalence on extraneous variables by randomly assigning participants to two or more groups. If enough participants are included to allow

FIGURE 8.4
Posttest-only
control-group design.

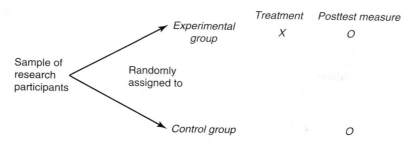

randomization to work, then, theoretically, all possible known and unknown extraneous variables are controlled (excluding those such as experimenter expectancies and any differential treatment the participants might receive during the experiment on any variable other than the independent variable). During the conduct of the experiment, the experimenter must treat all groups exactly the same except for the variation on the independent variable.

By including a randomized control group, many of the threats to internal validity discussed in Chapter 6 are controlled for, including history, maturation, testing, instrumentation, and regression artifact. These threats are controlled because the effects of these variables affect both the experimental and the control groups. For example, when participants are randomly assigned, each group should have the same percentage of extreme scores and, therefore, should demonstrate the same degree of regression toward the mean. Selection bias is naturally ruled out because random assignment has assured the equality of the experimental and control groups at the time of randomization. As stated earlier, randomization does not provide 100% assurance. It is, however, our *best* protection against the selection rival hypothesis.

As long as the extraneous variables affect both groups equally, any observed difference between the groups will not be due to these variables, and we can assume that the difference is due to the independent variable. Thus we can conclude that the independent variable is the cause of the different performance on the dependent variable. Remember, we want the groups to be identical on all variables except the independent variable. Note, however, that if any of the threats to internal validity act differentially, then the threat will remain. As discussed in Chapter 6, differential effects are also known as "additive and interactive effects." An effect acts differentially when it causes the groups to become different because the threat affects one group but not the other group.

For example, if the participants in the experimental group were treated in one session and the participants in the control group were treated in a different session, it is possible that certain events took place in one session that did not take place in the other. If a differential event did take place (e.g., laughter, a joke, or a comment about the purpose of the experimental procedure), there would be no way of eliminating its influence, and it might produce an effect that is picked up by the dependent variable for only one group. Such an event would have to be considered a possible cause for any significant difference noted between the groups, and it competes with the independent variable in explaining the difference between the groups' performance on the dependent variable.

Fortunately, the internal validity threats usually do not occur differentially (i.e., affect the groups differentially) when the participants are randomly assigned to the groups and when the experimenter treats the groups similarly during the experiment in every way except for the administration of the levels of the independent variable. For example, to control for instrumentation, it is required that the groups do not differ with regard to the observers or interviewers that collect the dependent variable data. Therefore, either the same observers or interviewers must be used for both groups (and "blinded" in that they do not know what group participants are in) or, if enough observers or interviewers are available, they should be randomly assigned to individual observation sessions. The key point is that random assignment typically ensures that the effect of extraneous variables are randomly distributed across the groups and thus not threatening the internal validity of the experiment.

Strengths and Weaknesses of the Posttest-Only Control-Group Design

At least two difficulties can be identified in the posttest-only control-group design. First, although randomization is the best control technique available for achieving equivalence, it does not provide complete assurance that the necessary equivalence has been attained. This is particularly true when the group of participants being randomized is small (e.g., less than 30 participants). If there is any doubt that random assignment will work, it is advisable to combine matching and statistical control along with the randomization technique.

Second, because the posttest-only control-group design lacks a pretest, it lacks the potential benefits of including a pretest, such as providing a way to check on the success of the randomization process (i.e., are the groups similar on the pretest measure?), and it lacks the increased "statistical power" associated with the inclusion of a pretest. When *statistical power* is increased, the researcher is more likely to detect a statistically significant difference between the groups if there is a true difference in the populations from which the groups were sampled. (This idea is demonstrated in Chapter 15 when we discuss a statistical technique called the *analysis of covariance*.) More advantages of including a pretest in an experiment are provided in the next section.

The most basic version of the posttest-only control-group design contains only two groups (i.e., an experimental group and a control group), but it illustrates the two key features of all strong between-participants design: inclusion of a control group and random assignment of participants to the groups. These features produce a very strong design for eliminating threats to internal validity. However, experiments are seldom confined to just two levels of variation of one independent variable. Instead, most studies use several levels of variation of the independent variable, resulting in more than two groups.

For example, let's say that a recent study found that college students who were assigned to monthly meetings with their advisor were more likely to complete

FIGURE 8.5
Posttest-only
control-group design
with three levels of
variation of the
independent variable.

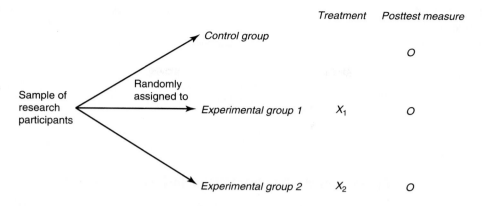

college. We might want to know if meeting each month was necessary for the program to be successful. To obtain information about how many advisor sessions are needed, the researcher could randomly assign students to three different groups that varied on the number of sessions received. In one experimental group, the participants would meet with their advisor once each month for a year. In a second experimental group, the participants would meet with their advisor once every 2 months, and a control group would be included that did not have any meetings with their advisor. The structure of this expanded posttest-only control-group design is depicted in Figure 8.5. This design includes more than one experimental group and it allows us to pose and address more specific research questions.

STUDY QUESTIONS 8.4

- **What is the structure of a posttest-only control-group design?**
- **What threats to internal validity are eliminated with this design, and how does the design control for these threats?**
- **What are some of the strengths and weaknesses of the posttest-only control-group design?**

Pretest–posttest control-group design
Administration of a posttest to two or more randomly assigned groups of participants after the groups have been pretested and administered the different levels of the independent variable

Pretest–Posttest Control-Group Design

You can see a depiction of the basic **pretest–posttest control-group design** in Figure 8.6. It is similar to the posttest-only control-group design except that the pretest–posttest control-group design includes pretest measurement before administration of the experimental and control conditions. Both of these designs are strong on internal validity and rule out all of the basic threats to internal validity. The internal validity of both designs are threatened only if one of the threats acts differentially (i.e., if the effect of the threat occurs on one group but not the other). Because of random assignment, however, these differential threats occur infrequently. Both designs are also similar in that additional experimental groups can be added to the basic two-group design versions.

FIGURE 8.6
Pretest–posttest
control-group design.

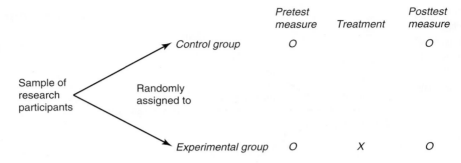

Advantages and Disadvantages of Including a Pretest

You might wonder why a researcher would add a pretest to the posttest-only control-group design to produce a pretest–posttest control-group design. There are several reasons why many researchers prefer to include a pretest in this design and other designs (Lana, 1969; Maxwell & Delaney, 2004; Selltiz et al., 1959). First, including the pretest measurement allows the researcher to check to see how well the randomization process worked. Although random assignment provides the greatest assurance possible of *initial comparability* of research participants, it is not infallible. When a pretest is included, the researcher does not have to assume that randomization worked properly; the researcher can check to see if the groups are similar on the dependent variable after random assignment but before the experimental conditions are introduced. If the researcher measures the participants on additional variables relevant to the study, initial comparability can also be checked on those variables (e.g., motivation, intelligence, attitudes).

Second, the inclusion of measurement of additional variables during the pretest also enables the researcher to check to see if the relationship between the independent variable and the dependent variable depends on the participants' status on other potentially important independent variables. For example, perhaps the treatment works well for men but not for women. If an additional variable (such as gender) "interacts" with the independent variable, the researcher will know that this additional variable must be added to the research design. When the new variable is added, the design becomes a factorial design, which is discussed later in the chapter.

Third, if a pretest is included, the researcher can determine if a ceiling effect is likely to occur (when pretest scores are examined before introducing the experimental conditions). A **ceiling effect** occurs when the participants' scores on the dependent variable are so high that there is little or no room left for improvement. For example, if a dependent variable had a maximum value of 100 and the average score for some participants was 98 or 99 on the pretest, then there would be little room left for improvement. If pretest data are examined prior to administration of the treatment, the researcher can eliminate the participants with extreme scores and conduct the experiment with those participants who have some possibility for improvement. If pretest scores are not examined until after administration of the treatment and no treatment effect is found, then pretest scores should be examined to determine if a ceiling effect might have occurred.

Ceiling effect
Situation where participants' pretest scores on the dependent variable are too high to allow for additional increases

Fourth, if the experimental and control groups are slightly different on the dependent variable measure at the pretest, the researcher can use a statistical technique called **analysis of covariance** to statistically control for these pretest differences. Not only does this statistical technique adjust for pretest differences, it also provides a more accurate and powerful test of the differences between the experimental and control group posttest scores. This means that if the experiment has an impact, this design is slightly more likely to pick up on the impact because of the inclusion of the pretest.

Fifth, perhaps the most common reason for pretesting is to gain an empirical demonstration of whether the treatment condition succeeded in producing a change in the research participants. The most direct way of gaining such evidence of *change* is to measure the difference between the pretest and posttest scores.

There is at least one potential difficulty when a pretest is used in the pretest–posttest control-group design and other designs. The participants might change in some way because they were given a pretest. Note, however, that because both groups were given the pretest, they both should be affected equally by taking the pretest; therefore, the internal validity of the design is not weakened. However, external validity can sometimes be weakened when a pretest is included in the design.

As you know from Chapter 6, external validity is the degree to which the results of a study generalize. The issue here is that when everyone in the experiment is given a pretest, the results might generalize best to people who have taken a pretest, and might not generalize as well to those who have not taken a pretest. Because this generalization problem does not exist in the posttest-only control-group design, the pretest–posttest control-group design can sometimes have slightly less external validity.

Many researchers believe that the advantages of including a pretest in the pretest–posttest control-group design outweigh this disadvantage. A key point in this section is that both the posttest-only control-group design and the pretest–posttest control-group design are very strong research designs, but they have slightly different strengths and weaknesses.

| **Analysis of covariance** A statistical procedure in which group means are compared after adjusting for pretest differences |

STUDY QUESTIONS 8.5

- **Diagram a pretest–posttest control-group design, and explain the components of this design.**
- **What threats to internal validity are eliminated with this design, and how does the design control for these threats?**
- **What are some of the strengths and weaknesses of including a pretest in the pretest–posttest control-group design?**

Within-Participants Designs

| **Within-participants design** All participants receive all conditions |

In a **within-participants design**, all research participants are members of all experimental conditions in the experiment. Within-participants designs are also called **repeated measures designs** because all participants are measured "repeatedly" (i.e., under each experimental condition). The basic within-participants design is

FIGURE 8.7
Within-participants posttest-only design with 15 participants.

Note: X_1 is condition 1, X_2 is condition 2, X_3 is condition 3, P stands for participant, and O stands for posttest measurement. Note that participants 1–15 are in all three treatment conditions.

$$X_1 \quad O \quad X_2 \quad O \quad X_3 \quad O$$

P_1	P_1	P_1
P_2	P_2	P_2
P_3	P_3	P_3
P_4	P_4	P_4
P_5	P_5	P_5
P_6	P_6	P_6
P_7	P_7	P_7
P_8	P_8	P_8
P_9	P_9	P_9
P_{10}	P_{10}	P_{10}
P_{11}	P_{11}	P_{11}
P_{12}	P_{12}	P_{12}
P_{13}	P_{13}	P_{13}
P_{14}	P_{14}	P_{14}
P_{15}	P_{15}	P_{15}

Repeated measures design
Another name for a within-participants design

Within-participants posttest-only design
All participants receive all conditions, and a posttest is administered after each condition is administered

the **within-participants posttest-only design** in which the participants are given a posttest measuring their performance on the dependent variable after they have been exposed to each experimental condition. This design is depicted in Figure 8.7.

Because of the likelihood of carryover effects when the same participants receive all experimental conditions, many researchers use the control technique discussed in Chapter 7 called *counterbalancing*. The idea of counterbalancing is to give the experimental conditions in different orders to different sets of participants. In this way, the researcher can average out basic (linear) carryover effects. A depiction of the within-participants posttest-only design with counterbalancing is shown in Figure 8.8. Notice that all of the participants still receive all of the experimental conditions in the counterbalanced version of the within-participants posttest-only design.

As an example of the within-participants posttest-only design is a study conducted by Mahoney, Taylor, Kanarek, and Samuel (2005) to test the effect of breakfast type on cognitive performance. Elementary school students participated in three within-participant sessions (on 3 different days). Each session consisted of one of three types of breakfast (cereal, oatmeal, no breakfast) followed by a series of cognitive tasks. Order of breakfast type was counterbalanced across the

FIGURE 8.8
Within-participants posttest-only design with counter-balancing for 15 participants.

$$X_1 \quad O \quad X_2 \quad O \quad X_3 \quad O \quad \longleftarrow \quad P_1, P_2, P_3, P_4, P_5$$

$$X_2 \quad O \quad X_3 \quad O \quad X_1 \quad O \quad \longleftarrow \quad P_6, P_7, P_8, P_9, P_{10}$$

$$X_3 \quad O \quad X_1 \quad O \quad X_2 \quad O \quad \longleftarrow \quad P_{11}, P_{12}, P_{13}, P_{14}, P_{15}$$

three sessions. Mahoney et al. found that the students performed worst in the no breakfast sessions and best in the oatmeal sessions. Because of the variability among different people, within-participants designs (where participants serve as their own control) are often the designs that are employed in research using cognitive or physiological measures.

Strengths and Weaknesses of Within-Participants Designs

As we have explained, in within-participants designs, the same people participate in *all* experimental conditions. Because of this, participants serve as their own control, and variables such as age, gender, and prior experience remain constant over the entire experiment. In other words, if all participants are in all conditions, the conditions can't differ because some kinds of people are in one condition but not in another. This is a powerful technique of control. Because the participants serve as their own control, they are perfectly matched in the various treatment conditions; this increases the sensitivity of the experiment. Therefore, within-participants designs are maximally sensitive to the effects of the independent variable.

Also, the within-participants design does not require as many participants as does the between-participants design. In the *within-participants* design, with all participants participating in all treatment conditions, the number of participants needed for an entire experiment is equal to the number of participants needed for one experimental treatment condition. In the *between-participants* design, the number of research participants needed equals the number of participants required for one treatment condition times the number of treatment conditions. If 25 participants are needed in each treatment condition and there are three treatment conditions, then only 25 participants are needed in a within-participants design, whereas 75 participants (25 times 3) are needed in the between-participants design. When participants are difficult to obtain, this within-participants design advantage is important.

With these advantages, you might think that within-participants designs would be used more than the between-participants designs. Actually, this is not always true because of the disadvantages that accompany the within-participants design. First, within-participants designs can be taxing on participants because they have to be present for multiple treatment conditions. Second, perhaps the most serious handicap is the confounding influence of a sequencing effect. Remember that a sequencing effect can occur when participants participate in more than one treatment condition. Because the primary characteristic of a within-participants design is that all participants participate in all experimental treatment conditions, a sequencing rival hypothesis is a real possibility. Fortunately, investigators can use the control technique of *counterbalancing* (shown in Figure 8.8) to help rule out the sequencing threat to internal validity. Unfortunately, as discussed in Chapter 7, counterbalancing controls only linear sequencing effects; if the sequencing effects are nonlinear (called *differential carryover effects*), then a confounding sequencing effect will remain.

As you can see, there are some problems associated with the within-participants design, and these problems are generally more difficult to control than those in the between-participants design. As a result, the within-participants design is not the most commonly used design.

- **Draw a diagram of the within-participants posttest-only design (with three levels of one independent variable) with and without counterbalancing.**
- **What are some strengths and weaknesses of the within-participants posttest-only design?**

Factorial Designs

Factorial design

Two or more independent variables are studied to determine their separate and joint effects on the dependent variable

Between-participants variable

Type of independent variable where different participants receive different levels of the independent variable

Within-participants variable

Type of independent variable where all participants receive all levels of the independent variable

Cell

Combination of levels of two or more independent variables

The designs covered thus far consider only one independent variable. However, in psychological research, we are frequently interested in the effect of two or more independent variables acting in concert. When there is more than one independent variable, a factorial design is the experimental design of choice. In a **factorial design**, two or more independent variables (at least one of which is manipulated) are simultaneously studied to determine their separate and interactive effects on the dependent variable. The independent variables in factorial designs can be **between-participants variables**, which is the type used in between-participants designs (i.e., participants experience only one level of the independent variable), **within-participants variables**, which is the type used in within-participants designs (i.e., participants experience all levels of the independent variable), or a combination of between and within-participants variables. In this section, we focus on a factorial design with two between-participants independent variables.

Figure 8.9 depicts the *design layout* (i.e., a picture showing logical structure) of a factorial design in which one of the independent variables has three levels (variable A) and the other has two levels (variable B). The levels of variable A are A_1, A_2, and A_3, and the levels of variable B are B_1 and B_2. There are six combinations of these two independent variables—A_1B_1, A_1B_2, A_2B_1, A_2B_2, A_3B_1, and A_3B_2. Each of these combinations is referred to as a **cell** in the design layout and represents an experimental condition. The number of cells in a design layout is obtained by multiplying the number of levels of the independent variables—in this case there are six cells ($3 \times 2 = 6$).

The participants would be randomly assigned to the six cells and would receive the appropriate treatment combination when the experiment is conducted. The participants randomly assigned to A_1B_1 receive the A_1 level of the first independent variable and the B_1 level of the second independent variable. In like manner, the

FIGURE 8.9

Factorial design with two independent variables.

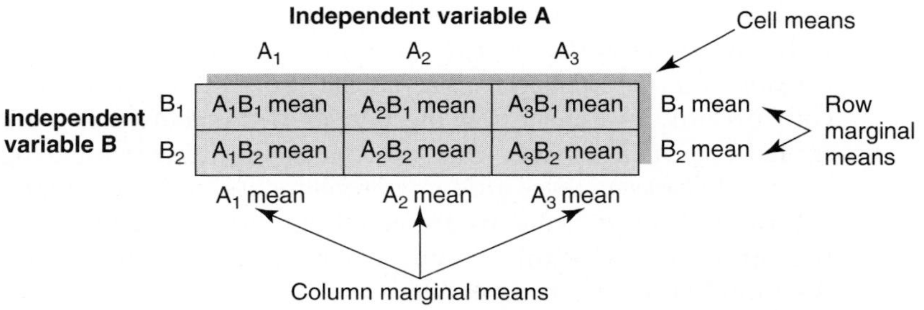

participants randomly assigned to the other cells receive the designated combination of the two independent variables. Once the experiment is conducted, the researcher obtains the two types of means shown in Figure 8.9: cell means and marginal means. A **cell mean** is the mean score of the participants in a cell. A **marginal mean** is the mean score of all participants receiving one level of an independent variable (ignoring or averaging across the levels of the other independent variable).

The factorial design allows the investigation of two types of effects: main effects and interaction effects. A **main effect** refers to the separate influence of each independent variable on the dependent variable. The term *main effect* did not arise in the previous designs in this chapter because only one independent variable existed (and therefore, only one main effect). However, more than one independent variable exists in a factorial design, and the separate effects of each independent variable must be identified. To distinguish the influence of the different independent variables, we refer to each one as a separate main effect. In a design with two independent variables, two main effects are investigated.

The factorial design also allows the investigation of interaction effects. An **interaction effect** is the joint or "interactive" effect of the independent variables. A **two-way interaction** effect occurs when the effect of one independent variable on the dependent variable varies at the different levels of the other independent variable. For example, perhaps the effect of caffeine consumption on the dependent variable test anxiety varies according to the amount of sleep someone has had. When you have two independent variables in your factorial design, you analyze the data for two main effects (one for each independent variable—such as caffeine consumption and amount of sleep) and one interaction effect (for the "interaction" of the two independent variables).

You might ask: Why not just conduct a separate experiment for each independent variable? The answer is that both separate experiments and the factorial design enable you to study the main effects, but only the factorial design enables you to study the interaction effect. It is very important to know whether independent variables interact. In a sense, the factorial design comes with a prize. By including the two independent variables in the same design, you learn about the main effects for each variable *and* you get a prize—you can determine if an interaction effect is present.

Let's make these concepts more concrete with an example. Let's say that we are interested in factors that affect driving performance. Our first independent variable (variable A) is caffeine consumption with the levels of low (A_1), medium (A_2), and high (A_3). The second independent variable (variable B) is sleep deprivation with the levels of not deprived (B_1) and deprived (B_2). Students are randomly assigned to each combination of these two independent variables (i.e., to each cell). The dependent variable is driving performance (operationalized as the number of correct maneuvers on the training course).

The cell and marginal means for this hypothetical experiment are provided in Figure 8.10. *To determine if there are any main effects, you compare the marginal means for each independent variable.* The marginal means for caffeine consumption are 2.2, 7.3, and 5.3, which suggests that (ignoring the sleep deprivation variable) driving performance is best with a medium level of caffeine consumption. The marginal means for sleep deprivation are 5.4 and 4.4, which suggest that (ignoring caffeine consumption) sleep deprivation leads to slightly lower driving performance.

Cell mean
The average score of the participants in a single cell

Marginal mean
The average score of all participants receiving one level of an independent variable

Main effect
The influence of one independent variable on the dependent variable

Interaction effect
The joint, combined, or "interactive" effect of two or more independent variables on the dependent variable

Two-way interaction
The effect of one independent variable on the dependent variable varies with the different levels of the other independent variable

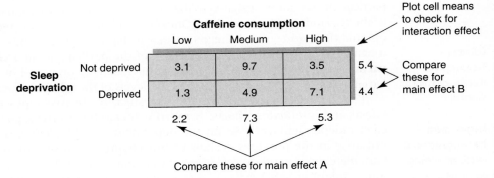

FIGURE 8.10
Tabular representation of data from experiment on driving performance.

Plot cell means to check for interaction effect

Caffeine consumption

		Low	Medium	High	
Sleep deprivation	Not deprived	3.1	9.7	3.5	5.4
	Deprived	1.3	4.9	7.1	4.4
		2.2	7.3	5.3	

Compare these for main effect B

Compare these for main effect A

According to these two sets of marginal means, it looks like there is a main effect for caffeine consumption and a main effect for sleep deprivation.

To determine if an interaction effect is present, construct a line plot of the cell means and visually inspect the results. Specifically, to determine if an interaction is present in the line graph, use these two rules:

- No interaction rule: If the lines are parallel, there is no interaction; interpret any main effects that are present.
- Interaction rule: If the lines are *not* parallel, there is an interaction; interpret the interaction effect, and do not interpret main effects.

The lines in Figure 8.11 are not parallel; therefore, the interaction present rule applies. You should interpret the interaction effect (not main effects). The interaction effect suggests that the relationship between caffeine consumption and driving

FIGURE 8.11
Line graph of cell means.

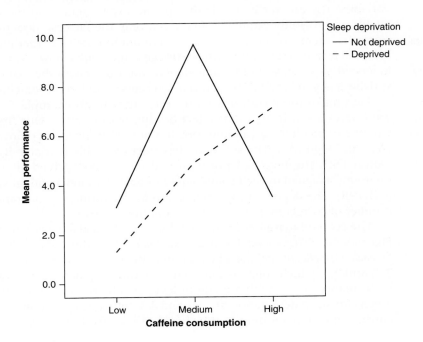

performance changes at the different levels of sleep deprivation. For participants who are sleep deprived, the best driving performance is obtained under high caffeine consumption, and low consumption has the lowest level of driving performance. For participants who are not sleep deprived, the best driving performance is obtained under medium caffeine consumption, and it appears that low and high consumption have about the same low level of driving performance. Notice that when an interaction is present, one cannot provide a simple answer to the question: "Which level of caffeine consumption provides the best performance?" The answer is that it depends on whether the participants are sleep deprived or not. It appears that both caffeine consumption and sleep deprivation influence driving performance; however, the causal impact is an interactive effect.

Now you know about cell means, marginal means, main effects, and interaction effects. Because these concepts are very important in psychological research, we demonstrate several additional possible outcomes from a two-factor experiment in Exhibit 8.1.

EXHIBIT 8.1

Examples of Main Effects and Interaction Effect

The concepts of main effects and interaction effects are very important in psychological research. We present several different outcomes that could accrue from an experiment having the design shown in Figure 8.9 (i.e., an experiment with three levels of variable A and two levels of variable B). Some of the outcomes presented represent interactions and others do not, so that you can see the difference in the two situations. We will set up a progression from a situation in which one main effect is significant to a situation in which both main effects and the interaction are significant. (Although significance is determined via statistical testing, you can assume that the effects we demonstrate are statistically significant.) The letters A and B continue to represent the two independent variables. If it helps you to understand the tables and graphs better by using "real" variables, you can use the variables we used earlier (i.e., A = caffeine consumption, B = sleep deprivation, and the dependent variable is driving performance). Table 8.1 and Figure 8.12 depict the various cases included in this exhibit.

Table 8.1 shows the cell means and marginal means. Each cell contains the mean score for all the participants in the cell. There are six cell means in each case. The means outside of each box are the *marginal means*, which are used to

determine if main effects are present. To determine if an interaction effect is present, the cell means are plotted in Figure 8.12 for each table from Table 8.1. Remember: If the lines in the plot of cell means are parallel, there is no interaction; if they are not parallel, there is an interaction.

Parts (a), (b), and (d) of Figure 8.12 represent situations in which one or both of the main effects are significant, but there is no interaction. In each case, the mean scores for the level of variation of at least one of the main effects differ. This can be seen from both the marginal means in the numerical examples presented in Table 8.1 and the graphs in Figure 8.12. Note also from Figure 8.12 that the lines for levels B_1 and B_2 are parallel in each of these (a), (b), and (d). In such a situation an interaction cannot exist, because an *interaction* means that the effect of one variable, such as B_1, depends on the level of the other variable being considered, such as A_1, A_2, or A_3. In each of these cases, the B effect is the same at all levels of A.

Part (c) depicts the classic example of an interaction. Neither main effect is significant, as indicated by the fact that the three-column means are identical and the two-row means are identical and reveal no variation in Table 8.1. However, if the variable A treatment effect is considered only for level B_1, we note that the scores systematically

(continued)

EXHIBIT 8.1 (continued)

TABLE 8.1

Tabular Presentation of Hypothetical Data Illustrating Different Kinds of Main and Interaction Effects
(Note: Cell means are inside the cells, and the marginal means are in the margins.)

	A_1	A_2	A_3	
B_1	10	20	30	20
B_2	10	20	30	20
	10	20	30	

(a) A is significant; B and the interaction are not significant

	A_1	A_2	A_3	
B_1	20	20	20	20
B_2	30	30	30	30
	25	25	25	

(b) B is significant; A and the interaction are not significant

	A_1	A_2	A_3	
B_1	30	40	50	40
B_2	50	40	30	40
	40	40	40	

(c) Interaction is significant; A and B are not significant

	A_1	A_2	A_3	
B_1	10	20	30	20
B_2	40	50	60	50
	25	35	45	

(d) A and B are significant; interaction is not significant

	A_1	A_2	A_3	
B_1	20	30	40	30
B_2	30	30	30	30
	25	30	35	

(e) A and the interaction are significant; B is not significant

	A_1	A_2	A_3	
B_1	10	20	30	20
B_2	50	40	30	40
	30	30	30	

(f) B and the interaction are significant; A is not significant

	A_1	A_2	A_3	
B_1	30	50	70	50
B_2	20	30	40	30
	25	40	55	

(g) A, B, and the interaction are significant

increase from level A_1 to A_3. In like manner, if only level B_2 is considered, then there is a systematic decrease from level A_1 to A_3. In other words, A *is* effective but in opposite directions for levels B_1 and B_2, or the effect of A depends on which level of B we are considering. Therefore, there is an *interaction*. We find graphs to be more helpful than tables in depicting interaction, but you should use whichever mode better conveys the information.

Parts (e) and (f) show examples of situations in which a main effect and an interaction are significant; part (g) shows a case in which both main effects and the interaction are significant. These illustrations exhaust the possibilities that exist for relationships in a factorial design having two independent variables. The exact nature of the main effects or the interaction may change, but one of these types of conditions will exist, unless you have no main effects and no interaction effect in which no effect would be significant in your experiment. Before we leave this section, one additional point needs to be made regarding the interpretation of significant main and interaction effects. Whenever either a main or an interaction effect *alone* is significant, you naturally have to interpret this effect. When *both* main and interaction effects are significant, however, and the main effect is contained in the interaction effect, then only the interaction effect is interpreted because the significant interaction effect qualifies the meaning that would arise from the main effect alone.

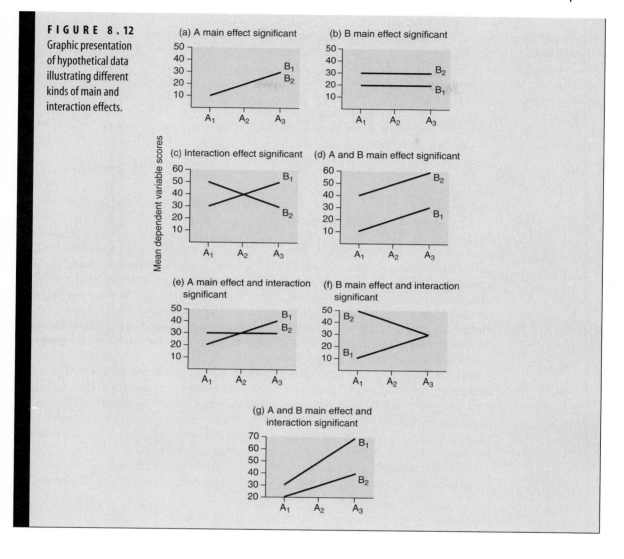

FIGURE 8.12
Graphic presentation of hypothetical data illustrating different kinds of main and interaction effects.

(a) A main effect significant

(b) B main effect significant

Mean dependent variable scores

(c) Interaction effect significant

(d) A and B main effect significant

(e) A main effect and interaction significant

(f) B main effect and interaction significant

(g) A and B main effect and interaction significant

STUDY QUESTIONS 8.7

- **Draw a diagram of a factorial design in which variable A has three levels and variable B has three levels.**
- **What is a main effect, and how does one determine if a main effect is present?**
- **What is an interaction effect, and how does one determine if an interaction is present?**

Factorial Designs Based on a Mixed Model

Many times in psychological research, there are several variables of interest, of which one or more would fit into a between-participants design and one or more would fit into a within-participants design. The factorial design can incorporate

Factorial design based on a mixed model
A factorial design that uses a combination of within-participants and between-participants independent variables

both between-participant and within-participant variables in one design, which produces a **factorial design based on a mixed model**. It's called a "mixed model" because it includes both between- and within-participants independent variables. The simplest form of such a design involves a combination of one between-participants variable and one within-participants variable. The between-participants variable requires a different group of research participants for each level of variation. The within-participants variable is constructed in such a way that all participants have to take each level of variation. When these two independent variables are included in the same scheme, it becomes a factorial design based on a mixed model, as illustrated in Figure 8.13.

In this design, participants are randomly assigned to the different levels of variation of the between-participants independent variable, but all participants take each level of variation of the within-participants independent variable. As with all factorial designs, the number of experimental conditions is equal to the product of the number of levels of the independent variables. For example, you might want to know if different types of motivational instructions are equally effective for easy, moderate, and difficult tasks. Motivational instruction is the between-participants variable because you assign participants to the three motivational instructions conditions, forming three groups. The within-participants independent variable is task difficulty, and each group will perform the easy, moderate, and difficult tasks. Because both of these independent variables (type of instructions and difficulty of task) have three levels, the number of treatment combinations is 9 (i.e., $3 \times 3 = 9$).

In this design, we are able to test for the effects produced by each of the two independent variables, as well as for the interaction between the two independent variables. We have the advantage of needing fewer participants because all participants take all levels of variation of one of the independent variables. Therefore, the number of participants required is only some multiple of the number of levels of the between-participants independent variable.

Our discussion of the factorial design based on a mixed model has been limited to the consideration of only two independent variables. However, as

FIGURE 8.13
Factorial design based on a mixed model with two independent variables for 10 participants.

Within-participants independent variable A

	A_1	A_2	A_3
B_1	P_1 P_2 P_3 P_4 P_5	P_1 P_2 P_3 P_4 P_5	P_1 P_2 P_3 P_4 P_5
B_2	P_6 P_7 P_8 P_9 P_{10}	P_6 P_7 P_8 P_9 P_{10}	P_6 P_7 P_8 P_9 P_{10}

Between-participants independent variable B

with all factorial designs, one can include as many independent variables as are considered necessary. Also, it is important to remember that you can include any combination of the between-participants type of independent variable and the within-participants type of independent variable in a factorial design. If you have a combination of at least one between-participants and one within-participants independent variable, then you have a factorial design based on a mixed model.

STUDY QUESTION 8.8 | **What are the characteristics of a factorial design based on a mixed model?**

Strengths and Weaknesses of Factorial Designs

So far, the discussion of factorial designs has been limited to those with two independent variables. There are times when it is advantageous to include three or more independent variables in a study. Factorial designs enable us to include as many independent variables as we consider important. Mathematically or statistically, there is almost no limit to the number of independent variables that can be included in a study.

Practically speaking, however, there are several difficulties associated with increasing the number of independent variables. First, there is an associated increase in the number of research participants required. In an experiment with two independent variables, each of which has two levels of variation, a 2 × 2 arrangement is generated, yielding four cells. If 15 participants are required for each cell, the experiment requires a total of 60 participants. In a three-variable design, with two levels of variation per independent variable, a 2 × 2 × 2 arrangement exists, yielding eight cells, and 120 participants are required in order to have 15 participants per cell. Four independent variables mean that 16 cells and 240 participants are required. As you can see, the required number of participants increases rapidly with an increase in the number of independent variables. This difficulty, however, does not seem to be insurmountable; many studies are conducted with large numbers of research participants.

A second problem with factorial designs incorporating more than two independent variables is the increased difficulty of simultaneously manipulating the combinations of independent variables. In an attitude study, it is harder to simultaneously manipulate the credibility of the communicator, type of message, gender of the communicator, prior attitudes of the audience, and intelligence of the audience (a five independent variable problem) than it is just to manipulate the credibility of the communicator and prior attitudes of the audience.

Three-way interaction
A two-way interaction that changes at the different levels of the third independent variable

A third complication arises when higher-order interaction effects are significant. We have explained the concept of an interaction for a factorial with two independent variables; this is called a two-way interaction. Designs with more than two independent variables have higher-order interactions effects. In a design with three independent variables, it is possible to have a three-way interaction. A **three-way interaction** (or a "triple" interaction) is present when a two-way interaction changes at the different levels of the third independent variable. In addition to the three-way interaction, in a design with three independent variables you might also have up to 3 two-way interactions (A × B, A × C, and B × C) and three main effects (for a total of seven effects). In a design with four independent variables, it is possible to have a four-way interaction (i.e., a three-way interaction changes at the different levels of the fourth independent variable). In addition to the four-way interaction, you might also have up to 4 three-way interactions, 6 two-way interactions, and 4 main effects (for a total of 15 effects)! Three-way interactions can be difficult to interpret, and interactions of an even higher order (e.g., four-way interactions) tend to become unwieldy.

In spite of these problems, factorial designs are very popular because of their overriding advantages when appropriately used. The following four advantages of factorial designs are adapted from Kerlinger and Lee (2000, pp. 371–372).

The first advantage is that factorial designs allow the experimenter to manipulate more than one independent variable simultaneously in an experiment, and therefore more precise hypotheses can be tested. For example, did a combination of three variables produce an effect? A second positive feature is that the researcher can control a potentially confounding variable by building it into the design as an independent variable. For example, if you are worried that an effect might be different for men and women, you can add gender to your design. The third advantage of the factorial design is that it enables the researcher to study the interactive effects of the independent variables on the dependent variable. This advantage is probably the most important because it enables us to hypothesize and test interactive effects. Testing main effects does not require a factorial design, but testing interactions does. It is this testing of interactions that lets researchers investigate the complexity of behavior and see that behavior is caused by the interaction of many independent variables.

STUDY QUESTION 8.9 | **What are some strengths and weaknesses of the factorial design?**

Choice/Construction of the Appropriate Experimental Design

It is your task to determine which research design is most appropriate for a particular research study. There are several factors to consider in making the design decision, including the nature of the research problem, the specific research question, the extraneous variables that must be controlled, and the relative advantages and disadvantages inherent in alternative designs. Experimental research is appropriate for research questions concerning cause and effect, and the randomized or strong designs are the best experimental designs available.

When you have a causal research question and are going to use an experimental design, you will usually find that one of the specific designs illustrated in this chapter will fit your needs. Sometimes, however, you might need to extend the designs we have presented and construct a more complex experimental design. To do this you will use the designs and design components provided in this chapter. When you read journal articles in your particular research area, you might find that some of the designs are more complex. Fortunately, you will also find that the designs were constructed using the components we have provided in this chapter.

If you need to construct a complex design, you should carefully examine the designs used in the prior research literature and determine why the more complex designs are used. Then, construct a similar a design for your research study that will be warranted in the research literature. Here are some considerations that are under your control when constructing an experimental research design: (1) Should I use a control group (2) Should I use multiple treatment comparison groups (comparing more than one active treatment)? (3) Should I use a pretest? (4) Should I use just one or multiple pretests (to get a stable baseline)? (5) Should I use just one or multiple posttests (to get a stable treatment effect or identify delayed outcomes)? (6) Should I use a within-participants or a between-participants independent variable, or should I use both? (7) Should I include multiple theoretically interesting independent variables in the design (as in factorial designs)? and (8) Should I include more than one dependent variable (to see how the treatment affects several different outcomes)?

If you become a psychologist, then, over time, you will become more and more adept at design selection and construction. For now, start with the major design types and specific designs presented in this chapter, but over time you must continue reading and learning from the published research literature. Keep taking more classes in research design and in statistics, and continue advancing your knowledge. To get you started, your next step after reading our book will be to read the more advanced book (published in 2002), *Experimental and Quasi-Experimental Designs for Generalized Causal Inference,* by Will Shadish, Tom Cook, and Don Campbell.

STUDY QUESTIONS 8.10	• **What are the design components used to construct an experimental design?** • **Select one of the experimental designs presented in this chapter, and discuss the components used and their purposes.**

Summary

The design of a research study is the basic outline of the experiment, specifying how the data will be collected and analyzed and how unwanted variation will be controlled. The purpose of an experimental design is to answer a question about cause and effect. A good experimental research design must satisfy two criteria. First, the design must test the causal hypotheses advanced. Second, extraneous variables must be controlled so that the experimenter can attribute the observed effects to the independent variable (i.e., to claim that A caused B). If you have the choice of several designs that will enable you to answer your research question, then you should select or construct the design that will provide maximum control over extraneous variables that can also explain the results; your goal is always to eliminate rival hypotheses.

Experimental designs can be viewed as falling on a continuum, with weak designs falling on or near one pole and strong or randomized designs falling on or near the other pole. Strong experimental designs provide the strongest evidence of cause and effect. Weak designs provide weak evidence of cause and effect. The center of the continuum includes moderately strong designs known as quasi-experimental designs. Quasi-experimental designs provide moderately strong evidence of cause and effect, and they are discussed in Chapter 10. The current chapter focuses on weak designs and strong designs.

The weak designs discussed are the *one-group posttest-only design* (administration of a posttest to a single group of participants after they have been given an experimental treatment condition), the *one-group pretest–posttest design* (administration of a posttest to a single group of participants after they have been pretested and given an experimental treatment condition), and the *posttest-only design with nonequivalent groups* (comparison of posttest performance of a group of participants who have been given an experimental treatment condition with a group that has not been given the experimental treatment condition). These weak designs usually do not provide the desired answers because they do not control for the influence of many extraneous variables that can affect the results.

Before listing the strong experimental designs, remember that when a between-participants independent variable is used, different sets of participants receive the different levels of the independent variable; when a within-participants independent variable is used, all participants receive all levels of the independent variable. The strong designs discussed include the between-participants *posttest-only control-group design* (the basic version has administration of a posttest to two randomly assigned groups of participants after one group has been administered the experimental treatment condition), the between-participants *pretest–posttest control-group design* (the basic version has administration of a posttest to two randomly assigned groups of participants after both groups have been pretested and one of the groups of participants has been administered the experimental treatment condition), the *within-participants posttest-only design* (all participants receive all treatments, and a posttest is administered after participants have been exposed to each experimental condition), *factorial designs* (two or more between-participants or two or more within-participants independent variables are used to study the separate and joint influence of the independent variables; if the independent variables are between-participants variables, then the participants are randomly assigned to the groups), and *factorial designs based on a mixed model* (includes at least one between-participants independent variable and at least one within-participants independent variable and is used to study the separate and joint influence of the independent variables). Factorial designs sometimes include pretests.

Strong experimental designs are especially strong for answering questions about cause and effect. Therefore, when you want to know if an independent variable causes changes in a dependent variable, you should select or construct strong experimental research designs.

Key Terms and Concepts

Analysis of covariance
Between-participants designs
Between-participants variable
Ceiling effect
Cell
Cell mean
Control group
Counterfactual
Experimental group
Factorial design based on a mixed
    model
Factorial design
Interaction effect
Main effect
Marginal mean
One-group posttest-only design

One-group pretest–posttest design
Posttest-only control-group design
Posttest-only design with nonequiva-
    lent groups
Pretest–posttest control-group design
Randomized designs
Repeated measures design
Research design
Strong experimental designs
Three-way interaction
Two-way interaction
Weak experimental designs
Within-participants design
Within-participants
    posttest-only design
Within-participants variable

Related Internet Sites

http://www.wadsworth.com/psychology_d/templates/student_resources/work shops/index.html

This site has several tutorials maintained by Wadsworth. When you get to this site, click on research methods workshops and then on the icon for True Experiments and Between versus Within Designs.

http://www.socialresearchmethods.net/kb/expfact.htm
This site provides instruction on factorial designs and interactions.

Practice Test

The answers to these questions can be found in Appendix.

1. The one-group posttest-only design, the one-group pretest–posttest design, and the posttest-only design with nonequivalent groups have in common
   a. Their frequent use by research psychologists
   b. The fact that they do not control for threats to internal validity
   c. The fact that they are all strong designs
   d. The fact that they are more typically used in animal (vs. human) research
   e. The fact that they do not use a control group

2. A control group is needed
   a. To control for some rival hypotheses
   b. To serve as a comparison
   c. To control for differential attrition effects
   d. To control for experimenter expectancy effects
   e. Both a and b are correct

3. The primary difference between a between-participants and a within-participants design is

a. The number of independent variables they can test

b. Whether they can test for the effect of an interaction

c. The number of main effects they can test

d. Whether the various treatment combinations use different participants or the same participants

e. The type of dependent variables that can be used

4. If I have studied the effect that three dosages—15, 30, and 60 mg—of the drug Cymbalta has on depressed people and people with an eating disorder and have found that the lower dosages are most effective with people with eating disorders and the higher dosages are most effective with people with depression, I have identified

a. An interaction between the drug dosage and the type of disorder

b. A main effect of drug dosage

c. A main effect of type of treatment

d. A main effect of both drug dosage and type of treatment

e. A design with three cells

5. If I have conducted an experiment that requires me to randomly assign 30 participants to two levels of one independent variable (15 in one condition and 15 in the other condition) and all 30 participants take all three levels of a second independent variable, I have used what type of design?

a. Pretest–posttest design

b. Simple randomized design

c. Factorial design

d. Within-participants posttest-only design

e. Factorial design based on a mixed model

Challenge Exercises

1. For each of the follow experimental briefs:

a. Identify the type of design used to test the hypothesis of the study

b. Explain why this design might have been used

c. Identify the threats to internal validity

Study A. College students are used to test the hypothesis that carbohydrate cravings increase as a person's level of depression increases. To test this hypothesis, the experimenter randomly assigns participants to three groups and then administers a mood-induction technique that will temporarily induce different types of moods. One version of the mood-induction technique is administered to one group to induce a depressed mood, another version is used to induce an elated mood in a second group, and a third version is administered to the third group to ensure that their mood does not change. After the mood-induction procedure has been administered to each group, the participants provide an assessment of the extent to which they experience carbohydrate cravings.

Study B. Hillary wants to find out if nicotine patches really help people quit smoking, so she identifies 100 people who have been smoking at least a pack of cigarettes a day for the past 10 years and want to quit. She has them all sign a form agreeing to stop smoking. She lets the participants decide if they want to be in the group that will wear the patch for a month or the group that will not wear the patch. At the end of the month, she monitors their cigarette smoking and finds that 35% of the individuals in the patch group quit smoking and 20% of the individuals in the no-patch group stopped smoking. Hillary concludes that the nicotine patches are effective in helping people quit or reduce their consumption of cigarettes.

Study C. Dr. Cane was interested in determining if there was an association between a person's gender and the tendency to report a false memory. To test this hypothesis, male and female participants were interviewed about a real emotional event that happened to them (a serious accident) between the ages of 4 and 10 and about a false event (getting lost). Two weeks later, these same individuals were interviewed about both events, and the interviewers attempted to elicit both memories using guided imagery, context reinstatement, and mild social pressure. The results of this experiment revealed that 100% of females and males recalled the real emotional event. However, 28% of females and 55% of males recalled the false event.

2. Basketball players naturally want to increase their accuracy in shooting foul shots so they hire a sports psychologist who hypothesizes that either anxiety reduction or mental imagery can help them. The sports psychologist randomly assigns 60 basketball players to 6 treatment conditions (10 in each condition). Each group of basketball players then shoots 20 free throws under 1 of 6 conditions formed by the two independent variables. The first independent variable is anxiety and has three levels—high, moderate, or low; the second independent variable is imagery and has two levels—imaging that the shot is going through the hoop or imaging that the shot is missing the hoop. The mean number of shots that are made by each group of basketball players is as follows

		Anxiety conditions		
		High	Moderate	Low
Imagery condition	Making shot	15	14	6
	Missing shot	9	12	17

a. Does there seem to be an anxiety main effect? If there is, what does it mean?
b. Does there seem to be an imagery main effect? If there is, what does it mean?
c. Does there seem to be an interaction? If there is, graph the interaction and explain what it means.

3. Assume that you wanted to examine the impact of classroom technology on class attendance of male and female students. Students are randomly assigned to a psychology class with either no technology, moderate technology, or extensive technology. This study produced the following data.

		Technology Use		
		None	Moderate	Extensive
Student sex	Male	30	55	75
	Female	38	60	28

a. Does there seem to be a technology main effect? If there is, what does it mean?
b. Does there seem to be a sex main effect? If there is, what does it mean?
c. Does there seem to be an interaction? If there is, graph the interaction and explain what it means.

CHAPTER

Procedure for Conducting an Experiment

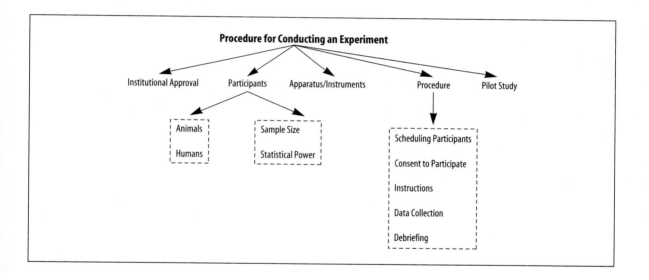

Raising a child with a disability challenges families to find the ways to best meet his or her needs. As the occurrence of autism has increased, so have the available therapies that often claim to be the one solution that parents need. Many of these therapies are expensive and have not been adequately researched. For example, a simple Web search resulted in the identification of a popular Web site detailing 19 different therapies for autism and a sponsored Web site featuring 38 therapies. Many therapies claim to be better than others, and some claim to be a simple one-shot cure for autism. Parents can order audiotapes, videotapes, vitamins, diets, and a host of other recommended therapies. In reality, autism takes many forms, and it is likely that multiple therapies might prove to be effective and some therapies might be effective with subsets of children. Sherer and Schreibman (2005) demonstrated this complexity when they identified children with autism who varied in their response to a treatment program. Although all of the children had autism and were similar in many ways, only some of them benefited from the therapy. Understanding which children will benefit from which therapy (and why) is crucial. But how do we know which therapies will last the test of time? How do we know which therapies are most effective for which forms of autism? Without this knowledge, how are parents to proceed? Research is needed to assess the effectiveness of different therapies and to determine what therapies work best with different children. For example, if you were going to conduct a study on the effectiveness of an autism therapy, you would have to determine the following: Where will you get a sample of individuals who are on the autism spectrum? Will you include individuals of any age, or will you limit your sample to a specific group such as preschoolers? Will you limit your sample to males or will you also include females? Where will you conduct the study? Who will assist in conducting the study? Who will train them? These are a few of the decisions that you will have to make prior to beginning data collection.

Introduction

Researchers design their studies to answer their research question. This means that they identify the relevant independent and dependent variables and attempt to control for extraneous variables. After these design and control decisions have been made, however, there are still many decisions to be made about conducting the experiment because the design provides only the framework of the study. Once established, this framework must be filled in and implemented. The researcher has to determine the kinds of participants to be used, from where they can be obtained, and how many should be asked to participate. If human participants are to be used, the researcher must determine what instructions and tasks will be given.

In this chapter, we discuss the issues that must be addressed to conduct the study. We address the issues in a general way because each study has its own unique characteristics; however, the discussion should provide the information you will need to conduct your own experimental research study. In fact, many of the principles in this chapter apply to any experimental and nonexperimental research study. That's because almost every study involves a research problem, research questions, a research plan (e.g., data collection, data analysis), and implementation of the plan. This chapter is about implementation of a research plan, especially for experimental research. We explain institutional approval, selection of participants and sample size, selection of appropriate instruments, scheduling participants, obtaining informed consent for participants, instructions, data collection, and debriefing. When you finish this chapter, you will understand the "nuts and bolts" of conducting an experiment.

Institutional Approval

If you are conducting a study that uses nonhuman animals as research participants, you must receive approval from the Institutional Animal Care and Use Committee (IACUC). If you are conducting a study that uses humans as research participants, you must receive approval from the Institutional Review Board (IRB). In either case, you must prepare a research protocol that details all aspects of the research, including the type of participants you propose to use and the procedures that will be employed in conducting the study. An example of a research protocol was presented in Exhibit 4.4 in Chapter 4. A detailed protocol is necessary because either the IACUC or the IRB must review your research protocol to determine if your research study is ethically acceptable.

The IACUC reviews research protocols to determine if animals will be used in appropriate ways. Specifically, the IACUC reviews research protocols to determine if the researcher is planning to employ procedures to help avoid or minimize pain and discomfort to the animals, use sedatives or analgesics in situations requiring more than momentary or slight pain, whether activities involving surgery will include appropriate preoperative and postoperative care, and whether methods of euthanasia are in accordance with accepted procedures. If the study procedures conform to acceptable practices, the IACUC will approve the study, and you can then proceed with data collection. If it does not approve the study, the committee will detail the questionable components, and the investigator can revise the study in an attempt to overcome the objections.

The IRB reviews research protocols to determine if humans will be treated in appropriate ways. The primary concern of the IRB is the welfare of the human participants. The IRB will review protocols to ensure that participants will provide informed consent for participation in the study and that the procedures will not harm the participants. This committee has particularly difficult decisions to make when a procedure involves the potential for harm. Some procedures, such as administering an experimental drug, have the potential for harming research participants. In such instances, the IRB must carefully consider the potential benefits that might accrue from the study relative to the risks to the participants. Thus the IRB frequently faces the ethical questions discussed in Chapter 4. Sometimes the board's decision is that the risks to the human participants are too great to permit the study; in other instances the decision is that the potential benefits are so great that the risks to the human participants are deemed to be acceptable. At times, the IRB decision seems to be partially dependent on the composition of the IRB—Kimmel (1991) has revealed that men and research-oriented individuals who worked in basic areas were more likely to approve research proposals than were women and individuals who worked in service-oriented contexts and were employed in applied areas.

Although there might be differences among IRB members with regard to the way ethical questions are resolved, the board's decision is final and the investigator must abide by it. If the IRB refuses to approve the study, the investigator must either redesign the study to overcome the objections of the IRB, supply additional information that will possibly overcome the objections of the IRB, or not conduct the study.

Receiving approval from the IRB or the IACUC is one of the important steps that investigators must accomplish in order to conduct their proposed research studies. Conducting research (experimental and nonexperimental) without such approval can cause investigators and their institutions to be severely reprimanded and jeopardize the possibility of receiving Public Health Service funding for future research projects. To receive approval from the appropriate review board, you must be able to describe in detail how you will conduct your research. In the next sections, we discuss the decisions that you must make about conducting your research. Let's start by considering who will participate in your research.

Research Participants

Psychologists investigate the behavior of organisms, and there are many organisms that can potentially serve as research participants. In most cases, the research question asked dictates the type of organism to be used. If, for example, a study is to investigate imprinting ability, then one must select a species, such as ducks, that demonstrates this ability. Much psychological research focuses on questions specific to humans such as human attitudes, emotions, cognitions, and behaviors. Therefore, humans are often the participants in psychological research.

Other than humans, precedent has established that the albino variant of the brown rat is the standard laboratory research animal. The use of the albino rat in infrahuman research has not gone without criticism. Lockard (1968) eloquently criticized the fact that psychologists focused too much attention on the use of this particular animal. Lockard argued that rather than using precedent as the primary guide for selecting a particular organism as a participant, one should look at the research problem and select the type of organism that is most appropriate for the research question.

Obtaining Animals (Rats)

Once a decision has been made about the type of organism to be used, the next question is where to get the participants. Researchers who use rats typically select from one of three strains: the Long-Evans hooded, the Sprague–Dawley albino, and the Wistar albino. The researcher must decide on the strain, sex, age, and supplier of the albino rats, because each of these variables can influence the results of the study.

Once the albino rats have been selected, ordered, and received, they must be maintained in the animal laboratory. The Animal Welfare Act, most recently amended in 2007, regulates the care, handling, treatment, and transportation of most animals used in research. The National Academy of Sciences Institute of Laboratory Animal Research (ILAR) developed a *Guide for the Care and Use of Laboratory Animals* (1996). The purpose of this guide is to assist scientific institutions in using and caring for laboratory animals in professionally appropriate ways. The recommendations in this publication reflect the policies of the National Institutes of Health and the American Association for the Accreditation of Laboratory Animal Care (AAALAC). Therefore, the guidelines in this manual are the ones that researchers should adhere to when caring for and using laboratory animals.

Obtaining Human Participants

Researchers selecting humans as their research participants must decide on the inclusion and exclusion criteria for their participants. For example, are you looking for human participants in a certain age group or with a certain disorder or a certain set of experiences? Your recruitment strategy will be partially determined by the type of participants that you need. For example, if you are conducting a study with homeless people, you might contact homeless shelters and visit areas that are known to be frequented by homeless individuals. Additionally, your recruitment strategy is influenced by your resources. In much psychological research with human participants, participants are recruited on the basis of convenience and availability.

A great deal of psychological research is conducted at colleges and universities, and many of these studies use students as participants. In most university settings, the psychology department has a participant pool consisting of introductory psychology students. These students are motivated to participate in a research study because they are frequently offered this activity as an alternative to some other course requirement, such as writing a brief paper. Participant pools provide a readily available supply of participants for the researcher. Participant pools can be operated in a number of ways, varying from a Web site that allows students to register and sign up to participate in research to announcements posted in a central departmental location informing students of research opportunities. While the participant pool that exists within psychology departments provides a convenient sample, there is a serious concern that the findings obtained from these participants are not generalizable to a noncollege student population. Consider the fact that college students are bright individuals, all of whom have graduated from high school but not from college. This represents a unique segment of the population.

Some studies require a noncollege student population. For example, a child psychologist who wishes to study kindergarten children usually will try to solicit the cooperation of a local kindergarten. Similarly, to investigate incarcerated criminals, one must seek the cooperation of prison officials as well as the criminals. When one has to draw research participants from sources other than a departmental participant pool, a new set of problems arises. Assume that a researcher is going to conduct a study using kindergarten children. The first task is to find a kindergarten that will allow the researcher to collect the data needed for the study. In soliciting the cooperation of the person in charge, the researcher must be as tactful and diplomatic as possible because many people are not receptive to psychological research. If the person in charge agrees to allow the researcher to collect the data, the next task is to obtain the parents' permission to allow their children to participate. This involves having parents sign permission slips that explain the nature of the research and the tasks required of their children. The children also should provide their assent to participate. Where an agency or school is involved, such as an institution for persons with intellectual disabilities, one might be required to submit a research proposal for the agency's research committee to review.

The Internet is a powerful tool for recruiting research participants. However, you must keep in mind that Internet users are a select group. Obviously, Internet users cannot represent people who do not have access to the Internet or who choose not to use the Internet. On the other hand, the Internet is capable of reaching individuals from other cultures and individuals who might be inaccessible due to time and cost constraints, such as individuals with disabilities. If you wanted to conduct a study investigating some aspect of unique populations such as identical twins, you could recruit such individuals via the World Wide Web or the Internet from online groups such as Mothers of Twins Clubs. Such online groups exist for many special populations. With the Internet, you have immediate access to a larger sample of individuals not confined to your geographic location.

Internet studies offer different challenges in terms of contacting and obtaining research participants. For example, if your strategy is to contact individuals and ask them to participate in your study, you must identify a mechanism for contacting these individuals. If the research participants belong to an organization or association, you could contact the organization or association and ask for a list of e-mail addresses of their members. You could also post a request to a selected number of e-mail lists, Usenet groups, or open discussion groups. Another mechanism is to purchase a list of e-mail users from Net-based white page services. The address of one such Internet address finder is http://www.iaf.net. There are also commercial services, such as Survey Sampling, http://www.surveysampling.com, that will identify and select specific samples of individuals for your study.

Alternatively, if your strategy is to post a research study on the Internet and have participants log on to the Web site and complete the study, you could post the study on one of several Web sites that specialize in advertising research opportunities. One of these sites is hosted by the Social Psychology Network, http://www.socialpsychology.org/addstudy.htm, and another is hosted by the American Psychological Society, http://psych.hanover.edu/research/exponnet.html.

After identifying the target participant population, the researcher must select individual participants from that group. Ideally, this should be done randomly. In a study investigating kindergarten children, a sample should be randomly selected from the population of all kindergarten children (e.g., in the United States or the area of interest to you). However, random selection from large dispersed populations is usually impractical. Therefore, human participants are generally selected on the basis of convenience, availability, and willingness to participate. The kindergarten children used in a study will probably be those who live closest to the university and who cooperate with the investigator.

Because samples are not usually randomly selected, the researcher might have a built-in bias in the data. For example, the children whose parents allow them to participate might perform differently than those whose parents restrict their participation. The participants who volunteer to participate in an Internet study might perform differently than those who do not. Because of the inability to select participants randomly, the investigator *must* report the nature of participant selection and assignment, in addition to the characteristics of the participants. This information will enable other investigators to replicate the experiment and assess the compatibility of the results.

STUDY QUESTIONS 9.1

- **What factors frequently determine the selection of research participants used in a study, and which is the most important factor that should be used?**
- **What problems might exist in using research participants who are not attending college?**

Sample Size

After you have decided which type of participants will be used in the research study and have obtained access to an accessible population of such participants, you must determine how many participants are needed to test the hypothesis adequately. This decision is based on issues such as the design of the study, the variability of the data, and the type of statistical procedure to be used. The relationship between the design of the study and sample size can be seen clearly by contrasting a single-case and a multiparticipant design. Obviously, a single-case design requires a sample size of one, so sample size is not an issue. In multiparticipant designs, however, the sample size is important because the number of participants used can theoretically vary from two to infinity. We usually want more than two participants, but it is impractical and unnecessary to use too many participants. As the number of participants within a study increases, the ability of our statistical tests to detect an effect of the independent variable increases; that is, the power of the statistical test increases. Power, therefore, is an important concept in determining sample size.

Power

Power
The probability of rejecting a false-null hypothesis

Power is defined as the probability of rejecting a false-null hypothesis. Any time we reject a false-null hypothesis, we are correctly saying that the treatment condition produced an effect. This is the type of decision we want to make. Therefore, a key point here is that we want power to be high, or, more specifically, by convention, *we want to have a power of at least 0.80* (which means we will correctly reject a false-null 80% of the time). Power increases as the number of participants increases. As the sample size increases, however, the cost in terms of both time and money also increases. From an economic standpoint, we would like a relatively small sample. Researchers must balance the competing desires of detecting an effect and reducing cost. They must select a sample size that is small enough to fit within their cost constraints but large enough to detect an effect produced by the independent variable. A power analysis seems to be the best method for resolving these competing desires and determining the appropriate sample size to use for a study.

Effect size
The magnitude of the relationship between two variables in a population

The power of a statistical test is determined by the alpha level, the sample size, and the effect size. The **effect size** is the magnitude of the relation between the independent and dependent variable in a population. You can identify the anticipated effect size based on a review of the literature in your research area. If there is little or no research in your area, Jacob Cohen (1992) offers starting points for what can be considered small, medium, and large effect sizes for several statistical indices. For example, for a correlation coefficient, he considers 0.10 to be small, 0.30 to be medium, and 0.50 as large in psychological research. For differences between means using the Cohen's *d* statistic, 0.20 is considered small, 0.50 is medium, and 0.80 is large. Don't worry about these numbers for now, because we explain correlation coefficients and Cohen's *d* in Chapter 14. For now, just think about effects as being small, medium, or large. We explain the concept of alpha level in Chapter 15—all you need to know for now is that in most psychological research *we use an alpha level of 0.05*. These three factors (alpha level, sample size, and effect size) are related so that, for a given level of power, when any two of them are known, the third is determined. Therefore, for a given power level, if you know (or can estimate) the effect size and you know the alpha level that you will use, you can identify the sample size needed.

Table 9.1 shows the number of research participants that you will need in your research study when power is 0.80 (which is recommended) for alpha levels of 0.01 and 0.05 for small, medium, and large effect sizes for several different statistical tests that you might use one day. We will show how to use Table 9.1 for two tests.

First, assume that you want to conduct an experiment, and you will want to determine if the difference between the treatment group mean and the control group mean is statistically significant. You have examined the prior literature, and it suggests that the effect size is medium. Following convention, you will use an alpha level of 0.05. To determine the sample size that you will need in your study, go to the table and find the number corresponding to "*t* test for two means," for a "medium" effect size, for an alpha of "0.05." The number is on the first line, and is 64. This is the number of participants that you need *in each of your two groups*. Therefore, you will need a total of 128 participants in your study sample.

T A B L E   9 . 1

Number of Research Participants Needed for Small, Medium, and Large Effect Sizes at Recommended Power of 0.80 for alpha = 0.01 and 0.05

		α				
		0.01			**0.05**	
Test	*Small*	*Medium*	*Large*	*Small*	*Medium*	*Large*
t test for two means[a]	586	95	38	393	64	26
Simple correlation (*r*)[b]	1,163	125	41	783	85	28
Analysis of variance[a]						
2 groups	586	95	38	393	64	26
3 groups	464	76	30	322	52	21
4 groups	388	63	25	274	45	18
5 groups	336	55	22	240	39	16
Multiple regression[b]						
2 predictors	698	97	45	481	67	30
3 predictors	780	108	50	547	76	34
4 predictors	841	118	55	599	84	38
5 predictors	901	126	59	645	91	42

[a]The sample size number is for each group. Multiply this number by the number of groups to determine the total sample sized needed.

[b]The sample size reported is the total sample sized needed.

Note: Effect size is the strength of relationship. Analysis of variance is used to compare two or more means for statistical significance. Multiple regression is used to predict or explain variance in a dependent variable using two or more independent variables (labeled "predictors" in table). Information from table was extracted from Cohen, 1992.

Second, let's assume that you want to determine the correlation between two variables. You have examined the literature, and it suggests that the effect size is medium. Following convention again, you use an alpha level of 0.05. Go to the table and find the number corresponding to "simple correlation" for a "medium" effect size for an alpha of "0.05." The number is on the second line, and it is 85. This is the *total number of participants* that you will need to in your study sample.

To learn more about this power and sample size, you should read the article from which we developed our Table 9.1. The author, Jacob Cohen (1992), explains the idea of power in more depth and explains what he means by small, medium, and large effect sizes. You will learn how to conduct significance testing in Chapter 15.

STUDY QUESTIONS 9.2
- **How should a researcher determine the sample size to use in a multiparticipant design?**
- **Using Table 9.1, how many research participants would you need in an experiment if you have two groups, you expect a medium effect size, and you want to use an alpha level of 0.01?**

Apparatus and/or Instruments

In addition to securing the appropriate number of research participants, the investigator must identify how the independent variable conditions will be presented and how the dependent variable will be measured. In some studies the presentation and manipulation of the independent variable requires the active participation of the investigator, and the measurement of the dependent variable involves the administration of a variety of psychological assessment instruments. For example, Nezu (1986) investigated the effectiveness of two different types of therapy in treating depression. These treatments required active intervention on the part of the experimenter, which meant that the investigator was actively participating in the manipulation of the independent variable. To assess the effectiveness of the two treatments, Nezu administered several different depression inventories. Consequently, psychological assessment instruments were used as the dependent variable measures.

In other studies, a specific type of apparatus must be used to arrive at a precise presentation of the independent variable and to measure the dependent variable. For example, assume that you are conducting a study in which the independent variable involves presenting words on a screen for different periods of time. You could try to control manually the length of time during which the words were presented, but because it is virtually impossible for a human to consistently present words for a very specific duration of time, a computer is typically used. Similarly, if the dependent variable is the recorded heart rate, you could use a stethoscope and count the number of times per minute a participant's heart beats. It is, however, much more accurate and far simpler to use an electronic means for measuring this kind of dependent variable. The use of such automatic recording devices also reduces the likelihood of making a recording error as a function of experimenter expectancies or some type of observer bias.

Microcomputers (i.e., personal computers) are used frequently in experimentation, both for the presentation of stimulus material and for the recording of dependent variable responses. The use of microcomputers in the laboratory gives the experimenter an extremely flexible tool. It can be programmed to present as many different independent variables and record as many different types of responses as your creativity will allow. In addition, the researcher is not tied to one specific computer. Rather, the role of the computer in stimulus presentation and recording of responses is preserved in the computer program, and this program is typically saved on a removable device, which enables the researcher to reconfigure any compatible computer at a moment's notice.

In addition to the use of microcomputers, advances in technology and interdisciplinary research have enabled psychologists to conduct research that would have been impossible several decades ago. For example, psychologists have been measuring brain waves for more than 50 years. However, it is only recently that we have used the measurement of brain waves, or the electroencephalograph (EEG), to study the way brain systems respond to various stimulus conditions such as written words. This research has progressed to the point where recordings are taken from a configuration of 80 or more electrodes placed on the scalp of a research participant's head (see Figure 9.1). This electrical activity of the brain is then transformed into a series of pictures, or maps of the brain, which depict the

FIGURE 9.1
Illustration of subject wearing the geodesic sensor net of 64 electrodes.
(From *Images of the mind* by Michael I. Posner & Marcus E. Raichle, © 1994 by Scientific American Library. Reprinted by permission of Henry Holt and Company, LLC.)

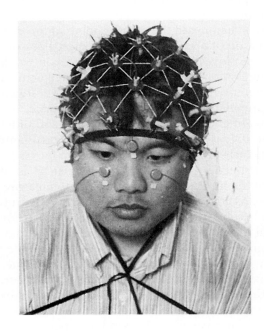

degree of activity of various areas of the brain. Areas of the brain that are very active are shown as bright spots and are interpreted as the areas that are stimulated by the independent variable that was presented, such as seeing a word presented on a computer screen.

To further confirm that the area identified by the EEG produced *brain maps* that do represent the brain area stimulated by the independent variable, psychologists have teamed up with physicians. Through this collaboration, research participants have had positron emission tomography (PET) and/or magnetic resonance imaging (MRI) scans while participating in an experiment and responding to the presentation of an independent variable such as word presentation. The areas that are found to be active in PET scans are also the same areas found to be active with the EEG brain maps, at least in terms of response to stimuli such as word presentation. Psychologists, particularly cognitive neuropsychologists, in collaboration with physicians, are increasingly combining the technological tools of brain imaging from EEG recordings and PET and MRI scan to investigate the brain systems involved in a variety of behavioral activities and disorders.

Because the apparatus for a given study can serve a variety of purposes, the investigator must consider the particular study being conducted and determine the type of apparatus that is most appropriate. One journal, *Behavioral Research Methods, Instruments, and Computers,* is devoted specifically to apparatus and instrumentation. If you have difficulty identifying an instrument or a computer program that will perform a certain function, you might find it helpful to consult this journal and the previous research conducted in your area of investigation.

Procedure

Prior to conducting your study, you need to plan and specify all of the procedural details that you will need to carry out. The events to take place in the experiment must be arranged so that they flow smoothly. You must carefully plan the whole experiment and specify the sequence in which each activity is to take place, laying down the exact procedure to be followed during data collection. For animal research, this means not only specifying the conditions of the laboratory environment and how the animals are going to be handled in the laboratory but also specifying how they are to be maintained in their maintenance quarters and how they are to be transferred to the laboratory. These are important considerations because such variables can influence the animals' behavior in the laboratory.

With human participants, the researcher must specify what the participants are to do, how they are to be greeted, and the type of nonverbal behavior (looking at the participants, smiling, using a particular tone of voice in reading instructions, etc.) as well as the verbal behavior in which the experimenter is to engage. In this section, we explain some of the procedural "nuts and bolts" for conducting your study.

Scheduling of Research Participants

Scheduling research participants in the experiment involves the consideration not only of when the researcher has time available but also of the type of participants being used. With rats, for example, there is the problem of the lighting cycle. As Sidowski and Lockard (1966, p. 10) have noted:

> Rats and other nocturnal animals are most active in the dark phase of the lighting cycle and do most of their eating and drinking then. From the animal's point of view, the light portion of the day is for sleeping and inactivity but may be interrupted by an experimenter who requires him to run or bar-press for food. It is unfortunate that the amount of lighting and the timing of the cycle are usually arranged for the benefit of the caretaker and not the animals or the experimenter.

Clearly, researchers must be aware of the implications of their scheduling decisions.

When scheduling human participants, there is a different set of issues to consider. First, the experiment must be scheduled at a time when the experimenter and the participants are available. Some participants will undoubtedly fail to show up, so it is often advisable to allow for limited rescheduling. Some participants who do not show up at the designated time will not want to be rescheduled. In such instances, the researcher will need to use replacement participants, and then replacement participants must be scheduled to substitute for those who drop out.

STUDY QUESTION 9.3

- **What issues need to be considered in scheduling human and animal research participants?**

Consent to Participate

Most studies require that you obtain each research participant's informed consent to participate in the study. However, as stated in Chapter 4, there are a number of limited circumstances in which the IRB might waive this requirement. It is very important that you understand that it is the IRB that makes the determination as to whether consent to participate can be waived in any study. Therefore, even if you think that it would be appropriate to waive consent, you must request such a waiver from the IRB, and they will make the decision. Additionally, if your research requires consent, the IRB must review and approve your consent form and consent procedure.

The consent process must inform each research participant of all aspects of the study that might influence his or her decision to participate. This information, included in the consent to participate form, is typically provided in written form. Ideally, a consent form should be written in simple, first-person, layperson's language. If the research participant is a minor, the parent or guardian must provide consent. If the minor is over the age of seven, he or she must give assent and the parent/guardian must provide consent. When minors are the research participants, a form written to their level of understanding must be provided.

The consent form should be prepared so that it includes the following elements:

1. What the study is about, where it will be conducted, the duration of the study, and when the research participant will be expected to participate should be specified.

2. The statement should list what procedures will be followed and whether any of them are experimental. In the description of the procedures, the attendant discomforts and risks should be spelled out.

3. Any benefits to be derived from participation in the study and any alternative procedures that might be beneficial to the participant should be identified.

4. If the research participant will receive any monetary compensation, this should be detailed, including the schedule of payments and the effect (if any) on the payment schedule in the event the participant withdraws from the study. If course credit is to be given, the statement should provide an explanation of how much credit will be received and whether the credit will still be given if the research participant withdraws from the study.

5. If the study involves responding to a questionnaire, participants should be informed that they can refuse to answer, without penalty, any questions that make them uncomfortable.

6. Studies that investigate sensitive topics such as depression, substance abuse, or child abuse should provide information on where assistance for these problems can be obtained, such as from counselors, treatment centers, and hospitals.

7. The participants must be told that they can withdraw from the study at any time without penalty.

8. The participants must be informed as to how the records and data obtained will be kept confidential.

As you can see, the consent form is quite involved, and its purpose is to provide research participants with complete information about the study so that they can make an intelligent and informed choice as to whether they want to participate. Exhibit 4.6 in Chapter 4 gives an illustration of a consent to participate form. Only after consent has been obtained can you proceed with the study.

STUDY QUESTION 9.4

• **What is the purpose of the consent form, and what information is included in this form?**

Instructions

When you conduct an experiment using human participants, you must prepare a set of instructions. This brings up such questions as "What should be included in the instructions?" and "How should they be presented?" Instructions must include a clear description of the research purpose, or disguised purpose, and the task that the research participants are to perform. Certain types of instructions might be ineffectual in producing the desired outcome. Instructions requesting that the research participant "pay attention," "relax," or "ignore distractions" are probably ineffective because research participants are constrained by other factors that limit their ability to adhere to the commands. Instructions sometimes request that the participants perform several operations at the same time. If this is not possible, then they will choose one of the possible operations to perform, and the experimenter will not know which choice was made. For example, if the participants receive the instruction to work quickly and accurately, they might concentrate on accuracy at the expense of speed, because both speed and accuracy cannot be achieved simultaneously. This means that the experimenter will not know which component of the instructions contributed most to the dependent variable measure. Similarly, vague instructions (e.g., instructions telling the participants to imagine, guess, or visualize something) allow the participants to place their own interpretations on the task. It is best to avoid such instructions whenever possible.

As you can see, instructions should be clear, unambiguous, and specific, but at the same time they should not be too complex because of the possibility of a memory overload (Sutcliffe, 1972). Beginning researchers often think that directions should be extremely terse and succinct. Although this style is good for writing the research report, in writing instructions one runs the risk that the participants will not grasp important points. Instructions should be very simple, down to earth, and, at times, even redundant. You might find it useful to include "warmup" trials as part of your instructions. These are pretest trials that are similar to those the participant would complete in the actual study. They are included to ensure that the research participant understands the instructions and the way they are to respond.

STUDY QUESTIONS 9.5

- **What purpose do the instructions to participants serve?**
- **What guidelines should be followed in preparing these instructions?**

Data Collection

Once you have scheduled your participants and received their informed consent, you are ready to collect data from the research participants. The primary rule to follow in this phase of the experiment is to adhere as closely as possible to the procedure that has been laid out. A great deal of work has gone into developing this procedure, and if it is not followed exactly, you run the risk of introducing contaminates into the experiment. If this should happen, you will not have the well-controlled study you worked so hard to develop, and you might not attain an answer to your research question.

Debriefing, or Postexperimental Interview

Once the data have been collected, there is a tendency to think that the job has been completed and the only remaining requirement (other than data analysis) is to thank the participants for their participation and send them on their way. However, the experiment does not—or should not—end with the completion of

**Postexperimental
interview**
An interview with the
participant following
completion of the
experiment, during
which all aspects of
the experiment are
explained and the
participant is allowed
to comment on the
study

data collection. In most studies, following data collection, there should be a debriefing or **postexperimental interview** with the participants that allows them to comment freely about any part of the experiment. The interview can also provide information regarding the participants' thinking or strategies used during the experiment, which can help explain their behavior.

Debriefing Functions

Tesch (1977) has identified three specific functions of debriefing. First, debriefings have an ethical function. In many studies, research participants are deceived about the true purpose of an experiment. Ethics dictate that we must undo such deceptions, and the debriefing session is the place to accomplish this. Some experiments will generate negative affect in the participants or, in some other way, create physical or emotional stress. The researcher must attempt to return the participants to their preexperimental state by eliminating any stress that the experiment has generated. Second, debriefings have an educational function. The typical rationale used to justify requiring the participation of introductory psychology students in experiments is that they learn something about psychology and psychological research. The third function of debriefing is methodological. Debriefings are frequently used to provide evidence regarding the effectiveness of the independent variable manipulation or of the deception. They are also used to probe the extent and accuracy of participants' suspicions and to give the experimenter an opportunity to convince the participants not to reveal the experiment to others. Sieber (1983) has added a fourth function. She states that participants should, from their participation in the study, derive a sense of satisfaction from the knowledge that they have contributed to science and society. The debriefing procedure should be designed to help bring about this belief.

How to Debrief

Given these functions of debriefing, how do we proceed? Two approaches have been used. Some investigators use a questionnaire approach, in which participants are handed a postexperimental questionnaire to complete. Others use a face-to-face interview, which seems to be the best approach because it is not as restrictive as a questionnaire.

If you want to probe for any suspicions that the participants might have had about the experiment, this is the first order of business. Social psychologists Aronson and Carlsmith (1968) believe that the researcher should begin by asking the participants if they have any questions. If so, the questions should be answered as completely and truthfully as possible. If not, the experimenter should ask the participants if all phases of the experiment—both the procedure and the purpose— were clear. Next, depending on the study being conducted, it might be appropriate to ask participants to describe how they felt during the experiment and whether they encountered any difficulties during the experiment.

If the experiment contained deception and the participants suspected that it did, they are likely to have revealed this fact by this time. If no suspicions have been revealed, the researcher can ask the participants if they thought there was more to the experiment than was immediately apparent. Such a question cues the participants that there must have been. Most participants will therefore say yes, so this should be followed with a question about what the participants thought was involved and how this might have affected their behavior. Such questioning will give the investigator additional insight into whether the participants had the experiment figured out and will also provide a perfect point for the experimenter to lead into an explanation of the purpose of the study. The experimenter can continue "the debriefing process by saying something like this: 'You are on the right track, we *were* interested in some problems that we didn't discuss with you in advance. One of our major concerns in this study is . . .'" (Aronson & Carlsmith, 1968, p. 71). The debriefing should then be continued in the manner suggested by Mills (1976). If the study involved deception, the reasons that deception was necessary should be included. The purpose of the study should then be explained in detail, as well as the specific procedures for investigating the research question. This means explaining the independent and dependent variables and how they were manipulated and measured. As you can see, the debriefing requires explaining the entire experiment to the participants.

The last part of the debriefing session should be geared to convincing the participants not to discuss any components of the experiment with others. This can be accomplished by asking the participants not to describe the experiment to others until after the date of completion of the data collection, pointing out that communicating the results to others might invalidate the study. If the study were revealed prematurely, the experimenter would not know that the results were invalid and the participants would probably not tell (Altemeyer, 1971), so the experimenter would be reporting inaccurate results to the scientific community. Aronson (1966) found that we can have reasonable confidence that the participants will not tell others; but Altemeyer (1971) has shown that if participants do find out, they will probably not tell the experimenter.

At this point you might wonder whether this debriefing procedure accomplishes the functions it is supposed to accomplish. The ethical function will be accomplished quite well if the procedures are followed. The educational function is fulfilled less completely in debriefing. Most investigators seem to think, or rationalize, that the educational function is served if the participants participate in the experiment and are told of its purpose and procedures during debriefing. However, data indicate that participants perceive psychological experiments to be most deficient in educational value, although they view debriefing in general to be quite effective (Smith & Richardson, 1983). The methodological function seems to be served well because participants have the opportunity to share their thoughts and experiences with the researcher.

It is questionable as to whether all the functions of debriefing are fulfilled when conducting an online research study. The most common and direct way of providing debriefing is to post the debriefing at the Web site on which the study is located. This way you can tailor the debriefing to the study you are conducting. It is even possible to make the debriefing material available to those who decide to terminate the study prior to completion by having a "leave the study" link button, or a pop-up window that executes when a person leaves a study. While these techniques will present the debriefing material, online research makes it difficult to engage in the desensitizing component of debriefing because it is difficult to assess the participant's psychological state and determine if an individual has been stressed by the study. It is also difficult to determine if any stress that has been created by the study has been reduced through debriefing, because it is difficult to receive feedback from the research participant.

STUDY QUESTIONS 9.6   • **What function is served by the postexperimental interview?**
                • **How should you proceed in conducting this interview?**

Pilot Study

Pilot study
An experiment that is conducted on a few participants prior to the actual collection of data

Before conducting an experiment, it is strongly recommended that you conduct a pilot study. A **pilot study** is a run-through of the entire experiment with a small number of participants. The pilot study can provide a great deal of information. If the instructions are not clear, this will show up either in the debriefing session or by virtue of the fact that the participants do not know what to do after the instructions have been read.

The pilot study can also indicate whether the independent variable manipulation produced the intended effect. For example, if you were trying to induce the emotion of surprise, debriefing can help to determine if fear, surprise, or some other state was actually generated. If none of the pilot participants report the particular emotion under study, then their help can be solicited in assessing why it was not generated, after which changes can be made until the intended state is reliably induced. In a similar manner, the sensitivity of the dependent variable can be checked. Pretesting might suggest that the dependent variable is too crude to reflect the effect of the manipulation and that a change would make it more appropriate.

The pilot study also gives the researcher experience with the procedure. At first, the experimenter will not be familiar with the sequence and therefore probably will not make a smooth transition from one part of the study to another. With practice, the researcher will develop fluency in carrying out the steps, which is required if constancy is to be maintained in the study. During the pilot study, the experimenter also tests the procedure. Too much time might be allowed for certain parts and not enough for others, the deception (if used) might be inadequate, and so on. If there are problems, the experimenter can identify them before any data are collected, and the procedure can be corrected.

If you are conducting an Internet-based study you should complete the online study tasks yourself as well as have a few pilot participants complete the tasks. Completing the study yourself will allow you to understand how it feels to be a participant, and having pilot participants complete the study will allow you to get feedback. Completing a pilot run of your online study will also show whether the study works properly in your browser and if the data are returned to you in a manner that is understandable and arranged in the desired way.

Many subtle factors can influence an experiment, and the pilot phase is the time to identify them. Pilot testing involves checking all parts of the experiment to determine if they are working appropriately. If a malfunction is isolated, it can be corrected without any damage to the experiment. If a malfunction is not spotted until after the data have been collected, it *might* have had an influence on the results of the study. If changes are made to the study after receiving IRB approval, the IRB must approve the intended changes.

STUDY QUESTIONS 9.7
- **What procedural issues must be specified prior to actual data collection?**
- **What purpose is served by a pilot study?**

Summary

Following completion of the study design, the investigator must make a number of additional decisions before beginning to collect data. The entire plan for the study must be presented to the appropriate review board for review. The investigator must decide on the type of organism to be used in the study. Although precedent is sometimes the determining factor guiding the selection of a particular organism, the research problem should be the main determinant. The organism that is best for investigating the research problem should be used when possible.

Once the question of type of organism has been resolved, the researcher needs to determine where these organisms can be attained. Infrahumans, particularly rats, are available from a number of commercial sources. Most human research participants used in psychological experimentation come from departmental participant pools, which usually consist of introductory psychology students. If the study calls for participants other than those represented in the participant pools, the investigator must locate an available source and make the necessary arrangements. One source that is used with increasing frequency is the Internet. In addition to identifying the source of research participants, the experimenter needs to determine how many participants should be used. A power analysis is used for determining sample size. Instructions must also be prepared for studies using human research participants. The instructions should include a clear description of the purpose (or disguised purpose) of the task required of the participants.

Next, the investigator must specify the procedure to be used in data collection—the exact sequence in which all phases of the experiment are to be carried out, from the moment the investigator comes in contact with the research participants until that contact terminates.

When the research participant arrives at the experimental site, the first task of the experimenter is to obtain the research participant's consent to participate in the study. This means that the participant must be informed of all aspects of the study that might affect his or her willingness to participate. Only after this information has been conveyed and the participant agrees to participate can the experimenter proceed with the study. Immediately following data collection, the experimenter must conduct a postexperimental interview, or debriefing session, with the participants. During this interview, the experimenter attempts to detect any suspicions that the participants might have had. In addition, the experimenter explains to the participants the reasons for any deceptions that might have been used, as well as the entire experimental procedure and purpose. It is helpful to conduct a pilot study to iron out unforeseen difficulties.

Key Terms and Concepts

Effect size
Pilot study

Postexperimental interview
Power

Related Internet Site

http://opl.apa.org
This site offers a number of classic studies in psychology in which students can participate. After participating in an online experiment, they can analyze the data collected as well as see the results of the data collected.

Practice Test

The answers to these questions can be found in Appendix.

1. The type of organism that should be used in research studies
   a. Should be determined by precedent
   b. Should be determined by the research question
   c. Is the type of organism available to the researcher
   d. Should be the type used in prior studies
   e. Is either rats or college students

2. Sample size should be determined by a combination of which of the following factors?
   a. Effect size, alpha level, power
   b. Effect size, alpha level, significance level
   c. Significance level, alpha power, straight power
   d. Alpha level, power, beta level
   e. Beta level, effect size, significance level

3. Which of the following journals will be helpful in identifying a specific piece of apparatus or computer program to assist in data collection?
   a. *Journal of Applied Psychology*
   b. *Psychological Methods*
   c. *Psychological Assessment*
   d. *Behavioral Research Methods, Instruments, and Computers*
   e. *Psychological Instrumentation and Computers*

4. If you have pretested your entire procedure on a few participants prior to actually collecting data you have
   a. Sampled your procedure
   b. Conducted a pilot study
   c. Conducted a postexperimental debriefing
   d. Tested the effectiveness of the independent variable manipulation
   e. Wasted participants that could have contributed to the study

5. What function does debriefing serve?
   a. Ethical function
   b. Educational function
   c. Methodological function
   d. Participant satisfaction from contributing to science
   e. All of the above are functions of debriefing

Challenge Exercise

1. Employment agencies are in the business of finding employment for individuals. One of the difficulties these agencies have is identifying individuals with the necessary skills to keep a job after they are placed. Let's assume that you are aware of this difficulty and you have developed a four-week course designed to teach individuals the skills they need to retain a job. Your four-week course consists of training in dealing with a boss, dealing with other difficult employees, dressing for the job, and other skills such as just ensuring that the worker arrives on time for work. The basic design you want to use is a simple posttest-only randomized design with a treatment and control group. With this as your research problem and experimental design, answer the following questions.
   a. What research participants do you plan to use, and how do you plan to obtain these participants?
   b. How many participants should you use? Identify how you would decide on the number of participants to use if you do not have sufficient information to identify the specific number.
   c. What factors do you have to take into consideration in presenting the treatment condition and control conditions and how will you implement these factors? What outcome measures will you use to test the effectiveness of the treatment condition?
   d. What type of approval is needed to enable you to conduct this study?
   e. Prepare a short consent form for this study.
   f. Prepare a short debriefing statement for this study.

CHAPTER 10

Quasi-Experimental Designs

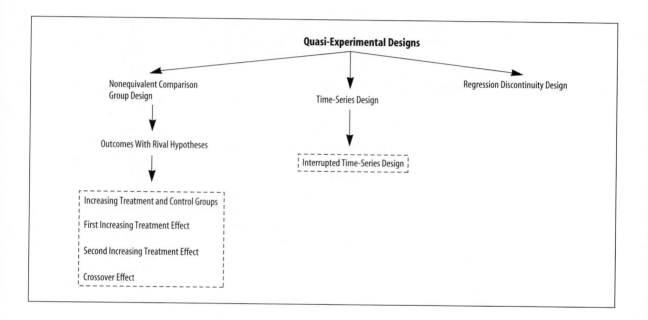

One of the most significant changes occurring in the life of many Americans during the last several decades of the twentieth century was the advent of the personal computer. In August 2000, 51% of all U.S. households had one or more computers and 41% had access to the Internet (Newburger, 2001). The Internet is a marvelous technological development, providing easy access to information and communication in a way unparalleled by anything we have known in the past. Unfortunately, there is some evidence (Kraut, Mukhopadhyay, Szczypula, Kiesler, & Scherlis, 1998) that the Internet is used primarily for communication—communication that could decrease in-person communication. This has led some researchers to ask questions about the behavioral and psychological effects of the Internet. These questions seem particularly important because of numerous reports of individuals becoming addicted to the Internet, an addiction that is leading to divorce, child neglect, job termination, debt, flunking out of school, and legal trouble.

Young (1996), for example, cites the case of a homemaker who initially spent a few hours per week scanning a variety of chat rooms. During the next 3 months, she continued to increase the time spent conversing or chatting online with other individuals, peaking at 50–60 hours per week. This obsession with participating in chat rooms eventually resulted in her reducing her involvement with her family, eliminating social activities, and ceasing to perform activities such as cooking, cleaning, and grocery shopping. The end result was that she became estranged from her two daughters and separated from her husband within 1 year of the purchase of her home computer.

The repeated occurrence of stories such as the one just mentioned and research (Kraut, Patterson, et al., 1998) demonstrating the negative social impact of extensive Internet use has led some individuals, such as Harvard psychologist Maressa Hecht Orzack (Potera, 1998), to develop a treatment for this problem. Dr. Orzack's approach is to treat Internet addiction like binge eating, where the client is taught to set limits, balance activities, and schedule time. It is appropriate, therefore, to ask the question: Is this treatment effective? On the basis of the material you have learned in previous chapters, you should realize that this research question is best answered using a strong experimental research design. A purposive sample of individuals meeting specified criteria for excessive Internet use could be randomly assigned to either a control group that did not receive Orzack's treatment or an experimental group that did receive the treatment. Following treatment, the two groups could be compared to determine if the experimental treatment group improved on the dependent variable of addiction more than the no-treatment control group.

The problem with using such an approach is that many treatment programs will not allow a researcher to come in and determine randomly whether a person can or cannot receive the treatment. Rather, the mission of treatment programs is to treat individuals, such as those with an addiction to the Internet, and they accept anyone who requests treatment. It would be unethical to do otherwise. This is one of the primary difficulties encountered in moving out of the laboratory and into the real world. Outside the laboratory setting, it is more difficult to use the strongest control technique, random assignment, to groups. But in such cases investigators need not throw up their hands and abandon the research. Rather, they can turn to the use of quasi-experimental designs— designs that enable researchers to investigate problems that preclude the use of procedures required by a randomized experimental design. For example, the researcher might work with the program administrator to allow construction of a control group (that is similar to the experimental treatment group) from the program's waiting list. Or the experimenter might determine whether multiple pretests and multiple posttests can be used with each participant. In this chapter, you will learn about some experimental design alternatives that do not involve random assignment.

Introduction

A **quasi-experimental design** is an experimental design that does not meet all the requirements necessary for controlling the influence of extraneous variables. Quasi-experimental designs always lack random assignment of participants to groups, which is found only in strong experimental designs discussed in Chapter 8. Fortunately, quasi-experimental designs are better at controlling extraneous variables than the weak designs discussed Chapter 8. It is helpful to view these three types of designs (weak, quasi, and strong) as falling on the continuum shown in Figure 10.1. The figure shows that quasi-experimental designs are neither the worst nor the best experimental designs. Quasi-experimental designs fall in-between the two poles.

You might ask whether it is possible to draw causal inferences from studies based on a quasi-experimental design, because such a design does not rule out the influence of all rival hypotheses. Making a causal inference from a quasi-experiment requires meeting the same basic requirements needed for any causal relationship. You must meet the following three conditions: (1) cause and effect must covary (i.e., there must be a relationship between the independent and dependent variables), (2) cause must precede effect (i.e., changes in the independent variable must precede changes in the dependent variable), and (3) rival hypotheses must be implausible (i.e., the relationship between the independent and dependent variables must not be due a confounding extraneous variable). The first two requirements (cause covarying with effect and cause preceding effect) are easy to handle in quasi-experiments, because, as in randomized experiments, the researcher (or researcher working with the program staff) actively manipulates the independent variable so that the cause precedes the effect (which is measured at posttest after the manipulation), and one simply analyzes the data to determine if a statistical relationship is present. However, the third requirement, ruling out rival hypotheses, is more difficult because random assignment is not possible in quasi-experiments. Therefore, one or more rival hypotheses or alternative explanations for the observed relationship between the independent and dependent variables frequently exist with quasi-experiments.

Causal inferences can be made using quasi-experimental designs, but these inferences are made only when data are collected that help render alternative explanations implausible. Furthermore, the evidence will usually be more suspect than evidence from a strong experimental design. Shadish et al. (2002) have identified three principles, presented in Table 10.1, to address rival explanations and show that they are implausible. Principle one requires the identification and study of all plausible threats to internal validity. Much of this chapter focuses on

FIGURE 10.1
Continuum of experimental research designs.

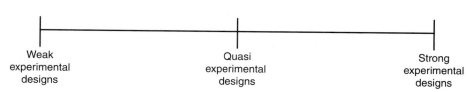

| Weak experimental designs | Quasi experimental designs | Strong experimental designs |

TABLE 10.1
Principles Used to Rule out Rival Explanations in Quasi-Experiments

1. *Identification and study of plausible threats to internal validity:* This principle involves identifying plausible rival explanations and then probing and investigating them to determine how likely it is that they can explain the covariation between the treatment and the outcome.

2. *Control by design:* This principle involves adding design elements, such as additional pretest time points or additional control groups, to either eliminate a rival explanation or obtain evidence about the plausibility of the rival explanation.

3. *Coherent pattern matching:* This principle can be used when a complex prediction can be made about a causal hypothesis, and there are few, if any, rival explanations that would make the same prediction. If the complex prediction is supported by the data, most rival explanations are eliminated. The more complex the prediction, the less likely it is that a rival explanation can explain the prediction and the more likely that the independent variable is producing the effect.

principle one strategies (i.e., identifying key threats and minimizing their effects through design and control strategies).

Principle two (i.e., control by design) involves the use of design components to control for plausible threats. As a review from the last chapter, here are the major **design components** that are usually available to a researcher: (1) control or comparison groups (zero, one, or more than one), (2) pretest (zero, one, or more than one), (3) posttest (one or more than one), (4) within-participants and/or between-participants independent variables, (5) inclusion of one or more theoretically interesting independent variables, and (6) measurement of one or more theoretically interesting dependent variables. You can view the quasi-experimental designs presented as design improvements upon the weak designs explained in Chapter 8. For example, you will see that the interrupted time-series design (a quasi-experimental design) discussed in this chapter is like the one-group pretest–posttest design (a weak design from Chapter 8) with additional pretests and posttests added. Likewise, nonequivalent comparison group design (a quasi-experimental design) is like the posttest-only design with nonequivalent groups (a weak design from Chapter 8) with a pretest added. You can also think of quasi-experimental designs as like strong designs with one or more components removed (typically random assignment to groups).

The third principle (i.e., coherent pattern matching) recommends the use of a pattern-matching strategy. This typically involves stating complex hypotheses about how multiple dependent variables will precisely change after an intervention. Stronger (i.e., more complex) hypotheses generally require stronger theory and are more easily falsifiable, which is what the philosopher Karl Popper (1902–1994) recommended (he called these "bold" hypotheses). For example, one might predict that after a treatment, the experimental treatment group will increase very much on one dependent variable, decrease very much on another dependent variable, and increase only slightly on yet another dependent variable, and, at the same time, the control group might be predicted to show no movement at all on any of the dependent variables. This would be a relatively complex pattern-matching type of hypothesis. To learn more about pattern matching, we

Design components
Structures and procedures used in constructing research designs

recommend Campbell (1966), Shadish et al. (2002), and Trochim and Donnelly (2008). In the remainder of the chapter we focus on principles one and two.

STUDY QUESTIONS 10.1

- **How does a quasi-experimental research design differ from a strong experimental research design?**
- **What are the requirements for making a strong claim of cause and effect?**
- **How are rival hypotheses ruled out in quasi-experimental designs?**

Nonequivalent Comparison Group Design

Nonequivalent comparison group design
A quasi-experimental design in which the results obtained from nonequivalent experimental and control groups are compared

The **nonequivalent comparison group design** is probably the most common of all quasi-experimental designs (Shadish et al., 2002). This design includes both an experimental and a control group, but participants are not randomly assigned. Because of the lack of random assignment, the participants in the control and experimental groups will not be equivalent on all variables, and this can affect the dependent variable. These uncontrolled variables operate as rival hypotheses to explain the outcome of the experiment, making these designs quasi-experimental designs. But when a better design cannot be used, some form of a nonequivalent comparison group design is frequently recommended.

The basic scheme, depicted in Figure 10.2, consists of giving an experimental group and a control group first a pretest and then a posttest (after the treatment condition is administered to the experimental group). The pre- to posttest changes of the two groups are then compared to determine if significant differences exist. The design appears similar to the pretest–posttest control-group experimental design. However, there is one important difference that makes one a *strong* experimental design and the other a *quasi*-experimental design. In the between-participants pretest–posttest control-group design, the participants are randomly assigned to the experimental and control groups, whereas in the nonequivalent comparison group design they are not. Thus, the nonequivalent comparison group design is what you would get if you took away the random assignment component from the between-participants pretest–posttest control-group design. The absence of random assignment is what makes the nonequivalent control-group design a quasi-experimental design.

The pretest component of the nonequivalent comparison group design is very important because it tells us how the groups compared initially. One can generally assume that the larger the difference between the groups on the pretest, the greater the likelihood of a strong selection bias (Shadish et al., 2002). If the pretest is not included, you will end up with the weak design discussed in the Chapter 8—the

FIGURE 10.2
Nonequivalent comparison group design. (*Note:* The dashed line indicates the lack of random assignment.)

	Pretest measure	Treatment	Posttest measure
Experimental group	O_1	X_1	O_2
Control group	O_1	X_2	O_2

posttest-only design with nonequivalent groups. From a design perspective, be sure to notice that the *nonequivalent comparison group design* presented here (a quasi-experimental design) is an improvement over the *posttest-only design with nonequivalent groups*, but is not as good as the *pretest–posttest control-group design* (a strong, randomized design). The point is to notice what happens when design components (such as pretests and random assignment) are added or subtracted from designs.

Pretesting allows for testing and examination of biases, such as those listed in Table 10.2, that often threaten the design. All of these threats to internal validity would have been minimized if the researcher could randomly assign participants, but that's not possible with the nonequivalent comparison group design. *Selection bias* is the most obvious result of the lack of random assignment—the groups likely will not be equivalent on all extraneous variables. Because participants are not randomly assigned, you cannot assume that the groups are equivalent; in fact, you should assume that the groups are "nonequivalent" on variables in addition to the independent variable. Remember, we want the groups to be different only on the levels of the independent variable. Given the presence of nonequivalent groups, participants might be more likely (1) to drop out of one group than from another group (called *selection-attrition bias* or differential attrition), (2) to mature at different rates in the different groups (called *selection-maturation bias* or differential maturation), (3) to be differently assessed by the measurement process in different groups (called *selection-instrumentation* or differential instrumentation), (4) to "regress-to-the-mean" at different rates in the different groups (called *selection-regression bias* or differential regression), and (5) to react differently to non–treatment-related events occurring between the pretest and posttest (called *selection-history bias* or differential history). The key point here is that we want differences between the groups at the posttest (on the dependent variable) to be due *only to the independent variable*, and we do not want differences (on the dependent variable) to be caused by group differences in extraneous variables such as attrition, maturation, operation of instruments,

TABLE 10.2

Possible Biases That Exist in the Nonequivalent Comparison Group Design

1. *Selection bias*—Because groups are nonequivalent, there will always be a potential selection bias. However, the pretest allows the exploration of the possible size and direction of the bias on any variables measured at pretesting.

2. *Selection-attrition bias*—The pretest allows examination of the nature of attrition to see if there is a difference between those that drop out or do not complete the experiment and those that do.

3. *Selection-maturation bias*—This might exist if one group of participants becomes more experienced, tired, or bored than those in the other group.

4. *Selection-instrumentation bias*—This might exist if the nonequivalent groups of participants start at different points on the pretest, particularly if the measuring instrument does not have equal intervals.

5. *Selection-regression bias*—This might exist if the two groups are from different populations, such as the experimental treatment group from a population of individuals with a reading disability and the comparison group from a population of individuals without a reading disability.

6. *Selection-history bias*—This might exist if an event occurring between the pretest and posttest affects one group more than the other group.

regression to the mean, or reactions to non–treatment events occurring during the experiment. Shadish et al. (2002) have pointed out that the possibility of an extraneous variable confounding the results of a study depends on the characteristics of the design as well as the pattern of results obtained from the study. Therefore, we now examine several possible patterns of results to see when threats can be considered more or less plausible.

STUDY QUESTIONS 10.2

- **Diagram the nonequivalent comparison group design, and explain why it is a quasi-experimental design.**
- **What are the major potential threats to internal validity when using this design?**

Increasing treatment and control groups
An outcome in which the experimental and the control groups differ at pretesting and both increase from pre- to posttesting, but the experimental group increases at a faster rate

Selection-maturation effect
Participants in one group experience a different rate of maturation than participants in another group

Outcomes with Rival Hypotheses

Outcome I: Increasing Treatment and Control Groups   In the **increasing treatment and control groups** pattern illustrated in Figure 10.3, the control group reveals a small positive change from pretest to posttest, but the experimental group increases at a faster rate. Prima facie, the pattern suggests that the experimental treatment was effective because the difference between the two groups increases from pretest to posttest. However, this outcome could have also occurred, for example, as a result of a selection-maturation, selection-history, or selection-regression effect.

A **selection-maturation effect** refers to the fact that one of the two groups of participants was selected in such a way that its participants were growing or developing at a faster rate than the participants in the other group. Since both groups are increasing, it seems plausible that maturation is occurring, and it would not be unlikely that differential maturation also were occurring because the groups are nonequivalent. The experimental group might progress faster because its members are more motivated than those in the control group. For example, children placed in an experimental preschool program might have been

FIGURE 10.3
Increasing treatment and control groups.

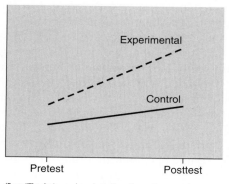

(From "The design and conduct of quasi-experiments and true experiments in field settings" by T. D. Cook & D. T. Campbell, 1976, in *Handbook of Industrial and Organizational Psychology*, edited by M. D. Dunnette. Copyright © Rand McNally Publishing Company.)

those who were showing an interest in reading and, therefore, their parents sought the educational opportunities to support their children's emerging skills. If this were the case, then the greater posttest increase could be accounted for by the fact that the selection procedure happened to place participants in the experimental group whose reading skills were already increasing more rapidly than the children in the control condition.

A second rival explanation of the increasing treatment effect shown in Figure 10.3 is a **selection-history effect** (Cook & Campbell, 1979). A general history effect, discussed in Chapter 6, is controlled in the nonequivalent comparison group design by inclusion of a control group. However, the design is still susceptible to a selection-history effect (i.e., a differential history effect), in which some event affects either the experimental or the control group, but not both (or affects one group more than the other group). Perhaps some significant event occurred between the pretest and posttest for the experimental group, but not for the control group. For example, in the experimental preschool example, perhaps the preschool served as reliable child care, which allowed the parents to find better jobs and increase their income, which led to increased educational opportunities in the home such as books and computers. This is something the researcher would need to consider carefully in the context of his or her particular research study, and to determine its plausibility.

Other rival explanations of the pattern shown in Figure 10.3 are possible. For example, a **selection-instrumentation effect** might occur if the measurement varied or operated differently for the two groups. You might be able to rule this out easily, however, after examining the measurement instruments and procedure used in the study. **Selection-attrition effect** also might have occurred if the groups became different because of participants dropping out. Careful examination of the characteristics and pretest scores of participants who dropped out would help determine the plausibility of this effect. A **selection-regression effect** appears unlikely because the experimental group started out higher on the pretest than the control group. One would have expected the lower scoring group to have shown greater upward regression to the mean.

Outcome II: First Increasing Treatment Effect   In the **first increasing treatment effect** pattern, illustrated in Figure 10.4, the control group shows no change from pretest to posttest, but the experimental group starts higher and shows significant positive change from pretest to posttest. Such a pattern suggests a positive treatment effect because one group changed and the other group showed no change at all. The lack of any control group change (in contrast to the experimental group) would need to be explained if a rival were to be identified. A selection-maturation effect is possible, but it seems unlikely because the control group shows no maturation at all. Selection-regression seems unlikely because the experimental group started out higher than the control group and should have shown less of an upward regression effect. Perhaps the most plausible threat is a selection-history effect. Perhaps a significant event happened (other than administration of the treatment) that affected the treatment group but not the control group. Or perhaps some event happened only for the experimental group that caused them to work

Selection-history effect
An extraneous event occurring between pretest and posttest influences participants in one group differently than participants in another group

Selection-instrumentation effect
Participants' scores in one group are affected by the process of measurement differently than participants in another group

Selection-attrition effect
Participants that drop out of one group are dissimilar to those in another group

Selection-regression effect
Participants in one group display a different rate of regression to the mean than participants in another group

First increasing treatment effect
An outcome in which the experimental and the control groups differ at pretesting, and only the experimental group's scores change from pre- to posttesting

FIGURE 10.4
First increasing treatment effect.

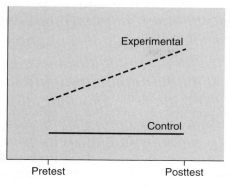

(From "The design and conduct of quasi-experiments and true experiments in field settings" by T. D. Cook & D. T. Campbell, 1976, in *Handbook of Industrial and Organizational Psychology*, edited by M. D. Dunnette. Copyright © Rand McNally Publishing Company.)

harder and show more improvement. The potential threats should be carefully examined in the context of the particular research study.

Second increasing treatment effect
An outcome in which the control group performs better than the experimental group at pretesting, but only the experimental group improves from pre- to posttesting

Outcome III: Second Increasing Treatment Effect   In the **second increasing treatment effect** pattern, illustrated in Figure 10.5, the control group shows no change from pretest to posttest, but the experimental group starts much lower and shows significant positive change from pretest to posttest. Before we can interpret the increase in performance of the experimental treatment group as being the result of the independent variable, we must consider potential rival hypotheses. The pattern shown in Figure 10.5 suggests the possibility of a selection-regression effect because the experimental group started out much lower and showed upward improvement. If the program is given to the children with unusually low scores on the pretest measure of the dependent variable and the control condition

FIGURE 10.5
Second increasing treatment effect.

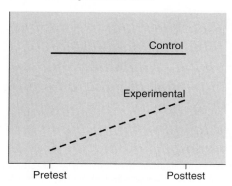

(From "The design and conduct of quasi-experiments and true experiments in field settings" by T. D. Cook and D. T. Campbell, 1976, in *Handbook of Industrial and Organizational Psychology*, edited by M. D. Dunnette. Copyright © Rand McNally Publishing Company.)

was given to average-scoring children, then one would expect regression to the mean only for the low-scoring children. This is a threat that you should be on the lookout for when examining evaluation research of compensatory programs. Because these programs are targeted at those with the most need, group selection might be based on especially low scores.

Crossover effect
An outcome in which the control group performs better at pretesting but the experimental group performs better at posttesting

Outcome IV: Crossover Effect   Figure 10.6 depicts the **crossover effect**, an experimental outcome in which the treatment group scores significantly lower than the control group at pretest but significantly higher at posttest. The control group doesn't change from pretest to posttest, but the experimental group shows a clear improvement from pretest to posttest. This outcome is much more readily interpreted than the other patterns and suggests that the program is quite effective. You would probably be especially pleased with this outcome. It renders many potential rival hypotheses implausible. Statistical regression can be ruled out because it is highly unlikely that the experimental treatment group's lower pretest scores would regress enough to become significantly higher than those of the control group on posttesting. Second, a selection-maturation effect is improbable because it is typically the higher-scoring pretest participants who gain faster on maturational factors.

The outcome pattern shown in Figure 10.6 provides the strongest evidence for effect of the independent variable. However, the pattern of results typically found in research will be more ambiguous. The researcher must take whatever pattern of results occurs, attempt to identify rival hypotheses that suggest why the relationship between the independent and dependent variable is due to some confounding extraneous variable, and then attempt to rule out the rival hypotheses. Full details of this entire process must be reported to the reader in the final research report.

FIGURE 10.6
Crossover effect.

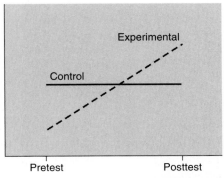

(From "The design and conduct of quasi-experiments and true experiments in field settings" by T. D. Cook and D. T. Campbell, 1976, in *Handbook of Industrial and Organizational Psychology*, edited by M. D. Dunnette. Copyright © Rand McNally Publishing Company.)

Ruling out Threats to the Nonequivalent Comparison Group Design

In an attempt to eliminate the potential impact of selection biases, researchers try to ensure the similarity of groups by either matching on variables that pose rival explanations or using statistical control procedures. For example, in a Head Start program, you might want to match on income, intelligence, parental involvement, and so forth. This list raises an important issue: it is often impossible to identify and match on all of the important variables. Matching equates the groups on the matched variables at the start of the experiment. Matching also should be carried out on the dependent variable, which is assumed to equate participants on additional variables. Unfortunately, one can never fully match, and matching is not a perfect replacement for the much stronger control technique of random assignment available in strong experimental research designs. Nonetheless, when random assignment is not possible, one should carefully examine the literature and local situation to determine the most important variables to use in matching.

One must be careful when matching, however, for the following two situations that can occur as a result of selection-regression effects. Assume that a researcher wants to match individuals from a disadvantaged population with individuals from an advantaged population. Assume that the average pretest performance score in the disadvantaged population is 44 and in the advantaged population is 88. Also assume that both populations' scores are normally distributed around the mean (where most scores are near the mean with far fewer scores at the extremes). This situation is shown in Figure 10.7.

In our first case, the experimenter decides to match on pretest scores by giving the program (i.e., the treatment) to disadvantaged individuals and locating individuals from the advantaged group *with similar pretest scores* to serve in the control group. To this, the researcher takes high-scoring disadvantaged individuals and finds matches from low-scoring advantaged individuals. The resulting treatment and control groups will have similar scores on the pretest and will appear to be fairly matched (equated on pretest scores). However, in this situation, the disadvantaged individuals will tend to regress downward from pretest to posttest (closer to the disadvantaged group average), and the advantaged individuals will tend to regress upward from pretest to posttest (closer to the advantaged group average), independently on any treatment effect. If the experimental condition is

FIGURE 10.7
Distributions of disadvantaged and advantaged groups. (*Note:* The darkened area shows high scoring disadvantaged and low scoring advantaged individuals used in matching.)

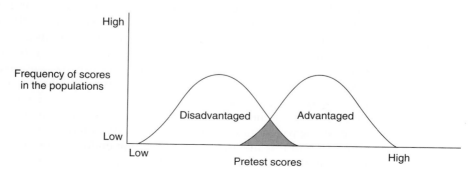

administered to the disadvantaged individuals (and the advantaged serve as controls), then finding a positive program effect becomes highly unlikely because the disadvantaged individuals must improve enough to overcome their own propensity to regress downward (to their group mean), and they must also offset the advantaged individuals' propensity to regress upward (to their group mean) in this situation. This use of individuals from opposite ends of preexisting groups works against finding a positive improvement due to the program, *even if the program is effective.*

Second, in our scenario, if the program was given to the low-scoring advantaged individuals (and high-scoring disadvantaged individuals served as controls), then *the program might appear effective, even if it was an ineffective program.* The key message is to be careful of selection–regression effects when matching participants from different populations because you might end up matching individuals that come from the opposite extremes of their respective groups. This can result in an effective treatment appearing to be ineffective or an ineffective treatment appearing to be effective!

Another strategy for equating groups is to attempt to determine what variables (other than your independent variable) your groups will likely differ on and measure those variables. Then, during data analysis, statistical control techniques can be used to adjust for pretest differences on the measured variables. Although this process can help somewhat, ultimately it fails because statistical control cannot fully equate the groups on all known and unknown variables. Also, statistical control techniques tend to be especially susceptible to measurement error on the pretest. To help deal with this problem, a statistical procedure known as *reliability adjusted analysis of covariance* (ANCOVA) is recommended (see Trochim & Donnelly, 2008). This approach and additional statistical approaches such as *propensity score matching* and *selection modeling* are beyond the scope of this book, but are discussed in more advanced books and articles (e.g., Rindskopf, 1992; Shadish et al., 2002).

Causal Inference from the Nonequivalent Comparison Group Design

The nonequivalent comparison group design, as we have just discussed, is susceptible to producing biased results because of the potential existence of a number of threats to internal validity. The existence of these potential threats suggests that the results obtained from this quasi-experimental design might be biased and different from what would be obtained from one of the randomized experimental designs. Heinsman and Shadish (1996) conducted a meta-analysis comparing the effect-size estimates from randomized experimental designs and the nonrandomized nonequivalent comparison group design to determine the extent to which similar results have been obtained from studies using these two designs. This analysis suggested that if the randomized experimental design and the nonequivalent comparison group design were equally well designed and executed, they yielded about the same effect size. In other words, the nonequivalent comparison group design gave about the same results as the randomized experimental design.

The result of this meta-analysis is a strong endorsement of the nonequivalent comparison group design. However, this strong endorsement exists only when the nonequivalent comparison group design is as well designed and executed as the randomized experimental design. As Heinsman and Shadish (1996) have pointed out, it is probably very difficult in many studies to design and execute the nonequivalent comparison group design as well as the randomized experimental designs. Therefore, in many studies, the nonequivalent comparison group design will give results that are difficult to interpret.

There seem to be two design components that researchers must focus on when designing and conducting quasi-experiments to strengthen internal validity. The first component focuses on the way participants are assigned to groups. To obtain unbiased results, experimenters must not let the participants self-select into groups or conditions. The more participants self-select into the treatment conditions, the more biased the results will be. The second component focuses on pretest differences. Big differences at the pretest will lead to big differences at the posttest. This means that the researcher should either try to reduce pretest differences by matching the comparison groups on variables correlated with the dependent variable or control for pretest differences by statistically adjusting the posttest scores for any pretest differences (e.g., using ANCOVA). If the experimenter focuses on these two design characteristics, the results obtained from the nonequivalent comparison group design will produce a closer approximation to a randomized experimental research design.

STUDY QUESTIONS 10.3

- **Identify and discuss the rival hypotheses that could explain the various outcomes that could occur in a nonexperimental comparison group design.**
- **Why is the crossover effect not readily explained by rival hypotheses?**
- **What design components should be used to reduce bias in quasi-experiments?**

Time-Series Design

In research areas such as psychotherapy and program evaluation, it is sometimes very difficult to find an equivalent group of research participants to serve as a control group. Is the *one-group pretest–posttest design* (discussed in Chapter 8) the only available design in such cases? Is there no means of eliminating some of the rival hypotheses that arise from this design? Fortunately, there is a means for eliminating some of these rival hypotheses, but to do so one must think of mechanisms other than using a control group.

Interrupted time-series design

A quasi-experimental design in which a treatment effect is assessed by comparing the pattern of pre- and posttest scores for a single group of research participants

Interrupted Time-Series Design

The **interrupted time-series design** requires the investigator to take a series of measurements with a single group both before and after the introduction of some treatment condition, as depicted in Figure 10.8. As shown in the figure, all of the participants are pretested a number of times and then posttested a number of times after or during exposure to the experimental treatment condition. The researcher plots the data for the dependent variable for all measurement points,

FIGURE 10.8
Interrupted
time-series design.

Multiple pretests	Treatment	Multiple posttests
$O_1 \, O_2 \, O_3 \, O_4 \, O_5$	X_1	$O_6 \, O_7 \, O_8 \, O_9 \, O_{10}$

before and after the treatment, and compares the before and after treatment patterns. The result of the treatment condition is indicated by a discontinuity in the recorded series of response measurements. For example, an effect is demonstrated when there is a change in the level and/or slope of the posttreatment responses as compared to the pretreatment responses.

Consider the study conducted by Lawler and Hackman (1969) in which they tried to identify the benefit derived from employee participation in the development of an employee incentive plan. Prior research had investigated a variety of payment plans and found that a given plan (say, a bonus plan) might be successful in one instance and not in another, indicating that the success of pay incentive plans is a function of multiple factors. Lawler and Hackman hypothesized that a particular pay incentive plan would be more effective if the employees participated in its development, as opposed to having a plan dictated by management. To assess the validity of this hypothesis, Lawler and Hackman had three work groups meet and develop a bonus incentive plan for reducing absenteeism. Absenteeism rates for the work groups were measured multiple times before and after the incentive plan was developed. The rates were converted to a percentage of the number of scheduled hours that the employees actually worked. The average percentage of scheduled hours worked for all participants appears in Figure 10.9. From this figure, you can see that there was a rise in this average percentage, and the rise

FIGURE 10.9

Mean attendance of the participative groups for the 12 weeks before the incentive plan and the 16 weeks after the plan. (*Note*: Attendance is expressed in terms of the percentage of hours scheduled to be worked that were actually worked.)

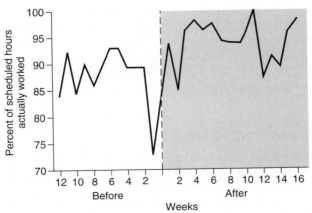

(From "Impact of employee participation in the development of pay incentive plans: A field experiment" by E. E. Lawler & J. R. Hackman, 1969, *Journal of Applied Psychology, 53,* 467–471. Copyright 1969 by the American Psychological Association. Reprinted by permission of the author.)

persisted over 16 weeks during which the data were collected. The program appears effective. Now it is necessary to ask two questions. First, did a statistically significant change occur following the introduction of the treatment condition? Second, can the observed change be attributed to the treatment condition?

The answer to the first question naturally involves tests of statistical significance; a test of statistical significance would indicate whether the difference in the pre and post patterns was greater than what would be expected by chance. However, before discussing tests of significance, we want to show why the *interrupted time series design* (which has multiple pretest and posttest measurements) is better than the *one-group pretest–posttest design* (which has a single pretest and a single posttest). We will examine the data that would have been obtained from the study by Lawler and Hackman (1969) and from a study conducted by Vernon, Bedford, and Wyatt (1924) if the researchers had used the one-group pretest–posttest design, which is a weak experimental design. To do this, we will only use the one data point immediately before the treatment is introduced and the one data point immediately after the treatment is introduced. The Vernon et al. study was concerned with investigating the influence of introducing a rest period on the productivity of various kinds of factory workers. Partial data for both studies, showing only the data point immediately before the treatment and the data point immediately after the treatment (to simulate a one-group pretest–posttest design), are presented in Figure 10.10 (the top line is for the Lawler and Hackman study, and the bottom line is for the Vernon et al. study). In *both* studies, the pretest-to-posttest pattern appears to support strongly the hypothesis that the experimental treatment condition produced a beneficial effect (both lines were low before treatment and were high after the treatment). Unfortunately, the one-group pretest–posttest design is a weak design. If you examine the full set of results for the Vernon et al. study (in Figure 10.11), you will see that the conclusion of program effect made from the use of only one point before and one point after the treatment was incorrect. The key message is that we need more than two data points (one pre and one post) when assessing the effects of a treatment for a single group.

FIGURE 10.10

A one-group pretest–posttest representation of a portion of the Vernon et al. (1924) data and Lawler and Hackman (1969) data.

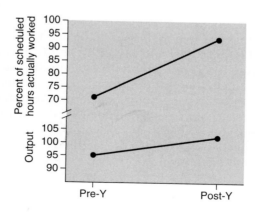

FIGURE 10.11

Effect of a ten-minute rest pause on worker productivity.

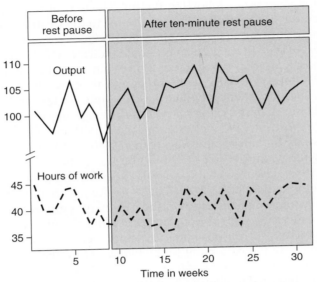

(Reprinted from *Two Studies of Rest Pauses in Industry* by H. M. Vernon, T. Bedford, & S. Wyatt, 1924. Medical Research Council, Industrial Fatigue Research Board No. 25. London: His Majesty's Stationery Office.)

In contrast to the one-group pretest–posttest design, when you have used an interrupted time-series design, visual inspection of the pre and post patterns is very helpful in determining whether an experimental treatment has a real effect and determining the pattern of an effect. Caporaso and Ross (1973) have presented a number of additional possible patterns of responses, shown in Figure 10.12. All of the pre and post data points shown in each line in Figure 10.12 would be used in an interrupted time-series design, but only the single points before and after the vertical line would have been used in a one-group pretest–posttest design. Examine each line in Figure 10.12 and try to determine if different conclusions about program effectiveness would have been obtained when all of the points are used versus when only the point before and the point after the treatment is used. When using all points before and after treatment, the first three patterns (A, B, and C) reveal no treatment effect but merely represent a continuation of a previously established pattern of behavior. However, if the one-group pretest–posttest approach had been used (i.e., examining only the one point before the treatment and the one point after the treatment), one would conclude that the treatment was effective in case A and case B (because it shows a clear increase) and that the treatment had a negative effect in case C (because it shows a decrease). All three of these conclusions would have been false! Using the interrupted time-series approach (i.e., using all the points in each line), lines D, E, F, and G suggest reliable changes in behavior, although line D represents only a temporary shift.

FIGURE 10.12
Possible pattern of behavior of a time-series variable.

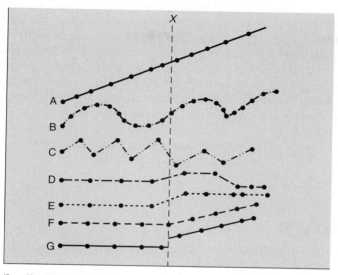

(From *"Quasi-Experimental Approaches: Testing Theory and Evaluating Policy"* by J. A. Caporaso & L. L. Ross, Jr. Copyright 1973 by Northwestern University Press. Reprinted by permission.)

This is the same conclusion one would have obtained using the one-group pretest–posttest approach; however, in these cases the interrupted time-series approach provided additional information about the longer-term pattern of posttest results (e.g., does it go up and stop? does it continue going up? does it go up and then decline?).

Now let us return to our original question of whether a statistically significant change in behavior follows the introduction of the treatment condition. Such a determination involves tests of statistical significance. The most widely used and most technically appropriate statistical test is to use an autoregressive integrated moving average (ARIMA) model (Box & Jenkins, 1970; Glass, Willson, & Gottman, 1975). Basically, this method consists of fitting a statistical model to the observed pattern of pre- and postresponse measures and testing it for statistical significance. Unfortunately, to make such an assessment using ARIMA requires many data points. Glass et al. (1975) recommend that at least 50 data points be obtained. This relatively large number of data points can typically be obtained when conducting experiments using animals. However, it frequently cannot be obtained when conducting research with humans. This difficulty has resulted in the relatively limited use of ARIMA statistical tests when analyzing time-series data. Fortunately, statistical procedures have been developed that can be used with as few as 10 data points (Bloom, 2003; Crosbie, 1993; Tryon, 1982). A valid statistical analysis can, therefore, be conducted on almost any study using a time-series analysis.

Lawler and Hackman's analysis of their data revealed a significant difference between the patterns of pre- and postresponse measures. This led them to conclude that a nonrandom change occurred following the introduction of the incentive plan. This brings us back to the second question: Can this significant change be attributed to the employees' participation in the incentive plan? *The primary source of weakness in the interrupted time-series design is its failure to control for the effects of history.* Considering Lawler and Hackman's study, assume that at about the same time the treatment condition was introduced, some extraneous event occurred that could also have led to an increase in the number of hours worked. Such an extraneous event would serve as a rival explanation for the nonrandom change. The investigator must consider all the other events taking place at about the same time as the experimental event and determine whether they might operate as plausible rival explanations that must be ruled out.

Regression Discontinuity Design

Regression discontinuity design
A design that assigns participants to groups based on their scores on an assignment variable and assesses the effect of a treatment by looking for a discontinuity in the groups regression lines

Assignment measure
Measure used to assign participants to experimental and control groups. Those with scores below the cutoff score are assigned to one group, and those with scores above the cutoff are assigned to the other group

The **regression discontinuity design** is a design that is used to determine whether a group of individuals meeting some predetermined criterion profit from receiving a treatment. This design, depicted in Figure 10.13, consists of measuring all participants on an **assignment measure** and then selecting a cutoff score based on this measure. All participants who score above the cutoff score receive the treatment, and all participants who score below the cutoff score do not receive the treatment. The opposite case also is used, where participants below the cutoff score get the treatment and participants above the cutoff score do not get the treatment. After the treatment is administered, the posttest measure is obtained and the two groups are compared on the outcome measure to determine whether the treatment was effective. For example, a researcher might measure college students on an English test that measures English deficiency, and assign those students with scores above the median deficiency to an English remediation program and use those with scores below the median as controls (Leake & Lesik, 2007). Although this might sound like a bad idea (i.e., to construct groups that are different at the start of the experiment), it actually works because the researcher knows the precise variable used for group assignment (Shadish et al., 2002). The participants are not allowed to self-select into the groups; the researcher fully controls participants' group assignment based on the selected cutoff score. Basically, the statistical procedure determines if there is a significant difference between the experimental and control groups' performance on the dependent variable (i.e., Is the difference between the two lines significantly different at the cutoff point in the graph?). For more information on the analysis of data from the regression discontinuity degign, see Shadish et al., (2002).

FIGURE 10.13

Structure of the regression discontinuity design. O_p is the assignment variable measure; C indicates the assignment measure cutoff score used to assign participants to conditions (where participants with scores above the cutoff are assigned to the treatment condition and participants with scores below the cutoff are assigned to the control condition); X refers to a treatment condition; and O_2 refers to the posttest measure of the outcome or dependent variable.

Experimental group	O_p	C	X	O_2
Control group	O_p	C		O_2

Pictorial depictions of results when no treatment effect is present and when a treatment effect is present will help you to see the idea clearly. Figure 10.14 illustrates the expected results when there is *no* treatment effect, and Figure 10.15 illustrates the expected results when there *is* a treatment effect. Both of these figures show the relationship between pretest and posttest scores for the treatment and control groups. The participants who scored higher than 50 on the preassignment variable received the treatment, and those scoring lower than 50 received the control condition. First look at Figure 10.14; you can see that there is no discontinuity in the regression line. There is a continuous increase of scores from a low of about 41 to a high of about 58, with a cutoff score of 50 separating the control group from the treatment group. The straight line pushed

FIGURE 10.14

Regression discontinuity experiment with no treatment effect.

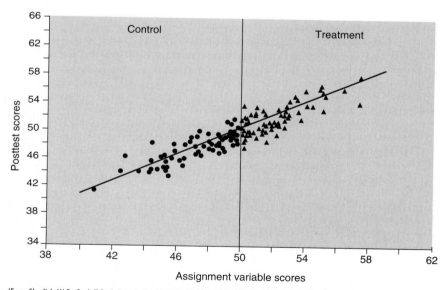

(From Shadish, W. R., Cook, T. D., & Campbell, D. T., 2002, *Experimental and quasi-experimental designs for generalized causal inference.* Copyright 2002. Houghton Mifflin Co. Used with permission.)

FIGURE 10.15
Regression discontinuity experiment with an effective treatment.

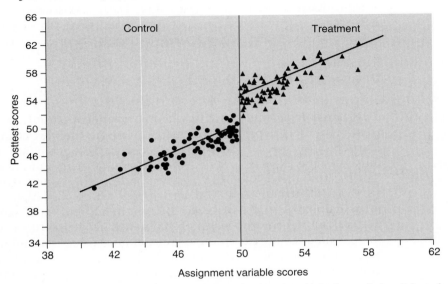

(From Shadish, W. R., Cook, T. D., & Campbell, D. T., 2002, *Experimental and quasi-experimental designs for generalized causal inference*. Copyright 2002. Houghton Mifflin Co. Used with permission.)

through the scores is the "regression line." This continuous regression line indicates that there was *no effect* of the treatment, because the scores of the people above the cutoff of 50 who received the treatment simply continued the same pattern of scores of people below the cutoff of 50 who did not receive the treatment. Now look at Figure 10.15. This figure shows a regression line for the people above the cutoff score of 50, which is not a continuation of the regression line that would be expected for people with a cutoff score below 50. In other words, there is a discontinuity of the regression line. This discontinuity indicates that the treatment had an effect, because if there were no treatment effect, there would be no discontinuity of the regression line, as illustrated in Figure 10.14.

The regression discontinuity design is an excellent design that can be used when researchers want to investigate the efficacy of some program or treatment but cannot randomly assign participants to comparison groups. However, there are a number of criteria, listed in Table 10.3, that must be adhered to for the design to effectively assess the effectiveness of a treatment condition. When these criteria are met, the regression discontinuity design is a very good design to use for testing the effect of a treatment condition and is typically more powerful than other quasi-experimental designs.

Any threat to the validity of the regression discontinuity design would have to cause a sudden discontinuity in the regression line that coincides with the cutoff. As Shadish et al. (2002) have pointed out, this is implausible, although possible. The primary threat that could produce such an effect is a differential history effect. This history effect would have to be one that affected only participants on

TABLE 10.3
Requirements of the Regression Discontinuity Design

- Assignment to comparison groups must be based only on the cutoff score.
- The assignment variable must be at least an ordinal variable, and it is best if it is a continuous variable. It cannot be a nominal variable such as sex, ethnicity, religious preference, or status as a drug user or nonuser.
- The cutoff score ideally should be located at the mean of the distribution of scores. The closer the cutoff score is to the extremes, the lower the statistical power of the design.
- Assignment to comparison groups must be under the control of the experimenter to avoid a selection bias. This requirement rules out most retrospective uses of the design.
- The relationship between the assignment and outcome variables (whether it is linear, curvilinear, etc.) must be known to avoid a biased assessment of the treatment effect.
- All participants must be from the same population. With respect to the regression discontinuity design, this means that it must have been possible for all participants to receive the treatment condition. This means that the design is not appropriate, for example, if the experimental participants are selected from one school and control participants from another.

one side of the cutoff (i.e., which makes it quite unlikely). Of the other threats to internal validity, differential attrition is about the only other serious threat (i.e., the participants dropping out from one group are different from those dropping out from the other group).

STUDY QUESTIONS 10.4
- **Describe the interrupted time-series design, and explain how rival hypotheses are eliminated in this design.**
- **What is the primary rival hypothesis that cannot be controlled when using the interrupted time-series design?**
- **Describe the regression discontinuity design.**
- **What rival hypotheses are not controlled in the regression discontinuity design?**

Summary

This chapter presented several quasi-experimental research designs, which represent approximations of strong experimental designs. Quasi-experimental designs are superior (for controlling extraneous variables) to the weak designs but not as good as the strong designs discussed in Chapter 8. Because of the difficulty of random assignment in field settings, quasi-experimental designs often are the best type of design available for use in field studies in which one wants to make causal inferences. The quasi-experimental designs presented are the nonequivalent comparison group design, the interrupted time-series design, and the regression discontinuity design.

The nonequivalent comparison group design is the one most frequently used. It is similar to the pretest–posttest experimental design (a strong design) except that the participants are *not* randomly assigned to the experimental and control groups, which means that we do not have the necessary assurance that the two groups of participants are equated. When using this design, researchers should attempt to determine the variables on which the treatment and control groups differ and then attempt to equate the groups on these variables using matching and/or statistical control techniques. However, this still does not assure us that the participants are equated on other extraneous variables not identified. The most common threats to internal validity of this design are provided in Table 10.2. Generally speaking, this design does give results that are of about the same average effect size as a randomized experiment when the two are equally well designed and executed.

The interrupted time-series design attempts to eliminate rival hypotheses without the use of a control group. In the interrupted time-series design, a series of measurements is taken on the dependent variable both before and after the introduction of some experimental treatment condition. The effect of that condition is then determined by examining the magnitude of the discontinuity produced by the condition in the series of recorded responses. The primary source of error in this design is a history effect.

The regression discontinuity design is used when the researcher can't give the treatment to all participants and can assign participants to groups based on their scores on an assignment variable. The effect of the treatment condition is determined by examining the regression line. A treatment effect is inferred if there is a discontinuity in the regression line.

Key Terms and Concepts

Assignment measure
Crossover effect
Design components
First increasing treatment effect
Increasing treatment and control groups
Interrupted time-series design
Nonequivalent comparison group
  design

Quasi-experimental design
Regression discontinuity design
Second increasing treatment effect
Selection-attrition effect
Selection-history effect
Selection-instrumentation effect
Selection-maturation effect
Selection-regression effect

Related Internet Sites

http://www.socialresearchmethods.net/kb/quasiexp.htm
This site provides a brief discussion of quasi-experimental design and has links to other designs such as the nonequivalent groups design and the regression discontinuity design as well as other issues relevant to this topic.

http://www.wadsworth.com/psychology_d/templates/student_resources/ workshops/_index.html
When this page appears, click on the "research methods workshops" link. Then click on "nonexperimental approaches," and this will bring you to a site that starts out with a brief description of some quasi-experimental designs.

http://www.socialresearchmethods.net/kb/quasioth.php
This link takes you to some additional quasi-experimental designs.

Practice Test   *The answers to these questions can be found in Appendix.*

1. The primary *difference* between a quasi-experimental design and a randomized experimental design is
   a. The number of independent variables that can be manipulated
   b. That randomized designs are more often used in field research
   c. The ability of the design to control for potential threats to internal validity
   d. The size of the treatment effect that can be expected

2. The primary threat to internal validity in the nonequivalent comparison group design is some form of a _____ effect.
   a. History
   b. Selection
   c. Testing
   d. Instrumentation

3. The outcome from a nonequivalent comparison group design that gives us the most confidence that the treatment produced the observed effect is
   a. An increasing treatment effect
   b. An effect in which both the experimental and control groups increase, but the experimental group increases more
   c. A crossover effect
   d. An effect in which the experimental group increases and the control group decreases

4. Most of the threats to internal validity are ruled out in the interrupted time-series design
   a. As a result of a discontinuity in the one point immediately before and the one point immediately after the treatment
   b. As a result of multiple posttests
   c. As a result of the multiple pretests and posttests
   d. As a result of the multiple pretests

5. A school superintendent wants to decrease the amount of truancy that exists in her school system. She assigns all those students who have missed coming to school an average of twice every week for the past year to participate in a program designed to make school more enjoyable and rewarding. The students with an average of less than twice a week will serve as controls. To test the effectiveness of this program she would probably use which design?
   a. Randomized experimental design
   b. Regression discontinuity design
   c. Nonequivalent comparison group design
   d. Time-series design

Challenge Exercises

1. For each of the following design briefs, identify
   a. The type of quasi-experimental design used
   b. The potential threat to internal validity that might exist in concluding that the treatment produced the observed effect

   A. The National Institutes of Health wanted to improve the research careers of promising young scientists by giving them a significant grant to allow them to devote time to their research careers. They requested and received applications from 100 scientists who were assistant professors and had been in their first job for less than 5 years. From this pool of 100 applicants, they selected the 25 most promising individuals in terms of number of publications, school from which they had received their terminal degree, and letters of recommendation. After 5 years had elapsed, they compared the performance of the 25 applicants who had received the award with the applicants who had not. It was found that the applicants who received the award were more productive in terms of number of publications, more of them had been promoted to associate professor, and their salary was higher than those who did not receive the award. Based on this evidence it was concluded that the program should be continued because it was a great success.

   B. MADD (Mothers against Drunk Drivers) has lobbied for tougher laws against drunk drivers for years. Assume that it was successful in convincing the legislators in your state to pass a tougher law against drunk drivers that required a mandatory jail sentence of at least 6 months, loss of driver's license for 5 years, and a fine of at least $10,000. You want to test the effect of this tougher law, so you record the number of people arrested and convicted for DUI (driving under the influence of alcohol) for 5 years prior to the passage of this law and for 5 years after passage of this law. You find that the number of arrests and convictions decreased after the law was passed, so you conclude that the tougher laws are effective.

   C. School systems frequently provide instruction and classes for individuals who are behind in particular subjects. You want to determine if a reading program is effective for children with reading difficulties, so you test all second-grade children on reading ability. The children who score below 30 on your test of reading ability are required to participate in the reading program. After these children have been in the reading program for a time, you again test all the second-grade children on reading ability. You find that the children given the program improved more than would be expected and conclude that it indicates that the program was effective.

2. A youth center wants to improve the family life for teenagers at risk for violence. One of the current programs that is being implemented is a type of therapy called Functional Family Therapy. To assess the effectiveness of this type of therapy in reducing violence among youth, two youth centers are

selected. One provides Functional Family Therapy to the families of teenagers who have been at the youth center and are being released back into the care of their parents; the other youth center continues its standard practice of follow-up and brief counseling of parents. For each teenager who is being released to his or her family, data are collected on the number of violent encounters with other teenagers, the law, and other family members for 1 month before and after the treatment program was initiated. The following shows four different outcomes that could occur.

a. Graph each outcome.
b. State whether the treatment condition seems to have been effective.
c. Identify the rival hypotheses that might explain the observed effect.

First Outcome:	Experimental group:	Pretest = 27	Posttest = 13
	Control group:	Pretest = 10	Posttest = 10
Second Outcome:	Experimental group:	Pretest = 16	Posttest = 4
	Control group:	Pretest = 10	Posttest = 27
Third Outcome:	Experimental group:	Pretest = 14	Posttest = 27
	Control group:	Pretest = 5	Posttest = 10
Fourth Outcome:	Experimental group:	Pretest = 4	Posttest = 13
	Control group:	Pretest = 15	Posttest = 15

CHAPTER 11

Single-Case Research Designs

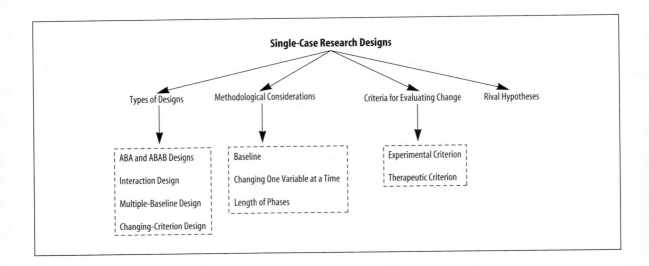

Dr. Kathleen Baynes of the University of California at Davis gave an intelligent businessman, H.W., a picture depicting a specific event and asked him to describe it. The following (cited in Gazzaniga, Ivry, & Mangun, 2002, p. 338) is the description provided by this individual. Read the description, and see if you can identify who is in the picture and what the people in the picture are doing.

First of all this is falling down, just about, and is gonna fall down and they're both getting something to eat . . . But the trouble is this is gonna let go and they're both gonna fall down . . . I can't see well enough but I believe that either she will have some food that's not good for you and she's to get some for her, too . . . and that you get it there because they shouldn't go up there and get it unless you tell them that they could have it. And so this is falling down and for sure there's one they're going to have for food and, and this didn't come out right, the, uh, the stuff that's uh, good for, it's not good for you but it, but you love, um mum mum (H.W. intentionally smacks lips) . . . and so they're . . . see that, I can't see whether it's in there or not . . . I think she's saying, I want two or three, I want one, I think, I think so, and so, so she's gonna get this one for sure it's gonna fall down there or whatever, she's gonna get that one and, and there, he's gonna get one himself or more, it all depends with this when they fall down . . . and when it falls down there's no problem, all they got to do is fix it and go right back up and get some more.

After reading this description we suspect that you are having a difficult time identifying the individuals and the activities they were engaged in. About the only thing you probably know is that something or someone was falling down and that food was involved. However, if you saw the picture you would see that it depicts a boy falling off a stool while reaching for cookies in a jar on a shelf and handing one to his sister. So what is missing from H. W.'s description? He accurately described a number of aspects of the scene, but he left out any reference to nouns. For example, he said "this" instead of "the stool" or "the chair"; he substituted "food" for "cookie" even though he knew it was a cookie, that it tasted good, and that it is considered bad for children; and he never mentioned the fact that the people in the picture were a male and female child.

This individual suffered from a stroke in his left hemisphere damaging an area called Wernicke's area, or a part of the cortex surrounding Wernicke's area, producing a disorder called *anomia*, the inability to name things or a difficulty in labeling objects. However, as his description indicates, comprehension is intact and speech is unaffected.

Cases such as this are relatively rare and provide glimpses into the operation of various areas of the brain, so scientists are very interested in using these individuals as research participants in investigations of brain structures that contribute to processes such as language. Because individuals with cortical damage in specific areas, such as Wernicke's area, are rare, investigations are typically limited to a single individual.

Introduction

Single-case research designs
Research design in which a single participant or a single group of individuals is used to investigate the influence of a treatment condition

Up to this point in the book, the designs that we discussed involved groups of different individuals. However, as the vignette at the beginning of this chapter reveals, there are times when large groups of individuals are not available to participate in an experiment. There are times when it is necessary to assess the effect of a treatment on a single individual. This means that we cannot use either random assignment or inclusion of a control group, which are the primary techniques typically used to control for the influence of rival hypotheses. How can we control for the influence of rival hypotheses when conducting an experiment on only one participant? The answer is to make use of single-case designs—designs constructed for use with only one participant and constructed in a manner that controls for the influence of many rival hypotheses.

Single-case research designs are designs that use only one participant or one group of individuals to investigate the influence of a treatment. The unique feature of these designs is the capacity to conduct experimental research with one participant or with one group of individuals such as a community, a group of employees, or a group of juveniles. Although single-case designs can be used with a group of participants as well as with a single participant, they are most frequently used with single participants. In discussing these designs, we focus attention on their use in experimentation with single participants.

This chapter presents the most frequently used single-case designs and demonstrates how each of them enables the investigator to assess the impact of an independent variable while at the same time controlling for the influence of rival hypotheses. The chapter concludes with a discussion of methodological issues that must be considered when designing a single-case research study.

History of Single-Case Designs

Encountering these designs for the first time, most people tend to equate them with case studies, but this is incorrect: Single-case designs experimentally investigate a treatment effect, whereas case studies provide an in-depth description of an individual or group of people. A brief look at the history of experimental psychology reveals that psychological research actually began with the intensive study of a single organism. Wundt's (1902) use of the method of introspection required a highly trained single participant. Ebbinghaus (1913) conducted his landmark studies on memory using only one participant—himself. Pavlov's (1928) basic findings were the result of experimentation with a single organism, a dog (see Exhibit 11.1), but were replicated on other organisms.

As you can see, single-case research was alive and well during the early history of psychology. However, in 1935, Sir Ronald Fisher published a book on experimental design that altered the course of psychological research. In it, Fisher laid the foundation for conducting and analyzing multiparticipant experiments. Psychologists quickly realized that the designs and statistical procedures elaborated by Fisher were very useful. With the publication of Fisher's (1935) work, psychologists turned from single-case studies toward multiparticipant studies.

The one notable exception to the multigroups tradition was B. F. Skinner (1953), his students, and his colleagues. They developed a general approach that has been labeled the *experimental analysis of behavior*. This method is devoted to experimentation with a single participant (or with only a few participants) on the premise that the detailed examination of a single organism under rigidly controlled conditions will yield valid conclusions about a treatment condition. The use of this approach led to the development of a variety of single-case experimental designs. Single-case designs are most commonly used today in research and practice areas that rely on applied behavior analysis. Applied behavior analysis is based on the principles of behavioral learning theory, especially operant conditioning. Two of the most prestigious journals publishing single-case research today are the *Journal of Experimental Analysis of Behavior* (started in 1958) and the *Journal of Applied Behavior Analysis* (started in 1968). Both of these journals were founded by the Society for the Experimental Analysis of Behavior.

EXHIBIT 11.1

Pavlov With His Laboratory Apparatus.

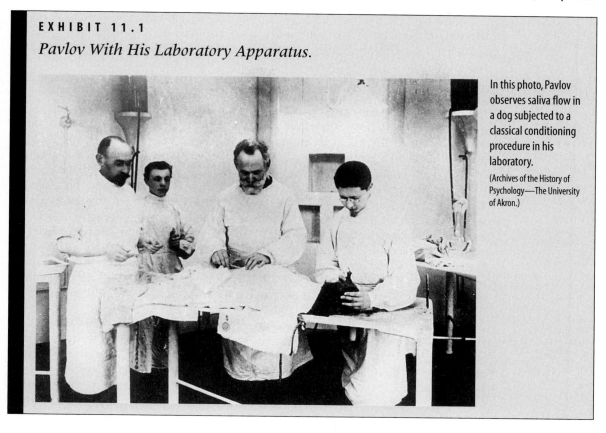

In this photo, Pavlov observes saliva flow in a dog subjected to a classical conditioning procedure in his laboratory.

(Archives of the History of Psychology—The University of Akron.)

STUDY QUESTIONS 11.1

- **What is a single-case design, and who is it used with?**
- **Discuss the history of single-case research.**
- **What theory of learning underlies much single-case research?**

Single-Case Designs

When planning an experimental study that uses only one participant, it is necessary to use some form of time-series design. Recall that the interrupted time-series design requires that repeated measurements be taken on the dependent variable both before and after the treatment condition is introduced. For example, assume we wanted to determine if caffeine was the cause of the emotional disturbance experienced by a truck driver. We could administer the caffeine and measure the participant's level of emotional stability, but then we would have no basis for determining whether the caffeine produced the effect because we would not know how stable the participant was when he was not consuming caffeine. Without such a comparison, it is impossible to infer any effect of the treatment condition.

What can we use as a basis of comparison in a single-case design? Because there is only one participant in the study, the comparison responses have to be the participant's own pretreatment responses. In other words, the investigator has to record the participant's responses before and after administration of the independent variable. In the caffeine experiment, we would have to record the participant's level of emotional stability prior to and after consuming caffeine. If we take only one pretreatment and posttreatment measure, we will have the analog of a one-group pretest–posttest design, which has many disadvantages. To overcome some of those problems (such as maturation and history), we must obtain multiple pretreatment and posttreatment measures. For example, we could measure the truck driver's level of emotional stability each day over a period of two weeks prior to consuming caffeine and while consuming caffeine. Now we have the analog of an interrupted time-series design using one participant, which furnishes a relatively continuous record of the organism's responses on the dependent variable emotional stability during the course of the experiment. Using this procedure, we would have a record of the truck driver's level of emotional stability over the course of the entire experiment. This technique is also experimental because it permits us to interject a planned intervention—a treatment condition such as caffeine—into the program. Consequently, it allows us to evaluate the effect of an independent variable.

Although the basic interrupted time-series design can be used in single-case research, we must remember that it is a quasi-experimental design. Taking repeated pretreatment and posttreatment measures of the dependent variable allows us to rule out many potential biasing effects, but it does not rule out the possibility of a history effect. The ability to detect a treatment effect with a time-series design hinges on the researcher's ability to determine what would have happened if the treatment condition had not been administered. This hypothetical situation of what would have happened to the treated participants had they not received the treatment is sometimes called the *counterfactual.* When using the interrupted time-series design, we collect both pretreatment and posttreatment measures of the dependent variable. In determining whether the treatment had any effect on behavior, we compare the posttreatment dependent variable measures to the pretreatment dependent variable measures (which is used as an estimate of the counterfactual) to see if there is a change. However, in this assessment, the underlying assumption is that the pattern of pretreatment measures would have continued if the treatment had not been applied. In other words, the pretreatment responses are used to forecast what the posttreatment responses would have been in the absence of the treatment. If this forecast is inaccurate, then we cannot adequately assess the effects of the treatment intervention. The basic time-series design, then, is limited in clearly identifying the influence of an experimental treatment effect.

STUDY QUESTION 11.2 | • **Explain the most basic time series design (interrupted time series design) and its limitations**

ABA and ABAB Designs

ABA design

A single-case design in which the response to the treatment condition is compared to baseline responses recorded before and after treatment

Baseline

The target behavior of the participant in its naturally occurring state or prior to presentation of the treatment condition

Reversal

Change of behavior back to baseline level after withdrawal of treatment

In order to improve on the basic time-series by generating stronger evidence of the causal effect of a treatment condition, the **ABA design** was developed. The ABA design, depicted in Figure 11.1, represents the most basic of the single-case research designs. As the name suggests, it has three separate conditions. The A condition is the baseline condition, which is where the target behavior (i.e., the dependent variable) is recorded in its freely occurring state. In other words, **baseline** refers to a given behavior as observed prior to presentation of any treatment. The baseline measure thus gives the researcher a frame of reference or counterfactual for assessing the influence of a treatment condition on the target behavior. The B condition is the experimental condition, where the treatment is deliberately imposed to try to alter the target behavior. Generally, the treatment condition is continued for an interval equivalent to the original baseline period or until some substantial and stable change occurs in the behaviors being observed.

After the treatment condition has been introduced and the dependent variable measured, the A condition is then reintroduced. The treatment condition is withdrawn, and whatever condition existed during baseline is reinstated. This second A condition is reinstituted in order to determine whether behavior will revert back to its pretreatment level. It is generally assumed that the effects of the treatment are reversible, but this is not always the case. *Reversal of the behavior back to its pretreatment level is the crucial element for demonstrating that the experimental treatment condition, and not some other extraneous variable, produced the change observed during the B phase of the experiment.* If the plan had included only two phases (A and B), as in the basic time-series design, rival hypotheses, such as history, could have existed. However, if the behavior reverts back to the original baseline level when the treatment conditions are withdrawn, rival hypotheses become less plausible.

Consider the study conducted by Walker and Buckley (1968). These researchers investigated the effect of using positive reinforcement to condition attending behavior in a nine-year-old boy named Phillip. A bright, underachieving child, Phillip was referred to the investigators because he exhibited deviant behavior that interfered with classroom performance. The investigators first took a baseline measure of the percentage of time that Phillip spent on his academic assignment. After the percentage of attending time had stabilized, the treatment condition was introduced, which consisted of enabling Phillip to earn points if no distraction occurred during a given time interval. These points could then be exchanged for a model of his choice. When Phillip had completed three successive ten-minute distraction-free sessions, the reinforcement of being able to earn points was withdrawn. Figure 11.2 depicts the results of this experiment. During the first baseline (A) condition, attending behavior was very low. When the treatment contingency (B) of being able to earn points was associated with attending behavior, percentage of attending behavior increased dramatically. When the

FIGURE 11.1
ABA design.

A	B	A
Baseline measure	Treatment condition	Baseline measure

FIGURE 11.2

Percentage of attending behavior in successive time samples during the individual conditioning program.

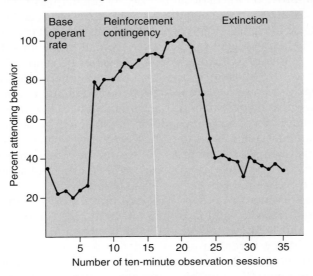

(From "The use of positive reinforcement in conditioning attending behavior" by H. M. Walker & N. K. Buckley, 1968, *Journal of Applied Behavior Analysis, 1*, p. 247. Copyright 1968 by the Society for the Experimental Analysis of Behavior, Inc.)

contingency was withdrawn and baseline conditions were reinstated (A), attending behavior dropped to its pretreatment level.

In this case, the ABA design seems to provide a rather dramatic illustration of the influence of the experimental treatment conditions. However, there are several problems with the ABA design (Barlow, Nock, & Hersen, 2008). First, the design ends with the baseline condition. From the standpoint of a therapist or other individual who desires to have some behavior changed, this is unacceptable because the benefits of the treatment condition are denied. Fortunately, this limitation is easily handled by adding a fourth phase to the ABA design in which the treatment condition is reintroduced. We now have an **ABAB design**, as illustrated in Figure 11.3. For example, in the study above, the treatment would be reinstated after the second baseline so that Phillip ends the study with the treatment phase (and better classroom performance). The participant thus leaves the experiment with the full benefit of the treatment condition.

A second potential problem with the ABA design is not so easily handled. As previously stated, one of the strengths of the ABA design is that it can demonstrate that the outcome variable reverts to the baseline level when the experimental treatment condition is withdrawn. Unfortunately, a reversal to baseline does not occur with all dependent variables. Failure to reverse might be due to a carryover effect across phases, whereby the treatment condition resulted in a relatively

ABAB design
Extension to ABA design to include reintroduction of the treatment condition

FIGURE 11.3
ABAB design.

A	B	A	B
Baseline measure	Treatment condition	Baseline measure	Treatment condition

permanent change in behavior. You will see in the future sections that a *multiple-baseline design* is better suited for studying interventions that might result in relatively permanent changes in behavior.

A third issue with the ABA design concerns a distinction between a reversal and a withdrawal ABA design. In discussing the ABA design, we have described **withdrawal**, in which the treatment condition is removed during the third (second A) phase of the design. Leitenberg (1973) states that the ABA withdrawal design should be distinguished from an ABA **reversal design**. The distinction occurs in the third (second A) phase of the ABA design. In the withdrawal design, the treatment condition is withdrawn; in the reversal design, the treatment condition is applied to an alternative but incompatible behavior. For example, assume that you were interested in using reinforcement to increase the play behavior of a socially withdrawn four-and-a-half-year-old girl, as were Allen, Hart, Buell, Harris, and Wolf (1964). If you followed the procedure used by these investigators, you would record the percentage of time the girl spent interacting with both children and adults during the baseline phase. During treatment (the B phase), praise would be given whenever the girl interacted with other children, and isolated play and interaction with adults would be ignored. During the third phase of the experiment (the second A phase), the true reversal would take place. Instead of being withdrawn, the contingent praise would be shifted to interactions with adults so that any time the child interacted with adults she would be praised, and interactions with other children would be ignored. This phase was implemented to see if the social behavior would increase to adults and decrease to children as the reinforcement contingencies shifted. Although the ABA reversal design can reveal rather dramatic results, it is more cumbersome and thus is used much less frequently than the more adaptable withdrawal design. Therefore, most of the single-case ABA and ABAB designs that you encounter will be of the withdrawal variety.

Withdrawal
Removal of the treatment condition

Reversal design
A design in which the treatment condition is applied to an alternative but incompatible behavior so that a reversal in behavior is produced

STUDY QUESTIONS 11.3

- **Diagram the ABA single-case research design, and explain how this design rules out confounding extraneous variables.**
- **Why is the ABA design often extended to an ABAB design?**
- **Under what circumstances are the ABA and ABAB designs ineffective in identifying a treatment effect?**
- **What is the difference between a reversal and a withdrawal of the treatment effect?**

Interaction Design*

A survey of the literature on single-case designs shows that researchers have extended the ABA and ABAB designs in a variety of ways. One intriguing and valuable extension is the use of an **interaction design** to identify the interactive effect of two or more independent variables. In discussing multiparticipant experimental designs in Chapter 8, we described an *interaction effect* as the situation that exists when the influence of one independent variable on the dependent variable

Interaction design
Single-case design used to identify interaction effects

*The interaction design is an advanced design that can be skipped without loss of continuity of the material.

Interaction effect in single-case research The combined influence of two or more independent variables

depends on the specific level of another independent variable. In a single-case design, we do not have that degree of flexibility. When we discuss an **interaction effect in single-case research**, we are referring to the combined influence of two or more independent variables. For example, we could investigate the interaction effect of a concrete reinforcement (giving of tokens) and verbal reinforcement (the experimenter saying "good").

In order to isolate the interactive effect of two variables from the effect that would be achieved by only one of these variables, it is necessary to analyze the influence of each variable separately and the two variables in combination. To complicate the issue further, we must do this by changing only one variable at a time. It is a cardinal rule in single-case research that you must change only one variable at a time. Thus the sequence in which we test for the influence of each variable separately and in combination must be such that the influence of the combination of variables (interaction effect) can be compared with the influence of each variable separately. Figure 11.4 illustrates this design. In sequence 1 (row 1), the researcher begins with an ABAB design logic to test the effect of B; then, B becomes the "baseline" to test the interactive/combined effect of BC compared to B, This logic is repeated in sequence 2 (row 2) to first test the effect of C and then the interactive/combined effect of BC compared to C. *The idea is to see if "BC combined" has a greater effect than "only B" and "only C."*

Here's an example. Let's say that we want to know if tokens, social praise, or the combination of tokens and praise is more effective for increasing on-task classroom behavior. In sequence 1, we establish the baseline (A). Then the effect of treatment B (tokens) is independently investigated, and then the combined influence of treatments B (tokens) and C (social praise) is compared to the influence of treatment B (tokens) alone. In like manner, in sequence 2, we establish the baseline, then the effect of treatment C (social praise) is independently investigated, and then the combined influence of treatments B (tokens) and C (social praise) is compared to treatment C (social praise) alone. In this way, it is possible to determine whether the combined influence of B and C was greater than that of either B or C alone. If it is, then an interactive effect exists. However, if the combined effect was greater than one of the treatment variables (C) but not the other (B), then an interactive effect does not exist because the effect can more parsimoniously be attributed to treatment B.

Investigating interaction effects can be complicated. First, at least two research participants are typically required. One person has to be tested using one sequence and another person has to be tested using the other sequence in Figure 11.4. Second, the interaction effect can be demonstrated only under conditions in which each variable alone (e.g., social praise) does *not* produce maximum increment in the dependent variable. However, understanding the combined role of independent variables is an important goal of research, and studying interaction effects is well worth the effort.

FIGURE 11.4
Single-participant interaction design.

	Baseline	*Single treatment*	*Baseline*	*Single treatment*	*Combined treatment*	*Single treatment*	*Combined treatment*
Sequence 1	A	B	A	B	BC	B	BC
Sequence 2	A	C	A	C	BC	C	BC

- **Diagram the interaction single-case research design.**
- **What is an interaction in a single-case design?**

Multiple-Baseline Design

One of the primary limiting features of the ABA design is its failure to rule out a history effect in situations where the dependent variable behavior does not revert to baseline level when the treatment condition is withdrawn. If you suspect that such a situation might exist, the multiple-baseline design is a logical alternative because it does not entail withdrawing a treatment condition. Therefore, its effectiveness does not hinge upon a reversal of behavior to baseline level.

Multiple-baseline design
A single-case design in which the treatment condition is successively administered to several target participants, target outcomes, or target settings

In the **multiple-baseline design**, depicted in Figure 11.5, baseline data are collected on the same behavior for two or more different individuals, on two or more different behaviors for the same individual, or on the same behavior across two or more different situations for the same individual. After the baseline data have been collected, the experimental treatment is *successively* administered to each target. By successive administration we mean the experimental treatment is administered to the first participant (or, alternatively, to the first behavior or situation); then, after a period of time, the treatment is also administered to the second participant (or, second behavior or second situation); and, then, after a period of time, the treatment is also administered to the third participant (or behavior or situation). If the target exposed to the experimental treatment changes while all others remain at baseline, this provides evidence for the efficacy of the treatment. It becomes increasingly implausible that rival hypotheses would influence each different target only at the time the treatment was administered.

Here's an example where the researchers (Van Houten, Van Houten, & Malenfant, 2007) used a multiple-baseline design to test the effectiveness of a program designed to increase helmet use by middle school students when riding their bicycles. Three schools were targeted, and baseline helmet use data were gathered at each school. The treatment program was introduced at one school at a time. As shown in Figure 11.6, increases in correct helmet use occurred when the helmet program was introduced in each school. When the campaign was introduced at the Bonita Springs Middle School, helmet use increased (but did not change at the other two schools). When the program was added at Riviera Middle School, helmet use increased (but remained low at Meadowlawn Middle School). Finally, when the campaign was added at Meadowlawn Middle School, helmet use was high at all three of the middle schools. This fingerprint or pattern of change provided evidence of the causal efficacy of the helmet advocacy program on helmet use by students.

FIGURE 11.5
Multiple-baseline design.

		T_1	T_2	T_3	T_4
	A	Baseline	Treatment		
Behaviors,	B	Baseline	Baseline	Treatment	
people, or	C	Baseline	Baseline	Baseline	Treatment
situations	D	Baseline	Baseline	Baseline	Baseline

FIGURE 11.6

The percentage of students wearing bicycle helmets correctly at all three middle schools.

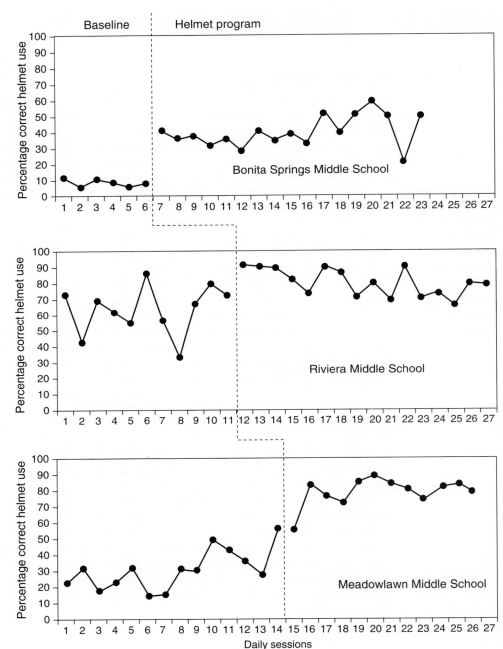

Although the multiple-baseline design avoids the problem of reversibility, it has a basic difficulty. For this design to be effective in evaluating the efficacy of the treatment condition, the target outcomes must not be interrelated. If the design uses several target participants, the participants must not communicate or interact (i.e., what is happening with one participant must be independent from what is happening with another participant). Or, if the design is used with several target outcome variables, the outcome variables must be independent (i.e., change in one variable must not naturally produce change in the other variable). Finally, if the design uses several target situations, the situations must be independent. The key point here is that there must not be **interdependence** of targets such that a change in one target naturally alters the other targets. This problem of interdependence is more common when the multiple-baseline design employs multiple variables with one participant. For example, a treatment to improve tardiness of an individual might target tardiness to school, tardiness to work, and tardiness to appointments. However, once the treatment is applied to tardiness to school, you might also observe changes in tardiness to work and appointments.

Interdependence
Violation of design assumption in which changing one target (participant, outcome, or setting) produces changes in the remaining targets

The problem of interdependence of targets is real and needs to be considered before the multiple-baseline design is selected because the strength of multiple baseline is the ability to demonstrate changes in the dependent variable that coincide with introduction of the treatment. If administering the experimental treatment to one target results in a corresponding change in the other targets, then when the experimental treatment is administered to the remaining targets, it will have less impact because the behavior has already been altered. In such a case, it is not clear what caused the change in behavior. We cannot always predict which variables are interdependent. Sometimes data exist on interdependence, but where none exist, the investigators must collect their own.

STUDY QUESTIONS 11.5
- **Diagram the multiple-baseline single-case research design.**
- **How are confounding extraneous variables ruled out in this design?**
- **What is meant by *interdependence of targets* in the context of this design?**

Changing-Criterion Design

Changing-criterion design
A single-case design in which a participant's behavior is gradually shaped by changing the criterion for success during successive treatment periods

The **changing-criterion design**, depicted in Figure 11.7, requires an initial baseline measure on a single target behavior (i.e., on a single dependent or outcome variable). Following this measure, an initial or starting criterion level of performance on the dependent variable is set, and the treatment condition is implemented. During this first treatment phase, if the participant successfully reaches the criterion level across several trials, the criterion level is increased for the next phase. When the experiment moves to the next successive phase, a new and more difficult criterion level is implemented, and the treatment condition is continued. When behavior reaches this new criterion level and is maintained across trials, the next phase, with its more difficult criterion level, is introduced. In this manner, each successive phase of the experiment requires a step-by-step increase in performance on the dependent variable: "Experimental control is

FIGURE 11.7

Changing-criterion design. T_1 through T_4 refer to four different phases of the experiment.

T_1	T_2	T_3	T_4
Baseline	Treatment and initial criterion	Treatment and criterion increment	Treatment and criterion increment

demonstrated through successive replication of change in the target behavior, which changes with each stepwise change in criterion" (Kratochwill, 1978, p. 66).

Himadi, Osteen, Kaiser, and Daniel (1991) provide a good illustration of the changing-criterion design in a study to reduce the delusional verbalizations of a 51-year-old white male with schizophrenia, chronic undifferentiated type. The content of the delusions involved grandiose and bizarre elements, including the beliefs that he was the son of Jesus and Mary, he controlled the U.S. government, he owned the U.S. Mint as well as a gold mine, and that his brain was surgically removed when he was an infant. To modify these delusional verbalizations, the investigators first obtained baseline data on the number of delusional answers given, over five baseline sessions, to 10 questions identified as reliably eliciting delusional answers. After collecting the baseline data, the treatment was applied. The treatment session consisted of asking the patient a question that had reliably elicited a delusional answer and instructing the patient to respond to the question "so that other people would agree with your answers." If a delusional answer was given, the experimenter provided an appropriate answer and had the patient model this answer, with the experimenter's assistance, until the patient could do so readily. After the patient provided the appropriate answer, he was given a reinforcer consisting of a cup of coffee. During the first phase, the treatment was applied to *two* questions, with the criterion being that the patient had to provide nondelusional responses to the two questions. After successfully reaching the desired criterion performance over five sessions, the criterion was increased, now requiring nondelusional responses to *four* delusion-eliciting questions. The results of this experiment, shown in Figure 11.8, reveal that the patient's performance improved as the criterion level was increased. This overall pattern of results is the desired "fingerprint" pattern. When a change in behavior parallels the criterion change so closely, it rather convincingly demonstrates the effect of the treatment contingency.

Hartmann and Hall (1976) indicate that the successful use of the changing-criterion design requires attention to three factors: the length of the baseline and treatment phases, the magnitude of change in the criterion, and the number of treatment phases or changes in the criterion. With regard to the length of the treatment and baseline phases, Hartmann and Hall state that the treatment phases should be of different lengths, or, if they are of a constant length, then the baseline phases should be longer than the treatment phases. This is necessary to ensure that the step-by-step changes in the participant's behavior are caused by the experimental treatment and not by some history or maturational variable that occurs simultaneously with the criterion change. With regard to the actual length of each treatment, the rule of thumb is that each treatment phase must be long enough to allow the behavior to change to its new criterion level and then to stabilize. If the behavior continues to fluctuate between the new and the old criterion level, stability has not been achieved.

FIGURE 11.8
A record of a behavioral training program to alter delusional responses to personal background questions. The horizontal lines reflect criterion levels.

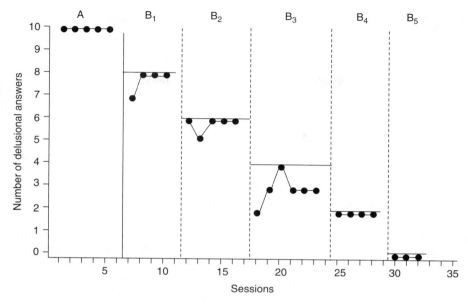

The second consideration is the magnitude of the criterion change. Naturally, it must be large enough so that a detectable change can occur. If the behavior is difficult to change, the criterion change should be small enough so that it can be achieved but still large enough to be noticed. If the behavior varies wildly, then the criterion change must be rather large in order to allow the experimenter to detect any change.

Hartmann and Hall (1976) state that two criterion changes might be adequate. This issue is, however, directly dependent on the number of replications that are required to demonstrate convincingly that the behavioral change is the result of the treatment condition. For this reason, Kratochwill (1978) recommends at least four criterion changes. When the participant's behavior is quite variable, Hall and Fox (1977) suggest including a reversal in one of the treatment phases. This reversal could consist of reverting back to baseline or to a former criterion level. Such a reversal would provide additional evidence of the influence of the treatment condition.

The changing-criterion design can be a useful design in studies that require shaping of behavior over a period of time (Hall & Fox, 1977). It is also useful in cases in which step-by-step increases in accuracy, frequency, duration, or magnitude are the therapeutic or research goals (Hartmann & Hall, 1976). For example, this would be the case in learning to read or write.

STUDY QUESTIONS 11.6

- **Diagram the changing-criterion design, and identify the type of situation in which this design would be appropriate to use.**
- **Discuss the factors of length of baseline and treatment phases, magnitude of change in the criterion, and the number of treatment phases as they relate to this research design.**

Methodological Considerations in Using Single-Case Designs

The preceding discussion of single-case research designs by no means represents an exhaustive survey, but we presented the most basic and commonly used designs. Regardless of which design is used, there are several common issues to consider when conducting a single-case study.

Baseline

Baseline has been defined as the target behaviors in their freely occurring state. Baseline data in single-case research is of critical importance. A prime concern is obtaining a **stable baseline** because the baseline data serve as the standard against which change induced by the treatment is assessed. A stable baseline is characterized by an absence of trend (or slope) in the data and only a slight degree of variability (Kazdin, 1992). An absence of trend (or slope) means that the baseline data should not demonstrate an increase or decrease over time. Although this is the ideal, sometimes it is impossible to eliminate a baseline trend.

Stable baseline
A set of responses characterized by the absence of trend and little variability

If the trend occurring during the baseline phase is opposite that which is expected during the treatment phase, the experiment can demonstrate that the treatment is powerful enough not only to produce an effect but also to reverse a previous trend. However, if the baseline trend is in the same direction as is expected from the treatment, it is difficult to draw an unambiguous conclusion regarding the influence of the treatment condition. In such a case, it is best to wait for the baseline to stabilize before introducing the treatment condition. If this cannot be done, one can resort to an alternating-treatments design in which the two treatments are designed to change the trend in opposite directions.

A stable baseline is also characterized by having little variability in the baseline data. Excessive variability during baseline, or other phases of a single-case design, can interfere with one's ability to draw valid conclusions about a treatment. However, the definition of excessive variability is relative because variability is excessive only if it interferes with one's ability to draw conclusions about the treatment effect, and drawing valid conclusions depends on many factors, such as the initial level of behavior during baseline and the magnitude of change when the intervention is implemented. When extreme fluctuations or unsystematic variations exist in the baseline data, one should check all components of the study and try to identify and control the sources of the variability. Sometimes the fluctuation can be traced to sources that are important to the validity of the experiment, such as unreliability in scoring the dependent variable. When the sources cannot be identified or controlled, one can artificially reduce the variability by averaging data points across consecutive days or sessions. This averaging substantially reduces variability and allows the effect of the treatment condition to be accurately assessed. However, it does distort the day-to-day pattern of performance.

There is one additional problem to be considered in obtaining baseline frequencies on humans: the potential reactive effect of the assessment on the behavior under study (Webb, Campbell, Schwartz, & Sechrest, 1966). The fact that baseline data are being taken might itself have an effect on the behavior. This was vividly demonstrated by McFall (1970) and Gottman and McFall (1972), who showed that monitoring one's own behavior can have a significant influence on that behavior. If one monitors frequency of smoking, one increases the number of cigarettes smoked, whereas if one monitors the frequency of not smoking, one smokes less.

Changing One Variable at a Time

A cardinal rule in single-case research is that only one variable can be changed from one phase of the experiment to the next (Barlow, Nock, & Hersen, 2008). Only when this rule is adhered to can the variable that produced a change in behavior be isolated. Assume that you want to test the effect of reinforcement on increasing the number of social responses emitted by a chronic schizophrenic. In an attempt to employ an ABA design, you first measure baseline performance by recording the number of social responses. Following baseline, you enroll your participant in a new day program and say "good" after each social response. At this point, you are violating the rule of one variable because you introduced a new day program *and* a reinforcement procedure. If the number of social responses increases, you will not know whether the change is due to the new day program or the reinforcement procedure. In fact, it might not be either variable independently but the combined (interactive) influence that is the catalyst. To isolate the separate and combined influences of the two variables, you would need an interaction design.

Length of Phases

Although there are few length of phases guidelines to follow, most experimenters advocate continuing each phase until some semblance of stability has been achieved. Although this is the ideal, in many clinical studies it is not feasible. In addition, following this suggestion leads to unequal phases, which Barlow, Nock, and Hersen (2008) consider to be undesirable. According to these investigators, unequal phases (particularly when the treatment phase is extended in time to demonstrate a treatment effect) increase the possibility of a confounding influence of history or maturation. For example, if the baseline phase consisted of recording responses for 7 days and the treatment phase lasted 14 days, we would have to entertain the possibility of a history or maturation variable affecting the data if a behavioral change did not take place until about the 7th day of the treatment phase. Because of such potential confounding influences, Barlow et al. suggest using an equal number of data points for each phase of the study.

Two other issues relate directly to the length of phases: carryover effects and cyclic variations (Barlow, Nock, & Hersen, 2008). Carryover effects in single-case ABAB designs usually appear in the second baseline phase of the study as a failure to reverse to original baseline level. When such effects do occur or are suspected, some single-case researchers (e.g., Bijou et al., 1969) advocate using short treatment condition phases (B phases) or a multiple-baseline design might be appropriate.

Barlow et al. (2008) also consider cyclic variations an important issue in the applied single-case literature. It is of paramount concern when participants are influenced by cyclic factors, such as monthly paychecks or cyclical physiological and psychological changes in bipolar participants. Where the data might be influenced by cyclical factors, it is advisable to extend the measurement period during each phase to incorporate the cyclic variation in both baseline and treatment phases of the study. If this is not possible, then the results must be replicated across participants that are at different stages of the cyclic variation or you must include participants not affected by the cyclical variation. If identical results are achieved across participants regardless of the stage of the cyclic variation, then meaningful conclusions can still be derived from the data.

STUDY QUESTION 11.7 | **List and then discuss the methodological issues that must be considered when designing a single-case study.**

Criteria for Evaluating Change

The single-case designs discussed in this chapter attempt to rule out the influence of extraneous variables by using strategies that should produce hypothesized "fingerprint" patterns of responses, which are quite different from the control techniques used in multiparticipant experimental research designs. Single-case designs use different criteria for evaluating treatment effects than do multiparticipant designs. The two criteria that are most commonly used in single-case research are an experimental criterion and a therapeutic criterion (Kazdin, 1978).

Experimental Criterion

Experimental criterion
In single-case research, repeated demonstration that a behavioral change occurs when the treatment is introduced

In single-case research, the **experimental criterion** requires repeated demonstration that a behavioral change occurs when the treatment is introduced. This often involves comparing the preintervention and postintervention behavior. The experimental criterion is met if scores on the dependent variable during the intervention phase do not overlap with scores on the dependent variable during the baseline phase or if the trend during baseline and intervention phases differs. In making this comparison, many experimenters using a single-case design do not employ statistical analysis, which is definitely a source of controversy, as illustrated in Exhibit 11.2. Additionally, many researchers rely on replicating the treatment effect over time as the experimental criterion of success. When it can be demonstrated that behavior repeatedly changes as the treatment conditions change, the experimental criterion would appear to have been fulfilled.

Therapeutic Criterion

Therapeutic criterion
Demonstration that the treatment condition has eliminated a disorder or has improved everyday functioning

The **therapeutic criterion** refers to the clinical or practical significance or value of the treatment effect for the participant. Does the treatment effect eliminate some disorder for the participant or does it enhance the participant's everyday

EXHIBIT 11.2

Analysis of Data Obtained From Single-Case Designs

In the past, when single-case research designs were conducted predominantly by Skinner, his colleagues, and his students, statistical analysis of single-case data was shunned. It was deemed to be unnecessary because the studies were conducted on infrahumans and sufficient experimental control of extraneous variables could be established to enable the experimental effect to be determined by visual inspection of the data.

As single-case designs have become more popular, some people have insisted on the need for statistical analysis of the data. This point of view is by no means universal, however.

The arguments against the use of statistical analysis are as follows:

1. Statistical analysis of the data provides evidence of a treatment effect only by demonstrating if the effect is statistically significant. It offers no evidence regarding the treatment's clinical effectiveness. For example, even though a treatment condition that was applied to reduce irrational thought patterns in schizophrenic individuals produces a statistically significant decline in such thought patterns, the patient might not have improved enough to operate effectively outside of an institutional setting.

2. Statistical tests hide the performance of the individual because they lump participants together and focus only on average scores. Consequently, a treatment condition that benefited only a few individuals might not achieve statistical significance and would therefore be considered ineffective when in fact it was beneficial for some individuals.

Two basic arguments support the use of statistical analysis:

1. Visual inspection of the data obtained from single-case designs will not provide an accurate interpretation when a stable baseline cannot be established. When data are not statistically analyzed, investigators must use the trend and the variability of the data to reach a conclusion as to whether the treatment condition produced an effect. If the baseline data and the treatment data have different trends or different levels of performance, then a decision is typically made that the treatment condition produced an effect, particularly if there is a stable baseline. However, if there is a great deal of variability in the data, it is difficult to interpret the data without statistical analysis. Statistical analysis can analyze extremely variable data more objectively than individuals.

2. Visual inspection of the data can lead to unreliable interpretation of the treatment effects. For example, Gottman and Glass (1978) found that the thirteen judges given data from a previously published study disagreed on whether the treatment effect was significant. Seven said a treatment effect existed, and six said it did not.

The proponents and opponents of statistical analysis each have valid points to make. However, doctrinaire positions that unequivocally advocate one strategy to the exclusion of the other seem to do more harm than good. When a stable baseline and limited variability can be achieved, statistical analysis probably adds little to the interpretation of the data. When they cannot, statistical analysis should be used in addition to visual analysis. Visual inspection and statistical analysis should be viewed as complementary tools in the development and verification of hypotheses using single-case designs.

functioning? This criterion is much more difficult to demonstrate than is the experimental criterion. For example, a self-destructive child might demonstrate a 50% reduction in self-destructive acts following treatment but still engage in fifty instances of such behavior every hour. Even though the experimental criterion has been satisfied, the child is still far from reaching a normal level of behavior.

In an attempt to resolve this problem, researchers have included a procedure known as social validation in some experiments. **Social validation** of a treatment effect consists of determining if the treatment effect has produced an important change in the way the client can function in everyday life. (E.g., after treatment, can a claustrophobic client ride in an elevator?) This validation is accomplished by either a social comparison method or a subjective evaluation method.

The **social comparison method** involves comparing the behavior of the client before and after treatment with the behavior of his or her nondeviant peers. If the participant's behavior is no longer distinguishable from that of the nondeviant peers, then the therapeutic criterion has been satisfied. The **subjective evaluation method** involves assessing whether the treatment has led to qualitative differences in how others view the participant. Individuals who normally interact with the participant and are in a position to assess the participant's behavior might be asked to provide a global evaluation of the client's functioning on an assessment instrument, such as a rating scale or a behavioral checklist. If this evaluation indicates that the client is functioning more effectively, then the therapeutic criterion is considered to have been satisfied. Each of these methods has its limitations, but both provide additional information regarding the therapeutic effectiveness of the experimental treatment condition.

STUDY QUESTION 11.8 | **Discuss the criteria that have been used for evaluating treatment effects in single-case research designs.**

Rival Hypotheses

The last methodological consideration applies to all psychological research. The researcher must continuously consider potential rival hypotheses for the experimental findings (e.g., experimenter expectancies, sequence effects, instructions). If a pattern of results appears to support your interpretation, you still must carefully consider whether another (rival) interpretation might be superior or might call into question your interpretation. For each of the single-case designs discussed, we have listed a number of requirements for proper usage; we have also listed several general methodological requirements for the conduct of single-case research. If any basic requirement is not met for one design, then you must select an alternative design. Sometimes you will need to construct more complicated designs than the ones discussed in this chapter to meet your particular research needs. Furthermore, if any additional threats creep into your experiment, you must be alert to identify them. Good research requires careful implementation of design and continuous observation and thought by the experimenter about what is happening and what it means.

| **What are some possible rival hypotheses for the findings from ABA and ABAB designs, interaction designs, multiple-baseline designs, and changing criterion designs?**

Summary

In conducting an experimental research study that uses only one participant, you must reorient your thinking because extraneous variables cannot be controlled by using a randomization control technique nor can they be handled by the inclusion of a control group. To begin to rule out the possible confounding effect of extraneous variables, you use a form of a time-series design. This means that multiple premeasures and postmeasures on the dependent variable are made in order to exclude potential rival hypotheses such as maturation and history. A commonly used single-case design is the ABA type, which requires the investigator to take baseline measures before and after the experimental treatment effect has been introduced. The experimental treatment effect is demonstrated by a change in behavior when the treatment condition is introduced and a *reversal* of the behavior to its pretreatment level when the experimental treatment condition is withdrawn. The success of this design depends on the reversal.

Many extensions of the basic ABA design have been made. The interaction design attempts to assess the combined or interactive effect of two or more variables. The influence of each variable is assessed separately and in combination. In addition, the influence of the combination of variables, or the interaction of the two or more variables, must be compared with that of each variable separately. This means that at least two participants must be used in the study.

A third type of single-case design is the multiple-baseline design. This design avoids the necessity for reversibility required in the ABA design by relying on the successive administration of the experimental treatment condition to different target participants (or target behaviors or target contexts). The influence of the treatment condition is revealed if a change in behavior occurs simultaneously with each successive introduction of the treatment condition. Although the multiple-baseline design avoids the problem of reversibility, it requires that target participants, behaviors, or contexts under study be independent.

The changing-criterion design is useful in studies that require the shaping of behavior over a period of time. This design requires that, following the baseline phase, a treatment condition is implemented and continued across a series of intervention phases. For each intervention phase, a stronger criterion level of performance is required in order for the participant to advance to the next intervention phase. The experimenter makes the criterion level progressively more difficult. In this way, behavior can gradually be shaped to a desired criterion level.

In addition to a basic knowledge of the single-case designs, you should also understand the methodological considerations required to appropriately implement the designs. These include the following:

1. *Baseline.* A stable baseline should be obtained, although some variation will always be found in the freely occurring target behaviors.

2. *Changing one variable at a time.* A cardinal rule in single-case research is that only one variable can be changed from one phase of the experiment to another.

3. *Length of phases.* Although there is some disagreement, many methodologists contend that the length of the phases should be kept equal.

4. *Criteria for evaluating change.* An experimental or a therapeutic criterion (or both) should be used to evaluate the results of a single-case design to determine whether the experimental treatment condition produced the desired effect.

5. *Rival hypotheses.* Alternative explanations of the findings should be considered, including the effect of variables such as instructions, experimenter expectancies, and sequencing effects.

Key Terms and Concepts

ABA design	Reversal
ABAB design	Reversal design
Baseline	Single-case research designs
Changing-criterion design	Social comparison method
Experimental criterion	Social validation
Interaction design	Stable baseline
Interaction effect in single-case research	Subjective evaluation method
Interdependence	Therapeutic criterion
Multiple-baseline design	Withdrawal

Related Internet Sites

http://seab.envmed.rochester.edu/jeab/ and **http://seab.envmed.rochester.edu/jaba/index.html**
These are the sites for two prominent journals that rely on single-case designs and analysis, the *Journal of the Experimental Analysis of Behavior* and the *Journal of Applied Behavior Analysis.*

http://www.msu.edu/user/sw/ssd/issd01.htm
This site discusses the basic single-case designs and other methodological issues such as the characteristics of single-case evaluation including how to determine whether a treatment is effective.

Practice Test

The answers to these questions can be found in Appendix.

1. Single-case research designs are a type of
   a. Time-series design
   b. Quasi-experimental design
   c. Multimodal design
   d. Mixed model design
   e. Case study

2. When the ABA cannot be used because the targeted behavior does not return to baseline after the treatment is implemented, a good alternative is to use the
   a. Changing-criterion design
   b. Interaction design
   c. Alternating treatments design
   d. Multiple-baseline design
   e. ABAB design

3. Which of the single-case designs would you use if you wanted to test the combined effect of two treatment conditions?
   a. ABA design
   b. Interaction design
   c. Multiple-baseline design
   d. Changing-criterion design
   e. Alternating treatments design

4. If you used the experimental criterion for evaluating the effectiveness of a treatment effect you would
   a. Ensure that the baseline behavior was stable before administering the treatment condition
   b. Determine whether the participant could function effectively in society after the treatment
   c. Determine whether the behaviors seen during baseline and treatment overlap
   d. Determine whether the trend of the behaviors during baseline and treatment differed
   e. Use both c and d

5. Rival hypotheses are ruled out in the single-case designs by
   a. The repeated measurements during baseline and following treatment
   b. The withdrawal of treatment in the ABA and ABAB designs
   c. The administration of the treatment condition at different times to different participants in the multiple-baseline design
   d. All of the above are correct

Challenge Exercises

1. Assume that you conducted a study using an ABA design in which you tested the effectiveness of turning off the television every time a ten-year-old boy sucked his thumb. Construct a graph depicting
   a. The effectiveness of the denial of watching TV on the reduction of thumb sucking
   b. A reduction in thumb sucking when the TV was turned off, but an inability to verify that the reduction in thumb sucking was due *only* to the turning off the TV

2. Assume you wanted to test the effectiveness of a specific treatment of stuttering. You identified three children who stuttered and used the multiple-baseline design to demonstrate that the treatment worked. Construct a graph depicting

   a. The effectiveness of the treatment
   b. An interdependence of behaviors that would reduce your ability to conclude that the treatment was effective

3. Assume that you wanted to evaluate the effectiveness of a program designed to help people get over their claustrophobia. This program consisted of having them give you $50. Each day they were able to stay in a small enclosed room for an additional ten minutes, you returned $10, until they were able to remain in there for a total of 50 minutes. On the first day that they stayed in the room for 10 minutes, they received $10. Then they had to stay in the room for 20 minutes to receive another $10, and so forth, until they were able to remain for 50 minutes and get the last $10.

   a. Construct a graph depicting the effectiveness of this strategy.
   b. Specify the type of design used.

4. Assume a mother came to you with the following problem. Every time her child was around other kids, he bit them severely. She did not know how to eliminate this problem and wanted your help. You suggest that a combination of reinforcement and punishment would probably work. As a researcher, design a study that will test the effectiveness of your suggestion. Construct a design using two participants that will test the effectiveness of the combined effects of reinforcement and punishment in eliminating children's biting of other children.

CHAPTER

Survey Research

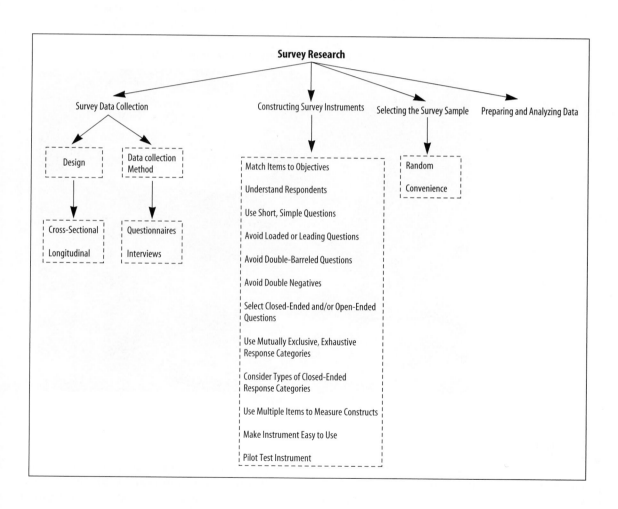

In 1936, the periodical *Literary Digest* set out to predict the winner of the presidential election. A sample of participants was selected from telephone directories and car registrations. This sample was surveyed to determine whom the participants would vote for in the 1936 election. Based on the results of this survey, the respected *Literary Digest* predicted that Alfred Landon would defeat Franklin Roosevelt by a wide margin. However, if you know your U.S. presidents, you know that Franklin Roosevelt won the election. In the 1948 election, Gallop and Roper polls predicted Thomas E. Dewey would defeat Harry Truman by a narrow margin. As seen in the famous picture below, the *Chicago Daily Tribune* ran the headline of "Dewey Defeats Truman." In the past 60 years, sampling theory and practice have advanced substantially. Today, we know that sample size is not the key issue for obtaining a representative sample; what is most important is that the correct *sampling method* is used.

A victorious Harry Truman shows off an incorrect newspaper, November 3, 1948.

Introduction

Survey research
A nonexperimental research method relying on questionnaires or interview protocols

Survey research is a widely used type of nonexperimental research. It is a research method where individuals fill out a questionnaire or are interviewed about their attitudes, activities, opinions, and beliefs. The questionnaire or interview protocol usually is standardized to present each research participant with the same stimulus (i.e., questions, directions). Survey research oftentimes is conducted with a sample selected from a target population of interest. Survey research can probe into a given state of affairs that exists at a given time as well as follow changes over time.

Probably the most widely known surveys are those conducted by the Gallup organization. Gallup polls are frequently conducted to survey the voting public's opinions on such issues as the popularity of the president or a given policy or to determine the percentage of individuals who might be expected to vote for a given candidate at election time. Surveys are initially conducted to answer the questions "how many" and "how much." But collection of frequency data is only a preliminary phase of the research in many studies. Researchers often want to answer the questions "who" and "why." Who votes for the Republican candidate, and who votes for the Democrat? Why do people buy a certain make of car or brand of product? Such information helps us to understand why a particular phenomenon occurred and increases our ability to predict what will happen.

For example, Table 12.1 presents the results to one question of a Gallup poll taken in 1998 concerning the drug Viagra. This question asked, "There is a new prescription drug on the market called Viagra. Without telling me the answer, specifically, do you know what this drug is used for or not?" The responses to this question revealed that 64% of the individuals polled knew what it was used for. However, this knowledge varied according to the background characteristics of the respondents. For example, men were more likely than women to be aware of the drug's use, older individuals were more likely than younger individuals, whites were more likely than nonwhites, individuals with higher education were more likely than individuals with lower education, individuals living in suburbs were more likely than those living in rural areas, and married were more likely than unmarried to be aware of the drug's use.

The most basic tenet of survey research is this: If you want to know what people think, then ask them. As you will learn in this chapter, the researcher's job is to make sure that questions are asked in ways that encourage participants to be honest and forthcoming. When feasible, participants' responses should be corroborated using additional strategies and data collection methods (e.g., observational and unobtrusive data). Because survey research data provide results based on correlations among variables, it is important to be very cautious in drawing conclusions about cause and effect unless the relationships are corroborated through experimental research.

Although psychology usually emphasizes experimental research for studying psychological phenomena because of its superiority for demonstrating cause-and-effect relationships, survey research also has a long and venerable tradition in psychology. For example, survey research was routinely used by famous psychologists such as Kurt Lewin (1890–1946), Rensis Likert (1903–1981), Floyd Henry Allport (1890–1978), and Muzafer Sherif (1906–1988). Today, survey research is an important part of many subfields in psychology, including social psychology, personality psychology, clinical psychology, industrial-organizational psychology, developmental psychology, community psychology, and cross-cultural psychology. Several APA journals regularly publishing research based on survey data are the *Journal of Applied Psychology, Journal of Personality*

TABLE 12.1

Response Obtained from a Gallup Poll to the Question "There is a new prescription drug on the market called Viagra. Without telling me the answer, specifically, do you know what this drug is used for or not?"

	Know its purpose? (%)		
	Yes	*No*	*No opinion*
National	64	33	3
Sex			
Male	69	29	2
Female	60	37	3
Age			
18–29 years	53	46	1
30–49 years	64	33	3
50–64 years	71	25	4
65 & older	70	27	3
Region			
East	74	23	3
Midwest	59	36	5
South	57	41	2
West	70	29	1
Community			
Urban	62	35	3
Suburban	70	28	2
Rural	54	42	4
Race			
White	67	30	3
Nonwhite	50	48	2
Education			
College postgraduate	89	11	0
Bachelor's degree only	76	22	2
Some college	66	31	3
High school or less	52	34	4
Ideology			
Liberal	63	35	2
Moderate	63	33	4
Conservative	66	32	2
Clinton approval			
Approve	64	33	3
Disapprove	64	33	3
Income			
$75,000 & over	64	14	2
$50,000 & over	77	21	2
$30,000–49,999	66	31	3
$20,000–29,000	62	35	3
Under $20,000	49	47	4
Marital status			
Married	67	29	4
Not married	60	38	2

and Social Psychology, Professional Psychology: Research and Practice, Psychology and Aging, Health Psychology, Psychology of Addictive Behaviors, and *Psychology of Religion and Spirituality.*

It is possible to mix major research approaches. For example, a researcher might include an experimental manipulation within a survey instrument, making it a cross between survey and experimental research. However, in this chapter we focus on standard survey research designs.

When Should One Conduct Survey Research?

Survey research is a research method that is applicable to a wide range of problems. It is also deceptively easy to use. The unsophisticated researcher might think that all that is needed is to construct a number of questions addressing the issue of interest and then get people to respond to these questions. However, completing these seemingly simple steps requires a lot of thought and work. Without this thought and work, the questions asked will elicit unreliable answers.

Survey research is the method of choice when you need to measure individuals' attitudes, activities, opinions, and beliefs. In Table 12.2, we show some of the types of survey questions that can be used in survey research. The purpose of the table is to show the wide range of information that can be collected thorough survey research. Survey research is helpful in exploratory, descriptive, predictive, and, in some cases, explanatory research.

When survey researchers measure attitudes, opinions, and beliefs using good measurement procedures, they are able to examine relationships among the variables, make predictions, and determine how subgroups differ. Survey research is also helpful when there is a need to track changes in beliefs over time. For example, social psychologists have tracked changes in stereotypes toward minority groups since the early 1900s, showing major changes in beliefs and how the beliefs relate to other variables (e.g., Gilbert, 1951; Karlins, Coffman, & Walters, 1969; Katz & Braly, 1933; Philogene, 2001). Survey research is also commonly used to collect data used to test theoretical models constructed by researchers based on past literature, experimental results, and other factors (e.g., Pettigrew et al., 2008). Survey research in psychology is also used for more purely predictive (Leffert et al., 1998) and descriptive purposes (Plous, 1996).

Strong survey research is based on random samples from populations. When this is the case, survey research is an especially useful research approach when one needs to make direct statistical generalizations about attitudes, opinions, and beliefs from a single sample to a population. This is the need in political polling, but it is also important when psychologists estimate the prevalence of social and psychological characteristics in populations. In this way, survey research provides a direct route to the external validity (i.e., population validity) of conclusions about people's attitudes, opinions, and beliefs.

T A B L E   1 2 . 2
Matrix of Kinds of Questions Asked in Survey Research

Question Domain	Time		
	Past (Retrospective)	Present	Future
Behaviors	When you were in elementary school, did you ever hit another child during a fight?	Do you regularly arrive at your research methods class more than 5 minutes late?	Are you going to vote in the in the next presidential election?
Experiences	What was it like being a member of a gang when you were a teenager?	What is it like being asked about your teenage gang membership?	If you become a parent one day, what experiences do you think you will most enjoy in that role?
Attitudes, opinions, beliefs, values	When you were 10 years old, did you believe in Santa Claus?	Do you think that you are a good person?	Do you think that you will become more politically conservative or more liberal as you get older?
Knowledge	When you were 10 years old, did you know the definition of experimental research?	What is the definition of experimental research?	Do you think you will know the definition of stratified random sampling at the end of this semester?
Background or demographic	What school did you attend when you were in the 10th grade?	What is your current age?	Do you plan to attend graduate school in psychology?

STUDY QUESTION 12.1 | • **What is survey research? When might survey research be needed in psychological research?**

Steps in Survey Research

Here are the typical steps in survey research: (1) plan and design the survey research study [e.g., determine what issues you want to survey, determine whether a cross-sectional or longitudinal design will be used, identify the target population, select the sample(s)], (2) construct and refine the survey instrument (this will vary slightly depending on whether you are using a questionnaire or an interview protocol), (3) collect the survey data, (4) enter and "clean" (i.e., locate and eliminate errors where possible) the data, (5) analyze the survey data, and (5) interpret and report the results. In Table 12.3, we have listed some key issues you must consider when you design your survey research study. We provide the knowledge and principles needed to design and conduct survey research in the remainder of this chapter.

TABLE 12.3
Issues in Designing a Survey Research Study

- What are the research objectives of the study (i.e., what do you want to find out?)
- Who is the target population?
- Will a cross-sectional or longitudinal design be used?
- What sampling method will you use?
- How big (i.e., number of participants) should the sample be?
- Can a previously used data collection instrument be found or will a new one have to be constructed?
- Will a questionnaire or interview be used?
- What specific method of data collection will be used (in-person, mail, telephone, or Internet)?
- Who will collect the survey data and how will they be trained?
- What is the time frame in which the survey will be conducted?

Cross-sectional and Longitudinal Designs

In Chapter 2, we discussed cross-sectional and longitudinal research designs. This distinction is especially important in survey research because selecting one of these designs is done in all survey research. We briefly review these designs here and extend them as typically applied in the survey research literature.

Cross-sectional studies
Data are collected during a single, brief time period

In **cross-sectional studies**, the survey data are collected from the research participants during a single, relatively brief time period (i.e., a period long enough to collect data from all the participants in the sample). The data are collected from the participants in the sample only once. Although the data are collected only once, they typically are collected from multiple groups or types of people in a cross-sectional survey (e.g., such as people from multiple age groups, from different socioeconomic classes, and with different accomplishments and abilities). For example, Whisman (2007) in "Marital Distress and DSM-IV Psychiatric Disorders in a Population-Based National Survey" collected and analyzed data from a national survey research study with a representative sample of English-speaking adults (18 years or older) in the United States. Whisman found that marital distress was associated with anxiety, mood, and substance disorders. Also, the association between marital distress and depression was stronger when one moved from younger to older age groups in the sample. In another cross-sectional survey, Plous (1996) surveyed APA members to determine members' attitudes toward the use of animals in research. The majority of respondents approved the use of animals, but wanted to eliminate or minimize the pain experienced by research animals and the number of animals euthanized.

In **longitudinal studies**, survey data are collected at more than one point in time. Longitudinal studies usually last multiple years. Although longitudinal studies include a minimum of two time points or data collection periods, data can be collected over as many time periods as warranted by the research questions. Longitudinal studies are expensive because data are collected over multiple years. Therefore, longitudinal studies are not always feasible when available resources and funds are limited and when results are needed more quickly. Several types of longitudinal research are discussed in the literature.

In the survey research literature, longitudinal studies are sometimes referred to as **panel studies** (also called *prospective studies*). In these studies, the researcher collects data from the same group of people at successive points over time. The same individuals (i.e., the "panel") are surveyed more than once over time. The individuals in a panel study usually include multiple ages. For example, Moskowitz and Wrubel (2005) used a longitudinal panel design to gain a more in-depth understanding of the meaning of having contracted HIV. To accomplish the purpose of this study, Moskowitz and Wrubel identified fifty-seven gay men, ranging in ages from 24 to 48, who tested positive for HIV. Then the researchers conducted bimonthly interviews over the course of two years to identify how these individuals appraised their HIV related changes over time.

One last distinction made in the survey research literature concerns what are called trend studies. In a **trend study** (also called *successive independent samples design*), the researcher takes independent samples from a general population over time and the same questions are asked. It is different from a longitudinal or panel design because different people are studied at each successive data collection period. An example of a national survey conducted with independent samples over time is the General Social Survey, which is conducted by the National Opinion Research Center (at the University of Chicago). Each year a different sample of U.S. citizens who are 18 years or older are asked questions about many social, psychological, and demographic variables. Other examples of national surveys conducted over time (annually) with independent samples are the National Survey on Drug Use and Health (e.g., Denisco, Chandler, & Compton, 2008) and the Monitoring the Future survey (e.g., Pampel & Aguilar, 2008).

Panel studies
Longitudinal study where data are collected from the same individuals at successive time points

Trend study
Independent samples are taken successively from a population over time and the same questions are asked

Selecting a Survey Data Collection Method

Another major decision you must make when designing a survey research study is whether you want to have your research participants complete a questionnaire or whether you want to interview them. In other words, you must decide on the type of **survey instrument** to be used for data collection. A **questionnaire** is a self-report data collection instrument that is filled out by research participants. Questionnaires traditionally are paper-and-pencil instruments, but they are increasingly being placed on the World Wide Web.

Survey instrument
Data collection instrument used in survey research such as a questionnaire or interview protocol

Questionnaire
Self-report data collection instrument filled out by research participants

Interview
Verbal self-report data are collected from interviewees by an interviewer

Interview protocol
Data collection instrument used by the interviewer

Face-to-face interview method
Survey method where participants are interviewed in a face-to-face setting

Telephone interview method
Survey method where interviews are conducted over the telephone

Random-digit dialing
Random sampling method frequently used with telephone interviewing

Mail questionnaire method
Survey method where questionnaires are sent to potential participants via regular mail

In an **interview**, a trained interviewer asks research participants (i.e., the interviewees) questions and records the responses. The survey instrument used in interviewing looks much like a questionnaire, but it is given a more specialized label of **interview protocol**. The primary difference between a questionnaire and an interview protocol is that a questionnaire must be written so that participants can easily complete it without the aid of anyone. An interview protocol is a survey instrument that has been put into a script-like format so that the interviewer can systematically read the questions and easily record participant responses. Interviews are generally preferred to questionnaires because the researcher has more control over data collection and can probe participants for follow-up responses.

There are several specialized methods for collecting survey data that we now explain, including face-to-face interviewing, telephone interviewing, mail questionnaires, group-administered questionnaires, and electronic questionnaires. Each has its own set of advantages and disadvantages, such as cost and response rate. The **face-to-face interview method**, as the name suggests, is a person-to-person interview, which typically involves going to the interviewee's home and obtaining responses by conducting a personal interview. This technique has the advantages of allowing the interviewer to clear up any ambiguities in the question asked and to probe for further clarification of responses if the interviewee provides an inadequate answer. This method generally provides a higher completion rate and more complete respondent information. The primary weakness of this method is that it is the most expensive. It is also possible that the interviewer might bias the responses. For example, an interviewer might (either consciously or unconsciously) spend more time and probe more effectively with an attractive or an especially interesting interviewee, resulting in biased results. Interviewer training can help interviewers learn how to conduct effective interviews to minimize any problems of this sort. Table 12.4 provides some practical tips for conducting interviews (most of which also apply to the telephone interviewing method).

With the **telephone interview method**, as the name suggests, the survey is conducted by means of a telephone interview. This method is significantly less expensive than the face-to-face interview (Groves & Kahn, 1979), and some data (Rogers, 1976) demonstrate that the information collected is comparable to that obtained in a face-to-face interview. This seems to be particularly true with the use of random-digit dialing. In some areas, 20–40% of customers elect not to list their phone numbers in telephone directories (Rich, 1977). Such unlisted numbers are accessible with the **random-digit dialing**. In this sampling method, telephone numbers are dialed through use of a random process, usually by a computer, which means that unlisted numbers are just as accessible as listed numbers. This results in an unbiased sample that will provide a representative sample if all of the participants selected agree to complete the survey. If a survey researcher has access to a computer-assisted telephone interview (CATI) system, the interviewer's questions are prompted on the computer screen and the interviewee's responses are put directly into the computer for analysis.

The **mail questionnaire method**, as the name suggests, involves sending questionnaires to interviewees through the mail and asking them to return the

TABLE 12.4
Conducting Effective Research Interviews

1. Make sure interviewers are trained.
2. Do background homework on interviewees.
3. Be sensitive to cultural differences.
4. Find a quiet and comfortable setting for the interview.
5. Explain purpose of interview.
6. Establish trust and rapport.
7. Discuss confidentiality of interview.
8. Follow the interview protocol exactly as explained during training.
9. Be empathetic and remain neutral to interviewee's statements.
10. Continually monitor yourself and the interviewee.
11. Be a good listener (i.e., the interviewee should be doing the talking not you).
12. Make sure the interviewee understands exactly what you are asking.
13. Provide sufficient time for responses.
14. Maintain control of the direction and focus of the interview (i.e. stay on topic).
15. Use probes and prompts for follow-up clarifications, detail, and explanation.
16. Demonstrate respect for the interviewee's valuable time.
17. Tape record interviewee responses if possible.
18. Take notes sparingly during interview.
19. Immediately after the interview, edit your notes and record any additional observations.

completed questionnaires, typically in stamped return envelopes provided by the organization conducting the survey. The primary advantage of this technique is its low cost. You can send a questionnaire anywhere in the world for the price of postage. However, a disadvantage is that most questionnaires are never returned. The return rate is typically 20–30% for the initial mailing (Nederhof, 1985), although the rate can be increased by use of techniques such as follow-up letters reminding survey respondents and enclosing another copy of the questionnaire.

Group-administered questionnaire method
Survey method where participants fill out the questionnaire in a group setting

Sometimes a researcher is able to use the **group-administered questionnaire method**. In this case, the researcher has the participants convene in a group setting. The researcher hands out the questionnaire and participants fill it out during the group session. This approach sometimes is used with organizational surveys when the participants are available in a single workplace. The advantage of this approach is that questionnaires are completed quickly and efficiently. Oftentimes, however, this is not a viable approach because participants are dispersed across locations.

Electronic survey
Survey conducted over the Internet

An **electronic survey** involves contacting people over the Internet and having them complete a survey instrument accessed on their computer. This type of survey has shown tremendous growth since the 1990s. Kaye and

Johnson (1999) identified over 2,000 Web-based surveys several years ago, and the use of electronic surveys continues to grow (Shannon, Johnson, Searcy, & Lott, 2002).

There are currently two types of electronic surveys: e-mail surveys and Web-based surveys. An **e-mail survey** consists of sending an e-mail message with an appeal to complete a survey instrument that is either a part of the message or is in an attached file. The person who receives the e-mail message completes the survey instrument and returns it to the sender. A **Web-based survey** is an electronic survey that is posted on the World Wide Web. Once the survey instrument is constructed and posted, respondents are identified and sent an e-mail message inviting them to participate in the research study. If they agree, they are given a link with an Internet address to the survey instrument. All they have to do is click on the link, which brings them to the Web site containing the survey instrument, which they then proceed to complete.

One variation of the Web-based survey that has recently been introduced is the pop-up survey (Llieva, Baron, & Healey, 2002). This type of survey appears in the browser's window while browsing various Web sites. The pop-up invites the Web browser to participate in the survey and to click on a link that brings them to the Web site containing the survey instrument. This type of survey has been viewed as a very positive contribution to Web site research (Llieva et al., 2002).

There are a number of significant advantages to conducting an electronic survey over other types of surveys. One of the major advantages is cost because electronic surveys do not require postage, printing costs, or involvement of interviewers. Anderson and Kanuka (2003) have estimated that electronic surveys cost about one-tenth of the cost of a comparable mail survey. Electronic surveys also have the advantages of having instant access to a wide audience, regardless of their geographical location, being fast, capable of having responses downloaded into a spreadsheet or a statistical analysis program, and being flexible in terms of layout because of the kinds of response formats that can be incorporated particularly with Web-based surveys. While electronic surveys have a number of advantages over other survey methods, they do have disadvantages. One disadvantage is the inability to ensure privacy and anonymity, particularly with e-mail surveys, because the respondent's e-mail address is generally included in his or her response. Another major disadvantage is that Web-based surveys often are sent to Internet lists or discussion groups, where the message asks members for their responses; this is a type of **volunteer sampling**, and it produces samples that might significantly differ from the population and, therefore, is inferior to random sampling methods that produce representative samples. There is evidence that e-mail surveys generate better response rates than Web-based surveys and are more likely to avoid multiple entries to the same survey by the same person (Llieva et al., 2002).

e-mail survey
Electronic survey where participants are contacted directly via e-mail, and the survey instrument is attached to the message

Web-based survey
Electronic survey where participants are contacted indirectly by posting an invitation to participate and a link to the survey instrument on the Internet

Volunteer sampling
Nonrandom sampling method where participants self-select into the sample

STUDY QUESTION 12.2 | • **What are the differences between cross-sectional and longitudinal designs? What are the characteristics of the different survey data collection methods?**

Constructing and Refining a Survey Instrument

In addition to deciding on the mode of data collection, it is necessary to construct a number of questions or survey items that will provide answers to your research questions. If an already validated survey instrument is available, we recommend that you use it because constructing a survey instrument requires a lot of work. Researchers can determine if an available instrument is appropriate by (1) determining what samples it has been used with and examining reliability and validity data across these samples and (2) evaluating the instrument based on the guidelines in this chapter. If the instrument has worked in the literature with similar samples, then use it. If it has not been tried with people similar to your sample, but it does follow the guidelines, then consider using it. If it is not constructed well, then don't use it. Now, we explain how to construct a survey instrument under the assumption that an already developed instrument is *not* available for your research project.

The survey instrument of data collection will be a *questionnaire* or an interview protocol. An interview protocol is highly similar to a questionnaire; essentially, it is a questionnaire that has been put into script format so that the interviewer can read the questions and record the responses. All of the principles of questionnaire construction discussed in this section apply equally to interview protocols. In particular, we explain the process of questionnaire construction through the use of the twelve principles that are listed in Table 12.5. You can find full-length books on survey instrument construction in Brace (2004), Dillman (2007), and Bradburn, Sudman, and Wansink (2004).

TABLE 12.5
Principles of Questionnaire Construction

1. Write items to match the research objectives.
2. Write items that are appropriate for the respondents to be surveyed.
3. Write short simple questions.
4. Avoid loaded or leading questions.
5. Avoid double-barreled questions.
6. Avoid double-negatives.
7. Determine whether closed-ended or open-ended questions are needed.
8. Construct mutually exclusive and exhaustive response categories for closed-ended questions.
9. Consider the different types of closed-ended response categories.
10. Use multiple items to measure complex or abstract constructs.
11. Make sure the questionnaire is easy to use from the beginning to the end.
12. Pilot test the questionnaire until it is perfected.

Principle 1. Write Items to Match the Research Objectives

Your research proposal will include your research purpose and research questions or objectives. When constructing a questionnaire, your task is to construct items that cover the different areas and content needed to fulfill your objectives. This involves determining what is essential and what is not needed. You should conduct an extensive review of the literature to make sure you have identified all areas that you need to cover in your questionnaire. It also means that you must write items that will work; that is, you must write items and construct a questionnaire that will have the psychometric properties of providing reliable and valid data. The issues of content and construct validity are especially relevant; that is, make sure you construct a set of items that represent the content domain of interest and make sure you measure each construct adequately. To obtain these desired properties, make sure you follow all of the remaining principles.

Principle 2. Write Items That Are Appropriate for the Respondents to be Surveyed

It is essential not to forget that it is your research participants, not you, who will be completing the questionnaire. If you are going to construct questionnaire items that will work with your particular respondents, you need to consider, empathetically, how your participants will view what you write. Don't use stilted or pretentious language. Think about the reading level and the demographic and cultural characteristics of your participants, and write items that are understandable and meaningful to them. Make sure to use natural and familiar language that is clear to both you and your research participants. This will help your participants feel relaxed and less threatened when filling out the questionnaire. It will also increase their motivation to complete the questionnaire.

Principle 3. Write Short, Simple Questions

Survey questionnaire items should be short, clear, and precise. This includes using simple language and avoiding jargon. Your goal is for everyone to easily understand the item and interpret what the question or item is addressing in the same way. If you have something complex to ask, you must find a simple and clear way to ask it. If you write items that are unambiguous and easy to answer, participants will clearly understand what is asked and their answers should be meaningful. Furthermore, participants will be likely to continue answering all the items on your questionnaire and not leave any blank responses.

Loaded term
A word that produces
an emotionally
charged reaction

Principle 4. Avoid Loaded or Leading Questions

Loaded and leading questions bias participants' responses. One form of bias comes when a "loaded" term is used in the item stem. A **loaded term** is a word that produces some sort of positive or negative emotion on the part of the respondent separate from any content value. For example, in politically conservative circles in the United States the term "liberal" came to take on connotations far beyond recommending progressive change. A liberal was sometimes depicted as someone with low morals and one who does not believe in individual responsibility. Because of the loaded nature of the word, researchers needed to use synonyms to *liberal* or, even better, to specify exactly what was meant (increasing spending on education, affirmative action, etc.). For example, it would be preferable to ask the question "What is your opinion of Barack Obama?" instead of "What is your opinion of the liberal Barack Obama?" because of the loaded word "liberal." The inclusion of one word can have a dramatic impact on participant responses. Here is the key point: If a particular word tends to evoke emotional feelings or stereotyped thoughts, then avoid using it.

Leading question
A question that suggests how the participants should answer

A **leading question** is slightly different. This refers to a question or item stem (i.e., the words in the question or item not including the response categories) that suggests to the participant how he or she should respond. Here is an example from Bonevac (1999):

> Do you believe that you should keep more of your hard-earned money or that the government should get more of your money for increasing bureaucratic government programs?
>
> ☐ Keep more of my hard-earned money.
>
> ☐ Give my money to increase bureaucratic government programs.
>
> ☐ Don't know/no opinion

This question is leading because it is suggesting to participants that they should select the response "keep more of my hard-earned money." Notice that this item also has some loaded words in it such as "bureaucratic" and "hard-earned."

Principle 5. Avoid Double-Barreled Questions

Double-barreled question
Asking about two or more issues in a single question

A **double-barreled question** asks two (or more) things in a single question, and must be avoided. A question such as "Do you agree that President Obama should focus his primary attention on the economy and foreign affairs?" How would you interpret the participant's response if he or she agreed? Would you claim the participant wanted attention applied to the economy, foreign affairs, or both? The question asks about two separate issues: the economy and foreign affairs. Each issue might elicit a different attitude, and combining them into one question makes it unclear which attitude or opinion is being assessed. If the word *and* or *or* appears in your question, check to make sure that you have not written a double-barreled question rather than just asking about a very specific situation.

Principle 6. Avoid Double Negatives

Double negative
A sentence construction that contains two negatives

A **double negative** is a sentence construction that includes two negatives. When asking participants whether they agree or disagree with statements, double negatives can easily occur. Here is an example:

> Do you agree or disagree with the following statement?
> Psychology professors should not be allowed to conduct research during their office hours.

In order to disagree with this statement you have to construct a double negative. You would have to form the response that you "do not think that psychology professors should not be allowed to conduct research during their office hours." When using agreement scales, the use of some double negatives might be unavoidable. If you do use an occasional double negative, you should underline the negative word or words to focus the participants' attention to the negative (e.g., we should have underlined "not" in our item stem provided above), and keep double negatives to a minimum.

Principle 7. Determine Whether Closed-Ended or Open-Ended Questions Are Needed

Open-ended question
A question that allows participants to respond in their own words

An **open-ended question** requires participants to come up with their own answer. Participants respond to open-ended questions in their own natural language, and they are not limited to a set of predetermined response categories. They can provide any response that they desire. For example, if you wanted to find out what people do when they feel depressed, you could ask an open-ended question such as "What do you do most often when you feel depressed?" Open-ended questions are valuable when the researcher needs to know what people are thinking or when the dimensions of a variable are not well defined. They are commonly used in exploratory or qualitative research. However, the responses to open-ended questions must be coded and categorized, which takes time.

Closed-ended question
A question where participants must select their answer from a set of predetermined response categories

A **closed-ended question** requires respondents to choose from a set of predetermined response alternatives provided by the researcher. For example, if you wanted to find out what people do when they feel depressed, you could ask the question as a closed-ended question as follows:

> What do you do most often when you feel depressed?
> ☐ Eat
> ☐ Sleep
> ☐ Exercise
> ☐ Talk to a close friend
> ☐ Cry

Generally, closed-ended questions are appropriate when the dimensions of a variable are known. In such an instance, the alternative responses can be specified, and the respondent can select among these alternatives. Closed-ended questions also provide more standardized data because all participants are exposed to the same response categories.

Mixed-question format

Includes a mixture of both closed- and open-ended response characteristics in a single item

An additional, **mixed-question format** also is possible for the question we used as an example above:

What do you do most often when you feel depressed?

☐ Eat

☐ Sleep

☐ Exercise

☐ Talk to a close friend

☐ Cry

☐ Other (Please Specify):_____

Principle 8. Construct Mutually Exclusive and Exhaustive Response Categories for Closed-Ended Questions

Mutually exclusive categories

Nonoverlapping response categories

When constructing response categories, it is important to construct the categories so that they do no overlap. **Mutually exclusive categories** do not overlap. Here is a set of response categories for annual income that is *not* mutually exclusive:

Please check the box that includes your current annual income in dollars:

☐ 25,000 or less

☐ 25,000 to 50,000

☐ 50,000 to 75,000

☐ 75,000 to 100,000

☐ 100,000 to 150,000

☐ 150,000 to 200,000

☐ 200,000 or more

Do you see the problem? What if your annual salary were $50,000 per year? There would be two possible categories for this amount because they are not mutually exclusive. Here are the *corrected,* mutually exclusive, categories:

Please check the box that includes your current annual income in dollars:

☐ Less than 25,000

☐ 25,000 to 49,999

☐ 50,000 to 74,999

☐ 75,000 to 99,999

☐ 100,000 to 149,999

☐ 150,000 to 199,999

☐ 200,000 or more

Exhaustive categories
Response categories that cover the full range of possible responses

It is also important to construct a set of response categories that includes a place for all possible responses. **Exhaustive categories** include a place for all possible responses. The set of annual income categories provided above were exhaustive because they included a place for all possible annual incomes. If you eliminate one of the categories in that set, they no longer would be exhaustive. For example, if you forgot to include the category "□ 250,000 or more," then someone earning $300,000 per year would have no place to record his or her response.

The key point is that it is important that your response categories are both mutually exclusive and exhaustive!

Principle 9. Consider the Different Types of Closed-Ended Response Categories

Rating Scales   When asking participants questions or measuring their reactions to statements, researchers usually prefer multichotomous rather than dichotomous response categories. Here is an item with a dichotomous response format measuring agreement:

I take a positive attitude toward myself.

□ Yes

□ No

Rating scale
An ordered set of response choices, such as a 5-point rating scale, measuring the direction and strength of an attitude

To increase variance and obtain a measure of intensity, a multichotomous response format, called a **rating scale,** is used by most researchers. Here is an example:

I take a positive attitude toward myself.

1	2	3	4	5
Strongly disagree	Disagree	Neutral	Agree	Strongly agree

This 5-point rating scale is superior to the dichotomous response format because it taps into two key dimensions of attitudes. It measures *direction* (positive or negative toward the attitudinal object) and *strength* or intensity of attitude. Some researchers prefer to exclude the center (neutral) category and to push respondents to "lean" in one direction or the other. Research suggests that when a shift is made to a 4-point scale by excluding the center point, the distribution of agree and disagree responses is not significantly affected (Converse & Presser, 1986; Schuman & Presser, 1996).

Anchor
Descriptors placed on points on a rating scale

When constructing the descriptors (called the **anchors**) for the points on 4-point and 5-point rating scales, you must make sure that the distance between each pair of descriptors or response categories is the same. For example, the distance between agree and strongly agree should be the same as between disagree and

EXHIBIT 12.1

Examples of Response Categories for Popular Rating Scales

Approval scale

1	2	3	4	5
Strongly disapprove	Disapprove	Neutral	Approve	Strongly approve

Satisfaction scale

1	2	3	4	5
Very dissatisfied	Somewhat dissatisfied	Neutral	Somewhat satisfied	Very satisfied

Amount Comparison scale

1	2	3	4	5
Much less	A little less	About the same	A little more	Much more

Similarity scale

1	2	3	4
Very much unlike me	Somewhat unlike me	Somewhat like me	Very much like me

Effectiveness scale

1	2	3	4
Not at all effective	Not very effective	Somewhat effective	Very effective

Performance scale

1	2	3	4
Excellent	Good	Fair	Poor

strongly disagree. However, the distance between somewhat agree and strongly agree would not be the same as between agree and strongly agree. Exhibit 12.1 provides a few examples of anchors for rating scales measuring various attitudinal dimensions.

Rating scales with more than four or five points are also commonly and effectively used in psychological research. Rating scales commonly vary from four to eleven points. Here is an example of a 7-point scale with the center and end points anchored with descriptors:

How would you rate the overall job performance of your supervisor?

1	2	3	4	5	6	7
Very low			Average			Very high

Some researchers use "10 point" scales because they assume many people think this way (i.e., on a 1-to-10 scale, how would you rate XYZ?). However, we recommend that a zero be included because some respondents will falsely assume that 5 is the center point between 1 and 10. The center point on a 1-to-10 scale is 5.5; the center point on a 0-to-10 scale is 5. We also recommend that you anchor the center with a descriptor to reduce individual differences in scale use. For example, on the 7-point scale shown above, we anchored the center point. If you are wondering how many points should be used on scaled response categories, we recommend that you use somewhere from 4 to 11 points (McKelvie, 1978; Nunnally, 1978).

Binary forced-choice approach
Participant must select from the two response choices provided with an item

Binary Forced Choice   Another response format sometimes used is the **binary forced-choice approach**. When using this approach, you do not have participants use rating scales to evaluate each attitudinal object. Instead, pairs of attitudinal objects are provided, and participants must select the ones that best fit their beliefs. For example, a popular instrument used to measure "normal" narcissism in personality and social psychological research is the Narcissistic Personality Inventory (NPI) (e.g., Foster & Campbell, 2007). Here is the introduction to the instrument followed by two of the items on the NPI:

> In each of the following pairs of attributes, choose the one that you MOST AGREE with. Mark your answer by writing EITHER A or B in the space provided. Only mark ONE ANSWER for each attitude pair, and please DO NOT skip any items.
>
> ____ 1. A I have a natural talent for influencing people.
>   B I am not good at influencing people.
> ____ 2. A I would do almost anything on a dare.
>   B I tend to be a fairly cautious person.

Although some research suggests that forced-choice format can reduce response sets (explained below), item level data analysis is difficult, and psychometricians generally recommend that binary forced-choice items be avoided (Anastasi & Urbina, 1997; Nunnally, 1978; Thorkildsen, 2005).

Ranking
Participants asked to put their responses in ascending or descending order

Rankings   Sometimes survey researchers ask participants to rank order their responses. A **ranking** indicates the importance or priority assigned to an attitudinal object. Rankings can be used with open-ended or closed-ended responses. For an open-ended example, you might ask "In your opinion, what are the three top psychology professors in your college?" Then you follow this up with a request to rank the top three professors. Rankings also are sometimes done with closed-ended items. Here is an example:

> The following five professors have been nominated for the Outstanding Teacher Award this academic year. Please fill in your <u>rank order</u> of these professors, where 1 is your most favorite and 5 is your least favorite:
>
> Ranks
> ____ Dr. John Doe
> ____ Dr. Sally Smiley
> ____ Dr. Tim Goodbody
> ____ Dr. Jill Lookgood
> ____ Dr. Lisa Shapely

As a general rule, you should not ask participants to rank more than three to five attitudinal objects at one time because ranking can be a difficult task. Additionally, rank ordering can be difficult to analyze statistically when your goal is to relate the ranking to other variables. Last, rank ordering can be achieved for a group of respondents without asking for ranks. You have participants rate each object on a rating scale (e.g., 5-point) and then you compare the group means for each object. You can then rank order the means from lowest to highest.

Checklist
Participants asked to check all response categories that apply

Checklists   Survey researchers sometimes provide a list of categories (a **checklist**) and ask participants to check the responses that apply to them. Unlike other response formats, the checklist is a multiple-response format because participants are told to check all categories that apply to them. Here is an example of a checklist type item:

During the past year, have you taken a course in any of the following subject areas? Check all that apply.

☐ Anthropology
☐ Economics
☐ History
☐ Political Science
☐ Psychology
☐ Sociology

Principle 10. Use Multiple Items to Measure Complex or Abstract Constructs

In the last section, we explained how to set up the response categories for the items on your questionnaire. Another key issue is how many items you need to measure psychological constructs adequately. Measurement is defined as "the assignment of numerals to objects or events according to rules" (Stevens, 1946). Rarely, however, is the use of a single item adequate to measure constructs of interest to psychologists. Single items can adequately measure constructs such as sex (via self-report of male or female), weight (e.g., measured on a scale), and ethnicity (self-report). However, most constructs of interest are more complex than sex and weight and, therefore, require multiple items for measurement. Examples of more complex constructs are self-esteem, intelligence, locus of control, statistic anxiety, dogmatism, and temperament. It is a maxim in psychological measurement that multiple items are needed to measure constructs. Multidimensional constructs (i.e., constructs that have two or more components or domains or dimensions such as intelligence) by definition require more than one item for measurement. Most unidimensional constructs (constructs that have only one dimension such as global self-esteem) also require multiple-item measurement because single-item measurement is notoriously unreliable (i.e., inconsistent and untrustworthy).

Semantic differential
Scaling method measuring the meanings that participants give to attitudinal objects

Semantic Differential   A **semantic differential** is a scaling technique that is used to measure the meaning that participants give to attitudinal objects or concepts and to produce semantic profiles (Osgood, Suci, & Tannenbaum, 1957).

Participants are asked to rate the attitudinal object provided in the item stem on a series of bipolar rating scales, with contrasting adjectives anchoring the left and right endpoints. A 7-point rating scale is the most popular, with only the endpoints anchored. For example, in an article entitled "Occupation and Social Experience: Factors Influencing Attitude Towards People with Schizophrenia," the researchers (Ishige & Hayashi, 2005) measured the participants' attitudes using 20 bipolar adjectives. Here are several of the adjective pairs they used: safe vs. harmful, bad vs. good, fierce vs. gentle, shallow vs. deep, active vs. inert, lonely vs. jolly, simple vs. complicated, dirty vs. clean, and distant vs. near. As you can see, the contrasting adjective pairs are composed of antonyms. If you need help locating antonyms for a descriptor, online dictionaries are readily available on the World Wide Web.

Traditionally, in semantic differential scaling, several contrasting adjective pairs are developed to address each of the following three dimensions directed toward the attitudinal object: activity, evaluation, and potency. For example, you might rate "juveniles" as high on activity (e.g., aggressive), unfavorable on evaluation, and high on potency (e.g., powerful). You might rate "books" as low on activity (e.g., passive), favorable on evaluation (if you like books), and average on potency. Politicians might be rated as average on activity, unfavorable on evaluation, and high on potency (i.e., powerful). You can easily find many examples of semantic differential scales by conducting a literature search using "semantic differential" as the search term.

Likert scaling

A multi-item scale is used to measure a single construct by summing each participant's responses to the items on the scale

Summated rating scale

Another name for Likert scaling

Likert Scaling The most frequently used multi-item approach to scaling is **Likert scaling**.[1] It is named after the famous social psychologist Rensis Likert (1903–1981) who, while working on his dissertation, first used this scaling approach (Likert, 1932; Seashore & Katz, 1982). (His last name is pronounced "LICK-ert," not "LIE-kert.") In Likert scaling, each participant rates multiple items designed to measure one construct; the respondent typically rates all of the items using a 4-, 5-, 6-, or 7-point rating (i.e., response) scale. A single score is obtained for each participant by summing his or her item scores. (Some researchers also divide the sum by the total number of items.) Because each participant's responses to the items measuring the single construct are summed, this type of scale is also known as a **summated rating scale**.

You can view a summated rating scale in Table 12.6. The scale shown is the Rosenberg Self-Esteem Scale, and it is composed of 10 items. Although the ten items in the Rosenberg Self-Esteem Scale measure self-esteem, five of the items (3, 5, 8, 9, and 10) are worded in the negative direction. Before a research participant's responses on the ten items are summed, the five negative item scores must be reversed. The participant's sum on the ten items (after appropriate reversals) can be divided by 10 if one prefers that the final range falls between 1 and 4 (rather than between 10 and 40).

---

[1]Some researchers use the term "Likert scale" to refer to any questionnaire item that uses a 5-point response scale. Most writers, including us, recommend that the term "Likert-type item" or the simpler "5-point rating scale" be used in this case instead of "Likert scale" (which more properly designates a multi-item summated scale).

TABLE 12.6
The Rosenberg Self-Esteem Scale

Circle one response for each of the following items.

	Strongly Disagree	Disagree	Agree	Strongly Agree
1. I feel that I am a person of worth, at least on an equal basis with others.	1	2	3	4
2. I feel that I have a number of good qualities.	1	2	3	4
*3. All in all, I am inclined to feel that I am a failure.	1	2	3	4
4. I am able to do things as well as most other people.	1	2	3	4
*5. I feel I do not have much to be proud of.	1	2	3	4
6. I take a positive attitude toward myself.	1	2	3	4
7. On the whole, I am satisfied with myself.	1	2	3	4
*8. I wish I could have more respect for myself.	1	2	3	4
*9. I certainly feel useless at times.	1	2	3	4
*10. At times I think I am no good at all.	1	2	3	4

*Items marked with an asterisk have reverse wording. Scores for the reverse wording items must be reversed before summing with responses to the other items. For the reverse wording items, convert a response of 1 to 4; convert 2 to 3; convert 3 to 2; and convert 4 to 1. After conversion, sum the 10 responses, and divide the sum by 10 for the final scale score for each participant.

Source: Morris Rosenberg's "Self-Esteem Scale" from pp. 325–327 of *Society and Adolescent Self Image*, 1989.

When researchers use summated rating scales to measure constructs, they should report a coefficient alpha value (also called "Cronbach's alpha"), which is an index of internal consistency reliability based on the data collected in the study being reported. The value of coefficient alpha should be 0.70 or higher if the scale is reliable.

Principle 11. Make Sure the Questionnaire Is Easy to Use From the Beginning to the End

A checklist for questionnaire construction is provided in Table 12.7. Please read the list carefully and be sure to check it when you construct your own questionnaire. We will address some of the issues below.

Ordering of Questions   The ordering, or sequencing, of the questions must always be considered. When the questionnaire includes both positive and negative items, it is generally better to ask the positive questions first. Similarly, the more important and interesting questions should come first to capture the attention of the respondent. Roberson and Sundstrom (1990) found that placing the important questions first and demographic questions (age, gender, income, etc.) last in an employee attitude survey resulted in the highest return rates. This practice of putting demographics *last* also is standard practice in professional survey research firms. You should start this last section with a lead-in like one of the

TABLE 12.7
Questionnaire Construction Checklist

1. Follow the 12 principles provided in Table 12.4.
2. Always put a title on your questionnaire.
3. Number the items or questions consecutively (starting with "1").
4. Include page numbers.
5. Use a standard font type (e.g., Times New Roman) with a readable font size (e.g., 12 point).
6. Provide clear instructions wherever needed.
7. Provide lead-ins for new or lengthy sections in the questionnaire.
8. Make sure the questionnaire has a professional and uncluttered appearance.
9. Carefully place each question or set of questions to ensure logic and flow from beginning to end.
10. Start the questionnaire with interesting, gentle questions.
11. Place demographic and other sensitive questions at the end of the instrument.
12. Avoid multiple-response questions.
13. List response categories for closed-ended questions vertically, rather than horizontally. An exception to this rule can be the horizontal presentation of a rating scale.
14. Use closed-ended response categories when appropriate responses are known.
15. Include some open-ended questions.
16. Do not use "fill-in" lines with open-ended questions; provide blank space in the response area.
17. Do not "break" questions (or instructions or lead-ins) across pages.
18. On multipage questionnaire, place "Please continue to next page" at the bottom of pages.
19. Always end the questionnaire with a "Thank you for completing this questionnaire."

following: "Last are some demographic questions that will be used for classification purposes only" or "To finish this questionnaire, we have a few questions about you."

Contingency Questions   It is a good idea to limit the number of contingency questions for paper-and-pencil questionnaires (i.e., questionnaires that participants fill out) because they increase the risk of error. A **contingency question** is an item that directs participants to different follow-up questions depending on their response. It allows the researcher to direct participants to the correct place within the questionnaire (if there is any deviation from everyone answering the next question). Here is an example of a contingency question:

> **Contingency question**
> An item directing the participant to different follow-up questions depending on the initial response

Question 43. What is your gender?

☐ Male → <u>IF MALE, GO TO QUESTION 45</u>

☐ Female → <u>IF FEMALE GO TO QUESTION 44</u>

The use of contingency questions is not problematic in interview protocols and questionnaires used in Web-based surveys because in the former, interviewers are trained to administer the interview protocol, and in the latter, skips can be programmed into the Web-based instrument to automatically send the participant to the correct questions.

Questionnaire Length   Many significant questions can be asked in any survey, but every data-gathering instrument has an optimal length for the population to which it is being administered. After a certain point, the respondents' interest and cooperation diminish. The survey researcher must therefore ensure that the questionnaire is not too long, even though some important questions might have to be sacrificed. It is impossible to specify the optimum length of any survey questionnaire because length is partially dependent on the topic and the method of data collection. As a general rule, telephone interviews should be no longer than fifteen minutes. However, a face-to-face interview might consume more time without making the interviewee feel uncomfortable. Questionnaires sent through the mail should be the shortest and easiest to complete; otherwise, potential participants will not fill them out and send them back.

Response Bias   A person can have several types of biases when responding to surveys. One of the most common is a **social desirability bias**. This bias occurs when people respond to a survey in a way that makes them look the best rather than responding as they really feel or believe. Survey researchers must constantly be aware of this type of bias affecting individuals' responses and construct instruments and interpret the results with this potential bias in mind. One strategy to minimize this bias is to make the data anonymous so that not even you, the researcher, can connect a name to a response. Then you can tell the participants that their responses will be anonymous. You must not ask for or allow participants to provide any identifying information (e.g., name, phone number, student number). After explaining that their responses will be anonymous, ask them to be open and honest in their answers. They should feel free to do this now, knowing that no one can connect their name with what they say. Another strategy is to use binary forced-choice response categories that have been equated on desirability. Respondents will have to pick one of two choices that are equally desirable. This approach is not used often because rating scales are more popular and easier to analyze than binary forced-choice response data.

Another type of bias is a specific **response set** or a tendency to respond in a specific manner to all questions. For example, a person might hesitate in giving extreme responses and tend to cluster his or her responses around a central choice. One strategy to minimize a tendency to select a center choice is to use an even number of response categories on rating scales rather than an odd number with a center point. Other individuals might be "yea-sayers," tending to agree with every statement. One strategy to minimize this is to break up questions into different types. For example, insert an open-ended question between a set of closed-ended items. Surveys instruments need to be constructed so that biases such as these are eliminated or at least minimized. Some researchers reverse items

---

Social desirability bias
Error occurring when participants try to respond in the way they think makes them look good

Response set
Tendency for a participant to respond in a particular way to a set of items

to help eliminate response sets. This approach can help, but it has also been shown to decrease the reliability of the items. Therefore, reversing items can come with a cost. In sum, you will need to think carefully and check empirically during pilot testing to determine the kinds of biases that might affect your data collection instrument and act accordingly.

Principle 12. Pilot Test the Questionnaire Until It Is Perfected

Pilot test

Testing for the proper operation of a data collection instrument before using it in the research study

We already have alluded to the importance of pilot testing. We can not stress enough how important it is to "try out," or **pilot test**, your data collection instrument (e.g., questionnaire, interview protocol). The purpose is to identify problems and fix them. Pilot testing must be done *before* you use the instrument in a research study. You can start pilot testing by testing out your questionnaire with colleagues and friends. Then you will need to pilot test it with individuals who are very similar to those who will be in your research study. Your pilot testing participants should be instructed to complete the instrument and to identify any ambiguous or unclear items, or any other problems they might have in completing the instrument. One especially useful strategy during pilot testing is to use the **think-aloud technique**, where participants verbalize their thoughts and perceptions while they engage in the activity of filling out the questionnaire. You might even decide to make audiotape or videotape recordings of the pilot test sessions for later review. It is also helpful to interview participants after they complete the questionnaire, discussing how it worked, what they thought it was about, if anything was confusing, and if anything irritated them. The ultimate purpose of pilot testing is to obtain an instrument that will work flawlessly when it is used in your research study.

Think-aloud technique

Participants verbalize their thoughts while engaged in an activity such as completing a questionnaire

STUDY QUESTION 12.3

- **What are the major principles of questionnaire construction? What are the key issues within each of the 12 principles?**

Selecting Your Survey Sample From the Population

Population

The full group of interest to the researcher

Sample

A subset of the population

After the survey instrument (i.e., the questionnaire or interview protocol) has been constructed, it must be administered to a group of individuals to obtain a set of responses that will provide answers to your research questions. There are many ways in which a researcher can select the participants who will be given the questionnaire. Most research projects involve selecting a sample of participants from a population of interest. A **population** refers to all the events, things, or individuals to be represented, and a **sample** refers to any number of individuals less than the population that is used to make the representation. The researcher makes generalizations about the population based on the sample results.

The manner in which this sample of participants is selected depends on the goals of the research project. If the research question focuses on exploring the relationship between variables and if direct, precise generalizations do not need to be made about the population, then a convenience sampling method might be

Convenience sampling
Use of people who are readily available, volunteer, or are easily recruited for inclusion in a sample

used. **Convenience sampling** is a nonprobability sampling method whereby the sample of participants selected is based on convenience and includes individuals who are readily available. For example, a significant amount of psychological research is conducted using introductory psychology students as participants because these students are conveniently available to researchers. The obvious advantage of using the convenience sampling technique is that participants can be obtained without spending a great deal of time or money. However, researchers usually want the results of their studies to generalize to "people in general" or at least to "a college student population." Making such a generalization from this sample of college students can be hazardous because the sample is composed of students volunteering for the study who have elected to take introductory psychology during the semester in which the study was conducted.

Responses to electronic surveys also represent a type of convenience sample because, in spite of the large number of individuals who are connected to the Internet, many people still are not connected or choose not to use the Internet (Solomon, 2001). Furthermore, participants in the final sample will include only those people who decide to respond to your e-mail invitation to participate in the survey research study. This means that any sample of responses to electronic surveys will be biased. Bias can be reduced by sampling from populations in which Internet access is extremely high, such as college students and university faculty within the United States, Canada, and Western Europe. However, even these populations might produce a biased sample because of differing levels of experience and comfort with Internet-based tools such as Web browsers. This is one of the primary reasons that electronic surveying, although attractive, should be used with caution (Solomon, 2001).

Random sampling
Selection of sample members using a statistically random process

When the research question requires an accurate depiction of the general population, a **random sampling** method must be used. As discussed in more detail in Chapter 5, there are several methods of random sampling, including simple random sampling, stratified sampling, and cluster sampling. We will review only simple random sampling in this chapter. An example of random sampling is seen in most presidential campaigns polls conducted to test the pulse of the voting public. These polls are taken to determine the popularity of the candidates as well as the influence of various issues, such as prior drug use, on the public's opinions of candidates. It is very important that the results based on the sample generalize to the population in political polling.

Sampling error
Variation of sample values from population values

When a true random sample of participants is obtained from the population, the results can be amazingly accurate. For example, in 1976, a *New York Times–CBS* poll correctly predicted that 51.1% of the voters would vote for Jimmy Carter and 48.9% for Gerald Ford (Converse and Traugott, 1986). The prediction was made using a sample of less than 2,000 individuals selected from almost 80 million voters. This perfectly accurate prediction was unusual, but it illustrates the accuracy with which the population responses can be predicted from a sample of just a few individuals, if these individuals are selected randomly. In virtually all polls such as this, there is **sampling error**, or random error, that arises from the fact that the sample results randomly vary slightly from the population characteristics.

However, this error is typically quite small and much smaller than it would be if any other sampling method were used.

This ability to generalize directly from the single sample to the population also is important in many survey research studies. This ability to generalize is a strength of survey research that is based on random samples. Experimental research rarely is based on random samples; however, this problem is dealt with because causal generalizations based on experimental research data are based on replication with multiple samples of different people, different places, and different times. What is of most importance in experimental research is random assignment, not random selection.[2]

Simple random sampling
A popular and basic equal probability selection method

When **simple random sampling** is used, every member of the population has an equal chance of being selected for the study. The advantage of this method is that it provides a sample of participants whose responses represent those of the general population; this type of sample is called a **representative sample**. One way of thinking about simple random sampling is to consider the "hat model." The idea is to write each person's name on a small piece of paper and put them into a hat. There must be one equally sized piece of paper for each person in the population. Next, shake up the pieces of paper in the hat and pull one piece out. The person whose name is on that piece of paper is in your sample. If you want a sample of size 100, then repeat this process 99 more times until you have your 100 people. (You do not put the piece of paper back into the hat once selected because you want to avoid sampling the same person more than once.) If you actually draw a random sample, a better method than the hat model is to give each person in the population a number (starting with 1 and ending with the number of people in the population) and then use a random number generator to indicate the numbers (i.e., people) randomly selected to be in the sample. As mentioned in Chapter 5, you will find useful random number generators here: http://randomizer.org and http://www.random. org. For more information on random sampling methods reread Chapter 5, or see books devoted to sampling (e.g., Henry, 1990; Kalton, 1993).

Representative sample
A sample that resembles the population

Preparing and Analyzing Your Survey Data

After you construct your data collection instrument, select your sample, and collect your survey data, you will be ready to enter your data into a statistical software program such as the popular program called SPSS. Quantitative (i.e., numerical data) are relatively easy to enter into SPSS; the data entry window looks and operates much like a spreadsheet. Once you enter the data, you must carefully check the

---

[2]Any sampling method that has this characteristic is called an equal probability of selection method (EPSEM). In addition to simple random sampling, there are other equal probability of selection methods such as proportionate stratified sampling, cluster sampling when clusters are of equal size (or PPS is used), and systematic sampling (when a random start is used). The key idea is that equal probability of selection methods produce representative samples, enabling the researcher to generalize from the sample directly to the population.

quality of your data. For example, if you used a 5-point rating scale, a response of "6" or "7" would not be valid. You would need to go back to the survey instrument to determine whether you made a data entry error that can be corrected. If not, this response would have to be coded as "missing." If you used a contingency question that directed only women to answer a question, then any responses to the question by men must be omitted (i.e., coded as missing). If you have any open-ended responses, you will need to examine the written responses for themes and categories, and if possible, you should assign codes to the themes/categories. Those codes will represent a nominal variable and can be entered into the data set and analyzed with the other data. Once you have carefully checked and "cleaned your data," you are ready for analysis. You will learn how to analyze data in Chapters 14 and 15.

Summary

Survey research is a nonexperimental research method relying on questionnaires or interview protocols for data collection. It is used when the research is interested in measuring individuals' attitudes, reported activities, opinions, and beliefs. Typically, the survey method relies on a sample of participants selected so that the researcher can generalize from the sample to the target population. Surveys can be conducted at a single time (cross-sectional) or at multiple time periods (longitudinal survey). The steps in survey research are shown in Table 12.3. Survey data collection methods include administering a survey instrument (i.e., a questionnaire) or conducting interviews (using an interview protocol). Popular survey data collection methods include face-to-face interviews, telephone interviews, mail questionnaires, and electronic surveys. Twelve principles of questionnaire construction are provided in Table 12.5. When constructing or evaluating a questionnaire, it is very important to make sure that all of the points in the questionnaire construction checklist (Table 12.7) are accurately followed.

Key Terms and Concepts

Anchor
Binary forced-choice approach
Checklist
Closed-ended question
Contingency question
Convenience sampling
Cross-sectional studies
Double negative
Double-barreled question
Electronic survey
e-mail survey
Exhaustive categories
Face-to-face interview method

Group-administered questionnaire method
Interview
Interview protocol
Leading question
Likert scaling
Loaded term
Longitudinal studies
Mail questionnaire method
Mixed-question format
Mutually exclusive categories
Open-ended question
Panel studies

Pilot test
Population
Questionnaire
Random sampling
Random-digit dialing
Ranking
Rating scale
Representative sample
Response set
Sample
Sampling error

Semantic differential
Simple random sampling
Social desirability bias
Summated rating scale
Survey instrument
Survey research
Telephone interview method
Think-aloud technique
Trend study
Volunteer sampling
Web-based survey

Related Internet Sites

http://www.isr.umich.edu/src

http://www.norc.uchicago.edu/

http://www.princeton.edu/~psrc/

http://www.irss.unc.edu/odum/jsp/home.jsp

http://gallup.com

http://www.ropercenter.uconn.edu/
These are some well-known survey research centers in the United States. They have many interesting materials and helpful links.

http://www.aapor.org/poll
Answers to frequently asked questions about surveys and polls.

http://www.spss.com/uk/SurveyTips.pdf
Excellent free guide on questionnaire and interview protocol construction.

http://www.amstat.org/sections/srms/whatsurvey.html
Link to brochures explaining survey research.

Practice Test

The answers to these questions can be found in Appendix.

1. A researcher wrote the following item stem for a five-point rating scale. "Don't you agree that the University needs a football team." What is the problem with this item?

   a. It uses unfamiliar language.
   b. It is a double-barreled question.
   c. It uses double negatives.
   d. It is a "leading" question.

2. Which of the following sets of closed-ended response categories has mutually exclusive categories?

a. 0–10, 10–20, 20–30, 30–40
b. 0–9, 10–19, 20–29, 30–39
c. 0–5, 5–10, 10–15, 15–20
d. 0, 1–3, 3–6, 6–9, 10 or more

3. A technique used to measure the meaning participants attach to various attitudinal objects or concepts is called:

a. The semantic differential technique
b. The nonanchored rating scale
c. The mutually exclusive response list
d. The checklist

4. According to your text, how many points should a rating scale have?

a. Five
b. Four
c. Ten
d. Somewhere from 4 to 11 points

5. A question that allows participants to respond in their own words is a:

a. Loaded question
b. Leading question
c. Double-barreled question
d. Open-ended question
e. Closed-ended question

Challenge Exercises

1. What is the problem(s) with this set of response categories to the question "What is your current age?"

1–5
5–10
10–20
20–30
30–40

2. How many points should be included on a rating scale? Why? (You can rely on our discussion as well as other discussions you might find on the Web.)

3. Think of an issue about which you wonder what people might think (e.g., attitudes toward research with animals, psychology students' understanding of the different specializations of applied psychology) and construct a ten-item questionnaire. Make sure that you include some demographic items at the end so that you would be able to check to see if the attitudes differ by group. Then evaluate your questionnaire according to the 19 checkpoints provided in Table 12.7 (Questionnaire Construction Checklist). Give yourself a numerical grade between 0% and 100% (where 100% means you properly followed all 19 checkpoints).

Qualitative and Mixed Methods Research

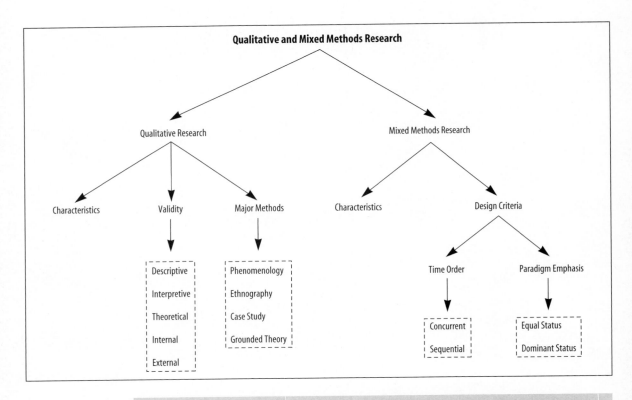

On April 29, 1999, two students, Eric Harris and Dylan Klebold, entered Columbine High School in Colorado killing 13 individuals and wounding numerous others before committing suicide. Evidently, the massacre was the result of long hours of detailed planning. Harris and Klebold had acquired a small arsenal of guns and ammunition and made numerous bombs in preparation for the massacre. After killing 12 students and one teacher, they both turned their guns on themselves and ended their lives.

The Columbine massacre leaves us asking how and why this even happened. Because the shooters killed themselves, we cannot ask them about their thinking. But research has pieced together the story of Columbine through the writings and activities of the shooters leading up to their deaths, interviews with their classmates, and documents that provide accounts of their activities. This compilation of diaries, interviews, and documents reflects qualitative research. Other killers who have not committed suicide have also been interviewed in depth and studied for their reasons and motivations. Just as importantly, a sometimes forgotten part of the Columbine massacre is the lives of the survivors of the event. What was their experience like? How did their lives change as a result of this terrible event?

Qualitative research offers an excellent way to dig deeply into the lives of individuals and groups to study the world as they see it from their perspectives. In this chapter, you will learn about qualitative methods for exploring the lives of particular individuals and particular groups. The qualitative approach to psychological research offers a complementary approach that adds to and enhances what is provided in quantitative research.

Introduction

Qualitative research
The type of research relying on qualitative research data

Mixed methods research
Type of research in which quantitative and qualitative data or approaches are combined in a single study

In Chapter 2, we briefly introduced qualitative research. At its most basic level, **qualitative research** is defined as the approach to empirical research that relies primarily on the collection of qualitative data (i.e., nonnumeric data such as words, pictures, images). In this chapter, we explain qualitative research in more detail. The majority of this textbook has focused on quantitative research (such as experiments and surveys) because the majority of psychological research is quantitative. Therefore, you now know a great deal about quantitative research. Qualitative research does, however, have a long-standing and important place in psychological research (Camic, Rhodes, & Yardley, 2003; Smith, 2008; Willig & Stainton-Rogers, 2008). The third type of research, **mixed methods research**, combines ideas and approaches from quantitative and qualitative research (Johnson, Onwuegbuzie, & Turner, 2007). We will explain this type of research after explaining qualitative research in more detail.

Table 13.1 shows the key differences among quantitative, qualitative, and mixed methods research. Some of what you have learned about quantitative research is shown in the first column. For example, quantitative research focuses on testing hypotheses, and obtaining results that can be generalized broadly. Quantitative journal articles usually include quite a few numbers and statistical test results. Notice how qualitative research differs from quantitative research in the table. Qualitative research is much more focused on individual people and single, local groups for intensive case study, and there is little interest in obtaining results that are broadly generalizable. Additional differences are shown in the table. Finally, you will notice in Table 13.1 that mixed methods research is based on a combination or mixture of the characteristics of quantitative and qualitative research.

In the remainder of this chapter, we will explain qualitative and mixed methods research.

TABLE 13.1

Characteristics of Quantitative, Qualitative, and Mixed Research Approaches*

	Quantitative Research	Qualitative Research	Mixed Research
Scientific Emphasis	Confirmation and falsification. Focuses on *testing* hypotheses and theories.	Exploratory. Focuses on *generating* hypotheses and theories.	Equal emphasis. Combines hypothesis/theory generation and testing.
View of the World	Mental processes and behavior are regular and predictable.	Mental processes and behavior are situational, dynamic, social, contextual, and personal.	Thought and behavior contain predictable and particularistic/contextual elements.
Primary View of Reality	Objective (material, physical, causal).	Subjective.	Combination of objective, subjective, and intersubjective.
Research Objectives	Explain (cause and effect), control, predict, description of characteristics of populations.	Explore, particular description, depth of understanding, social "construction" of reality.	Combination of objectives.
Research Purpose	Find general and complex laws of thought and behavior.	Describe and understand particular groups and individuals in particular contexts.	Integrate the general and the particular.
Data	Quantitatively measured variables (numbers).	Words, text, images, documents.	All data types are relevant; quantitative and qualitative data are both used in a single study.
Results	Generalizable findings.	Particularistic findings and claims.	Attempts to integrate general and particular, and produce "practical theory."
Final Report	Statistical results (with significance testing of correlations, differences between means) with discussion of results.	Narrative with rich contextual description and many direct quotations.	Mixture of statistics and qualitative data reporting.

*Although this chapter covers qualitative and mixed research, we have included the characteristics of quantitative research for comparative purposes.

Major Characteristics of Qualitative Research

Michael Patton (2002) has done a good job of summarizing the characteristics of qualitative research. Patton's list of the twelve major characteristics of qualitative research is shown in Table 13.2. Not all qualitative research studies have all 12 of the characteristics, but studying his list will give you a good feel for features usually associated with qualitative research. The 12 key terms are highlighted in italics in the table.

Research Validity in Qualitative Research

We pointed out in Chapter 6 that *research validity* refers to the correctness or truthfulness of the inferences that are or can be made from the results of a research study. The validity of qualitative research findings has sometimes been questioned. For example, qualitative research has been criticized for a lack of rigor and for producing findings

TABLE 13.2
Twelve Major Characteristics of Qualitative Research

Design Strategies

1. *Naturalistic inquiry*—Studying real-world situations as they unfold naturally; nonmanipulative and noncontrolling; openness to whatever emerges (lack of predetermined constraints on findings).

2. *Emergent design flexibility*—Openness to adapting inquiry as understanding deepens and/or situations change; the researcher avoids getting locked into rigid designs that eliminate responsiveness and pursues new paths of discovery as they emerge.

3. *Purposeful sampling*—Cases for study (e.g., people, organizations, communities, cultures, events, critical incidences) are selected because they are "information rich" and illuminative, that is, they offer useful manifestations, of the phenomenon of interest; sampling, then, is aimed at insight about the phenomenon, not empirical generalization from a sample to a population.

Data-Collection and Fieldwork Strategies

4. *Qualitative data*—Observations that yield detailed, thick description; inquiry in depth; interviews that capture direct quotations, about people's personal perspectives and experiences; case studies; careful document review.

5. *Personal experience and engagement*—The researcher has direct contact with and gets close to the people, situation, and phenomenon under study; the researcher's personal experiences and insights are an important part of the inquiry and critical to understanding the phenomenon.

6. *Empathic neutrality and mindfulness*—An empathic stance in interviewing seeks vicarious understanding without judgment (neutrality) by showing openness, sensitivity, respect, awareness, and responsiveness; in observation it means being fully present (mindfulness).

7. *Dynamic systems*—Attention to process; assumes change as ongoing whether focus is on an individual, an organization, a community, or an entire culture; therefore, mindful of and attentive to system and situation dynamics.

Analysis Strategies

8. *Unique case orientation*—Assumes that each case is special and unique; the first level of analysis is being true to, respecting, and capturing the details of the individual cases being studied; cross-case analysis follows from and depends on the quality of individual case studies.

9. *Inductive analysis and creative synthesis*—Immersion in the details and specifics of the data to discover important patterns, themes, and interrelationships; begins by exploring, then confirming, guided by analytical principles rather than rules, ends with a creative synthesis.

10. *Holistic perspective*—The whole phenomenon under study is understood as a complex system that is more than the sum of its parts; focus on complex interdependencies and system dynamics that cannot meaningfully be reduced to a few discrete variables and linear, cause-effect relationships.

11. *Context sensitivity*—Places findings in a social, historical, and temporal context; careful about, even dubious of, the possibility or meaningfulness of generalizations across time and space; emphasizes instead careful comparative case analyses and extrapolating patterns for possible transferability and adaptation in new settings.

12. *Voice, perspective, and reflexivity*—The qualitative analyst owns and is reflective about her or his own voice and perspective; a credible voice conveys authenticity and trustworthiness; complete objectivity being impossible and pure subjectivity undermining credibility, the researcher's focus becomes balance-understanding and depicting the world authentically in all its complexity while being self-analytical, politically aware, and reflexive in consciousness.

Source: From M. Q. Patton, *Qualitative Research and Evaluation Methods*, 3rd ed., pp. 40–41, copyright 2002 by Sage Publications, Inc.

Researcher bias
Only noticing data that support one's prior expectations

Reflexivity
Thinking critically about one's interpretations and biases

Negative-case sampling
Searching for cases that challenge one's expectations or one's current findings

Descriptive validity
The factual accuracy of the account reported by the researcher

Investigator triangulation
Use of multiple investigators to collect and interpret the data

that are dependent upon the particular researcher conducting the study. In this section, we explain how strong qualitative research can be conducted.

One threat to watch out for is **researcher bias**, which might take the form of searching out and only confirming one's preconceived notions. Although it is true that many qualitative studies have been conducted that lack validity and rigor, this does not have to be the case. Two strategies for reducing researcher bias are **reflexivity** (i.e., constantly attempting to identify your potential biases and discerning how you can minimize their effects) and **negative-case sampling** (i.e., attempting to locate and examine cases that disconfirm your prior expectations). Table 13.3 includes 15 important validity strategies that are used during the conduct of a qualitative research study to help shift it from a study of questionable value to a high-quality research study for meeting its purpose. We now briefly explain some of the validity strategies and the types of validity that are of particular relevance in qualitative research (based on the work of Joseph Maxwell, 1992, 2005).

Descriptive Validity One purpose of qualitative research is to provide an accurate description of a particular phenomenon, situation, or group. Therefore, descriptive validity is important. **Descriptive validity** is present to the degree that the account reported by the researcher is accurate and factual. One very useful validity strategy for obtaining descriptive validity is **investigator triangulation** (i.e., the use of multiple investigators to collect and interpret the data). By using multiple investigators, the description is less likely to be based on a single researcher's perspective. When multiple researchers agree about the descriptive

TABLE 13.3
Validity Strategies That Should Be Used in Qualitative Research

Strategy	Description
Data triangulation	The use of multiple data sources to help understand a phenomenon.
Extended fieldwork	To provide for both discovery and validation researchers should collect data in the field over an extended time period.
External audit	Using outside experts to assess the study quality.
Investigator triangulation	The use of multiple investigators (i.e., multiple researchers) in collecting, analyzing, and interpreting the data.
Low-inference descriptors	The use of description phrased very close to the participants' accounts and researcher's field notes. Verbatims (i.e., direct quotations) are a commonly used type of low-inference descriptors.
Methods triangulation	The use of multiple research methods to study a phenomenon.
Negative-case sampling	Attempting to select cases that disconfirm the researcher's expectations and generalizations.
Participant feedback	The feedback and discussion of the researcher's interpretations and conclusions with the actual participants and other members of the participant community for verification and insight.
Pattern matching	Predicting a series of results that form a distinctive pattern and then determining the degree to which the actual results fit the predicted pattern or "fingerprint."

Strategy	Description
Peer review	Discussion of the researcher's interpretations and conclusions with other people. This includes discussion with a disinterested peer (e.g., with another researcher not directly involved). This peer should be skeptical and play the devil's advocate, challenging the researcher to provide solid evidence for any interpretations or conclusions. Discussion with peers who are familiar with the research can also help provide useful challenges and insights.
Reflexivity	Involves self-awareness and critical self-reflection by the researcher on his or her potential biases and predispositions as these might affect the research process and conclusions.
Researcher-as-detective	A metaphor characterizing the qualitative researcher as he or she searches for evidence about causes and effects. The researcher develops an understanding of the data through careful consideration of potential causes and effects and by systematically eliminating rival explanations or hypotheses until the final case is made beyond a reasonable doubt. The detective can utilize any of the strategies listed here.
Rule out alternative explanations	Making sure that you have carefully examined evidence for competing or rival explanations and that yours is the best explanation.
Theory triangulation	The use of multiple theories and perspectives to help interpret and explain the data.
Triangulation	Cross-checking information and conclusions through the use of multiple procedures or sources. When the different procedures or sources are in agreement you have corroboration.

Interpretive validity
Accurately portraying the participants' subjective viewpoints and meanings

Participant feedback
Member checking to see if participants agree with the researcher's statements, interpretations, and conclusions

Low-inference descriptors
Descriptions that are very close to participants' words or are direct verbatim quotes

Theoretical validity
Degree to which the theory or explanation fits the data

details of the account provided in a qualitative research report, readers can place more faith in that account.

Interpretive Validity The second type of validity for qualitative research focuses on the primary purpose of qualitative research, which is to *report how people subjectively think and feel about phenomena*. **Interpretive validity** is present to the degree that the researcher accurately portrays the *meanings given by the participants* to what is being studied. Your goal here is to "get into the heads" of your participants and accurately document *their viewpoints and meanings*. One useful validity strategy for interpretive validity is to obtain **participant feedback**; this process is also called "member checking." The strategy is to discuss your findings with your research participants to determine if they agree with your interpretations of their viewpoints, and then, based on that feedback, make modifications so that you represent their meanings and ways of thinking. Another useful validity strategy is the use of **low-inference descriptors** in your report; this means that you should phrase your description of the participants' thinking in language that is very close to the participants' accounts and to your field notes taken during the research study. This means that the researcher should include quite a few quotes in the report to demonstrate points made.

Theoretical Validity Maxwell calls the third type of validity **theoretical validity**. It is present to the degree that the theoretical explanation provided by the researcher accurately fits the data. Four validity strategies provided

Extended fieldwork
Spending enough time in the field to fully understand what is being studied

Theory triangulation
The use of multiple theories or perspectives to aid in interpreting the data

Pattern matching
Construction and testing of a complex hypothesis

Peer review
Discussing your interpretations with one's peers and colleagues

Ideographic causation
A single intentional action for a particular person in a local situation with an observable result

Nomological causation
The standard view of causation in science; refers to causal relationships among variables.

Researcher-as-detective
Metaphor applied to researcher looking for the local cause of a single event

Methods triangulation
Use of multiple research methods or methods of data collection

Data triangulation
Use of multiple sources of data

in Table 13.3 are especially helpful for obtaining theoretical validity. The first strategy is **extended fieldwork**, which means that the researcher should collect data in the field over an extended period of time. The second strategy is **theory triangulation**, which involves the consideration of multiple theories and multiple perspectives to help interpret and understand the qualitative data. Out of this, a fuller explanation is expected to result. The third strategy is **pattern matching**. This is a hypothesis-testing strategy in which the researcher makes a unique and complex prediction (rather than a very simple prediction) and determines whether it is supported. That is, did the "fingerprint" pattern of results that the researcher predicted actually occur? If it does, the theory will have significant predictive power. The fourth strategy that is especially relevant for theoretical validity is **peer review**. This requires you to discuss your interpretations, conclusions, and explanations with your peers or colleagues who can provide a different perspective. If you are deeply involved in a qualitative study, the use of objective outsiders, who are not deeply involved in the study, can be quite helpful in providing a fresh perspective.

Internal Validity   The definition of internal validity is the same as it was for quantitative research. It's the degree to which a researcher is justified in concluding that an observed relationship is *causal*. However, the issue of causation is treated quite differently in qualitative research. In most of the science of psychology, the goal is to understand how variables are causally related and how the world operates. Qualitative research is much less concerned with the *general* human world; it focuses on studying very small, *particular* contexts in the world. Therefore, rather than attempting to state how the human world operates in general, the goal is to describe how a particular group operates in a particular place, and sometimes the qualitative researcher is interested in what caused a particular event in a particular context. We call this particularistic notion of causation **ideographic causation**. It amounts to making a very specific and local claim. For example, you might say that your car wouldn't start this morning because the battery was dead or because it ran out of gas. In other words, ideographic causation is a commonsense notion of causation used in very limited and particularistic circumstances. Ideographic causation is contrasted with **nomological causation**, which is of primary interest to quantitative psychology.

At least three of the validity strategies in Table 13.3 are especially relevant to the issue of causation in qualitative research. The first strategy is called **researcher-as-detective**, which involves carefully thinking about cause and effect and examining each possible "clue" and then drawing a conclusion. The second strategy is called **methods triangulation**, which involves the use of multiple data collection methods, such as interviews, questionnaires, and observations in investigating an issue to determine if the same conclusion is reached via the different methods. The third strategy is **data triangulation**, which involves the use of multiple data sources, such as interviews with different types of people or using observations in different settings. The idea is that you should not limit yourself to a single data source if you want to draw an accurate conclusion about what event or events caused a particular outcome.

External Validity   The definition of external validity is the same as it was for quantitative research. It is still the degree to which you can *generalize* your results to other people, settings, and times. This type of validity is the least utilized in qualitative research because qualitative researchers usually are *not* interested in making generalizations. Remember, the key purpose of qualitative research is to explore and describe a *particular* phenomenon in a particular place with a particular person or group of people.

| **Naturalistic generalization** Generalization, based on similarity, made by the reader of a research report |

When qualitative researchers consider external validity, they usually focus on a type of generalizing called **naturalistic generalization**, which refers to generalization based on similarity of the people and context reported in the study and the people and context to which the generalization is made. This type of generalization fits the qualitative research perspective because it is not the researcher that makes this generalization. Rather, it is the reader of the article or report that decides when and how to generalize. When making a naturalistic generalization, you would look at your clients or people you are working with and generalize to them to the degree that they are similar to the people in the qualitative research report.

To enable naturalistic generalizations, the qualitative research report should include the details about the participants and context necessary so that readers will be in the position to make naturalistic generalizations. If you ever consider making the more traditional sort of generalization from a qualitative research study, a strategy is to generalize the finding only when it has been shown in many studies. You are able to generalize when a research result has been shown with different types of people, at different times, and in different settings. One more type

| **Theoretical generalization** Generalization of a theoretical explanation beyond the particular research study |

of potential generalization is called **theoretical generalization**. This involves generalizing the theory generated in a study [such as a grounded theory (GT) research result]. Even if the particulars do not generalize, the main ideas and the process observed might generalize. However, before this generalization can legitimately be made, the theory must be tested with new research participants.

STUDY QUESTION 13.1 | **How is "validity" established in qualitative research? What kinds of strategies are used to help establish validity in qualitative research?**

Four Major Qualitative Research Methods

We have discussed qualitative research as a broad form of research. It turns out that there are at least four major qualitative research methods that are variations on the broad type of qualitative research discussed thus far. They are phenomenology, ethnography, grounded theory, and case study research. Each of these more specialized methods has its own unique origins and unique conceptual vocabulary. Sometimes a researcher will utilize one of these more specialized methods. At other times, the researcher might mix the approaches to meet his or her particular research circumstances and needs.

Phenomenology

The first major approach to qualitative research, **phenomenology**, involves the description of an individual's, or group of individuals', conscious *experience* of a phenomenon such as the death of a loved one, a counseling session, an illness, winning a championship football game, or experiencing a specific emotion such as guilt, anger, or jealousy. Here's the key question addressed via phenomenological research: *What is the meaning, structure, and essence of the lived experience of this phenomenon for a particular individual or for many individuals?* The researcher attempts to gain access to each participant's **life world**, which is the research participant's inner world of subjective experience. Your life world is where you have your "lived experiences"; it is where your immediate consciousness exists; it's where you feel, and sense, and have "inner talk." This area is also known as your *phenomenal space.*

This research method has a long history in psychology, but its founding is usually attributed to the philosopher Edmund Husserl (1859–1938). It's Husserl who coined the term *Lebenswelt,* which is German for "life-world." Husserl thought that all individuals would experience the same phenomenon in the same way if all other factors (preconceptions, learned feelings) were removed or "bracketed" out of the representation. Many later phenomenologists would argue that individuals and groups can experience the same phenomenon (e.g., death of a loved one) differently. Regardless of your position on this issue, phenomenological research always involved "getting inside of people's heads" to see how *they* experience things.

Phenomenology has been used extensively in psychology and related fields. This is the case because oftentimes it is important to document how people subjectively experience their situations, from their perspectives. In a study of children with pediatric cancer, Fochtman (2008) argued that "Only when clinicians truly understand the meaning of this illness to the child can they design nursing interventions to ease suffering and increase quality of life in children and adolescents with cancer" (p. 185). Here are a few phenomenological experiences that have been studied in psychology and related fields: obsessive-compulsive disorder (Garcia et al., 2009; Wahl, Salkovskis, & Cotter, 2008), addiction (Gray, 2004), racism (Beharry & Crozier, 2008), sexual abuse (Alaggia & Millington, 2008), psychotic symptoms in narcolepsy (Fortuyn et al. 2009), life satisfaction (Thomas & Chambers, 1989), and the meaning of aging (Adams-Price, Henley, & Hale, 1998).

Phenomenological Data Collection and Data Analysis How do phenomenologists collect and analyze data and develop a description of an individual's or group of individuals' experience of a phenomenon? The phenomenological research method involves getting each participant to focus on his or her phenomenal space and to describe the experience (current or from memory) on its own terms. The participant must give the experience his or her full attention. The primary qualitative method of data collection used by phenomenologists is in-depth interviews, although open-ended questionnaires are also commonly used (where participants write about their experiences).

In the following example of phenomenological research, we briefly explain the process of data analysis and report writing. The study, conducted by Riemen (1986), investigated the phenomenon of caring and noncaring interactions with nurses *from the perspective of patients*. To investigate this phenomenon, Riemen interviewed nonhospitalized individuals over the age of 18 who had a prior inter-action with a nurse. The interviewer requested that each research participant think about their experiences with one or more caring and noncaring nurses. They were asked to describe how they felt during these interactions with nurses. From the interviews, Riemen searched for **significant statements** (i.e., a few words or a phrase, a sentence, or a few sentences) that had particular relevance to the phenomenon being studied. When attempting to determine if a statement is significant, you should ask yourself questions such as (a) "Is the statement descrip-tive of the experience?" and (b) "Does the statement appear to be something that is meaningful to the participant in expressing his or her experience?" These state-ments are usually written verbatim (word for word) or as close as possible to the participants' words. Some caring statements identified by Riemen were "listened well," "empathetic," and "talked to me about things other than illness." Some noncaring statements included "I felt as though my hands were being slapped," "didn't want to talk," and "she looked at the equipment instead of me."

> **Significant statements** Words, phrases, or sentence length participant statements that the researcher thinks vividly communicate the participant's experience

Once the significant phrases and statements were extracted from the tran-scribed data, Riemen constructed a list of the meanings of the statements. Riemen determined the meanings by reading, rereading, and reflecting on the statements of the research participants. Riemen's goal was to empathetically arrive at the research participants' meanings of their statements. For example, some of Riemen's formulated meanings of the significant statements about caring nurses were "Nurse's voluntary and unsolicited return to the client was highly indicative of a caring attitude" and "Nurse's caring made him feel comfortable, relaxed, secure, and in good hands, as though he was being taken care of by a family member." Meaning given to some noncaring statements included "The nurse's attitude of lack of interest in her as a person is interpreted by the client as the nurse viewing nursing as 'only a job,'" or "The nurse who does not pay any attention to the client's needs but views nursing as a job is perceived by the client as noncaring" (in Creswell, 1998, pp. 286–287). Next, the formulated "meaning" statements are organized into clusters or themes. Riemen formulated the clusters of "nurse's exis-tential presence," "client's uniqueness," and "consequences" for the caring cluster. Last, a summary description of the **essence** or phenomenological structure of the phenomenon is produced by integrating the statements, their meaning, and the clusters they formed.

> **Essence** Phenomenological structure of the experience

Phenomenological Report Writing   The final report of a qualitative pheno-menological study is written in narrative form. It should include a detailed description of the participants in the study and the data collection methods used to obtain the data. The strategy of data analysis should be provided. If any validity checks were used, they should be explained. For example, one useful validity strategy is called member checking, where the researcher asks the participants if the significant statements, meanings, and phenomenological summary accurately express their views. Once validated, the significant statements and meanings should be described in some detail (including tables when needed). The results also should include a rich description of the essential or common characteristics of the experience. Sometimes, differences will be identified across types of participants, which will be reported.

Here is the essence or phenomenological structure reported by Riemen (1986) in describing participants' experience of a caring nurse.

> In a caring interaction, the nurse's existential presence is perceived by the client as more than just a physical presence. There is the aspect of the nurse giving of oneself to the client. This giving of oneself may be in response to the client's request, but it is more often a voluntary effort and is unsolicited by the client. The nurse's willingness to give of oneself is primarily perceived by the client as an attitude and behavior of sitting down and really listening and responding to the unique concerns of the individual as a person of value. The relaxation, comfort, and security that the client experiences both physically and mentally are an immediate and direct result of the client's stated and unstated needs being heard and responded to by the nurse. (in Creswell, 1998, p. 289)

Here is the description of the essence or structure of the participants' experience of a noncaring nurse:

> The nurse's presence with the client is perceived by the client as a minimal presence of the nurse being physically present only. The nurse is viewed as being there only because it is a job and not to assist the client or answer his or her needs. Any response by the nurse is done with a minimal amount of energy expenditure and bound by the rules. The client perceives the nurse who does not respond to this request for assistance as being noncaring. Therefore, an interaction that never happened is labeled as a noncaring interaction. The nurse is too busy and hurried to spend time with the client and therefore does not sit down and really listen to the client's individual concerns. The client is further devalued as a unique person because he or she is scolded, treated as a child, or treated as a nonhuman being or an object. Because of the devaluing and lack of concern, the client's needs are not met and the client has negative feelings; that is, he or she is frustrated, scared, depressed, angry, afraid, and upset. (in Creswell, 1998, p. 289)

Ethnography

Ethnography
Qualitative research method that focuses on the discovery and description of the culture of a group of people

The second major approach to qualitative research is ethnography. **Ethnography** refers to the discovery and description of the culture of a group of people or of a cultural event. Ethnography originated in the discipline of anthropology in the late nineteenth century, and the core concept relied upon by ethnographers is culture. A **culture** is the system of shared beliefs, values, practices, language, norms, rituals, and material things that group members use to understand their

Culture
The shared beliefs, values, practices, language norms, rituals, and material things that the members of a group use to interpret and understand their world

Shared beliefs
Statements or conventions that people sharing a culture hold to be true or false

Shared values
Culturally defined standards about what is good or bad or desirable or undesirable

Norms
Written and unwritten rules specifying how people in a group are supposed to think and act

Holism
Idea that a whole, such as a culture, is more than the sum of its individual parts

Emic perspective
The insider's perspective

Etic perspective
The researcher's external or "objective outsider" perspective

world. **Shared beliefs** are cultural statements or conventions that cultural members hold to be true or false. **Shared values** are culturally defined conceptions of what is good or bad or desirable or undesirable. **Norms** are the unwritten and written rules that specify appropriate group behavior. Embedded in the concept of culture is the idea of **holism**, which is the idea that the whole is greater than the sum of its parts. Culture sometimes is divided into *nonmaterial culture* (e.g., the shared language, beliefs, norms, values, and practices) and *material culture* (e.g., the material thing created by a culture such as clothes, flags, buildings, art). The foundational question in ethnography is this: *What are the cultural characteristics of this group of people or of this cultural scene?* The job of the ethnographer is to enter a group or scene and document the cultural characteristics.

Culture is often thought of as being associated with very large groups of individuals such as the Japanese, Mexican, or American. However, the concept of culture can also be used on a much smaller scale. We can study macro (i.e., large) or micro (i.e., small) cultures. Berg (1998) has even pointed out that a distinction is sometimes made between microethnography and macroethnography. At the macro level we might study the cultural characteristics of Japanese adolescents or the Ohio Amish. On the micro level, we might study the cultural characteristics of a street gang, a motorcycle group, a therapeutic setting, or even the emergent culture in a research methods class of 20 students and a teacher. The difference in the two is the scope of the investigation. Obviously, studying the culture of Japanese adolescents has a greater scope than studying a particular therapeutic setting. However, regardless of the scope of the investigation, the primary concern is with describing the culture of the people in the targeted setting. Similar to phenomenology (and virtually all qualitative research), the focus of ethnography is on depicting the culture from the insider's perspective (called the **emic perspective**). At the same time, the research also focuses on the "objective outsider's" perspective (called the **etic perspective**). In short, the researcher must balance the emic *and* etic perspectives when producing a valid ethnography.

Ethnography can help psychologists better understand the many cultural groups and cultural settings with which they work, as well as in studying how interventions might interact with cultural variables. Here are a few examples of ethnographic research used in areas related to psychology: cultural adaptations of HIV prevention interventions among adults with severe mental illness (Wainberg et al., 2007), ethnography of deinstitutionalized but seriously mentally ill patients (Newton et al., 2000), ethnography of a job training program (Hull & Zacher, 2007), depressive children in a hospital unit undergoing dialysis (Walters, 2008), low-income mothers' child safeguarding practices (Olsen, Bottorff, Raina, & Frankish, 2008), ethnography of human relationships in cyberspace (Carter, 2005), ethnography of an online chat room (Shoham, 2004), and ethnography of African great apes (King, 2004).

Ethnographic Data Collection Methods   Now let's take a look at how an ethnographer studies a cultural setting. One method of data collection commonly used by ethnographers is in-depth interviews (also called "ethnographic interviews") with members of the group being investigated. For example, Smith, Sells, and Clevenger (1994) conducted an ethnographic study of reflective team meetings in a family therapy setting. To acquire information about the micro culture in this therapeutic setting, Smith et al. conducted in-depth interviews with eleven couples and their therapists. They were interviewed at least twice over a four-month period, and the interviews lasted up to two hours.

Participant observation is also very important in ethnographic research. **Participant observation** is the method of data collection in which the researcher becomes an active participant in the group he or she is investigating. Ellen (1984) describes the ethnographic process as subjective soaking or becoming immersed in the culture being studied. This immersion is accomplished primarily through participant observation and face-to-face interactions with members of the culture. For example, Schouten and McAlexander (1995), in their ethnographic study of the subculture of consumption of Harley-Davidson bikers, not only went to rallies of the Harley Owners Group but also eventually bought Harley-Davidson bikes and the appropriate clothing, such as black boots, and used the bikes for their everyday transportation. Marquart (1983), in his study of the social control system that existed in the Texas Department of Corrections (TDC), went through the training program to become a prison guard and was employed as one for 18 months in the maximum-security unit. During this period of time, he interacted with, interviewed, and observed the behaviors of the prison guards and inmates as he patrolled the cell blocks, showers, and dining halls, searched for weapons, and broke up fights. By entering, participating, leaving, and reflecting, the ethnographer is able to understand and document the insider's perspective (i.e., the emic perspective) and the objective outsider's perspective (i.e., the etic perspective).

Entry, Group Acceptance, and Fieldwork   One of the first tasks that must be accomplished when using the participant observation method is to gain entry to the group you wish to study. In some instances, this is very easy. For example, if you wanted to conduct an ethnographic study of fraternity or sorority rush week, you might do so by actually participating in rush week, either as a bona fide participant or under the guise of wanting to belong to a sorority or fraternity. During rush week, you would not only be a participant in the process, but you would also be observing and taking notes on the behavior and activity of other students involved in this process.

In other instances, entry to the group or culture is not as easily accomplished. Gaining access to a local teenage street gang would, in most instances, be a rather difficult process. Similarly, access to elite groups, such as the super rich, is often very difficult because these individuals set up barriers to maintain their privacy and actively avoid scrutiny. Marquart, for example, had to get the approval of the TDC and the superintendent of the unit at which he was employed in order to conduct his study.

Before gaining entry into a group, you must decide whether this entry will be covert or overt. In some instances, the entry must be covert because this is the only way in which the research can be conducted. For example, Humphreys' (1970) study of casual homosexual encounters in a public restroom could not

Participant observation
Data collection method in which the researcher becomes an active participant in the group being investigating

have been conducted if he had formally announced his identity as a researcher. However, covert entry is generally looked down upon by Institutional Review Boards because of the lack of informed consent. Therefore, most participant observation is overt, such as in Marquart's study mentioned above and in Schouten and McAlexander's study of Harley-Davidson bikers, also mentioned above. However, even when entry is overt, you might have to get past **gatekeepers**, individuals who operate to protect, either formally or informally, the members of a group. Marquart, for example, had to secure the permission and approval of the warden of the prison unit in which he was employed. Even when gatekeepers provide their approval, there frequently must be acceptance by the members of the group before honest and valid information can be obtained.

One of the difficulties with collecting data through participant observation is that your presence can create a **reactive effect** in which your presence alters the behavior of the group members. Marquart had to earn the trust of each inmate before the inmate would reveal his control techniques. Suspicion and paranoia run rampant in a prison environment. It would be virtually impossible for an unknown researcher to walk into a prison and expect the inmates or the guards to divulge their informal system of control. When Schouten and McAlexander (1995) first gained entry to a Harley-Davidson motorcycle group, they "were treated politely by some, standoffishly by others, and overly gregariously by others, but no one treated us as if we really belonged there" (p. 46). It was only after they stopped and rendered assistance to one of the members who had mechanical problems with his bike that an initial bond was formed and they began to be indoctrinated into the ways of the group and eventually treated as one of the members.

In classical ethnography, the data collection process is called **fieldwork**. On the one hand, the researcher must *not* be **ethnocentric** during interactions with others in the culture (i.e., you must not judge others based on your cultural standards). On the other hand, the researcher must avoid **going native**, which would happen if you identified so completely with the group being studied that you could no longer take the perspective of an objective outsider. The insider and outsider roles must *both* be negotiated. During fieldwork, the researcher collects information on the patterns of behavior and social relations among the members of a group primarily through observing the behavior of the group members and listening to what they say. The researcher also interacts in face-to-face conversations and sometimes conducts interviews.

What you see and hear and think during fieldwork are recorded in your **fieldnotes**. The setting and context also should be richly described in the fieldnotes. You might also take photographs of surroundings and note the clothing worn by the group members. In the Harley-Davidson study, Schouten and McAlexander took pictures of the members' dress and appearance (see Figure 13.1). When the researcher has moments to reflect and when he or she leaves the group, fieldnotes must be finished, checked, and edited and notes must be written about his or her emerging interpretations and what kinds of data that should be collected during the next field entry period. Through this back-and-forth process between insider and outsider roles, the ethnographer produces an "objective" ethnography that also reflects the inner world of the culture.

Gatekeepers
Group members who control a researcher's access to the group

Reactive effect
Nontypical behavior of participants because of the presence of the researcher

Fieldwork
A general term for data collection in ethnographic research

Ethnocentric
Judgment of people in other cultures based on the standards of your culture

Going native
Overidentification with the group being studied so that one loses any possibility of objectivity

Fieldnotes
Notes taken by the researcher during (or immediately after) one's observations in the field

FIGURE 13.1
Example of dress and appearance of Harley-Davidson bikers.

(Photograph courtesy of Harley-Davidson Photograph & Imaging. Copyright H-D.)

Data Analysis and Report Writing As data are collected, they should be analyzed for themes, patterns, and meanings. You have to make some sense of the volumes of information that are collected. Throughout the process, the data should be checked for their validity. Once the themes, meanings, and patterns have been identified and validated, the ethnographer writes a narrative account that provides a description and interpretation of the culture being studied. This narrative report might include the characteristics of the group, how members of the group interact with one another, what the group has in common, what some of the group's norms and rituals are, and what the group's identity is. Schouten and McAlexander's (1995) narrative report of their ethnographic study of Harley-Davidson bikers first discussed the structure of the Harley-Davidson biker groups and then proceeded to present a narrative of the core values of the biker groups, such as the feeling of personal freedom and machismo surrounding the Harley-Davidson culture. The narrative report should also discuss how one becomes transformed into a group member and how, once a person has become a member, he or she expresses commitment and transmits to others the material and nonmaterial culture identified with being a member of the group. The final ethnography (i.e., the report) should provide a rich and holistic description of the culture of the group under study.

Case Study Research

Case study
Qualitative research method in which the researcher provides a detailed description and account of one or more cases

The third major approach to qualitative research is case study research. A **case study** is defined as the intensive and detailed description and analysis of one or more cases. A **case** is a bounded system such as a person, a group, an organization, an activity, a process, or an event. In the definition, "system" refers to a holistic entity that includes a set of interrelationships among the elements comprising the case. By "bounded," we mean that most cases have a boundary identifying what the case is and what it is not. Case study research also frequently emphasizes the

Case
A bounded system

environment in which the case exists. Here's the foundational question in case study research: *What are the characteristics of this single case or of these comparison cases?*

Case study research has a long history in psychology. Clinical case studies are especially common in clinical and counseling psychology. To give you a feel for topics studied via case study research, here are a few examples: client-centered therapy for a client that experienced severe childhood abuse (Murphy, 2009), experience of residents with severe mental illness in an inner-city recovery-housing building (Whitley, Harris, & Drake, 2008), barriers to help seeking for patients with dysthymia (i.e., chronic mild depression) (Svanborg et al., 2008), long-term integrative psychotherapy with a patient with schizophrenia (Lysaker et al., 2007), comparative case study of U.S. and Malawi soccer teams (Guest, 2007), moral development in a college fraternity (Mathiasen, 2005), and a test of the self-medication hypothesis for clients experiencing social phobia (Shepherd & Edelmann, 2007).

Data Collection in Case Study Research   Multiple sources and methods of data collection are used in case study research. For example, case study data might come from in-depth interviews, documents, questionnaires, test results, and archival records. Contextual and life history data are also collected in case study research to contextualize the case and to aid in understanding the causal trajectories that might have influenced the case. Quantitative data are also sometimes used in case study research, but remember that if both qualitative and quantitative data are utilized, then it should be called a mixed methods case study rather than a qualitative case study.

Case Study Designs   There are several types of case studies: intrinsic, instrumental, and collective (Stake, 1995). An **intrinsic case study** is an in-depth description of a particular individual, organization, or event conducted for the purpose of understanding that particular case. There is no interest in generalizing. Exhibit 13.1 provides a description of an intrinsic case study of an individual who had, for many years, been in and out of the mental health care system and later engaged in autocastration. This brief summary of the case study describes a unique event that was important in this person's life and provides some understanding of possible reasons for the autocastration.

Intrinsic case study
Case study in which the researcher is only interested in understanding the individual case

An **instrumental case study** is a case study conducted to provide insight into an issue or to develop, refine, or alter some theoretical explanation. It is undertaken to understand something more general than just the particular case. The specific case is not as important as gaining an understanding of the phenomenon or event. For example, right after the Columbine tragedy, the media and mental health care professionals studied the life histories of Eric Harris and Dylan Klebold to try to understand why they became killers. They looked at the type of behavior engaged in by these two and revealed that they had become obsessed with the violent video game Doom. Doom is an interactive game in which players try to rack up the most kills. Harris and Klebold had been arrested in January of the previous year for breaking into a commercial van and stealing electronics. They were both enamored of Nazi culture and would berate their classmates in German. Harris and Klebold were taunted as outcasts by some student groups. Their classroom

Instrumental case study
Case study in which the researcher studies a case in order to understand something more general than the particular case

EXHIBIT 13.1

A Case Study of Autocastration

Meyer and Osborne (1982) described a case study of a twenty-nine-year-old male who castrated himself with a kitchen knife while immersed in the ocean because he thought the cool water would act as an anesthetic. He then returned home and handed his testicles to his mother, an act that he thought would return to her the life she had given him at birth. Subsequent in-patient psychiatric treatment revealed that this man had been emotionally disturbed during most of his childhood. When he was 17, he withdrew from social activities and was diagnosed as suffering from psychotic depression. Visual hallucinations were frequent, and he had the persistent delusion that he was draining his brain of nuclear material when he masturbated. During this time, he frequented prostitutes and engaged in homosexual activities. These sexual exploits increased his feelings of guilt, anxiety, and depression. He considered suicide but chose castration instead because it would destroy the object of his guilt. The autocastration was interpreted by the case's therapist as a substitute for suicide.

writing assignments took on a more violent tone. These data were not examined because of an interest in describing the event of the killings at Columbine High School. Rather, they were examined to understand why the killings took place and to help develop an understanding that would apply in other times and places.

Collective case study
Study of multiple cases for the purpose of comparison

Comparative case study
Another name for a collective case study

A **collective case study** (also called a **comparative case study**) involves the extensive study of two or more individual cases. For example, a researcher might conduct a case study of three individuals with mild mental retardation who are placed in a general education class, or examine several astronauts' descriptions and experiences of being in space, or compare several cases of a rare clinical syndrome. When multiple cases are studied, the primary purpose is to understand the phenomenon or event comparatively, and often, the purpose is instrumental rather than intrinsic. For example, Hippocrates (1931), Posidonius (cited in Roccatagliata, 1986, p. 143), and others have provided case study descriptions of multiple individuals who suffered from seasonal affective disorder. These collective case studies provided information about a general phenomenon that afflicts many people and provided verification of the hypothesis that when a person is afflicted with this condition, he or she will usually experience depression in the winter months. Collective case studies, therefore, can provide some information that can be generalized to other cases. However, this generalization is limited because the few cases investigated will likely represent a biased sample. Ultimately, generalizing from one or several cases is possible only when there is no variability in the manifestation of the phenomenon being studied.

Cross-case analysis
Case study analysis in which cases are compared and contrasted

Case Study Data Analysis and Report Writing   The key idea in case study data analysis is that each case must be intensively analyzed as a separate entity. This involves analyzing the case as a system that has parts but also is a unified whole operating in an environment. The analyst must also relate the case to the research question(s). (This point is true of all research.) In a collective or comparative case study, the analyst goes one step further by also conducting a **cross-case analysis**. This means that multiple cases are compared and contrasted and the researcher looks for similarities (or patterns that cut across the cases) and differences.

The case study report should reflect the insider view of each case as well as the objective outsider viewpoint. The final report should provide a deep understanding of each case and also provide rich (i.e., vivid and detailed) and holistic (i.e., describing the whole and its parts) description of each case and the context in which it is embedded. If the goal is to inform the research literature beyond an understanding of the particular case, then the case should be integrated into the broader literature on the topic or phenomenon that was studied. Finally, it is very important that the report discuss the validity strategies (see Table 13.3) that were used to help produce a valid and trustworthy case study.

Grounded Theory

Grounded theory
Methodology for generating and developing a theory that is grounded in the particular data

Theory
An explanation of how and why something operates as it does

The fourth major approach to qualitative research is called grounded theory. **Grounded theory** is defined as a general methodology for generating and developing a theory that is "grounded" in empirical data (Bryant & Charmaz, 2007; Strauss & Corbin, 1998). A **theory** is an explanation of "How" and "Why" something operates. The focus is on inductively generating a theory to describe and explain a phenomenon or process. Grounded theory was originally formulated by two sociologists Barney Glaser and Anselm Strauss (1967), but today it is used in most social, behavioral, and clinical sciences. Here's the foundational question addressed in grounded theory research: *What theory or explanation emerges from an analysis of the data collected about this phenomenon?*

In Chapter 1, we defined *induction* as an inquiry starting from the specific or particular and moving to the more abstract and general. We also discussed the difference between the *logic of discovery* and the *logic of justification* (page 18); the former emphasizes the inductive process of starting with particular empirical data, and the latter emphasizes the more deductive process of starting with a general theory or a hypothesis and deducing the consequences that should occur and then testing the hypothesis with newly collected data to determine if it is supported. Here is a relatively simple way to think about the process: The logic of discovery focuses on theory *generation,* and the logic of justification focuses on theory *testing.* Grounded theory is the qualitative research approach that is specifically developed for discovering or generating a theory or explanation from empirical data.

According to the founders (i.e., Glaser and Strauss), there are four key characteristics of a good grounded theory. First, the newly constructed grounded theory should *fit* the data. Here's the question: "Does the theory correspond to real-world data?" Second, the theory must provide *understanding* of the phenomenon. Here's the question: "Is the theory clear and understandable to researchers and practitioners? Third, the theory should have some *generality.* Here's the question: "Is the theory abstract enough to move beyond the specifics in the original research study?" Fourth, the theory should contribute to some *control* of the phenomenon. Here's the question: "Can the theory be applied to produce real-world results?"

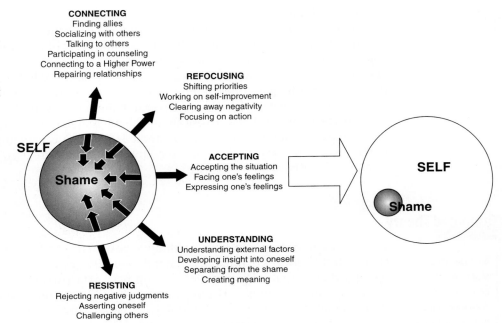

FIGURE 13.2
Grounded theory model of rebuilding of the self. The arrows extending outward from the self represent the expansive and enhancing forces of the five main sub-processes on the self. The inward arrows represent their effect on shrinking and externalizing the shame from the core self.

(From Van Vilet, 2008.)

Here are some examples of grounded theory (GT) research. Van Vilet (2008) used GT to document how adults who have experienced severe shame experiences bounced back to reproduce a positive self. The process included factors such as connecting, refocusing, accepting, understanding, and resisting. The depiction of their GT model is shown in Figure 13.2. Boyd and Gumley (2007) used GT to understand how clients experienced persecutory paranoia and how these beliefs affected their behavior. The core experience category was fear and vulnerability, which included confusion and uncertainty and self under attack. These processes led to engagement in the use of safety systems, of which paranoid behavior was a key defensive system. Schraw, Wadkins, and Olafson (2007) documented the process of academic procrastination among college students. Procrastination had positive (cognitive efficiency and peak experiences) and negative (fear of failure and postponement) dimensions. Operating in varying contexts (e.g., unclear directions, deadlines, and lack of incentives), procrastination led to the use of cognitive and affective coping mechanisms, which led to consequences for the students' quality of life and quality of work.

Data Collection in Grounded Theory Research   Any type of data collection is legitimate in grounded theory, but interviews are the most common, followed by observations. Data collection and analysis continue throughout a grounded theory study. This process is continuous because the researcher must enter the mode of "theory generator" and "theoretician," which requires creative and

Theoretical sensitivity
Researcher is effective in understanding what kinds of data need to be collected and what aspects of already collected data are important for theory development

descriptive skills and the use of empirical data. Using the jargon of grounded theory, during the collecting and analyzing of data, a researcher needs **theoretical sensitivity**. This just means that the researcher must be sensitive about what data are important when developing the grounded theory and to use this insight to know when and what kind of additional data need to be developed to construct the theory.

Grounded Theory Data Analysis and Report Writing   Grounded theory relies on a three-stage data analysis process that includes three steps. In the first stage, called **open coding**, you read the transcribed data (transcribed fieldnotes, interviews, open-ended questionnaires), and mark important ideas and concepts with a word or several words that describe the material more succinctly. In the second stage, called **axial coding**, you decide which concepts are the most important and begin trying to order them so that one phenomenon leads to another. In the third stage, called **selective coding**, you put the finishing touches on your explanation of the phenomenon. Your focus is on the main idea of your explanation (called "story line"), and you put the finishing touches on your "grounded theory." We showed the visual depiction of a grounded theory in Figure 13.2, and we depict another in Figure 13.3. Using the jargon of grounded theory, the grounded theory process (of collecting and analyzing data and depicting the visual model of your

Open coding
First stage of data analysis in GT; it's the most exploratory stage

Axial coding
Second stage of data analysis in GT; focus is on making concepts more abstract and ordering them into the theory

FIGURE 13.3
Grounded theory model of clients engaging in therapy.
(From Ward, 2005.)

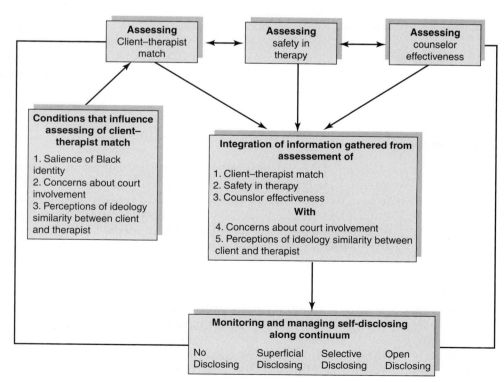

Selective coding
Third and final stage of data analysis in GT in which the theory is finalized

Theoretical saturation
Occurs when no new information relevant to the GT is emerging from the data and the GT has been sufficiently validated

theory) is "complete" when **theoretical saturation** occurs. Theoretical saturation is present when no new concepts are emerging from additional data, the theory makes sense of the data, and the theory is well validated.

The final report should include a detailed description of the topic and procedures as in any research study. The concepts found in the data should be presented and defined, and examples clarifying each concept should be provided. This usually requires inclusion of participant quotations for clarity and evidence. Most importantly, the report must include a clear description of the grounded theory. An important part of this description is a visual depiction of the grounded theory model that was developed from the data (such as the model shown in Figure 13.2).

In Figure 13.3, we provide the depiction of the grounded theory developed by Ward (2005). Ward focused on how African American clients experienced and interacted with therapists in a community mental health agency. As shown in the figure, the clients made continual assessments. They assessed the client–therapist match (which was affected by three factors shown in the figure), they assessed their personal safety in therapy, and they evaluated the ongoing effectiveness of the therapy. This information was cognitively integrated by the clients, and this integrative mediating process affected client self-disclosure during therapy sessions. Model building of this sort is an important part of science, whether it is done through grounded theory or some other approach. Grounded therapy offers one way to conduct this initial theory-building process. Remember, however, that it is essential that grounded theory models be tested (and modified as needed) with new data in order to improve the models and to justify one's belief that the models are correct and can be applied beyond the original research participants.

STUDY QUESTION 13.2 | **What are the characteristics of each of the four major methods of qualitative research? What topic might one investigate with each qualitative method, and why?**

Mixed Research

Compatibility thesis
Position that quantitative and qualitative research methods and philosophies can be combined

As defined above, *mixed methods research* is the research approach in which quantitative *and* qualitative data or techniques are combined or mixed in a single research study or in a set of closely related studies. Mixed methods research is the third major research methodology, but it is also the newest methodology (after quantitative research and qualitative research) and, therefore, is the least developed at present. Mixed methods research as discussed here has only recently been systematically and formally developed (Johnson et al., 2007; Tashakkori & Teddlie, 2003). Although much of its potential still is to be realized in practice, mixed methods research often offers an attractive approach to research because it can be used to strengthen both quantitative and qualitative research. Some of the strengths and weaknesses that have been proposed are listed in Table 13.4.

Proponents of mixed methods research typically adhere to a compatibility thesis and follow the philosophy of pragmatism. In this context, the **compatibility thesis** is the idea that quantitative and qualitative methods are

TABLE 13.4

Strengths and Weaknesses of Mixed Methods Research

Strengths:

- Can provide multiple sources of evidence
- Can reduce alternative explanations of a finding
- Can help provide multiple types of validity in a single study
- Can elucidate divergent aspects of a phenomenon
- Can provide fuller, deeper, more complex, and more comprehensive explanation
- Can provide both an emic perspective (i.e., insider's perspective) *and* the etic perspective (i.e., objective outsider's perspective)
- Can identify mediating mechanisms and moderating factors for later testing
- Can help connect theory to practice (i.e., general to specific)
- Can compensate for the weaknesses of one method by the systematic inclusion of another method
- Can provide stronger inferences
- Can illuminate subjective meaning that can be missed in purely quantitative research
- Can be used to check the implementation of a study (including its meaning to the participants)
- Can be used to check the operation and meaning of measurement instruments
- Can provide rich, detailed, subjective data *and* objective quantitative data in the same study
- Can add an exploratory dimension to theory/hypothesis testing research (or vice versa)

Weaknesses:

- Requires skill in both quantitative and qualitative research by a single researcher or the use of a mixed research team
- Can be more time consuming and expensive
- Because it's a new methodology, many design, implementation, and analysis procedures remain to be fully worked out

Pragmatism

Philosophy focusing on what works as the criterion of what should be viewed as tentatively true and useful in research and practice

complementary and can be used effectively together in a single research study. That is, quantitative and qualitative research approaches can be used together in a single research study to address a single research question or a set of related research questions. The philosophy of **pragmatism** (which is a part of the philosophy of naturalism discussed in Chapter 1) provides empirical justification for the use of mixed approaches to the degree that they work in practice and produce desired outcomes. According to this philosophy, it is an "empirical question" whether combining or mixing quantitative and qualitative approaches is justified in practice.

Mixed Methods Designs

Mixed methods (MM) research designs can be based on many different design factors. However, we present a relatively simple design typology that can be used as the starting point for constructing your mixed methods design. Our design

Time order
One of the two dimensions used in MM design matrix; its levels are concurrent and sequential

Paradigm emphasis
One of the two dimensions used in MM design matrix; its levels are equal status and dominant status

scheme classifies design on two dimensions. The first dimension is **time order**, and it has two levels: *concurrent* (the quantitative and qualitative parts are conducted at approximately the same time) and *sequential* (the quantitative and qualitative parts are conducted one after another). The second dimension is **paradigm emphasis**, and it has two levels: *equal status* (the quantitative and qualitative approaches are given equal emphasis) and dominant status (one approach is given primary emphasis).

The two dimensions of time order and paradigm emphasis produce a 2-by-2 design matrix shown in Figure 13.4. The design matrix includes nine specific designs.

In order to understand the designs, you must first understand the notation. Here is an explanation of the notation:

- QUAN and quan both stand for quantitative research.
- QUAL and qual both stand for qualitative research.
- Capital letters denote priority or increased weight or emphasis.
- Lowercase letters denote lower priority or weight or emphasis.
- A plus sign (+) indicates the concurrent conduct of the quantitative and qualitative parts (e.g., collection of data).
- An arrow (→) represents a sequential conduct of the quantitative and qualitative parts (e.g., collection of data).

Now we will use the notation. Here is a design: qual→QUAN. Using the notation, you can see that this refers to a quantitative dominant status, sequential mixed methods design. The overall study would be primarily quantitative in emphasis, and the qualitative part would precede the quantitative part or phase. A researcher might use this design to explore the factors related to employees leaving an organization. Based on the factors identified in the exploratory phase with employees who have left the organization and on the relevant turnover research literature, the researcher could construct a structured questionnaire for predicting turnover in the organization. Then, in phase two, the researcher could

FIGURE 13.4
The mixed methods design matrix.

Paradigm Emphasis	Time Order: Concurrent	Time Order: Sequential
Equal status	QUAL + QUAN	QUAL → QUAN QUAN → QUAL
Dominant status	QUAL + quan QUAN + qual	QUAL → quan qual → QUAN QUAN → qual quan → QUAL

select a random sample of employees (or use all employees if the organization is not too large) and have the sample participants complete the instrument. Then the organizational researcher could start testing the predictive validity of the instrument by checking to see if it accurately predicts turnover during the next six months. In this example, the quantitative part was primary and the qualitative part was supportive. The qualitative part also occurred first because it was a sequential design.

There are eight more designs in Figure 13.4, which is far too many to memorize. However, to use the figure, you just need to answer two questions: (1) To best meet your research objective, should you operate largely within one methodological paradigm or treat them equally? (2) Should you conduct the phases of your study concurrently (i.e., at roughly the same time) or sequentially? After answering those two questions, look at the appropriate cell in Figure 13.4 and determine which design will best fit your research needs.

When deciding how to structure the quantitative and qualitative parts of your study, you will need to think about three key issues. First, you must determine what kind of quantitative and qualitative data will best address your research question(s). Second, try to use a mixture or combination of quantitative and qualitative methods that has *complementary strengths and nonoverlapping weaknesses*. This second point provides a logic for your design so that you don't just randomly put together quantitative and qualitative elements. Third, always remember that mixed research is not an excuse to rely on weak quantitative or weak qualitative methods.

In conclusion, it is important to understand that you are not limited to the mixed methods designs provided here. Our designs were provided to get you started. You should feel free to mix and match other characteristics into a mixed methods research design that best fits your needs. Your goal, always, is to answer your research question(s) and to design a study that will help you to do that well. There is much more that we could have discussed here. Currently, the second edition of the *Handbook of Mixed Methods Research* is being produced (Tashakkori & Teddlie, in press) and will be out about the same time as our textbook. This handbook will provide the latest and best resource for additional information about mixed methods designs, sampling strategies, validity strategies, and so forth. Again, however, if you construct a mixed methods design that addresses your research question(s) and conduct both parts well, then you will be okay for your first mixed methods study. It is essential however that you use quantitative, qualitative, and mixed methods research validity strategies during the conduct of your study, and you must at some point integrate the quantitative and qualitative findings if you are to call your study a mixed methods research study.

STUDY QUESTION 13.3 | **What is mixed methods research? What are the basic designs?**

Summary

Most of this book focuses on quantitative research. However, this chapter explains qualitative research and mixed methods research. The differences between these three major methodologies are summarized in Table 13.1. Most simply, however, quantitative research relies on quantitative data, qualitative research relies on qualitative data, and mixed methods research relies on quantitative and qualitative data. Patton's 12 major characteristics of qualitative research are summarized in Table 13.2. The major types of validity in qualitative research are *descriptive validity* (factual accuracy of the account provided by the researcher), *interpretive validity* (degree to which the researcher accurately portrays the participants' subjective viewpoints and meanings), and *theoretical validity* (degree to which the theory or explanation developed fits the data). Qualitative research treats internal validity differently than quantitative research. Qualitative research is only interested in local or *ideographic causation.* Quantitative research is focused on general or lawlike or *nomological causation.* The traditional and primary purpose of science is to understand nomological causation. Regarding external validity, qualitative research is usually *not* interested in making generalizations. When they speak of generalizing, qualitative researchers recommend *naturalistic generalizations*—this occurs when a reader of a research report generalizes from the people in the study to other people based on their similarity. Table 13.3 shows the validity strategies that should be used in qualitative research to help obtain the various types of validity and produce a strong qualitative study rather than a weak or flawed qualitative study.

Four major qualitative research methods were discussed next. First, *phenomenology* is the qualitative approach in which the researcher attempts to understand and describe how one or more research participants subjectively experience a phenomenon such as the death of a loved one. The most commonly used method of data collection is in-depth interviews. Second, *ethnography* is the qualitative approach that focuses on the discovery and description of the *culture* of a group of people. The focus can also be on describing cultural scenes. It is important that the ethnographer understand and depict the *emic* (i.e., the insider's) perspective *and* the *etic* (i.e., the objective outsider's) perspective. Ethnographic interviews and participant observation are commonly used methods of data collection in ethnographic research. Third, *case study research* is the qualitative research method in which the researcher provides a detailed description and account of one or more cases. Three case study designs are *intrinsic case studies* (where the focus is only on the particular case), *instrumental case studies* (where the focus is on understanding something more than just the case), and *collective* or *comparative case studies* (where the focus is on comparing cases). Fourth, *grounded theory* is the methodology for generating and developing a theory that is grounded in the particular data. It is helpful for discovery, when little is known about a topic or process.

Mixed methods research was also covered. Mixed methods research is the type of research in which quantitative and qualitative data or approaches are combined in a single study. A major strength of mixed methods research is that it can combine the strengths of quantitative and qualitative research and minimize their weaknesses (through combination) in a single research study. Its primary weakness is that it is more difficult to conduct (because you must be an expert in both quantitative and qualitative research) and is more expensive. Additional strengths and weaknesses of mixed methods research are summarized in Table 13.4. A 2-by-2 matrix of mixed methods research designs was presented.

Key Terms and Concepts

Axial coding
Case
Case study
Collective case study
Comparative case study
Compatibility thesis
Cross-case analysis
Culture
Data triangulation
Descriptive validity
Emic perspective
Essence
Ethnocentric
Ethnography
Etic perspective
Extended fieldwork
Fieldnotes
Fieldwork
Gatekeepers
Going native
Grounded theory
Holism
Ideographic causation
Instrumental case study
Interpretive validity
Intrinsic case study
Investigator triangulation
Life world
Low-inference descriptors
Methods triangulation

Mixed methods research
Naturalistic generalization
Negative-case sampling
Nomological causation
Norms
Open coding
Paradigm emphasis
Participant feedback
Participant observation
Pattern matching
Peer review
Phenomenology
Pragmatism
Qualitative research
Reactive effect
Reflexivity
Researcher bias
Researcher-as-detective
Selective coding
Shared beliefs
Shared values
Significant statements
Theoretical generalization
Theoretical saturation
Theoretical sensitivity
Theoretical validity
Theory
Theory triangulation
Time order

Related Internet Sites

http://www.phenomenologycenter.org/index.html
This site has a wealth of information about phenomenology.

http://www.groundedtheory.com/
Web site of one of the founders of grounded theory.

http://www.lcweb.loc.gov/folklife/other.html
Resources for ethnography.

http://writing.colostate.edu/guides/research/casestudy/pop2f.cfm
Case study research links.

http://www.qualitativeresearch.uga.edu/QualPage/
Lots of materials on qualitative research are found at this link.

http://mmr.sagepub.com/
Link to the *Journal of Mixed Methods Research*.

Practice Test   *The answers to these questions can be found in Appendix.*

1. Which of the following is characteristic of qualitative research?

    a. Operational measures of constructs
    b. Context sensitivity
    c. Importance of generalization to populations
    d. A priori hypotheses

2. Which of the following is characteristic of qualitative research?

    a. Interpersonal distance from participants
    b. Control of variables
    c. Statistical analysis
    d. Personal contact and insight

3. The primary method of data collection used in phenomenological research is:

    a. In-depth interviews
    b. Participant observation
    c. Analysis of standardized tests
    d. Multiple methods

4. The disciplinary origin of ethnography is:

    a. Psychology
    b. Education
    c. Anthropology
    d. Philosophy

5. The purpose of a grounded theory study is to:

    a. Describe cultural characteristics
    b. Inductively generate a theory
    c. Describe one or more individuals' experiences of a phenomenon
    d. Describe one or more cases in depth

6. Which is true about this design: QUAL→QUAN

    a. It is an equal-status concurrent mixed methods research design
    b. It is an equal-status sequential mixed methods research design
    c. It is a dominant-status concurrent mixed methods research design
    d. It is a dominant-status sequential mixed methods research design

Challenge Exercises

1. A researcher wants to understand why people are willing to handle snakes as a part of their church activities in several rural churches in Tennessee, Alabama, and Georgia.

    How would you study this phenomenon? (HINT: Apply ideas and concepts from qualitative and or mixed methods research.)

2. Locate a published qualitative or mixed methods research journal article, and answer the following questions:

    a. What was the research about?

    b. What qualitative research method did the researcher use? Give some detail to document this.

    c. Summarize the research findings.

    d. What is your personal evaluation of this research article?

    e. What are the primary strengths of this article?

    f. What are the primary weaknesses of this article?

    g. What would be a good follow-up study? (HINT: Perhaps a study that eliminates the weaknesses you identified would be a good follow-up study.)

CHAPTER 14

Descriptive Statistics

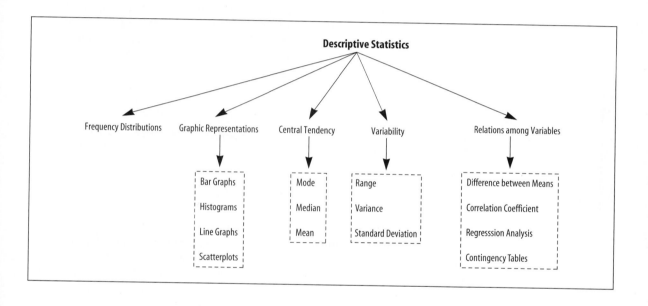

In this vignette, we demonstrate how statistical analysis, if not conducted properly, can deceive people. Our example is based on a real case of purported gender discrimination at the University of California, Berkeley, several decades ago. The example is written up in *Science* (Bickel, 1975). The data shown below refer to men and women admitted to graduate school in the Department of Psychology at a hypothetical university. Take a moment to examine the data in Exhibit 14.1. Notice that 55% of the men who applied to this department were admitted to graduate school, but only 45% of the women who applied were admitted. Let's assume that their qualifications were the same. If this were the case, one might conclude that gender discrimination has occurred because men had a much higher rate of acceptance than women.

EXHIBIT 14.1

	Number Applied	Number Admitted	Percentage Admitted
Men	180	99	55
Women	100	45	45

Now, assume that the 280 students applying to the Psychology Department applied to two different graduate programs; each student applied either to the doctoral program in clinical psychology or the doctoral program in experimental psychology. The researcher decides to break down the data separately for each program, and obtains the two tables in Exhibit 14.2. What do you see in these tables? We now see that women (not men) had the higher acceptance rates in both degree programs! If there is any discrimination, it is in favor of the women applicants. What's going on?

EXHIBIT 14.2

	Clinical Psychology Program				Experimental Psychology Program		
	Number Applied	Number Admitted	Percentage Admitted		Number Applied	Number Admitted	Percentage Admitted
Men	60	9	15%	Men	120	90	75
Women	60	12	20%	Women	40	32	80

The overall data (Exhibit 14.1) suggested one conclusion, but when the data were more carefully analyzed (they were "disaggregated"), a completely different conclusion became apparent. How could it be that opposite conclusions are suggested in the two exhibits based on the same data? The answer is that a statistical phenomenon known as *Simpson's Paradox* has occurred. It happened because the women tended to apply to the program that was harder to get into, but the men tended to apply to the program that was easier to get into. The aggregated (Exhibit 14.1) suggested one conclusion, but the disaggregated (Exhibit 14.2) data produce an opposite and more accurate conclusion. The moral of this story is to be cautious when you examine and interpret descriptive data and to always look at the data critically and in multiple ways until you are able to draw the most warranted conclusion.

Introduction

The opening vignette to this chapter reveals the importance of intelligent statistical analysis of data in psychological research. During the conduct of a research study, the researcher collects the data on the variables of interest and then enters the data into a statistical software program such as SPSS or SAS. Statistical software makes the process of quantitative data analysis much simpler than in years past because the program does all of the calculations. Statistics, for research psychologists, are tools that assist in making sense of the research results and in making decisions in the face of uncertainty.

FIGURE 14.1
Major Divisions of the field of statistics.

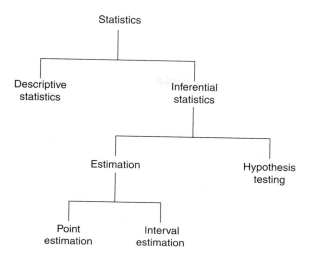

The field of statistics can be divided into the two broad categories called descriptive statistics and inferential statistics. In **descriptive statistics**, the goal is to describe or summarize your research data. This allows you to make sense of your set of data and to make the key characteristics easily understandable to others. In **inferential statistics**, the goal is to go beyond the immediate set of data and to infer characteristics of populations based on your sample data. As you can see in Figure 14.1, inferential statistics can be subdivided into estimation and hypothesis testing, and estimation can be subdivided into point and interval estimation.

In this chapter, we will explain descriptive statistical analysis, and in Chapter 15, we will explain inferential statistical analysis. We assume no prior knowledge of the material, and both chapters are written so that everyone can understand the material. Our discussion requires very little mathematical background, so don't worry! We focus on showing you what statistical procedures to select to understand your data and on how to interpret and communicate your results.

Descriptive statistics
The type of statistical analysis focused on describing, summarizing, or explaining a set of data

Inferential statistics
The type of statistical analysis focused on making inferences about populations based on sample data

Descriptive Statistics

Data set
A set of data, where the rows are "cases" and the columns are "variables"

Descriptive statistics starts with a set of data (called a **data set**). The researcher uses descriptive statistics to understand and summarize the key numerical characteristics of the data set. For example, you might calculate the averages of your experimental and control group scores in an experiment. Or if you conducted a survey, you might want to know the frequencies for each question. You might also want to use graphs to pictorially communicate some of your results. In the next chapter, which is on inferential statistics, you will learn how to determine if the difference between the experimental and control groups means is statistically significant and if other observed results are statistically significant. In this chapter, we focus on taking whatever set of data you currently have and showing how to summarize the key characteristics of the data. Here is the key question in descriptive statistics: How can I communicate the important characteristics of my data? One way would be to supply a printout of all of your data, but that would be very inefficient. We can communicate much better than that!

We have included a data set in Table 14.1 that we will use in several places in this chapter. We refer to this data set as the "college graduate data set." We will hypothetically say that these data came from a survey research study that you conducted with 25 recent college graduates. In the questionnaire used to collect the data, you asked participants about their starting salaries, undergraduate GPA, college major (you only surveyed three majors), gender, the SAT scores they had when they entered college, and the number of days they believe they missed during college. The goal in this survey research study was to determine what variables predicted the starting salaries of psychology, philosophy, and business majors.

Take a moment now to examine the data set shown in Table 14.1. Notice that it includes four quantitative variables (salary, GPA, SAT scores, days of school missed)

TABLE 14.1

Hypothetical Data Set for Nonexperimental Research for 25 Recent College Graduates

Person	Salary	GPA	Major	Gender	SAT	Days
1	24,000	2.5	1	0	1,110	36
2	25,000	2.5	1	0	1,100	26
3	27,500	3.0	1	0	1,300	31
4	28,500	2.4	2	1	1,100	18
5	30,500	3.0	2	0	1,150	26
6	30,500	2.9	2	1	1,130	18
7	31,000	3.1	1	0	1,180	16
8	31,000	3.3	1	0	1,160	11
9	31,500	2.9	2	0	1,170	25
10	32,000	3.6	1	0	1,250	12
11	32,000	2.6	1	1	1,230	26
12	32,500	3.1	2	0	1,130	21
13	32,500	3.2	2	1	1,200	17
14	32,500	3.0	3	1	1,150	14
15	33,000	3.7	1	0	1,260	29
16	33,500	3.1	2	1	1,170	21
17	33,500	2.7	2	1	1,140	22
18	34,500	3.0	3	0	1,240	14
19	35,500	3.1	3	0	1,330	16
20	36,500	3.5	2	1	1,220	0
21	37,500	3.4	3	1	1,150	4
22	38,500	3.2	2	0	1,270	10
23	38,500	3.0	3	1	1,300	0
24	40,500	3.3	3	1	1,280	5
25	41,500	3.5	3	1	1,330	2

Note: For the categorical variable "major," 1 = psychology, 2 = philosophy, and 3 = business. For the categorical variable "gender," 1 = male and 2 = female.

and two categorical variables (college major and gender). This data set is set up in the standard format in which cases are shown in rows and variables are shown in columns. When you have data, you can enter them into a spreadsheet such as Excel (which can be used by a statistical program such as SPSS) or you can directly enter your data in the "spreadsheet" feature in SPSS. We used the popular statistical program SPSS for most of the analyses in this and the next chapter. Most universities provide access to SPSS or another statistical program in their computer labs.

Frequency Distributions

Frequency distribution

Data arrangement in which the frequencies of each unique data value is shown

One basic way to represent the data values for a variable is to use a frequency distribution. A **frequency distribution** is a systematic arrangement of data values in which the unique data values are rank ordered and the frequencies are provided for each of these values. Oftentimes, the percentages for each frequency are also included in a frequency distribution. The first column shows the unique data values for the variable, the second column the frequencies for each of these values, and the third column the percentages.

For example, look at Table 14.2. This is the frequency distribution of the variable *starting salary* from our college graduate data set. You can see that in column 1 the

TABLE 14.2
Frequency Distribution of Staring Salary

(1) Starting Salary	(2) Frequency	(3) Percentage
24,000.00	1	4.0
25,000.00	1	4.0
27,500.00	1	4.0
28,500.00	1	4.0
30,500.00	2	8.0
31,000.00	2	8.0
31,500.00	1	4.0
32,000.00	2	8.0
32,500.00	3	12.0
33,000.00	1	4.0
33,500.00	2	8.0
34,500.00	1	4.0
35,500.00	1	4.0
36,500.00	1	4.0
37,500.00	1	4.0
38,500.00	2	8.0
40,500.00	1	4.0
41,500.00	1	4.0
	$N = 25$	100.0%

Note: column 2 shows the "frequency distribution," and column 3 shows the "percentage distribution."

lowest salary is $24,000 and the highest is $41,000. The frequencies are shown in column 2. The most frequently occurring salary for our sample of recent college graduates was $32,500; three of the 25 recent graduates had this starting salary. The third column shows the percentage distribution. Four percent of the 25 cases had a salary of $24,000, and 8% of the cases had a salary of $32,000.

Graphic Representations of Data

Graphs are pictorial representations of data. Graphs can be used for one variable or for more than one variable. Although not frequently used in published research, some researchers like to use graphs to help communicate the nature of their data. For example, program evaluators often include graphs in their reports because their clients often like to see graphic representations of the data.

Bar Graphs

Bar graph
Graph that uses vertical bars to represent the data values of a categorical variable

One simple graph is a **bar graph**, which uses vertical bars to represent the data. Bar graphs are used with categorical variables. In Figure 14.2, you can see a bar graph of the categorical variable *college major* from our college graduate data set. Notice that the horizontal axis shows the three categories in the variable, and the frequencies of each category are shown on the vertical axis. The bars provide graphical representations of the frequencies of the three majors in our data set. Eight of the recent graduates were psychology majors, ten were philosophy majors, and seven were business majors. You can easily convert these numbers into percentages if you so desire: 32% were psychology majors (8 divided by 25), 40% were philosophy majors (10 divided by 25), and 28% were business majors (7 divided by 25).

FIGURE 14.2
A bar graph of undergraduate major.

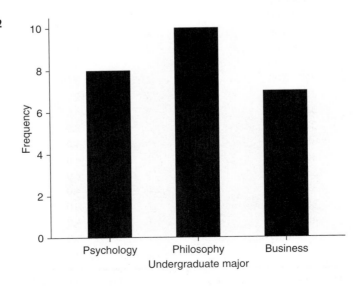

Histograms

Histogram
Graph depicting
frequencies and
distribution of a
quantitative
variable

Bar graphs are used when you have a categorical variable. Histograms are used for quantitative variables. A **histogram** is a presentation of a frequency distribution in bar format. It has the advantage over a frequency distribution in that it more clearly shows the shape of the distribution of values. You can see the histogram for starting salary (from our college graduate data set) in Figure 14.3. Notice that, in contrast to bar graphs, the bars in histograms are placed next to each other with no space in between.

Line Graphs

Line graph
A graph relying on
the drawing of one
or more lines

A useful way to graphically depict the distribution of a quantitative variable is to construct a line graph. A **line graph** is a graph that relies on the drawing of one or more lines. You can see the line graph of starting salary in Figure 14.4. Line graphs are also useful to visually show and aid in the interpretation of interaction effects in experiments (as well as other types of research).

Let's say that you conducted an experiment to test a new social skills training program that you have developed. You use a pretest–posttest control group design (i.e., you randomly assigned your participants to the treatment and control groups and measured the performance of both of these groups before and after the treatment group received social skills training). Your dependent variable is the number of appropriate social interactions the participants performed, which you measured at the pretest and again at the posttest. The independent variable is training (training vs. no training). The data from your experiment are shown in Table 14.3.

FIGURE 14.3
Histogram of starting salary.

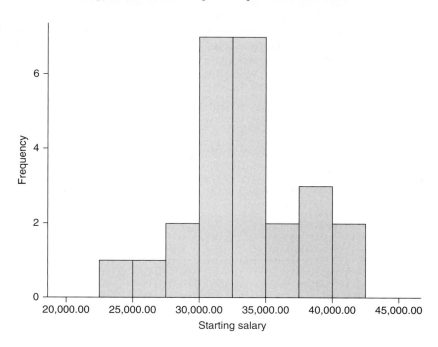

FIGURE 14.4
Line graph of starting
salary.

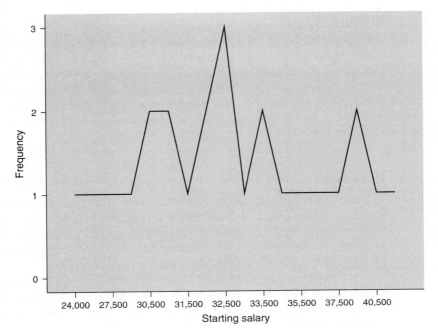

TABLE 14.3
**Hypothetical Data Set for Experimental Research Study Examining
the Effectiveness of Social Skills Training**

Person	Pretest Scores	Treatment Condition	Posttest Scores
1	3	1	4
2	4	1	4
3	2	1	3
4	1	1	2
5	1	1	2
6	0	1	0
7	2	1	2
8	4	1	4
9	4	1	4
10	3	1	4
11	2	1	3
12	5	1	5
13	3	1	3
14	3	1	3
15	2	2	4
16	3	2	5
17	1	2	2

Person	Pretest Scores	Treatment Condition	Posttest Scores
18	2	2	4
19	1	2	2
20	2	2	4
21	2	2	3
22	3	2	5
23	5	2	6
24	2	2	4
25	4	2	2
26	4	2	5
27	2	2	4
28	5	2	6

Note: pretest = number of appropriate interactions at beginning of the experiment; posttest = number of appropriate interactions after the experimental intervention; treatment condition = 1 for received social skills training and 2 for did not receive social skills training.

Some of the results of this hypothetical experiment are shown in Figure 14.5. We have used a line graph to show what happened in your research study. Looking at the line graph you can see that both groups started low on the number of appropriate skills they exhibited. That is, everyone was low on the dependent variable at the start of the experiment. At the end of the study, after the treatment group received social skills training, we see a very different result; the participants in the treatment group have higher scores than the participants in the control group. The graph shows that the number of appropriate social skills demonstrated

FIGURE 14.5
Line graph of results from pretest–posttest control group design studying effectiveness of social skills treatment.

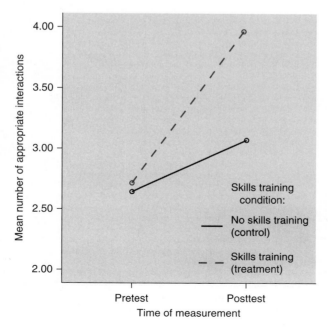

increased for the treatment group, but not (or very little) for the control group. In short, this line graph is what you had hoped for because it shows that your treatment seems to work. Actually, there is one more step. You must also determine if the result is statistically significant. We will show you how to get this piece of information in the next chapter.

Scatterplots

Scatterplot

A graphical depiction of the relationship between two quantitative variables

A **scatterplot** is a graph used to depict the relationship between two quantitative variables. By convention, we always put the dependent variable on the vertical axis and the independent or predictor variable on the horizontal axis. The dots within the graph represent the cases (i.e., participants) in the data set.

You can see a scatterplot of the two quantitative variables grade point average and starting salary in Figure 14.6. Following agreed-upon convention in research, we put the independent (predictor) variable on the horizontal axis and the dependent variable on the vertical axis. You can see in the scatterplot that there appears to be a positive relationship between GPA and starting salary, because as GPA increases, starting salary also increases. When you have a positive relationship, the data values tend to start at the bottom left side of the graph and end at the top right side.

The scatterplot of days of school missed during college and starting salary is shown in Figure 14.7. You can see in this scatterplot that there appears to be a negative relationship between days missed and starting salary because as days missed increases starting salary decreases. With a negative relationship, the data values tend to start at the top left side of the graph and end at the lower right side.

FIGURE 14.6
A scatterplot of starting salary by college GPA.

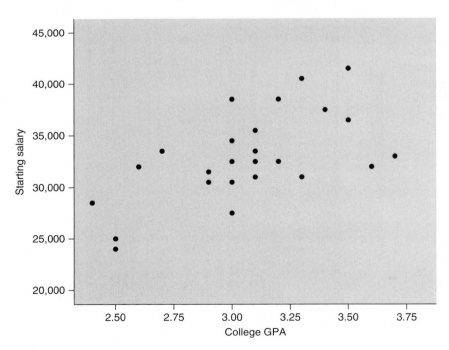

FIGURE 14.7
Depiction of a
negative
relationship.

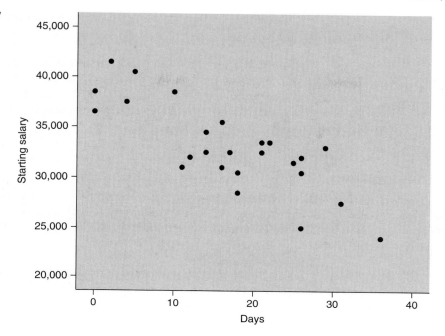

STUDY QUESTION 14.1 **What is descriptive statistics? What are the techniques (discussed thus far) for describing variables? When are these techniques used?**

Measures of Central Tendency

Measure of central tendency
Numerical value expressing what is typical of the values of a quantitative variable

One of the most important ways to describe and understand data is to obtain measures of central tendency. A **measure of central tendency** is the single numerical value that is considered most typical of the values of a quantitative variable. For example, your college GPA is the value expressing what is typical for your grades. The three most common measures of central tendency are the mode, the median, and the mean.

Mode

Mode
The most frequently occurring number

The most basic, and the crudest, measure of central tendency is the mode. The **mode** is the most frequently occurring number for a variable. For example, in the following set of numbers

0, 2, 3, 4, 5, 5, 5, 7, 8, 8, 9, 10

the mode is 5 because 5 is the most frequently occurring number. Five occurs three times. If there is a tie for the most frequently occurring number, then you would need to report both and point out that the data for the variable are bimodal.

For practice, determine the mode for the following set of numbers:

1, 2, 2, 5, 5, 7, 10, 10, 10

If you said 10, then you are right. Notice that the mode in this case is not a very good indicator of the central tendency of the data. If the data are normally distributed where most people fall toward the center of the distribution of numbers, then the mode works much better than in this case. In practice, research psychologists rarely use the mode.

Median

Median
The center point in an ordered set of numbers

The **median** is the center point in a set of numbers that has been arranged in ascending or descending order. If you have an odd number of numbers, the median is the middle number. For example, in the following numbers

1, 2, 3, 4, 5

the median is 3. If you have an even number of numbers, the median is the average of the two centermost numbers. (Remember, you must put the numbers in order before locating the center number of numbers.) For example, in the following numbers

1, 2, 3, 4

the median is 2.5 because 2.5 is the average of the two centermost numbers (i.e., the average of 2 and 3 is 2.5). An interesting property of the median is that it is not affected by the size of the highest and lowest numbers. For example, the median of 1, 2, 3, 4, 5 is the same as the median of 1, 2, 3, 4, 500. In both cases the median is 3!

Mean

Mean
The arithmetic average

The **mean** is the name researchers use to refer to the arithmetic average. You already know how to calculate the mean (i.e., the average). The average of 1, 2, and 3 is 2, right? Here is what you actually did when you calculated the mean: $(1 + 2 + 3)/3$. Psychologists sometimes refer to the mean as $\bar{X}$ (called X bar). Here is our formula for getting the mean:

$$\text{Mean} = \frac{\sum X}{n}$$

The formula is easy if you note that "X" stands for the variable you are using, "n" is the number of numbers you have, and "Σ" is a sum sign (it says to add up the numbers that follow it). In our simple case where the three values of our variable are 1, 2, and 3, the formula is applied as follows:

$$\text{Mean} = \frac{\sum X}{n} = \frac{1 + 2 + 3}{3} = \frac{6}{3} = 2$$

Psychologists frequently calculate the means for the groups that they want to compare, such as the mean performance level for treatment and control groups. Take a moment to look again at Figure 14.5. Each of the four points in the graph is a group mean. The four points are the means for the treatment and the control groups at the pretest and the means for these two groups at the posttest. We plotted the means to help you interpret the results of the experiment. Those results suggest that the treatment worked: at the pretest the means for the treatment and the control groups were low, but following the intervention, the mean for the treatment group was much higher and the mean for the control group showed little change.

Measures of Variability

Measure of variability
Numerical value expressing how spread out or how much variation is present in the values of a quantitative variable

In the previous section, you learned about the measures of central tendency which tell you what is typical for a variable. However, it is also important to find out how much your data values are spread out (i.e., how different they are). That is, you want to know how much variability is present. A **measure of variability** is defined as a numerical index that provides information about how spread out or how much variation is present in a variable.

If all of the data values for a variable were the same, then there is no variability. For example, there is no variability in these numbers:

4, 4, 4, 4, 4, 4, 4, 4, 4, 4

There is variability in these numbers:

1, 2, 3, 3, 4, 4, 4, 6, 8, 10

The more different your numbers, the more variability you have. Now, let's test your understanding of variability. Which of the following sets of data have the most variability present?

Data for group one: 44, 45, 45, 45, 46, 46, 47, 47, 48, 49

Data for group two: 34, 37, 45, 51, 58, 60, 77, 88, 90, 98

As you can see, the data for group two have more variability than group one. Sometimes when there is little variability in a group, we say that the scores are homogeneous. When the scores show a lot of variability, we say that the scores are heterogeneous.

Now we introduce you to three of the types of variability that psychologists might examine in their data. We examine the range, the variance, and the standard deviation.

Range

Range
The highest number minus the lowest number

The simplest measure of variability, but also the most crude, is the range. The **range** is the highest (i.e., largest) number minus the lowest (i.e., smallest) number in a set of numbers. Here is the formula:

Range $= H - L$

where

H is the highest number, and

L is the lowest number.

For example, in the data for group one shown in the previous section above, the range is equal to 5 (49 minus 44). Now take a moment and determine the range for the data for group two shown above. If you said the range is 64, you are correct. The highest number is 98 and the lowest is 34, and the difference between these two numbers is 64. The range is a crude index of variability because it takes into account only two numbers (the highest and the lowest). Now we introduce you to the measures of variability that research psychologists more frequently use.

Variance and Standard Deviation

The two most popular measures of variability are the variance and the standard deviation. They are superior to the range because they take into account all of the data values for a variable. They both provide information about the dispersion or variation around the mean value of a variable.

Variance
The average deviation of data values from their mean in squared units

The **variance** is the average deviation of the data values from their mean in "squared units." The variance is popular because it has nice mathematical properties. To turn the variance into more meaningful units, you can obtain the **standard deviation**. To calculate the standard deviation, you take the square root of the variance (i.e., you put the value of the variance into your calculator and press the square root key). The standard deviation (i.e., the square root of the variance) is an approximate indicator of the average distance that your data values are from their mean. (If you have a mean of 5 and a standard deviation of 2, then the data values tend to be approximately 2 units above or below 5.) For the variance and the standard deviation, the larger the value, the greater the data are spread out; the smaller the value, the less the data are spread out.

Standard deviation
The square root of the variance

We show you how to calculate the variance and standard deviation in Table 14.4. We wanted the variance and standard deviation of the numbers 2, 4, 6, 8, and 10. As shown in Table 14.4, the variance of these five numbers is 8, and the standard deviation is 2.83. In other words, the average distance of the numbers from their mean in squared units is 8, and the approximate average distance of the numbers from their mean in regular units is 2.83. If the numbers would have been more spread out, the variance and standard deviations would have been bigger; if the numbers had been less spread out, the variance and standard deviations would have been smaller.

Normal Distribution
A theoretical distribution that follows the 68, 95, 99.7 percent rule

68, 95, 99.7 percent rule
Rule stating percentage of cases falling within 1, 2, and 3 standard deviations from the mean on a normal distribution

Standard Deviation and the Normal Curve. If the data were fully normally distributed, the standard deviation would have additional meaning. Examine the standard normal distribution in Figure 14.8, and you will see that the normal curve or **normal distribution** has a bell shape; it is high in the middle and it tapers off to the left and the right. If the data were fully normally distributed, then you would be able to apply the "**68, 95, 99.7 percent rule**." This rule says that 68% of the cases fall within one standard deviation from the mean, 95% fall

T A B L E   1 4 . 4
Calculating the Variance and Standard Deviation

	(1)	(2)	(3)	(4)
	(X)	$(\bar{X})^*$	$(X - \bar{X})$	$(X - \bar{X})^2$
	2	6	−4	16
	4	6	−2	4
	6	6	0	0
	8	6	2	4
	<u>10</u>	6	<u>4</u>	<u>16</u>
	30		0	40
	↑			↑
Sums	ΣX			$\Sigma (X - \bar{X})^2$

Steps:
(1) Insert your data values in the *X* column.

(2) Calculate the mean of the values in column 1, and place this value in column 2. In our example, the mean is 6.

$$\bar{X} = \frac{30}{5} = 6.$$

(3) Subtract the values in column 2 from the values in column 1, and place these into column 3.

(4) Square the numbers in column 3 (i.e., multiply the number by itself), and place these in column 4. (Note: you can ignore the minus signs in column 3 because a negative number multiplied by a negative number produces a positive number.)

(5) Insert the appropriate values into the following formula for the variance:

$$\text{Variance} = \frac{\Sigma (X - \bar{X})^2}{n}$$

where
$\Sigma (X - \bar{X})^2$ is the sum of the numbers in column 4, and *n* is the number of numbers

In this example, the variance $= \dfrac{\Sigma (X - \bar{X})^2}{n} = \dfrac{40}{5} = 8$

(6) The standard deviation is the square root of the variance $(SD = \sqrt{\text{variance}})$. In this example, the variance is 8 (see step 5), and the standard deviation is 2.83 (i.e., the square root of 8 = 2.83).

within two standard deviations, and 99.7% fall within three standard deviations. Actually, the rule is a slight approximation because the more exact percentages are 68.26, 95.44, and 99.74, but the rule is easy to remember, and it is a very close approximation.

In practice, it is important to understand that sample data are never fully normally distributed in the sense of perfectly matching the normal distribution

FIGURE 14.8
Areas under the
normal distribution.

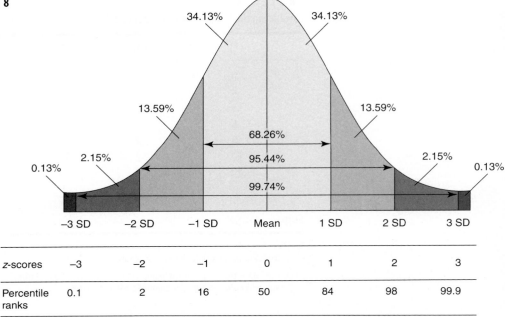

z-scores	−3	−2	−1	0	1	2	3
Percentile ranks	0.1	2	16	50	84	98	99.9

described here. That's because we have described what also can be called the theo-retical normal distribution. The theoretical normal distribution is what researchers are referring to when they report the degree to which their data are normally distributed. The normal distribution also has many applications in more advanced statistics courses.

z-scores: The last concept covered in this section is that researchers sometimes like to convert their observed data into a type of standardized scores called **z-scores**. These scores are the values for a variable that have been transformed from their original "raw scores" into a new "standardized" metric that has a mean of zero and a standard deviation of one. This is convenient because the data values now can be interpreted in terms of how far they are from their mean. If a data value is +1.00, one can say that this value falls one standard deviation above the mean, a value of +2.00 means it falls two standard deviations above the mean, a value of −1.5 means it falls one and a half standard deviations below the mean, and so on. "Standardized units" or "z-scores" were used with the normal curve just shown in Figure 14.8.

You can easily standardize your data using the following formula:

$$z\text{-score} = \frac{\text{raw score} - \text{mean}}{\text{standard deviation}} = \frac{X - \bar{X}}{SD}$$

To use this formula, you need the raw scores that you wish to convert to z-scores and you need to know the mean and standard deviation for the raw scores. For example, take the set of scores used in Table 14.4: 2, 4, 6, 8, 10. In Table 14.4, we showed that the mean of these five numbers was 6, and the standard deviation (which we

z-score
A score that has been transformed into standard deviation units

calculated in the table) was 2.83. Therefore, we can convert any or all of these numbers into z-scores. Here is the conversion of the last number, 10, to a z-score:

$$z\text{-score} = \frac{\text{raw score} - \text{mean}}{\text{standard deviation}} = \frac{10 - 6}{2.83} = \frac{4}{2.83} = 1.413$$

Therefore, the z-score for the number 10 is 1.41; this says that the value of 10 falls 1.41 standard deviations above the mean of its variable. Here is the conversion of the first number, 2, to a z-score:

$$z\text{-score} = \frac{\text{raw score} - \text{mean}}{\text{standard deviation}} = \frac{2 - 6}{2.83} = \frac{-4}{2.83} = -1.413$$

Therefore, the number 2 is 1.413 standard deviations *below* the mean. The negative sign indicates that that the number is below the mean.

You will recall that when we defined z-scores, we stated that for any set of z-scores the mean will always be zero and the standard deviation will be one. You can trust us or you can easily check us. Here are all of the z-scores for our set of five numbers: −1.413, −.707, 0, +.707, +1.413. You can see that the average of these numbers is zero. Next, to see if their standard deviation is equal to one, use the procedure shown in Table 14.4, and calculate the standard deviation of this set of z-scores. By the way, we checked, and yes, it worked. The key point here is that *you can take any set of numbers, convert the numbers to z-scores, and they will always have a mean of zero and a standard deviation of one.* This helps psychologists when they want to compare scores across different variables and different data sets and when they want to know how far a data value falls above or below the mean.

STUDY QUESTION 14.2 | **What are central tendency and variability? What are some measures of each of these? What are their strengths and weaknesses?**

Examining Relationships Among Variables

Rarely is a psychologist interested in a single variable. Psychologists typically are interested in determining whether independent and dependent variables are related. They use independent (or predictor) variables to "explain variance" in dependent (or outcome) variables. Determining what independent variables predict or cause changes in dependent variables is perhaps the primary goal of science. Then practitioners can apply this knowledge to produce changes in the world such as use new psychotherapy techniques to reduce mental illness or to determine how to predict who is "at risk" for future problems so that early interventions can be started.

In this last section, we will describe several approaches used to examine relationships among two or more variables. The vast majority of the time the dependent variable in psychological research is a quantitative variable (e.g., response time, performance level, level of neuronal activation). Therefore, most of the indexes of relationship described here are used for quantitative dependent variables. We will explain one exception in which you have a categorical dependent variable and a categorical independent (or predictor variable).

Unstandardized and Standardized Difference Between Group Means

When you have a quantitative dependent variable and a categorical independent variable, your first evidence on whether these variables are related is obtained by calculating the means on the dependent variable for each group making up the categorical variable and then comparing those means. The most direct and simplest way to determine the magnitude of difference between two means is to subtract one mean from another and examine the size of the difference. This is called the **unstandardized difference between means** because you use the natural units of the data. Then you make the decision about whether the difference between the means is large or small.

Unstandardized difference between means
The difference between two means in the variables' natural units

For example, in our college graduate data set, the mean (i.e., the average) starting salary for males is $34,791.67, and the mean starting salary for females is $31,269.23. Therefore, the unstandardized difference between these two means is $34,791.67 minus $31,269.23, which is $3,522.44. This appears to us to be a sizable difference between the two means. Another way of making this point is to state that "there appears to be a sizable relationship between gender and starting salary" in our data. In the next chapter, we will teach you how to determine if the difference between the means is "statistically significant"; for now, we are just interested in showing how to obtain descriptive information about your data.

To aid in deciding how different the group means are, the difference between the means is often transformed into a standardized measure. For group means, **Cohen's d** is a popular standardized measure of the difference between the means. Cohen's d is one of many effect size indicators that researchers use. An **effect size indicator** is a standardized measure of the magnitude or strength of a relationship between variables. We will tell you about some additional effect size indicators later; for now, we will focus on how to obtain Cohen's d. Here is the formula:

Cohen's d
The difference between two means in standard deviation units

Effect size indicator
Index of magnitude or strength of a relationship or difference between means

$$d = \frac{\text{mean difference}}{\text{standard deviation}} = \frac{M_1 - M_2}{SD}$$

where

M_1 is the mean for group 1

M_2 is the mean for group 2

SD is the standard deviation of either group (traditionally it's the control group's standard deviation in an experiment; some researchers prefer a pooled standard deviation)

As a rough starting point for interpreting d, Cohen defined effect sizes of $d = .2$ as "small," $d = .5$ as "medium," and $d = .8$ as "large." When you first start interpreting the sizes of Cohen's d, you can start with Cohen's criteria of .2, .5, and .8, but with experience you will learn how to adjust your interpretation based on additional information, such as the size of differences provided in published research on your topic.

Now let's calculate Cohen's d to compare the average male and female incomes from our college student data set. Gender is the categorical independent or predictor variable, and starting salary is the quantitative dependent variable. The mean starting salary for males is $34,791.67 and that for females is $31,269.23.

The unstandardized difference between the means is $3,522.44. Using a statistical program (i.e., SPSS), we determined that the standard deviation for females is $4,008.40. Now we have the three pieces of information needed to use the formula for Cohen's d. We have the two group means, and we have the standard deviation for the group we chose as our comparison group (i.e., females). Hear are the three pieces of information plugged into the formula.

$$d = \frac{M_1 - M_2}{SD} = \frac{\$34{,}791.67 - \$31{,}269.23}{\$4{,}008.40} = \frac{\$3{,}522.44}{\$4{,}008.40} = .88$$

Cohen's d is .88. This says that the mean starting salary for men is .88 standard deviations above the mean for females. Using Cohen's criteria for interpretation, one would consider this a "large" difference between the means. It is important to note, however, that Cohen did not want researchers to mindlessly use his criteria. In some research studies, a smaller Cohen's d would be considered a large or important effect. In this case, we agree that the value of .88 seems to be a large standardized difference between male and female salaries. For one more practice example, go to Exhibit 14.3 where we use Cohen's d to interpret the means plotted in Figure 14.5 for our experiment on the effectiveness of social skills training.

Correlation Coefficient

When you have a quantitative dependent variable and a quantitative independent variable, you need to either obtain a correlation coefficient or a regression coefficient. In this section, we explain the idea of a correlation coefficient. By definition, a **correlation coefficient** is a numerical index ranging from −1.00 to +1.00 that indicates the strength and direction of the linear relationship between two variables. The absolute size of the number indicates the strength of the correlation and the sign (positive or negative) indicates the direction of relationship. The endpoints, −1.00 and +1.00, stand for "perfect" correlations because they are the strongest possible correlations; zero indicates no correlation at all. Therefore, as you move away from zero in either direction, the correlation becomes stronger; stated differently, the closer you are to zero, the weaker the correlation. These ideas are depicted in Figure 14.9.

Here is a quick test of your understanding: "Which correlation is stronger, +.20 or +.70?" The latter is stronger because +.70 is farther away from zero. Which of these correlations is stronger, −.20 or −.70? It is the latter because −.70 is farther away from zero. Here's a trick question: "Which correlation is stronger +.50 or −.70?" It is the latter because −.70 is farther from zero. When judging the relative *strength* of two correlation coefficients, ignore the sign and determine which number is farther from zero. Another way of saying this is to take the absolute value of the number (i.e., if the sign is negative then change it to positive) and see which number is bigger.

You are probably wondering, "What is the difference between correlation coefficients that have a negative sign and those that have positive sign?" The issue here is that of the *direction* of relationship between the variables. When the sign is

Correlation coefficient Index indicating the strength and direction of linear relationship between two quantitative variables

EXHIBIT 14.3

Using Cohen's d *in a Pretest–Posttest Control-Group Experimental Research Design*

Earlier we described an experiment where the researcher randomly assigned participants to the treatment and control groups. The levels of the independent variable were treatment condition and control condition. The purpose of the treatment was to improve the social skills of the participants. The dependent variable of social skills was operationalized as the number of appropriate interactions in a 1-hour observation session. The treatment and control group participants were measured on the dependent variable at the pretest and again at the posttest (i.e., after the treatment had been administered to the treatment group).

Figure 14.5 depicts a line graph of the pretest means for the treatment and control groups and the posttest means for the treatment and control group. As you look at that line graph, it appears that the treatment worked because after the intervention the social skills performance of the treatment group improved quite a bit more than that for the control group. That is, at the pretest, the two groups' means were similar, suggesting that random assignment to the groups worked well, but after the treatment, the two groups' means became different. It appears that the treatment group did much better after social skills training, but the control group changed by only a small amount.

We now show how to calculate Cohen's *d* for the two pretest means and for the two posttest means. First, using the statistical package SPSS to do our calculations, we found that at the pretest the mean social skills performance for the experimental group (M_1) was 2.71, the pretest mean for the control group (M_2) was 2.64, and the standard deviation (*SD*) for the control group was 1.39. Using these three pieces of information, you can calculate Cohen's *d* as follows:

$$d = \frac{M_1 - M_2}{SD} = \frac{2.71 - 2.64}{1.39} = \frac{0.07}{1.39} = .05$$

Second, using SPSS at the posttest we found that at the posttest the mean social skills performance for the experimental group (M_1) was 4.00, the posttest mean for the control group (M_2) was 3.07, and the standard deviation (*SD*) for the control group was 1.27. Using these three pieces of information, you can calculate Cohen's *d* as follows:

$$d = \frac{M_1 - M_2}{SD} = \frac{4.00 - 3.07}{1.27} = \frac{0.93}{1.27} = .73$$

Interpreting these data, it appears that the difference between the means was very small at the pretest. The standardized mean difference measured by Cohen's *d* was .05, which means the treatment group was only .05 of a standard deviation larger than the control group mean. Cohen defined .2 as a small difference, and our calculated value of 05 is much smaller than .2. This supports our earlier observation that the means were barely different at the pretest. Conversely, at the posttest Cohen's *d* was .73, which indicates the experimental group mean was .73 standard deviation units above the control group mean. Using Cohen's criteria, .73 is a moderately large difference (it is .73 standard deviations better than the control group's mean).

Although the results just presented appear to support the efficacy of the social skills training, we still cannot trust this experimental finding. The big problem is that the observed differences between the means might represent nothing more than random or chance fluctuation in the data. In the next chapter on inferential statistics, we will check to see if this difference is statistically significant. If it is statistically significant, we will be able to conclude that difference between the posttest means (adjusting for the small differences at the pretest) is real (i.e., not just a random fluctuation but an actual difference that is due to the treatment). For now, we can only state that based on our descriptive analysis of the data, it appears that the experimental treatment was successful in improving participants' social skills.

FIGURE 14.9
Strength and direction
of a correlation
coefficient.

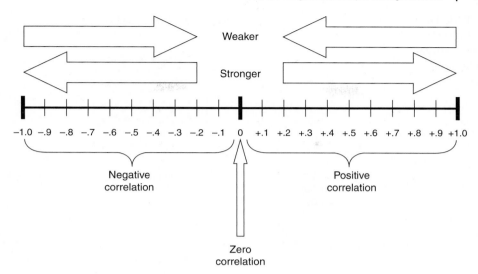

Negative correlation
Correlation in which
values of two variables
tend to move in
opposite directions

Positive correlation
Correlation in which
values of two variables
tend to move in the
same direction

negative, you have a **negative correlation** (which means the values of the two variables tend to move in *opposite* directions); conversely, when the sign is positive, you have a **positive correlation** (which means the two variables tend to move in the *same* direction). You can see some diagrams of correlations of different strengths and directions in Figure 14.10.

Here is an example of a negative correlation: the more hours students spend partying the night before an exam, the lower their test grades tend to be. This correlation would be negative because as the values on hours spent partying go *up*, the values on test grades tend to go *down* (i.e., they move in opposite directions). As an example of a positive correlation, the more hours students spend studying for a test, the higher their test grades tend to be. This correlation would be positive because as the values on hours spent studying go *up*, test grades tend to go *up* (they move in the same direction).

In short, with a negative correlation the variables move in the opposite direction, and with a positive correlation the variables move in the same direction. Here is a checkpoint question: "Is the correlation between education and income positively or negatively correlated?" It is positive because the two variables tend to move in the same direction; as years of schooling increases, income also tends to increase. Here's another checkpoint question: "Is the correlation between amount of caffeine consumption and degree of sleepiness positively or negatively correlated?" It's negative because as caffeine consumption increases, people generally become less sleepy.

One way to visually determine the direction of the relationship between two variables is to construct a scatterplot. Take a moment to examine Figure 14.6 (on page 398), and you will see the scatterplot of college GPA and starting salary. The scatterplot shows that as college GPA increases, starting salary also tends to increase. In this case, the correlation coefficient is +.61 which is a moderately strong positive correlation. Now examine Figure 14.7 (on page 399), and you will see the scatterplot

FIGURE 14.10
Correlations of
different strengths
and directions.

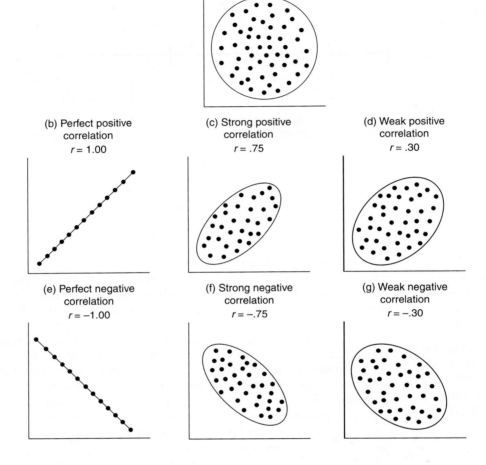

of days missed during college and starting salary. This scatterplot shows that as the number of days missed during college increases, starting salary tends to *decrease*. In this case, the correlation coefficient is −.81 which indicates a strong negative correlation.

An additional way to understand the concept of correlation is to examine one of the definitional formulas and to use the formula to calculate a correlation coefficient on a small set of data. To learn how to do this, read Exhibit 14.4.

In this section, we have explained the *Pearson correlation* coefficient, and there is a caveat you need to know. The Pearson correlation coefficient works only if your data are linearly related. All of the depictions in Figure 14.10 were linear relationships. In contrast, Figure 14.11 shows a **curvilinear relationship** (i.e., a curved relationship). If you calculate the Pearson correlation coefficient on a curved relationship, it generally will tell you that your variables are not related, when in fact they are related. You would draw an incorrect conclusion about the relationship.

Curvilinear relationship
A nonlinear (curved) relationship between two quantitative variables

EXHIBIT 14.4

How to Calculate the Pearson Correlation Coefficient

Earlier we showed how to obtain z-scores and pointed out that a z-score tells you how far a data value is from the mean of its variable. For example, you learned that a z-score of +2.00 says that the score is two standard deviations above the mean, and a z-score of −2.00 says the score is two standard deviations below the mean. To use the following formula for calculating the correlation coefficient, you need to first convert your independent variable (X) and dependent variable (Y) data values to z-scores. Then the following formula is straightforward because you just need to multiply the scores, add them up, and divide them by the number of cases. By dividing the sum by n, you are obtaining the average of the multiplied z-scores

Here's the formula:

$$r = \frac{\text{Sum of the cross products of the z-scores}}{\text{Number of cases}} = \frac{\Sigma(z_X z_Y)}{n}$$

where

Σ tells you to sum what is on its right in the formula

Z_X is the z-score of the value of the X or independent variable

Z_Y is the z-score of the value of the Y or dependent variable

n is the number of cases

With a positive relationship, some cases have low X and low Y values and some have high X and high Y values (see picture "a"). This pattern provides a positive value for the numerator of the formula, which tells you that the relationship is positive. With a negative relationship, some cases have low X and high Y values and some have high X and low Y values (see picture "b"). This pattern provides a negative value for the numerator of the formula, which tells you that

the relationship is negative. This idea is shown in the following pictures:

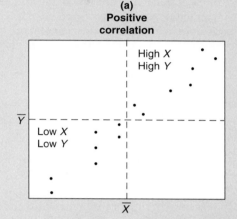

(a)
Positive correlation

High X
High Y

$\overline{Y}$

Low X
Low Y

$\overline{X}$

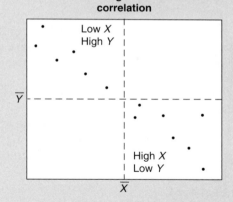

(b)
Negative correlation

Low X
High Y

$\overline{Y}$

High X
Low Y

$\overline{X}$

Although researchers do not calculate correlation coefficients by hand these days (because they use computer programs such as SPSS), it is helpful to calculate the correlation coefficient once to get a better feel for how the numerical value is produced. Therefore, below is a table showing how to calculate the correlation between two variables, X and Y, using the formula just presented above. Our X variable will be the same X variable used earlier when we calculated z-scores. We use a Y variable that is strongly correlated. At the end of the chapter, we list a practice exercise where you can apply this procedure to obtain your own correlation coefficient. Here are the data for number of hours spent studying (i.e., the X variable): 2, 4, 6, 8, 10. Here are the data for test grades (i.e., the Y variable): 50, 73, 86, 86, 98.

Step 1. Convert the X and Y variable scores to z-scores. We already obtained the z-scores for the X variable when we introduced the concept of z-scores. Here are those z-scores: $-1.413, -.707, 0,$ $+.707, +1.413$. Using that same procedure, here are the z-scores for variable Y: $-1.750, -.343,$ $.453, .453, 1.187$.

Step 2. Calculate the sum of the cross products of the z-scores (i.e., $\sum Z_X Z_Y$). A three-column procedure works well for this step:

z-scores for variable X	z-scores for variable Y	Cross products of z-scores
$\downarrow$	$\downarrow$	$\downarrow$
Z_X	Z_Y	$Z_X Z_Y$
-1.413 ←times→	-1.750 equals→	2.473
$-.707$	$-.343$	$.243$
0	$.453$	0
$.707$	$.453$	$.320$
1.413	1.187	1.677

$$\sum Z_X Z_Y = 4.713$$

This is the sum you need for the formula.

Step 3. Divide the sum of the third column (i.e., $\sum Z_X Z_Y$) by the number of cases (i.e., n).

$$r = \frac{\sum Z_X Z_Y}{n} = \frac{4.713}{5} = .943$$

The correlation between hours spent studying (X) and test grades (Y) is +.943. Therefore, the two variables are very strongly correlated. As the number of hours spent studying increases, so does test grades.

If your two variables result in a curved relationship, you need to use a technique called **curvilinear regression** (see Pedhazur, 1997, pp. 520–535). This technique fits the appropriate statistical model and indicates the strength of the relationship.

Curvilinear regression
The type of regression analysis that can accurately model curved relationships

Partial Correlation Coefficient Partial correlation is a technique that is widely used in areas of psychology where the use of experiments for some problems sometimes is difficult. Some of these fields are personality, social, and developmental psychology. Good, strong theory is required to use partial correlation because the researcher must know the variable(s) that he or she needs to control for. For example,

FIGURE 14.11
A curvilinear relationship.

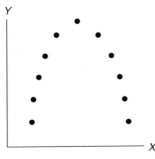

in applied social psychology the researcher might want to study the relationship between the number of hours spent viewing or playing violence (via television and other media such as movies and games) and the number of aggressive acts performed. In this case, the researcher would want to control for variables such as personality type, school grades, and exposure to violence in the family and neighborhood to make sure that the relationship between observed and performed violence was not due to those factors. This sort of nonexperimental research has built on Albert Bandura and his colleagues' classic experimental research showing that children act aggressively after being exposed to an adult model acting aggressively (Bandura, Ross, & Ross, 1963).

Partial correlation coefficient

The correlation between two quantitative variables controlling for one or more variables

The value of the **partial correlation coefficient** indicates the strength and direction of relationship between two variables after controlling for the influence of one or more other variables. Just like with the Pearson correlation coefficient, the partial correlation coefficient has a range of -1.00 to $+1.00$, where zero indicates there is no relationship and the sign indicates the direction of the relationship (see Figure 14.9). The key difference is that the partial correlation coefficient indicates the relationship between two variables after controlling for another variable. Because researchers use statistical programs to calculate partial correlation coefficients, we will not provide a formula in this section. However, if you are curious how to calculate the partial correlation coefficient (or the regression coefficients discussed in the next section), we recommend these two excellent books Cohen, Cohen, West, and Aiken (2003) and Pedhazur (1997).

Regression analysis

Use of one or more quantitative independent variables to explain or predict the values of a single quantitative dependent variable

The correlation coefficient obtained in partial correlation is called the "partial" correlation coefficient because the technique statistically removes or "partials" out the influence of the other variables statistically controlled for. Although this technique of statistical control can be useful, it does not work perfectly. One of the most important points of this textbook that you must not forget is that *the best way (by far) to eliminate the influence of confounding variables in psychological research is to randomly assign participants to groups and conduct an experiment.*

Simple regression

Regression analysis with one dependent variable and one independent variable

Regression Analysis

When all of your variables are quantitative, the technique called regression analysis is often appropriate.[1] **Regression analysis** is a set of statistical procedures used to explain or predict the values of a dependent variable based on the values of one or more independent or predictor variables. The two main types of regression analysis are called **simple regression**, in which there is a single independent or predictor variable, and **multiple regression**, in which there are two or more independent or predictor variables.

Multiple regression

Regression analysis with one dependent variable and two or more independent variables

---

[1]Although categorical independent variables can be used in regression analysis, we prefer to treat regression as the special case of the general linear model where all of the independent variables (IVs) are quantitative. ANOVA would be the special case of the GLM in which the IV(s) are categorical, and ANCOVA would be the special case in which there is a mixture of categorical and quantitative IVs. In all of these cases, the DV is quantitative.

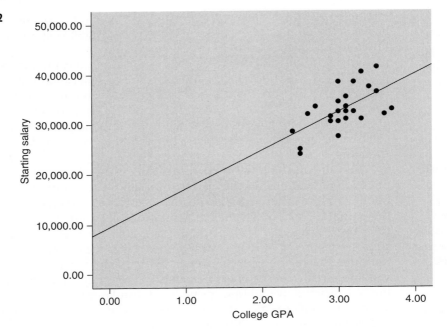

The basic idea of regression analysis is to obtain the **regression equation**. This equation defines the **regression line** that best fits the pattern of observations in your data. Although regression analysis can be used with curvilinear data, we only discuss linear relationships in this book. You can see a regression line in Figure 14.12, which is the scatterplot of college GPA and starting salary with the regression line inserted.

You might remember from your high school algebra class that the two important characteristics of a line are the slope and the Y-intercept. The slope tells you how steep the line is, and the Y-intercept tells you where the line crosses the Y axis (i.e., the vertical axis). These are two of the components of the regression equation for a regression line as follows:

$$\hat{Y} = b_0 + b_1 X_1$$

where

$\hat{Y}$ (called Y-hat) is the predicted value of the dependent variable

b_0 is the Y-intercept

b_1 is the slope (it's called the regression coefficient), and

X_1 is the single independent variable

Now we provide the regression equation for the regression line shown in Figure 14.12. The dependent variable (Y) is starting salary, and the independent or predictor variable (X_1) is GPA. You will be glad to know that researchers rarely, if ever, calculate the regression equation by hand! Instead, they use statistical programs such as SPSS or SAS (which is exactly what we did). Here is the regression equation:

$$\hat{Y} = \$9,405.55 + \$7,687.48(X)$$

Y-intercept
The point at which a regression line crosses the Y (vertical) axis

The **y-intercept** is defined as the point where the regression line crosses the Y-axis. In our regression equation, the y-intercept is $9,405.55. Therefore, the regression line shown in Figure 14.12 crosses the Y-axis at exactly $9,405.55. This is the predicted starting salary if a person had a GPA of 0 (i.e., an F average).

Regression coefficient
The slope or change in Y given a one unit change in X

The **regression coefficient** is defined as the predicted change in the dependent variable (Y), given a one-unit change in the independent variable (X). The regression coefficient or slope in our example is $7,687.48. This regression coefficient says that starting salary is expected to increase by $7,687.48 for every one unit increase in GPA (or decrease by $7,687.48 for every one unit decrease in GPA). For example, a student with a 3 on the GPA variable (i.e., a B) is predicted to start at a salary of $7,687 *more* than a student with a 2 (i.e., a C). We used the traditional grading scale (A = 4, B = 3, C = 2, D = 1, F = 0).

The regression equation can be used to obtain predicted values for the dependent variable for specific values of the independent variable. For example, let's see what the predicted starting salary is for a student with a college GPA of 3 (i.e., a B average):

$$\hat{Y} = \$9,405.55 + \$7,687.48(3.00) \quad \text{We inserted the GPA value of 3.00.}$$

$$\hat{Y} = \$9,405.55 + \$23,062.44 \quad \text{We multiplied } \$7,687.48 \text{ by } 3.00$$

$$\hat{Y} = \$32,467.99 \quad \text{We added } \$9,405.55 \text{ and } \$23,062.44$$

The expected starting salary is $32,467.99. As an exercise, you should use the equation and determine the predicted starting salary for someone with a C average (i.e., a GPA value of 2). Just insert a 2 into the equation and solve it. You will find that the predicted starting salary is $24,780.51. Notice that the difference between the starting salary for someone with a C and a B is equal to the value of the regression coefficient (i.e., $32,467.99 minus $24,780.51 is $7,687.48). That confirms our statement that the regression coefficient shows the change in the dependent variable, given a one unit change in the independent variable.

Multiple regression is similar to simple regression except that it uses two or more independent or predictor variables. A multiple regression equation includes one regression coefficient for each independent variable. An important and highly useful difference between the simple regression and multiple regression is that the multiple regression coefficient shows the relationship between the dependent variable and the independent variable *controlling for the other independent variable(s) in the equation*. This is analogous to the idea discussed above with partial correlation, and, not surprisingly, the multiple regression coefficient is called the **partial regression coefficient**.

Partial regression coefficient
The regression coefficient in a multiple regression equation

In simple regression, the relationship examined via the regression coefficient is analogous to a Pearson correlation, which does not control for any confounding variables; in multiple regression, the relationship is analogous to partial correlation in which one or variables are "partialled" out or "controlled for." The difference in the actual values of the correlation and regression coefficients is that the correlation coefficient is in standardized units that vary from -1.00 to $+1.00$, and the regression coefficient is in natural units. For example, the partial correlation coefficient expressing the relationship between starting salary and GPA controlling for SAT scores is $+.559$ (suggesting a moderately strong positive relationship), and the partial regression coefficient is $5,488.71$ (which says that controlling for SAT scores, each unit change in GPA is predicted to lead to a $5,488.71$ change in income).

Using the data from our hypothetical college student data set, we used SPSS to provide the following multiple regression equation that is based on the dependent variable of starting salary and the predictor variables of GPA and high school SAT:

$$\hat{Y} = -\$2,617.28 + \$5,488.71(X_1) + \$17.79(X_2)$$

where

X_1 is grade point average, and

X_2 is high school SAT

The first partial regression coefficient in the above regression equation is $5,488.71$, which says that after controlling for SAT scores, starting salary increases by $5,488.71$ for each one-unit increase in GPA. The second partial regression coefficient is 17.79, which says that after controlling for GPA, starting salary increases by 17.79 for each one-unit increase in SAT. According to this equation, it is important to do well on your SATs and GPA![2]

If you would like to obtain a predicted starting salary using our multiple regression equation, you insert the values for GPA and SAT and solve for Y-hat. Here is an example where we checked for the predicted starting salary for a B student who had a 1100 on her SAT:

$\hat{Y} = -\$2,617.28 + \$5,488.71(3) + \$17.79(1100)$
We inserted a 3 for grade and 1100 for SAT

$\hat{Y} = -\$2,617.28 + \$16,466.13 + \$17.79(1100)$
We multiplied $5,488.71 times 3

$\hat{Y} = -\$2,617.28 + \$16,466.13 + \$19,569.00$
We multiplied $17.79 times 1100

$\hat{Y} = \$38,652.41$
We added the three numbers

---

[2]If you want to determine which of the variables in a multiple regression is more strongly related to starting salary (controlling for the other variables in the equation), take the values for "part correlation" for each variable from the SPSS printout and square them; then just see which one is bigger. This index is called the *semi-partial correlation squared.* It tells you the amount of variance in the DV that is uniquely explained by the IV. The variable that explains more variance is the more important variable.

The predicted starting salary is $38,652.41. You can put any other valid values into this regression equation for GPA and SAT and obtain the predicted starting salary.

Contingency Tables

Contingency table
Table used to examine the relationship between categorical variables

When you have a categorical dependent variable and a categorical independent variable, one basic technique it to construct a contingency table (also called cross-tabulation). A **contingency table** is a table displaying information in cells formed by the intersection of two or more categorical variables. In a two-dimension contingency table, which is what we explain here, there are only two variables; the rows represent the categories of one of the variables and the columns represent the categories of the other variable. Depending on your needs, various types of information can be placed into the cells of a contingency table, such as cell frequencies, cell percentages, row percentages, and column percentages. You can see a contingency table with cell frequencies in Table 14.5(a) and a contingency table with column percentages in the cells in Table 14.5(b). Remember, our data for this example (just like our other examples) are hypothetical; we constructed the data set to make the example instructive and interesting.

Look at the contingency Table 14.5(a). You can see that the column variable is gender (i.e., female or male). The row variable is personality type. People with type-A personality are more likely to be impatient, competitive, irritable, high achieving, engage in multitasking, and feel a sense of urgency. People with type-B personality are more likely to be cooperative, less competitive, more relaxed, more patient, more satisfied, and easygoing. The research question is whether there is a relationship between gender and personality types. The cells in Table 14.5(a) contain cell frequencies. Do you think that you see a relationship between gender and personality type based on your examination of Table 14.5(a)? That is, does gender

TABLE 14.5
Personality Type by Gender Contingency Tables

(a) Contingency Table Showing Cell Frequencies (Hypothetical data)

		Gender	
		Female	Male
Personality	Type A	2972	2460
Type	Type B	1921	971
		4893	3431

(b) Contingency Table Showing Column Percentages (based on the data in Part (a))

		Gender	
		Female	Male
Personality	Type A	60.7%	71.7%
Type	Type B	39.3%	28.3%
		100%	100%

seem to predict personality type? Do not look at Table 14.5(b) yet! Do you think that women tend to be type-A more than men tend to be type-A?

Although it is important to report cell frequencies, it is very difficult to determine how the two variables are related based on cell frequencies alone. In Table 14.5(b), we have calculated what are called column percentages for females and males. To obtain a column percentage, divide the cell frequency by the total frequency for the column (and then move the decimal point so that you have a percentage). For example, there are 2972 females in column one, and there are a total of 4893 females. This column percentage is 2972 divided by 4893, which is .607, or in percentage form it is 60.7%. The number of females in the other cell is 1921; therefore, this percentage is 39.3%. Notice that these two column percentages add up to 100%. In the table, we also calculated the column percentages for men.

Now look at Table 14.5(b), and try to determine if gender and personality type are related. When we converted the raw numbers to column percentages, we obtained group **rates**. The correct way to read this table is to compare across the columns. On reading the table this way, one can see that 60.7% of females were type-A, but 71.7% of the men were type-A. In other words, men had a greater rate of type-A personality than women. Now let's look at type-B personality. The rates for type-B personality are 39.3% for females and 28.3% for men; therefore, women have a higher rate of type-B personality than men. That's how these two variables are related with our hypothetical data.

Generally speaking, we recommend that you make your predictor variable the column variable and make your dependent variable the row variable. Then calculate column percentages and compare the rates across the rows. That's what we did in Table 14.5(b). In order to correctly read a contingency table, you need to remember these two simple rules:

- If the percentages are calculated down the columns, then compare across the rows.

- If the percentages are calculated across the rows, then compare down the columns.

These rules should come in handy because rates are frequently reported in the news and are frequently used in some types of research (e.g., epidemiology), and now you will know how rates are obtained and how the comparisons should be made. For more advanced research, you can extend the ideas presented by adding another (a third) independent or predictor variable. To do this you would construct the two-way table within the categories of the additional variable. But we will leave that for a more advanced course on data analysis.

Rates
The percentage of people in a group that have a particular characteristic

STUDY QUESTION 14.3 | **What are the techniques for describing relationships between variables? When is each technique used?**

Summary

The purpose of descriptive statistics is to describe and summarize the characteristics of a set of data. Many of the procedures in this chapter are demonstrated with the data set provided in Table 14.1. That data set includes four quantitative variables (starting salary, GPA, SAT scores, and number of school days missed in college) and two categorical variables (college major and gender). Variables are often summarized one at a time, but multivariable descriptive analyses also are important. Descriptive procedures discussed in this chapter include frequency distributions, graphics (bar graphs, histograms, line graphs, and scatterplots), measures of central tendency (mean, median, mode), measures of variability (range, variance, standard deviation), and the analysis of relationships among two or more variables (unstandardized difference between two means, effect size indicators, correlation coefficients, partial correlation coefficients, simple and multiple regression, and contingency tables). When your independent variable is categorical and your dependent variable is quantitative, group means are compared to see how the variables are related. When your independent and dependent variables are both categorical, use a contingency table to examine the relationship. When your independent and dependent variables are both quantitative, the data are plotted in a scatterplot, a correlation coefficient is computed, or a regression analysis is conducted.

Key Terms and Concepts

68, 95, 99.7 percent rule
Bar graph
Cohen's *d*
Contingency table
Correlation coefficient
Curvilinear regression
Curvilinear relationship
Data set
Descriptive statistics
Effect size indicator
Frequency distribution
Histogram
Inferential statistics
Line graph
Mean
Measure of central tendency
Measure of variability
Median
Mode
Multiple regression

Negative correlation
Normal distribution
Partial correlation coefficient
Partial regression coefficient
Positive correlation
Range
Rates
Regression analysis
Regression coefficient
Regression equation
Regression line
Scatterplot
Simple regression
Standard deviation
Unstandardized difference
   between means
Variance
y-intercept
z-score

Related Internet Sites

http://www.statsoft.com/textbook/stathome.html
This is an online statistics book. You can also look up the concepts in this chapter.

http://www.stat.tamu.edu/~west/applets
This site explains many of the ideas of statistical analysis.

http://wise.cgu.edu
This site includes lots of statistics-related learning materials, including "applets" that demonstrate statistics.

http://www.stat.tamu.edu/spss.php
This is another excellent source of learning materials to supplement this chapter.

Practice Test

The answers to these questions can be found in Appendix.

1. What is the median of the following set of scores: 18, 11, 12, 10, 9?
   a. 10
   b. 11
   c. 18
   d. 12

2. The standard deviation is
   a. A measure of variability in squared units
   b. A measure of central tendency
   c. The square root of the variance
   d. All of the above

3. In a normal distribution, 99.7% of the scores fall between z-scores of
   a. −1 thru +1
   b. −2 thru +2
   c. −3 thru +3
   d. 0 thru +3

4. On the normal curve, the mean, median, and mode are ____.
   a. The same
   b. Different
   c. The mean is greater than the mode
   d. The mean is less than the mode

5. In a simple regression, the regression coefficient tells you
   a. The mean of the variable
   b. The point where the regression line crosses the X-axis
   c. The amount of change in the dependent variable per unit change in the independent variable
   d. The amount of change in the independent variable per one unit change in the dependent variable

6. In graphing the frequencies of a single variable, which axis indicates the frequencies?

   a. *X* or abscissa
   b. *Y* or ordinate

7. A contingency table is

   a. A frequency distribution for a single variable
   b. A table displaying information in cells formed by the intersection of two or more categorical variables.
   c. A table containing correlation coefficients
   d. A normal curve representation of two variables

Challenge Exercises

1. What is the standard deviation of the following data?

Here is the information you will need:

$$\text{Variance} = \frac{\sum (X - \bar{X})^2}{n}$$

Note: The standard deviation is the square root of the variance.

X
1
3
1
2
2
3

   a. 1.67
   b. .67
   c. .82
   d. .89

2. Let's suppose we are predicting score on a training posttest from number of years of education and the score on an aptitude test given before training. Here is the regression equation

$$\hat{Y} = 25 + .5X_1 + 10X_2,$$

where X_1 = years of education, and X_2 = aptitude test score.

What is the predicted score for someone with 10 years of education and an aptitude test score of 5?

a. 25
b. 50
c. 35
d. 80

3. You will recall that we claimed that when you convert a set of numbers into z–scores, the new converted set of numbers will have a mean of zero and a standard deviation of 1. Check to see if our claim was correct by converting the following scores into z-scores: 1, 2, 21, 22, 48, 59, 91, 100.

CHAPTER 15

Inferential Statistics

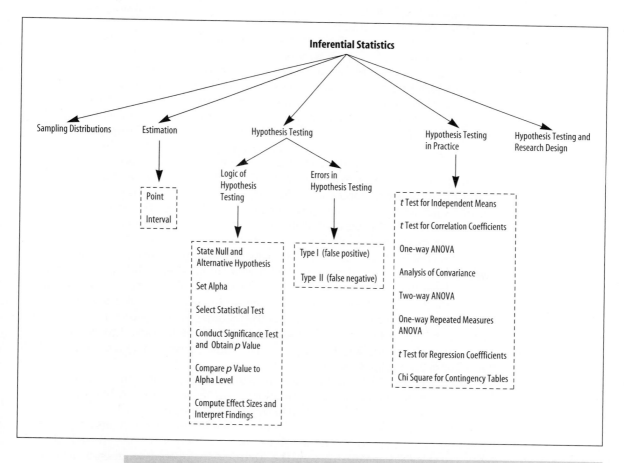

Lenard Hebert, a 40-year-old recovering drug addict, started using drugs during his tour as a marine in Vietnam in 1967. Thus began a 25-year history of doing whatever drug was most popular. When he returned home in the 1970s, he "did strictly reefer. A good militant did natural, herbal things. Then I went disco. I snorted cocaine for

423

ten years. It was chic because it was so expensive." When crack appeared on the drug scene, Hebert switched from cocaine and turned his apartment into a crack den. This ultimately led to his downfall. Just before he arrived at the Phoenix House, a residential drug treatment center, he had been sleeping in abandoned cars and shelters for the homeless (Hurley, 1989). Hebert's story resembles that of thousands of Americans who have been engaged in drug abuse.

Because of the devastating effects of drugs on society, there has been an ongoing attempt to find effective treatments as well as to identify factors that predispose individuals to drug abuse. Although it might seem that everyone would be equally predisposed to drug abuse, there is actually a lot of variability. If the predisposing factors could be identified, extra efforts could be directed toward helping individuals at risk to abuse drugs. The best way to combat drug abuse is through effective prevention.

One researcher who has focused attention on prevention is Susan Schenk. Schenk's efforts in this area began rather serendipitously while she was a graduate student at Concordia University in Montreal. She had designed a drug study that required the use of about 40 rats. Because she did not have the funds to purchase the rats, she did what all resourceful graduate students do: she scrounged. Another graduate student had just completed a study on the effects of social interactions on rats from the time of weaning to about nine weeks of age. Because he no longer had any use for the rats, he let Schenk use them in her drug study. Much to her surprise, these rats did not demonstrate the expected drug effect. Schenk speculated that this was because the rats had been provided with an enriched social environment (burrows, tubes, extensive handling by the experimenter, access to other rats, etc.) rather than being housed alone in the typical sterile environment of a rectangular steel cage. She decided to conduct a study investigating the role of environmental factors in drug abuse.

To investigate the role of environment in drug abuse, Schenk, Lacelle, Gorman, and Amit (1987) housed rats either in isolation or four to a cage for a period of six weeks. They then inserted catheters into the rats' jugular veins and trained them to press a lever that would give them an infusion of 1.0 mg/kg of cocaine. After the rats had learned to press the lever to get cocaine, both groups were observed on three different occasions to determine the number of times they pressed the lever during a 3-hour test period. On one occasion, each lever press delivered a 1.0 mg/kg infusion of cocaine; on another occasion, a 0.5 mg/kg dose; and on the third occasion, a 0.1 mg/kg dose.

After Schenk completed this study, she had data consisting of the number of times the rats in the two housing conditions made lever presses to obtain the various amounts of cocaine. She had to somehow use the data to get an answer to her research question of whether the type of environment in which rats are reared influences the extent to which they abuse cocaine. The way in which she did this was to statistically analyze her data. The statistical analysis she conducted revealed that rats reared in isolation were more likely to abuse cocaine than those reared in an enriched environment.

Introduction

In the last chapter, we described descriptive statistics, which are used to describe and summarize the numerical characteristics of a set of data. In inferential statistics, researchers attempt to go beyond their data. As shown in Figure 14.1, the two major divisions within inferential statistics are *estimation* and *hypothesis testing*. In estimation, the goal is to estimate the value of population parameters. In hypothesis testing, the goal is to test hypotheses about population parameters.

In inferential statistics, researchers use **sample** data to make generalizations about **populations**. If you calculate a numerical index such as a mean or a correlation coefficient on sample data, it is called a **statistic**. If you were able to calculate a numerical index (such as a mean or a correlation coefficient) using the data from an entire population, it would be called a population **parameter**. The goal in inferential statistics is to understand population parameters. Researchers must use sample data to understand populations, however, because it is rarely feasible to collect data from everyone in the population of interest. Random sampling is assumed in inferential statistics, because these samples follow the laws of probability and allow researchers to make warranted claims about population parameters. Researchers use different symbols to represent statistics and parameters. For example, if you calculated the mean annual income in a sample, the mean is symbolized with $\overline{X}$ ("*X*-bar"), but if you calculated the mean with the entire population, it is symbolized with the Greek letter μ ("mu"). Researchers use symbols like this to help them keep information about samples and populations separate. Interestingly, the convention is to use Roman letters to represent sample statistics, but to use Greek letters to represent population parameters. Perhaps that's why some students say "statistics is like Greek to me"! In Table 15.1, we list several symbols commonly used in inferential statistics.

Sample
The set of cases selected from the population

Population
The full group to which one wants to generalize

Statistic
A numerical index based on sample data

Parameter
A numerical characteristic of a population

TABLE 15.1

Commonly Used Symbols for Sample Statistics and Their Associated Population Parameters

Numerical Index	Sample Statistic	Population Parameter
Mean	$\overline{X}$ (*X* bar)	μ (mu)
Standard deviation	*SD*	σ (sigma)
Variance	SD^2	σ^2 (sigma squared)
Correlation coefficient	*r*	ρ (rho)
Proportion	*p*	π (pi)
Regression coefficient	*b*	β (beta)*

*Beta has two other common uses not to be confused with the population regression coefficient, including the standardized regression coefficient for sample data, and $1 - \beta$, which is used to symbolize the statistical power of a significance test.

Sampling Distributions

Inferential statistics relies on "sampling distributions" for making probability statements about population parameters based on sample data. A sampling distribution is not something you would ever have to construct yourself, but it is useful to understand the concept. A **sampling distribution** is the theoretical probability distribution of the values of a sample statistic that would result from all possible samples of a particular size drawn from a population.

Sampling distribution
The theoretical probability distribution of the values of a statistic that would result if you selected all possible samples of a particular size from a population

To make this idea more concrete, here is how a **sampling distribution of the mean** could be constructed: draw a random sample from the population, calculate and write down the value of the income sample mean. Then, draw another random sample, calculate and write down the value of this sample mean. Continue this process an infinite number of times or until all possible samples of a particular size (e.g., 30 people per sample) have been recorded. Then display all of the sample means obtained. If you construct a line graph of all of these sample means, you will have a depiction of your sampling distribution of the mean. You can see the picture of a sampling distribution of the mean that we constructed in Figure 15.1. In our hypothetical *sampling distribution of the mean*, the average is $76,000 and the standard error is $10,000.

Sampling distribution of the mean
The theoretical probability distribution of the means of all possible samples of a particular size selected from a population

You need to notice two key characteristics of the sampling distribution shown in Figure 15.1, where the mean income (i.e., $\overline{X}$) was determined for an infinite number of random samples. First, the average of all the sample means provided in our sampling distribution of the mean is equal to the true population mean (i.e., μ). This happens when random sampling, which is an "unbiased" sampling process, is used to obtain the participants for the samples. In this example, the average of all the sample means is $76,000, which is also the true mean income in the entire population.

Second, notice that the sample value of the mean income (i.e., $\overline{X}$) for a particular sample is rarely the exact same value as the population mean (i.e., μ). The means of the samples vary around the true population mean. Moreover, you can see that these

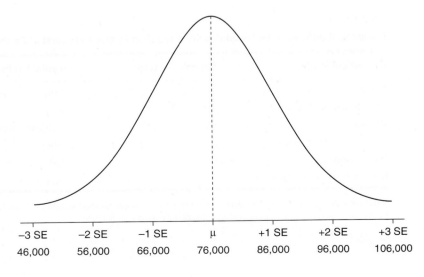

FIGURE 15.1
Hypothetical sampling distribution of the mean for income variable. SE stands for standard error.

−3 SE	−2 SE	−1 SE	μ	+1 SE	+2 SE	+3 SE
46,000	56,000	66,000	76,000	86,000	96,000	106,000

sample means follow a normal distribution, which indicates that most of the sample means are relatively close to the population mean and sample means with values very far from the population mean are uncommon. Because the sampling distribution of the mean is a normal distribution, the sample means follow the "68, 95, 99.7% rule" (defined in the last chapter). That is, 68% of the sample means in the sampling distribution of the mean are within one standard deviation of the true population mean, 95% are within two standard deviations, and 99.7% are within three standard deviations. Rather than using the term "standard deviation" like we just did, however, **standard error** is the term that is used to refer to the standard deviation of a sampling distribution. The standard error is a special kind of standard deviation; *it's the standard deviation of a sampling distribution.* Now look at Figure 15.1 one more time. Since the population mean is $76,000 and the standard error is $10,000, you can see that 68% of the sample means fall between $66,000 and $86,000 (i.e., $76,000 plus or minus one standard error, which is $10,000), 95% fall between $56,000 and $96,000 (i.e., $76,000 plus or minus two standard errors, which is $20,000), and 99.7% fall between $46,000 and $106,000 (i.e., $76,000 plus or minus three standard errors, which is $30,000).

Standard error
The standard deviation of a sampling distribution

Although we have used the example of constructing a sampling distribution for sample means, a sampling distribution can be constructed for any sample statistic. For example, you could have a sampling distribution of the correlation coefficient and a sampling distribution of the regression coefficient. In hypothesis testing, discussed later, researchers rely on sampling distributions of "test statistics." A **test statistic** is a sample statistic (e.g., difference between means, correlation coefficient, regression coefficient) that has been converted into a statistic that follows a known sampling distribution that is convenient to work with for obtaining probability values and testing hypotheses. Some commonly used sampling distributions for test statistics are the z distribution, t distributions, F distributions, and chi-square (i.e., χ^2) distributions.

Test statistic
A statistic that follows a known sampling distribution and is used in significance testing

Fortunately you will never have to construct a sampling distribution! In practice you select only one sample, and the computer package you use to analyze your data estimates the appropriate sampling distribution for you. The key point here is that the values of sample statistics such as means, percentages, correlation coefficients, and test statistics vary around the true population value in a known, probabilistic way. This is why empirical research claims are always probabilistic (i.e., statements of what is probably true) rather than certain or absolute.

Estimation

Estimation
The branch of inferential statistics focused on obtaining estimates of the values of population parameters

Estimation is one of the two major types of inferential statistics. In **estimation**, your goal is to answer this question: "Based on my random sample, what is my estimate of the population parameter?"

You can provide two kinds of "estimates" using your sample data. First, you can use the value of the statistic in your sample, such as the mean, to estimate the population value. For example, if you were estimating the mean income in a population, you would take the mean value of the participants' income in your sample (e.g., perhaps it is $50,000) and use it as your best guess of the population mean (i.e., the average income of everyone in the population). This is called point estimation because you use one number in your sample to estimate the one number (point) of interest in the population. In **point estimation**, researchers use the value of a sample statistic as the estimate of the value of a population parameter.

You will recall from our discussion of sampling distributions that sample statistics (such as the mean) jump around from sample to sample and that the value of the sample statistic rarely is *exactly* the same as the value of the population parameter. Because of this probabilistic nature of sample statistics, researchers usually prefer to use interval estimation. In **interval estimation**, the researcher puts a confidence interval around the point estimates. For example, if the mean income in a sample is $49,000, the researcher might use a statistical program (such as SPSS or SAS) to obtain an interval estimate (also called a confidence interval) around the sample mean of $49,000. Perhaps the "95% confidence interval" is "$44,000 to $54,000."

A **confidence interval** is a range of numbers inferred from the sample that has a certain probability or chance of including the true population value. When the researcher uses a 95% confidence interval, he or she can be 95% confident that the interval includes the population parameter because this type of confidence interval will capture or include the true population parameter 95% of the time. This idea is demonstrated in Figure 15.2. Notice in the figure that 19 of the 20 (i.e., 95%) of the confidence intervals captured the true population mean, but one (i.e., 5%) missed the population mean. We set the figure up this way so that you can see that the confidence the researcher has is in the long-term process of constructing confidence intervals, not in a single interval.

We pointed out that 95% confidence intervals capture the true population value 95% of the time. If a researcher uses a 99% confidence interval, then this type of interval will include the true population value 99% of the time, and a 68% confidence interval will include the true value 68% of the time. You might wonder, why not just use a 99% confidence interval so that the researcher can be more confident. The answer is that this increased confidence (e.g., moving from 95% to 99% confident) comes with a cost. The 99% interval will have to be wider (i.e., less precise) than a 95% interval on a set of data. That's why 95% confidence intervals are popular in research; it offers a reasonable compromise.

For a concrete example, we will calculate the confidence intervals for the variable "starting salary" from the college student data set provided in the last chapter (see Table 14.1, page 392). The sample mean for starting salary is $32,960.00. Here are several confidence intervals calculated with those data:

- 99% confidence interval: $30,533.85 to $35,386.15 (the width is $4,852.60)
- 95% confidence interval: $31,169.71 to $34,750.29 (the width is $3,580.58)
- 90% confidence interval: $31,475.93 to $34,444.70 (the width is $2,968.77)
- 68% confidence interval: $32,079.13 to $33,840.87 (the width is $1,761.74)

As you can see, the confidence intervals became narrower as we decreased the level of confidence. Here is the tradeoff: If you want to have a precise confidence interval (i.e., a narrow interval), then you have to use an interval that allows less

---

Point estimation
Use of the value of a sample statistic as one's estimate of the value of a population parameter

Interval estimation
Placement of a range of numbers around a point estimate

Confidence interval
An interval estimate inferred from sample data that has a certain probability of including the true population parameter

F I G U R E   1 5 . 2
Sampling distribution
of the mean and
illustration of the
95% confidence
intervals for
20 samples.

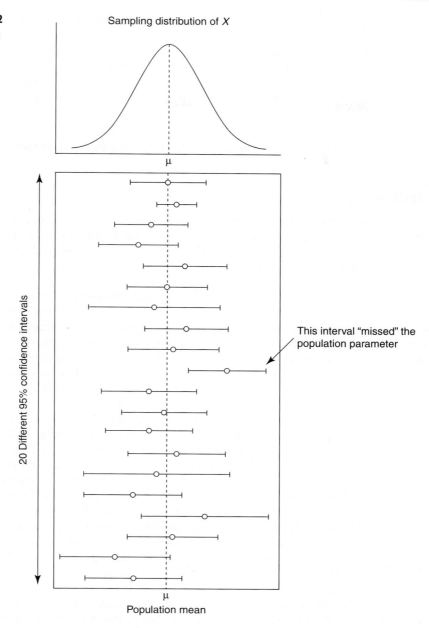

Sampling distribution of *X*

μ

20 Different 95% confidence intervals

This interval "missed" the
population parameter

μ
Population mean

confidence of including the population parameter. In this example, we didn't
know the population mean because we had only one sample to work with. You
could make claims with varying levels of confidence using the above intervals. For
example, we are 95% confident that the interval ranging from $31,169.71 to
$34,750.29 will include the true population mean. Remember, however, that our

confidence is in the long-term process—95% of the time, 95% confidence intervals will include the true population parameter.

There is one additional factor that you need to know that affects the width of a confidence interval—it's the sample size. The larger the sample size, the more precise (i.e., the narrower) your confidence interval. So if you need a precise (i.e., narrow) confidence interval, then make sure that you include many participants in your research study.

STUDY QUESTION 15.1 | **What is statistical estimation? What are the two types of estimation?**

Hypothesis Testing

Hypothesis testing
The process of testing a predicted relationship or hypothesis by making observations and then comparing the observed facts with the hypothesis or predicted relationship; the branch of inferential statistics focused on determining when the null hypothesis can or cannot be rejected in favor of the alternative hypothesis

Null hypothesis
Typically the hypothesis of no difference between means or no relationship in the population

Alternative hypothesis
The logical opposite of the null hypothesis

Hypothesis testing is the branch of inferential statistics concerned with how well sample data support a null hypothesis and when the null hypothesis can be rejected. Unlike estimation, in which the researcher has no clear hypothesis about the population parameter, in hypothesis testing the researcher states the null and alternative hypotheses and then uses the data to determine what decision should be made about these hypotheses. The **null hypothesis** is a statement about a population parameter; typically, it states that there is no relationship between the independent and dependent variables in the population.[1] The **alternative hypothesis** is the logical opposite of the null hypothesis (i.e., stating that there *is* a relationship between the independent and dependent variables in the population).

You can think of the null hypothesis as the hypothesis the researcher hopes to "nullify" because when you reject this hypothesis you conclude that there is a relationship or pattern in the world. A primary goal of science is to identify relationships and patterns in the natural world (especially causal relationships). Hypothesis testing is sometimes called "null hypothesis significance testing" (NHST) because it is the null hypothesis that is directly tested, not the alternative hypothesis. Although the null hypothesis is directly tested in hypothesis testing, your decision about the null hypothesis logically determines your decision about the alternative hypothesis because the alternative hypothesis is the logical opposite of the null hypothesis. If you reject the null hypothesis, you can claim that the data support the alternative hypothesis and claim that a pattern has been found in the world.

To make the concepts of null and alternative hypotheses more concrete, examine Table 15.2 where you can see several examples of research questions, null hypotheses, and alternative hypotheses. The table also shows how the statistical hypotheses are written using Greek symbols for the population parameters. The null and alternative hypotheses are written using population parameters because the researcher is interested in the population (not the sample) in inferential statistics. Later in this chapter, we test the null hypotheses shown in the Table 15.2.

---

[1]We focus only on the "nil" null hypothesis, which is the hypothesis of no difference between means or no relationship between variables. The nil null hypothesis is by far the most commonly tested null hypothesis. However, one does not have to test a "no difference" null hypothesis. For more information on this issue, see Cohen (1994) and Thompson (2006).

TABLE 15.2

Examples of Null and Alternative Hypotheses in Inferential Statistics

Research Question	Verbal Null (H_0) Hypothesis	Symbolic H_0 Hypothesis	Verbal Alternative (H_1) Hypothesis	Symbolic H_1 Hypothesis
Survey research examples:				
Do males or females have a higher starting salary?	The male and female population means are not different.	$H_0: \mu_M = \mu_F$	The male and female population means are different.	$H_1: \mu_M \neq \mu_F$
Is there a correlation between GPA (*X*) and starting income (*Y*)?	The population correlation between GPA and starting income is equal to zero.	$H_0: \rho_{XY} = 0$	The population correlation between GPA and starting income is not equal to zero.	$H_1: \rho_{XY} \neq 0$
Do psychology, philosophy, and business majors have different starting incomes?	Students majoring in psychology, philosophy, and business have the same mean starting income.	$H_0:$ $\mu_{Psy} = \mu_{Phil} = \mu_{Bus}$	At least two of the population means are different.	$H_1:$ Not all equal
Experimental research examples:				
Does participation in social skills training condition produce higher skills performance for experimental training program participants compared to no treatment control participants?	Controlling for pretest differences, there is no skills performance difference between the hypothetical populations of people receiving the treatment and people not receiving the treatment.	$H_0: \mu_{Train} = \mu_{No\,Train}$	The two population means are different.	$H_1:$ $\mu_{Train} \neq \mu_{No\,Train}$
Does participation in health program produce a reduction in participants' weight?	There is no difference in weight for the hypothetical treatment population at pretest and posttest.	$H_0:$ $\mu_{Pretest} = \mu_{Posttest}$	The pretest and posttest population means are different.	$H_1:$ $\mu_{Pretest} \neq \mu_{Posttest}$

According to the *logic of hypothesis testing*, you start by assuming that an effect is *not* present or that there is *no* true relationship between your independent and dependent variables, and then you determine whether the data warrant rejection of the null hypothesis. The data provide the evidence for evaluating the null hypothesis. Although the researcher states the null hypothesis, which can be tested via hypothesis testing, the researcher ultimately hopes to reject the null hypothesis and accept the alternative hypothesis. This might seem a little backward (i.e., testing a hypothesis that you hope to reject), but that's how hypothesis testing works—we can only directly test the null hypothesis. Statements about the alternative hypothesis are made on the basis of logic—if the null is very likely *not* true, then the researcher logically concludes that the alternative very likely *is* true.

Here's an example using the variables gender and starting salary from the data provided in Table 14.1. We will assume that the data make up a sample that was randomly selected from the population. In this example, we are interested in whether males or females have higher mean starting salaries in the populations of male and female recent college graduates. Here are the null and alternative hypotheses:

Null hypothesis: H_0: $\mu_M = \mu_F$

Alternative hypothesis: H_1: $\mu_M \neq \mu_F$

When you have a random sample and wish to engage in hypothesis testing, you will always know if your *sample* means differ (just calculate the means and see if they're different), but the key question is whether the means are different enough for you to reject the null hypothesis and conclude that the difference is *not just due to chance*. The goal in hypothesis testing is to make claims about *population parameters* based on sample data. The above null hypothesis says the average starting salaries for males and females are the same in their respective populations. The alternative hypothesis says the male and female population means are *not* the same (i.e., they are different).

Here are the sample means calculated from the data set provided in Table 14.1:

- The average starting salary for males ($\bar{X}_M$) is \$34,791.67.
- The average starting salary for females ($\bar{X}_F$) is \$31,269.23.

In the sample data, males earn more than females. However, when we discussed sampling distributions, you learned that the values of sample statistics (such as means and correlation coefficients) vary from sample to sample because of chance variation. In hypothesis testing, we are trying to determine whether the difference between the sample means should be viewed as random variation (i.e., "chance"), or if the difference is large enough, we should conclude that the difference is not just due to chance variation. If you conclude that the difference is not a chance difference, you are concluding that there is a *real* or true difference in the populations from which the data were selected.

You need to learn how to determine whether you can reject the null hypothesis and accept the alternative hypothesis. After stating the null and alternative hypotheses, you must decide what alpha level you want to use. The **alpha level** (also called the **level of significance**) is set by the researcher at some small value (typically .05), and it is the point at which the researcher would conclude that the observed value of the sample statistic is sufficiently rare *under the assumption of a true null hypothesis* that he or she would reject the null hypothesis. The alpha level is set by the researcher *before* he or she analyzes the data. By convention, alpha is usually set at .05. If you set alpha at .05, you will incorrectly reject the null hypothesis only 5% of the time or less. That is, you will only conclude 5% of the time that there is a relationship in the population, when there

Alpha level
The point at which one would reject the null hypothesis and accept the alternative hypothesis

Level of significance
Another name for alpha level

really is not a relationship. We will label this error a "Type I" error, and it is an error that researchers hope to avoid.

Next, you input the data into a statistical program such as SPSS or SAS and run the appropriate statistical test. (Aren't you glad you don't have to do the mathematics by hand!) When the means for two groups of people are being compared, the most common statistical test is the **independent samples *t* test**. It's called a *t* test because it relies on the *t* distribution as its sampling distribution. The *t* distribution serves as the sampling distribution for the *t* test *under the assumption that the null hypothesis is true*. As shown in Figure 15.3, the *t* distribution looks a lot like a normal curve; it's just a little flatter and a little more spread out than the normal curve. Just like the normal curve, the *t* distribution has a mean of zero, is symmetrical, is higher in the center, and has a "left tail" and a "right tail" that represent rare events. In the figure, we have marked that area in the sampling distribution that would be rare (called the **critical region**) if we used an alpha level of .05. The critical region marks the 5% of the area in that sampling distribution that would be rare if the true difference between the means was zero. *If the null hypothesis is true*, the sample statistic will only fall in the tails of the sampling distribution (in Figure 15.3) 5% of the time, and the sample statistic will fall in the noncritical region of this sampling distribution 95% of the time. This knowledge is important, because if the value of your sample statistic falls in the critical region, you would claim that it is a rare event, and this would enable you to reject the null hypothesis. Generally speaking, *t* statistic values greater than +2.00 or less than −2.00 are rare events. The statistical program will determine the value of your *t* test statistic.

Rather than rely on the value of the *t* statistic, however, researchers use a more convenient indicator, called the **probability value** (or **p value**). The *p* value is a value between 0 and 1, and it indicates the proportion of the area in the sampling distribution that lies at or beyond the value of your test statistic value. The closer the *p* value is to zero, the less likely your test result would be *if the null hypothesis were true*. Therefore, a very small *p* value provides the evidence you need to reject the null hypothesis. A very small *p* value means that the value of your sample statistic would be a rare event if the null hypothesis were true. The exact point at

Independent samples *t* test
The significance test of the difference between two means that uses the *t* probability distribution

Critical region
The area on a null hypothesis sampling distribution where the observed value of the statistic, if it fell in this area, would be considered a rare event

Probability value
The likelihood of the observed value (or a more extreme value) of a statistic, if the null hypothesis were true

_p_ value
A shorter name for probability value

FIGURE 15.3
A *t* distribution of test statistic values for difference between two means. The critical region is darkened and is in the tails of the *t* distribution. The *t* distribution is a family of curves that depend on the sample size. The one shown here illustrates the typical shape and the critical region and noncritical regions.

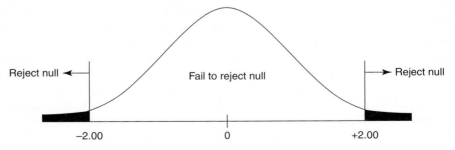

which you will decide to reject the null hypothesis will be determined by the alpha level that you chose to use in your research study.

Putting these ideas together, here is the key hypothesis testing decision rule that you must remember: *if the p value is less than (or equal to) the alpha level, then reject the null hypothesis and tentatively accept the alternative hypothesis.* If you chose an alpha level of .05, then the rule takes this more precise form: *if the p value is less than (or equal to) .05, then reject the null hypothesis and tentatively accept the alternative hypothesis.* When researchers reject the null hypothesis, they are warranted in making the claim that their research finding is **statistically significant**, which means the finding (e.g., such as an observed difference between two means) is very likely a real relationship (i.e., not due to chance). In inferential statistics, we make probability-based claims. We never make absolute claims.

Now, (using the **independent samples *t* test**) we can complete our test of the null hypothesis about the starting salaries of male and female recent college graduates. We are using the **independent samples *t* test**. Following convention, we set our alpha level at .05. We entered the data into the statistical package SPSS, ran the independent samples *t* test, and found that the value on the *t* distribution for our test statistic was 2.18. More importantly, the *p* value was equal to .04. *This p value (.04) is less than our alpha level (.05), so we reject the null hypothesis and tentatively accept the alternative hypothesis.* The difference between the sample means ($34,791.67 and $31,269.23) is statistically significant. We conclude that the observed difference between the sample means is not merely the result of chance. We conclude that the two population means are different.

When you reject the null hypothesis and accept the alternative hypothesis, all you can claim is that the population means are not the same. Remember, the null hypothesis said that the population means were exactly the same, and when you reject the null, you conclude that the population means are not equal and that the finding is statistically significant. Oftentimes we are also interested in whether the finding is practically significant. **Practical significance** (also called **clinical significance**) is a subjective but carefully considered decision made by the researcher about whether the difference between the means or the observed relationship is "big enough to matter" for practical decisions (e.g., to continue the line of research, to make policy decisions, or to make clinical recommendations).

To aid in making judgments about practical significance, researcher frequently use what are called **effect size indicators**. An effect size indicator is a measure of the magnitude or strength of a relationship. It tells you how big an effect or difference between means is present. There are many different effect size indicators, such as Cohen's *d*, partial eta squared (η^2), omega squared (ω^2), and the amount of variance explained by one or more independent variables. We touch on several of these in this chapter. For example, Cohen's *d* for our two starting salaries of $34,791.67 and $31,269.23 is equal to .88, which is large using Cohen's criteria provided in the last chapter. The mean for males is .88 standard deviations higher than the mean for females. The **partial eta squared** effect size indicator tells you how much variance in the dependent variable is uniquely explained by the independent or predictor variable. In our example, eta squared is .17; therefore, 17% of the variance in starting salary is explained by the predictor variable gender.

Statistically significant
Conclusion that an observed finding would be very unlikely if the null hypothesis were true

Independent samples *t* test
Used to determine if the difference between the means of two groups is statistically significant

Practical significance
Claim made when a statistically significant finding seems large enough to be important

Clinical significance
A type of practical significance

Effect size indicators
An index of magnitude or strength of relationship

Partial eta squared
The amount of variance in the dependent variable uniquely explained by a single categorical independent variable

The gender and income example just completed was a survey research example. Hypothesis testing is even more commonly used in experimental research. We now use the logic of hypothesis testing using part of a data set provided in the last chapter in Table 14.3 (page 396). In this example, the researcher conducted an experiment to test a new social skills training program to determine if the program caused an improvement in the social skills of participants in the experimental condition. The independent variable is training (social skills training condition vs. no training control condition). The dependent variable is the number of appropriate social interactions the participants performed during the period of experimenter observation. For now, let's assume the researcher used a *posttest-only control-group design*. That is, the researcher randomly assigned the participants to the experimental (training) and control (no training) groups, administered training to the participants in the experimental group, and then measured both groups on the dependent variable (number of appropriate social interactions). The data are provided in Table 14.3 in the columns labeled "treatment condition" and "posttest scores"; we are ignoring the "pretest scores" data column for now, but will use it in a later example.

At the posttest (i.e., after the treatment was administered to the experimental group, but not to the control group), the mean number of appropriate social interactions for the experimental-group participants was 4.00 and the mean for the control-group participants was 3.07. It would appear that the treatment was successful because the participants receiving the social skills training performed more appropriate interactions than the control participants. However, the question in an experiment is whether the difference between the groups is greater than would be expected based on chance. We want to know whether the difference between the means (4.00 and 3.07) is statistically significant.

Following convention, we set our alpha level at .05. We entered the data into the statistical package SPSS, ran the independent samples *t* test, and found that the value on the *t* distribution for our test statistic was 1.87. More importantly, the *p* value was equal to .07. *This p value (.07) is greater than our alpha level (.05), so we fail to reject the null hypothesis.* The difference between the experimental- and control-group means is not statistically significant. Because the difference was not significant, we did not calculate a measure of effect size. We conclude that the observed difference between the means in our experimental research data is probably just a chance (i.e., random) variation. We can *not* conclude that the two population means are the same as stated in the null hypothesis. If a finding is *not statistically significant*, then you do not claim that your data support the null hypothesis. You must simply state that you "failed to reject the null hypothesis" and move on to a new experiment.

Directional Alternative Hypotheses

Sometimes a researcher will state an alternative hypothesis in a directional form rather than in a nondirectional form during statistical testing. That is, the researcher will want to test the hypothesis that one population mean is greater than (or less than) another. A **nondirectional alternative hypothesis** is an alternative hypothesis that includes a not equal to sign ($\neq$). A **directional alternative hypothesis** contains either a greater than sign (>) or a less than sign (<).

Nondirectional alternative hypothesis
An alternative hypothesis that includes the "not equal to sign" ($\neq$)

Directional alternative hypothesis
An alternative hypothesis that includes a "less than sign" (<) or a "greater than sign" (>)

For example, the researcher in the previous example used the following traditional hypotheses for our testing procedure:

Null hypothesis: H_0: $\mu_{Training} = \mu_{No\ Training}$

Alternative hypothesis: H_1: $\mu_{Training} \neq \mu_{No\ Training}$

The researcher tested the null hypothesis, stating that the two population means are equal, and used the nondirectional alternative hypothesis, stating that the means are not equal.

The researcher in the previous example could have used the following set of hypotheses:

Null hypothesis: H_0: $\mu_{Training} \leq \mu_{No\ Training}$

Alternative hypothesis: H_1: $\mu_{Training} > \mu_{No\ Training}$

You can see that the alternative hypothesis says that skills training population mean is greater than the control-group population mean. In other words, a directional alternative hypothesis was stated. The null hypothesis also changes so that all possible outcomes were included in the two hypotheses. The null hypothesis still has the equality sign in it (i.e., the sign $\leq$ means less than or *equal* to).

The researcher could have also stated this set of hypotheses:

Null hypothesis: H_0: $\mu_{Training} \geq \mu_{No\ Training}$

Alternative hypothesis: H_1: $\mu_{Training} < \mu_{No\ Training}$

Once again, a directional alternative hypothesis was given. This time, however, the alternative hypothesis states that the skills training population mean is less than the control-group population mean.

The use of directional alternative hypotheses is controversial. Although the use of directional alternative hypotheses slightly increases the **statistical power** of the hypothesis test (i.e., the researcher is slightly more likely to reject the null when it is false), this gain in sensitivity of the test comes with a serious drawback. If the researcher uses a directional alternative hypothesis and a large difference is found in the *opposite* direction, he or she can *not* conclude that a relationship exists in the population. That's the rule of directional hypothesis testing—even if you find a large difference you must conclude that the difference is not statistically significant if it's in the opposite direction from the one you hypothesized. This conclusion would appear to go against one of the major tenets of scientific research, which is to conduct scientific research that allows for the discovery of how the natural world operates. Directional alternative hypotheses in significance testing tend to suppress the discovery function of scientific research.

Because of this major drawback to using directional alternative hypotheses, most researchers use nondirectional alternative hypotheses in statistical testing, just as we did above when we conducted our *t* tests. This is the case even if the researcher's "research hypothesis" or actual theory-based prediction is directional (expects one group to be greater). In fact, if a researcher has used a *directional* alternative hypothesis in a statistical hypothesis testing procedure, he or she is required to tell you; if

Statistical power
The probability of rejecting the null hypothesis when it is false

the researcher does not state the type of alternative hypothesis used, the reader will assume that it was a nondirectional alternative hypothesis.

Review of the Logic of Hypothesis Testing

Hypothesis testing is a systematic activity. Every time you conduct a hypothesis test, you follow the steps summarized in Table 15.3. Perhaps the most important points in hypothesis testing are the two decision-making rules:

- Rule 1: If the *p* value (which is obtained from the computer printout and is based on your empirical research results) is less than or equal to the alpha level (researchers usually select the .05 level), then reject the null hypothesis and tentatively accept the alternative hypothesis. Conclude that the finding is *statistically significant* (i.e., the observed difference between means or observed relationship is not just due to chance fluctuations).

- Rule 2: If the *p* value is greater than the alpha level, then the researcher cannot reject the null hypothesis. The researcher can only claim to "fail to reject" the null hypothesis and conclude that the finding is *not statistically significant*.

Logic of hypothesis testing
The five steps in the process of significance testing

If you commit these two rules to memory, the rest of the material in this chapter will be easier than you might expect, because these rules are at the core of hypothesis testing. Now you should review the six steps in hypothesis testing summarized in Table 15.3. These steps form the **logic of hypothesis testing** (also called the *logic of significance testing*).

TABLE 15.3
Steps in Hypothesis Testing with Decision-Making Rules

Step 1. State the null and the alternative hypotheses.

Step 2. Set the alpha level (i.e., level of significance). (Psychologists usually set the alpha level at .05.)

Step 3. Select the statistical test to be used (e.g., *t* test, ANOVA, regression analysis).

Step 4. Conduct the statistical test and obtain the *p* value.

Step 5. Compare *p* value to the alpha level (i.e., level of significance), and apply either decision rule 1 or decision rule 2.

	Decision Rule 1:
If:	*p* value is ≤ alpha level*
Then:	Reject the null hypothesis and tentatively accept the alternative hypothesis.
Conclusion:	The research finding is statistically significant.

	Decision Rule 2:
If:	*p* value is > alpha level
Then:	Fail to reject the null hypothesis.
Conclusion:	The research finding is not statistically significant.

Step 6. Compute effect size, interpret findings, make judgment of practical significance of results.

*The issue of what to do when *p*=alpha is a matter of some controversy. We recommend the convention provided by the late Jacob Cohen that a *p* value of .00 to .05 is sufficiently small to reject the null, but .051–1.00 is not sufficiently small to reject the null. For example, using Cohen's rule .0504 would be statistically significant because it rounds to .05, but .0505 is not because it rounds to .051.

Hypothesis-Testing Errors

Because samples rather than complete populations are used in inferential statistics, hypothesis testing can sometimes provide the wrong answer. Hypothesis testing relies on sampling distributions in guiding decisions, and the resulting decisions reflect the laws of probability. The decisions made are usually correct, but sometimes they are incorrect. The four possible outcomes of hypothesis testing are shown in Table 15.4.

Across the top of Table 15.4, you can see the two possible conditions existing in the natural world—either the null hypothesis is true or it is false. Across the rows of the table, you can see the two possible decisions the researcher can make—the researcher can either reject or fail to reject the null hypothesis. Crossing these two dimensions produces the possible hypothesis testing outcomes. We are most concerned with the two errors that can occur. They are called Type I and Type II errors.

Type I error
Rejection of a true null hypothesis

A **Type I error** occurs when the researcher rejects a true null hypothesis. If the null hypothesis is true (i.e., the independent and dependent variables are not related), then you do not want to reject it—if you do reject it, you have made a Type I error. A Type I error is called a "false positive" because the researcher falsely concludes that there is a relationship in the world (i.e., in the population). The researcher makes an incorrect claim of statistical significance. Here's an analogy. In medicine, the null hypothesis states that "the patient is well," and the alternative hypothesis says the patient is not well (i.e., ill). A false-positive error would occur if the doctor concludes that a patient has the illness, when the patient really does not have the illness. The doctor has claimed that a well person is sick (although the doctor thinks the correct decision was made).

Type II error
Failure to reject a false null hypothesis

A **Type II error** occurs when the researcher fails to reject a false null hypothesis. If the null hypothesis is false, then you want to reject it. This type of error is called a "false negative" because the researcher falsely concludes that there is no relationship in the population when there *is* a relationship. The researcher makes an incorrect claim of nonstatistical significance. The researcher should be claiming that the finding is statistically significant, but he or she concludes that the finding is not statistically significant. Continuing the medical analogy, a false-negative error occurs when the doctor concludes that the patient does not have the disease when the patient really does have it. The doctor has claimed that a sick person is well (although the doctor thinks the correct decision was made).

TABLE 15.4
The Four Possible Outcomes of Statistical Hypothesis Testing

		Actual status of the null hypothesis	
		Null is true	Null is false
Researcher's Decision	Reject the null	Type I error (false positive)	Correct decision
	Fail to reject the null	Correct decision	Type II error (false negative)

Researchers want to avoid Type I and II errors. Researchers traditionally have been more concerned about avoiding Type I errors. You can make fewer Type I errors by using a more stringent alpha level. If you use an alpha level of .05, you are willing to make a false-positive (Type I) error 5% of the time. If you use the more stringent alpha level of .01, you will, at most, make a Type I error 1% of the time.

One might think, "Why not just use a more stringent alpha level so I can make fewer Type I errors?" The problem is that when you use a more stringent alpha level, you simultaneously increase your likelihood of making a Type II error, which you do not want. Because of this tradeoff, we generally recommend using the .05 alpha level rather than a .01 or .001 level *unless you have a strong reason for needing to minimize risk of a Type I error in your particular research study.* The good news is that there is a way to reduce the likelihood of making a Type II error, and it does not increase the likelihood of making Type I errors—increase the number of participants in your research study. If you use more participants, you will make fewer Type II errors.

In Chapters 5 and 9, we explained how to determine the sample size that you will need for your research study.

STUDY QUESTION 15.2 | **What is statistical "hypothesis testing"? When is it used? What is its logic?**

Hypothesis Testing in Practice

In this section of the chapter, we do something very practical. We show you how to use several different statistical analysis techniques that will allow you to analyze data from most of the experimental and survey research designs discussed in this book. We already have discussed (page 434) the *independent samples t test* for comparing two group means (see page 434). All of the examples in this section are different, but they have one important thing in common—in every case we will use the same logic of hypothesis testing shown in Table 15.3. In each case, we will show the null and alternative hypotheses, set the alpha level at .05, obtain the *p* value, and determine if the relationship is statistically significant. We will also provide an effect size indicator in each example to determine the strength of the relationship.

In short, we will be following the six steps in hypothesis testing summarized in Table 15.3. You should review the steps now and along the way, and convince yourself that we are doing the same process again and again. When writing up the results of your significance testing in a research report, you must tell the reader the alpha level used for each test. If you use one standard level (as is customary) for all of your tests, you simply need to make the following statement one time at the beginning of the analysis: An alpha level of .05 was used for all statistical tests. You can take that as our statement for all of our significance tests that follow.

The *t* Test for Correlation Coefficients

Correlation coefficients show the strength and direction of the relationship between two quantitative variables. In the last chapter, we examined the correlation between GPA and starting salary using the recent college graduates data set (Table 14.1), and we showed that the correlation was .61. This is a moderately strong positive correlation in the sample data. The scatterplot also suggested a moderately strong positive correlation (Figure 14.6, page 398). We know that there is a relationship in the sample data, but the key question is whether the observed relationship is big enough to reject the null hypothesis and conclude that the observed relationship is *not just due to chance*. The goal in hypothesis testing is to make a claim about the population parameter (i.e., the correlation in the population) based on the sample data. We now determine whether we can conclude that the correlation of .61 between GPA and starting salary should be viewed as real relationship in the population or whether it should be viewed as nothing more than chance variation.

t **test for correlation coefficient**
Statistical test used to determine if a correlation coefficient is statistically significant

The *t* **test for correlation coefficients** is the statistical test used to determine whether an observed correlation coefficient is statistically significant. It's called the "*t* test" for a correlation coefficient because the test statistic used follows the *t* distribution. Therefore, SPSS uses the appropriate *t* distribution as the sampling distribution to test the null hypothesis that there is no correlation present in the population from which the data came.

Here are the null and alternative hypotheses used to test our correlation coefficient for statistical significance:

Null hypothesis: H_0: $\rho_{\text{GPA-SS}} = 0$

Alternative hypothesis: H_1: $\rho_{\text{GPA-SS}} \neq 0$

Recall that ρ is the Greek letter rho, and it refers to the population correlation coefficient. The null hypothesis says there is no correlation between GPA and starting salary in the population, and the alternative hypothesis says there is a correlation. For all of our significance tests, we set alpha at .05—that's the point at which we will consider our sample statistic value rare if the null hypothesis were true.

We entered the data into SPSS, and ran the *t* test for correlation coefficients. The value of the *t* statistic was 3.69, and, more importantly, the *p* value was .001. Because the *p* value is less than the alpha level, we use Rule 1 in Table 15.3—we reject the null hypothesis and tentatively accept the alternative hypothesis. The correlation between GPA and starting salary is statistically significant. We believe there is a real correlation between these variables in the population from which the sample data were selected.

Using APA style, one could write up this result as follows:

The moderately strong correlation between GPA and starting salary was statistically significant, $r(23) = .61$, $p = .001$.

Degrees of freedom
The number of values that are "free to vary"; it's used when computing a statistic to be used in inferential statistics

The number in the parentheses is called the **degrees of freedom** (*df*) for the significance test. The degrees of freedom are obtained on the SPSS printout. For the correlation coefficient the degrees of freedom is the total number of cases minus two (i.e., $n - 2$). We had 25 cases, so the degrees of freedom was 23 (i.e., $25 - 2 = 23$). The number after the first equals sign is the correlation coefficient, and the number after the second equals sign is the *p* value.

Because the correlation is positive, we conclude that as GPA goes up, starting salaries for recent college graduates tend to go up. Interestingly, a correlation coefficient can be viewed as an effect size indicator because it is a standardized measure of relationship, and a correlation of .61 suggests a moderately strong relationship.

An additional effect size indicator can be obtained by *squaring the correlation coefficient*, which tells you how much variance in the dependent variable is explained by the independent or predictor variable. In this case, .61 squared (i.e., .61 times .61) is equal to .37. Changing the proportion .37 to a percentage, you can see that 37% of the variance in starting salary is explained by GPA. This suggests a strong relationship, and one would be inclined to conclude that this relationship is practically significant in addition to statistically significant.

We are not convinced, however, that there are not additional variables that explain starting salary, and we would want to control for those variables before we conclude that GPA is important. Using our data set, we could obtain the correlation between GPA and starting salary, controlling for the other quantitative variables in our data set by calculating a partial correlation coefficient.

One-Way Analysis of Variance

One-way analysis of variance
Statistical test used when you have one quantitative DV and one categorical IV

ANOVA
Abbreviation for analysis of variance.

One-way analysis of variance (also called *one-way ANOVA*) is used to compare two or more group means for statistical significance. More specifically, it is used when you have one quantitative dependent variable and one categorical independent or predictor variable. (Two-way ANOVA is used when you have two categorical independent variables, three-way ANOVA is used when you have three categorical independent variables, and so forth.) The test statistic used in the analysis of variance follows the F distribution, rather than the t distribution used in our previous tests. The F distribution is a probability distribution that is usually skewed to the right.

Once again we use data from the recent college graduate data set provided in Table 14.1. We use starting salary as the dependent variable and college major as the categorical independent/predictor variable. The three levels of college major were 1 = psychology, 2 = philosophy, and 3 = business. The research question is whether there is a statistically significant difference in the starting salaries of psychology, philosophy, and business students.

Here are the statistical hypotheses under consideration:

Null hypothesis: H_0: $\mu_{Psych} = \mu_{Phil} = \mu_{Bus}$
Alternative hypothesis: H_1: Not all equal

The null hypothesis states that the psychology, philosophy, and business mean starting salaries are the same in their respective populations of new college graduates. The alternative hypothesis states that the population means are not all the same; at least two of the means are different from one another. The alternative hypothesis does not state which two of the population means are different from one another.

We used the SPSS program to get our numerical results. The F value was equal to 11.05. When there is no difference between the means, the F value tends to be near the value of 1.00, so you can see that this F value seems large. Because the F distribution is skewed to the right, this value of 11.05 falls in the right tail of the distribution. When the calculated value of a test statistic falls in the far right tail of the sampling distribution, the p value will be small. Our p value was equal to .00048, which is indeed small. Because our p value of .00048 is less than our alpha level of .05, we reject the null hypothesis and tentatively accept the alternative hypothesis (i.e., we applied Rule 1 from Table 15.3). We conclude that the relationship between college major and starting salary is statistically significant. The effect size indicator eta-squared was .50, which means 50% of the variance in starting salary is explained by college major. Because the effect size indicator is large, we conclude that the strength of the relationship is strong.

When you reject a null hypothesis in analysis of variance that has *three or more* means, you know that at least two of the means are different. You do not, however, know which means are significantly different. We conclude that at least two of the college major means are significantly different and that follow-up tests are needed to determine which means are significantly different. In the next section, we will determine which of the means are significantly different.

Using APA style, you can write up the results as follows:

A one-way analysis of variance was conducted to determine if the relationship between college major and starting salary was statistically significant. The ANOVA was significant, $F(2, 22) = 11.05$, $p < .001$, $\eta^2 = .50$. The strength of the relationship, assessed with η^2, was strong, with college majors accounting for 50% of the variance in starting salary.

All of the information in the write-up was available on the SPSS printout. The first number in the parentheses (i.e., 2) is the *between groups degrees of freedom*, which is the number of groups minus one. Our independent variable (college major) had three groups; therefore, the *df* was equal to 3 minus 1, which is 2. The second number in the parentheses is the *error degrees of freedom*, which is the number of participants in the study minus the number of groups. We had 25 participants and three groups; therefore, this was equal to 25 minus 3, which is 22. Notice that we reported $p < .001$ rather than giving an exact p value. *According to APA guidelines, researchers should report exact p values; the exception is when the* p *value is greater than .05 or smaller than .001; otherwise we report the exact* p *value in our write-ups.*

Post Hoc Tests in Analysis of Variance

Post hoc tests
Follow-up test to one-way ANOVA when the categorical IV has three or more levels; used to determine which pairs of means are significantly different

One-way analysis of variance tells the researcher whether the relationship between a categorical independent or predictor variable and a quantitative dependent variable is statistically significant. If your categorical variable has only two levels, then a statistically significant outcome is interpretable; just look to see which mean is larger and conclude that mean is significantly larger than the other mean. If you have three or more means, however, a statistically significant outcome for the one-way analysis of variance must be followed up with **post hoc tests** to determine which of the means are significantly different. College major was significantly related to starting salary; however, since college major has three levels, we conduct post hoc tests to determine which of the means are significantly different.

You might think that you could just do an independent samples *t* test for each pair of the means to determine which differences are statistically significant.

Unfortunately, you can't conduct multiple t tests like this because doing so would inflate the probability of making a Type I error (a false-positive error). Many post hoc tests are available in SPSS that control for this problem, and they will provide adjusted (i.e., corrected) p values for the researcher to use. Some popular post hoc tests are the Tukey test, the Newman–Keuls test, the Sidak test, and the Bonferroni test. The researcher selects the test(s) he or she wants to use from a menu in SPSS. All of the tests just mentioned are fine, but they will give you slightly different p values. We will use the Bonferroni post hoc test procedure now.

Here are the three sample mean incomes for the three college majors from our previous one-way analysis of variance:

- Average starting salary for recent graduates majoring in psychology is $29,437.50.

- Average starting salary for recent graduates majoring in philosophy is $32,800.00.

- Average starting salary for recent graduates majoring in business is $37,214.29.

We already know from the one-way analysis of variance that at least two of these means are statistically significant. The question in post hoc testing is which means are significantly different from each other? We must check for statistical significance because the observed differences between these means could be due to chance.

First, we checked to see whether the psychology and philosophy means were significantly different. The Bonferroni-adjusted p value (obtained from the SPSS printout) was .11. Our selected alpha level is .05. Our p value (.11) is greater than the alpha level (.05); therefore we use Rule 2. We fail to reject the null hypothesis (that the population means are the same) and conclude that the observed difference between the two means is *not statistically significant.* We can't say whether the psychology or philosophy mean is larger in the population. When we fail to reject the null hypothesis, we also cannot conclude that the population means are exactly the same.

Second, we checked to see whether the psychology and business major means were significantly different. The Bonferroni-adjusted p value (obtained from the SPSS printout) was .0003. Our selected alpha level is .05. Our p value (.0003) is less than the alpha level (.05); therefore, we use Rule 1. We reject the null hypothesis (that the population means are the same) and conclude that the difference between the two means is statistically significant. We are warranted in concluding that business majors have, on average, a higher starting salary than psychology majors in the population. Cohen's d is 2.25, which is very large. The business major mean is 2.25 standard deviations higher than the psychology mean. If we found this result, we would conclude that it is practically significant in addition to being statistically significant.

Third, we checked to see whether the philosophy and business major means were significantly different. The "Bonferroni-adjusted" p value was .03. Our selected alpha level is .05. Our p value (.03) is less than the alpha level (.05); therefore, we use Rule 1. We reject the null hypothesis and conclude that the difference between the two means is statistically significant. We are warranted in concluding that business majors have, on average, a higher starting salary than philosophy majors in the population. The difference between the two means is $4,414.29, and Cohen's d is 1.50, which is very large. The business major mean is 1.5 standard deviations higher than the philosophy major mean. If we found this result, we would conclude that it is practically significant in addition to being statistically significant.

Using APA style, you could write up the results as follows:

> Follow-up tests were conducted to determine which of the means were significantly different. Bonferroni-adjusted p values were used to control for inflated Type I error rate. The difference between the starting salaries of psychology ($M = 29,437.50$, $SD = 3,458.30$) and business ($M = 37,214.29$, $SD = 3,251.37$) graduates was statistically significant ($p < .001$). The difference between the starting salaries of philosophy ($M = 32,800$, $SD = 2,945.81$) and business ($M = 37,214.29$, $SD = 3,251.37$) graduates also was statistically significant ($p = .03$). The difference between the starting salaries of psychology and philosophy graduates was not significant ($p > .05$).

Analysis of Covariance

<div class="margin-note">

Analysis of covariance
Statistical test used when you have a one quantitative DV and a mixture of categorical and quantitative IVs (the quantitative IV is called a "covariate")

ANCOVA
Abbreviation for analysis of covariance

</div>

Analysis of covariance (also called **ANCOVA**) is used when you have a quantitative dependent variable and a mixture of categorical and quantitative independent variables. In the case discussed in this section, we have one categorical independent variable and one quantitative independent variable called a "covariate." ANCOVA can be thought of as an extension of ANOVA in that like ANOVA, it has one or more categorical independent variables, but unlike ANOVA, it also has one or more covariates added into the analysis.

If you are able to add a covariate that is strongly related to your dependent variable to an analysis of variance model, then you will increase the sensitivity (i.e., statistical power) of the test of the categorical independent variable. This means you are less likely to make a Type II error when testing the effect of the categorical independent variable.

ANCOVA is the statistical test used for experimental designs that have pretests and more than one group, such as the pretest–posttest control-group design and the nonequivalent comparison-group design. It is also used with the factorial design if you include a pretest in the design. The test statistic used in ANCOVA follows the F probability distribution just as was the case in ANOVA.

Now we will demonstrate ANCOVA by reanalyzing the social skills training experimental data, that previously found a nonsignificant difference between the experimental and control groups. In that example, we did not include the pretest data and chose just to see if the skills training and control group means were significantly different at the posttest—using the independent samples t test, we found that the p value was .07, which was greater than the alpha level of .05, so we failed to reject the null hypothesis. ANOVA can also be used to compare two posttest group means, and it provided us with an equivalent nonsignificant p value (.07). We were forced to conclude that the treatment was not effective.

Now we will include the pretest data and appropriately analyze all the data from the hypothetical pretest–posttest control-group design. The data for 28 cases are provided in Table 14.3 (page 396). When we were ignoring the pretest data, the null hypothesis stated that the posttest means for the skills training and control groups were the same in the population. In ANCOVA, the null hypothesis is slightly different; it states that the posttest means that *have been adjusted for pretest differences* are the same. Here are the hypotheses tested in ANCOVA:

Null hypothesis: H_0: $\mu_{\text{ADJ-Skills Training}} = \mu_{\text{ADJ-No Training}}$

Alternative hypothesis: H_1: $\mu_{\text{ADJ-Skills Training}} \neq \mu_{\text{ADJ-No Training}}$

The only new feature of these hypotheses is that we inserted "ADJ" to convey that we now are testing adjusted means rather than means unadjusted for pretest differences.

We used the SPSS computer program to obtain our results.[2] The test statistic used in ANCOVA for the differences between the group means relies on the F distribution. The F value was 8.38, and more importantly, the p value was .008. Based on this p value, we apply Rule 1. Because the p value (.008) is less than the alpha level (.05), we reject the null hypothesis, tentatively accept the alternative hypothesis, and conclude that the difference between the skills training and control-groups means is statistically significant. We calculated Cohen's d for these two group means earlier (see Exhibit 14.3) and found that it was equal to .73, which is moderately large. When we ran the ANCOVA analysis, we also had SPSS report partial eta-squared, and it was equal to .251; changing the proportion (.251) to a percentage (25.1%), we conclude that 25% of the variance in skills performance is explained by the experimental treatment, which is impressive. We conclude that social skills training causes an increase in participants' performance on the social skills test and that this effect is practically significant.

Using APA style, you could write up the results as follows:

We conducted a one-way analysis of covariance to determine whether the difference between the treatment and control-group means was statistically significant after adjusting for pretest differences between the groups. The difference between the adjusted skills training mean ($M = 3.97$, $SE = .21$) and the adjusted control-group mean ($M = 3.10$, SE = .21) was statistically significant $F(1, 25) = 8.38$, $p = .008$, $\eta^2 = .25$. The strength of the relationship, assessed with η^2, was moderately strong, with the treatment variable accounting for 25% of the variance in social skills performance.

In this and a previous example, we have analyzed the data from our social skills experiment. When we did not include the pretest in the analysis, the p value was .07, and we failed to reject the null hypothesis. When we included the pretest and conducted an ANCOVA, the p value was .008, and we rejected the null hypothesis. This makes a point we stated earlier: ANCOVA is usually more sensitive (i.e., has higher statistical power) in testing the difference between means. In this case, we conclude that the means are significantly different (based on the ANCOVA results) and that our earlier test, which resulted in the failure to reject the null hypothesis,

---

[2]We first checked to make sure we had not violated the homogeneity of slopes assumption by checking the interaction between the categorical independent variable and the covariate. Because this p value was greater than .05, we did not violate the assumption; therefore, we dropped the interaction term and ran the standard ANCOVA.

was a Type II error. This is one reason we recommend including pretests in experimental designs. We list several reasons for including a pretest in Chapter 8.

Two-Way Analysis of Variance

Two-way analysis of variance (also called *two-way ANOVA*) is used when you have a quantitative dependent variable and two categorical independent variables. We will demonstrate two-way ANOVA using the set of hypothetical data provided in Table 15.5. These data are for another experiment testing the effectiveness of our skills training program. These new data include the variable gender. Therefore, we have two categorical independent variables this time: treatment condition (skills training vs. control) and gender (male vs. female). We explained in Chapter 8 that a factorial experimental design includes at least two independent variables (at least one of which is manipulated), and participants are randomly assigned to the groups (on at least one IV). In our experiment, the training variable is the manipulated variable; obviously gender is not manipulated by the experimenter! Because the training independent variable is manipulated and participants were randomly assigned to the groups making up this variable, stronger cause and effect conclusions can be drawn about the treatment than about the nonmanipulated variable gender.

TABLE 15.5
Hypothetical Data Set For Posttest-Only Factorial Design Featuring Social Skills Training By Gender

Participant	Posttest Scores	Treatment Condition	Gender
1	2	1	1
2	4	1	1
3	3	1	1
4	2	1	1
5	2	1	1
6	0	1	1
7	2	1	1
8	4	1	2
9	4	1	2
10	4	1	2
11	3	1	2
12	5	1	2
13	2	1	2
14	2	1	2
15	8	2	1
16	6	2	1
17	6	2	1
18	6	2	1
19	4	2	1
20	5	2	1

(continued)

Participant	Posttest Scores	Treatment Condition	Gender
21	3	2	1
22	4	2	2
23	6	2	2
24	3	2	2
25	4	2	2
26	3	2	2
27	3	2	2
28	5	2	2

Note: The dependent variable is number of appropriate social interactions measured at posttest; the manipulated independent variable is skills training (1 = treatment vs. 2 = control); the nonmanipulated independent variable is gender (1 = male vs. 2 = female).

We explained in Chapter 8 that in a factorial experiment with two independent variables you test for a main effect for each independent variable and you test for an interaction effect. A main effect is the separate effect of an independent variable, and an interaction effect is present when the effect of one independent variable varies at the different levels of the other independent variable.

To save space (and save you some reading), we will state the null hypotheses verbally rather than writing them out. The null hypothesis for treatment condition says the population means of skills trained and the not-trained participants are equal. The null hypothesis for gender says that population means of males and females are the same. Last, the null for the interaction states that in the population there is no interaction between treatment condition and gender.

Here are the empirical results:

- Treatment condition main effect: F value = 15.51; p value = .001
- Gender main effect: F value = .021; p value = .885
- Interaction effect: F value = 7.68; p value = .011

Using an alpha level of .05, the treatment condition main effect is statistically significant, the gender main effect is not statistically significant, and the treatment-by-gender interaction effect is statistically significant.

When the interaction effect is statistically significant, the rule is to focus interpretation on the interaction effect rather than main effects. To aid in interpreting this statistically significant interaction effect, we plotted the cell means in Figure 15.4. The interaction plot shown in Figure 15.4 suggests that the skills training program works better for males than for females. This observation was found to be warranted by the follow-up significance tests.

Here is an APA style presentation of the results:

A 2×2 ANOVA was conducted to evaluate the effects of skills training and gender. The analysis yielded a statistically significant skills training main effect, $F(1, 24) = 15.51$, $p = .001$, $\eta^2 = .393$, and a statistically significant interaction between treatment and gender, $F(1, 24) = 12.89$, $p = .01$, $\eta^2 = .242$. The gender main effect

FIGURE 15.4
Interaction plot for
factorial skills training
experiment.

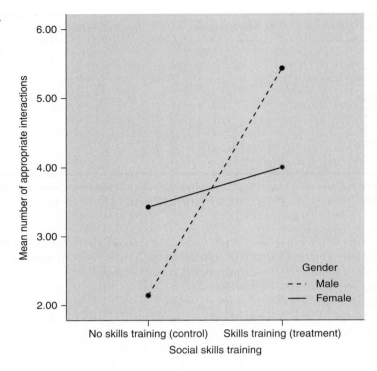

was not significant, $p > .05$. Examination of the interaction plot suggested that the training program worked better for men than for women. Men had a mean performance of 2.14 in the control group and a mean of 5.43 in the skills training condition, representing an unstandardized difference of 3.29 and a Cohen's d of 2.69. This difference was large and statistically significant ($p < .001$). Women had a mean performance of 3.43 in the control group and a mean of 4.00 in the skills training condition, representing an unstandardized difference of .57 and a Cohen's d of .63. This difference was not statistically significant ($p > .05$). We conclude that the skills training treatment worked better for men than for women.

When you examine the interaction plot in Figure 15.4, you might see additional features that you want to check for statistical significance. That's fine, but for each comparison between means, you will need to obtain the p value and determine if the difference is statistically significant. If the difference is not statistically significant, you are probably looking at chance variation, and no claims about the observed difference is warranted.

One-way repeated measures analysis of variance
Statistical test used when you have one quantitative DV and one repeated measures IV

One-Way Repeated Measures Analysis of Variance

One-way repeated measures analysis of variance (also called *one-way repeated measures* ANOVA) is used when you have one quantitative dependent variable and one within-participants independent variable. With a within-participants independent variable, the same participants are measured more than once. This is the appropriate analytical procedure for a repeated measures design as well as for the one-group pretest–posttest designs (and several variants of these designs) discussed in Chapter 8.

We demonstrate this analysis with a set of data from a one-group pretest–posttest design with two rather than the traditional one posttest. We call these posttests the immediate and delayed posttests. The treatment in our hypothetical experiment is a health program designed to reduce participants' weight by participation in a structured diet program administered over a one-month period. The participants meet with the researcher four times during the month long program. The weight of all participants (the dependent variable) is measured at the beginning of the program (pretest), at the end of the program (immediate posttest), and again one month after completion of the program (delayed posttest). The data for this hypothetical experiment are provided in Table 15.6.

Here are the null and alternative hypotheses:

Null hypothesis: H_0: $\mu_{\text{Pretest}} = \mu_{\text{Immediate Posttest}} = \mu_{\text{Delayed Posttest}}$
Alternative hypothesis: H_1: Not all equal

The null hypothesis says that the population means at the three different times for the group of participants are equal (i.e., the weight of the people is the same at all three times, which would suggest no program impact). The alternative hypothesis says at least two of the means are significantly different.

We used SPSS to obtain the statistical results. The F value was 24.38, but more importantly, the p value was less than .001. Because the p value is less than the alpha level (of .05), we reject the null hypothesis and conclude that at least two of the means are significantly different. However, we don't know which of the three means plotted in Figure 15.5 are significantly different, so we conducted post hoc tests.

TABLE 15.6

Hypothetical Data for One-Group Pretest–Posttest Design with Immediate and Delayed Posttest

Participant	Pretest	Immediate Posttest	Delayed Posttest
1	222	223	222
2	156	154	153
3	142	139	138
4	225	221	220
5	159	153	155
6	275	270	269
7	301	297	294
8	268	261	258
9	212	210	209
10	189	186	185

Note: The within-participants independent variable is time (pretest, immediate posttest, delayed posttest), and the dependent variable is weight.

FIGURE 15.5
Plot of means for
one-group
pretest–posttest
design with immediate
and delayed posttests.

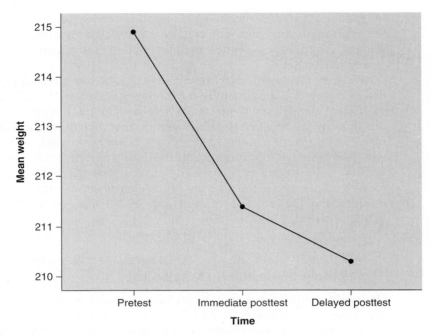

Here are the three sample means for weight in this study:

- Mean weight at pretest is 214.9 pounds.
- Mean weight at immediate posttest is 211.4 pounds.
- Mean weight at delayed posttest is 210.3 pounds.

When examining the three means, it appears that the program was successful, on average, in reducing participants' weights. The immediate posttest suggests that the program was successful (it's lower than the pretest), and the delayed posttest suggests that the program success continued one month later. These observations were tested via post hoc tests. First, the mean difference between the participants' weight at pretest and immediate posttest is 3.5 (i.e., 214.9–211.4) pounds. The Bonferroni-adjusted p value for the significance test of this difference was .003. Because .003 is less than the alpha level (.05), we conclude that the difference between the participants' pretest and immediate posttest weights is statistically significant. Second, the difference between the participants' weight at pretest and delayed posttest is 4.6. The Bonferroni-adjusted p value for this difference was .001. Because .001 is less than the alpha level, we conclude that the difference between the participants' pretest and delayed posttest weights is statistically significant. Third, the difference between the participants' weight at immediate posttest and delayed posttest is 1.1. The Bonferroni-adjusted p value for this difference was .095. Because .095 is greater than the alpha level, we conclude that the difference between the participants' pretest and delayed posttest weights is not statistically significant.

We also obtained a measure of effect size for the three comparisons. Cohen's *d* for the pretest to immediate posttest change was .06, which suggests a small improvement in weight. Cohen's *d* for the pretest to delayed posttest change was equal to .08, which also suggests a small improvement. Cohen's *d* for the immediate posttest to delayed posttest change was equal to .02, which also suggests a small improvement. We conclude that the weight loss program produces a statistically significant weight loss, but the weight reduction is small.

Here is an APA style presentation of the results:

A one-way repeated measures ANOVA was conducted with weight as the dependent variable and time (pretest, immediate posttest, and delayed posttest) as the within-participants independent variable. The time main effect was statistically significant, $F(2, 18) = 24.38$, $p < .001$. To interpret this main effect, we conducted three post hoc tests and obtained Bonferroni-adjusted p values. First, the difference between the pretest ($M = 214.90$, $SD = 54.35$) and immediate posttest ($M = 211.40$, $SD = 53.79$) weights was statistically significant, $p = .003$, indicating a significant improvement from pretest to immediate posttest. Second, the difference between the pretest ($M = 214.90$, $SD = 54.35$) and delayed posttest ($M = 210.30$, $SD = 52.88$) weights also was statistically significant, $p = .001$, indicating a significant improvement from pretest to delayed posttest. Third, the difference between the immediate posttest ($M = 211.40$, $SD = 53.79$) and delayed posttest ($M = 210.30$, $SD = 52.88$) weights was not significant, $p > .05$. Overall, the results show that the statistically significant improvement in pretest weight found at the immediate posttest continued to the delayed posttest measurement. Cohen's *d* was only .06 for the pretest to immediate posttest change and .08 for the pretest to delayed posttest change. The weight losses resulting from the program were statistically significant but relatively small in size.

The *t* test for Regression Coefficients

t test for regression coefficients
Statistical test used to determine if a regression coefficient is statistically significant

In the last chapter, we introduced regression analysis. In *simple regression*, the researcher analyzes the relationship between one quantitative dependent variable and one quantitative independent or predictor variable.[3] In *multiple regression*, the researcher analyzes the relationship between one quantitative dependent variable and two or more quantitative independent or predictor variables. The **t test for regression coefficients** uses the *t* distribution to test the significance of the regression coefficients obtained in regression analysis. Regression coefficients express the relationship between an independent variable and the dependent

[3]Although regression analysis can be used with categorical independent variables, we prefer to operationalize regression as working with quantitative independent variables, ANOVA as working with categorical independent variables, and ANCOVA as working with a mixture of categorical and quantitative independent variables. All of these analytic techniques are "special cases" of the general liner model (GLM).

variable (controlling for any other independent variables included in the regression equation).

We will now take the multiple regression equation from the last chapter and test the two regression coefficients for statistical significance. Here is that regression equation once again:

$$\hat{Y} = -\$2,617.28 + \$5,488.71(X_1) + \$17.79(X_2)$$

where

$\hat{Y}$ is the predicted value for starting salary,

X_1 is college GPA,

X_2 is high school SAT scores,

$\$-2,617.28$ is the Y-intercept,

$\$5,488.71$ is the value of the regression coefficient for X_1. It expresses the relationship between grade point average and starting salary (controlling for SAT scores), and

$\$17.79$ is the value of the regression coefficient for X_2. It expresses the relationship between high school SAT and starting salary (controlling for GPA).

Our goal is to see if these two regression coefficients are statistically significant. Before a researcher is justified in interpreting a regression coefficient from his or her data, it must be checked for statistical significance. That's because the coefficient found on the sample data might simply be due to chance (i.e., sampling error). If a regression coefficient is statistically significant, the researcher can conclude that there is a high probability of a real relationship in the population and proceed to interpret the coefficient observed in the sample data.

Our first research question is about the first regression coefficient ($\$5,488.71$):

Research question 1: Is the relationship between GPA and starting salary (controlling for SAT) statistically significant?

Here are the statistical hypotheses for this research question:

Null hypothesis: H_0: $\beta_{YX1.X2} = 0$
Alternative hypothesis: H_1: $\beta_{YX1.X2} \neq 0$

The null hypothesis says that the population regression coefficient is equal to zero (i.e., there is no relationship in the population). The alternative hypothesis says that the population coefficient is nonzero (i.e., there is a relationship in the population).

Semi-partial correlation squared
The amount of variance in the dependent variable uniquely explained by a single quantitative independent variable

Using SPSS, we found that the t value was 3.16, and the p value was .005. Our p value (.005) was less than our alpha level (.05); therefore, we reject the null hypothesis, tentatively accept the alternative hypothesis, and conclude that the relationship expressed in this regression coefficient is statistically significant. The appropriate effect size indicator for a regression coefficient is called the **semi-partial correlation squared** (symbolized sr^2); it is equal to .169, which means 16.9% of the variance in starting salary is uniquely explained by GPA. We would conclude that this relationship between SAT and starting salary is statistically significant and practically significant.

Our second research question is about the second regression coefficient ($17.79):

Research question 2: Is the relationship between SAT and starting salary (controlling for GPA) statistically significant?

Here are the statistical hypotheses for this research question:

Null hypothesis: H_0: $\beta_{YX2.X1} = 0$

Alternative hypothesis: H_1: $\beta_{YX2.X1} \neq 0$

Using SPSS we found that the t value was 3.88, and the p value was .001. Our p value (.001) was less than our alpha level (.05); therefore, we reject the null hypothesis, tentatively accept the alternative hypothesis, and conclude that the relationship expressed in this second regression coefficient is statistically significant. The effect size indicator semi-partial correlation squared was equal to .255, which means that 25.5% of the variance in starting salary is uniquely explained by SAT scores. We would conclude that this relationship between SAT and starting salary is statistically significant and practically significant.

We have concluded that both of the predictor variables are important predictors of starting salary. However, you might also want to compare the two predictor variables for relative importance (i.e., which variable is more important?). Because GPA uniquely explained 16.9% of the variance in starting salary and SAT explained 25.5%, we conclude that SAT is a more important variable than GPA for predicting starting college students' starting salary.

Here is a brief APA style write-up of the results of our regression analysis:

A multiple regression was conducted to determine how well the starting salaries of recent college graduates is predicted by SAT scores and college GPA. The overall model including both predictor variables was statistically significant, $F(2, 22) = 18.49$, $p < .001$. The multiple correlation squared (R^2) for the full model was .63, indicating that 63% of the variance in starting salary was explained by the two predictor variables. Starting salary was significantly predicted by GPA ($\beta = .435$, $p = .005$) and GRE ($\beta = .535$, $p = .001$). college GPA uniquely accounted for 25.5% of the variance in starting salary ($sr^2 = .255$), and SAT uniquely accounted for 16.9% of the variance in starting salary ($sr^2 = .169$). We conclude that both predictor variables were important, but GPA was a stronger predictor than SAT.

Rather than using the regular (i.e., unstandardized) regression coefficients (i.e., $5,488.71 for GPA and $17.79 for SAT, which are symbolized by "b") in the write-up, we followed convention and used the standardized regression coefficients that are symbolized with the Greek letter beta (i.e., β). These values were available on the SPSS printout. When a regression equation has many predictor variables, the results are usually presented in tables.

Chi-Square Test for Contingency Tables

The **chi-square test for contingency tables** is used to determine whether a relationship observed in a contingency table is statistically significant. In the last chapter, we explained that contingency tables are used for studying the relationship between two or more categorical variables. We also demonstrated "how to read a contingency table." A key point was that you need to percentage your contingency table correctly if you hope to see a relationship in the table. We provided you with the following two rules:

- If the percentages are calculated down the columns, then compare across the rows.
- If the percentages are calculated across the rows, then compare down the columns.

We now construct a contingency table using the categorical variables gender and college major provided in the college student data set (Table 14.1). Our research question is whether gender is related to college major. The 2-by-2 contingency table produced by the statistical program SPSS is shown in Table 15.7. Take a moment to examine the Table 15.7 and use the appropriate rule to determine if there appears to be a relationship—the percentages are calculated down the columns, so compare across the rows. Indeed, there appears to be a relationship. Looking at the first row, you will see that 53.8% of females, but only 8.3% of males, are psychology majors. Females are more than six times as likely (53.8/8.3 = 6.5) to be psychology majors (i.e., females have a far higher rate than males of majoring in psychology). Looking at the second row, 30.8% of females and 50% of males are philosophy majors. Males are more than one-and-a-half (50.0/30.8 = 1.6) times as likely as females to be philosophy majors. Looking at the third row, you will see that males are more than two-and-a-half (41.7/15.4 = 2.7)

TABLE 15.7
Contingency Table of College Major by Gender

			Gender		Total
			Female	Male	
Undergraduate major	Psychology	Count	7	1	8
		% within Gender	53.8%	8.3%	32.0%
	Philosophy	Count	4	6	10
		% within Gender	30.8%	50.0%	40.0%
	Business	Count	2	5	7
		% within Gender	15.4%	41.7%	28.0%
Total		Count	13	12	25
		% within Gender	100.0%	100.0%	100.0%

times as likely as females to be business majors. Clearly the variables gender and undergraduate major appear to be related in the sample data. But the key question before you that can justifiably interpret these results is this: "Is the observed relationship statistically significant?"

The null hypothesis is that there is no relationship between gender and undergraduate major in the population from which the sample data were randomly selected. The alternative hypothesis is that there is a relationship. The probability distribution used for contingency tables is the chi-square (χ^2) distribution. The computed value of the test statistic for our contingency table was 6.16, and the p value was .046. Our p value (.046) is less than our alpha level (.05); therefore, we conclude that the relationship is statistically significant. We used the effect size indicator called *Cramer's V* to determine the strength of the relationship. The size of this effect size indicator can be interpreted like the size of a correlation coefficient. Our Cramer's V was .496, which suggests that the relationship between gender and college major was moderately strong. We conclude that the relationship between gender and college major is statistically and practically significant.

Here is a brief APA style write-up of the results of our chi-square analysis:

> A two-way contingency table analysis was conducted to determine whether gender and college major were related. These variables were found to be significantly related, Pearson χ^2 (2, N = 25) = 6.16, p = .046, Cramer's V = .50. Based on Cramer's V, we conclude that the strength of relationship is moderately strong.

Other Significance Tests

You have come a long way! There are additional significance tests that we could discuss, but the logic would be same as the logic of hypothesis testing that you now understand. The logic is summarized in Table 15.3, and you use this logic every time you want to determine if a relationship or difference between means is statistically significant. The key step is to obtain the p value and determine if it is less than (or equal to) or greater than the alpha level. If it's the former, the finding is statistically significant, and the researcher concludes that he or she is very likely observing a real relationship. If it's the latter, the finding is not statistically significant, and the researcher concludes that he or she is probably just observing chance variation. Remember to always obtain an effect size indicator to help determine how strong the effect or relationship is for statistically significant findings.

STUDY QUESTION 15.3 | **What are the statistical tests discussed thus far? How do these statistical tests differ (in terms of the types of variables)?**

Hypothesis Testing and Research Design

We have demonstrated null hypothesis significance testing with hypothetical survey research and experimental research data. In the following list, "IV" stands for independent or predictor variable and "DV" stands for dependent variable. We have demonstrated the following statistical tests:

- *t* test for independent samples (use with one categorical IV and one quantitative DV)
- *t* test for correlation coefficients (use with one quantitative IV and one quantitative DV)
- One-way ANOVA (use with one categorical IV and one quantitative DV)
- Post hoc tests for ANOVA (use with categorical IV(s) resulting in three or more groups, and one quantitative DV)
- ANCOVA (use with mixture of quantitative and categorical IVs and one quantitative DV)
- Two-way ANOVA (use with two categorical IVs and one quantitative DV)
- One-way repeated measures ANOVA (it's like regular ANOVA except that the IV is a within-participants variable rather than a between-participants variable)
- *t* test for regression coefficients (use with quantitative IV(s) and one quantitative DV)
- Chi-square test for contingency tables (use when all variables are categorical)

We used the same logic of hypothesis testing summarized in Table 15.3 with all of the tests. When you read about a finding being statistically significant in research articles assigned to you for class, you will know the logic that was used.

In earlier chapters, we covered several experimental research designs, and we want you to know what statistical test to use for each design. This chapter has demonstrated significance testing for the following experimental research designs:

- posttest-only control-group design
- pretest–posttest control-group design
- factorial design
- one-group pretest–posttest design

In Tables 15.8, 15.9, and 15.10 we list the three major categories of experimental research designs along with the appropriate statistical procedures. This will enable you to connect the concepts of design and analysis.

TABLE 15.8

Statistical Analysis for Weak Experimental Research Designs

Design	Analysis Procedure
One-group posttest-only design	Descriptive and correlational statistics
One-group pretest–posttest design	Paired *t* test or one-way repeated measures ANOVA
Posttest-only design with nonequivalent groups (with two groups)	Independent *t* test or one-way ANOVA
Posttest-only design with nonequivalent groups (with more than two groups)	One-way ANOVA (with follow-up tests as needed)

T A B L E   1 5 . 9

Statistical Analysis for Strong Experimental Research Designs

Design	Analysis Procedure
(a) Between-Participants Designs	
Posttest-only control group design (with two groups)	Independent samples *t* test or one-way ANOVA
Posttest-only control group design (with more than two groups)	One-way ANOVA (with post hoc tests as needed)
Pretest–posttest control group design (with two groups)	One-way ANCOVA or mixed model ANOVA
Pretest-posttest control group design (with more than two groups)	One-way ANCOVA (with post hoc tests as needed) or mixed model ANOVA (with post hoc tests as needed)
Between participants factorial design (with two independent variables and no pretest)	Two-way ANOVA (with post hoc tests as needed)
Between participants factorial design (with two independent variables and pretest)	Two-way ANCOVA (with post hoc tests as needed)
(b) Within-Participants Designs	
Within-participants posttest-only design (with two conditions)	Paired *t* test or one-way repeated measures ANOVA
Within-participants posttest-only design (with more than two conditions)	One-way repeated measures ANOVA (with post hoc tests as needed)
Within-participants factorial design (with two within-participants independent variables)	Two-way repeated measures ANOVA (with post hoc tests as needed)
(c) Factorial design based on a mixed model	
Factorial design based on a mixed model	Two-way mixed model ANOVA (with post hoc tests as needed)

T A B L E   1 5 . 1 0

Statistical Analysis for Quasi-experimental Research Designs

Design	Analysis Procedure
Nonequivalent comparison-group design (with two groups)	One-way ANCOVA or reliability corrected ANCOVA or mixed model ANOVA
Nonequivalent comparison-group design (with more than two groups)	One-way ANCOVA (with post hoc tests as needed) or reliability corrected ANCOVA (with post hoc tests as needed) or mixed model ANOVA (with post hoc tests as needed)
Interrupted time-series design	Autoregressive integrated moving average (ARIMA) model for long series with 50 points or more; for short series, see Bloom (2003), Crosbie (1993), and Tryon (1982)
Regression-discontinuity design	ANCOVA on adjusted scores (Shadish, Cook & Campbell, 2002)

Summary   This chapter introduces readers to inferential statistics, which is the branch of statistics that focuses on making inferences about population parameters based on sample data. The theory of inferential statistics is based on the concept of sampling distributions. A sampling distribution is the theoretical probability distribution that would result if you took all possible samples of a particular size from a population and calculated the sample statistic (e.g., such as a mean, standard deviation, or correlation coefficient) value for each of the samples. That would result in a lot of values, but it would demonstrate that the values vary around the true population parameter and follow a known distributional form (such as a normal curve). In practice you would never have to conduct this process, and you would select only one sample in your research study; statistical packages are used to estimate the values of the relevant sampling distributions for your analyses.

Two major branches in the field of inferential statistics are *estimation* (in which you use your sample data value(s) to estimate the population data value(s)) and *hypothesis testing* (in which you determine how likely your observed result such as a difference between two group means would be if there were no difference between the group means in the population). The chapter goes into depth in explaining the logic of hypothesis testing (which is summarized into five key steps as shown in Table 15.3). Perhaps the most important idea in hypothesis testing is that you reject the null hypothesis (that there is no relationship in the population) when the *p* value (which is based on your sample data) is less than the alpha level. Psychologists typically set the alpha level (also called the level of significance) at .05; therefore, if the *p* value is less than (or equal to) .05, the researcher rejects the null hypothesis (of no relationship) and accepts the alternative hypothesis (that there *is* a relationship in the population). If the *p* value is greater than .05, the researcher will "fail to reject" the null hypothesis.

The chapter demonstrates how to use the logic of hypothesis testing for each of the following statistical tests:

1. Independent samples *t* test—used when you have 1 quantitative DV and 1 categorical IV with just two levels

2. *t* test for correlation coefficients—used when your IV and DV are both quantitative

3. One-way ANOVA—used when you have 1 quantitative DV and one categorical IV (with two or more levels)

4. Post hoc tests in one-way analysis of variance—used when the categorical IV has 3 or more levels and you need to know which pairs of group means are significantly different

5. ANCOVA—used when you have 1 quantitative DV and a mixture of categorical and quantitative IVs. In the traditional case of ANCOVA, you have 1 quantitative DV, 1 categorical IV, and 1 quantitative IV (which is called a covariate)

6. Two-way ANOVA—used when you have 1 quantitative DV and 2 categorical IVs

7. One-way repeated measures ANOVA—used when you have 1 quantitative DV and your 1 IV is a repeated measures variable (it's also called a within-participants or within-subjects variable)

8. *t* test for regression coefficients—used when you have 1 quantitative DV and one or more quantitative IVs[3]

9. Chi-square test for contingency tables—used when all of your variables are categorical

Understanding these statistical analyses is simplified by realizing that *you follow the same five steps of hypothesis testing for all of the tests*. Therefore, make sure that you understand and memorize the five steps (i.e., Table 15.3) and the concepts listed in the steps (i.e., null hypothesis, alternative hypothesis, alpha level, and *p* value). Tables 15.8–15.10 list the appropriate statistical tests used with the research designs discussed in earlier chapters.

Key Terms and Concepts

Alpha level
Alternative hypothesis
Analysis of covariance
ANCOVA
Chi-square test for contingency tables
Clinical significance
Confidence interval
Critical region
Degrees of freedom
Directional alternative hypothesis
Effect size indicators
Estimation
Hypothesis testing
Independent samples *t* test
Interval estimation
Level of significance
Logic of hypothesis testing
Nondirectional alternative hypothesis
Null hypothesis
One-way analysis of variance
One-way repeated measures analysis of variance

Parameter
Partial eta squared
Point estimation
Population
Post hoc tests
Practical significance
Probability value
p value
Sample
Sampling distribution
Sampling distribution of the mean
Semi-partial correlation squared
Standard error
Statistic
Statistical power
Statistically significant
t test for correlation coefficient
t test for regression coefficients
Test statistic
Two-way analysis of variance
Type I error
Type II error

Related Internet Sites

http://www.stat.sc.edu/rsrch/gasp/
This site provides the basic data analysis procedures needed to analyze data collected from most psychological studies. This site includes the *t* test, regression, and one-way ANOVA, as well as other descriptive statistical procedures. Nine educational procedures are also included to assist in teaching statistics online.

http://www.sportsci.org/resource/stats/errors.html
This Internet site gives a discussion of Type I and Type II errors.

http://onlinestatbook.com/stat_sim/
This site provides demonstrations of significance tests.

http://www.statsoft.com/textbook/stathome.html
This is an online statistics book. You can also look up the concepts in this chapter.

http://statpages.org/
This is a link to many free statistical tools

Practice Test   *The answers to these questions can be found in Appendix.*

1. The null and alternative hypotheses in ANOVA (as in any hypothesis testing procedure) refer to _____.
   a. Sample statistics
   b. Population parameters
   c. Sampling parameters
   d. None of the above

2. If you conducted a study in which you randomly assigned people to two groups and tested them on a measure of attention, which statistical test would you use to determine whether the two groups differed on the measure of attention?
   a. Two-way analysis of variance
   b. One-way analysis of variance
   c. Independent *t* test
   d. Simple regression
   e. B and C are both true

3. At a minimum, how many significance tests are conducted for a standard two-way ANOVA?
   a. 3
   b. 2
   c. 1
   d. 4

4. In hypothesis testing, the "probability of the observed result of your statistic or a more extreme result, if the null hypothesis were true" is called the _____, and the "cutoff the researcher uses to decide when to reject the null hypothesis" is called the _____ _____.
   a. Alpha level, *p* value
   b. *p* value, alpha level
   c. Probability value, significance level
   d. Both *b* and *c* are true because the terms used are synonyms

5. If you have conducted your statistical analysis and the results state that you can reject the null hypothesis but this, in fact, is incorrect, you have
   a. Made a Type I error
   b. Made a calculation error
   c. Made a Type II error
   d. Used the wrong statistical test
   e. Stated the wrong hypothesis

6. What significance level is most commonly used by psychologists?

a. .5

b. .1

c. .01

d. .05

Challenge Exercises

1. The following data are from a hypothetical experiment in which independent variable A is some prior knowledge of statistics (where A_1 = has prior knowledge, A_2 = does not have prior knowledge) and independent variable B is gender (where B_1 = females, B_2 = males). Twenty males are randomly assigned to the two conditions in variable A, and 20 females also are randomly assigned to the two conditions in variable A. There are 10 individuals in each cell of the table below, which shows the cell means. Graph (i.e., plot) the cell means from following data. *Assume that any differences in the means (for main effects or interaction effect) are statistically significant.*

	B_1	B_2	
A_1	8	6	7
A_2	2	4	3
	5	5	

a. Are there any main effects present? If yes, what main effect(s) is/are present?

b. Is there a two-way interaction between independent variables A and B? If yes, what does this interaction mean (i.e., interpret the interaction).

2. What statistical analysis procedure would be appropriate in each of the following situations? Assume your independent variables are between-participants independent variables.

a. You have one quantitative dependent variable and one categorical independent variable.

b. You have one quantitative dependent variable and two categorical independent variables.

c. You have one quantitative dependent variable and three categorical independent variables.

d. You have one quantitative dependent variable and one categorical independent variable and quantitative independent variable/covariate.

e. You have one quantitative dependent variable (DV) and one quantitative independent variable.

CHAPTER

16

Preparing the Research Report for Presentation or Publication

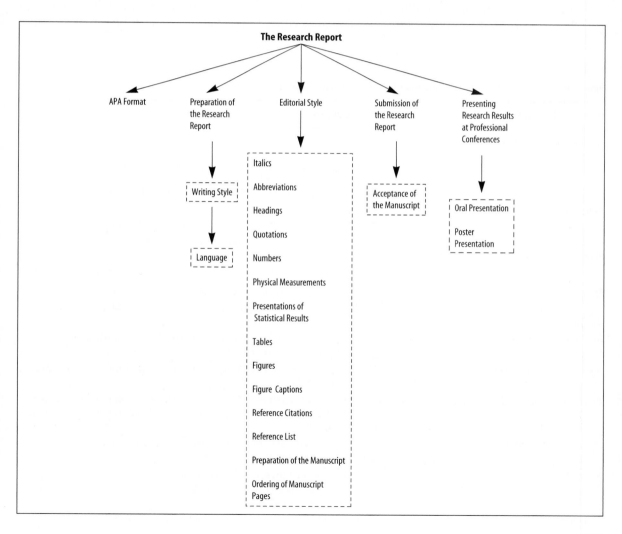

Introduction

Throughout this book, we have presented the steps involved in the research process and discussed in detail the intricacies of each. A thorough presentation was made to enable you to conduct a sound scientific research study. As a scientist, however, you have a responsibility not only to conduct a well-designed and well-executed study but also to communicate the results of the study to the rest of the scientific community. Your study might have answered a very significant research question, but the results are of limited value unless they are made public. The primary mechanism for communicating results is through professional journals. Within the field of psychology, the Association for Psychological Science (APS) publishes four journals, and the American Psychological Association (APA) journal programs include 58 journals and a magazine. Table 16.1 highlights many of these journals and illustrates that these journals cover a wide variety of areas and provide an outlet for studies conducted within just about any field of interest. There

TABLE 16.1

American Psychological Association and Association for Psychological Science Journals

Name of Journal	Area Covered
American Psychological Association Journals	
American Psychologist	Contains archival documents and articles focusing on current issues in psychology, issues relating to the science and practice of psychology, and the contribution psychology makes to public policy
Behavioral Neuroscience	Contains original studies in anatomy, chemistry, endocrinology, genetics, pharmacology, and physiology as they relate to behavioral neuroscience
Clinician's Research Digest: Briefings in Behavioral Science	Provides monthly reviews and highlights of the most relevant articles of nearly 100 journals
Developmental Psychology	Publishes articles relating to human development across the life span
Emotion	Publishes articles on all aspects of emotional processes
Experimental and Clinical Psychopharmacology	Publishes research integrating pharmacology and behavior
Health Psychology	Devoted to furthering an understanding of the relationship between behavioral principles and physical health or illness
Journal of Abnormal Psychology	Publishes articles relating to the determinants, theories, and correlates of abnormal behavior
Journal of Applied Psychology	Publishes articles that contribute to our understanding of any applied area of psychology except clinical and applied experimental or human factors psychology
Journal of Comparative Psychology	Contains behavioral studies that relate to evolution, development, ecology, control, and functional significance of various species
Journal of Consulting and Clinical Psychology	Contains research investigations pertaining to development, validity, and use of various techniques for diagnosing and treating disturbed behavior in all populations
Journal of Counseling Psychology	Contains articles pertaining to evaluation, application, and theoretical issues related to counseling

American Psychological Association Journals (continued)

Journal of Educational Psychology	Publishes studies and theoretical papers pertaining to education such as learning and cognition
Journal of Experimental Psychology: Animal Behavior Processes	Publishes experimental and theoretical studies on animal behavior
Journal of Experimental Psychology: Applied	Focuses on studies that bridge practically oriented problems and psychological theory
Journal of Experimental Psychology: General	Publishes integrative articles of interest to all experimental psychologists
Journal of Experimental Psychology: Human Perception and Performance	Focuses on perception, planning and control of physical actions and related cognitive processes
Journal of Experimental Psychology: Learning, Memory, and Cognition	Contains original studies on all cognitive processes
Journal of Family Psychology	Focuses on the study of family systems and processes and on problems such as marital and family abuse
Journal of Personality and Social Psychology	Contains articles on all areas of personality and social psychology
Neuropsychology	Publishes articles on the relation between the brain and human cognitive, emotional, and behavioral function
Professional Psychology: Research and Practice	Focuses on the practice of psychology
Psychological Assessment	Publishes articles on assessment techniques
Psychological Bulletin	Publishes evaluative and integrative reviews of substantive issues in scientific psychology
Psychological Methods	Devoted to the development and dissemination of methods for collecting, analyzing, understanding, and interpreting psychological data
Psychological Review	Publishes articles that make a theoretical contribution to psychology
Psychology and Aging	Publishes articles on the physiological and behavioral aspects of adult development and aging
Psychology of Addictive Behaviors	Publishes articles on alcoholism, drug use and misuse, eating disorders, tobacco and nicotine addiction, and other compulsive behaviors
Psychology, Public Policy, and Law	Focuses on the link between psychology as a science and public policy and legal issues
Rehabilitation Psychology	Publishes articles focusing on the psychological and behavioral aspects of rehabilitation

Association for Psychological Science Journals

Psychological Science	The flagship research journal of APS–publishes articles of interest across all areas of psychology
Current Directions in Psychological Science	Contains reviews spanning all areas of psychology and its applications
Psychological Science in the Public Interest	Publishes definitive assessments of topics in which psychological science might have the potential to inform and improve the well-being of society
Perspectives on Psychological Science	Publishes theoretical statements, literature reviews, viewpoints or opinions, research presentations, and scholarship

are other journals that also publish the results of psychological studies. In order to facilitate the clear communication of research results, the APA has published a manual (American Psychological Association, 2010) that gives a standardized format for authors to follow when preparing research reports. Because many periodicals instruct their authors to prepare their manuscripts according to the style specified in the APA manual, this is the format we present here for writing a research report.

Prior to preparing a report on a study that you have completed, you must ask yourself if the study is important enough to justify publication. Would others be interested in it, and, more important, would it influence their work? As a general rule, you should never conduct a study you don't think is publishable. If you think the study is significant, you must decide whether it is well designed. For example, you must ask yourself whether you have built in the controls needed to eliminate the influence of rival hypotheses. If you can satisfy yourself with regard to the quality of the research design and the significance of the results, then you are justified in proceeding with the preparation of the research report.

The APA Format

The structure of the research report is very simple and tends to follow the steps one takes in conducting a research study. To illustrate the function and format of the research report, an article that was published in the *Journal of Abnormal Psychology* is reproduced on the following pages, using the format required when an article is submitted for publication.[1] Each section of the research report also includes an explanation of the content that should be included in that section. This explanation might include some recommendations that are not illustrated in the research report, because each study will not include all the elements listed in the publication manual (American Psychological Association, 2010).

When reading through each section of the research report and then when writing your own report, you should remember the purpose of the research report. The primary goal is to report as precisely as possible what you did, including a statement of the problem investigated, the methods used to investigate the problem, the results of your investigation, and any conclusions you might have reached. Is there any criterion you can use to determine whether you have clearly and explicitly reported your study? The criterion of replication is probably the most important. If another investigator can read your research report and precisely replicate your study, then chances are good that you have written a clear and complete report.

The following sample research report was prepared according to the guidelines specified in the APA publication manual. This type of research report could be submitted to a journal such as the *Journal of Consulting and Clinical Psychology* or *Behavior Therapy*.

[1]"Sadder and less accurate? False memory for negative material in depression" by J. Joormann, B. A. Teachman and I. H. Gotlib, 2009, *Journal of Abnormal Psychology, 118*, 412–417. Copyright by the American Psychological Association.

Page number The page number should appear in the upper right-hand corner of all manuscript pages. All pages should be numbered consecutively, beginning with the title page.

Running head The running head is an abbreviated title typed flush left at the top of the first (title) page and on all subsequent pages. It is typed in all uppercase letters. It is an abbreviated title of not more than 50 characters in length, counting letters, punctuation, and spaces between words.

Authors' names and institutional affiliations The names of the authors in the order of their contribution to the study appear immediately below the title typed in upper- and lowercase letters and centered on the page. The preferred form is to list first name, middle initial, and last name, with titles and degrees omitted. The institutional affiliation when the study was conducted is centered under the author's name on the next double-spaced line. Authors with no institutional affiliation should list the city and state of residence. Authors from different institutions should be typed on separate lines.

Sadder and Less Accurate?

False Memory for Negative Material in Depression

Jutta Joormann

University of Miami

Bethany A. Teachman

University of Virginia

Ian H. Gotlib

Stanford University

Title The title should be centered on the upper half of the first page of the manuscript and typed in upper- and lowercase letters. It should state the main topic of the study and concisely identify the variables or theoretical issues under investigation. A typical title should be no more than 12 words.

Author Note The label "Author Note" is centered on the title page below the author affiliation and typed in upper- and lowercase letters. This note is used to identify each author's institutional affiliation and to provide acknowledgments, disclaimers, and point of contact. Each paragraph should start with an indent. The first paragraph identifies the departmental affiliation of each author or the city and state if there is no institutional affiliation—country should be provided if outside the United States. The second paragraph states the author affiliation if subsequent to the time of the study. The third paragraph identifies the grants or other support received for the study as well as any acknowledgments for assistance given in the conduct or completion of the study. The fourth and last paragraph identifies the person to contact for correspondence regarding the manuscript including the mailing address and e-mail of that person.

Author Note

Jutta Joormann, Department of Psychology, University of Miami; Bethany A. Teachman, Departme[nt] ment of Psychology, S

This research was MH59259 to Ian H. G[otlib] thank Lindsey Sherde[l] Storbeck and Gerald C

Correspondence c[oncerning] Department of Psycho[logy] mann@psy.miami.edu

Abstract

Previous research has demonstrated that induced sad mood is associated with increased accuracy of recall in certain memory tasks; the effects of clinical depression, however, are likely to be quite different. We used the Deese-Roediger-McDermott (DRM) paradigm to examine the impact of clinical depression on erroneous recall of neutral and/or emotional stimuli. Specifically, we presented DRM lists that were highly associated with negative, neutral, or positive lures and compared participants diagnosed with Major Depressive Disorder (MDD) and nondepressed control (CTL) participants on the accuracy of their recall of presented material and their false recall of never-presented lures. Compared with CTL participants, MDD participants recalled fewer words that had been previously presented but were more likely to falsely recall negative lures; there were no differences between MDD and CTL participants in false recall of positive or neutral lures. These findings indicate that depression is associated with false memories of negative material.

Keywords: depression, memory, cognition, emotion, bias

Abstract The abstract is a one-paragraph comprehensive summary of the contents of the research report typically ranging from 90 to 290 words in length. It is typed on a separate page, with the word Abstract centered at the top of the page in upper- and lowercase letters and no paragraph indentation for the first paragraph. The abstract of an empirical study should include a brief statement of the problem, a summary of the method used (including a description of the participants, instruments, or apparatus), the procedure, the results (including statistical significance levels), effect sizes, and any conclusions and implications.

FALSE MEMORY IN DEPRESSION 3

Sadder and Less Accurate? False Memory for Negative

Material in Depression

Mood states and emotions affect memory in various ways. Mood-induction studies, for example, have demonstrated that negative affect is associated with increased accuracy in retrieval (Storbeck & Clore, 2005), while positive mood states are associated with decreases in processing capacity (Mackie & Worth, 1989) and reduced processing motivation (Wegener & Petty, 1994), resulting in less accurate recall (Ruder & Bless, 2003). At the same time, research on mood-congruency suggests that affective states increase the accessibility of mood-congruent material (Bower, 1981). Understanding this complex interaction of mood and memory is important given its critical role in emotion regulation and emotional disorders.

Individual differences in mood-congruent memory and in the accessibility of mood-incongruent material have been proposed to predict the ability to regulate negative mood states (Joormann & Siemer, 2004; Joormann, Siemer, & Gotlib, 2007). Indeed, depression, by definition a disorder characterized by difficulty regulating negative mood states, is associated with two distinct but related memory impairments.

First, difficulties in cognitive control (i.e., focal attention to relevant stimuli and inhibition of irrelevant material) result in memory deficits for non-emotional material (Burt, Zembar, & Niederehe, 1995; Hertel, 2004). In a series of studies, Hertel and her collaborators (Hertel, depression-related imp found primarily in free attention is not well co ory deficits, depressed pressed people in stru situations (Hertel, 200 opportunity to rumina that might explain wh depressed group. Unco

Introduction The text of the research report begins on a new page with the title of the paper typed at the top center of the page. The introductory text is not labeled because of its position in the paper. The introduction is funnel shaped in the sense that it is broad at the beginning and narrow at the end. It should begin with a very general introduction to the problem area and then start to narrow by citing the results of prior works that have been conducted in the area and that bear on the specific issue that you are investigating, leading into a statement of the variables to be investigated. In citing prior research, do not attempt to make an exhaustive review of the literature. Cite only those studies that are directly pertinent, and avoid tangential references. This pertinent literature should lead directly into your study and thereby show the continuity between what you are investigating and prior research. You should then state the purpose of your study and your hypothesis. The introduction should give the reader the rationale for the given investigation, explaining how it fits in with, and is a logical extension of, prior research.

FALSE MEMORY IN DEPRESSION 4

Thus, performance deficits in free recall in depression likely do not reflect a generalized deficit, but might be due instead to depression-related deficits in cognitive control.

Second, negative affect associated with depressive disorders makes mood-congruent material more accessible and mood-incongruent material less accessible, a finding that is consistent with predictions from schema and network theories of emotion (see Mathews & MacLeod, 2005). Indeed, biased memory for negative, relative to positive, information represents perhaps the most robust cognitive finding associated with major depression (Blaney, 1986; Matt, Vazquez, & Campbell, 1992). In a meta-analysis of studies assessing recall performance, Matt and colleagues found that people with major depression remember 10% more negative than positive words. Nondepressed control participants, in contrast, demonstrated a memory bias for positive information in 20 of 25 studies. Importantly, the effects of mood on memory may help explain why depressed people are caught in a vicious cycle of increasingly negative mood and enhanced accessibility of negative material that maintains or exacerbates negative affect and hinders emotion regulation. This process is likely to be different in non-clinical samples, in which negative mood frequently leads to enhanced recall of mood-*incongruent* material, a finding commonly interpreted as stemming from efforts to repair negative mood (Parrott & Sabini, 1990; Rusting & DeHart, 2000).

Previous studies of mood and memory have focused almost exclusively on the number of items that are correctly recalled. It is important to recognize, however, that there are different errors of memory: people can forget stimuli that they have seen, and they can 'remember' items that they have not seen. This latter error, often termed a 'commission error' or 'false memory,' has rarely been investigated in depression. Interestingly, results of research examining mood and memory in non-clinical samples and findings from studies of mood-congruent biases in depressed samples lead to different predictions regarding the production of false memories in MDD. If negative affect is generally associated with more careful processing and greater accuracy than is positive affect (e.g., Ruder & Bless, 2003), as suggested by mood Clore, 2005), depress memories. On the oth control (e.g., Hertel, material, as suggested cognitive theories of produce more false m negative stimuli.

To test these comp mott (DRM; Roediger pants. In the DRM task list, each word is highl referred to as the criti lure could include 'cast see these lists, they te (Roediger & McDermot equal to, and often gre instructions to particip sion possibility of false 2007; see Roediger, Wa

In fact, unlike false recall in other paradigms, participants typically recall the critical lures with a high degree of confidence and state that they recalled the word because they actually remember seeing or hearing it, and not just because it seemed familiar (see Roediger & McDermott, 1995; 2000).

To date, few researchers have examined individual differences in DRM performance and the effects of emotional states on DRM recall. Storbeck and Clore (2005) recently demonstrated that non-clinical individuals in a negative mood state were less likely to recall critical lures than were participants who had undergone a positive mood induction, a finding consistent with predictions of greater accuracy due to item-specific processing in sad moods. It is important to note, however, that Storbeck and Clore used only one negative list and that their sample was unselected, so presumably did not have chronic activation of negative material. In the only published study to examine false memory in a diagnosed depressed sample, Moritz, Glaescher, and Brassen (2005) used a variant of the DRM design and reported a non-significant trend that depression was associated with an increased production of false memory for negative material. These findings are intriguing, but difficult to interpret because Moritz et al. presented only four lists in total (only one of which was depression-relevant) and tested recognition rather than recall. This is important because memory biases in depression have been found most consistently in free recall tasks (Hertel, 2000). Moreover, because their lists were not part of the original set of DRM lists, it is difficult to compare their findings to other studies using the DRM task. All of these factors have been shown to influence the size of DRM effects (see Roediger et al., 2001), and may explain Moritz et al.'s non-significant trend.

In the current study, we used a classic DRM paradigm and analyzed recall separately for lists that were associated with positive, negative, and neutral lures.

FALSE MEMORY IN DEPRESSION   7

We hypothesized that, given their chronic activation of negative material, depressed participants would 'recall' more negative, but not more positive or neutral, critical lures than would nondepressed control participants

Method

Participants

Participants were solicited from two outpatient psychiatry clinics and through advertisements posted within the community. We excluded individuals if they were not fluent in English, were not between 18 and 60 years of age, or if they reported severe head trauma or learning disabilities, psychotic symptoms, bipolar disorder, or alcohol or substance abuse within the past six months. Trained interviewers administered the Structured Clinical Interview for the DSM-IV (First, Spitzer, Gibbon, & Williams, 1996) to eligible individuals during their first study session. Interrater reliability was high: $k = .93$ for the MDD diagnosis, and .92 for the "nonpsychiatric control" diagnosis (i.e. according to the DSM-

Participants were criteria for MDD. T

Method The purpose of the method section is to tell the reader exactly how the study was conducted. This is the part of the research report that must directly satisfy the criterion of replication. If another investigator could read the method section and replicate the study you conducted, then you have adequately described it. Stating exactly how you conducted the study is necessary so that the reader can evaluate the adequacy of the research and the reliability and validity of the results. In order to facilitate communication, the method section is typically divided into subsections: participants or subjects; apparatus or materials; and procedure. Deviation from this format might be necessary if the experiment is complex or a detailed description of the stimuli is called for. In such instances, additional subsections, might be required to help readers find specific information.

Participants or subjects The participants subsection should identify the demographic characteristics of the research participants, such as their age, sex and ethnic or racial group. Any other pertinent information regarding the participants should also be included, such as eligibility and exclusion criteria, the number of participants that were selected for the study but did not complete it (and why), and any inducements that were given to encourage participation. You should also state how the sample size was determined (e.g. power analysis). If animals were used, their genus, species, strain number, and supplier should be specified, in addition to their gender, age, weight, and physiological condition.

FALSE MEMORY IN DEPRESSION   8

current diagnosis and no history of any Axis I disorder. Participants also completed the Beck Depression Inventory-II (BDI; Beck, Steer, & Brown, 1996), a 21-item, self-report measure of the severity of depressive symptoms and the 22-item Ruminative Response Scale (RRS, Nolen-Hoeksema & Morrow, 1991) to examine how participants tend to respond to sad feelings and symptoms of dysphoria. Fifty-two individuals (25 currently diagnosed with MDD, 27 never-disordered controls) participated in this study.

Materials

We presented 40 lists, each containing 15 words. Thirty-five of the 40 lists were taken from McDermott and Watson (2001). We added to this the happy list and the sad list used by Storbeck and Clore (2005) and created three additional lists using valence, arousal, frequency, and association norms. To assess false memory separately for neutral, negative, and positive lures, we compared valence ratings for critical lures from these lists to the Affective Norms of English words (ANEW; Bradley & Lang, 1999), which lists valence and arousal ratings for over 1000 English adjectives, verbs, and nouns on 9-point scales (1: not at all arousing/very negative to 9: very arousing/very positive). Because 11 of the 40 critical lures are not included in the ANEW, we obtained ratings from 12 undergraduate and graduate students using scales that were identical to the ANEW (full details on the ratings and lists may be obtained from the first author).

Apparatus, materials, measures, and instruments In this subsection, the reader can learn what apparatus or materials were used. Sufficient detail should be used to enable the reader to obtain comparable equipment. In addition, the reader should be told why the equipment was used. Any mention of commercially marketed equipment should be accompanied by the firm's name and the model number or, in the case of a measuring instrument such as an anxiety scale, a reference that will enable the reader to obtain the same scale. Custom-made equipment should be described; in the case of complex equipment, a diagram or photograph might need to be included.

FALSE MEMORY IN DEPRESSION 9

Of the 40 lures associated with the lists, we identified 3 as positive, 3 as negative, and 34 as neutral. Combining ANEW ratings with our ratings, the positive lures had an average valence rating of $M = 7.67$ ($SD = 0.55$) and an average arousal rating of $M = 5.43$ ($SD = 0.96$); the negative lures had an average valence rating of $M = 2.87$ ($SD = 2.18$) and an average arousal rating of $M = 4.43$ ($SD = 0.26$). The remaining (neutral) lures had an average valence rating of $M = 5.20$ ($SD = 1.46$) and an arousal rating of $M = 4.63$ ($SD = 1.33$). As expected, the three types of critical lures differed significantly in their valence ratings, $F(2,37) = 7.91$, $p < .01$, but importantly, did not differ in arousal, word frequency, or average word length, all $Fs < 1$, ns.

Design and Procedure

The false recall paradigm was modeled after Storbeck and Clore (2005). All words were presented in the same order, with the first word of each list being most strongly associated with the critical lure, and associative strength decreasing throughout the list. The sequence of the lists was randomized for each participant. The words were presented for 250 ms each with a 32-ms inter-stimulus-interval.

Participants were tested individually within a week after their initial diagnostic interview. They read instructions on a computer screen telling them to remember as many words as poss[...] They were further inf[...] list, and that they wou[...] they could remember. [...]

Procedure
In the procedure subsection, the reader is told exactly how the study was executed, from the moment the participant and the experimenter came into contact to the moment their contact was terminated. Consequently, this subsection represents a step-by-step account of what both the experimenter and the participant did during the study. This section should include any instructions or stimulus conditions presented to the participants and the responses that were required of them, as well as any control techniques used (such as randomization or counterbalancing). In other words, you are to tell the reader exactly what both you and the participants did and how you did it. After reading the procedure subsection, the reader should understand the research design used as well as how the research design was implemented to answer the research question.

FALSE MEMORY IN DEPRESSION 10

instructions, we cautioned participants not to guess during the recall task. All participants began with the 'King' list as a practice trial. After each list, a tone signaled the start of the memory test. Participants were given a booklet to write down the words they recalled. After 45 s another tone signaled the end of the recall period and the start of the presentation of the next list. This procedure was repeated for all 40 lists.

Results

Participant Characteristics

Demographic and clinical characteristics of the two groups of participants are presented in Table 1. The two groups did not differ significantly in age, $t(50) < 1$, or education, $t(46) = 1.41$, $p > .05$; as expected, MDD participants had significantly higher BDI

Results The purpose of the results section is to summarize the collected data and the analysis performed on these data. All APA journals expect, at minimum, a reporting of the hypothesis tested and their effect size and confidence intervals. Inferential tests (e.g., t tests, F tests, and chi-square measures) should be accompanied by the value of the test statistic, the degrees of freedom, probability value, effect size, and direction of the effect. The exact probability (p value) should be reported. Sufficient descriptive statistics (e.g., means, standard deviation) should be included to ensure the understanding of the effect being reported. In illustrating the direction of a significant effect (nonsignificant effects are not elaborated on for obvious reasons), you need to decide on the medium that will most clearly and economically serve your purpose. If a main effect consisting of three groups is significant, your best approach is probably to incorporate the mean scores for each of these groups into the text of the report. If the significant effect is a complex interaction, the best approach is to summarize your data by means of a figure or a table, which is placed on a separate page at the end of the research report. If you do use a figure or table (a decision that you must make), be sure to tell the reader, in the text of the report, what data it depicts. Then give a sufficient explanation of the presented data to make sure that the reader interprets them correctly. When means are reported, always include an associated measure of variability, such as standard deviation or mean square error. In writing the results section, there are several things you should not include. Individual data are not included unless a single-case study is conducted. Statistical formulas are not included unless the statistical test is new, unique, or in some other way not standard or commonly used.

scores than did CTL participants, $t(50) = 16.23$, $p < .01$. MDD participants also had higher scores on the RRS, $t(50) = 9.35$, $p < .01$. Five participants in the MDD group were diagnosed with current comorbid anxiety disorders (1 with current and lifetime Social Anxiety Disorder (SAD) and Post Traumatic Stress Disorder (PTSD), 2 participants with current and lifetime SAD and lifetime PTSD, and 1 participant with current and lifetime PTSD, 1 participant was diagnosed with lifetime PTSD but no current comorbid condition). No other current or lifetime comorbid diagnoses were observed in our sample.

Accurate Recall of Presented Words

To examine whether the MDD and CTL participants differed in their recall of words from the lists, we first examined the mean percentages of correctly recalled words per list (see Ta[...]
(ANOVA) examining c[...]
factor and valence of[...]
tor. This analysis yiel[...]
$\eta^2 = .14$, and valence,[...]
significant interaction[...]
Although MDD partici[...]
than did CTL participa[...]
itive: $t(50) = 3.15$, p [...]
ference was most pro[...]
indicating that the de[...]
depressed counterpar[...]
CTL participants reca[...]
from the positive, $t(2$[...]

$d = 1.05$, lists, which did not differ from each other, $t(26) < 1$, ns. In contrast, MDD participants recalled significantly fewer words from the positive, $t(24) = 4.25$, $p < .05$, $d = .87$, and negative, $t(24) = 6.14$, $p < .05$, $d = 1.25$, lists than they did from the neutral lists; they did not differ in their recall for words from positive and negative lists, $t(24) = 1.40$, $p > .05$, $d = .29$.

Mean Error Production

To investigate group differences in the number of errors on the memory test, we examined whether MDD and CTL participants differed in the average number of words per list they falsely recalled, excluding the critical lures (see Table 1). The group by valence ANOVA conducted on the mean number of errors per list type (excluding lures) yielded only a main effect of valence, $F(2,100) = 169.11$, $p < .01$, $\eta^2 = .77$. Participants made more errors on the neutral lists than they did on the positive, $t(51) = 15.88$, $p < .01$, $d = 4.45$, and negative, $t(51) = 17.14$, $p < .01$, $d = 4.80$, lists, which did not differ from each other, $t(51) = 1.08$, $p > .05$, $d = .22$.

Critical lures

Finally, and most importantly, to examine false recall of the critical lures, we conducted a two-way (group by valence) ANOVA on the probability of recalling critical lures. Neither the main effect of group, $F(1,50) = 1.89$, nor the main effect of valence, $F(2,100) = 1.94$, was significant, both $ps > .05$. The critical interaction of group and valence, however, was significant, $F(2,100) = 3.47$, $p < .05$, $\eta^2 = .06$ (see Figure 1). Follow-up tests indicated that the MDD and the CTL participants did not differ in their probability of recalling positive, $t(50) < 1$, or neutral, $t(50) = 1.36$, lures, both $ps > .05$; as predicted, however, the MDD participants falsely recalled a significantly greater number of critical lures from the negative lists than did the CTL participants, $t(50) = 2.20$, $p < .05$, $d = .63$.[1]

FALSE MEMORY IN DEPRESSION   13

Discussion The purpose of the discussion section of the research report is to interpret and evaluate the results obtained, giving primary emphasis to the relationships between the results and the hypotheses of the study. Begin the discussion by stating whether the hypothesis of the study was or was not supported. Following this statement, you should interpret the results, telling the reader what you think they mean. In doing so, you should attempt to integrate your research findings with the results of prior research. This interpretation should include a consideration of potential bias, threats to internal validity, and other limitations and weaknesses. In general, the discussion should answer the following questions: (1) What does the study contribute, (2) how has it helped solve the study problem, and (3) what conclusions and theoretical implications can be drawn from the study?

Discussion

The present study was designed to investigate whether clinical depression is associated with increased false recall of neutral and/or emotional material. Compared to control participants, depressed participants falsely recalled a higher proportion of negative lures. Importantly, no group differences were obtained for recall of positive and neutral lures, indicating that the higher propensity for false recall in depression does not reflect a general deficit, but instead, is specific to the processing of negative material. Depressed participants also demonstrated less accurate recall than did their nondepressed counterparts for previously presented items, especially those from the positive lists. Thus, even though depressed participants exhibited a general deficit in recall, consistent with prior literature (e.g. Burt et al., 1995), they were also more likely to recall negative lures that had not been presented to them.

Our findings have important clinical and theoretical implications. If depressed people are more prone than are their nondepressed counterparts to produce false memories for negative material, the impact of memory on emotion dysregulation in this disorder is likely to be even more powerful than had been postulated. In fact, the present findings suggest that the effects of clinically significant depression are quite different from th

reported that induced

lures, participants dia

negative affect, exhibi

When discussing the shortcomings, you should mention only the flaws that might have had a significant influence on the results obtained. You should accept a negative finding as such and offer a post hoc explanation. You should not attempt to explain it as being due to some methodological flaw (unless, as might occasionally occur, there is a very good and documented reason why a flaw did cause the negative finding).

FALSE MEMORY IN DEPRESSION   14

How can we explain this difference between induced negative mood and MDD in accuracy of 'recall?' The primary theoretical account of false memories is the activation-monitoring framework proposed by Roediger et al. (2001). Through spreading activation, semantic activation processes during encoding of a list can bring to mind items that are related to the list but that were not presented. Indeed, the stronger the initial activation, the higher the probability for false recall. The activation of these items, however, is not sufficient to lead to false memory. A second process, monitoring, can affect the false memory effect by selecting items at recall that the participant does not remember seeing even though they seem familiar. Thus, the activation-monitoring framework proposes that the probability of false recall is a function of the strength of activation of never-presented but related items and the monitoring process at retrieval. Storbeck and Clore (2005) added a variant of the DRM paradigm to their study that allowed them to investigate whether mood influences accessibility of lures at encoding or monitoring at recall. They concluded that critical lures were less likely to be accessible in the negative mood group than in the positive mood group, but that mood state did not affect monitoring at retrieval.

Unlike transient negative mood, however, depression may have unique effects at both the activation and monitoring phases. Specifically, depression may be associated with increased activation of negative lures at encoding because of its more chronic accessibility of negative material and/or with reduced monitoring at retrieval. To examine this issue systematically, it will be important in future research to assess these processes, in a single study, in depressed and nondepressed participants and in nondepressed individuals who are put in a negative mood state. With respect to effects at retrieval, recent studies suggest that the monitoring process is closely related to working memory and that poor working memory is associated with increased recollection of critical lures (e.g., Peters, Jelicic, Verbeek, & Merckelbach, 2007). Importantly, previous studies have identified depression-associated deficits in working memory and cognitive control (Joormann & Gotlib, 2008), suggesting that reduced monitoring in depression is likely. If it was only monitoring that was deficient, however, depressed participants would be expected to have a greater overall number of false memories than would control pa[...]

negative material sugg[...]

impairment in monito[...]

accessibility of negativ[...]

Consistent with th[...]

mood is associated wi[...]

over-general and abst[...]

ciated with deficits in[...]

between people in a n[...]

fore, also be due to im[...]

Future research is cle[...]

memory in depression[...]

We should note tw[...]

to use as many of the [...]

the task in order that our findings could readily be compared to other DRM studies, we used three positive, three negative and 34 neural lists. The relatively small number of positive and negative lists was also due to the inherent difficulties in constructing novel, high-quality DRM lists. Although this design choice somewhat limits direct comparison of false recall of neutral versus emotional lures, our main hypotheses focused on between-group comparisons of the original DRM neutral and emotional material, making this limitation less critical. As a related point, the lists were not constructed to be matched on valence, arousal, and word frequency, although, importantly, the critical lures from these lists did meet these criteria. Second, it should be kept in mind that the MDD and CTL participants likely differed on other characteristics, such as personality/temperament. For example, previous studies have demonstrated that individual differences in neuroticism are associated with biases in memory (Chan, Goodwin, & Harmer, 2007; Ruiz-Callabero & Bermudez, 1995). Thus, while we took care to recruit clinically depressed participants with few comorbid conditions, future research is needed to investigate whether group differences in personality or temperament may have contributed to the current results.

Taken together, the current findings suggest a 'double whammy' for memory biases in depression: depressed people recall more negative and less positive information from an event than actually occurred and simultaneously 'recall' negative information that did not occur. Increased accessibility of negative material and deficits in cognitive control may thus affect the use and effectiveness of mood regulation strategies by increasing ruminative responses to negative affect and by enhancing difficulties in using mood-incongruent memories to repair mood. Examining the treatment implications of altering the increased accessibility of negative material and subsequent impairment in monitoring will be critical next steps to try to break depression's vicious cycle of increasingly harmful cognition and negative mood.

References

American Psychiatric Association. (1994). *Diagnostic and statistical manual of mental disorders (4th ed.)*. Washington, DC: Author.

Beck, A. T. (1976). *Cognitive therapy and the emotional disorders*. New York: International Universities Press.

Beck, A. T., Steer, R. A., & Brown, G. K. (1996). *Manual for the Beck Depression Inventory-II*. San Antonio, TX: Psychological Corporation.

Blaney, P. H. (1986). Affect and memory: A review. *Psychological Bulletin, 99*, 229–246.

Bower, G. H. (1981). Mood and memory. *American Psychologist, 36*, 129–148.

Bradley, M. M., & Lang, P. J. (1999). *Affective norms for English words (ANEW): Technical Manual and Affective Ratings*. Gainesville, FL: The Center for Research in Psychophysiolo

Burt, D. B., Zembar, M
A meta-analysis of
Bulletin, 117, 285

Chan, S., Goodwin, G.,
students have neg
37, 1281–1291.

First, M. B., Spitzer, R.
Interview for DSM
DC: American Psyc

Hertel, P. T. (2000). Th
memory. In D. L. M
in research and th

The purpose of the reference section, as you might expect, is to provide an accurate and complete list of all the references cited in the text of the report. All the listed references in the text must be cited and presented in alphabetical order using a hanging indent format. This means the first line of each reference is set flush left and subsequent lines are indented.

Hertel, P. T. (2004). Memory for emotional and nonemotional events in depression: A question of habit? In D. Reisberg & P. Hertel (Eds.), *Memory and emotion* (pp. 186–216). New York: Oxford University Press.

Joormann, J., & Gotlib, I. H. (2008). Updating the contents of working memory in depression: Interference from irrelevant negative material. *Journal of Abnormal Psychology, 117*, 206–213.

Joormann, J., & Siemer, M. (2004). Memory accessibility, mood regulation and dysphoria: Difficulties in repairing sad mood with happy memories? *Journal of Abnormal Psychology, 113*, 179–188.

Joormann, J., Siemer, M., & Gotlib, I. H. (2007). Mood regulation in depression: Differential effects of distraction and recall of happy memories on sad mood. *Journal of Abnormal Psychology, 116*, 484–490.

Jou, J., & Foreman, J. (2007). Transfer of learning in avoiding false memory: The roles of warning, immediate feedback, and incentive. *The Quarterly Journal of Experimental Psychology, 60*, 877–896

Mackie, D. M., & Worth, L. T. (1989). Processing deficits and the mediation of positive affect in persuasion. *Journal of Personality and Social Psychology, 57*, 27–40.

Mathews, A., & MacLeod, C. (2005). Cognitive vulnerability to emotional disorders. *Annual Review of Clinical Psychology, 1*, 167–195.

Matt, G. E., Vazquez, C., & Campbell, W. K., (1992). Mood-congruent recall of affectively toned stimuli: A meta-analytic review. *Clinical Psychology Review, 12*, 227–255.

McDermott, K., & Watson, J. (2001). The rise and fall of false recall: The impact of presentation duration. *Journal of Memory and Language, 45*, 160–176.

Moritz, S., Glaescher, J., & Brassen, S. (2005). Investigation of mood-congruent false and true memory recognition in depression. *Depression and Anxiety, 21*, 9–17.

Parrott, W. G., & Sabini, J. (1990). Mood and memory under natural conditions: Evidence for mood incongruent recall. *Journal of Personality & Social Psychology, 59*, 321–336.

Peters, J. V., Jelicic, M., Verbeek, H., & Merckelbach, H. (2007). Poor working memory predicts false memories. *European Journal of Cognitive Psychology, 19*, 231–232.

Roediger, H. L., III, & McDermott, K. B. (2000). Tricks of memory. *Current Directions in Psychological Science, 9*, 123–127.

Roediger, H.L., III, & McDermott, K. (1995). Creating false memories: *Remembering words not presented in lists. Journal of Experimental Psychology: Learning, Memory, and Cognition, 21*, 803–814.

Roediger, L., III, Watson, J., McDermott, K., & Gallo, D. (2001). Factors that determine false recall: A multiple regression analysis. *Psychonomic Bulletin & Review, 8*, 385–407.

Ruder, M., & Bless, H. (2003). Mood and the reliance on the ease of retrieval heuristic. *Journal of Personality and Social Psychology, 85*, 20–32.

Ruiz-Caballero, J., & Bermúdez, J. (1995). Neuroticism, mood, and retrieval of negative personal memories

Rusting, C. L., & DeHa mood: Consequenc *Psychology, 78*(4)

Storbeck, J., & Clore, C memory. Mood and

Watkins, E. (2008). Co *Bulletin, 134*, 163

Wegener, D. T., & Petty The hedonic contir *66*, 1034–1048.

Footnote

[1]This group difference remained significant when we excluded MDD participants diagnosed with a current comorbid condition, $t(45) = 2.14$, $p < .05$. False recall was not significantly correlated with measures of rumination (RRS) or BDI scores.

Footnotes Footnotes are numbered consecutively, with a superscript Arabic numeral, in the order in which they appear in the text of the report. Most footnotes are content footnotes, containing material needed to supplement the information provided in the text. Footnotes are also used to acknowledge copyright permission. Footnotes appear at the bottom of the page on which it was discussed. You can also place footnotes on a separate page after the References. When placed on a separate page, type the word "Footnotes" at the top of the page *centered* in upper- and lowercase letters. The first line of each footnote is indented five spaces or one-half inch, and the superscript numeral of the footnote should appear in the space just preceding the beginning of the footnote. Footnotes are typed in the order in which they are mentioned in the text.

Table 1

Characteristics of participants, proportion of correctly recalled words, and mean error rates

	Group	
	MDD	CTL
N (N female)	25 (14)	27 (19)
Age	32.56 (8.33)	31.29 (10.69)
Years of education	15.42 (2.53)	16.22 (2.26)
% Caucasian	65	66
% income <$50.000	77	70
BDI	27.48 (11.48)	1.19 (1.99)
RRS	56.97 (12.51)	31.13 (6.80)
Recall: % Corre		
Recall: % Corre		
Negative		
Recall: % Corre		
Mean Errors Po		
Mean Errors N		
Mean Errors N		

Note. Standard deviat
Disorder; CTL = Contr

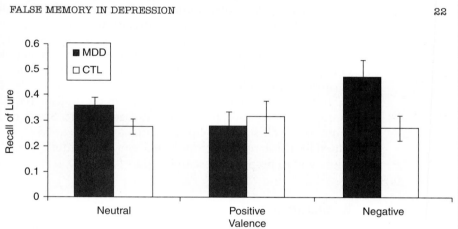

FIGURE 1

Probability of recalling critical neutral, positive, or negative lures in the DRM task in participants with Major Depressive Disorder (MDD) and control participants (CTL). Error bars represent one standard error.

Preparation of the Research Report

In the preceding section you saw an example of the way a research report must be prepared in order to be submitted for possible publication in a psychological journal. Although the essence of the report was discussed in the marginal notes, there are still many style rules that must be considered.

The APA *Publication Manual* presents the stylistic requirements authors must adhere to in the preparation of manuscripts submitted for possible publication in APA journals as well as many non-APA journals. These explicit stylistic requirements have gone through a number of changes to reflect the maturing nature of the language of psychology. As such, they have evolved along with psychology. The first set of requirements was published as a seven-page writer's guide in the February 1929 issue of the *Psychological Bulletin.* This document was succeeded in 1944 by a 32-page document. In 1952, the 1944 document was expanded to 60 pages and carried the title *Publication Manual.* New revisions followed in 1957, 1967, 1974, 1983, 1994, and 2001. The current 2010 revision reflects updated information on manuscript preparation.

Since the publication of the 2001 edition of the *Publication Manual,* many changes have been made in the publishing world, and the 2010 edition of the *Publication Manual* reflects not only the new standards in publishing but also the new practices in information dissemination, which range from blogs and personal Web postings to articles published in online databases. An additional change made in the 2010 edition of the *Publication Manual* was the decision to emphasize general principles that should be adhered to in the preparation of a manuscript because of the wide use of the *Publication Manual* in fields other than psychology.

In the following pages, we summarize the stylistic requirements that are most frequently used in preparing the research report. Space does not permit the presentation of all stylistic requirements, and the *Publication Manual* should be consulted for those requirements that are not presented here. Those presented should allow you to prepare a research report for class.

Writing Style

If you have decided that the study you have conducted is important enough to prepare a research report, you must prepare that research report in a manner that clearly communicates to the reader. Good writing is a craft and an art that requires thoughtful concern for the presentation and language used. Good writing is usually a developmental process that is acquired over time and requires continuous effort.

However, for the student who has difficulty writing, we recommend an excellent book by W. Strunk, Jr., and E. B. White, *The Elements of Style.* This book is a classic and has the virtue of being short. For assistance in reasoning and writing clearly, we recommend J. T. Gage's *The Shape of Reason,* and for additional assistance in preparing your research, R. L. Rosnow and M. Rosnow's *Writing Papers in Psychology* is excellent. C. A. Hult's book, *Researching and Writing in the Social Sciences,* is also an excellent reference. Finally, some years ago H. F. Harlow published a very humorous commentary on the content and style of a research report in the

Journal of Comparative and Physiological Psychology. (See the References for bibliographic data on all these titles.) We now provide some general principles elaborated on in more detail in the APA *Publication Manual* (2010).

To clearly communicate the essence of a research report, you must have an orderly presentation of ideas. There must be a continuity of words, concepts, and thematic development from the beginning to the end of the report. This continuity can be achieved by the use of punctuation marks to show the relationship between ideas and by the use of transitional words, such as *then, next, therefore,* and *however.* However, some transitional words (e.g., *while* and *since*) create confusion and should be used cautiously. *Since* is often incorrectly used in place of *because.* Scientific writing requires precision, and use of these transitional terms should be limited and correct.

The preparation of the research report requires a smoothness and economy of expression. Smoothness of expression is achieved by avoiding ambiguity and the insertion of the unexpected, shifting topics, tense, or person, all of which add to the confusion of the reader. By being consistent with verb tenses, smooth expression is enhanced. Economy of expression is achieved by being frugal with words. This means eliminating redundancy, wordiness, jargon, evasiveness, overuse of the passive voice, circumlocution, and clumsy prose as well as overly detailed descriptions of any part of the research report such as participants or procedures.

With respect to writing, we want to make a number of points that might assist you. Some people have trouble getting started. They sit down at a computer or with a pencil and pad of paper, and the words or ideas just do not develop. In such instances you can use one of two approaches. Rosnow and Rosnow (1992) suggest that you begin with the section you feel will be easiest to write. For example, this might be the method section because you should already know details such as the characteristics of the research participants you tested and the procedure followed in testing them. Once you have begun writing this section, you might find that other sections such as the introduction are easier to write. The other technique is to force yourself to begin writing a section even if you don't like what you are saying. This technique has the advantage of getting something down on paper and giving you something to work with and revise. It also forces you to move beyond the beginning point, which might cause the ideas to begin flowing. To use this technique, you must accept the fact that your first draft is just that. Seldom if ever should you consider the first draft the final product. Rather, you should produce the first draft and then revise it. This process should continue until you are satisfied with the final product.

When you have completed the final product, you should let it rest for several days and then reread it. This rereading several days later should result in additional revisions, because the time lapse should allow you to approach the paper more objectively and identify sections that need work.

In preparing the research report, make sure that you avoid plagiarism. *Plagiarism* means that you are kidnapping another person's ideas or efforts and passing them off as your own. In several sections of the research report, particularly the introduction, you must make use of others' work. When you do so, make sure that you give them credit.

Language

The language used to communicate the results of research should be free of demeaning attitudes and biased assumptions. The APA *Publication Manual* provides three guidelines—specificity, sensitivity to labels, and acknowledging participation—that should be followed to achieve the goal of unbiased communication.

Specificity　When referring to a person or people, you should choose accurate and clear words that are free from bias. When in doubt, err in the direction of being more rather than less specific. For example, if you are describing age groups, it is better to provide a specific age range (e.g., *ages 8 to 12*) instead of a broad category (e.g., *under 12*). The range of *people at risk* is too broad. It is preferable to identify the risk and the people involved (e.g., *children at risk for sexual abuse*). Similarly, *gender* is preferred when referring to men and women as a social group rather than *sex* because *sex* can be confused with sexual behavior.

Labels　The preferences of the participants in any study must be respected, and they should be called what they prefer to be called. This means avoiding labels when possible and avoiding categorizing participants as objects (e.g., *the elderly*) or equating participants with their conditions (*depressives* or *stroke victims*). One way to avoid such labels is to use adjectival forms such as *gay men* or *stroke patients*. Another option is to place the person first followed by a descriptive phrase (e.g., *individuals with a diagnosis of major depression*). Similarly, sensitivity should be given to any suggestion that one group is better than or is the standard against which another is to be judged. For example, it would be inappropriate to contrast *depressed individuals* with *normal individuals*, thus stigmatizing the depressed people. A more appropriate contrast would be between *depressed* and *nondepressed* individuals.

Participation　Writing about the research participants should be done in such a way that acknowledges their participation and conforms to the traditions of your field. Although a specific descriptive term such as *children* or *women* could and have been used to provide specific information about the research participants, most studies use the general term *participants* or *subjects*. When discussing actions taken by research participants, use the active voice to acknowledge the activity in which they engaged. For example, state that "the participants *completed* the MMPI" instead of "the MMPI was administered to the participants." By using the active voice you are acknowledging the individuals' voluntary and active participation in the research study.

Specific Issues　All research reports should avoid writing in a way that reflects demeaning attitudes and biased assumptions. Keeping these in mind, specific attention should be given to the following issues.

Gender.　Participants should be described in such a way that avoids ambiguity in sex identity or gender role. This means that you should avoid using *he* to refer to both sexes or *man* or *mankind* to refer to people in general. The words *people, individuals,* or *persons* can be substituted without losing meaning or clarity of expression.

Sexual Orientation.   Use the term *sexual orientation* rather than *sexual preference* because the sexual orientation of a person is not chosen, although the sex of the partner of choice might be. This means that the term *homosexual* should be replaced with terms such as *gay men, lesbians, bisexual men,* and *bisexual women* for people who have this identity.

Racial and Ethnic Identity.   When referring to racial and ethnic groups, it is important to remember that designations can become dated and sometimes negative. Therefore, it is important to be sensitive to the participants' preferred designation. For example, *Black* and *African American* are both acceptable terms, but the research participants might have a preference for one of these terms. In general, you should be more, versus less, specific with the term used to identify participants' racial and ethnic identify. Precision or specificity seems to be particularly important when designating the ethnic group of participants because the acceptable designation might depend on where a person is from (e.g., *Hispanic, Latino, or Chicano*). If proper nouns are used to designate a racial or ethnic group (e.g., *Black* or *White*), make sure that they are capitalized.

Disabilities.   When describing individuals with disabilities, it is important to maintain their integrity as human beings. This means that you should avoid language that equates them with their condition. The most appropriate guideline to use is to make sure that you do not focus on the person's disability but to use "people-first" language. For example, rather than using descriptors such as depressives, stroke victims, or brain damaged to describe research participants, identify them as "individuals with depression" or "persons with brain damage." In general, do not reduce the study participants to deficient individuals.

Age.   The general rule to follow regarding age is to be specific in describing the age of participants and avoid open-ended definitions, such as *over 65.* Individuals under the age of 12 can be referred to as *boys* and *girls,* and individuals aged 13 to 17 can be referred to as *young men* and *young women* or *female adolescent* or *male adolescent.* Persons 18 and older should be referred to as *men* and *women. Older adults* is an acceptable term, whereas *elderly* and *senior* are not.

The issues discussed in this section focus on ensuring that biased communication does not enter the research report. The publication manual also recognizes the need to avoid historical and interpretive inaccuracies. It is necessary to avoid misrepresenting past ideas in an effort to avoid language bias. This means that the original language contained in past manuscripts should be maintained with a comment regarding its prior use.

Editorial Style

Editorial style refers to the rules or guidelines used by a publisher to ensure a clear, consistent presentation of published material. These rules specify the construction of many of the elements included in a research report such as tables and figures as well as the uniform use of punctuation and abbreviations. Here we list and discuss some of these rules. The *Publication Manual* lists many other rules and guidelines and should be consulted if you have questions about any other style issue not presented here.

Italics   The general guideline is to use italics infrequently. Consult the *Publication Manual* if you think it would be appropriate to use italics.

Abbreviations   Use abbreviations sparingly. Generally speaking, abbreviate only when the abbreviations are conventional and likely to be familiar to the reader (such as IQ) or if you can save considerable space and avoid cumbersome repetition. In all instances, the Latin abbreviations *cf.* (compare), *e.g.* (for example), *etc.* (and so forth), *i.e.* (that is), *viz.* (namely), and *vs.* (versus, against) are to be used only in parenthetical material. The exception to this rule is the Latin abbreviation *et al.,* which can be used in the text of the manuscript. The unit of time *second* is abbreviated *s* rather than *sec.* Units of time such as *day, week, month,* and *year* are never abbreviated. There are many other abbreviations that can be used in a research report. For many other abbreviations, you should consult the *Publication Manual* (2010).

Headings   Headings serve to outline the manuscript and to indicate the importance of each topic. There are five different levels of headings that can be used in a manuscript. They have the following top–down progression: (level 1) centered main heading, boldface in upper- and lowercase letters; (level 2) flush left-side heading, boldface, upper- and lowercase letters; (level 3) indented side heading, boldface, lowercase paragraph heading ending with a period; (level 4) indented, boldface, italicized, lowercase paragraph heading ending with a period; (level 5) indented, italicized, lowercase paragraph heading ending with a period. For paragraph headings (i.e., levels 3, 4, and 5), the written paragraph material starts on the same line as the heading. Remember that all headings are not used in every manuscript but start each section with the highest heading level (level 1). Also, you should have at least two subsection headings within any section. If you cannot use at least two subsections, then avoid using a subsection heading.

If four levels of headings are needed, use level 1, level 2, level 3, and level 4 as follows:

Experiment 1

Method

   Procedure.

   Mode of stimulus presentation.

The number of levels needed will depend on the complexity and length of your manuscript. If you need only one level, then use a level 1 heading. If two levels are needed, then use a level 1 and level 2 heading, and so forth.

Quotations   A quotation of fewer than 40 words should be inserted into the text and enclosed with double quotation marks. Quotations of 40 or more words should be displayed in a freestanding block of lines without quotation marks. The author, year, and specific page from which the quotation is taken should always be included.

Numbers   The general rule about expressing numbers in the text is to use words to express any number that begins a sentence as well as any number below 10. Use numerals to express all other numbers. There are several exceptions to this rule. For example, numbers should always be used to represent dates, time, and age. The APA *Publication Manual* should be consulted for these exceptions. A second rule to follow in stating numbers is to use Arabic, and not Roman, numerals.

Physical Measurements   All physical measurements are to be stated in metric units. If a measurement is expressed in nonmetric units, it must be accompanied, in parentheses, by its metric equivalent.

Presentation of Statistical Results   When presenting the results of statistical tests in the text, provide enough information to allow the reader to corroborate the results. Although what counts as sufficient information depends on the statistical test and analysis selected, in general, when reporting inferential statistics, it means including information about the magnitude or value of the test, the degrees of freedom, the probability level, the direction of the effect and associated effect size or confidence intervals. For example, a t and F test could be reported as follows:

$t(36) = 4.52, p = .04, d = .54, 95\% \text{ CI } [0.29, 0.95]$

$F(3, 52) = 17.35, p = .02, \text{est } \omega^2 = .06$

Such common statistical tests as t and F tests are not referenced, and the formulas are not included in the text. Referencing and formulas are included only when the statistical test is new, rare, or essential to the manuscript, as when the article concerns a given statistical test.

   After the results of a statistical test are reported, descriptive statistical data such as means and standard deviations must be included to clarify the meaning of a significant effect and to indicate the direction of the effect.

Tables   Tables are expensive to publish and therefore should be used only when they can convey and summarize data more economically and clearly than can a lengthy discussion in text. Tables should be viewed as informative supplements to the text. Although each table should be intelligible by itself, it should also be an integral part of the text. As a supplement, only the table's highlights should be discussed in text. If you decide to use tables, number them with Arabic numerals in the order in which they are mentioned in the text.

   In preparing the table, you can use the tables presented in the sample article as guides. Each table should have a brief title that clearly describes the data it contains. This title and the word *Table* and its number are typed flush with the left margin and at the top of the table. Each column and row of data within the table should be given a heading that identifies, as briefly as possible, the data contained in that row or column.

   The *Publication Manual* provides additional detail regarding the heading that can be used in the construction of a table. You should consider the readability of the table when deciding on whether to single- or double-space the table content. When expressing numerical values in the table, carry each data point to the number of decimal places needed to express the precision of the measurement and place a dash to indicate missing data.

Tables can be used to present many different types of data. The *Publication Manual* discusses a large variety of different types of tables and gives illustrations of many of these tables. If you need help in organizing the table you wish to construct, you should consult the *Publication Manual.*

When writing the manuscript, you should refer to the table somewhere in the text. This reference should tell what data are presented in the table and briefly discuss the data. When referring to a table, identify it by name, as in *the data in Table 3.* Do not use a reference such as *the above table* or *the table on page 12.*

After you have constructed a table, use the following checklist to ensure that you have constructed it according to the specifications listed in the *Publication Manual.*

- Is the table necessary?
- Does the table belong in the print version of the manuscript or can it be placed in an online supplemental file? There are times when it would be more appropriate to provide the data in a supplemental file and inform the reader as to where this file can be obtained.
- Are tables that present comparable data presented in a consistent manner?
- Is the title brief and explanatory?
- Does a column heading exist for each column?
- Is there an explanation for all abbreviations and for any special italics, dashes, boldface, and special symbols?
- Do the notes have the appropriate order of (1) general note, (2) specific note, and (3) probability note?
- Have all vertical rules (lines) been eliminated?
- Do all major point estimates have confidence intervals reported, and is the same confidence level used for all tables?
- Are all probability levels correctly identified for statistical significance tests conducted?
- Has any copyrighted table reproduced been given full credit, and has permission been received from the copyright holder?
- Have you referred to the table in the text?

Figures   Figures are any illustration other than a table and might be a chart, graph, photograph, drawing, or any other depiction. Although tables are preferred for the presentation of quantitative information, figures give an overall view of the pattern of results but require the reader to estimate values. There are, however, times when figures can convey a concept more effectively than a table, such as when an interaction is described. If you are considering using a figure, ask yourself the following questions:

- Will the figure add substantially to the understanding of the manuscript?
- Will a figure most efficiently present the information?
- What type of figure will most efficiently convey the information?

If you don't think the figure would add substantially to the understanding of the manuscript but might enrich its understanding, you can place the figure in an online supplemental materials archives. Typically a figure is included in a manuscript only when it is necessary to illustrate some complex theoretical formulation, the flow of participants in an experiment, or the representation of empirical result from a complex interaction.

When constructing a figure you should aim for simplicity, clarity, continuity, and information value. This means that any figure should augment the text and present only essential facts that are easy to read and understand, with all elements of the figure clearly labeled and explained. When constructing a figure, remember to distinguish between error bars and confidence intervals when these are used.

Figure Legends and Caption Both legends and captions are included in any figure. Legends are used to explain the symbols in the figure and are, therefore, an integral part of the figure. All legends should be placed within the figure.

A figure caption is both an explanation of the figure and the figure title. The caption should be a brief descriptive phrase that is placed directly below the figure. This descriptive phrase should explain the figure. Following the descriptive phrase should be any additional information needed to clarify the figure such as an explanation of any symbols, error bars, or probability values.

Figure Preparation As a general rule, all figures should be computer generated using professional graphics software. Although the requirements might differ slightly from one publisher to another, make sure that the resolution used is sufficient to produce a high-quality image. In general, lettering should be no smaller than 8 points and no larger than 14 points. Preparation of some figures, such as electrophysiological, radiological, and other biological data, presents challenges because of the complexity of the data, and the lack of a single convention for presentation of these data. Again, the primary guideline to follow is to make sure the presentation is done clearly and completely. After completing the figure, you can use the following checklist to help ensure that it communicates effectively and adheres to APA style and formatting conventions.

- Is the figure necessary?
- Has it been presented in a clear, simple format free of extraneous detail?
- Is the title descriptive of the content?
- Have all components of the figure been clearly labeled?
- Are all figures mentioned in the manuscript?
- Has a sufficiently high resolution been used to permit accurate reproduction?

Reference Citations In the text of the research report, particularly in the introductory section, you should have placed your research study in the context of prior research by citing the researchers who have influenced you and the studies that suggest the need for the study you have conducted. In citing this work, you need to give these other individuals credit for the ideas that you have used. In doing so, you must avoid plagiarism or presenting others' ideas as yours. This means that any paraphrasing, quoting, or describing another's idea that might have influenced your thinking needs to receive credit. When quoting another source, you should always provide the author(s) name, year, and page or paragraph number (for nonpaginated material) of the quoted source. Quoted sources of fewer than 40 words should be inserted into the text of the manuscript enclosed by quotation marks as follows:

> Jones (2010) has stated that "the way to handle missing data is to . . ." (p. 275), which is consistent with the recommendations of others.

Quotations for more than 40 words should be displayed in a block quotation or a freestanding block of text that is indented an additional half inch. There are no quotation marks on this indented block quotation as follows:

> The consumption of a carbohydrate-rich diet has an effect on the synthesis of central serotonin. Consumption of a carbohydrate-rich diet increases the ratio or tryptophan to the other large neutral amino acids resulting in more tryptophan crossing the blood–brain barrier increasing its availability for synthesis to central serotonin. (Neuro, 1999, p. 547)

If you are quoting material without pagination as might exist in online material, provide the author, year, and number of the paragraph in which it appears (e.g., para. 4)

If you are paraphrasing material or referring to another's idea, you must provide the author(s) name and the year of the source. In addition, the APA *Publication Manual* encourages you to provide a page or paragraph number to assist the reader in locating the relevant material. However, this is only a suggestion and not a firm style guideline.

When citing references in the text of a manuscript, the APA format uses the author–date citation method, which involves inserting the author's surname and the publication date at the appropriate point, as follows:

> Doe (1999) investigated the . . .

or

> It has been demonstrated (Doe, 2002) . . .

or

> A positive relationship has been demonstrated (Doe, 2002).

With this information, the reader can turn to the reference list and locate complete information regarding the source. Multiple citations involving the same author are arranged in chronological order:

> Doe (1997, 1999, 2001, 2002)

Multiple citations involving different authors are arranged alphabetically, as follows:

> Several studies (Doe, 2003; Kelly, 2002; Mills, 2002) have revealed . . .

If a citation includes more than two but fewer than six authors, all authors should be cited the first time the reference is used. Subsequent citations include only the name of the first author, followed by the words *et al.* and the year the article was published. If six or more authors are associated with a citation, only the surname of the first author followed by *et al.* is used for all citations.

You should consult the APA *Publication Manual* if you encounter references from other sources, such as works with no author, authors with the same surname, or personal communications.

Reference List   All citations in the text of the research report must be accurately and completely cited in the reference list so that it is possible for readers to locate the works. This means that each entry should include the name of the author, year of publication, title, publishing data, and any other information necessary to identify the reference. All references are to appear in alphabetical order, typed double-spaced with a hanging indent on a separate page with the word *References* centered at the top of the page in upper- and lowercase letters.

The general form of a reference is as follows for a periodical, book, and book chapter:

Canned, I. B., & Rad, U. B. (2002). Moderating violence in a peaceful society. *Journal of Violence and Peace Making, 32,* 231–234.

Wind, C. (2001). *Why children hurt.* New York: Academic Publishers.

Good, I. M. (2003). Moral development in violent children. In A. Writer and N. Author (Eds.), *The anatomy of violent children* (pp. 134–187). Washington, DC: Killer Books.

Electronic publishing is currently the rule rather than the exception. While it has increased the efficiency of the publication process and enhanced the sharing of research results, it has created some confusion or difficulty in establishing a specific method of referencing such material. This difficulty has been compounded by the fact that it is sometimes difficult to determine if an online version of an article is the final version or an advanced online version. As a general rule, the APA *Publication Manual* recommends that you reference online material as you would a fixed-media source and then add as much electronic retrieval information as you can to try to ensure that others can also locate the source you cited.

One fact about material appearing on the Internet is that it is prone to being moved, deleted, or restructured, resulting in a broken or nonworking address. In an attempt to solve this problem, publishers of scholarly material have begun using the digital object identifiers (DOI) system. The DOI system provides a persistent means of identifying and managing information placed on digital networks. This system, implemented by registering with agencies such as CrossRef, provides two critical functions. The first involves assigning each published manuscript a specific identifier and a corresponding routing system that will direct the reader to the content of the corresponding manuscript regardless of where it exists. The second function is to provide a linking mechanism that allows click-through access to each referenced manuscript.

To use this system, publishers assign a DOI to each published article. Once the DOI is assigned, you can use it to link to the content of the article. The DOI of a manuscript is typically located on the first page of an electronic journal article and on the first page of an APA journal next to the copyright notice. The *Publication Manual* recommends that you include the DOI when providing references to citations that have this identifier as follows:

> Hammerstein, J. R. (2010). The effectiveness of fatigue in predicting depression relapse. *Journal of Significant Depression Research, 104*, 225–267. doi:10.1087/15836542880

If the source you are referencing was published prior to the use of the DOI, you naturally cannot include it in the reference. If you are referencing an online article that was published prior to the addition of DOI, provide the home page URL of the source you are referencing as follows:

> Hammerstein, J. R. (2005). The effectiveness of fatigue in predicting depression relapse. *Journal of Significant Depression Research, 8*, 22–50. Retrieved from http://jaba.lib.edu.au/articles.html.

Many other items could be included in a reference list such as book chapters, brochures, monographs, magazine articles, and many types of information retrieved from the Internet. If you have included a source not mentioned here or if you have a variation of a source mentioned here and are not sure how it should be presented, you should consult the APA *Publication Manual.*

Preparation of the Manuscript for Submission You should use a uniform typeface and font size to provide a readable manuscript and to allow the publisher to estimate its length. The APA *Publication Manual* recommends that you use a Times New Roman typeface with a 12-point font size. When preparing the text, double-space all material including title, headings, footnotes, author notes, references, and figure captions. Never use single or one-and-a-half spacing except in tables and figures. Margins should be at least 1 in. at the top, bottom, and both sides of each page and justify only the left side of the page with the right-side margin uneven or ragged.

Ordering of Manuscript Pages The pages of the manuscript should be arranged as follows:

1. *Title page.* This is a separate page (numbered page 1) and includes the title, author's name, institutional affiliation, running head, and author's notes.
2. *Abstract.* This is a separate page, numbered page 2.
3. *Text of the manuscript.* The text begins on page 3 and continues on consecutive pages through the completion of the discussion section.
4. *References.* References begin on a separate page.
5. *Footnotes.* Footnotes also begin on a new page, unless they are placed at the bottom of the page on which they are discussed.
6. *Tables.* Begin on a separate page.
7. *Figures.* Begin on a separate page.

Submission of the Research Report for Publication

If you have conducted an independent research project and completed the preparation of a research report (aside from the laboratory reports that you might have prepared in this class), you must now decide whether to submit it to a journal for possible publication. Earlier in this chapter, we stated that no study should be undertaken if you do not believe it is potentially worthy of publication. But even if at the outset you believe that the study you are conducting is worthy of publication, you might change your mind once the study is completed and you have prepared the research report. Therefore, at this stage you must make a final decision whether to submit the manuscript to a journal. This final decision should be based on your judgment of the significance and quality of the study. Frequently it is valuable to have a colleague read and provide a critique of the article before you submit it for possible publication. A colleague presents a new perspective and can evaluate the worth of the article and its potential problems more critically and objectively.

If both you, as the author, and a colleague agree that the manuscript should be submitted for publication, you must then select the journal to which you are going to submit the article. Journals vary both in the percentage of submitted manuscripts they accept and in the types of articles that they will publish. From Table 16.1, you can see that each journal focuses on a different subject area. You must select a journal that publishes articles on subjects similar to yours. In making this selection, you must also decide whether your manuscript makes a contribution significant enough to warrant possible publication in one of the most prestigious journals. In the field of psychology, the APA and APS journals are generally considered the most prestigious as well as some of the most difficult to get into. Many of these journals accept only about 15% of the manuscripts submitted to them.

Once you have selected the appropriate journal, send the required number of copies of the manuscript to the journal editor, with a cover letter stating that you are submitting the manuscript for possible publication in that journal. The cover letter should give the journal editor information regarding (1) whether the manuscript has been presented at a scientific meeting, (2) if other closely related manuscripts have been published or submitted to other journals, (3) the title, length, and number of tables, and figures, and (4) a statement verifying that the treatment of animal or human participants was in accordance with APA ethical standards. If you desire a masked review, you should request this in the cover letter. Finally, you should include your telephone number, fax number, e-mail address, and address for future correspondence. Once the journal editor receives the manuscript, either electronically or by first-class mail, he or she assigns it a number and usually within forty-eight hours sends an acknowledgment of receipt to the author.

At this point, the control of the manuscript is out of your hands and in the hands of the journal editor. The journal editor typically sends the manuscript to several individuals who are knowledgeable regarding the topic of your study, and they review the manuscript and reach a decision about its acceptability. Their comments are returned to the journal editor, who makes the final decision. This decision can be a rejection, an acceptance, or an acceptance pending approval of recommended revisions. This last is the most typical mode of acceptance. The whole process typically takes 2 to 3 months.

If you get an outright acceptance—a very rare occurrence—you can celebrate. If you get a provisional acceptance—acceptance pending approval of recommended revisions—you can evaluate the recommendations and attempt to conform to them. Once the revisions have been made, you must resubmit the manuscript, which is then reevaluated by the journal editor. The editor might elect to accept the manuscript at this point, send it out for another review, or request additional revisions. If you get a rejection, try to evaluate the reviewers' comments regarding their reasons for rejecting the manuscript. If you agree with the reviewers' comments, you might reevaluate the manuscript and decide that it really was not worthy of publication. Alternatively, you might disagree with the reviewers' comments and believe that the manuscript still warrants publication. In this case, you should find another journal that focuses on the subject matter of your study and then start the process over. As you can see, the process of getting an article published is time consuming, involves a lot of work, and is subject to the approval and recommendation of your peers. Many studies are never published. Although the procedure just outlined has its flaws, it is probably the best that can be established to ensure that only high-quality research is published.

Acceptance of the Manuscript

After an article has been accepted for publication, the journal editor sends the corresponding authors two forms: a copyright transfer form that transfers the copyright of the published article to the journal and an author certification form with which authors accept responsibility for the contents of the published article and indicate agreement on the order of authorship.

The final version of the accepted manuscript will be edited by both the journal editor and a copy editor to correct any errors, to ensure conformation to APA stylistic requirements, or to clarify expression. After the manuscript is copyedited, it is sent back to the author for review. The author must review any changes to ensure that the meaning or content of the manuscript has not been altered. Typically, the author is requested to have the copyedited manuscript returned within forty-eight hours.

After you have returned the copyedited version of the manuscript, it is set in type. The typesetter then sends you the manuscript and two sets of typeset proofs. You are to read these proofs and make sure that they correspond to the copyedited version of the manuscript. At this stage, you cannot make any changes in the content of the manuscript. Any changes are limited to production errors and to updates of references, citations, or addresses. The original proofs and the manuscript are to be sent back to the Production Editor within forty-eight hours. Once you have sent the proofs back, you have completed your role in the publication process. The only thing you have to do is wait and see the manuscript in print, which typically takes about 4 to 6 months.

Presenting Research Results at Professional Conferences

The ultimate goal of a research study is to communicate the results by having the written report of the study published in a scholarly journal. However, many times the results of a research study are presented at one of the numerous conferences that are held each year. These conferences include the national meetings of the APA and the Association for Psychological Science, the regional meetings of various psychological associations (e.g., the Southeastern Psychological Association, SEPA), and various international meetings. Also, a number of colleges and universities host conferences that are geared toward undergraduate research. The common thread running through all these conferences is that their primary activity is the presentation of research conducted by psychologists. Typically these conferences put out a call for submissions of research studies. Researchers who wish to present their findings submit a written report or an abstract of a report of their research study to a designated individual, who in turn sends the submissions out for review. The selected reviewers review the submissions and recommend the acceptance or rejection of the submission. If the submission is accepted, it is placed on the program for the meeting, and the researcher who sent in the submission is obligated to attend the meeting and present the results of his or her research study. This presentation can take the form of an oral presentation or a poster presentation.

Oral Presentation

If you are scheduled to make an oral presentation of your research at a professional conference, make sure that you read and follow the guidelines that you will receive, because there are a number of restrictions that dictate what can be done during the oral presentation. Typically, the oral presentations by individuals conducting research on similar topical areas are grouped together for a session that usually lasts about one hour. Each person has 15 minutes to make his or her presentation and answer any questions. Because time has to be allowed for questions, you should make sure that your presentation does not exceed 12 minutes, and, because you have only 12 minutes to present the results of your research, the preparation for the presentation differs from a written report that you would prepare for publication. Here are some recommendations for the preparation of an oral presentation:

- Concentrate on only one or two points. Keep reminding the audience of the central theme by relating each section to that theme. In other words, tell the audience what you are going to say, and then say it.
- Omit most of the specifics of the research design because this will probably be too much detail for the listener to follow.
- Focus on the following points:
  1. State what you studied
  2. State why you studied it
  3. State how you studied it—give a general description of your research design

4. State what you found

5. State the implications of your results

- Do not read your presentation, because this tends to be boring. Instead, talk to the audience as if you were having a conversation with them. This means that you must know your topic well and have the presentation rehearsed. It is better to have notes from which you can talk in a conversational tone than to read from a prepared document

- If you include audio–visual presentations, make sure they are readable and comprehensible from a distance.

- Practice giving the presentation to others to ensure that you stay within your time limit and that everything flows smoothly.

- Being prepared will make your presentation most informative to your audience and will allow you to feel most confident, especially if this is your first presentation.

Poster Presentation

If you are scheduled to make a poster presentation of your research at a professional conference, you should read the directions that you will receive carefully because different associations have specific requirements, such as the size of the poster and the recommended font size. A poster presentation consists of presenting your research as a poster at a specific session on that topic or theme along with many other individuals at the same time. This means that you need to prepare a visual presentation of your research and present it as a poster that anyone can see and read. After you have placed the visual presentation of your research on the poster, you are to remain by the poster for the duration of the poster session, which is typically one hour. It is important that you bring a number of written copies of your research report to give to interested individuals. The advantage of this procedure is that you can discuss your research with interested individuals who walk by and read your poster, and they can get a copy of your research that they can take home with them. In this way, you increase your chances of finding other individuals with similar interests. As a result of these conversations, you might develop new research ideas and might even meet individuals with whom you will collaborate on subsequent research projects.

Here are some tips that you can use in preparing your poster:

- The layout of the poster is important and should flow naturally from the introduction to the results and conclusion. Figure 16.1 presents one possible layout.

- When preparing the poster, use a typeface that is easy to read, such as Times New Roman. Do not try to get fancy because this will generally reduce readability.

- Use a font size that is large enough to read from a distance of about ten feet. A font size of 24-pt. or greater should be sufficient.

FIGURE 16.1
Template for a poster presentation.

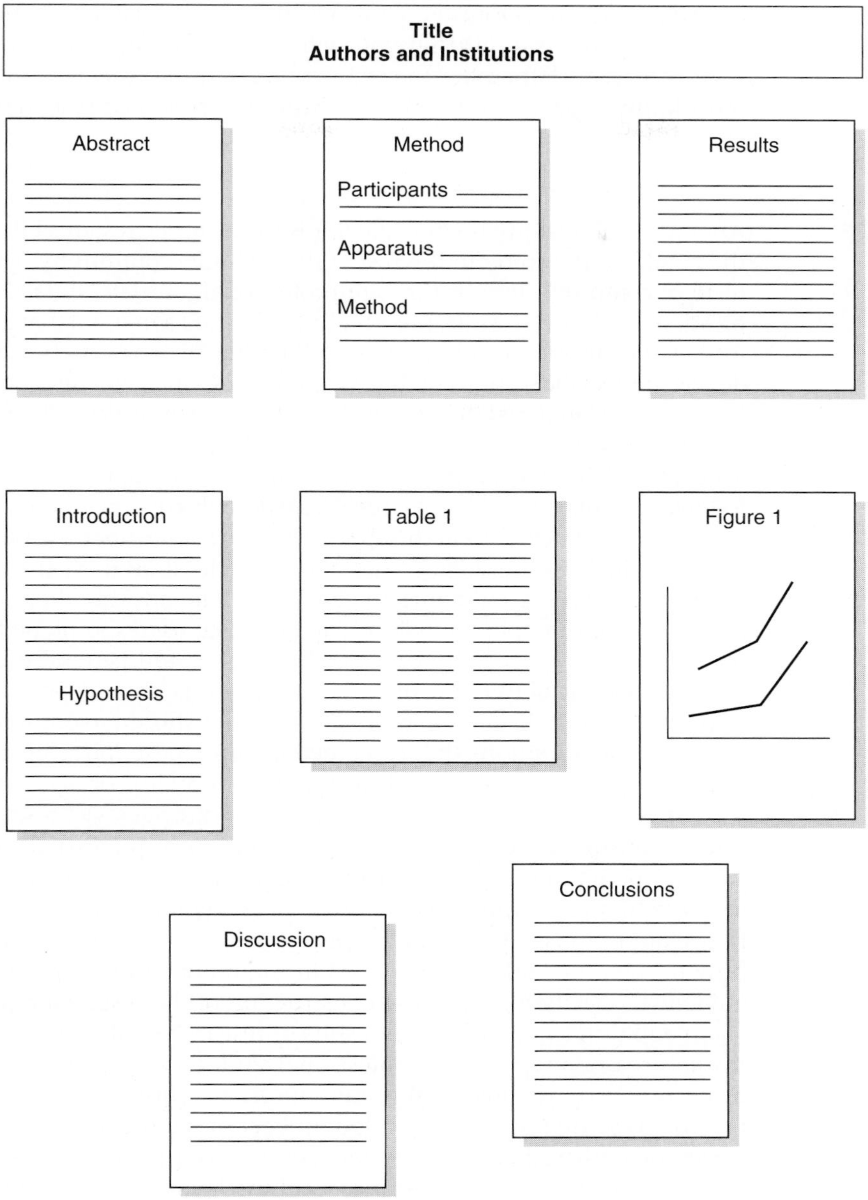

- Make your points with as few words as possible.
- If you can present the various sections of your poster on one large poster board, this is desirable. If not, then mount each page of your poster on a backing using an attractive color. Make sure that you bring pins to mount your poster to the bulletin board that will be available.

After you have mounted your poster to the available bulletin board, relax and enjoy the conversations that you will have with individuals who wish to discuss your research. Remember that you conducted the research, so you will have the most knowledge about it and will be the expert on this research study.

Summary

After a research study is completed, it is the author's responsibility to communicate the results of the study to the rest of the scientific community. The primary mechanism of communication is through professional journals. To facilitate clear communication of research results, the APA has published a manual that gives a standardized format for authors to follow when preparing their research reports. This manual details the specific sections of the research report and gives directions and suggestions for the type of material that is to be included in each section. The main sections of the research report are the title; abstract; introduction; method section, which includes a description of the participants, any materials or apparatus, and the procedure followed in collecting the data; results section; discussion section; and references.

In preparing the research report, there are a number of stylistic requirements that should be adhered to. The writing style should clearly communicate the essence of the research report. In general, this means that there must be a smoothness and economy of expression. The language used should be free of bias, which means that the words chosen must be specific and generally free of labels. Any communication about the research participants should be done in a way that acknowledges their participation. The writing should avoid demeaning attitudes and biased assumptions that can creep in when describing a person's sex identity, sexual orientation, racial or ethnic identity, disability, or age.

The APA *Publication Manual* specifies an editorial style, a set of rules or guidelines to ensure a clear, consistent presentation of published material. There are rules for when to use italics and abbreviations; how to list headings of various topics; how to present numbers, physical measurements, and statistical results; when to use quotations, tables, and figures; how to construct the tables and figures; and how to reference other works cited in the report. In general, there are rules and guidelines specifying the entire construction of the research report.

In addition to reporting the results of research studies in professional journals, results are often reported at professional conferences. These reports are either oral or poster presentations. Oral presentations are short and should be focused on a few points so that the audience does not get overwhelmed with the specifics of the design or statistical analysis. Poster presentations should be prepared so that they are easily read from some distance, and the layout of the poster should naturally flow from the introduction to the conclusion.

Key Terms and Concepts

Abstract
Apparatus, materials, measures, and instruments
Author note

Authors' names and institutional affiliations
Discussion
Footnotes

Introduction
Method
Page number and header
Participants
Procedure

References
Results
Running head
Title

Related Internet Sites

http://www.psychology.org
This site provides links to other sites that should assist students in writing papers using the APA format. To find the sites relating to APA style, use this site to search for the related links by doing an *APA style* search.

http://www.apastyle.org
This is the site maintained by the American Psychological Association and contains information about the *Publication Manual*. It also has links to Style Tips, What's New in the publication manual, and answers to some frequently asked questions.

http://www.vanguard.edu/faculty/ddegelman/index.cfm?doc_id=796
This Web site provides a list of the core elements of APA style that can be used as a guide in writing or checking a written research report.

http://www.apastyle.org/learn/
This Web site has links to tutorials focusing on the essential components required in writing a manuscript that corresponds to APA requirements.

Appendix A

Answers to Practice Tests

Chapter 1
1. a   2. b   3. b   4. b   5. d

Chapter 2
1. a   2. c   3. a   4. d   5. a   6. b

Chapter 3
1. a   2. e   3. d   4. e   5. b

Chapter 4
1. b   2. a   3. c   4. e   5. b

Chapter 5
1. a   2. a   3. c   4. d   5. d   6. b

Chapter 6
1. e   2. b   3. b   4. d   5. b   6. a

Chapter 7
1. a   2. d   3. a   4. e   5. c

Chapter 8
1. b   2. e   3. d   4. a   5. e

Chapter 9
1. b   2. a   3. d   4. b   5. e

Chapter 10
1. c   2. b   3. c   4. c   5. b

Chapter 11
1. a   2. d   3. b   4. c   5. d

Chapter 12
1. d   2. b   3. a   4. d   5. d

Chapter 13
1. b   2. d   3. a   4. c   5. b   6. b

Chapter 14
1. b   2. c   3. c   4. a   5. c   6. b   7. b

Chapter 15
1. b   2. e   3. a   4. b   5. a   6. d

Glossary

A

ABA design—A single-case design in which the response to the treatment condition is compared to baseline responses recorded before and after treatment

ABAB design—Extension to ABA design to include reintroduction of the treatment condition

Accessible population—The population of research participants that is practically available to the investigator

Active consent—Verbally agreeing and signing a form consenting to participate in research

Active deception—Deliberately misleading research participants by giving them false information

Additive and interactive effects—Differences between groups is produced because of the combined effect of two or more threats to internal validity

Alpha level—The point at which one would reject the null hypothesis and accept the alternative hypothesis

Alternative hypothesis—The logical opposite of the null hypothesis

Analysis of covariance—A statistical procedure in which group means are compared after adjusting for pretest differences; statistical test used when you have a one quantitative DV and a mixture of categorical and quantitative IVs (the quantitative IV is called a "covariate")

Anchor—Descriptors placed on points on a rating scale

ANCOVA—Abbreviation for analysis of covariance

ANOVA—Abbreviation for analysis of variance

Animal rights—The belief that animals have rights similar to humans and should not be used in research

Animal welfare—Improving the laboratory conditions in which animals live and reducing the number of animals used in research

Anonymity—Keeping the identity of the research participant unknown

Archived research data—Data (usually quantitative) originally used for a different research project

Assent—Agreement from a minor to participate in research after receiving an age-appropriate explanation of the study

Assignment measure—Measure used to assign participants to experimental and control groups. Those with scores below the cutoff score are assigned to one group, and those with scores above the cutoff are assigned to the other group

Attrition—Loss of participants because they don't show up or they drop out of the research study

Automation—The technique of totally automating the experimental procedures so that no experimenter–participant interaction is required

Axial coding—Second stage of data analysis in GT; focus is on making concepts more abstract and ordering them into the theory

B

Bar graph—Graph that uses vertical bars to represent the data values of a categorical variable

Baseline—The target behavior of the participant in its naturally occurring state or prior to presentation of the treatment condition

Between-participants designs—Groups are produced by random assignment, and the different groups are exposed to the different levels of the independent variable

Between-participants variable—Type of independent variable where different participants receive different levels of the independent variable

Biased sample—A nonrepresentative sample

Binary forced-choice approach—Participant must select from the two response choices provided with an item

Blind technique—A method whereby knowledge of each research participant's treatment condition is kept from the experimenter

C

Carryover effect—A sequencing effect that occurs when performance in one treatment condition affects performance in another treatment condition

Case—A bounded system

Case study—Qualitative research method in which the researcher provides a detailed description and account of one or more cases

Categorical variable—Variable that varies by type or kind

Causal description—Description of the consequences of manipulating an independent variable

Causal explanation—Explaining the mechanisms through which a causal relationship operates

Causation—A term whose meaning is debated by philosophers, but in everyday language implies that manipulation of one event produces another event

Cause—The factor that makes something else exist or change

Cause-and-effect relationship—Relationship in which changes in one variable produce changes in another variable

Ceiling effect—Situation where participants' pretest scores on the dependent variable are too high to allow for additional increases

Cell—Combination of levels of two or more independent variables

Cell mean—The average score of the participants in a single cell

Census—Collection of data from everyone in the population

Changing-criterion design—A single-case design in which a participant's behavior is gradually shaped by changing the criterion for success during successive treatment periods

Checklist—Participants asked to check all response categories that apply

Chi-square test for contingency tables—Statistical test used to determine if a relationship observed in a contingency table is statistically significant

Clinical significance—A type of practical significance

Closed-ended question—A question where participants must select their answer from a set of predetermined response categories

Cluster—A collective type of unit that includes multiple elements

Cluster random sampling—Sampling method where clusters are randomly selected

Coefficient alpha—The most frequently used index of internal consistency

Cohen's *d*—The difference between two means in standard deviation units

Cohort-sequential design—Design that combines cross-sectional and longitudinal elements by following two or more age groups over time

Collective case study—Study of multiple cases for the purpose of comparison

Comparative case study—Another name for a collective case study

Compatibility thesis—Position that quantitative and qualitative research methods and philosophies can be combined

Complete counterbalancing—Enumerating all possible sequences and requiring different groups of participants to take each of the sequences

Concurrent probing—Obtaining a participant's perceptions of the experiment after completion of each trial

Concurrent validity—Degree to which test scores obtained at one time correctly relate to the scores on a known criterion obtained at approximately the same time

Concurrent verbal report—A participant's oral report of the experiment, which is obtained as the experiment is being performed

Confidence interval—An interval estimate inferred from sample data that has a certain probability of including the true population parameter

Confidentiality—Not revealing information obtained from a research participant to anyone outside the research group

Confounding—Occurs when extraneous variable co-occurs with the independent variable and affects the dependent variable

Confounding extraneous variable—An extraneous variable that co-occurs with the independent variable and affects the dependent variable

Confounding variables—An extraneous variable that if not controlled for will eliminate the researcher's ability to claim that the IV causes changes in the DV

Constancy—The influence of an extraneous variable is same on all of the independent variable groups

Construct validity—The extent to which a construct is adequately represented by the measures used in a research study

Content-related evidence or content validity—Judgment by experts of the degree to which items, tasks, or questions on a test adequately represent the construct

Contingency question—An item directing the participant to different follow-up questions depending on the initial response

Contingency table—Table used to examine the relationship between categorical variables

Control—(1) A comparison group, (2) elimination of the influence of extraneous variables, or (3) manipulation of antecedent conditions to produce a change in mental processes and behavior

Control group—The group of participants that does not receive the active treatment condition and serves as a standard of comparison for determining whether the treatment condition produced any causal effect

Convenience sampling—Use of people who are readily available, volunteer, or are easily recruited for inclusion in a sample

Convergent validity evidence—Validity evidence based on the degree to which the focal test sores correlate with independent measures of the same construct

Correlation coefficient—Index indicating the strength and direction of linear relationship between two quantitative variables

Correlational research—Nonexperimental research study based on describing relationships among variables and making predictions

Counterbalancing—A technique used to control sequencing effects

Counterfactual—What the experimental group participants' responses would have been if they had *not* received the treatment

Criterion-related validity—Degree to which scores predict or relate to a known criterion such as a future performance or an already-established test

Critical region—The area on a null hypothesis sampling distribution where the observed value of the statistic, if it fell in this area, would be considered a rare event

Cronbach's alpha—Another name for coefficient alpha

Cross-case analysis—Case study analysis in which cases are compared and contrasted

Crossover effect—An outcome in which the control group performs better at pretesting but the experimental group performs better at posttesting

Cross-sectional study—Study conducted at a single time period, and data are collected from multiple groups; data are collected during a single, brief time period

Culture—The shared beliefs, values, practices, language norms, rituals, and material things that the members of a group use to interpret and understand their world

Curvilinear regression—The type of regression analysis that can accurately model curved relationships

Curvilinear relationship—A nonlinear (curved) relationship between two quantitative variables

Cyclical variation—Any type of systematic up-and-down movement on the dependent variable over time

D

Data set—A set of data

Data triangulation—Use of multiple sources of data

Debriefing—A postexperimental discussion or interview about the details of the study, including an explanation for the use of any deception

Deception—Giving the participant a bogus rationale for the experiment

Deduction—A reasoning process that involves going from the general to the specific

Degrees of freedom—The number of values that are "free to vary"; it's used when computing a statistic to be used in inferential statistics

Dehoaxing—Debriefing the participants about any deception that was used in the experiment

Demand characteristics—Any of the cues available in an experiment, such as instructions, rumors, or setting characteristics, that influence the responses of participants

Dependent variable—Variable that is presumed to be influenced by one or more independent variables

Description—The portrayal of a situation or phenomenon

Descriptive research—Research that attempts to describe some phenomenon, event, or situation

Descriptive statistics—The type of statistical analysis focused on describing, summarizing, or explaining a set of data

Descriptive validity—The factual accuracy of the account reported by the researcher

Desensitizing—Eliminating any undesirable influence that the experiment might have had on the participant

Design components—Structures and procedures used in constructing research designs

Determinism—The belief that mental processes and behaviors are fully caused by prior natural factors

Differential attrition—In a multigroup design, groups become different on an extraneous variable because of differences in the loss of participants across the groups

Differential carryover effect—A treatment condition affects participants' performance in a later condition in one way and in another way when followed by a different condition

Differential history—The groups in a multigroup design experience different history events that result in differences on the dependent variable

Differential influence—When the influence of an extraneous variable is different for the various groups

Direct effect—An effect of one variable directly on another variable; depicted as a single arrow in a path model

Directional alternative hypothesis—An alternative hypothesis that includes a "less than sign" ($<$) or a "greater than sign" ($>$)

Discoverability—The assumption that it is possible to discover the regularities that exist in nature

Discriminant validity evidence—Validity evidence based on the degree to which the focal test scores do *not* correlate with measures of *different* constructs

Disproportional stratified sampling—Stratified sampling where the sample proportions are made to be *different* from the population proportions on the stratification variable

Documents—Personal and official documents that were left behind

Double-barreled question—Asking about two or more issues in a single question

Double-blind placebo method—Neither the experimenter nor the research participant is aware of the treatment condition administered to the participant

Double negative—A sentence construction that contains two negatives

Duhem–Quine principle—States that a hypothesis cannot be tested in isolation from other assumptions

E

Ecological validity—The degree to which the results of a study can be generalized across settings or environmental conditions

Effect size indicator—Index of magnitude or strength of a relationship or difference between means

Effect—The difference between what would have happened and what did happen when a treatment is administered

Effect size—The magnitude of the relationship between two variables in a population

Electronic survey—Survey conducted over the Internet

Element—The basic unit selected

e-mail survey—Electronic survey where participants are contacted directly via e-mail, and the survey instrument is attached to the message

Emic perspective—The insider's perspective

Empirical adequacy—Present when theories and hypotheses closely fit empirical evidence

Empiricism—The acquisition of knowledge through experience

Equal probability of selection method (EPSEM)—Sampling method in which each individual element has an equal probability of selection into the sample

Equating the groups—Using control strategies to make the influence of extraneous variables constant across the independent variable groups so that the only systematic *difference* between the groups is due to the influence of the independent variable

Equivalent-forms reliability—Consistency of a group of individuals' scores on two versions of the same test

Essence—Phenomenological structure of the experience

Estimation—The branch of inferential statistics focused on obtaining estimates of the values of population parameters

Ethical dilemma—The investigator's conflict in weighing the potential cost to the participant against the potential gain to be accrued from the research project

Ethnocentric—Judgment of people in other cultures based on the standards of your culture

Ethnography—Qualitative research method that focuses on the discovery and description of the culture of a group of people

Etic perspective—The researcher's external or "objective outsider" perspective

Event sampling—Observations are recorded every time a particular event occurs

Exhaustive categories—Response categories that cover the full range of possible responses

Existing or secondary data—Collection of data that were left behind or originally used for something different than the current research study

Experimental criterion—In single-case research, repeated demonstration that a behavioral change occurs when the treatment is introduced

Experimental group—The group of participants that receives the treatment condition that is intended to produce an effect

Experimental research—The research approach in which one attempts to demonstrate cause-and-effect relationships by manipulating the independent variable

Experimenter attributes—Biasing experimenter effects attributable to the physical and psychological characteristics of the researcher

Experimenter effects—Actions and characteristics of researchers that influence the responses of participants

Experimenter expectancies—Biasing experimenter effects attributable to the researcher's expectations about the outcome of the experiment

Explanation—Determination of the cause or causes of a given phenomenon

Extended fieldwork—Spending enough time in the field to fully understand what is being studied

External validity—Degree to which the study results can be generalized to and across other people, settings, treatments, outcomes, and times

Extraneous variable—Variable that might compete with the IV in explaining the outcome

F

Face validity—Prima facie judgment of whether the items appear to represent the construct and whether the test or instrument looks valid

Face-to-face method—Survey method where participants are interviewed in a face-to-face setting

Factor analysis—A statistical analysis procedure used to determine the number of dimensions present in a set of items

Factorial designs—Two or more independent variables are studied to determine their separate and joint effects on the dependent variable

Factorial design based on a mixed model—A factorial design that uses a combination of within-participants and between-participants independent variables

Falsificationism—A deductive approach to science that focuses on falsifying hypotheses as the key criterion of science

Field experiment—An experimental research study that is conducted in a real-life setting

Fieldnotes—Notes taken by the researcher during (or immediately after) one's observations in the field

Fieldwork—A general term for data collection in ethnographic research

First increasing treatment effect—An outcome in which the experimental and the control groups differ at pretesting, and only the experimental group's scores change from pre- to posttesting

Focus group—Collection of data in a group situation where a moderator leads a discussion with a small group of people

Frequency distribution—Data arrangement in which the frequencies of each unique data value is shown

Frequency distribution control—A matching technique that matches groups of participants by equating the overall distribution of the chosen variable

G

Gatekeepers—Group members who control a researcher's access to the group

Going native—Overidentification with the group being studied so that one loses any possibility of objectivity

Grounded theory—Methodology for generating and developing a theory that is grounded in the particular data

Group-administered questionnaire method—Survey method where participants fill out the questionnaire in a group setting

Group counterbalancing—Administering different sequences to different groups of participants

H

Histogram—Graph depicting frequencies and distribution of a quantitative variable

History—Any event that can produce the outcome, other than the treatment condition, that occurs during the study before posttest measurement

Holism—Idea that a whole, such as a culture, is more than the sum of its individual parts

Homogeneity—The degree to which a set of items measures a single construct

Hypothesis—The best prediction or a tentative solution to a problem

Hypothesis testing—The process of testing a predicted relationship or hypothesis by making observations and then comparing the observed facts with the hypothesis or predicted relationship; the branch of inferential statistics focused on determining when the null hypothesis can or cannot be rejected in favor of the alternative hypothesis

I

Ideographic causation—A single intentional action for a particular person in a local situation with an observable result

Incomplete counterbalancing—Enumerating fewer than all possible sequences and requiring different groups of participants to take each of the sequences

Increasing treatment and control groups—An outcome in which the experimental and the control groups differ at pretesting and both increase from pre- to posttesting, but the experimental group increases at a faster rate

Independent samples *t* test—The significance test of the difference between two means that uses the *t* probability distribution

Independent variable—Variable that is presumed to cause changes in another variable

Indirect effect—An effect occurring through a mediating variable

Induction—A reasoning process that involves going from the specific to the general

Inferential statistics—The type of statistical analysis focused on making inferences about populations based on sample data

Informed consent—Informing the research participant of all aspects of the study that might influence his or her willingness to volunteer to participate

Instrumental case study—Case study in which the researcher studies a case in order to understand something more general than the particular case

Instrumentation—Changes from pretest to posttest in the assessment or measurement of the dependent variable

Interaction design—Single-case design used to identify interaction effects

Interaction effect in single-case research—The combined influence of two or more independent variables

Interaction effect—The joint, combined, or "interactive" effect of two or more independent variables on the dependent variable

Interdependence—Violation of design assumption in which changing one target (participant, outcome, or setting) produces changes in the remaining targets

Internal consistency reliability—Consistency with which items on a test measure a single construct

Internal validity—The correctness of inferences made by researchers about cause and effect

Internet experiment—An experimental study that is conducted over the Internet

Interobserver agreement—The percentage of time that different observers' ratings are in agreement

Interpretive validity—Accurately portraying the participants' subjective viewpoints and meanings

Interrater reliability—The degree of consistency or agreement between two or more scorers, judges, observers, or raters

Interrupted time-series design—A quasi-experimental design in which a treatment effect is assessed by comparing the pattern of pre- and posttest scores for a single group of research participants

Interval estimation—Placement of a range of numbers around a point estimate

Interval scale—A scale of measurement with equal intervals of distance between adjacent numbers

Interview protocol—Data collection instrument used by the interviewer

Interviews—Data collection method in which an interviewer asks the interviewee a series of questions, often with prompting for additional information

Intrasubject counterbalancing—Administering the treatment conditions to each individual participant in more than one order

Intrinsic case study—Case study in which the researcher is only interested in understanding the individual case

Intuition—An approach to acquiring knowledge that is not based on a known reasoning process

Investigator triangulation—Use of multiple investigators to collect and interpret the data

K

Known groups validity evidence—Degree to which groups that are known to differ on a construct actually differ *according to the test* used to measure the construct

L

Laboratory experiment—An experimental research study that is conducted in the controlled environment of a laboratory

Laboratory observation—Observation conducted in lab setting set up by the researcher

Leading question—A question that suggests how the participants should answer

Level of significance—Another name for alpha level

Life world—A person's subjective inner world of experience

Likert scaling—A multi-item scale is used to measure a single construct by summing each participant's responses to the items on the scale

Line graph—A graph relying on the drawing of one or more lines

Loaded term—A word that produces an emotionally charged reaction

Logic of discovery—The inductive or discovery part of the scientific process

Logic of hypothesis testing—The five steps in the process of significance testing

Logic of justification—The deductive or theory-testing part of the scientific process

Logical positivism—A philosophical approach that focused on verifying hypotheses as the key criterion of science

Longitudinal study—Data are collected at two or more points in time

Low-inference descriptors—Descriptions that are very close to participants' words or are direct verbatim quotes

M

Mail questionnaire method—Survey method where questionnaires are sent to potential participants via regular mail

Main effect—The influence of one independent variable on the dependent variable

Manipulation—Active intervention by researcher that is expected to produce changes in the dependent variable

Marginal mean—The average score of all participants receiving one level of an independent variable

Matching variable—The extraneous variable used in matching

Matching—Using any of a variety of techniques for equating participants on one or more variables

Maturation—Any physical or mental change that occurs with the passage of time and affects dependent variable scores

Mean—The arithmetic average

Measure of central tendency—Numerical value expressing what is typical of the values of a quantitative variable

Measure of variability—Numerical value expressing how spread out or how much variation is present in the values of a quantitative variable

Measurement—The assignment of symbols or numbers to something according to a set of rules

Median—The center point in an ordered set of numbers

Mediating variable—Variable that occurs between two other variables in a causal chain; it's an intervening variable

Meta-anlaysis—A quantitative technique for describing the relationship between variables across multiple research studies

Method of data collection—Technique for physically obtaining the data to be analyzed in a research study

Method of difference—If groups are equivalent on every variable except for one, then that one variable is the cause of the difference between the groups

Methods triangulation—Use of multiple research methods or methods of data collection

Mixed methods research—Type of research in which quantitative and qualitative data or approaches are combined in a single research study

Mixed sampling—Use of a combination of quantitative and qualitative sampling methods

Mixed-question format—Includes a mixture of both closed- and open-ended response characteristics in a single item

Mode—The most frequently occurring number

Moderator variable—Variable that changes or "moderates" the relationship between other variables

Multidimensional construct—Construct consisting of two or more dimensions; contrasted with a unidimensional construct

Multiple-baseline design—A single-case design in which the treatment condition is successively administered to several target participants, target outcomes, or target settings

Multiple operationalism—Using multiple measures to represent a construct

Multiple regression—Regression analysis with one dependent variable and two or more independent variables

Mutually exclusive categories—Nonoverlapping response categories

N

Natural manipulation research—Type of research in which the independent variable approximates a naturally occurring manipulation, but it is not manipulated by the researcher

Naturalism—Position popular in behavioral science stating that science should justify its practices according to how well they work rather than according to philosophical arguments

Naturalistic generalization—Generalization, based on similarity, made by the reader of a research report

Naturalistic observation—Observation conducted in real-world situations

Negative correlation—Correlation in which values of two variables tend to move in opposite directions

Negative-case sampling—Searching for cases that challenge one's expectations or one's current findings

Nominal scale—The use of symbols, such as words or numbers, to classify or categorize measurement objects into groups or types

Nomological causation—The standard view of causation in science; refers to causal relationships among variables

Nondirectional alternative hypothesis—An alternative hypothesis that includes the "not equal to sign" ($\neq$)

Nonequivalent comparison group design—A quasi-experimental design in which the results obtained from nonequivalent experimental and control groups are compared

Nonexperimental quantitative research—Type of quantitative research in which the independent variable is not manipulated by the researcher

Nonnumerical data—Data that consist of pictures, words, statements, clothing, written records or documents, or a description of situations and behavior

Normal Distribution—A theoretical distribution that follows the 68, 95, 99.7 percent rule

Normal science—The period in which scientific activity is governed and directed by a single paradigm

Norming group—The reference group upon which reported reliability and validity evidence is based

Norms—Written and unwritten rules specifying how people in a group are supposed to think and act

Null hypothesis—Typically the hypothesis of no difference between means or among the variables being investigated or of no relationship in the population

Numerical data—Data consisting of numbers

O

Objectivity—Goal in science to eliminate or minimize opinion or bias in the conduct of research

Observation—Researcher watches and records events or behavioral patterns of people

One-group posttest-only design—Administration of a posttest to a single group of participants after they have been given an experimental treatment condition

One-group pretest–posttest design—Design in which a treatment condition is interjected between a pretest and posttest of the dependent variable

One-stage cluster sampling—Clusters are randomly selected and all the elements in the selected clusters constitute the sample

One-way analysis of variance—Statistical test used when you have one quantitative DV and one categorical IV

One-way repeated measures analysis of variance—Statistical test used when you have one quantitative DV and one repeated measures IV

Open coding—First stage of data analysis in GT; it's the most exploratory stage

Open-ended question—A question that allows participants to respond in their own words

Operational definition—Defining a concept by the operations used to represent or measure it

Operationalism—Representing constructs by a specific set of operations

Operationalization—Campbell's term for an operational definition; the way a construct is represented and measured in a particular research study

Order effect—A sequencing effect arising from the order in which the treatment conditions are administered to participants

Ordinal scale—A rank order measurement scale

Outcome validity—The degree to which the results of a study can be generalized across different but related dependent variables

P

p **value**—A shorter name for probability value

Panel studies—Longitudinal study where data are collected from the same individuals at successive time points

Paradigm—A framework of thought or beliefs by which reality is interpreted

Paradigm emphasis—One of the two dimensions used in MM design matrix; its levels are equal status and dominant status

Parameter—A numerical characteristic of a population

Partial blind technique—A method whereby knowledge of each research participant's treatment condition is kept from the experimenter through as many stages of the experiment as possible

Partial correlation coefficient—The correlation between two quantitative variables controlling for one or more variables

Partial eta squared—The amount of variance in the dependent variable uniquely explained by a single categorical independent variable

Partial regression coefficient—The regression coefficient in a multiple regression equation

Participant feedback—Member checking to see if participants agree with the researcher's statements, interpretations, and conclusions

Participant observation—Data collection method in which the researcher becomes an active participant in the group he or she is investigating.

Participant reactivity to the experimental situation—Research participants' motives and tendencies that affect their perceptions of the situation and their responses on the dependent variable

Passive consent—Consent is received from a parent or guardian by not returning the consent form

Passive deception—Withholding information from the research participants by not giving them all the details of the experiment

Path analysis—Type of research in which a researcher hypothesizes a theoretical causal model and then empirically tests the model

Pattern matching—Construction and testing of a complex hypothesis

68, 95, 99.7 percent rule—Rule stating percentage of cases falling within 1, 2, and 3 standard deviations from the mean on a normal distribution

Peer review—Discussing your interpretations with one's peers and colleagues

Periodicity—Problematic situation in systematic sampling that can occur if there is a cyclical pattern in the sampling frame

Phenomenology—Qualitative research method where the researcher attempts to understand and describe how one or more participants experience a phenomenon

Physical data—Any material thing created or left behind by humans that might provide clues to some event or phenomenon

Pilot study—An experiment that is conducted on a few participants prior to the actual collection of data

Pilot test—Testing for the proper operation of a data collection instrument before using it in the research study

Placebo Effect—Improvement due to partcipants' expections for improvement rather than the actual treatment

Plagiarism—Using work produced by someone else and calling it one's own

Point estimation—Use of the value of a sample statistic as one's estimate of the value of a population parameter

Population validity—Degree to which the study results can be generalized to and across the people in the target population

Population—The full group of interest to the researcher, to which one wants to generalize, and from which the sample is selected

Positive correlation—Correlation in which values of two variables tend to move in the same direction

Positive self-presentation—Participants' motivation to respond in such a way as to present themselves in the most positive manner

Post hoc tests—Follow-up test to one-way ANOVA when the categorical IV has three or more levels; used to determine which pairs of means are significantly different

Postexperimental inquiry—An interview of the participant after the experiment is over

Postexperimental interview—An interview with the participant following completion of the experiment, during which all aspects of the experiment are explained and the participant is allowed to comment on the study

Posttest-only control-group design—Administration of a posttest to two or more randomly assigned groups of participants that receive the different levels of the independent variable

Posttest-only design with nonequivalent groups—Design in which the performance of an experimental group is compared with that of a nonequivalent control group at the posttest

Power—The probability of rejecting a false-null hypothesis

Practical significance—Claim made when a statistically significant finding seems large enough to be important

Pragmatism—Philosophy focusing on what works as the criterion of what should be viewed as tentatively true and useful in research and practice

Precision control—A matching technique in which each participant is matched with another participant on selected variables

Prediction—The ability to anticipate the occurrence of an event

Predictive validity—Degree to which scores obtained at one time correctly predict the scores on a criterion at a later time

Pretest–posttest control-group design—Administration of a posttest to two or more randomly assigned groups of participants after the groups have been pretested and administered the different levels of the independent variable

Privacy—Having control of others access to information about you

Probabilistic causes—A weaker form of determinism that indicates regularities that usually but not always occur

Probability value—The likelihood of the observed value (or a more extreme value) of a statistic, if the null hypothesis were true

Proportional stratified sampling—Stratified sampling where the sample proportions are made to be the *same* as the population proportions on the stratification variable

Proximal similarity—Generalization to people, places, settings, and contexts that are similar to those described in the research study

Pseudoscience—Set of beliefs or practices that are not scientific but claim to be scientific

Psychological experiment—Objective observation of phenomena that are made to occur in a strictly controlled situation in which one or more factors are varied and the others are kept constant

PsycINFO—An electronic bibliographic database of abstracts and citations to the scholarly literature in psychology

Purpose of random assignment—To produce two or more equivalent groups for use in an experiment

Purpose of random selection—To obtain a representative sample

Purposive sampling—A researcher specifies the characteristics of the population of interest and then locates individuals who have those characteristics

Q

Qualitative research—Interpretive research approach relying on multiple types of subjective data and investigation of people in particular situations in their natural environment; the type of research relying on qualitative research data

Quantitative research study—A research study that is based on numerical data

Quantitative variable—Variable that varies by degree or amount

Quasi-experimental design—A research design in which an experimental procedure is applied but all extraneous variables are not controlled

Questionnaire—Self-report data collection instrument filled out by research participants

Quota sampling—A researcher decides on the desired sample sizes or quotas for groups identified for inclusion in the sample, followed by convenience sampling from the groups

R

Random assignment—Randomly assigning a sample of individuals to a specific number of comparison groups

Random-digit dialing—Random sampling method frequently used with telephone interviewing

Random sampling—Selection of sample members using a statistically random process

Random selection—Selection of participants using a random sampling method

Randomization—Control technique that equates groups of participants by ensuring every member an equal chance of being assigned to any group

Randomized counterbalancing—Sequence order is randomly determined for each individual.

Randomized designs—Between-participants designs in which participants are randomly assigned to groups

Range—The highest number minus the lowest number

Ranking—Participants asked to put their responses in ascending or descending order

Rates—The percentage of people in a group that have a particular characteristic

Rating scale—An ordered set of response choices, such as a 5-point rating scale, measuring the direction and strength of an attitude

Ratio scale—A scale of measurement with rank ordering, equal intervals, and an absolute zero point

Rationalism—The acquisition of knowledge through reasoning

Reactive effect—Nontypical behavior of participants because of the presence of the researcher

Reality in nature—The assumption that the things we see, hear, feel, smell, and taste are real

Reflexivity—Thinking critically about one's interpretations and biases

Regression analysis—Use of one or more quantitative independent variables to explain or predict the values of a single quantitative dependent variable

Regression artifacts—Effects that appear to be due to the treatment but are due to regression to the mean

Regression coefficient—The slope or change in Y given a one unit change in X

Regression discontinuity design—A design that assigns participants to groups based on their scores on an assignment variable and assesses the effect of a treatment by looking for a discontinuity in the groups regression lines

Regression equation—The equation that defines a regression line

Regression line—The line of "best fit" based on a regression equation

Regression toward the mean—A synonym for regression artifacts

Reliability—The consistency or stability of scores

Reliability coefficient—Type of correlation coefficient used as an index of reliability

Repeated measures design—Another name for a within-participants design

Replication—The reproduction of the results of a study in a new study

Representative sample—A sample that resembles the population

Research design—The outline, plan, or strategy used to investigate the research problem

Research ethics—A set of guidelines to assist the researcher in conducting ethical research

Research hypothesis—The predicted relationship among the variables being investigated

Research misconduct—Fabricating, falsifying, or plagiarizing the proposing, performing, reviewing, or reporting of research results

Research problem—An interrogative sentence that states the relationship between two variables

Research program—Lakatos's term for a paradigm. It includes a set of "hard-core" beliefs and an outer "protective belt" of additional beliefs

Research validity—Truthfulness of inferences made from a research study

Researcher bias—Only noticing data that support one's prior expectations

Researcher-as-detective—Metaphor applied to researcher looking for the local cause of a single event

Response rate—The percentage of people selected to be in a sample and who participate in the research study

Response set—Tendency for a participant to respond in a particular way to a set of items

Retrospective verbal report—An oral report in which the participant retrospectively recalls aspects of the experiment

Reversal—Change of behavior back to baseline level after withdrawal of treatment

Reversal design—A design in which the treatment condition is applied to an alternative but incompatible behavior so that a reversal in behavior is produced

Revolutionary science—A period in which scientific activity is characterized by the replacement of one paradigm with another

S

Sacrifice groups—Groups of participants who are stopped and interviewed at different stages of the experiment

Sample size calculator—A statistical program used to provide a recommended sample size

Sample—A subset of the population; the set of cases or elements selected from the population

Sampling—The process of drawing a sample from a population

Sampling distribution—The theoretical probability distribution of the values of a statistic that would result if you selected all possible samples of a particular size from a population

Sampling distribution of the mean—The theoretical probability distribution of the means of all possible samples of a particular size selected from a population

Sampling error—Variation of sample values from population values

Sampling frame—A list of all the elements in a population

Sampling interval—The population size divided by the desired sample size; it's symbolized by the letter k

Scatterplot—A graphical depiction of the relationship between two quantitative variables

Science—The most trustworthy way of acquiring reliable and valid knowledge about the natural world

Search engine—A software program that seeks out Web pages stored on servers throughout the World Wide Web

Seasonal variation—Values on the dependent variable vary by season

Second increasing treatment effect—An outcome in which the control group performs better than the experimental group at pretesting, but only the experimental group improves from pre- to posttesting

Selection—Production of nonequivalent groups because a different selection procedure operates across the groups

Selection-attrition effect—Participants that drop out of one group are dissimilar to those in another group

Selection–history—The groups are exposed to the same history event, but they react differently because they were not equated

Selection-history effect—An extraneous event occurring between pretest and posttest influences participants in one group differently than participants in another group

Selection–instrumentation—The groups react to changes in instrumentation differently because they were not equated

Selection-instrumentation effect—Participants' scores in one group are affected by the process of measurement differently than participants in another group

Selection–maturation—The groups undergo different rates of maturation because they were not equated

Selection-maturation effect—Participants in one group experience a different rate of maturation than participants in another group

Selection–regression artifact—The groups show different amounts of regression to the mean, because they were not equated

Selection-regression effect—Participants in one group display a different rate of regression to the mean than participants in another group

Selection–testing—The groups react to the pretest differently, because they were not equated

Selective coding—Third and final stage of data analysis in GT in which the theory is finalized

Semantic differential—Scaling method measuring the meanings that participants give to attitudinal objects

Semi-partial correlation squared—The amount of variance in the dependent variable uniquely explained by a single quantitative independent variable

Shared beliefs—Statements or conventions that people sharing a culture hold to be true or false

Shared values—Culturally defined standards about what is good or bad or desirable or undesirable

Significant statements—Words, phrases, or sentence length participant statements that the researcher thinks vividly communicate the participant's experience

Simple random sampling—A popular and basic equal probability selection method

Simple regression—Regression analysis with one dependent variable and one independent variable

Single-case research designs—Research design in which a single participant or a single group of individuals is used to investigate the influence of a treatment condition

Snowball sampling—Each sampled person is asked to identify other potential participants with the inclusion characteristic

Social comparison method—A social validation method in which the participant is compared with nondeviant peers

Social desirability bias—Error occurring when participants try to respond in the way they think makes them look good

Social validation—Determination by others that the treatment condition has significantly changed the participant's functioning

Specificity of the research question—The preciseness with which the research question is stated

Stable baseline—A set of responses characterized by the absence of trend and little variability

Standard deviation—The square root of the variance

Standard error—The standard deviation of a sampling distribution

Statistic—A numerical index based on sample data

Statistical conclusion validity—The validity of inferences made about the covariation between the independent and dependent variables

Statistical control—Control of measured extraneous variables during data analysis.

Statistical power—The probability of rejecting the null hypothesis when it is false

Statistically significant—Conclusion that an observed finding would be very unlikely if the null hypothesis were true; the observed relationship is probably *not* due to chance

Stratification variable—The variable on which the population elements are divided for the purpose of stratified sampling

Stratified random sampling—Division of population elements into mutually exclusive groups and then selection of a random sample from each group

Strong experimental designs—Designs that effectively control extraneous variables and provide strong evidence of cause and effect

Subjective evaluation method—A social validation method in which others' views of the participants are assessed to see whether those others perceive a change in behavior

Summated rating approach—Another name for Likert scaling

Survey instrument—Data collection instrument used in survey research such as a questionnaire or interview protocol

Survey research—A nonexperimental research method relying on questionnaires or interview protocols

Systematic sampling—The sampling method where one determines the sampling interval (k), randomly selects an element between 1 and k, and then selects every kth element

T

t **test for correlation coefficient**—Statistical test used to determine if a correlation coefficient is statistically significant

Target population—The large population to which the researcher would like to generalize the study results

Telephone interview method—Survey method where interviews are conducted over the telephone

Temporal validity—The degree to which the results can be generalized across time

Testing effect—Changes in a person's score on the second administration of a test resulting from having previously taken the test

Tests—Standardized or researcher-constructed data collection instruments designed to measure personality, achievement, and performance

Test–retest reliability—Consistency of a group of individuals' scores on a test over time

Test statistic—A statistic that follows a known sampling distribution and is used in significance testing

Theoretical generalization—Generalization of a theoretical explanation beyond the particular research study

Theoretical saturation—Occurs when no new information relevant to the GT is emerging from the data and the GT has been sufficiently validated

Theoretical sensitivity—Researcher is effective in understanding what kinds of data need to be collected and what aspects of already collected data are important for theory development

Theoretical validity—Degree to which the theory or explanation fits the data

Theory triangulation—The use of multiple theories or perspectives to aid in interpreting the data

Theory—A group of logically organized and deductively related laws; an explanation of how and why something operates as it does

Therapeutic criterion—Demonstration that the treatment condition has eliminated a disorder or has improved everyday functioning

Think-aloud technique—A method that requires participants to verbalize their thoughts as they are performing the experiment

Third variable problem—Occurs when observed relationship between two variables is actually due to a confounding extraneous variable

Three-way interaction—A two-way interaction that changes at the different levels of the third independent variable

Time order—One of the two dimensions used in MM design matrix; its levels are concurrent and sequential

Time-interval sampling—Observations are recorded during preselected time intervals

Treatment variation validity—The degree to which the results of a study can be generalized across variations in the treatment

Trend study—Independent samples are taken successively from a population over time and the same questions are asked

Triangulation—Use of multiple data sources, research methods, investigators, and/or theories/perspectives to cross-check and corroborate research data and conclusions

Two-stage cluster sampling—Clusters are randomly selected, and a random sample of elements is drawn from each of the selected clusters

Two-way analysis of variance—Statistical test used when you have one quantitative DV and two categorical IVs

Two-way interaction—The effect of one independent variable on the dependent variable varies with the different levels of the other independent variable

Type I error—Rejection of a true null hypothesis

Type II error—Failure to reject a false null hypothesis

U

Unstandardized difference between means—The difference between two means in the variables' natural units

V

Validation—Gathering of evidence regarding the soundness of inferences made from test scores

Validity coefficient—The type of correlation coefficient used in validation research

Validity—Accuracy of inferences, interpretations, or actions made on the basis of test scores

Variable—A characteristic or phenomenon that can vary across or within organisms, situations, or environments

Variance—The average deviation of data values from their mean in squared units

Volunteer sampling—Nonrandom sampling method where participants self-select into the sample

W

Weak experimental designs—Designs that do not control for many extraneous variables and provide weak evidence of cause and effect

Web-based survey—Electronic survey where participants are contacted indirectly by posting an invitation to participate and a link to the survey instrument on the Internet

Withdrawal—Removal of the treatment condition

Within-participants design—All participants receive all conditions

Within-participants posttest-only design—All participants receive all conditions, and a posttest is administered after each condition is administered

Within-participants variable—Type of independent variable where all participants receive all levels of the independent variable

Y

Y-intercept—The point at which a regression line crosses the Y (vertical) axis

Yoked control—A matching technique that matches participants on the basis of the temporal sequence of administering an event

Z

z-score—A score that has been transformed into standard deviation units

References

Ackermann, R. J. (1989). "The new experimentalism." *British Journal for the Philosophy of Science, 40,* 185–190.

Adair, J. G., Dushenko, T. W., & Lindsay, R. C. L. (1985). Ethical regulations and their impact on research practice. *American Psychologist, 40,* 59–72.

Adair, J. G., & Spinner, B. (1981). Subjects' access to cognitive processes: Demand characteristics and verbal report. *Journal for the Theory of Social Behavior, 11,* 31–52.

Adams-Price, C., Henley, T., & Hale, M. (1998). Phenomenology and the meaning of aging for young and old adults. *International Journal of Aging & Human Development, 47,* 263–277.

Aebi, M., Metzke, C., & Steinhausen, H. (2009). Prediction of major affective disorders in adolescents by self-report measures. *Journal of Affective Disorders, 115*(1), 140–149.

Alaggia, R., & Millington, G. (2008). Male child sexual abuse: A phenomenology of betrayal. *Clinical Social Work Journal, 36,* 265–275.

Allen, K. E., Hart, B., Buell, J. S., Harris, F. R., & Wolf, M. M. (1964). Effects of social reinforcement on isolate behavior of a nursery school child. *Child Development, 35,* 511–518.

Altemeyer, R. A. (1971). Subject pool pollution and the postexperimental interview. *Journal of Experimental Research in Personality, 5,* 79–84.

American Psychological Association. (1953). *Ethical standards of psychologists.* Washington, DC: Author.

American Psychological Association. (2002). *Ethical principles of psychologists and code of conduct.* Washington, DC: Author.

American Psychological Association. (2010). *Publication Manual of the American Psychological Association* (6th ed.). Washington, DC: Author.

Anastasi, A., & Urbina, S. (1997). *Psychological testing.* Upper Saddle River, NJ: Prentice Hall.

Anderson, R. E., Franckowiak, S., Christmas, C., Walston, J., & Crespo, C. (2001). Obesity and reports of no leisure time activity among older Americans: Results from the third national health and nutrition examination survey. *Educational Gerontology, 27,* 297–306.

Anderson, T., & Kanuka, H. (2003). *E-research: Methods, strategies, and issues.* Boston: Houghton Mifflin.

Aronson, E. (1966). Avoidance of inter-subject communication. *Psychological Reports, 19,* 238.

Aronson, E., & Carlsmith, J. M. (1968). Experimentation in social psychology. In G. Lindzey & E. Aronson (Eds.), *The handbook of social psychology* (2nd ed.). Reading, MA: Addison-Wesley.

Ayer, A. J. (Ed.). (1959). *Logical positivism.* New York: Free Press.

Baldwin, E. (1993). The case for animal research in psychology. *Journal of Social Issues, 49,* 121–131.

Baltes, P. B., Reese, H. W., & Nesselroade, J. R. (1977). *Life-span developmental psychology: Introduction to research.* Monterey, CA: Wadsworth Publishing Co.

Bandura, A., Ross, D., & Ross, S. A. (1966). Imitation of film-mediated aggressive models. *Journal of Abnormal and Social Psychology, 66*(1), 3–11.

Bannister, D. (1966). Psychology as an exercise in paradox. *Bulletin of British Psychological Society, 19,* 21–26.

Barber, T. X., & Silver, M. J. (1968). Fact, fiction, and the experimenter bias effect. *Psychological Bulletin Monograph, 70,* 1–29.

Barlow, D. H., Nock, M. K., & Hersen, M. 2008. *Single case experimental designs: Strategies for studying behavior change* (3rd ed.). Boston, MA: Allyn and Bacon.

Beck, A. T., Ward, C. H., Mendelson, M., Mock, J., & Erbaugh, J. (1961). An inventory for measuring depression. *Archives of General Psychiatry, 4,* 561–571.

Beckman, L., & Bishop, B. R. (1970). Deception in psychological research: A reply to Seeman. *American Psychologist, 25,* 878–880.

Beharry, P., & Crozier, S. (2008). Using phenomenology to understand experiences of racism for second-generation South Asian women. *Canadian Journal of Counselling, 42,* 262–277.

Berg, B. L. (1998). *Qualitative research methods for the social sciences.* Boston: Allyn & Bacon.

Berscheid, E., Baron, R. S., Dermer, M., & Libman, M. (1973). Anticipating informed consent: An empirical approach. *American Psychologist, 28,* 913–925.

Bickel, P. J. (1975). Sex bias in graduate admissions: Data from Berkeley. *Science, 187,* 398–404.

Bijou, S. W., Peterson, R. F., Harris, F. R., Allen, K. E., & Johnston, M. S. (1969). Methodology for experimental studies of young children in natural settings. *Psychological Record, 19,* 177–210.

Birnbaum, M. H. (2001). *Introduction to behavioral research in the Internet.* Upper Saddle River, NJ: Prentice Hall.

Blascovich, J., Spencer, S. J., Quinn, D., & Steele, C. (2001). African Americans and high blood pressure: The role of stereotype threat. *Psychological Science, 12,* 225–229.

Bloom, H. S. (2003). Using 'short' interrupted time-series analysis to measure the impacts of whole-school reforms. *Evaluation Review, 27,* 3–49.

Bonevac, D. (1999). *Simple logic.* Fort Worth, TX: Harcourt Brace.

Booth-LaForce, C. & Oxford, M. L. (2008). Trajectories of social withdrawal from grades 1 to 6: Prediction from early parenting, attachment, and temperament. *Developmental Psychology, 44,* 1298–1313.

Boring, E. G. (1954). The nature and history of experimental control. *American Journal of Psychology, 67,* 573–589.

Boris, M., & Mandel, F. S. (1994). Foods and additives are common causes of the attention deficit hyperactive disorder in children. *Annals of Allergy, 72,* 462–468.

Box, G. E. P., & Jenkins, G. M. (1970). *Time-series analysis: Forecasting and control.* San Francisco, CA: Holden-Day.

Boyd, T., & Gumley, A. (2007). An experiential perspective on persecutory paranoia: A grounded theory construction. *Psychology and Psychotherapy: Theory, Research and Practice, 80,* 1–22.

Brace, I. (2004). *Questionnaire design: How to plan, structure, and write survey material for effective market research.* London: Kogan Page.

Bracht, G. H., & Glass, G. V. (1968). The external validity of experiments. *American Educational Research Journal, 5,* 437–474.

Bradburn, N., Sudman, S., & Wansink, B. (2004). *Asking questions: The definitive guide to questionnaire design—for market research, political polls, and social and health questionnaires.* San Francisco, CA: Jossey-Bass.

Bradley, A. W. (1978). Self-serving bias in the attribution process: A reexamination of the fact or fiction question. *Journal of Personality and Social Psychology, 36,* 56–71.

Brady, J. V. (1958). Ulcers in "executive monkeys." *Scientific American, 199,* 95–100.

Brainard, J. (2000, December, 8). As U.S. releases new rules on scientific fraud, scholars debate how much and why it occurs. *The Chronicle of Higher Education, 47*(15), p. A26.

Bridgman, P. W. (1927). *The logic of modern physics.* New York: Macmillan.

Bryant, A., & Charmaz, K. (Eds.) (2007). *The Sage handbook of grounded theory.* Los Angeles: Sage.

Camic, P. M., Rhodes, J. E., & Yardley, L. (2003). *Qualitative research in psychology: Expanding perspectives in methodology and design.* Washington, DC: American Psychological Association.

Campbell, D. T. (1966). Pattern matching as an essential in distal knowing. In K. R. Hammond (Ed.), *The psychology of Egon Brunswik* (pp. 81–106). Austin, TX: Holt, Rinehart, and Winston.

Campbell, D. T. (1969). Prospective: Artifact and control. In R. Rosenthal & R. L. Rosnow (Eds.), *Artifact in behavioral research.* New York: Academic Press.

Campbell, D. T. (1986). Relabeling internal and external validity for applied social scientists. In W. M. K. Trochim (Ed.), Advances in quasi-experimental design and analysis (pp. 66–77). *New Directions for Program Evaluation, 31.* San Francisco, CA: Jossey-Bass.

Campbell, D. T. (1988). Definitional versus multiple operationalism. In E. S. Overman (Ed.), *Methodology and epistemology for social science: Selected papers.* Chicago: University of Chicago Press.

Campbell, D. T., & Kenny, D. A. (1999). *A primer on regression artifacts.* New York: Guilford.

Campbell, D. T., & Stanley, J. C. (1963). *Experimental and quasi-experimental designs for research.* Chicago: Rand McNally.

Campbell, K. E., & Jackson, T. T. (1979). The role of and need for replication research in social psychology. *Replications in Social Psychology, 1,* 3–14.

Caporaso, T. A., & Ross, L. L., Jr. (1973). *Quasi-experimental approaches: Testing theory and evaluating policy.* Evanston: Northwestern University Press.

Carlopia, J., Adair, J. G., Lindsay, R. C. L., & Spinner, B. (1983). Avoiding artifact in the search for bias: The importance of assessing subjects' perceptions of the experiment. *Journal of Personality and Social Psychology, 44*, 693–701.

Carlston, D. E., & Cohen, J. L. (1980). A closer examination of subject roles. *Journal of Personality and Social Psychology, 38*, 857–870.

Carter, D. (2005). Living in virtual communities: An ethnography of human relationships in cyberspace. *Information, Communication, & Society, 8*(2), 148–167.

Centers for Disease Control and Prevention. (2001). *Helicobacter pylori and peptic ulcer disease.* Retrieved December 4, 2001, from http://www.cdc.gov/ulcer/history.htm

Chalmers, A. F. (1999). *What is this thing called science?* (3rd ed.). Indianapolis, IN: Hackett.

Chouinard, R., & Roy, N. (2008). Changes in high-school students' competence beliefs, utility value and achievement goals in mathematics. *British Journal of Educational Psychology, 78*, 31–50.

Christensen, L. (1977). The negative subject: Myth, reality or a prior experimental experience effect. *Journal of Personality and Social Psychology, 35*, 392–400.

Christensen, L. (1981). Positive self-presentation: A parsimonious explanation of subject motives. *The Psychological Record, 31*, 553–571.

Christensen, L. (1988). Deception in psychological research: When is its use justified? *Personality and Social Psychology Bulletin, 14*, 664–675.

Christensen, L., Krietsch, K., White, B., & Stagner, B. (1985). The impact of diet on mood disturbance. *Journal of Abnormal Psychology, 94*, 565–579.

Cochran, W. G., & Cox, G. M. (1957). *Experimental designs.* New York: Wiley.

Cohen, J. (1992). A power primer. *Psychological Bulletin, 112*, 155–159.

Cohen, J. (1994). The earth is round (*p* < .05). *American Psychologist, 49*, 997–1003.

Cohen, J., Cohen, P., West, S. G., & Aiken, L. S. (2003). *Applied multiple regression/correlation analysis for the behavioral sciences.* Mahwah, NJ: Lawrence Erlbaum.

Conrad, H. S., & Jones, H. E. (1940). A second study of familial resemblances in intelligence. *39th yearbook of the National Society for the Study of Education* (pp. 97–141). Chicago: University of Chicago Press.

Converse, J. M., & Presser, S. (1986). *Survey questions: Handcrafting the standardized questionnaire.* Newbury Park, CA: Sage.

Converse, P., & Traugott, M. (1986). Assessing the accuracy of polls and surveys. *Science, 234*, 1094–1098.

Cook, T. D., & Campbell, D. T. (1979). *Quasi-experimentation: Design and analysis for field settings.* Chicago: Rand McNally.

Copi, I. M., & Cohen, C. (2005). *Introduction to logic* (12th ed.). Upper Saddle River, NJ: Pearson.

Cowley, G. (2002, September 16). The science of happiness. *Newsweek, 140*(12) 46–48.

Creswell, J. W. (1998). *Qualitative inquiry and research design.* Thousand Oaks, CA: Sage.

Cronbach, L. J. (1990). *Essentials of psychological testing.* New York: Harper & Row.

Crosbie, J. (1993). Interrupted time-series analysis with brief single-subject data. *Journal of Consulting and Clinical Psychology, 61*, 966–974.

Davidson, R. (1986). Source of funding and outcome of clinical trials. *Journal of General Internal Medicine, 1*, 155–158.

Denisco, R. A., Chandler, R. K., & Compton, W. M. (2008). Addressing the intersecting problems of opioid misuse and chronic pain treatment. *Experimental and Clinical Psychopharmacology, 16*, 417–428.

Denzin, N. K., & Lincoln, Y. S. (Eds.). (1994). *Handbook of qualitative research.* Thousand Oaks, CA: Sage.

DePaulo, B. M., Dull, W. R., Greenberg, J. M., & Swaim, G. W. (1989). Are shy people reluctant to ask for help? *Journal of Personality and Social Psychology, 56*, 834–844.

Diener, E., & Crandall, R. (1978). *Ethics in social and behavioral research.* Chicago: University of Chicago Press.

Dillman, D. A. (2007). *Mail and internet surveys: The tailored design method.* Hoboken, NJ: Wiley.

Dorfman, D. D. (1978). The Cyril Burt question: New findings. *Science, 201*, 1177–1186.

Ebbinghaus, H. (1913). *Memory, a contribution to experimental psychology.* 1885. Translated by H. A. Ruger & C. E. Bussenius. New York: Teachers College, Columbia University.

Ellen, R. F. (1984). *Ethnographic research.* New York: Academic Press.

Ellickson, P. L. (1989). *Limiting nonresponse in longitudinal research: Three strategies for school-based studies* (Rand Note N-2912-CHF). Santa Monica, CA: Rand Corporation.

Ellickson, P. L., & Hawes, J. A. (1989). An assessment of active versus passive methods for obtaining parental consent. *Evaluation Review, 13*, 45–55.

Erdfelder, E., Faul, F., & Buchner, A. (1996). GPOWER: A general power analysis program. *Behavior Research Methods, Instruments, & Computers, 28*, 1–11.

Ericsson, K. A., & Simon, H. A. (1980). Verbal reports as data. *Psychological Review, 87*, 215–251.

Festinger, L. (1957). *A theory of cognitive dissonance.* Evanston, IL: Row, Peterson.

Festinger, L., & Carlsmith, J. M. (1959). Cognitive consequences of forced compliance. *Journal of Abnormal and Social Psychology, 58*, 203–211.

Feyerabend, P. K. (1975). *Against method: Outline of an anarchistic theory of knowledge.* London: New Left Books.

Fields, D. L. (2002). *Taking the measure of work: A guide to validated scales for organizational research and diagnosis.* Thousand Oaks, CA: Sage.

Fillenbaum, S. (1966). Prior deception and subsequent experimental performance: The faithful subject. *Journal of Personality and Social Psychology, 4*, 532–537.

Fisher, C. B., & Fyrberg, D. (1994). Participant partners: College students with the costs and benefits of deception research. *American Psychologist, 49*, 417–427.

Fisher, R. A. (1935). *The design of experiments* (1st ed.). London: Oliver and Boyd.

Fochtman, D. (2008). Phenomenology in pediatric cancer nursing research. *Journal of Pediatric Oncology Nursing, 25*(4), 185–192.

Folkman, S. (2000). Privacy and confidentiality. In B. D. Sales & S. Folkman (Eds.), *Ethics in Research with Human Participants.* Washington, DC: American Psychological Association.

Fortuyn, H., Lappenschaar, G., Nienhuis, F., Furer, J., Hodiamont, P., Rijnders, C., et al. (2009). Psychotic symptoms in narcolepsy: Phenomenology and a comparison with schizophrenia. *General Hospital Psychiatry, 31*(2), 146–154.

Foster, J. D., & Campbell, W. K. (2007). Are there such things as "Narcissists" in social psychology? A taxometric analysis of the Narcissistic Personality Inventory. *Personality and Individual Differences, 43*, 1321–1332.

Fuller, R. L., Luck, S. J., McMahon, R. P., & Gold, J. M. (2005). Working memory consolidation is abnormally slow in schizophrenia. *Journal of Abnormal Psychology, 114*, 279–290.

Gadlin, H., & Ingle, G. (1975). Through the one-way mirror: The limits of experimental self-reflection. *American Psychologist, 30*, 1003–1009.

Gallup, G. G., & Suarez, S. D. (1985). Alternatives to the use of animals in psychological research. *American Psychologist, 40*, 1104–1111.

Garcia, A., Freeman, J., Himle, M., Berman, N., Ogata, A., Ng, J., et al. (2009). Phenomenology of early childhood onset obsessive compulsive disorder. *Journal of Psychopathology and Behavioral Assessment, 31*(2), 104–111.

Gardner, G. T. (1978). Effects of federal human subjects regulations on data obtained in environmental stressor research. *Journal of Personality and Social Psychology, 36*, 628–634.

Gathercole, S. E., & Willis, C. S. (1992). Phonological memory and vocabulary development during the early school years: A longitudinal study. *Developmental Psychology, 28*, 887–898.

Gazzaniga, M. S., Ivry, R. B., & Mangun, G. R. (2002). *Cognitive neuroscience: The biology of the mind* (2nd ed.). New York: W. W. Norton & Co.

Gholson, B., & Barker, P. (1985). Kuhn, Lakatos, and Laudan: Applications in the history of physics and psychology. *American Psychologist, 7*, 755–769.

Gilbert, G. M. (1951). Stereotype persistence and change among college students. *Journal of Abnormal and Social Psychology, 46*, 245–254.

Gilgun, J. F., Daly, K., & Handel, G. (Eds.). (1992). *Qualitative methods in family research.* Thousand Oaks, CA: Sage.

Glaser, B. G., & Strauss, A. L., (1967). *The discovery of grounded theory: Strategies for qualitative research.* New York: Aldine De Gruyter.

Glass, G. V., Willson, V. L., & Gottman, J. M. (1975). *Design and analysis of time series.* Boulder, CO: Laboratory of Educational Research Press.

Gold, R. (1958). Roles in sociological field observations. *Social Forces, 36*, 217–223.

Gottman, J. M., & Glass, G. V. (1978). Analysis of interrupted time-series experiments. In T. R. Kratochwill (Ed.), *Single subject research: Strategies for evaluating change.* New York: Academic Press.

Gottman, J. M., & McFall, R. M. (1972). Self-monitoring effects in a program for potential high school dropouts: A time-series analysis. *Journal of Consulting and Clinical Psychology, 39*, 273–281.

Gray, M. (2004, October). Philosophical Inquiry in Nursing: An Argument for Radical Empiricism as a Philosophical

Framework for the Phenomenology of Addiction. *Qualitative Health Research, 14*(8), 1151–1164.

Groves, R. M., & Kahn, R. L. (1979). *Surveys by telephone: A national comparison with personal interviews.* New York: Academic Press.

Gubrium, J. F., & Sankar, A. (Eds.). (1993). *Qualitative methods in aging research.* Thousand Oaks, CA: Sage.

Guest, A. M. (2007). Cultural meanings and motivations for sport: A comparative case study of soccer teams in the Unites States and Malawi. *Online Journal of Sport Psychology, 9*(1), 1–19.

Gunsalus, C. K. (1993). Institutional structure to ensure research integrity. *Academic Medicine, 68*(9 Suppl.), 533–538.

Haber, E. (1996). Industry and the university. *Nature Biotechnology, 14,* 441–442.

Hainer, C. (1999, February 17). Face it: Your features reveal inner truths. *USA Today,* p. 9D.

Hall, R. V., & Fox, R. W. (1977). Changing-criterion designs: An alternative applied behavior analysis procedure. In C. C. Etzel, G. M. LeBlanc, & D. M. Baer (Eds.), *New developments in behavioral research: Theory, method, and application* (in honor of Sidney W. Bijou). Hillsdale, NJ: Lawrence Erlbaum Associates.

Hanson, R., & Morton-Bourgon, K. (2009, March). The accuracy of recidivism risk assessments for sexual offenders: A meta-analysis of 118 prediction studies. *Psychological Assessment, 21*(1), 1–21.

Hare-Mustin, R. T., & Marecek, J. (Eds.). (1990). *Making a difference: Psychology and the construction of gender.* New Haven: Yale University Press.

Hartmann, D. P., & Hall, R. V. (1976). A discussion of the changing criterion design. *Journal of Applied Behavior Analysis, 9,* 527–532.

Hashtroudi, S., Parker, E. S., DeLisi, L. E., & Wyatt, R. J. (1983). On elaboration and alcohol. *Journal of Verbal Learning and Verbal Behavior, 22,* 164–173.

Heidbreder, E. (1933). *Seven Psychologies.* New York: The Century Co.

Heinsman, D. T., & Shadish, W. R. (1996). Assignment methods in experimentation: When do nonrandomized experiments approximate answers from randomized experiments. *Psychological Methods, 1,* 154–169.

Henry, G. T. (1990). *Practical sampling.* Thousand Oaks, CA: Sage.

Hermelin, E., Lievens, F., & Robertson, I. (2007, December). The validity of assessment centres for the prediction of supervisory performance ratings: A meta-analysis. *International Journal of Selection and Assessment, 15*(4), 405–411.

Hertel, P. T. (1998). The relationship between rumination and impaired memory in dysphoric moods. *Journal of Abstract Psychology, 107,* 166–172.

Hertel, P. T., & Rude, S. S. (1991). Depressive deficits in memory: Focusing attention improves subsequent recall. *Journal of Experimental Psychology: General, 120,* 301–309.

Hilgartner, S. (1990). Research fraud, misconduct, and the IRB. *IRB: A Review of Human Subjects Research, 12,* 1–4.

Hippocrates. (1931). Aphorisms. In *Hippocrates* (W. H. S. Jones, Trans.). (pp. 128–129). Cambridge, MA: Harvard University Press.

Hogan, J. D. (1994). G. Stanley Hall and company: Observations on the first 100 APA Presidents. *Annals of the New York Academy of Sciences, 727,* 133–138.

Holden, C. (1987). NIMH finds a case of "serious misconduct." *Science, 235,* 1566–1567.

Holder, A. R. (1993). Research records and subpoenas: A continuing issue. *IRB: A Review of Human Subjects Research, 15,* 6–7.

Holmes, D. S. (1973). Effectiveness of debriefing after a stress-producing deception. *Journal of Research in Personality, 7,* 127–138.

Holmes, D. S. (1976a). Debriefing after psychological experiments: I. Effectiveness of postdeception dehoaxing. *American Psychologist, 31,* 858–867.

Holmes, D. S. (1976b). Debriefing after psychological experiments: II. Effectiveness of postexperimental desensitizing. *American Psychologist, 31,* 868–875.

Holmes, D. S., & Bennett, D. H. (1974). Experiments to answer questions raised by the use of deception in psychological research: I. Role playing as an alternative to deception; II. Effectiveness of debriefing after a deception; III. Effect of informed consent on deception. *Journal of Personality and Social Psychology, 29,* 358–367.

Hull, G. A., & Zacher, J. (2007). Enacting identities: An ethnography of a job training program. *Identity: An International Journal of Theory and Research, 7*(1), 71–102.

Humphreys, L. (1970). *Tearoom trade.* Chicago: Aldine.

Hurley, D. (1989, July/August). Cycles of craving. *Psychology Today,* 54–58.

Institute of Laboratory Animal Research, Commission on Life Sciences, National Research Council. (1996).

Guide for the care and use of laboratory animals. Washington, DC: The National Academy Press.

Ishige, N., & Hayashi, N. (2005). Occupation and social experience: Factors influencing attitude towards people with schizophrenia. *Psychiatry and Clinical Neurosciences, 59,* 89–95.

Johnson, R. B., Onwuegbuzie, A. J., & Turner, L. A. (2007). Toward a definition of mixed methods research. *Journal of Mixed Methods Research, 1*(2), 112–133.

Johnson, R. F. Q. (1976). The experimenter attributes effect: A methodological analysis. *Psychological Record, 26,* 67–78.

Jones, J. H. (1981). *Bad blood: The Tuskegee syphilis experiment.* New York: Free Press.

Kalton, G. (1983). *Introduction to survey sampling.* Thousand Oaks, CA: Sage.

Karlins, M, Coffman, T. L., & Walters, G. (1969). On the fading of social stereotypes: Studies in three generations of college students. *Journal of Personality and Social Psychology, 13,* 1–16.

Kassin, S. M., & Kiechel, K. L. (1996). The social psychology of false confessions: Compliance, internalization, and confabulation. *Psychological Science, 7*(3), 125–128.

Katz, D., & Braly, K. (1933). Racial stereotypes of one hundred college students. *Journal of Abnormal Psychology, 28,* 280–290.

Katz, J. (1992). Psychophysiological contributions to phantom limbs. *Canadian Journal of Psychiatry, 37,* 282–298.

Kaye, B. K., & Johnson, T. J. (1999). Research methodology: Taming the cyber frontier. *Social Science Computer Review, 17,* 323–337.

Kazdin, A. E. (1978). Methodological and interpretive problems of single-case experimental designs. *Journal of Consulting and Clinical Psychology, 46,* 629–642.

Kazdin, A. E. (1980). *Research design in clinical psychology.* New York: Harper & Row.

Kazdin, A. E. (1992). *Methodological issues and strategies in clinical research.* Washington, DC: American Psychological Association.

Keller, E. F. (1984). Feminism and science. In S. Harding & J. F. O'Barr (Eds.), *Sex and scientific inquiry.* Chicago: University of Chicago Press.

Kelman, H. C. (1967). Human use of human subjects. *Psychological Bulletin, 67,* 1–11.

Kelman, H. C. (1968). *A time to speak.* San Francisco, CA: Jossey-Bass.

Kelman, H. C. (1972). The rights of the subject in social research: An analysis in terms of relative power and legitimacy. *American Psychologist, 27,* 989–1016.

Kennedy, J. L., & Uphoff, H. F. (1939). Experiments on the nature of extrasensory perception: III. The recording error criticism of extra-chance scores. *Journal of Parapsychology, 3,* 226–245.

Keppel, G., & Zedeck, S. (1989). *Data analysis for research designs: Analysis of variance and multiple regression/correlation approaches.* New York: W. H. Freeman.

Kerlinger, F., & Lee, H. (2000). *Foundations of behavioral research* (4th ed.). Fort Worth, TX: Harcourt College Pub.

Kerlinger, F. N. (1973). *Foundations of behavioral research.* New York: Holt, Rinehart and Winston.

Key, B. W. (1980). *The clam-plate orgy and other subliminal techniques for manipulating your behavior.* Englewood Cliffs, NJ: Prentice-Hall.

Kihlstrom, J. F. (1995). On the validity of psychology experiments. *APS Observer* (9), 10–11.

Kimmel, A. J. (1991). Predictable biases in the ethical decision making of American psychologists. *American Psychologist, 46,* 786–788.

Kimmel, A. J. (1996). *Ethical issues in behavioral research.* Cambridge, MA: Blackwell Publishers.

Kimmel, A. J. (1998). In defense of deception. *American Psychologists, 53,* 803–805.

King, B. J. (2004). Towards an ethnography of African great apes. *Social Anthropology, 12*(2), 195–207.

Kish, L. (1995). *Survey sampling.* Hoboken, NJ: Wiley.

Knight, J. A. (1984). Exploring the compromise of ethical principles in science. *Perspectives in Biology and Medicine, 27,* 432–441.

Krantz, J. H., Ballard, J., & Scher, J. (1997). Comparing the results of laboratory and World-Wide Web samples on the determinants of female attractiveness. *Behavioral Research Methods, Instruments, & Computers, 29,* 264–269.

Kratochwill, T. R. (1978). Foundations of time-series research. In T. R. Kratochwill (Ed.), *Single subject research: Strategies for evaluating change.* New York: Academic Press.

Kraut, R., Mukopadhyay, T., Szczypula, J., Kiesler, S., & Scherlis, W. (1998). Communication in information: Alternative uses of the Internet in households. In *Proceedings of the CHI 98* (pp. 368–383). New York: ACM.

Kraut, R., Patterson, M., Lundmark, V., Kiesler, S., Mukopadhyay, T., & Scherlis, W. (1998). A social technology that reduces social involvement and psychological well-being? *American Psychologist, 53,* 1017–1031.

Kuhn, T. S. (1962). *The structure of scientific revolutions.* Cambridge, MA: Harvard University Press.

Lakatos, I. (1970). Falsification and the methodology of scientific research programs. In I. Lakatos & A. Musgrave (Eds.), *Criticism and the growth of knowledge* (pp. 91–196). Cambridge, England: Cambridge University Press.

Lana, R. E. (1969). Pretest sensitization. In R. Rosenthal & R. L. Rosnow (Eds.), *Artifact in behavioral research.* New York: Academic Press.

Larsson, B., & Sund, A. M. (2008). Prevalence, course, incidence, and 1-year prediction of deliberate self-harm and suicide attempts in early Norwegian school adolescents. *Suicide and Life-Threatening Behavior, 38,* 152–165.

Latané, B. (1981). The psychology of social impact. *American Psychologist, 36,* 343–356.

Laudan, L. (1977). *Progress and its problems.* Berkeley: University of California Press.

Lawler, E. E., III, & Hackman, J. R. (1969). Impact of employee participation in the development of pay incentive plans: A field experiment. *Journal of Applied Psychology, 53,* 467–471.

Leak, G. K. (1981). Student perception of coercion and value from participation in psychological research. *Teaching of Psychology, 8,* 147–149.

Leake, M., & Lesik, S. A. (2007). Do remedial English programs impact first-year success in college? An illustration of the regression-discontinuity design. *International Journal of Research and Method in Education, 30,* 89–99.

Leffert, N., Benson, P. L., Scales, P. C., Sharma, A. R., Drake, D. R., & Blyth, D. A. (1998). Development assets: Measurement and prediction of risk behaviors among adolescents. *Applied Developmental Science, 2,* 209–230.

Leikin, S. (1993). Minors' assent, consent, or dissent to medical research. *IRB: A review of human subjects research, 15,* 1–7.

Leitenberg, H. (1973). The use of single-case methodology in psychotherapy research. *Journal of Abnormal Psychology, 82,* 87–101.

Lethbridge, R., & Allen, N. (2008, October). Mood induced cognitive and emotional reactivity, life stress, and the prediction of depressive relapse. *Behaviour Research and Therapy, 46,* 1142–1150.

Levine, J. M. (2000). Groups: Group processes. In A. Kazdin (Ed.), *Encyclopedia of psychology.* Washington, DC & New York: American Psychological Association and Oxford University Press.

Likert, R. (1932). A technique for the measurement of attitudes. *Archives of Psychology, 22*(140), 1–55.

Llieva, J., Baron, S., & Healey, N. M. (2002). Online surveys in marketing research: Pros and cons. *International Journal of Marketing Research, 44,* 361–375.

Lockard, R. B. (1968). The albino rat: A defensible choice or a bad habit? *American Psychologist, 23,* 734–742.

Logue, A. W., & Anderson, Y. D. (2001). Higher-education administrators: When the future does not make a difference. *Psychological Science, 12,* 276–281.

Lysaker, P. H., Davis, L. W., Jones, A. M., & Beattie, N. L. (2007). Relationship and technique in the long-term integrative psychotherapy of schizophrenia: A single case study. *Counselling & Psychotherapy Research, 7*(2), 79–85.

Maddox, T. (1997) *Tests: A comprehensive reference for assessment in psychology, education, and business.* Austin, TX: Pro Ed.

Mahoney, C. R., Taylor, H. A., Kanarek, R. B., & Samuel. P. (2005). Effect of breakfast composition on cognitive processes in elementary school children. *Physiology and Behavior, 85,* 635–645.

Marquart, J. W. (1983). *Cooptation of the kept: Maintaining control in a southern penitentiary.* Unpublished doctoral dissertation, Texas A&M University, Texas.

Marques, J. F. (1998). Raiders of the lost reference: Helping your students do a literature search. *APS Observer, 11,* 30–35.

Martinson, B. C., Anderson, M. S., & de Vries, R. (2005). Scientists behaving badly. *Nature, 420,* 739–740.

Marx, M. H. (1963). *Theories in contemporary psychology.* New York: Macmillan.

Masling, J. (1966). Role-related behavior of the subject and psychologist and its effects upon psychological data. *Nebraska Symposium on Motivation, 14,* 67–103.

Mathiasen, R. E. (2005). Moral development in fraternity members: A case study. *College Student Journal, 39,* 242–252.

Maxwell, J. A. (1992). Understanding and validity in qualitative research. *Harvard Educational Review, 62,* 279–299.

Maxwell, J. A. (2005). *Qualitative research design: An interactive approach.* Thousand Oaks, CA: Sage.

Maxwell, S. E., & Delaney, H. D. (2004). *Designing experiments and analyzing data: A model comparison perspective.* Mahwah, NJ: Lawrence Erlbaum.

McFall, R. M. (1970). Effects of self-monitoring on normal smoking behavior. *Journal of Consulting and Clinical Psychology, 35,* 135–142.

McGuigan, F. J. (1963). The experimenter: A neglected stimulus object. *Psychological Bulletin, 60,* 421–428.

McKelvie, S. (1978). Graphic rating scales: how many categories? *British Journal of Psychology, 69,* 185–202.

McLoughlin, J. A., & Nall, M. (1988). Teacher opinion of the role of food allergy on school behavior and achievement. *Annals of Allergy, 61,* 89–91.

Mellgren, R. L., Seybert, J. A., & Dyck, D. G. (1978). The order of continuous, partial and nonreward trials and resistance to extinction. *Learning and Motivation, 9,* 359–371.

Messick, S. (1995). Validity of psychological assessment: Validation of inferences from persons' responses and performances as scientific inquiry into score meaning. *American Psychologist, 50,* 741–749.

Meyer, R. G., & Osborne, Y. V. H. (1982). *Case studies in abnormal behavior.* Boston: Allyn and Bacon.

Miles, M. B., & Huberman, A. M. (1994). *Qualitative data analysis: An expanded sourcebook.* Thousand Oaks, CA: Sage.

Milgram, S. (1964a). Group pressure and action against a person. *Journal of Personality and Social Psychology, 69,* 137–143.

Milgram, S. (1964b). Issues in the study of obedience: A reply to Baumrind. *American Psychologist, 19,* 848–852.

Miller, A. G. (1972). Role playing: An alternative to deception? A review of the evidence. *American Psychologist, 27,* 623–636.

Miller, D. C. (1991). *Handbook of Research Design and Social Measurement.* Newbury Park, CA: Sage.

Miller, E. (1999). Positivism and clinical psychology. *Clinical Psychology and Psychotherapy, 6,* 1–6.

Mills, J. (1976). A procedure for explaining experiments involving deception. *Personality and Social Psychology Bulletin, 2,* 3–13.

Monster experiment. (2001, June 11). *Mobile Register,* p. 2A.

Moskowitz, J. T., & Wrubel, J. (2005). Coping with HIV as a chronic illness: A longitudinal analysis of illness appraisals. *Psychology & Health, 20,* 509–531.

Murphy, D. (2009). Client-centered therapy for severe childhood abuse: A case study. *Counseling & Psychotherapy Research, 9*(1), 3–10.

Musch, J., & Reips, U. (2000). A brief history of Web experimenting. In M. H. Birnbaum (Ed.), *Psychology experiments on the Internet.* New York: Academic Press.

Nederhof, A. J. (1985). A comparison of European and North American response patterns in mail surveys. *Journal of the Market Research Society, 27,* 55–63.

Neergaard, L. (1999, May 16). Sex and medicine: Prescribing drugs based on gender. *Mobile Register,* pp. 6A–7A.

Newburger, C. (2001). Home computers and Internet use in the United States: August 2000. *Current Population Reports,* U.S. Census Bureau, U.S. Department of Commerce. Retrieved November 23, 2002, from www.census.gov/prod/2001pubs/p23-207.pdf

Newton, L, Rosen, A., Tennant, C., Hobbs, C., Lapsley, H. M., & Tribe, K. (2000). Deinstitutionalisation for long-term mental illness: An ethnographic study. *Australian and New Zealand Journal of Psychiatry, 34,* 484–490.

Nezu, A. M. (1986). Efficacy of a social problem-solving therapy approach for unipolar depression. *Journal of Consulting and Clinical Psychology, 54,* 196–202.

Nicks, S. D., Korn, J. H., & Mainieri, T. (1997). The rise and fall of deception in social psychology and personality research, 1921–1994. *Ethics & Behavior, 7,* 69–77.

Nolen-Hoeksema, S., & Morrow, J. (1991). A prospective study of depression and posttraumatic stress symptoms after a natural disaster: The 1989 Loma Prieta earthquake. *Journal of Personality and Social Psychology, 61,* 321–336.

Nosek, B. A., Banaji, M. R. & Greenwald, A. G. (2002). E-research: Ethics, security, design, and control in psychological research on the Internet. *Journal of Social Issues, 58,* 161–176.

Nunnally, J. (1978). *Psychometric theory.* New York: McGraw-Hill.

Office for Protection from Research Risks [OPRR]. (2001, December 13). Protection of human subjects: Title 45, Code of federal regulations *45* (Part 46). Washington, DC: U.S. Government Printing Office.

Office for Protection from Research Risks, Protection of Human Subjects, National Commission for the Protection of Human Subjects of Biomedical and Behavioral Research. (1979). *The Belmont Report: Ethical principles and guidelines for the protection of human subjects of research* (pp. 887–809). Washington, DC: U.S. Government Printing Office.

Olsen, L., Bottorff, J. L., Raina, P., & Frankish, C. J. (2008). An ethnography of low-income mothers' safeguarding efforts. *Journal of Safety Research, 39*, 609–616.

Orne, M. T. (1962). On the social psychology of the psychological experiment: With particular reference to demand characteristics and their implications. *American Psychologist, 17*, 776–783.

Orne, M. T. (1973). Communication by the total experimental situations: Why is it important, how is it evaluated, and its significance for the ecological validity of findings. In P. Pliner, L. Kramer, & T. Alloway (Eds.), *Communication and affect.* New York: Academic Press.

Ortmann, A., & Hertwig, R. (1997). Is deception acceptable? *American Psychologist, 52*, 746–747.

Osgood, C. E., Suci, G. J., & Tannenbaum, P. J. (1957). *The measurement of meaning.* Urbana, IL: University of Illinois Press.

OSTP (2005). *Federal Policy on Research Misconduct.* Retrieved September 2005 from www.ostp.gov/html/001207_3.html

Pampel, F. C., & Aguilar, J. (2008). Changes in smoking, 1976–2002: A time-series analysis. *Youth and Society, 39*, 453–479.

Pappworth, M. H. (1967). *Human guinea pigs: Experimentation on man.* Boston: Beacon Press.

Pasternak, D., & Cary, P. (1995, September 18). Tales from the crypt: Medical horror stories from a trove of secret cold-war documents. *U.S. News & World Report*, pp. 70, 77.

Patton, M. Q. (1990). *Qualitative evaluation and research methods.* Thousand Oaks, CA: Sage.

Patton, M. Q. (2002). *Qualitative research and evaluation methods.* Thousand Oaks, CA: Sage.

Pavlov, I. P. (1928). *Lecture on conditioned reflexes* (W. H. Gantt, Trans.). New York: International.

Pedhazur, E. J. (1997). *Multiple regression in behavioral research: Explanation and prediction.* Fort Worth, TX: Harcourt Brace.

Peters, T. J., & Eachus, J. I. (2008). Achievind equal probability of selection under various random sampling strategies. *Paediatric and Perinatal Epidemiology, 9*, 219–224.

Pettigrew, R. F., Christ, O., Wagner, U., Meertens, R. W., van Dick, R., & Zick, A. (2008). Relative deprivation and intergroup prejudice. *Journal of Social Issues, 64*, 385–401.

Pfungst, O. (1965). *Clever Hans (the horse of Mr. Von Osten): A contribution to experimental, animal, and human psychology* (C. L. Rahn, Trans.). New York: Holt, Rinehart and Winston (Originally published 1911).

Philogene, G. (2001). Stereotype fissure: Katz and Braly revisited. *Social Science Information, 40*, 411–432.

Picou, J. S. (1996). Compelled disclosure of scholarly research: Some comments on high stakes litigation. *Law and Contemporary Problems, 59*, 149–157.

Pihl, R. D., Zacchia, C., & Zeichner, A. (1981). Follow-up analysis of the use of deception and aversive contingencies in psychological experiments. *Psychological Reports, 48*, 927–930.

Plous, S. (1996). Attitudes toward the use of animals in psychological research and education: Results from a national survey of psychologists. *American Psychologist, 51*, 1167–1180.

Polanyi, M. (1963). The potential theory of absorption. *Science, 141*, 1010–1013.

Polanyi, M., & Sen, A. (2009). *The tacit dimension.* Chicago: University of Chicago Press.

Popper, K. R. (1968). *The logic of scientific discovery.* London: Hutchinson and Co.

Posner, M. I., & Raichle, M. E. (1994). *Images of the mind.* New York: W. H. Freeman & Co.

Potera, C. (1998). Trapped in the web. *Psychology Today, 31*, 66–72.

Proctor, R. W., & Capaldi, E. J. (2001). Improving the science education of psychology students: Better teaching of methodology. *Teaching of Psychology, 28*, 173–181.

Regan, P. C., & Llamas, V. (2002). Customer service as a function of shopper's attire. *Psychological Reports, 90*, 203–204.

Reips, U. (2000). The Web experiment method: Advantages, disadvantages, and solutions. In M. H. Birnbaum (Ed.). *Psychology experiments on the Internet.* New York: Academic Press.

Resnick, J. H., & Schwartz, T. (1973). Ethical standards as an independent variable in psychological research. *American Psychologist, 28*, 134–139.

Rich, C. L. (1977). Is random digit dialing really necessary? *Journal of Marketing Research, 14*, 300–305.

Richards, M., Hardy, R., & Wadsworth, M. (1997). The effects of divorce and separation on mental health in a national UK birth cohort. *Psychological Medicine, 27*, 1121–1128.

Riemen, D. J. (1986). The essential structure of a caring interaction: Doing phenomenology. In P. M. Munhall & C. J. Oiler (Eds.), *Nursing research: A qualitative perspective*. Norwalk, CT: Appleton Century Crofts.

Rindskopf, D. (1992). The importance of theory in selection modeling: Incorrect assumptions mean biased results. In H. Chen & P. H. Rossi (Eds.), *Using theory to improve program and policy evaluations* (pp. 179–191). New York: Greenwood Press.

Ring, K., Wallston, K., & Corey, M. (1970). Mode of debriefing as a factor affecting reaction to a Milgram type obedience experiment: An ethical inquiry. *Representative Research in Social Psychology, 1*, 67–88.

Roberson, M. T., & Sundstrom, E. (1990). Questionnaire design, return rates, and response favorableness in an employee attitude questionnaire. *Journal of Applied Psychology, 75*, 354–357.

Robinson, J. P, Shaver, P. R., & Wrightsman, L. S. (1991). *Measures of personality and social psychological attitudes*. New York: Academic.

Roccatagliata, G. (1986). *A history of ancient psychiatry*. Westport, CT: Greenwood Press.

Rogers, T. F. (1976). Interviews by telephone and in person: Quality of responses and field performance. *Public Opinion Quarterly, 40*, 51–65.

Rosenberg, M. J. (1969). The conditions and consequences of evaluation apprehension. In R. Rosenthal & R. L. Rosnow (Eds.), *Artifact in behavioral research*. New York: Academic Press.

Rosenthal, R. (1966). *Experimenter effects in behavioral research*. New York: Appleton-Century-Crofts.

Rosenthal, R. (1978). How often are our numbers wrong? *American Psychologist, 33*, 1005–1007.

Rosnow, R. L. (1997). Hedgehogs, foxes and the evolving social contract in science: Ethical challenges and methodological opportunities. *Psychological Methods, 2*, 345–356.

Rosnow, R. L. (2002). The nature and role of demand characteristics in scientific inquiry. *Prevention & Treatment, 5*, Article ID 37.

Rosnow, R. L., & Rosenthal, R. (1998). *Beginning behavioral research*. Upper Saddle River, NJ: Prentice-Hall, Inc.

Rosnow, R. L., & Rosnow, M. (1992). *Writing papers in psychology* (2nd ed.). New York: Wiley.

Rugg, E. A. (1975). *Ethical judgments of social research involving experimental deception*. Unpublished doctoral dissertation, George Peabody College for Teachers, Nashville, TN.

Sales, B. D., & Folkman, S. (2000). *Ethics in research with human participants*. Washington, DC: American Psychological Association.

Sanders, G. S., & Simmons, W. L. (1983). Use of hypnosis to enhance eyewitness accuracy: Does it work? *Journal of Applied Psychology, 68*, 70–77.

Schenk, S., Lacelle, G., Gorman, K., & Amit, Z. (1987). Cocaine self-administration in rats influenced by environmental conditions: Implications for the etiology of drug abuse. *Neuroscience Letters, 81*, 227–231.

Schoenthaler, S. J. (1983). The Los Angeles probation department diet–behavior program: An empirical analysis of six institutional settings. *International Journal of Biosocial Research, 5*, 88–98.

Scholtz, J. A. (1973). Defense styles in suicide attempters. *Journal of Consulting and Clinical Psychology, 41*, 70–73.

Schouten, J. W., & McAlexander, J. H. (1995). Subcultures of consumption: An ethnography of the new bikers. *Journal of Consumer Research, 22*, 43–61.

Schraw, G., Wadkins, T., & Olafson, L. (2007). Doing the things we do: A grounded theory of academic procrastination. *Journal of Educational Psychology, 99*(1), 12–25.

Schuman, H., & Presser, H. (1996). *Questions and answers in attitude surveys: Experiments on question form, wording, and content*. Thousand Oaks, CA: Sage.

Sears, R. R., Whiting, J. W. M., Nowlis, V., & Sears, P. S. (1953). Some child-rearing antecedents of aggression and dependence in young children. *Genetic Psychology Monographs, 47*, 135–234.

Seashore, S. E., & Katz, D. (1982). Obituary: Rensis Likert (1903–1981). *American Psychologist, 37*, 851–853.

Seeman, J. (1969). Deception in psychological research. *American Psychologist, 24*, 1025–1028.

Seligman, M. E. P. (2002). *Authentic happiness: Using the new positive psychology to realize your potential for lasting fulfillment*. New York: Free Press.

Selltiz, C., Jahoda, M., Deutsch, M., & Cook, S. W. (1959). *Research methods in social relations*. New York: Holt.

Severson, H. H., & Ary, D. V. (1983). Sampling bias due to consent procedures with adolescents. *Addictive Behaviors, 8*, 433–437.

Shadish, W. R., Cook, T. D., & Campbell, D. T. (2002). *Experimental and quasi-experimental designs for generalized causal inference*. Boston, NY: Houghton Mifflin.

Shadish, W. R., & Reis, J. (1984). A review of studies of the effectiveness of programs to improve pregnancy outcome. *Evaluation Review, 8*, 747–776.

Shannon, D. M., Johnson, T. E., Searcy, S., and Lott, A. (2002). Using electronic surveys: Advice from survey professionals. *Practical Assessment, Research and Evaluation, 8.* Retrieved September 10, 2002, from http://ericae.net/pare/getvn.asp?v=8&n=1

Sharpe, D., Adair, J. G., & Roese, N. J. (1992). Twenty years of deception research: A decline in subjects' trust? *Personality and Social Psychology Bulletin, 18,* 585–590.

Shepherd, R. M., & Edelmann, R. J. (2007). Social phobia and the self medication hypothesis: A case study approach. *Conselling Psychology Quarterly, 20,* 295–307.

Sherer, M. R., & Schreibman, L. (2005). Individual behavioral profiles and predictors of treatment effectiveness for children with autism. *Journal of Consulting and Clinical Psychology, 73,* 525–538.

Shoham, A. (2004). Flow experiences and image making: An online chat-room ethnography. *Psychology & Marketing, 21,* 855–882.

Sidowski, J. B., & Lockard, R. B. (1966). Some preliminary considerations in research. In J. B. Sidowski (Ed.), *Experimental methods and instrumentation in psychology.* New York: McGraw-Hill.

Sieber, J. E. (1983). Deception in social research: III. The nature and limits of debriefing. *IRB: A Review of Human Subjects Research, 5*(3), 1–4.

Sieber, J. E., & Stanley, B. (1988). Ethical and professional dimensions of socially sensitive research. *American Psychologist, 43,* 49–55.

Sieber, J. E., Iannuzzo, R., & Rodriguez, B. (1995). Deception methods in psychology: Have they changed in 23 years? *Ethics and Behavior, 5,* 67–85.

Silverman, D. (1993). *Interpreting qualitative data: Methods for analyzing talk, text, and interaction.* Thousand Oaks, CA: Sage.

Skinner, B. F. (1953). *Science and human behavior.* New York: Macmillan.

Skinner, B. F. (1956). A case history in scientific method. *American Psychologist, 11,* 221–223.

Smith, J. A. (Ed.). (2008). *Qualitative psychology: A practical guide to research methods.* Los Angeles: Sage.

Smith, S. S., & Richardson, D. (1983). Amelioration of deception and harm in psychological research: The important role of debriefing. *Journal of Personality and Social Psychology, 44,* 1075–1082.

Smith, T. E., Sells, S. P., & Clevenger, T. (1994). Ethnographic content analysis of couple and therapist perceptions in a reflecting team setting. *Journal of Marital and Family Therapy, 20,* 267–286.

Smucker, B., S., Earleywine, M., & Gordis, E. B. (2005). Alcohol consumption moderates the link between cannabis use and cannabis dependence in an Internet survey. *Psychology of Addictive Behaviors, 19,* 212–216.

Society for Research in Child Development. (2003). *Ethical standards for research with children.* Retrieved March 12, 2003, from http://www.sred.org/about.html#standards

Soliday, E., & Stanton, A. L. (1995). Deceived versus nondeceived participants' perceptions of scientific and applied psychology. *Ethics & Behavior, 5,* 87–104.

Solomon, D. J. (2001). Conducting Web-based surveys. *Practical Assessment, Research and Evaluation, 7*(19) [Online]. Retrieved September 10, 2002, from http://ericae.net/pare/getvn.asp?v=7&n=19

Stake, R. E. (1995). *The art of case study research.* Thousand Oaks, CA: Sage.

Stevens, S. S. (1946). On the theory of scales of measurement. *Science, 103,* 677–680.

Strauss, A., & Corbin, J. (1998). *Basics of qualitative research: Techniques and procedures for developing grounded theory.* Thousand Oaks, CA: Sage.

Stulemeijer, M., van der Werf, S., Borm, G. F., & Vos, P. E. (2008). Early prediction of favourable recovery 6 months after mild traumatic brain injury. *Journal of Neurology, Neurosurgery & Psychiatry, 79,* 936–942.

Sutcliffe, J. P. (1972). On the role of "instructions to the subject" in psychological experiments. *American Psychologist, 27,* 755–758.

Svanborg, C., Rosso, M. S., Lützen, K., Bäärnhielm, S., & Wistedt, A. A. (2008). Barriers in the help-seeking process: A multiple-case study of early-onset dysthymia in Sweden. *Nordic Journal of Psychiatry, 62*(8), 346–353.

Taffel, C. (1955). Anxiety and the conditioning of verbal behavior. *Journal of Abnormal and Social Psychology, 51,* 496–501.

Tashakkori, A., & Teddlie, C. (Eds.) (2003). *Handbook of mixed methods in social and behavioral research.* Thousand Oaks, CA: Sage.

Teddlie, C., & Tashakkori, A. (2009). *Foundations of mixed methods research: Integrating quantitative and qualitative techniques in the social and behavioral sciences.* Thousand Oaks, CA: Sage.

Tedeschi, J. T., Schlenker, B. R., & Bonoma, T. V. (1971). Cognitive dissonance: Private ratiocination or public spectacle. *American Psychologist, 26,* 685–695.

Terror at rush hour. (2005, July 18). Terror at rush hour. *Newsweek,* pp. 29–36.

Tesch, F. E. (1977). Debriefing research participants: Though this be method there is madness to it. *Journal of Personality and Social Psychology, 35*, 217–224.

Thayer, H. S. (Ed.). (1953). *Newton's philosophy of nature: Selections from his writings.* New York: Hafner.

Thomas, L., & Chambers, K. (1989, September). Phenomenology of life satisfaction among elderly men: Quantitative and qualitative views. *Psychology and Aging, 4*(3), 284–289.

Thompson, B. (2006) *Foundations of behavioral statistics: An insight based approach.* New York, NY: Guilford.

Thorkildsen, R. A. (2005). *Fundamentals of measurement in applied research.* Boston: Pearson.

Thorne, S. B., & Himelstein, P. (1984). The role of suggestion in the perception of satanic messages in rock-and-roll recordings. *Journal of Psychology, 116*, 245–248.

Trochim, W. M. K. (2001). *The research methods knowledge base.* Cincinnati, OH: Atomic Dog.

Trochim, W. M. K., & Donnelly, J. P. (2008). *The research methods knowledge base.* Mason, OH: Cengage Learning.

Tryon, W. W. (1982). A simplified time-series analysis for evaluating treatment interventions. *Journal of Applied Behavior Analysis, 15*, 423–429.

Tunnell, G. B. (1977). Three dimensions of naturalness: An expanded definition of field research. *Psychological Bulletin, 84*, 426–437.

Turner, L. A., & Johnson, R. B. (2003). A model of mastery motivation for at-risk preschoolers. *Journal of Educational Psychology, 95*, 495–505.

U.S. Department of Agriculture. (1989, August 21). Animal welfare: Final rules. *Federal register.*

U.S. Department of Agriculture. (1990, July 16). Animal welfare: Guinea pigs, hamsters and rabbits. *Federal Register.*

U.S. Department of Agriculture. (1991, February 15). Animal welfare: Standards; final rule. *Federal Register.*

Underwood, B. J. (1959). Verbal learning in the educative process. *Harvard Educational Review, 29*, 107–117.

Unger, R., & Crawford, M. (1992). *Women and gender.* New York: McGraw-Hill.

Van Houten, R. Van Houten, J., & Malenfant, J. E. L. (2007). Impact of a comprehensive safety program on bicycle helmet use among middle-school children. *Journal of Applied Behavior Analysis, 40*, 239–247.

Van Vilet, K. J. (2008). Shame and resilience in adulthood: A grounded theory study. *Journal of Counseling Psychology, 55*, 233–245.

Vernon, H. M., Bedford, T., & Wyatt, S. (1924). *Two studies of rest pauses in industry* (Medical Research Council, Industrial Fatigue Research Board Report No. 25.) London: His Majesty's Stationery Office.

Vokey, J. R., & Read, D. (1985). Subliminal messages: Between the devil and the media. *American Psychologist, 40*, 1231–1239.

Wagner, R. K., Torgesen, J. K., Laughon, P., Simmons, K., & Rashotte, C. A. (1993). Development of young readers' phonological processing abilities. *Journal of Educational Psychology, 85*, 83–103.

Wahl, K., Salkovskis, P., & Cotter, I. (2008). 'I wash until it feels right' the phenomenology of stopping criteria in obsessive-compulsive washing. *Journal of Anxiety Disorders, 22*, 143–161.

Wainberg, M. L., González, M. A., McKinnon, K., Elkington, K. S., Pinto, D., Mann, C. G., Mattos, P. E. (2007). Targeted ethnography as a critical step to inform cultural adaptations of HIV prevention interventions for adults with severe mental illness. *Social Science & Medicine, 65*, 296–308.

Walker, H. M., & Buckley, N. K. (1968). The use of positive reinforcement in conditioning attending behavior. *Journal of Applied Behavior Analysis, 1*, 245–250.

Walster, E. (1964). The temporal sequence of post-decision processes. In L. Festinger (Ed.), *Conflict, decision, and dissonance.* Stanford: Stanford University Press.

Walters (2008). An ethnography of a children's renal unit: Experiences of children and young people with long-term renal illness. *Journal of Clinical Nursing, 17*, 3103–3114.

Ward, E. C. (2005). Keeping it real: A grounded theory study of African American clients engaging in counseling at a community mental health agency. *Journal of Community Psychology, 52*, 471–481.

Webb, E. J., Campbell, D. T., Schwartz, R. D., & Sechrest, L. (1966). *Unobstructive measures: Nonreactive research in the social sciences.* Chicago: Rand McNally.

Whewell, W. (1967). *The philosophy of the inductive sciences* (Vol. 2). New York: Johnson Reprint. (Original work published 1847).

Whisman, M. A. (2007). Marital distress and DSM-IV psychiatric disorders in a population-based national survey. *Journal of Abnormal Psychology, 116*, 638–643.

Whitley, R., Harris, M., & Drake, R. E. (2008). Safety and security in small-scale recovery housing for people with severe mental illness: An inner-city case study. *Psychiatric Services, 59*, 165–169.

Willig, C., & Stainton-Rogers, W. (Eds.) (2008). *The Sage handbook of qualitative research in psychology.* Los Angeles: Sage.

Wilson, T. D. (1994). The proper protocol: Validity and completeness of verbal reports. *American Psychological Society, 5,* 249–252.

Wilson, V. L. (1981). Time and the external validity of experiments. *Evaluation and Program Planning, 4,* 229–238.

Wittorf, A., Wiedemann, G., Buchkremer, G., & Klingberg, S. (2008, February). Prediction of community outcome in schizophrenia 1 year after discharge from inpatient treatment. *European Archives of Psychiatry and Clinical Neuroscience, 258*(1), 48–58.

Woodworth, R. S., & Sheehan, M. R. (1964). *Contemporary schools of psychology* (3rd ed.). New York: Ronald Press.

Wundt, W. (1902). *Outlines of psychology* (Trans., 2nd ed.). Oxford: Engelmann.

Yeo, R. (2003). *Defining science: William Whewell, natural knowledge and public debate in early Victorian Britain.* Cambridge, UK: Cambridge University Press.

Young, K. S. (1996). Psychology of computer use: XL. Addictive use of the Internet: A case that breaks the stereotype. *Psychological Reports, 79,* 899–902.

Zimney, G. H. (1961). *Method in experimental psychology.* New York: Ronald Press.

Index